Lecture Notes in Computer Science   16342

Founding Editors

Gerhard Goos
Juris Hartmanis

The series Lecture Notes in Computer Science (LNCS), including its subseries Lecture Notes in Artificial Intelligence (LNAI) and Lecture Notes in Bioinformatics (LNBI), has established itself as a medium for the publication of new developments in computer science and information technology research, teaching, and education.

LNCS enjoys close cooperation with the computer science R & D community, the series counts many renowned academics among its volume editors and paper authors, and collaborates with prestigious societies. Its mission is to serve this international community by providing an invaluable service, mainly focused on the publication of conference and workshop proceedings and postproceedings. LNCS commenced publication in 1973.

Martin Schrepp · Matthias Rauterberg

Editors

HCI International 2025 – Late Breaking Papers

27th International Conference on
Human-Computer Interaction, HCII 2025
Gothenburg, Sweden, June 22–27, 2025
Proceedings, Part XII

Springer

Editors
Martin Schrepp
SAP SE
Walldorf, Germany

Matthias Rauterberg
Eindhoven University of Technology
Eindhoven, The Netherlands

ISSN 0302-9743
ISSN 1611-3349 (electronic)
Lecture Notes in Computer Science
ISBN 978-3-032-13163-8
ISBN 978-3-032-13164-5 (eBook)
https://doi.org/10.1007/978-3-032-13164-5

This Springer imprint is published by the registered company Springer Nature Switzerland AG
The registered company address is: Gewerbestrasse 11, 6330 Cham, Switzerland

If disposing of this product, please recycle the paper.

Foreword

The HCI International (HCII) conference was founded in 1984 by Gavriel Salvendy (Purdue University, USA, Tsinghua University, P.R. China, and University of Central Florida, USA) and the first event of the series, "1st USA-Japan Conference on Human-Computer Interaction", was held in Honolulu, Hawaii, USA, on 18–20 August. Since then, HCI International has been held jointly with several Thematic Areas and Affiliated Conferences, with each one under the auspices of a distinguished international Program Board and under one management and one registration. Twenty-seven HCI International Conferences have been organized so far (every two years until 2013, and annually thereafter).

Last year, we celebrated 40 years since the establishment of the HCII conference, which has been a hub for presenting groundbreaking research and novel ideas and collaboration for people from all over the world. Over the years, this conference has served as a platform for scholars, researchers, industry experts, and students to exchange ideas, connect, and address challenges in the ever-evolving HCI field. The conference has evolved itself, adapting to new technologies and emerging trends, while staying committed to its core mission of advancing knowledge and driving change.

The 27th International Conference on Human-Computer Interaction, HCI International 2025 (HCII 2025), was held as an 'on-site' conference at the Gothia Towers Hotel and Swedish Exhibition & Congress Centre, in Gothenburg, Sweden, on June 22–27, 2025, with the additional option for 'on-line' participation. It incorporated the 21 thematic areas and affiliated conferences listed below.

A total of 7972 individuals from academia, research institutes, industry, and government agencies from 92 countries submitted contributions. 1430 papers and 355 posters (as short research papers) were included in the volumes of the proceedings published just before the start of the conference. Additionally, 439 papers and 104 posters were included in the volumes of the proceedings published after the conference, as "Late Breaking Work". The contributions thoroughly cover the entire field of human-computer interaction, highlight the evolving role of computers in diverse contexts, and demonstrate how HCI research is shaping and improving user experiences across a wide range of domains, influencing technological progress and its effective integration into various sectors. The volumes constituting the full set of the HCII 2025 conference proceedings are listed on the following pages.

I would like to thank the Program Board Chairs and the members of the Program Boards of all thematic areas and affiliated conferences for their contribution towards the high scientific quality and overall success of the HCI International 2025 conference. Their manifold support including paper reviews (via a single-blind review process, with a minimum of two reviews per submission), session organization, and their willingness to act as goodwill ambassadors for the conference is most highly appreciated.

This conference would not have been possible without the continuous and unwavering support and advice of Gavriel Salvendy, founder, General Chair Emeritus, and Scientific Advisor. For his outstanding efforts, I would like to express my sincere appreciation to Abbas Moallem, Communications Chair and Editor of HCI International News.

September 2025   Constantine Stephanidis

HCI International 2025 Thematic Areas and Affiliated Conferences

- HCI: Human-Computer Interaction Thematic Area
- HIMI: Human Interface and the Management of Information Thematic Area
- EPCE: 22nd International Conference on Engineering Psychology and Cognitive Ergonomics
- AC: 19th International Conference on Augmented Cognition
- UAHCI: 19th International Conference on Universal Access in Human-Computer Interaction
- CCD: 17th International Conference on Cross-Cultural Design
- SCSM: 17th International Conference on Social Computing and Social Media
- VAMR: 17th International Conference on Virtual, Augmented and Mixed Reality
- DHM: 16th International Conference on Digital Human Modeling & Applications in Health, Safety, Ergonomics & Risk Management
- DUXU: 14th International Conference on Design, User Experience and Usability
- C&C: 13th International Conference on Culture and Computing
- DAPI: 13th International Conference on Distributed, Ambient and Pervasive Interactions
- HCIBGO: 12th International Conference on HCI in Business, Government and Organizations
- LCT: 12th International Conference on Learning and Collaboration Technologies
- ITAP: 11th International Conference on Human Aspects of IT for the Aged Population
- AIS: 7th International Conference on Adaptive Instructional Systems
- HCI-CPT: 7th International Conference on HCI for Cybersecurity, Privacy and Trust
- HCI-Games: 7th International Conference on HCI in Games
- MobiTAS: 7th International Conference on HCI in Mobility, Transport and Automotive Systems
- AI-HCI: 6th International Conference on Artificial Intelligence in HCI
- MOBILE: 6th International Conference on Human-Centered Design, Operation and Evaluation of Mobile Communications

Conference Proceedings – Full List of Volumes

1. LNCS 15766, Human-Computer Interaction — Part I, edited by Masaaki Kurosu and Ayako Hashizume
2. LNCS 15767, Human-Computer Interaction — Part II, edited by Masaaki Kurosu and Ayako Hashizume
3. LNCS 15768, Human-Computer Interaction — Part III, edited by Masaaki Kurosu and Ayako Hashizume
4. LNCS 15769, Human-Computer Interaction — Part IV, edited by Masaaki Kurosu and Ayako Hashizume
5. LNCS 15770, Human-Computer Interaction — Part V, edited by Masaaki Kurosu and Ayako Hashizume
6. LNCS 15771, Human-Computer Interaction — Part VI, edited by Masaaki Kurosu and Ayako Hashizume
7. LNCS 15772, Human-Computer Interaction — Part VII, edited by Masaaki Kurosu and Ayako Hashizume
8. LNCS 15773, Human Interface and the Management of Information: Part I, edited by Hirohiko Mori and Yumi Asahi
9. LNCS 15774, Human Interface and the Management of Information: Part II, edited by Hirohiko Mori and Yumi Asahi
10. LNCS 15773, Human Interface and the Management of Information: Part III, edited by Hirohiko Mori and Yumi Asahi
11. LNAI 15776, Engineering Psychology and Cognitive Ergonomics: Part I, edited by Don Harris and Wen-Chin Li
12. LNAI 15777, Engineering Psychology and Cognitive Ergonomics: Part II, edited by Don Harris and Wen-Chin Li
13. LNAI 15778, Augmented Cognition, Part I, edited by Dylan D. Schmorrow and Cali M. Fidopiastis
14. LNAI 15779, Augmented Cognition, Part II, edited by Dylan D. Schmorrow and Cali M. Fidopiastis
15. LNCS 15780, Universal Access in Human-Computer Interaction: Part I, edited by Margherita Antona and Constantine Stephanidis
16. LNCS 15781, Universal Access in Human-Computer Interaction: Part II, edited by Margherita Antona and Constantine Stephanidis
17. LNCS 15782, Cross-Cultural Design: Part I, edited by Pei-Luen Patrick Rau
18. LNCS 15783, Cross-Cultural Design: Part II, edited by Pei-Luen Patrick Rau
19. LNCS 15784, Cross-Cultural Design: Part III, edited by Pei-Luen Patrick Rau
20. LNCS 15785, Cross-Cultural Design: Part IV, edited by Pei-Luen Patrick Rau
21. LNCS 15786, Social Computing and Social Media: Part I, edited by Adela Coman and Simona Vasilache

85. CCIS 2772, HCI International 2025 — Late Breaking Posters: Part II, edited by Constantine Stephanidis, Margherita Antona, Stavroula Ntoa, George Margetis and Gavriel Salvendy
86. CCIS 2773, HCI International 2025 — Late Breaking Posters: Part III, edited by Constantine Stephanidis, Margherita Antona, Stavroula Ntoa, George Margetis and Gavriel Salvendy

https://2025.hci.international/proceedings

27th International Conference on Human-Computer Interaction (HCII 2025)

The full list with the Program Board Chairs and the members of the Program Boards of all thematic areas and affiliated conferences of HCII 2025 is available online at:

http://www.hci.international/board-members-2025.php

HCI International 2026 Conference

The 28th International Conference on Human-Computer Interaction, HCI International 2026, will be held jointly with the affiliated conferences at the Montréal Convention Centre (Palais des congrès de Montréal), in Montreal, Canada, 26–31 July 2026. It will cover a broad spectrum of themes related to Human-Computer Interaction, including theoretical issues, methods, tools, processes, and case studies in HCI design, as well as novel interaction techniques, interfaces, and applications. The proceedings will be published by Springer (part of Springer Nature) in a multi-volume set. More information will become available on the conference website: https://2026.hci.international/.

General Chair
Constantine Stephanidis
University of Crete and ICS-FORTH
Heraklion, Crete, Greece
Email: general_chair@2026.hci.international

https://2026.hci.international/

Contents

Technology-Driven Cultural Shifts: AI, Metaverse, and Digital Society

User Experience in Product and Service Design

Exploring the Influence of Social Capital on the Perception and Use of COVID-19 Apps in New York State: A Qualitative Secondary Analysis of Focus Group Data

Yvonne Appiah Dadson$^{(\boxtimes)}$ ⓘ, Prabin Sharma ⓘ, DeeDee Bennett-Gayle ⓘ, and Xiaojun Yuan ⓘ

University at Albany, State University of New York, New York 2222, NY, USA
{ydadson,psharma6,dmbennett,xyuan}@albany.edu

Abstract. The widespread adoption of COVID-19 contact tracing and vaccination applications was critical to pandemic response efforts, yet social determinants influencing public uptake remain inadequately understood. While extant literature has predominantly examined individual attitudes and technological characteristics, social capital's contribution to application adoption decisions has received insufficient scholarly attention. This investigation explores how distinct dimensions of social capital influenced COVID-19 application adoption among New York State residents. A qualitative secondary analysis utilized focus group data from 63 residents aged 18+ years. Employing social capital theory, transcripts were systematically coded examining bonding (family/intimate ties), bridging (community networks), and linking (institutional relationships) social capital. A notable paradox emerged whereby individuals receiving greatest social support concurrently encountered significant adoption obstacles. These findings challenge conventional health behavior paradigms emphasizing familial influence, demonstrating institutional credibility dominated COVID-19 application adoption. Public health strategies should prioritize institutional partnerships over individual-focused campaigns.

Keywords: Social capital · COVID-19 contact tracing apps · Vaccination apps · Digital health · Health behavior

1 Introduction

The COVID-19 pandemic presented unmatched challenges to global health, demanding revolutionary solutions to stop the virus's spread. Digital contact tracing and vaccination apps offered beneficial tools to support traditional public health interventions, supported by research [1–3]. These apps aimed to precisely recognize and promptly notify people of the potential exposure to the virus, which was speed up the through distribution of vaccines [4, 5]. The success of these interventions relied greatly on public adoption along with continued use, which proved challenging [6–9].

M. Schrepp and M. Rauterberg (Eds.): HCII 2025, LNCS 16342, pp. 3–21, 2026.
https://doi.org/10.1007/978-3-032-13164-5_1

Studies explored what affects how often people use contact tracing and vaccination apps. Research shows that uptake is influenced by individual factors such as perceived benefits and risks, [4, 10], trust in government and health authorities [11, 12] and privacy and security concerns [13, 14]. App design, functionality, interoperability and other key technical factors were also cited as key factors [15, 16]. Many scholars acknowledge that, besides individual attitudes and behaviors, many detailed social and contextual factors considerably affect how these apps were adopted and used [15, 17].

Social capital referred to as the resources and benefits enclosed within social networks and relationships [18–20] may affect the adoption of health technologies [21, 22]. Social capital, including trust, norms, social support, − collaboration, information sharing, and behavioral change [23, 24]. Digital health interventions may succeed or fail depending on social capital influencing people's understanding, opinions, and plans regarding contact tracing and vaccination apps and their use [25, 26].

However, existing studies on the effect of social capital on contact tracing and vaccination app adoption and usage are few and produce varying results. Most studies have concentrated on individual factors. These studies used strict quantitative surveys or precisely designed experiments. This approach might not fully catch the complex and fast-developing nature of social capital in many real-world contexts [4, 14]. Further research is necessary to grasp the effect of social capital on people's opinions, experiences and actions concerning these apps and how this effect connects to larger social, cultural, and political issues [15, 17]. This study examines the role of social capital in the adoption and use of several contact tracing apps, along with several vaccination apps, using focus group data, to address this gap. Focus groups offer a meaningful method for gaining detailed understandings into people's subjective experiences, opinions and social interactions; they also allow for exploration of several complex contextual factors influencing health behaviors [27]. This study uses social capital theory to analyze focus group discussions to:

1. Identify social capital dimensions critical to understanding contact tracing and vaccination app experiences.
2. Investigate how social capital dimensions' influence participants' app adoption attitudes, intentions, and behaviors.
3. Examine social capital related barriers and facilitators to app adoption and use

This study expands our understanding of social determinants of health technology adoption and the role of social capital in health decisions. It also offers important implications for public health policy, app design and community engagement by providing a detailed view of how social capital affects the adoption of contact tracing and vaccination apps. Also, the study advances digital health research by showing how qualitative focus groups can illuminate the complex and dynamic processes of social capital, and this improves both methodological and theoretical approaches.

2   Literature Review

2.1   Social Capital: Concepts and Dimensions

Social capital, a multidimensional concept [18–20] is a widely studied topic in sociology, political science, economics, and public health. While there is no single definition, social capital generally refers to the resources and benefits embedded in social networks and relationships, easily accessed for individual or collective action [28, 29]. Information, large influence, strong social support and shared standards and values which are some of these important resources, take many forms and considerably encourage cooperation, trust and reciprocity among people and groups [19, 20].

Scholars have studied social capital at the individual, community and social levels [30, 31]. Social capital, individually, refers to the benefits as well as resources people obtain through their personal social networks and relationships. These include bonding social capital (i.e., strong ties with similar others) along with bridging social capital (i.e., weak ties with diverse others) [19, 32]. Social capital at the community level consists of important social structures namely trust, norms and wide-ranging networks that facilitate effective collaboration for meaningful mutual benefit [19]. At the societal level, social capital refers to institutions, relationships and norms that deeply shape the quality and quantity of a society's social interactions [33].

Social capital is a multidimensional concept including structural, cognitive, and relational components [24, 34]. The structural dimension reveals the interactions and connections among individuals and groups. This includes the extent, density and diversity of social networks, as well as the presence of some formal and informal social institutions [18, 20]. Shared understandings, norms and values form the cognitive dimension; this common framework helps us interpret and navigate several social relationships such as trust, reciprocity, and social cohesion [19, 35]. The relational dimension describes the nature and strength of social ties and interactions, including social support, influence and identification, affecting motivation and capacity for collective action [24, 32].

These multiple linked dimensions of social capital mutually reinforce one another, operating within several diverse social contexts and at multiple analytical levels [33, 36]. In some social networks, the structure itself can make it easier to develop cognitive and relational dimensions, like trust and social support, by offering opportunities for repeated interactions and exchanges [20, 34]. Cognitive and relational factors affect the development and strength of social networks, influencing people's willingness and ability to participate in relationships and group activities [24, 34].

2.2   Social Capital and Health Behaviors

Research increasingly shows that social capital considerably effects many aspects of health behaviors, such as physical activity, diet, substance use, mental well-being and the management of chronic illnesses [23, 31, 37]. Studies indicate that individuals and communities with higher social capital tend to have better health outcomes due to the protective and promotive effects of social support, influence, and resource access [38, 39]. For instance, some studies indicate a positive correlation between social capital and physical activity, particularly in terms of social participation, support, and neighborhood social cohesion [40, 41]

While social capital at the community level (such as trust and social cohesiveness) had conflicting results, a comprehensive systematic review by Haughton McNeill et al. [42] found that social support and social networks were consistently linked to greater levels of physical activity among adults. Similarly, Chen et al. [43] meta-analysis study discovered that social capital, specifically, social support and participation was positively correlated with physical activity in older individuals, with the benefits being strongest for walking and leisure activities. Dietary practices and outcomes, including the consumption of fruits and vegetables, dietary diversity, and obesity, have also been associated with social capital [44, 45]. For example, a study by Dean et al. [46] discovered that among African American adults in rural communities, higher levels of community social capital as indicated by social cohesion and neighborhood attachment were linked to increased consumption of fruits and vegetables. In a different study, Poortinga [45] discovered that among adults in England, social capital at the individual level as determined by civic engagement, social support, and trust was negatively connected with obesity and positively connected with healthy eating habits.

Studies indicate that individuals and communities with higher social capital tend to have better health outcomes due to the protective and promotive effects of social support, influence, and resource access. Depending on its features and circumstances, social capital has been demonstrated to have both protective and risk-enhancing effects in relation to substance use [47, 48]. Weitzman and Chen [47], for instance, discovered that among American college students, lower rates of binge drinking were linked to higher levels of social capital as indicated by volunteerism, community trust, and informal social control. The study did discover, however, that some types of social capital, like belonging to a fraternity or sorority and hanging out with friends, were linked to increased rates of binge drinking. This suggests that the health effects of social capital might vary depending on the customs and behaviors of one's social networks.

An essential factor in determining mental health and well-being is social capital, especially when it comes to social integration, support, and a sense of belonging [31, 49]. According to a systematic review by De Silva et al. [50], there was a consistent correlation between improved mental health outcomes, like lower levels of anxiety and depression, and individual-level cognitive social capital (like trust and a sense of belonging) and structural social capital (like social networks and social participation). Social capital, especially in the form of social support and social cohesion, was found to be positively associated with mental well-being among older adults in another systematic review by Ehsan and De Silva [49]. The effects were stronger for the relational and cognitive aspects of social capital.

Lastly, it has been discovered that social capital is important for managing chronic diseases and self-care practices such taking medications as prescribed, keeping track of oneself, and using healthcare services [51, 52]. For instance, a study conducted by Kanamori et al. [52] discovered that among African American individuals with type 2 diabetes, improved glycemic control and self-care practices were linked to greater levels of social capital, as indicated by social support and neighborhood social cohesion.

In addition to highlighting the need for additional research that considers the dimensions, levels, and mechanisms of social capital in various health contexts, these studies also demonstrate the complex and context-dependent ways in which social capital can influence health behaviors and outcomes. According to these studies, social capital can influence one's health in both positive and negative ways, depending on the norms, beliefs, and behaviors of one's communities and social networks [29, 53]. Since social capital has varying effects on different social groups and situations, initiatives that seek to use it to promote health should take these factors into account [36, 54].

2.3 Social Capital and Health Technology Adoption

As digital health interventions grow more common and significant, the significance of social capital in the adoption and use of health technology has drawn more attention in recent years [55, 56]. Wearable technology, telemedicine platforms, and mobile health apps are examples of health technologies that can enhance access to care, encourage healthy habits, and assist self-management [57, 58]. However, a number of technological, social, and individual barriers, including low health literacy, privacy concerns, and usability issues, frequently limit the effectiveness and uptake of these technologies [59–61]. Through influencing people's attitudes, intentions, and behaviors about these innovations, social capital has been found to be a significant component that can either help or impede the adoption and usage of health technology [62, 63].

Existing research has indicated that social capital, specifically in the form of social support and influence, can raise people's perceptions of the utility and usability of health technologies as well as their awareness, interest, and trust in them [64, 65] A study by Chowdhury et al. [62], for instance, discovered that social influence and support were important indicators of telemedicine service acceptance in Indian rural communities.

Social capital can also act as a barrier to the adoption and use of health technologies, particularly when one's social networks have competing expectations, beliefs, or norms [66, 67]. Huygens et al. [66] discovered that the attitudes and actions of family members and healthcare professionals affected older adults' use of self-management apps, potentially promoting or discouraging their use of technology. The social acceptability and stigma of using a mental health app were also identified by Yardley et al. [67] as significant concerns for youth, underscoring the significance of considering the larger social and cultural environment in which health technologies are used.

The study proposed that societal norms and attitudes that can prevent the adoption of mental health apps, like the stigma attached to getting care for mental health issues, should be addressed by initiatives that try to encourage their adoption. The complexity and dynamic nature of social capital's effects on the use and adoption of health technologies are illustrated by these studies, underscoring the need for additional research that considers the specific dimensions, mechanisms, and settings of social capital in the context of digital health. To guarantee the relevance, acceptability, and sustainability of digital health interventions, these studies also emphasize the significance of including communities and social networks in their design, implementation, and evaluation [55].

2.4 Contact Tracing and Vaccination Apps

Contact tracing apps, which use Bluetooth or GPS to alert exposed individuals, and vaccination apps, which use QR codes or digital certificates to verify and record vaccination status, are emerging as promising tools to control the spread of COVID-19 and facilitate the rollout of vaccines [68, 69]. These apps speed up case identification and make monitoring and vaccination distribution easier, which complements conventional public health measures [1–3]. However, persistent engagement, interoperability with health systems, and public penetration are critical factors that affect the efficacy of apps [70, 71].

A number of technological, personal, and societal obstacles have made it challenging to achieve adequate adoption [4]. The most important of them are privacy and security issues around the gathering and use of personal data, which call for strong governance, user control, and data minimization [13, 69, 72]. Two important factors influencing app adoption are perceived benefits and trust. People are more inclined to utilize apps if they think the technology benefits them and their communities and they have faith in the organizations that are sponsoring them [12, 26, 73]. However, in many situations, adoption has been hampered by pre-existing suspicion of the government and health institutions, as well as contradicting and false information [74].

Contact tracing and vaccination app adoption are shaped by intricate social and structural elements in addition to these individual factors. How technologies are viewed and utilized is influenced by social norms, cultural values, beliefs, and behaviors [15, 75]. Limited digital access and abilities, coupled with past experiences of exclusion and discrimination that engender mistrust, are additional obstacles that marginalized groups frequently encounter [14, 17]. Additionally, app deployment has been politicized in many countries due to political division and conflicting narratives surrounding public health policies [76, 77].

In the United States, where apps were voluntarily released and mostly at the state level, partisan differences probably contributed to the disparate adoption of these apps [60, 78]. Given these socio-technical complexities, qualitative and context-specific research is required to explore the ways in which individual attitudes and behaviors interact with social and structural elements to influence the adoption of apps in real-world contexts [15, 17]. Social capital theory provides a useful framework for this investigation, clarifying how social network-based resources and limitations can either help or impede app adoption and long-term use.

2.5 Social Capital Theory

The study is guided by the social capital theory, which offers a strong theoretical framework for investigating the ways in which social networks, connections, and resources impact the adoption and use of contact tracing and vaccination apps throughout the COVID-19 pandemic. Although the concept of social capital and its connection to health behaviors and technology adoption were introduced in the preceding sections, this section goes into greater detail about the specific propositions and insights of social capital theory that guide the study's focus group data analysis and interpretation. Bridging the gap between micro and macro levels of study, social capital theory links individual experiences and behaviors to more extensive societal structures and processes, which is one of its main advantages [36, 79]. The adoption and use of health technologies, like contact tracing and vaccination apps, are shaped by a complex interplay of factors that include individual attitudes and beliefs, interpersonal relationships and networks, community norms and resources, and societal institutions and policies. This multi-level perspective is especially helpful in understanding these effects [21, 80].

The social capital theory provides several important insights and assertions that help direct the examination of how social factors influence the uptake of vaccination apps and contact tracing during the COVID-19 epidemic. Above all, the theory posits that the degree of trust, reciprocity, and shared norms inside people's social networks will impact their willingness and capacity to use these apps [20, 39]. Individuals may be more inclined to view the apps as valid and helpful resources for preserving community health in areas with high levels of trust and a strong feeling of shared responsibility. In contrast, people might be more reluctant or resistant to using applications in situations where there is mistrust or contradicting norms [21, 73].

Social capital theory emphasizes how social influence and information flows shape attitudes and behaviors around health technologies [81, 82]. While those in isolated or fragmented networks might have less access to pertinent information and assistance, people who are a part of dense, cohesive networks might be more likely to be exposed to encouraging messages and role models for app adoption [83]. The theory also posits that, based on their attitudes and actions, opinion leaders and other powerful figures in social networks can either encourage or discourage the use of apps [84, 85].

According to Bourdieu [18] and Lin [79], social capital theory emphasizes how social networks and resources are unevenly dispersed throughout social groups and situations. This insight is especially important for comprehending how current social disparities and inequalities, such as those pertaining to race, ethnicity, socioeconomic status, and digital access, may influence the adoption and use of contact tracing and vaccination apps [12, 21]. Disadvantaged communities may struggle more to adopt apps because they often lack the necessary social support and resources, as suggested by Gilbert et al. [86] and Warschauer [87]. Social capital theory points out the fast-developing nature of social capital. Its effects and forms differ across groups, time and place, depending on the context [53, 88]. This perspective points out the meaningful need to explore how social capital might differentially affect app adoption. Considering local conventions, cultural values and past experiences, this exploration should include multiple communities and social groups [63, 89].

Furthermore, the pandemic's effect on social networks and their resources, their mobilization, the stress they underwent and their evolving responses to the crisis, reveals a concomitant, fluid transformation in social capital's influence on app usage [90]. Highly effective contact tracing apps, along with thorough vaccination apps, can greatly influence social capital as well as community resilience.

3   Methodology

This study revisited 2021 focus group data from a mixed-methods investigation of COVID-19 mobile app adoption and public perception in New York State, undertaking a secondary qualitative analysis. Focus groups gather diverse perspectives on the subjective experiences, opinions and social interactions of many people, thus illuminating the complex contextual influences on health behaviors [27, 91]. From a social capital perspective, several social resources, including trust, standards and support, influence attitudes and behaviors toward contact tracing and vaccination apps. Sixty-three New York residents aged 18 and older participated in the original study. Participants were selected using readily available convenience sampling methods. This yielded an important diverse sample. Participants were stratified by age, race/ethnicity and socioeconomic status to guarantee a diverse representation of viewpoints and promote all-embracing engagement. Sixteen focus groups, each comprising between six and eight participants, were conducted using Zoom to investigate experiences with the pandemic, opinions on and use of digital health technologies and the social and contextual factors influencing health behaviors.

Using a codebook created especially for this study, two coders independently coded the focus group transcripts for this secondary analysis. The primary themes in the codebook are social capital bonding, bridging, and linking social capital dimensions, social capital barriers, and social capital facilitators, to allow for a more thorough examination of the data, each major subject is further broken down into subcategories. The two coders systematically analyzed the data, precisely reviewing focus group transcripts and applying the appropriate codes from the codebook to precisely targeted sections of text. This allows for a far more thorough examination of diverse aspects and multiple levels of social capital.

4 Results

With an emphasis on the Excelsior Pass, the focus group discussions revealed several key themes about how different dimensions and expressions of social capital affected participants' participants' perceptions, intentions and behaviors regarding COVID-19 contact tracing and vaccination apps during the pandemic in New York State. Drawing from the systematic coding of the transcripts using NVivo, the findings are structured regarding three dimensions of social capital namely bonding, bridging and linking social capital followed by social capital facilitators and barriers. The concise notation: *[Pseudonym, Age Range, Gender, Race] is used to display the participant quotes. Anonymity is preserved while context is provided by following italicized quotes with bracketed demographic information.

The results section includes a breakdown of responses by type of social capital. As shown in Fig. 1, the majority of the participants mentioned comments that were coded as linking social capital (nearly 50%). The least popular form of social capital was bonding social capital (slightly over 10%).

4.1 Bonding Social Capital:The Complex Role of Close Relationships

Participants' perception and use of the COVID-19 app were significantly influenced by their personal friendships and close family ties. The networks of close friends and family members of the participants, which represent bonding social capital, had complicated and occasionally conflicting effects on their opinions of the apps. The percentage of

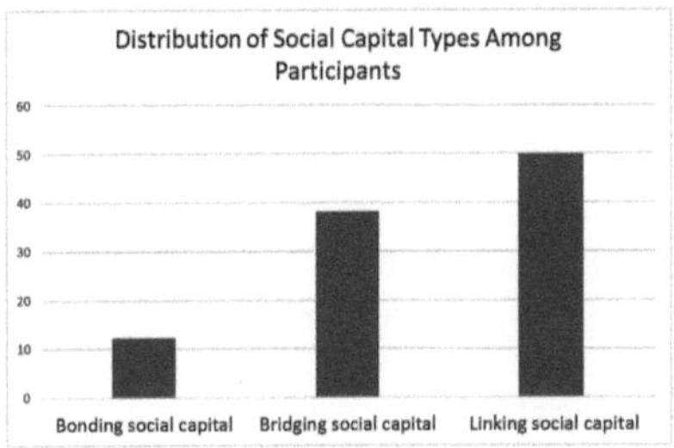

Fig. 1. Distribution of coded responses by social capital type.

responses coded as bonding social capital. As noted in Fig. 1, this was the least coded type of social capital, only 20 interview participants mentioned friends or personal ties that acted as a facilitator or barrier in their perception and use of the COVID-19 apps.

There was an interesting demographic pattern among participants who mentioned bonding social capital: the vast majority were middle-aged adults between 18–24 years of age. There were no such obvious characteristics among those who did not mention bonding social capital (Fig. 2).

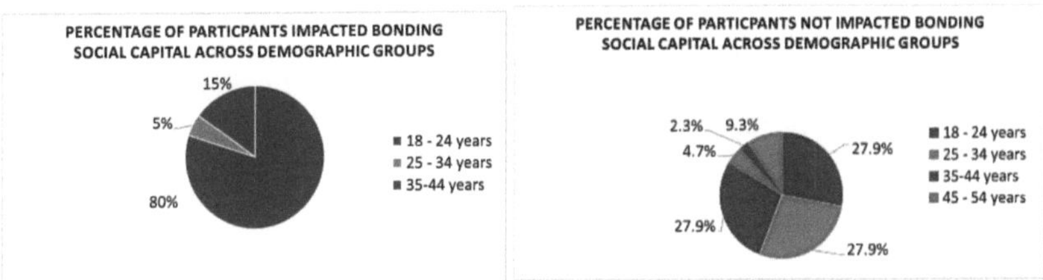

Fig. 2. a) pie chart on the left shows the percentage of coded responses that mentioned bonding social capital by age group. b) pie chart on the right shows the percentage of participants whose responses were not coded as bonding social capital.

While strong relationships often facilitaed app use, they sometimes created resistance, highlighting the double-edged nature of tight social bonds. Participants mentioned the potential for mobile apps in general to facilitate bonding social capital (such as Life360) and for COVID-19 specific apps. Below are a couple of quotes in italics with anonimyzed participant information in brackets.

I have a grandma of my own who she doesn't go out but she she's in a critical health and so if I knew about contact tracing, I bet I would have at times protected her were better if I used it [Rita, 18–24 years old, Non-Binary, Hispanic]

I only heard about it because I had dinner at Christmas with my family. A family member had it. My father-in-law who was much older than me, and probably less tech savvy than me, but I had no idea it exists [Kenya, 18-24 years old, Female, White]

Family Influence and Support: Trust and Expectations. Many participants disclosed how their close friends and family helped them download and use the apps. To other participants, these apps represented a crucial tool to safeguard their loved ones. Similarly, others believed that using the app would help prevent her family from contracting COVID-19. Additionally, other participants considered using the apps a small sacrifice for the peace of mind of keeping their vulnerable family members healthy.

> *My mom has this [Excelsior Pass]. She actually told me to download it when she first got it because she's always had her vaccine card on her phone. And it's just been way helpful. [Tiana,18 to 24 years old, Unassigned, Other]*

> *One of my friends told me about it, and I was like that's so convenient because I was always worried about losing my vaccine card, so I just downloaded and didn't think twice" [Farrah 18 to 24 years old, Female, White]*

Family-Based Resistance. The same tightknit ties also revealed the potential for conflicting beliefs within immediate networks to hinder app acceptance. The potential for bonding social capital to operate as a double-edged sword was made clear by this glaring difference of opinion that festered among even the closest of ties. In some families, it motivated a common goal to embrace interventions, while in others, it created barriers of resistance.

> *I never really went out and then neither did my family, so I kind of just turn it off because I knew it wasn't going anywhere [Elliot 18 to 24 years old, Male, White]*

> *I didn't, really know anyone else who did it so it's like I feel like I wouldn't even like help me, because no one I know has it. [Gretchen, 18 to 24 years, Female, White]*

4.2 Bridging Social Capital: Information Flow and Community Networks

Bridging social capital, in the form of weaker ties across participants' communities and social groups, played a notable role in spreading awareness and information about the contact tracing and vaccination apps. There were considerably more responses coded as bridging social capital. Only sixteen participants did not mention anything related to their communities or social groups.

There were considerable age-related differences between the people who reported bridging social capital and those who did not. Approximately 57% of participants aged 18–24 mentioned how bridging social capital affected their decision to use the apps. Almost half of the people who did not mention bridging social capital were 35–44 years of age (47.4%), see Fig. 3b.

Institutional Connections and Information Diffusion. Participants' affiliations with educational institutions like universities facilitated app use. Also, weak ties provided participants with valuable information and resources they may not have encountered in their immediate circles. The effectiveness of institutional outreach efforts via bridging ties was not always consistent.

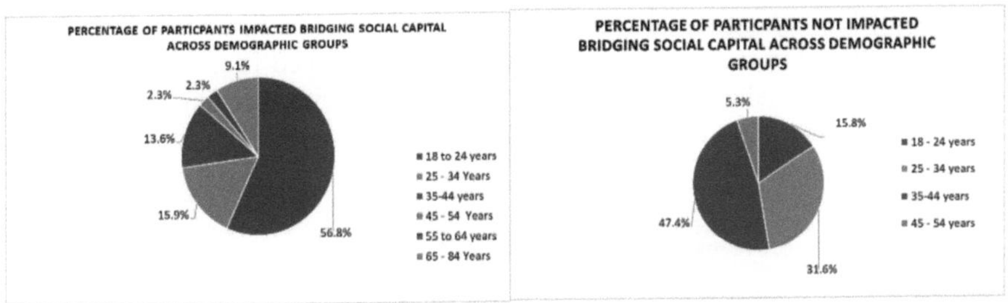

Fig. 3. a) pie chart on the left shows the percentage of coded responses that mentioned bridging social capital by age group. b) pie chart on the right shows the percentage of participants whose responses were not coded as bridging social capital.

The university at Albany sent out a big email everyone basically promoting this app telling everyone to get it [Dennis, 18 to 24 years old, Male, White]

The first time I use my Excelsior pass was actually for an event at the Albany Public Library, there was a gala, and at the check in, they scanned my pass. [Kenya, 18 to 24 years old, Female, White]

However, the lack of broad awareness emerged as a significant issue:

I'm surprised with how many people don't have it. My husband doesn't have it... I was expecting more venues and restaurants and just places to require it. Like I was all excited to get to use it. [Kenya, 18 to 24 years old, Female, White]

4.2.1 Community Awareness and Social Norms

The spread of information and establishment of norms through community networks significantly influenced app adoption. Some participants described how knowledge and use patterns differed across communities:

In New York, I was in the Bronx, and I went to school, I was in school in downtown Manhattan. For my area where I live, they didn't really have too many or like advertise too many contact tracing apps or things. [Angela, 18 to 24 years old, Nonbinary, Black or African American]

Honestly, I didn't hear what contact tracing apps before, like summer of last year, when I got a job with NYC. So, before that, I've never, I've never heard about them or saw them anywhere. [Charlie, 18 to 24 years old, Male, Black or African American]

4.3 Linking Social Capital: Government Trust and Institutional Relationships

Linking social capital, reflecting participants' relationships with government and health institutions, emerged as a critical factor shaping perceptions of COVID-19 apps. Trust in these institutions played a key role in willingness to adopt the apps. Twenty respondents did not mention anything related to linking social capital. Age-related trends were also identified in linking social capital. Respondents who placed importance on being impacted by bridging social capital were primarily (57%) aged 18–24 (Fig. 4a). On the other hand, almost half of the respondents who did not mention any bridging social capital fall into the 35–44 age range (Fig. 4b).

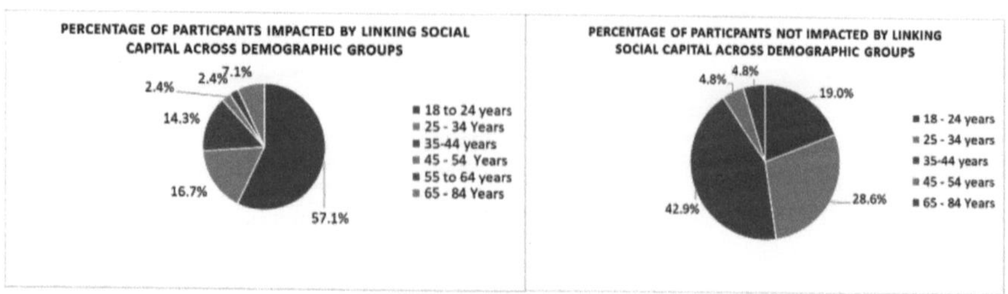

Fig. 4. a) pie chart on the left shows the percentage of coded responses that mentioned linking social capital by age group. b) pie chart on the right shows the percentage of participants whose responses were not coded as linking social capital.

Government and Policy Ties. Participants' trust in government institutions played a crucial role in their willingness to adopt the apps. This trust often stemmed from a belief in the competence and effectiveness of government institutions in handling the pandemic. Participants also revealed how official mandates and support from trusted institutions facilitated app adoption.

> *I wouldn't distrust them more than I would many other applications, especially with at least the COVID Alert New York app. It's run partially by the New York State Department of Health, which is a trustworthy organization. [Evan, 18 to 24 years old, Male, White]*

> *I feel that the New York State government has really done their due diligence in terms of getting the information out there, making sure that people are aware of what's going on, and also providing the necessary resources.[Nancy,65-84 years old, Female, Black or African American]*

4.4 Social Capital Facilitators and Barriers: Influence, Collective Care, Transparency

As noted in the previous sections, while many participants mentioned bridging, linking or bonding social capital, there were differences in context. Some mentioned social capital as a facilitator for their use of COVID-19 related apps. While others mentioned it as a barrier. Figure 5 shows the percentage of participants whose responses reflected a position that their social capital influenced their use as facilitator (5a) or barrier (5b).

More participants in the 18–24-year-old group (~65%) felt that social capital was more of a facilitator than a barrier, same for the 65–84-year-old group (11%). This trend was reverse for participants in the 25–34-year-old and 35–44-year-old groups, where more participants in these ages felt social capital was a barrier rather than a facilitator.

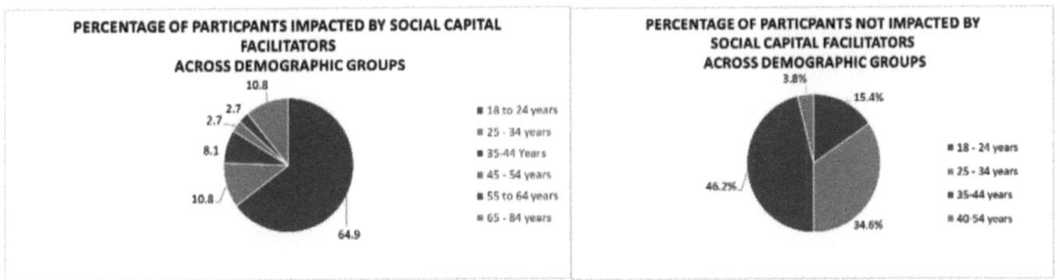

Fig. 5. a) pie chart on the left shows the percentage of coded responses that mentioned social capital as a facilitator by age group. b) pie chart on the right shows the percentage of participants that mentioned social capital as a barrier.

There was an imperceptible difference between social capital as a facilitator or barrier for the 45–54 groups, with less responses coded.

5 Discussion

In this qualitative study of 64 participants who discussed the use of COVID-19 related apps, three types of social capital were found among the themes coded, bonding, bridging and linking social capital. Linking social capital was coded the most among participants, indicating a strong influence on the participants relationships with the government and health institutions were an important factor influencing their perception of COVID-19 related apps. This aligns with previous research, indicating a strong relationship between political party affiliation and perception of COVID-19 apps [73]. Also, given that these apps were developed by government agencies, government perception may be a bigger influence than if they were developed by private third parties. Policy makers, and health-related app developers should consider the leverage the organization developing the app will have in potentially swaying public perception of the app.

Interestingly, bonding social capital had a limited influence on the participants perception of the COVID-19 apps. The sense of belonging with family and friends and the impact they have on the use of COVID-19 apps. Among participants, this type of social capital strongly shaped the perception of 18–24-year-old group.

While coding analysis indicates that these three different types of social capital influenced how the participants perceived the COVID-19 vaccination and contact tracing apps, the content of the response coded reveal their attitude, intention and behaviors. Many participants reflected on their non-use impacting family members, or how the proactive use by family and loved ones prompted their own use. Connections through school, work or for recreation influenced a number of participants to use at least one of the COVID-19 apps. Public perception on the government-led roll out of the apps also influenced behaviors.

The more interesting finding was when context of the responses coded social capital as a facilitator or barrier. Aligned with previous research on social capital and COVID-19 apps, demographics may influence the adoption of this technology as networks, resources, and other disparities are unevenly dispersed [21, 27, 30, 90]. In this study, differences in age range were more pronounced. Linking social capital emerged as the predominant adoption influence (49.8%), followed by bridging (38.1%) and bonding (12.1%) social capital. Age-stratified analysis revealed young adults (18–24 years) were most susceptible to institutional influence (57%) while experiencing highest social encouragement (65%) and barriers (56%). Middle-aged participants (35–44 years) demonstrated concentrated family influence (80%).

6   Conclusion

This study explores how social capital shapes people's perceptions and adoption of COVID-19 contact tracing and vaccination apps. By looking beyond individual attitudes and technological features, the findings show how trust in institutions, community networks, and family ties all play a role in health technology decisions. Notably, linking social capital — the connections people have with institutions — emerged as the strongest influence on adoption, particularly among young adults. At the same time, the study discovers a surprising pattern, that is, individuals with the greatest social support also encountered major barriers to adoption. It kind of shows the complexity and importance of these findings.

Acknowledgments. This study was supported by the University at Albany, SUNY President's COVID-19, and Minority Health Disparities Seed Funding Program of UAlbany. Gratitude is also extended to all reviewers for their constructive comments.

References

1. Abueg, M., et al.: Modeling the effect of exposure notification and non-pharmaceutical interventions on COVID-19 transmission in Washington state. npj Digit. Med. **4**(1), 49 (2021). https://doi.org/10.1038/s41746-021-00422-7

2. Anglemyer, A., et al.: Digital contact tracing technologies in epidemics: a rapid review. Cochrane Database Syst. Rev. **2020**(8) (2020). https://doi.org/10.1002/14651858.CD013699

3. Shahroz, M., et al.: COVID-19 digital contact tracing applications and techniques: a review post initial deployments. Trans. Eng. **5**, 100072 (2021). https://doi.org/10.1016/j.treng.2021.100072

4. Altmann, S., et al.: Acceptability of app-based contact tracing for COVID-19: cross-country survey study. JMIR Mhealth Uhealth. **8**(8), e19857 (2020). https://doi.org/10.2196/19857

5. Osmanlliu, E., Rafie, E., Bédard, S., Paquette, J., Gore, G., Pomey, M.-P.: Considerations for the design and implementation of COVID-19 contact tracing apps: scoping review. JMIR Mhealth Uhealth. **9**(6), e27102 (2021). https://doi.org/10.2196/27102

6. Cho, H., Ippolito, D., Yu, Y.W.: Contact tracing Mobile apps for COVID-19: privacy considerations and related trade-offs. ar Xiv. (2020). https://doi.org/10.48550/ARXIV.2003.11511

7. Jonker, M., De Bekker-Grob, E., Veldwijk, J., Goossens, L., Bour, S., Rutten-Van Mölken, M.: COVID-19 contact tracing apps: predicted uptake in the Netherlands based on a discrete choice experiment. JMIR Mhealth Uhealth. **8**(10), e20741 (2020). https://doi.org/10.2196/20741

8. Munzert, S., Selb, P., Gohdes, A., Stoetzer, L.F., Lowe, W.: Tracking and promoting the usage of a COVID-19 contact tracing app. Nat. Hum. Behav. **5**(2), 247–255 (2021). https://doi.org/10.1038/s41562-020-01044-x

9. Pandit, J.A., Radin, J.M., Quer, G., Topol, E.J.: Smartphone apps in the COVID-19 pandemic. Nat. Biotechnol. **40**(7), 1013–1022 (2022). https://doi.org/10.1038/s41587-022-01350-x

10. Caserotti, M., Girardi, P., Rubaltelli, E., Tasso, A., Lotto, L., Gavaruzzi, T.: Associations of COVID-19 risk perception with vaccine hesitancy over time for Italian residents. Soc. Sci. Med. **272**, 113688 (2021). https://doi.org/10.1016/j.socscimed.2021.113688

11. Abate, B.B., Tilahun, B.D., Yayeh, B.M.: Global COVID-19 vaccine acceptance level and its determinants: an umbrella review. BMC Public Health. **24**(1), 5 (2024). https://doi.org/10.1186/s12889-023-17497-4

12. Walrave, M., Waeterloos, C., Ponnet, K.: Adoption of a contact tracing app for containing COVID-19: a health belief model approach. JMIR Public Health Surveill. **6**(3), e20572 (2020). https://doi.org/10.2196/20572

13. Horvath, L., Banducci, S., James, O.: Citizens' attitudes to contact tracing apps. J Exp Polit Sci. **9**(1), 118–130 (2022). https://doi.org/10.1017/XPS.2020.30

14. Sharma, S., Singh, G., Sharma, R., Jones, P., Kraus, S., Dwivedi, Y.K.: Digital health innovation: exploring adoption of COVID-19 digital contact tracing apps. IEEE Trans. Eng. Manag. **71**, 12272–12288 (2024). https://doi.org/10.1109/TEM.2020.3019033

15. Amann, J., Sleigh, J., Vayena, E.: Digital contact-tracing during the Covid-19 pandemic: an analysis of newspaper coverage in Germany, Austria, and Switzerland. PLoS One. **16**(2), e0246524 (2021). https://doi.org/10.1371/journal.pone.0246524

16. Hoffman, A.S., Jacobs, B., Van Gastel, B., Schraffenberger, H., Sharon, T., Pas, B.: Towards a seamful ethics of Covid-19 contact tracing apps? Ethics Inf. Technol. **23**(S1), 105–115 (2021). https://doi.org/10.1007/s10676-020-09559-7

17. Rowe, F., Ngwenyama, O., Richet, J.-L.: Contact-tracing apps and alienation in the age of COVID-19. Eur. J. Inf. Syst. **29**(5), 545–562 (2020). https://doi.org/10.1080/0960085X.2020.1803155

18. Bourdieu, P.: The forms of capital. In: Handbook of Theory and Research for the Sociology of Education (1986)

19. Putnam, R.D.: Bowling alone: America's declining social capital: originally published in journal of democracy 6 (1), 1995. In: Crothers, L., Lockhart, C. (eds.) Culture and Politics, pp. 223–234. Palgrave Macmillan US, New York (2000). https://doi.org/10.1007/978-1-349-62965-7_12

20. Coleman, J.S.: Social Capital in the Creation of human capital. Am. J. Sociol. **94**(1), S95–S120 (1988) Accessed: Jun. 09, 2025. [Online]. Available: http: //www.jstor.org/stable/2780243

21. Hargittai, E., Redmiles, E.M.: Will Americans Be Willing to Install COVID-19 Tracking Apps? (2020). https://doi.org/10.5167/UZH-192829

22. Nunes, A., Limpo, T., Castro, S.L.: Acceptance of Mobile health applications: examining key determinants and moderators. Front. Psychol. **10**, 2791 (2019). https://doi.org/10.3389/fpsyg.2019.02791

23. Berkman, L.F., Glass, T., Brissette, I., Seeman, T.E.: From social integration to health: Durkheim in the new millennium. Soc. Sci. Med. **51**(6), 843–857 (2000). https://doi.org/10.1016/S0277-9536(00)00065-4

24. Nahapiet, J., Ghoshal, S.: Social capital, intellectual capital, and the organizational advantage. Acad. Manag. Rev. **23**(2), 242 (1998). https://doi.org/10.2307/259373

25. Bradshaw, E.L., et al.: Information safety assurances increase intentions to use COVID-19 contact tracing applications, regardless of autonomy-supportive or controlling message framing. Front. Psychol. **11**, 591638 (2021). https://doi.org/10.3389/fpsyg.2020.591638

26. Kostka, G., Habich-Sobiegalla, S.: In times of crisis: public perceptions towards COVID-19 contact tracing apps in China, Germany and the US. SSRN J. (2020). https://doi.org/10.2139/ssrn.3693783

27. Kitzinger, J.: Qualitative research: introducing focus groups. BMJ. **311**(7000), 299–302 (1995). https://doi.org/10.1136/bmj.311.7000.299
28. N. Lin, "Building a Network Theory of Social Capital'. (1999). [Online]. Available: https://faculty.washington.edu/matsueda/courses/590/Readings/Lin%20Network%20Theory%201999.pdf
29. Portes, A.: Social capital: its origins and applications in modern sociology. Annu. Rev. Sociol. **24**(1), 1–24 (1998). https://doi.org/10.1146/annurev.soc.24.1.1
30. Baum, F.E., Ziersch, A.: Social capital. J. Epidemiol. Community Health. **57**(5), 320–323 (2003). https://doi.org/10.1136/jech.57.5.320
31. Kawachi, I., Berkman, L.: Social ties and mental health. J. Urban Health: Bull. N. Y. Acad. Med. **78**(3), 458–467 (2001). https://doi.org/10.1093/jurban/78.3.458
32. Szreter, S., Woolcock, M.: Health by association? Social capital, social theory, and the political economy of public health. Int. J. Epidemiol. **33**(4), 650–667 (2004). https://doi.org/10.1093/ije/dyh013
33. Grootaert, C., Van Bastelar, T.: Understanding and measuring social capital: a multidisciplinary tool for practitioners. In: Directions in Development. World Bank, Washington, DC (2013)
34. Uphoff, N.: Understanding Social Capital: Learning from the Analysis and Experience of Participation. (2005). [Online]. Available: https://api.semanticscholar.org/CorpusID:151208453
35. Fukuyama, F. (ed.): Trust: the social virtues and the CREATION of prosperity. Int. J. World Peace. **14**(1), 84–87 (1997) Accessed: Jun. 09, 2025. [Online]. Available: http://www.jstor.org/stable/20752121
36. Halpern, D.: Social capital. Polity, Cambridge, UK ; Malden, MA (2005)
37. Villalonga-Olives, E., Kawachi, I.: The measurement of social capital. Gac. Sanit. **29**(1), 62–64 (2015). https://doi.org/10.1016/j.gaceta.2014.09.006
38. Abbott, S., Freeth, D.: Social capital and health: starting to make sense of the role of generalized trust and reciprocity. J. Health Psychol. **13**(7), 874–883 (2008). https://doi.org/10.1177/1359105308095060
39. Burt, R.S.: The network structure of social capital. Res. Organ. Behav. **22**, 345–423 (2000). https://doi.org/10.1016/S0191-3085(00)22009-1
40. Ball, K., Cleland, V.J., Timperio, A.F., Salmon, J., Giles-Corti, B., Crawford, D.A.: Love thy neighbour? Associations of social capital and crime with physical activity amongst women. Soc. Sci. Med. **71**(4), 807–814 (2010). https://doi.org/10.1016/j.socscimed.2010.04.041
41. Carlson, J.A., et al.: Interactions between psychosocial and built environment factors in explaining older adults' physical activity. Prev. Med. **54**(1), 68–73 (2012). https://doi.org/10.1016/j.ypmed.2011.10.004
42. Haughton McNeill, L., Wyrwich, K.W., Brownson, R.C., Clark, E.M., Kreuter, M.W.: Individual, social environmental, and physical environmental influences on physical activity among black and white adults: a structural equation analysis. Ann. Behav. Med. **31**(1), 36–44 (2006). https://doi.org/10.1207/s15324796abm3101_7
43. Chen, T., Dai, M., Xia, S.: Perceived facilitators and barriers to intentions of receiving the COVID-19 vaccines among elderly Chinese adults. Vaccine. **40**(1), 100–106 (2022). https://doi.org/10.1016/j.vaccine.2021.11.039
44. Allen, J.D., et al.: Pathways between acculturation and health behaviors among residents of low-income housing: the mediating role of social and contextual factors. Soc. Sci. Med. **123**, 26–36 (2014). https://doi.org/10.1016/j.socscimed.2014.10.034
45. Poortinga, W.: Social relations or social capital? Individual and community health effects of bonding social capital. Soc. Sci. Med. **63**(1), 255–270 (2006). https://doi.org/10.1016/j.socscimed.2005.11.039

46. Dean, W.R., Sharkey, J.R., Johnson, C.M.: Food insecurity is associated with social capital, perceived personal disparity, and partnership status among older and senior adults in a largely rural area of Central Texas. J. Nutr. Gerontol. Geriatr. **30**(2), 169–186 (2011). https://doi.org/10.1080/21551197.2011.567955
47. Weitzman, E.R., Chen, Y.-Y.: Risk modifying effect of social capital on measures of heavy alcohol consumption, alcohol abuse, harms, and secondhand effects: national survey findings. J. Epidemiol. Community Health. **59**(4), 303–309 (2005). https://doi.org/10.1136/jech.2004.024711
48. Wen, M.: Social capital and adolescent substance use: the role of family, school, and neighborhood contexts. J. Res. Adolesc. **27**(2), 362–378 (2017). https://doi.org/10.1111/jora.12299
49. Ehsan, A.M., De Silva, M.J.: Social capital and common mental disorder: a systematic review. J. Epidemiol. Community Health. **69**(10), 1021–1028 (2015). https://doi.org/10.1136/jech-2015-205868
50. De Silva, M.J., McKenzie, K., Harpham, T., Huttly, S.R.A.: Social capital and mental illness: a systematic review. J. Epidemiol. Community Health. **59**(8), 619–627 (2005). https://doi.org/10.1136/jech.2004.029678
51. Fu, Y., Zhang, S., Guo, X., Lu, Z., Sun, X.: Socioeconomic status and quality of life among older adults with hypertension in rural Shandong, China: a mediating effect of social capital. Front. Public Health. **11**, 1248291 (2023). https://doi.org/10.3389/fpubh.2023.1248291
52. Kanamori, S., et al.: Social participation and the prevention of functional disability in older Japanese: the JAGES cohort study. PLoS One. **9**(6), e99638 (2014). https://doi.org/10.1371/journal.pone.0099638
53. Moore, S., Kawachi, I.: Twenty years of social capital and health research: a glossary. J. Epidemiol. Community Health. **71**(5), 513–517 (2017). https://doi.org/10.1136/jech-2016-208313
54. Kawachi, I.: Commentary: reconciling the three accounts of social capital. Int. J. Epidemiol. **33**(4), 682–690 (2004). https://doi.org/10.1093/ije/dyh177
55. McGorry, P.D., Coghill, D., Berk, M.: Mental health of young Australians: dealing with a public health crisis. Med. J. Aust. **219**(6), 246–249 (2023). https://doi.org/10.5694/mja2.52047
56. Wang, T., Guo, X., Wu, T.: Social capital and digital divide: implications for Mobile health policy in developing countries. J. Healthcare Eng. **2021**, 1–13 (2021). https://doi.org/10.1155/2021/6651786
57. Holtz, B., Lauckner, C.: Diabetes management via Mobile phones: a systematic review. Telemed. E-Health. **18**(3), 175–184 (2012). https://doi.org/10.1089/tmj.2011.0119
58. Lupton, D.: Health promotion in the digital era: a critical commentary. Health Promot. Int. **30**(1), 174–183 (2015). https://doi.org/10.1093/heapro/dau091
59. Bennett Gayle, D., (Jenny) Yuan, X., Dadson, Y.A., Edwards, N.K.: Contact tracing Mobile applications in New York: a qualitative study on the use and privacy perceptions. ISCRAM. (2022) Conference, [Online]. Available: https://idl.iscram.org/files/gayle/2023/2552_Gayle_etal2023.pdf
60. Bennett Gayle, D., Dadson, Y., Goodarzi, M., Yuan, X.: COVID-19 Mobile applications for vaccination in New York state (NYS). In: Presented at the Hawaii International Conference on System Sciences (2025). https://doi.org/10.24251/HICSS.2025.432
61. X. Yuan, D. Bennett Gayle, E. S. Jung, and Y. A. Dadson, "COVID-19 contact tracing Mobile applications in New York state (NYS): an empirical study," in HCI International 2023 – Late Breaking Papers, vol. 14059, H. Degen, S. Ntoa, and A. Moallem, Eds., in Lecture Notes in Computer Science, , Cham: Springer Nature Switzerland, 2023, pp. 505–524. doi:https://doi.org/10.1007/978-3-031-48057-7_32.

62. Chowdhury, A., Baig, A.H., Chakraborty Subrata, R.G.: Conceptual Framework for Tele-health Adoption in Indian Healthcare. [Online]. Available: https://opus.lib.uts.edu.au/bit stream/10453/137441/1/Conceptual%20framework%20for%20telehealth%20adoption% 20in%20Indian%20healthcare.pdf

63. Eriksson, M.: Social capital and health – implications for health promotion. Glob. Health Action. **4**(1), 5611 (2011). https://doi.org/10.3402/gha.v4i0.5611

64. Baskerville, N.B., Dash, D., Wong, K., Shuh, A., Abramowicz, A.: Perceptions toward a smoking cessation app targeting LGBTQ+ youth and Young adults: a qualitative framework analysis of focus groups. JMIR Public Health Surveill. **2**(2), e165 (2016). https://doi.org/10.2196/publichealth.6188

65. Latkin, C.A., Davey-Rothwell, M.A., Knowlton, A.R., Alexander, K.A., Williams, C.T., Boodram, B.: Social network approaches to recruitment, HIV prevention, medical care, and medication adherence. JAIDS J. Acq. Immune Defici. Syn. **63**(Supplement 1), S54–S58 (2013). https://doi.org/10.1097/QAI.0b013e3182928e2a

66. Huygens, M.W.J., Vermeulen, J., Swinkels, I.C.S., Friele, R.D., Van Schayck, O.C.P., De Witte, L.P.: Expectations and needs of patients with a chronic disease toward self-management and eHealth for self-management purposes. BMC Health Serv. Res. **16**(1), 232 (2016). https://doi.org/10.1186/s12913-016-1484-5

67. Yardley, L., Morrison, L., Bradbury, K., Muller, I.: The person-based approach to intervention development: application to digital health-related behavior change interventions. J. Med. Internet Res. **17**(1), e30 (2015). https://doi.org/10.2196/jmir.4055

68. Ferretti, L., et al.: Quantifying SARS-CoV-2 transmission suggests epidemic control with digital contact tracing. Science. **368**(6491), eabb6936 (2020). https://doi.org/10.1126/science.abb6936

69. Morley, J., Cowls, J., Taddeo, M., Floridi, L.: Ethical guidelines for COVID-19 tracing apps. Nature. **582**(7810), 29–31 (2020). https://doi.org/10.1038/d41586-020-01578-0

70. Boudreaux, B., DeNardo, M., Denton, S., Sanchez, R., Feistel, K., Dayalani, H.: Data Privacy during Pandemics: a Scorecard Approach for Evaluating the Privacy Implications of COVID-19 Mobile Phone Surveillance Programs. RAND Corporation (2020). https://doi.org/10.7249/RRA365-1

71. Colizza, V., et al.: Time to evaluate COVID-19 contact-tracing apps. Nat. Med. **27**(3), 361–362 (2021). https://doi.org/10.1038/s41591-021-01236-6

72. Kolasa, K., Mazzi, F., Leszczuk-Czubkowska, E., Zrubka, Z., Péntek, M.: State of the art in adoption of contact tracing apps and recommendations regarding privacy protection and public health: systematic review. JMIR Mhealth Uhealth. **9**(6), e23250 (2021). https://doi.org/10.2196/23250

73. Kaspar, K.: Motivations for social distancing and app use as complementary measures to combat the COVID-19 pandemic: quantitative survey study. J. Med. Internet Res. **22**(8), e21613 (2020). https://doi.org/10.2196/21613

74. Dzandu, M.D., Pathak, B., De Cesare, S.: Acceptability of the COVID-19 contact-tracing app – does culture matter? Gov. Inf. Q. **39**(4), 101750 (2022). https://doi.org/10.1016/j.giq.2022.101750

75. Parker, M.J., Fraser, C., Abeler-Dörner, L., Bonsall, D.: Ethics of instantaneous contact tracing using mobile phone apps in the control of the COVID-19 pandemic. J. Med. Ethics. **46**(7), 427–431 (2020). https://doi.org/10.1136/medethics-2020-106314

76. Bates, G., Titi, M., Dickson-Gomez, J., Young, S., Keval, A., Meurer, J.: Navigating misinformation and political polarization of COVID-19: interviews with Milwaukee, Wisconsin county public health officials. Front. Public Health. **11**, 1215367 (2023). https://doi.org/10.3389/fpubh.2023.1215367

77. Hart, P.S., Chinn, S., Soroka, S.: Politicization and polarization in COVID-19 news coverage. Sci. Commun. **42**(5), 679–697 (2020). https://doi.org/10.1177/1075547020950735

78. Grossman, G., Kim, S., Rexer, J.M., Thirumurthy, H.: Political partisanship influences behavioral responses to governors' recommendations for COVID-19 prevention in the United States. Proc. Natl. Acad. Sci. USA. **117**(39), 24144–24153 (2020). https://doi.org/10.1073/pnas.200 7835117

79. Lin, N.: Inequality in social capital. Contemp. Sociol. **29**(6), 785 (2000). https://doi.org/10. 2307/2654086

80. Trang, S., Trenz, M., Weiger, W.H., Tarafdar, M., Cheung, C.M.K.: One app to trace them all? Examining app specifications for mass acceptance of contact-tracing apps. Eur. J. Inf. Syst. **29**(4), 415–428 (2020). https://doi.org/10.1080/0960085X.2020.1784046

81. Centola, D.: An experimental study of Homophily in the adoption of health behavior. Science. **334**(6060), 1269–1272 (2011). https://doi.org/10.1126/science.1207055

82. Rogers, E.M., Singhal, A., Quinlan, M.M.: Diffusion of innovations 1. In: Stacks, D.W., Salwen, M.B., Eichhorn, K.C. (eds.) An Integrated Approach to Communication Theory and Research, 3rd edn, pp. 415–434. Routledge (2019). https://doi.org/10.4324/978020371075 3-35

83. Valente, T.W.: Social network thresholds in the diffusion of innovations. Soc. Networks. **18**(1), 69–89 (1996). https://doi.org/10.1016/0378-8733(95)00256-1

84. Dearing, J.W.: Applying diffusion of innovation theory to intervention development. Res. Soc. Work. Pract. **19**(5), 503–518 (2009). https://doi.org/10.1177/1049731509335569

85. Valente, T.W., Davis, R.L.: Accelerating the diffusion of innovations using opinion leaders. Ann. Am. Acad. Pol. Soc. Sci. **566**(1), 55–67 (1999). https://doi.org/10.1177/000271629956 600105

86. Gilbert, K.L., Quinn, S.C., Goodman, R.M., Butler, J., Wallace, J.: A meta-analysis of social capital and health: a case for needed research. J. Health Psychol. **18**(11), 1385–1399 (2013). https://doi.org/10.1177/1359105311435983

87. Warschauer, M.: Technology and Social Inclusion: Rethinking the Digital Divide. The MIT Press (2003). https://doi.org/10.7551/mitpress/6699.001.0001

88. Carpiano, R.M.: Toward a neighborhood resource-based theory of social capital for health: can Bourdieu and sociology help? Soc. Sci. Med. **62**(1), 165–175 (2006). https://doi.org/10. 1016/j.socscimed.2005.05.020

89. Wang, H., Schlesinger, M., Wang, H., Hsiao, W.C.: The flip-side of social capital: the distinctive influences of trust and mistrust on health in rural China. Soc. Sci. Med. **68**(1), 133–142 (2009). https://doi.org/10.1016/j.socscimed.2008.09.038

90. Ling, R.S., Fortunati, L., Goggin, G., Lim, S.S., Li, Y. (eds.): The Oxford Handbook of Mobile Communication and Society The Oxford Handbooks Series. NY, United States of America: Oxford University Press, New York (2020)

91. Morgan, D.L.: Focus groups. Annu. Rev. Sociol. **22**(1), 129–152 (1996). https://doi.org/10. 1146/annurev.soc.22.1.129

Revolutionizing Household Finance:
A User-Centered Platform for Holistic Financial Management

Henglong Dang[1]([✉]) [iD] and Fang Ding[2] [iD]

[1] Independent Researcher, Bellevue, WA 98006, USA
danghenglong@gmail.com
[2] Brandeis University, Waltham, MA 02453, USA

Abstract. The increasing complexity of household financial management has been exacerbated by the fragmented architecture of existing digital financial tools. Although discrete applications support budgeting, expenditure tracking, forecasting, and account oversight, a critical gap remains: the absence of a unified platform that facilitates integrated financial planning and collaborative familial governance. This study introduces a comprehensive digital solution aimed at remedying this deficiency through a consolidated user interface augmented by predictive analytics.

Consequently, this paper delineates and assesses a holistic platform that directly ameliorates the functional fragmentation. Empirical inquiries, encompassing quantitative (N = 342 survey) and qualitative (N = 35 interviews) methodologies, discerned salient disutility points, revealing significant cognitive burden and a low satisfaction (2.7/5) with extant applications. An iterative prototype developmental trajectory, progressing from low-fidelity schematics to a high-fidelity interactive simulacrum, was informed by key dissatisfactions identified in the initial user research and insights from iterative usability validation cycles. Subsequent comparative performance assessment corroborated the platform's integrative schema, with a mean satisfaction of the proposed prototype of 84.2 out of 100 (SD = 7.9). Through synthesis of rigorous empirical methodologies with sophisticated algorithmic prognostications and resilient cooperative functionalities, this platform furnishes a pragmatic resolution, establishing a scalable archetypal framework for holistic, human-centered financial applications, augmenting the state of the art of financial management applications.

Keywords: Predictive Analytics · Fintech · Human-Centered Design · Financial Management · Functional Fragmentation

1 Context and Literature Review

1.1 Fragmentation in Contemporary Financial Tools

In the rapidly evolving domain of personal finance, households are increasingly reliant on digital tools to manage complex financial needs. However, rather than simplifying oversight, this proliferation of applications has resulted in fragmented ecosystems and

M. Schrepp and M. Rauterberg (Eds.): HCII 2025, LNCS 16342, pp. 22–40, 2026.
https://doi.org/10.1007/978-3-032-13164-5_2

limited UX coherence. Most U.S. adults concurrently use multiple financial management tools, contributing to workflow inefficiencies and elevated cognitive burden [1].

This phenomenon, herein referred to as functional fragmentation, encompasses the dispersion of essential financial tasks—such as budgeting, expense tracking, forecasting, and collaboration—across disparate, non-integrated systems. Households typically adopt distinct platforms to satisfy their complex financial management tasks, such as Mint for expense tracking, You Need a Budget (YNAB) for envelope budgeting, Robinhood for investment monitoring, and Prism for bill reminders, without a comprehensive application unifying these functions [2, 3]. This functional fragmentation is exacerbated by a lack of robust cross-tool integrations, preventing a unified view of an individual's or family's complete financial landscape, encompassing checking, credit, and investment accounts [4], with data silos and incompatible APIs frequently necessitating manual reconciliation efforts that increase user burden [5].

A review of 170 financial tools found that while many specialize in specific functions, they typically omit broader planning capabilities and shared-use features, thus failing to support complex household dynamics [6]. Predictive modeling features—such as dynamic "what-if" simulations or cash flow forecasts—are similarly absent in most tools, which tend to focus on retrospective visualizations over predictive guidance [7, 8]. Fewer than one-fourth of reviewed budgeting applications support forward-looking planning or envelope-style logic [9].

Beyond functional limitations, collaborative support remains underdeveloped. Shared budgets, role-specific permissions, and asynchronous notifications are rarely implemented, undermining coordination amongst multi-user households, co-parenting families, and those with irregular income streams [10]. The absence of adaptive configurations, including customizable roles or multilingual support, limits these systems' relevance across diverse financial contexts [11].

1.2 UX Challenges and Behavioral Gaps

User experience deficiencies further intensify cognitive burden. Inconsistent navigation patterns, unclear terminologies, redundant settings across modules, and non-intuitive instructions further impeded novice users from effectively utilizing said tools [12]. These challenges often compel users to revert to analog workarounds, including spreadsheets and manual CSV reconciliations. The inconsistency across tool interfaces hinders effective and sustained engagement, particularly when tools do not reflect users' actual financial behaviors.

These UX breakdowns can be framed within broader cognitive theories. Skumowski and Xu [4] revised cognitive load theory to emphasize the role of extraneous cognitive load in multi-modal digital environments, asserting that fragmented platforms heighten mental strain through excessive context switching. Behavioral models further confirm that financial applications fail to integrate nudging principles effectively. While features such as push-based reminders or visual goals can reinforce behaviors [13], few systems link them to calendar-based or scenario-based planning. Stefanov [14] (2024) additionally demonstrated the benefits of embedded tools like real-time financial health indicators, barcode scanning, and transaction clustering—capabilities still rare amongst mainstream providers.

1.3 Review of Existing Applications

Despite rapid market expansion, current financial management applications continue to exhibit a functionally narrow scope. Sindell [15] (2003) traced the early trajectory of personal finance software, showing how initial innovations emphasized account management and tax preparation rather than long-term planning or social use cases. Subsequent evaluations by Dewi and Gunawan [16] (2019) found that even amongst popular apps like Wallet and Monefy, critical budgeting components such as flexible debt scheduling and savings goal modeling remain underdeveloped. Similarly, Pavlova and Kuskov [17] (2022) argued that most financial applications lack cross-platform synchronization and account integration, especially for users juggling multiple banking products.

Stríček and Andrisková [18] (2015) demonstrated that many dashboards embedded within financial tools are non-interactive or lack the real-time responsiveness needed for effective decision-making, limiting their value to passive reporting functions. Complementing this, Dunwoody's patent on dashboard behavior modeling at IBM outlines how static dashboards fail to account for differing user contexts, reducing utility for multi-user households or shifting income streams [19]. These limitations are quantifiable: Tarigan [20] (2023) reported weak ISO 9241-11 compliance amongst top-rated apps, particularly when tested by non-technical or novice users.

1.4 The Role of Human-Centered Design in FinTech

As these system-level gaps accumulate, there has been a corresponding turn toward Human-Centered Design (HCD) within the FinTech domain. HCD frameworks emphasize iterative design, participatory feedback, and social inclusivity—elements crucial for building applications that adapt to user diversity. In the "Seven Grand Challenges of HCI," Stephanidis et al. [21] (2019) underscored the necessity of accounting for social, anticipatory, and behavior-aware features in complex domains like finance. Applied studies provide evidence that HCD practices not only improve UX metrics but also enhance user retention and emotional satisfaction. For instance, Gretalita [22] (2017) used Kansei Engineering to develop emotionally resonant interfaces for youth, improving both satisfaction and usage rates.

Additionally, Handayani [23] (2024) highlighted how millennial users prioritize personalization and feedback loops but often disengage when transparency and data control are absent. These studies reinforce the value of embedding user behavior modeling and emotional design into the core structure of financial applications.

1.5 Summary of Gaps and Conceptual Contributions

The literature collectively emphasizes a series of unmet needs in personal finance systems. Current tools disproportionately favor retrospective accounting over proactive planning, offer minimal collaborative support, and ignore the social and cognitive realities of multi-user households. Moreover, while applications collect behavioral data, they seldom translate it into adaptive UX strategies or predictive capabilities.

This study aims to address these deficiencies by proposing and evaluating a high-fidelity prototype that unifies budgeting, forecasting, and shared access within a cohesive, anticipatory platform. Drawing from empirical user research and grounded in HCD methodology, the system contributes not only a technical proof of concept but also a set of design principles relevant to the HCI community. It articulates a model of predictive, collaborative, and context-sensitive financial tooling that reflects emerging needs in both theory and practice.

2   Methodologies and Design

2.1   User Research Strategy and Data Collection

The study employed a sequential exploratory mixed-methods design grounded in Human-Centered Design principles and structured across three interconnected phases: (1) empirical user inquiry,[1] (2) iterative system design, and (3) comparative usability benchmarking. The goal was to extract actionable user insights, convert them into functional requirements, and validate them through iterative testing and comparative analysis.

The initial empirical phase utilized a quantitative online survey (N = 342), designed in Typeform and deployed over a three-week period through targeted outreach on Reddit, LinkedIn, and Facebook finance communities. The 28-item questionnaire was structured across four domains: demographic characteristics, digital tool usage, perceived limitations of current systems, and aspirational features. The demographic section collected data on age, major income sources (e.g., salary, freelance, gig work), and financial roles within households (e.g., sole decision-maker, shared responsibility) (see Fig. 1). The second domain addressed the current digital finance ecosystem. Respondents were asked to identify and rank the tools they regularly used, report on usage frequency, and indicate the degree of satisfaction across various dimensions using a 5-point Likert scale. The third section focused on unmet needs, such as disjointed data flows, insufficient predictive capabilities, and limitations in collaborative functionalities or privacy controls. For example, users were queried on their ability to simulate income variability, configure role-specific permissions, or receive event-triggered notifications with current tools. The final domain prompted participants to describe ideal features or functionalities missing from their current toolsets. Feedback from this pilot led to iterative adjustments in scale formatting, item clarity, and question ordering for the subsequent qualitative phase.

To deepen contextual understanding and supplement quantitative patterns, semi-structured interviews were conducted with a purposively selected subset of 35 survey respondents. Criteria for selection included demonstrable dissatisfaction with current tools as depicted in the quantitative phase, diversity in financial roles, and willingness to participate in subsequent study phases. Each interview, conducted via Zoom and lasting

---

[1] Prior to data collection, participants were informed of the study's objectives, voluntary nature, data usage, and anonymization procedures. All respondents provided explicit consent before participating in surveys or interviews. As the research involved no collection of Personally Identifiable Information (PII) and exclusively relied on self-reported behavioral data, it was exempt from formal Institutional Review Board approval under prevailing ethical guidelines for social and behavioral research. Nonetheless, the study adhered to rigorous ethical standards consistent with the ACM Code of Ethics and Research Integrity Principles in HCI.

approximately 30 min, was designed to elicit nuanced, narrative-driven insights that expanded upon the survey findings.

The interview protocol was structured around four thematic dimensions. First, participants were asked to describe their current financial tool ecosystems in detail, articulating which platforms they used, the purposes each served, and the manual workarounds they had adopted to bridge system limitations—such as regular CSV exports, copy-pasting balances, or sharing screenshots to coordinate with partners. Second, interviewees elaborated on specific pain points encountered during financial management tasks. These narratives contextualized aspects of extant applications that sow significant aversion from the users.

Third, participants were asked to reflect on their adaptive strategies and behavioral improvisations. These included the use of offline ledgers during international travel, reliance on verbal coordination with less digitally literate household members, or periodic manual audits to reconcile app data. Finally, interviews transitioned into forward-looking discussions in which participants were prompted to articulate desired features, describe their ideal financial interface, and evaluate hypothetical functionalities such as shared dashboards, forecasting simulations, or modular permissions. These qualitative responses directly informed the specification of system requirements and design priorities.

Findings from both the survey and interviews were synthesized into a consolidated set of functional and experiential requirements that the prototype would incorporate. These underpinned the creation of a low-fidelity prototype that underwent three rounds of formative usability testing with 12 participants per cycle, employing think-aloud protocols. Task-based feedback and observational data guided iterative design refinements, culminating in a high-fidelity interactive prototype developed in Figma, as elaborated in subsequent sections.

Sampling Method and Participant Demographics. A non-probabilistic voluntary sampling strategy was employed, with an emphasis on diverse financial identities and household structures. The inclusion criteria required that participants: (1) be over the age of 18; (2) use at least one digital finance tool regularly; (3) participate in financial decision-making within an individual or shared context.

Participants represented a heterogeneous population ($N = 342$) across income types and living arrangements. Some noteworthy demographic statistics of the participants include: 41.2% reported income from self-employment or freelancing; 28.9% managed shared budgets (e.g., couples, roommates, family households); 17.8% acted as financial guardians or managed finances on behalf of others; 52.6% self-identified as millennials and 36.7% as Gen Z. Geographic diversity included participants from North America, Europe, Southeast Asia, East Asia, and South America.

Major income sources and number of platforms participants used, as self-reported, are highlighted in Fig. 1. This demographically and economically diverse cohort facilitated exploration of edge-case needs, such as irregular income planning, multilingual UI expectations, and multi-currency budgeting.

Recruitment materials were disseminated via digital flyers, direct messages, and embedded posts in community groups. All materials included a brief study overview, time commitment estimates, incentive details, and a screening questionnaire to ensure inclusion criteria were met.

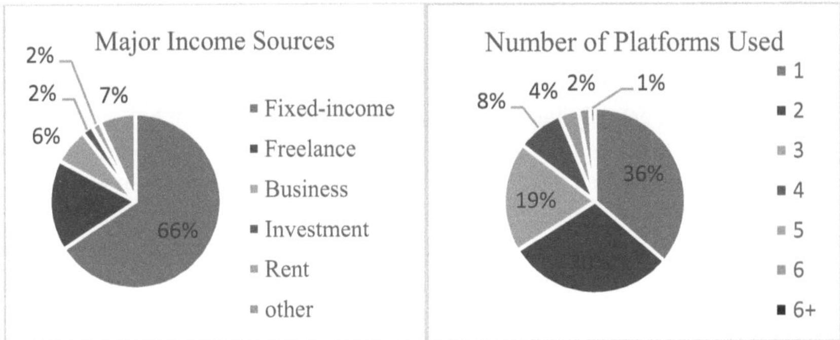

Fig. 1. Self-Reported Major Income Sources and Number of Platforms used.

2.2 Data Analysis: Descriptive and Inferential Statistics

Quantitative survey data were analyzed for descriptive and inferential statistical processing. Responses from 342 participants were curated for incomplete answers, valueless inputs and missing values, resulting in a final dataset of 331 complete responses (96.8% completion rate). Descriptive analyses were first conducted to explore distributions across demographic variables, financial roles, tool usage frequency, and satisfaction metrics.

Amongst respondents, 64.3% reported using two or more financial applications concurrently, while 34.5% reported using at least three. The average self-reported satisfaction score with their current digital finance tools was 2.7 out of 5 (SD = 1.1), with the lowest satisfaction among freelancers (mean = 2.3) and co-managing couples (mean = 2.4). A one-way ANOVA test confirmed a statistically significant difference in satisfaction across income groups ($F(2, 328) = 5.84$, $p < .01$), suggesting that financial volatility may intensify perceived tool inadequacy.

Likert-scale (5 points) assessments revealed that the most valued features were the ability to simulate future financial states (M = 4.64, SD = 0.51), role-based permissions for shared finances (M = 4.42, SD = 0.68), and a consolidated dashboard view (M = 4.37, SD = 0.73). Pearson correlation analysis showed a strong positive relationship between the number of tools used and reported cognitive fatigue ($r = 0.58$, $p < 0.001$), affirming the hypothesis that tool fragmentation contributes to user burden.

To further analyze user pain points, an Exploratory Factor Analysis (EFA) was performed using principal axis factoring with Promax Rotation on 14 pain-related scale items. Sampling adequacy was verified via the Kaiser-Meyer-Olkin measure (KMO = 0.84), and Bartlett's test of sphericity was significant ($\chi^2(91) = 973.24$, $p < .001$). The analysis yielded three factors explaining 71.2% of the variance: (1) integration friction, (2) forecasting insufficiency, and (3) collaboration difficulty. These dimensions were reflected strongly in both the quantitative and qualitative findings.

2.3 Qualitative Data Collection

Participants agreed to screen-share while performing a routine, non-sensitive financial management task, such as logging expenses, updating a shared budget, or reviewing month-end statements using applications that they constantly employed. These sessions lasted approximately 30 min each and were conducted synchronously over Zoom. During these sessions, instances of backtracking within interfaces, hesitation in locating functions, and reliance on non-digital systems (e.g., checking a paper bill before updating an app) were documented. For example, one participant using Mint navigated through five separate screens to verify account totals, while another toggled between a spreadsheet and WhatsApp to confirm shared grocery payments. These observational findings served two roles: they validated recurrent interview themes around functional fragmentation and inefficiency, and they exposed subtle usability breakdowns—such as inconsistent iconography or the absence of contextual prompts—which informed interaction design decisions during the wireframing process.

2.4 User Research Findings

Usability-Related Insights. The user research surfaced several persistent usability challenges across the ecosystem of personal finance tools currently in use identified in existing literature. A dominant issue was the burden imposed by fragmented user flows. Participants frequently described having to alternate between multiple applications to complete core financial tasks—such as logging expenses, viewing forecasted balances, and updating shared budgets—which introduced navigational friction and decision fatigue. In survey responses, 71.6% of users reported that switching between tools "often disrupted" their budgeting routines, and 65.1% stated that the process of reconciling information manually—particularly at the end of the month—was "mentally exhausting."

Participants also identified inconsistencies in user interface design as a recurring usability barrier. Disparate visual taxonomies and inconsistent terminology—particularly around financial planning constructs like "goals," "plans," or "envelopes"—complicated their navigation and comprehension across tools. Several users reported compensating with custom spreadsheets or external templates to reimpose clarity and structure. One participant, during a screen-sharing session, navigated through five nested menus in Mint just to locate a recurring bill, illustrating interface inefficiency.

Collectively, these findings reveal an ecosystem marked by friction, fragmentation, and a disconnect between system architecture and user mental models. They affirm the importance of unified dashboards, scenario-based planning, and intuitive, consistent UI hierarchies in mitigating cognitive overload and improving user satisfaction.

Mental Models and Task-Flow Patterns. The study revealed that many users approached personal finance with predictive mental models—expecting their tools not only to reflect past behavior but to offer foresight into future outcomes. However, most existing systems lag behind in this regard, relying primarily on retrospective data visualization. Survey results showed that 82.4% of participants desired tools that could simulate the financial impact of a decision, such as altering rent obligations, adjusting freelance hours, or modifying monthly discretionary spending. In interviews, users often described mental metaphors such as "financial GPS," "weather forecast," or "look-ahead budgeting," pointing to a cognitive preference for temporal visualization tools that are rarely implemented in mainstream applications.

The absence of temporal scaffolding was particularly detrimental for users with volatile income streams. Freelancers and gig workers, in particular, expressed frustration at not being able to visualize income gaps over multi-week spans or compare actual vs. anticipated income trends. Similarly, co-managing households lacked adequate representations of shared financial states. Couples frequently defaulted to verbal or informal systems (e.g., weekly sync-ups or shared Google Docs) to maintain coordination, revealing a misalignment between mental models and tool functionality. This misfit suggests a design imperative to reorient interface logic around proactive and context-aware task flows.

Comparison to Established UX Patterns. When mapped against established UX design heuristics, especially those outlined by Nielsen [24] (1994) and expanded for HCI systems by Stephanidis et al. [21] (2019), current financial applications exhibited numerous deficiencies. Heuristic breaches included "visibility of system status" (e.g., delayed transaction syncing), "user control and freedom" (e.g., inability to undo or redo inputs in shared budgets), and "recognition rather than recall" (e.g., non-standard iconography for financial categories). In the comparative evaluation of Mint, Pocket-Smith, Spendee, and YNAB, none of the applications fulfilled more than 7 out of 10 basic usability heuristics in testing scenarios involving multi-user financial tasks.

Participants praised certain isolated features—such as YNAB's philosophy of forward-looking allocation and PocketSmith's rudimentary cash flow projections—but indicated that these were either buried in unintuitive settings or incompatible with collaborative workflows. Additionally, the absence of onboarding personalization, scenario-based walk-throughs, or behavioral feedback loops limited the capacity of these tools to adapt to evolving user goals. This misalignment suggests an opportunity for systems that integrate anticipatory guidance, collaborative UX flows, and behavioral nudging into their core design logic. Table 1 summarizes key findings from the user research.

Table 1. Summary of Key User Research Findings and Relevant Implications.

Category	Specific Findings	Literature Connection	New Contribution	Design Implication
Functional Fragmentation	71.6% users reported tool-switching; 65.1% found manual reconciliation exhausting. EFA identified "integration friction" as a primary factor.	Confirms [1–5] on fragmentation and data silos.	Quantified cognitive burden ($r = .58$, $p < .001$) of fragmentation.	Need for unified dashboards, reduced context-switching, and cognitive integration.

(*continued*)

Table 1. (*continued*)

Category	Specific Findings	Literature Connection	New Contribution	Design Implication
Predictive Analytics	Desired simulation functions; Predictive forecasting systems	Reinforces [7–9] on lack of predictive features.	User-driven metaphors for foresight, revealing a cognitive preference for proactive guidance.	Proactive, anticipatory guidance; design for temporal visualization.
Collaborative Gaps	Defaulted to verbal/informal systems. Only 18.6% reported role-based permissions. EFA identified "collaboration difficulty" as a prominent factor.	Aligns with [6, 10, 11] on limited collaborative support.	Preference for asynchronous, context-embedded coordination (comment threads, activity logs) over real-time co-editing.	Design for asynchronous workflows, granular permissions, and transparent shared accountability.
Inclusive Design Gaps	Tools assumed "single-user, single-income mental model"; Exclusion of irregular expenses.	Expands on [6] regarding lack of support for complex household dynamics.	Detailed analysis of the limitations of the "single-user, single-income" model and specific needs of diverse household structures.	Develop socially-aware financial systems that accommodate diverse financial structures.

2.5 Design Process

Ideation and Conceptual Exploration. Following the consolidation of user research findings, the design process began with a structured ideation phase intended to translate empirically derived user needs into actionable design opportunities. This phase drew heavily on methodologies from contextual design and interaction scenario mapping, with the goal of producing an interface paradigm that supports proactive, collaborative, and cognitively lightweight financial management.

Initial exploration centered around three high-level constructs extracted from user insights: forecasting literacy, collaborative awareness, and contextual simplification. Forecasting literacy referred to the need for users to develop an intuitive grasp of temporal cash flow and scenario planning. Collaborative awareness focused on providing visibility and transparency within multi-user financial environments, while contextual simplification targeted the reduction of cognitive load through progressive disclosure and anticipatory UI design. These constructs were cross-referenced with behavioral science models and UX heuristics to ensure theoretical robustness. Ideation outputs included design sketches, low-fidelity storyboards, interaction sequences, and proto-personas with varied financial contexts.

Low-Fidelity and Mid-Fidelity Mockups. The conceptual ideas were translated into a suite of low-fidelity wireframes using Figma, representing key user flows such as shared budget creation, income forecasting, debt prioritization, and transaction categorization. The early wireframes prioritized information architecture, interaction logic, and screen transition flows. These were followed by mid-fidelity mockups that incorporated foundational visual design principles such as spacing, color hierarchy, and typography consistent with accessibility guidelines (WCAG 2.1 Level AA). Selected sample wireframes are presented in Fig. 2.

These prototypes were organized into five primary functional modules: (1) a consolidated dashboard showing financial overviews, upcoming bills, and savings trajectories; (2) a dynamic "scenario planner" that allowed users to simulate income or expense fluctuations; (3) a collaborative ledger with role-specific access modes (e.g., viewer, contributor, admin); (4) an activity log for transaction history and shared edits; and (5) a notification center integrating proactive alerts and spending nudges. Emphasis was placed on interaction fluidity and minimizing modal interruptions. Mockups were then annotated with user goals, backend logic dependencies, and interface state transitions. Selected low-fidelity wireframes are appended below, depicting representative pages.

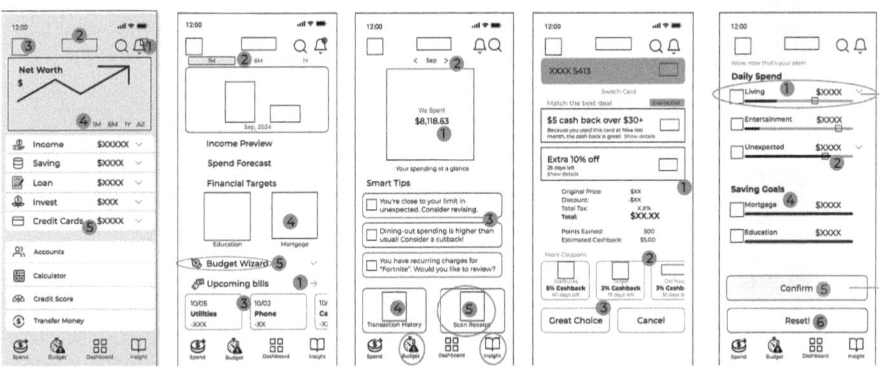

Fig. 2. Selected Representative Screenshots of low-fidelity wireframes.

User-Driven Design Decisions. Design decisions throughout the prototyping lifecycle were heavily informed by user feedback gathered during interviews, usability tests, and observation sessions. A recurring insight from earlier phases—that user struggled to match financial behaviors with static budgeting categories—led to the inclusion of customizable tagging and rule-based automation, allowing users to define recurring logic (e.g., "any deposit tagged as 'freelance' triggers a savings reallocation of 20%").

Similarly, the lack of real-time feedback in traditional tools informed the decision to design anticipatory notifications, such as alerts for upcoming bill-pay gaps or threshold warnings for overspending in volatile categories. This design element was modeled on behavioral finance principles, particularly the notion of "pre-commitment nudges," which have been shown to increase follow-through on financial goals.

In response to users' frustrations with shared expense coordination, the system incorporated annotated edit logs and comment threads on transactions, enabling asynchronous communication without leaving the application. These features were critical for co-parenting and roommate scenarios, where asynchronous task delegation and transparency are essential.

Iterative Refinements. The prototype underwent three rounds of iterative refinement, each informed by structured usability sessions conducted remotely with a diverse user cohort. Participants engaged in task-based walkthroughs (e.g., setting up a joint budget, simulating a 30% income drop, logging a transaction on behalf of a family member), followed by post-task debriefs to elicit impressions of usability, clarity, and cognitive effort.

Feedback from the first round led to simplification of onboarding flows, clearer visual separation between individual and shared financial zones, and redesigned button hierarchies to reduce decision complexity. The second round prompted improvements in microinteraction timing (e.g., animation delays, button press feedback) and recalibrated default alert settings to be less intrusive. The final round focused on refining edge-case handling and error recovery (e.g., reversing incorrect entries, restoring deleted budgets).

By the conclusion of this iterative cycle, the prototype was consistently rated as "highly usable" across several metrics. Participants reported reduced task completion times and increased confidence in forecasting accuracy and collaborative clarity compared to their existing tools. These results were subsequently validated in the evaluation phase detailed in Sect. 3.

2.6 Prototype Implementation

The prototype included five functional modules that aligned with core user needs identified during the research phase. The Dashboard Overview consolidated real-time account balances, budget status, and future cash flow projections. It also displayed contextual alerts for overspending risks or upcoming financial obligations. The Scenario Planner enabled users to simulate alternate income or expense trajectories using adjustable sliders, dropdowns, and time-range selectors. These simulations dynamically recalculated projected cash flows and updated visual indicators using D3.js-based SVG graphs. Selected high-fidelity prototypes are included below (Fig. 3).

Fig. 3. Selected Representative Screenshots for high-fidelity prototypes.

The Collaborative Ledger supported co-editing of transaction histories, category labeling, and note threading. Edits were version-controlled and time-stamped, with a change log accessible to all contributors. Users could tag transactions, attach receipts, or request clarification from household members using inline comments. Role-specific permissions dictated whether a user could initiate changes, approve edits, or view restricted categories (e.g., personal discretionary funds within a joint budget).

The Permissions and Role Management module allowed users to configure access hierarchies within shared accounts. This module included granular settings such as "read-only access to monthly reports" or "edit access limited to grocery and utility categories." Finally, the Notification and Alerts Engine allowed users to set behavioral triggers (e.g., income drops, overspending events, approaching goal targets), with notification delivery via push, email, or in-app modals. All events were logged in an Activity Feed, supporting auditability and retrospective review.

3 Prototype Evaluation and Discussion

3.1 Evaluation Objectives

The evaluation aimed to assess the prototype's effectiveness in facilitating financial management tasks, with a focus on three core areas: usability, predictive forecasting, and collaborative functionality. Usability was evaluated through task efficiency, cognitive load, and user satisfaction, examining whether the system reduced friction compared to existing tools. Forecasting assessment focused on the system's ability to help users simulate income or expense changes and interpret projected outcomes—especially for users with irregular incomes. Collaborative features, including role-based permissions and shared ledger mechanics, were evaluated to determine their effectiveness in improving coordination and reducing friction in joint financial management. Together, these objectives sought to validate both functional performance and user alignment, while also exploring the broader utility of anticipatory, multi-user platforms in personal finance contexts.

3.2 Participants

The usability evaluation involved 16 participants (8 females, 8 male), aged between 23 and 56 (M = 35.1, SD = 6.4), representing a spectrum of financial roles and digital literacy levels. Participants were recruited through voluntary sampling from online financial communities and prior study respondents with the same inclusion criteria as the user research.

The cohort included five freelance professionals with variable monthly earnings, four individuals in co-managed household budgets, and seven users responsible for personal budgeting within fixed-income contexts. Three participants managed finances for dependents or partners, and eight had prior experience using tools such as YNAB or PocketSmith. This purposive sampling strategy allowed the evaluation to target a diverse set of usage contexts, including those most sensitive to breakdowns in collaboration and forecasting accuracy.

3.3 Evaluation Methods

The evaluation phase employed a task-based usability testing protocol supplemented by both quantitative performance metrics and qualitative user feedback. Testing was conducted remotely with a cohort of 16 participants selected to represent a cross-section of target user groups, including individual budgeters, co-managing couples, and freelancers with irregular income. Each session lasted approximately 45 min and was conducted over Zoom with screen sharing and think-aloud protocols enabled.

Task Design: Representative User Scenarios. Participants were asked to complete a set of five representative tasks, each designed to simulate real-world financial workflows that the prototype aimed to improve. These tasks were selected based on high-frequency user behaviors and recurring breakdowns identified in earlier phases of the study. The task list included: (1) create a shared household budget by assigning categories, contributors, and custom thresholds; (2) simulate a sudden 30% income reduction for a freelancer and identify the month in which the user would first encounter a cash flow deficit; (3) log a shared expense and leave a comment tagging another user for clarification; (4) adjust a forecast scenario to visualize the impact of delaying a major payment by two weeks; (5) resolve a conflicting transaction entry using the activity feed and edit history. Each task was prefaced with a contextual narrative, allowing participants to approach the prototype with goal-directed reasoning. Tasks were counterbalanced to avoid ordering effects and minimize learning bias.

Metrics and Feedback: Quantitative and Qualitative Measures. Quantitative metrics were collected to evaluate task performance. These included time-on-task, number of clicks, error rates (e.g., misclassification of expenses, failed permission settings), and completion success. Additionally, participants completed the System Usability Scale (SUS) immediately after the session to capture perceived usability. The mean SUS score across all users was 84.2 (SD = 7.9), indicating excellent usability by industry standards.

Qualitative data were captured through real-time verbalizations during the sessions and follow-up feedbacks. Participants were asked to reflect on perceived friction, mental effort, interface clarity, and the plausibility of adopting the tool in real-world contexts. Specific attention was paid to moments of hesitation, confusion, or praise during interaction, with screen recordings used to identify and analyze critical events post hoc.

3.4 Evaluation Results

Quantitative Findings. Participants demonstrated a high degree of task success, with 94% average task completion across the five core scenarios. The mean time-on-task was 3.4 min (SD $= 1.1$) per task, with the income forecasting and scenario adjustment tasks taking slightly longer due to exploratory interactions. The observed error rate was low (mean $= 0.47$ errors per task), primarily concentrated in permission misconfigurations during shared budget setup.

System Usability Scale (SUS) yielded a mean score of 84.2 (SD $= 7.9$), placing the prototype within the "excellent" range. Users rated the interface highest on dimensions of clarity, visual feedback, and system status visibility, and lower—though still favorable—on discoverability of advanced configuration features. Table 2 summarizes implementations of features in the prototype in response to the user demand identified in the user research and corresponding benefits, showcasing the influences of the user research.

Table 2. User Research Insights to Design Decisions Mapping

User Research Insights	Design Feature	Prototype Module	Rationale/Benefit
Struggled with static budgeting categories and desired flexibility.	Customizable tagging & rule-based automation.	Collaborative Ledger / Dashboard	Allows users to define recurring logic, reducing manual effort and increasing flexibility.
Lack of real-time feedback and proactive guidance in traditional tools.	Anticipatory notifications & behavioral nudges.	Notification & Alerts Engine	Provides proactive guidance and reinforces financial goals, improving follow-through.
Cumbersome shared expense coordination, relying on external systems.	Annotated edit logs & comment threads on transactions.	Collaborative Ledger	Enables asynchronous communication and transparency, crucial for multi-user households.

(continued)

Table 2. (continued)

User Research Insights	Design Feature	Prototype Module	Rationale/Benefit
Desire for a unified financial overview and reduced context-switching burden.	Consolidated Dashboard Overview.	Dashboard Overview	Reduces context-switching and provides a holistic, real-time financial view.
Desire for predictive financial planning and simulation capabilities.	Dynamic Scenario Planner.	Scenario Planner	Empowers users to simulate financial impacts and make informed decisions.
Absence of granular permissions and shared accountability in existing tools.	Collaborative Ledger with Role-Specific Permissions.	Collaborative Ledger / Permission Management	Supports diverse household structures and shared accountability with customizable access.

3.5 Qualitative Insights and Key Lessons Learned

The qualitative findings from think-aloud protocols and post-task interviews offered critical insights into both the efficacy and areas for refinement of the prototype. Participants responded positively to the scenario planning module, frequently characterizing it as "confidence boosting" and "more transparent than spreadsheets." The ability to visualize projected financial states through forecasting curves was described as instrumental in "demystifying" the effects of uncertain income or upcoming obligations.

The collaborative ledger received consistent praise for its transparency and auditability. Users appreciated the system's capacity to maintain a clear activity trail, although three participants requested deeper integration with existing platforms such as Venmo or Zelle to facilitate streamlined transaction verification. Some usability friction was observed during the onboarding process, particularly regarding interpretation of the role-based hierarchy and configuration of notification settings. Nonetheless, most users acclimated quickly following a brief guided introduction.

A key takeaway was the validation of the prototype's anticipatory and collaborative orientation. Multiple participants indicated that the tool successfully consolidated functions they had previously attempted to replicate manually through spreadsheets, messaging threads, or hybrid tool combinations. This supports the core premise that a predictive, shared, and context-sensitive financial system can effectively address gaps prevalent in existing applications.

Several lessons emerged with implications for both future design refinements and broader HCI research in personal finance. Foremost among these was the importance of progressive disclosure in forecasting interfaces. While participants generally valued predictive functionality, some exhibited initial hesitancy when engaging with the scenario planning module—particularly those unfamiliar with modeling income volatility. This finding suggests that onboarding workflows should scaffold exposure to complex forecasting features, potentially through stepwise tutorials or guided presets that incrementally introduce higher levels of configurability.

Another significant insight pertained to collaboration paradigms. Users expressed a strong preference for asynchronous, context-embedded coordination mechanisms—such as editable comment threads, role-specific edit rights, and persistent activity logs—over real-time co-editing. This reflects the nature of financial decision-making in households, where collaborators often operate with differing schedules, responsibilities, and digital fluency. Accordingly, financial interfaces should support asynchronous workflows that align with users' temporal and cognitive rhythms rather than mimic patterns from workplace collaboration tools.

Visual temporal mapping emerged as a critical enabler of financial cognition. Participants consistently noted that graphically rendered projections aided in identifying shortfalls, reallocating funds, and optimizing discretionary expenditures. However, some requested finer temporal granularity (e.g., weekly versus monthly views), indicating the need for adjustable forecasting intervals to accommodate different budgeting styles and planning horizons.

Finally, the absence of live data integration was perceived as a limiting factor. Despite simulated import features, participants emphasized the continued burden posed by fragmented ecosystems and the desire for seamless interoperability with banking, peer-to-peer payment, and tax preparation systems. Although the current architecture allows for such extensions, future versions should prioritize direct API integrations to enhance realism and reduce manual data consolidation.

4 Discussion

The findings of this study affirm that anticipatory and collaborative financial management tools—when designed with user-centered rigor—can offer meaningful improvements over incumbent systems. By centering user mental models, minimizing context-switching, and embedding forecasting logic into everyday tasks, the prototype was able to mediate some of the most persistent pain points in digital finance. The high task completion rates and favorable usability scores observed across diverse participant profiles support the viability of such systems for real-world adoption.

This study also contributes to broader HCI discourse by operationalizing the design of anticipatory interfaces in the personal finance domain. While the field has seen growing interest in behavior-aware systems and proactive assistance, their application to everyday financial decision-making remains underexplored. The scenario planner and collaborative ledger developed here serve as functional instantiations of these theoretical ideals, demonstrating that financial systems can evolve beyond passive tracking into active planning environments.

Importantly, the prototype also exposed the limitations of monolithic tool design in contexts of shared responsibility and shifting financial conditions. The success of features like role-based permissions and threaded transaction communication points to the need for finer granularity in user agency—not only in who sees what, but in how systems scaffold shared accountability, reduce interpersonal friction, and support negotiation. These insights suggest that financial technologies must evolve to accommodate social configurations that are more dynamic, relational, and distributed than current single-user paradigms assume.

Finally, the iterative process used in this study reinforces the value of integrated research-through-design methodologies in FinTech contexts. By grounding technical development in empirical insight and continuously feeding evaluation back into refinement cycles, the project demonstrates how design artifacts can serve both as practical tools and epistemic vehicles for advancing interactive system theory.

5 Conclusion

5.1 Summary of Contributions

This research has presented the design and formative evaluation of a prototype for a unified personal finance management system that addresses a central limitation in contemporary FinTech ecosystems: the fragmentation of essential functionalities across non-integrated applications. Guided by human-centered design principles and grounded in empirical user inquiry, the study identified systemic usability challenges—such as tool-switching fatigue, forecasting limitations, and coordination breakdowns in multi-user households—and operationalized these into a cohesive, anticipatory design framework. The prototype synthesized expense tracking, predictive modeling, collaborative budgeting, and behavioral nudging into a single interactive system. While not intended as a production-grade product, the prototype functions as a validated proof of concept, demonstrating technical feasibility, usability, and conceptual innovation through structured mixed-method evaluation.

5.2 Broader Implications, Limitations, and Next Steps

The central contribution of this work lies in its reimagining of personal finance systems through the lens of anticipatory, collaborative design. By unifying functionalities traditionally dispersed across modular tools, the prototype challenges the dominant architecture of financial software and offers a human-centered alternative aligned with real-world cognitive workflows, social coordination needs, and behavioral triggers. It contributes to HCI scholarship by articulating new interaction models that prioritize shared agency, role-based permissions, and scenario-based planning—elements often absent in both commercial systems and research prototypes.

Nonetheless, several limitations qualify these findings. First, the evaluation was conducted in a controlled, remote setting using simulated data, limiting ecological validity. Second, while the participant pool was demographically diverse, it skewed toward digitally literate users, potentially underrepresenting accessibility concerns in less tech-fluent populations. Third, real-time banking integrations (e.g., Plaid, Yodlee) were simulated using mock datasets due to institutional and security restrictions. As a result, features such as automated transaction syncing and live balance forecasting were not operable. Additionally, the current system architecture lacks embedded machine learning algorithms for personalized financial modeling or anomaly detection, which remain targets for future development. Performance scalability under concurrent usage and mobile-first deployment also remains untested.

Future work will prioritize the implementation of a fully operational system with live financial API integrations, advanced forecasting models, and adaptive onboarding for diverse financial roles. A longitudinal field study is planned to assess behavioral impact over time, measuring financial goal attainment, collaborative efficacy, and sustained engagement. These efforts are not only technological upgrades but also research opportunities to deepen the design theory of predictive and multi-user financial interfaces in HCI.

To encapsulate, this work contributes both an empirical foundation and conceptual roadmap for advancing the state of the art of personal finance technologies. It affirms the value of human-centered design in aligning technological capabilities with the dynamic, distributed, and cognitively complex nature of household financial management.

Disclosure of Interests. The authors have no competing interest to declare that are relevant to the content of this article.

References

1. Mitchell, J., Li, X., Steel, D., Decker, P.: Financial characteristics of mobile banking and payment users in the United States. J. Global Business Insights. **9**, 1–13 (2024). https://doi.org/10.5038/2640-6489.9.1.1262
2. Agarwal, S., Zhang, J., Zou, X.: Household finance. In: Oxford Research Encyclopedia of Economics and Finance (2022). https://doi.org/10.1093/acrefore/9780190625979.013.430
3. Mehra, A., Srihari Hulikal Muralidhar, Sambhav Satija, Anupama Dhareshwar, O'Neill, J.: Prayana. CHI '18: Proceedings of the 2018 CHI Conference on Human Factors in Computing Systems. 1–13 (2018). doi:10.1145/3173574.3173963.
4. Skulmowski, A., Xu, K.M.: Understanding cognitive load in digital and online learning: a new perspective on extraneous cognitive load. Educ. Psychol. Rev. **34**, 171–196 (2021). https://doi.org/10.1007/s10648-021-09624-7
5. Grable, J.E., Kwak, E.-J.: 2 personal finance: a policy and institutional perspective. In: De Gruyter eBooks, pp. 17–34 (2022). https://doi.org/10.1515/9783110727692-002
6. Torno, A., Werth, O., Nickerson, R.C., Breitner, M.H., Muntermann, J.: More than Mobile banking – a taxonomy-based analysis of mobile personal finance applications. In: Twenty-Fifth Pacific Asia Conference on Information Systems (PACIS) (2021)
7. Gade, S.: The household financial management during the Covid pandemic – a comparative analysis. ECS Trans. **107**, 7131–7141 (2022). https://doi.org/10.1149/10701.7131ecst
8. Nweje, U., Taiwo, M.: Leveraging Artificial Intelligence for Predictive Supply Chain management, Focus on How AI-driven Tools Are Revolutionizing Demand Forecasting and Inventory Optimization. https://www.researchgate.net/publication/387903364_Leveraging_Artificial_Intelligence_for_predictive_supply_chain_management_focus_on_how_AI-driven_tools_are_revolutionizing_demand_forecasting_and_inventory_optimization. Last Accessed 19 May 2025. https://doi.org/10.30574/ijsra.2025.14.1.0027
9. Alenazi, M., Sas, C.: Creating and managing transactions and budgets: analysis of marketplace descriptions and functionality review of budgeting apps. Interact. Comput. (2024). https://doi.org/10.1093/iwc/iwae041

10. Vladimir Glukhov, Timofeeva, E.: Personal finance as indicator of economic status the individual. Middle East J. Sci. Res. **13**, 26–33 (2013). https://doi.org/10.5829/idosi.mejsr.2013.13.sesh.1406

11. Vines, J., Dunphy, P., Monk, A.: Pay or delay. Proceedings of the SIGCHI Conference on Human Factors in Computing Systems. CHI 14, 501–510 (2014). doi:10.1145/2556288.2556961.

12. Lewis, M., Perry, M.: Follow the Money. In: Proceedings of the 2019 CHI Conference on Human Factors in Computing Systems - CHI '19, pp. 1–13 (2019). https://doi.org/10.1145/3290605.3300620

13. Susanto, A., Chang, Y., Ha, Y.W.: Determinants of continuance intention to use the smartphone banking services: an extension to the expectation-confirmation model. Ind. Manag. Data Syst. **116**, 508–525 (2016)

14. Stefanov, T., Stefanova, M., Varbanova, S., Temelkov, S.: Personal Finance Management Application. TEM J., 2065–2075 (2024). https://doi.org/10.18421/tem133-34

15. Sindell, K.: Personal Finance. https://www.researchgate.net/publication/262326672_Personal_finance. Last Accessed 1 June 2025

16. Dewi, L., Gunawan, R.: Studi Komparasi Alat bantu Pengelola Keuangan Pribadi Berbasis mobile: comparative study mobile based personal financial management assistance. Jurnal Teknologi dan Terapan Bisnis (JTTB). **2**, 34–41 (2019). https://doi.org/10.0301/jttb.v2i1.55

17. Pavlova, A.I., Kuskov, N.S.: Developing the structure of a web application for personal finance accounting. Krasnoyarsk Sci. **11**, 96–106 (2022). https://doi.org/10.12731/2070-7568-2022-11-3-96-106

18. Stríček, I., Andrisková, I.: Dashboard usability in financial modeling. CBU Int. Conf. Proc. **3**, 020–027 (2015). https://doi.org/10.12955/cbup.v3.579

19. Dunwood, K.S.: Cross-User Dashboard Behavior Analysis and Dashboard Recommendations. (2017).

20. Tarigan, D.D., Meysawati, M., Fauziah, Agusten, D.: Analisis perbandingan penggunaan aplikasi fintech dana dan ovo berbasis ISO 9241–11 menggunakan metode "Statistical Product And Service Solution (SPSS).". Jurnal Ilmiah Teknik. **3**, 01–09 (2023). https://doi.org/10.56127/juit.v3i1.1103

21. Stephanidis, C., Salvendy, G., Antona, M., Chen, J.Y.C., Dong, J., Duffy, V.G., Fang, X., Fidopiastis, C., Fragomeni, G., Fu, L.P., Guo, Y., Harris, D., Ioannou, A., Jeong, K. (Kate), Konomi, S., Krömker, H., Kurosu, M., Lewis, J.R., Marcus, a., Meiselwitz, G.: Seven HCI Grand Challenges. Int. J. Hum.-Comput. Interact. 35, 1229–1269 (2019). doi:https://doi.org/10.1080/10447318.2019.1619259.

22. Gretalita, N.W.M., Suzianti, A., Ardi, R.: Visual usability design of financial personal assistant application. In: Proceedings of the 2017 International Conference on Information Technology - ICIT 2017, pp. 142–147 (2017). https://doi.org/10.1145/3176653.3176700

23. Handayani, T., Rahardian, R.L., Utami, E.Y., Riyanti, A., Rizani, A.: Fintech analysis of personal finance app usage among millennials. Journal of economic education and entrepreneurship Studies. **5**, 150–162 (2024). https://doi.org/10.62794/je3s.v5i2.2299

24. Nielsen, J.: 10 Heuristics for User Interface Design. https://www.nngroup.com/articles/ten-usability-heuristics/. Last Accessed 2 June 2025.

EmoGen: An Emoji-Based Interactive App to Support Emotion Expression via Generative Music (Exploring Usability and Emotional Resonance in Symbolic Music Interaction)

Jiayuan Guo[1], Zhaolin Lu[1], Jinyuan Guo[2], Weihan Chen[1], Tian Yuan[1], and Yue Zhang[3](✉)

[1] Design Cognition and Computing Research Center, School of Design and Arts, Beijing Institute of Technology, Beijing 100081, China
{jiayuan.guo,zhaolin.lu,3120231889,3220242698}@bit.edu.cn

[2] Division of Natural and Applied Sciences, Duke Kunshan University, Kunshan 215316, China
jg601@duke.edu

[3] School of Architecture and Art, Hefei University of Technology, Hefei 230009, China
zhangyue@hfut.edu.cn

Abstract. Emojis offer an intuitive and affective means of emotional communication in digital environments. However, existing AI-driven music generation systems often rely on text-based inputs, which may be cognitively demanding and less precise in conveying emotions. This study presents EmoGen, an emoji-based interactive application that supports emotional expression in generative music. Users select emojis across five categories: emotion, scene, object, style, and instrument, which are mapped to text prompts for customized music generation with audiovisual feedback. A mixed-method evaluation with eight participants (aged 21–48) was conducted, using the System Usability Scale (SUS) and thematic analysis of interview data. Results showed high emotional alignment between user inputs and generated music (mean = 7.12–7.88/10) and strong usability (SUS = 80.9). Qualitative feedback highlighted use cases such as emotional journaling, event-based music creation, and mood-based self-care. The evaluation results suggest that EmoGen supports active emotional exploration through symbolic musical interaction, externalizing the externalization of emotions into personalized soundscapes. This work demonstrates how intuitive emoji-based interfaces can enhance emotional resonance and contribute to emotional interaction design in generative music systems.

Keywords: Musical expression · Emoji · Generative music · Human computer interaction · User experience · System usability

---

J. Guo, Z. Lu, and J. Guo—Equal contribution.

1   Introduction

Music serves as a universal medium of entertainment and expression, a method capable of transmitting emotions and meanings across geographic, social, and cultural boundaries as well as allowing people to feel emotional resonance [15]. It has become an indispensable emotional bridge in people's daily lives [3]. In recent years, the rapid development of generative artificial intelligence (AI) technology has gradually transformed music creation and consumption processes. Systems such as Suno AI[1] exemplify this transformation by generating personalized music based on textual descriptions, thereby making music creation simple and efficient [43]. Through algorithmic generation of melodies, lyrics, harmonies, and rhythms, AI technology has revitalized music creation, enabling widespread participation in musical expression [21]. Despite these advancements, natural language-based music generation continues to face significant challenges, including complex creation processes, difficulties in conceptualizing ideas, and limitations in intuitively conveying intentions and emotions [43]. These obstacles hinder the widespread adoption and everyday use of AI-generated music [11].

Within computer-mediated communication (CMC), simple but effective visual elements such as stickers, emoji, and emoticons are commonly used to convey emotions or states rather than multiple words or long sentences [35]. Research has demonstrated that in certain scenarios, a single visual image can convey multiple meanings more subtly and effectively than words, and can make the process of expressing emotions more efficient [45]. In this context, emojis (emoticons), as a widely adopted graphical communication tool, offer a new possibility for music-generation interaction [34]. Their intuitive, emotional, and polysemantic features can simplify the complex input process and have unique advantages in expressing emotions and intentions [39]. Research by Chen et al. [10] has established that emojis enhance communication accuracy, efficiency, and enjoyment while adding richer emotional dimensions to information exchange [14]. However, the potential application of emojis in AI music generation remains largely unexplored, with no current products leveraging emojis for personalized music creation, enhanced user experience, or improved emotional alignment between music and creators.

To address this gap in AI music generation interaction, we designed and developed **EmoGen**, an emoji-based interactive music application that facilitates emotion expression through generative music. **EmoGen** enables users to convey their emotional states through the selection of emojis representing emotions, listening contexts, scenario elements, music styles, and instruments. The system then employs AI-driven music generation techniques, including text-to-lyrics and text-to-music models, to create music and lyrics based on the selected emojis. We conducted both qualitative and quantitative evaluations to assess EmoGen's effectiveness in supporting emotional expression through generative music and its overall usability [40].

---

[1] https://suno.com/.

This study aims to introduce a novel emoji-based interaction approach designed to enhance emotional expression in music generation, offering a more flexible, personalized, and engaging experience. The key contributions of this work are: 1) the introduction of an innovative emoji-based interactive application for controlling AI-generated music, providing an open-source tool for exploratory music experience research; 2) an exploration of emoji-based interaction's potential to facilitate emotional expression through generative music; and 3) the development of a structured emoji set supporting five key components of music generation.

2   Research Background

2.1   Emoji-Based Interaction

Emoji is a two-part Japanese word, with "E" meaning image and "moji" meaning character [38]. It refers to a class of emoticons originally created to express emotions or represent elements of objects [5]. Emojis are now widely used on cell phones, computers, and mobile devices for daily communication, have become an essential tool for expressing emotions online. Previous research in the fields of computer-mediated communication (CMC) and human-computer interaction (HCI) has sparked significant interest in understanding the perception and application of emojis [1].

Previous studies have revealed that emojis not only help to enhance emotion expression and personalized communication but also improve relationship management and communication efficiency in social interactions [20]. Its unique, fun, and emotion-conveying ability makes it surpass traditional text on many occasions, especially in special groups and cross-media creations, demonstrating its unique application value [19]. Research has shown that emojis play a crucial role in social communication, particularly in expressing emotions and managing interpersonal relationships [33]. For example, individuals predominantly utilize emojis for social purposes, with the emotional connotations of emojis significantly influencing the social context [12]. Some people use emojis instead of or in addition to textual messages to manage their interpersonal relationships in social communication [24], and they believe that emoji have a higher degree of personalization, better emotion expression, and their sense of humor can bring a better user experience [44].

Researchers in the field of Human-Computer Interaction (HCI) have expanded on the aforementioned characteristics of emojis in interpersonal communication, leveraging their advantages over plain text to investigate their potential for emotion expression in human-computer interaction. Wang et al. [41] capitalized on the expressive strengths of emojis to develop an interactive, emoji-based application aimed at assisting autistic children in articulating their emotions and fostering bidirectional social interactions. Namikawa et al. [28] proposed a communication technology design that utilizes the fun and ambiguity of emojis as an alternative to facial expressions in video calls to prevent sloppy and incorrect emotion transfer and facilitate communication. Qiu et al.

[32] used input elements such as emoji, images, and humming to create a cross-media music creation system that enables users to create music easily, even without a background in specialized music knowledge. However, this system does not provide sufficient user interaction for users to explore and express emotions in music generation.

2.2   Generative Music Interaction

Despite the continuous development of research methods for music-emotion matching, traditional text-based input and music element matching remain limited to the user's known music preferences, and there are still instances where the user's emotional information is vague or cannot be expressed through text [18]. Previous research has tried and explored different forms to solve the above problems. For example, music can only be searched by inputting precise text for matching at first, but with the development of technology, some methods utilize specific elements (e.g., melody, beat, and lyrics) that constitute the music for searching [22]. Several studies proposed different approaches to enable effective music retrieval when users have no clear preferences for specific music or struggle to express their emotional states in words.

For example, Park et al. [30] proposed a music retrieval system that utilizes image-based inputs and hybrid text interactions, while also conducting comparative evaluations of user experiences across different input modalities for emotion-based music matching. Louie et al. [27] explored how more expressive generative models and more controllable user interfaces influence the experience of music creators and the emotional expressiveness of their works as perceived by listeners. Their findings suggest that these two factors play complementary roles in enhancing user control and expressive capability in human-AI collaborative music creation. Dubnov et al. [13] proposed an interactive framework for musical improvisation that integrates generative models and symbolization methods to enhance human-AI co-creation. They further investigated the use of reinforcement learning to optimize improvisational interactions in music generation.

Building on these findings and drawing from research on emoji use in computer-mediated communication (CMC) and human-computer interaction (HCI), we developed **EmoGen**-a novel interactive application for emotion-driven music generation. **EmoGen** provides users with an intuitive way to experience and listen to music, enabling them to explore and express emotions seamlessly.

3   Methods and Design

3.1   Design Goals

Building upon prior research on affectivity in human-computer interaction for experiential use [17], as well as preliminary interviews with users who frequently listen to or create music, we derived three design goals. *First*, the application aims to directly link emoji-based input to AI-driven music generation, eliminating the need for text input and thereby making emotional expression more intuitive and accessible. *Second,* unlike traditional applications focused on retrieving or selecting pre-existing music, our design emphasizes customized input from each user, enabling the AI model to generate music that is uniquely tailored to their emotional states with greater accuracy. *Lastly,* we aim to enhance emotional alignment, enjoyment, and overall user experience in the processes of music creation and listening through emoji-based interactions [29].

3.2   System Architecture

Figure 1 shows the system architecture containing four main steps: emoji selection, prompt generation, music generation, and lyrics display. By multi-modal collaboration, this system optimizes the interactive experience from visual input to emotional output and provides the users with an accurate, intriguing, and efficient experience of music creation. The design joins multi-framework capabilities and technologies to ensure a fluent and efficient transmission from emojis to music.

Specifically, the user interface is developed using built-in physics simulation functions and behavioral script structure in the Unity 2D engine. Users select emojis based on their feelings from an interface where emoji icons are represented as stackable circular graphics with a simulated gravity environment. The selection is adjustable during this phase. After selection, the emojis are mapped into corresponding textual descriptions based on a predefined lookup table (Table 1) and inputted into prompts. These prompts include specific requirements for AI lyrics and music generation, such as making sure that the selected emojis are mentioned in lyrics while preferred musical styles and instruments are emphasized in rhythm composition if they do not appear directly in lyrics.

The system then employs Python scripts using Chrome WebDriver to automate the music generation process on Sonauto.ai's webpage by imitating user behavior. The script will simulate a virtual user clicking the input box on the webpage in the local browser and entering the prompt. After detecting that generation is complete by scanning for certain buttons, the script navigates to the lyrics page and then copies lyrics to the Streaming Assets file. Finally, the captured lyrics are displayed and matched back to emojis to associate the lyrics with the selected emojis.

The source code for the implementation described in this paper is publicly available on GitHub at https://github.com/ryanG1296/emoji_music_generator.

3.3   Emoji Selection

This design categorizes the input emojis into two types, emotion-based emojis and object-based emojis. Emotion-based emojis are used to determine the main emotional tone of the song and are used to express the user's current emotion or desired emotion of the music. We use the most common "yellow face" emoji as the basis, based on its compactness and familiarity, which makes it easier for

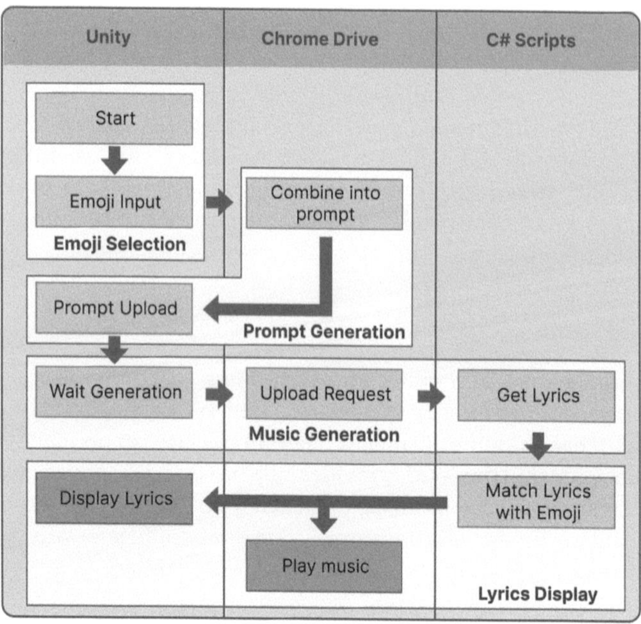

Fig. 1. Technical workflow of system architecture.

users to understand the emotions expressed. Based on Plutchik's eight basic emotion model [31], which maps emotions across different quadrants of emotional intensity and arousal, we selected and redrew 25 emojis covering each category of basic emotions. These emojis were made available for users to freely mix and match, allowing them to construct complex and nuanced emotional states, thereby enabling more layered and expressive emotional input.

Object-based emojis are used as a way to enrich music information, such as the scenarios where the music is used, what things or sounds users want to appear in the lyrics and music, and the instruments they want to use. Based on the summary of users' music-using scenarios in the preliminary interviews, 115 Apple Color Emoji patterns are extracted from the list of Apple iPhone Emoji provided by Emojipedia[2] and used as object emoji, such as sunsets, fireworks, and ocean waves, to help users better describe the background of the music and the content contained in it. The musical instrument category icons use self-drawn, easy-to-distinguish, and eye-catching patterns.

In general, users prefer to use emoticons that they can understand [9]. Given that emojis have been shown to have cognitive differences in different groups, for example, emojis were used differently in young and older groups, with young people using emojis more frequently to express emotions [16]. Was et al. [42] made a reminder for researchers designing with emoji that it is important to better understand how the target population understands and interprets emoji before

---

[2] https://emojipedia.org/.

starting the design. Therefore, during the prototyping process, we conducted a user perception test on the selected emojis representing various emotional tendencies.

3.4 Emoji Test

A total of 38 participants (15 males and 23 females) were recruited from individuals who regularly engage in online messaging and frequently use emojis. All participants were from mainland China, distributed across multiple provinces and cities, and ranged in age from 18 to 55 years (M = 30.34, SD = 11.61), to ensure a broad coverage of different regions, age groups, and genders. The test was administered anonymously through an online questionnaire platform.

The questionnaire consisted of two parts. In the first part, participants were presented with each emoji image and asked to provide a short description of their perceptions through open-ended questions. They subsequently rated the emotional tendency of each emoji using a five-point Likert scale ranging from 1 (very negative) to 5 (very positive). In the second part, participants were asked to identify any emojis they found incomprehensible or ambiguous and to further elaborate on the emotional perception conveyed by these symbols. The results, including word frequency statistics (proxemics summarized) and emotional tendency scores after excluding difficult-to-interpret emojis, are presented in Table 1. These results were used as emotional labels for corresponding emoji inputs in the music generation model, ensuring greater accuracy in the emotion mapping process.

3.5 User Interface Design

The interface design of **EmoGen** is based on convenient and efficient mobile requirements, emphasizing the fun and ease of use in the interactive process of music generation, allowing users to explore and create freely. The user interface of **EmoGen** consists of several pages (Fig. 2), including a start guide, emoji input for controlling music generation, loading music generation, playing music, and lyrics display.

The launch interface introduces users to the main features and usage of the application. Upon confirmation, the system transitions to the emoji input section, which consists of five independent pages: *Emotion, Scene, Element, Musical Style*, and *Instrument*. These pages allow users to select the emotions they wish to express, the intended music scenario, preferred elements, music style, and favored instruments. During the emoji selection process, users interact with dynamic emoji icons, and their selected emojis are displayed at the top of the screen. Users can freely navigate between pages to add or remove emojis, with no restrictions on the number of selections. By combining different emoji icons, users can construct a nuanced emotional profile to convey to the system.

After completing the emoji input, users proceed to the music generation interface. The system converts the selected emojis into information tags and transmits them to the API of the AI music generation model. A progress bar

Table 1. Mapping of Emoji Icons and Perceived Emotions

Emoji	Emotional Score	Comments
	4.03	Happy
	2.13	Sad
	1.50	Crying
	2.79	Surprised
	4.37	Satisfied
	3.26	Surprised
	2.00	Hard
	4.74	Kiss
	4.55	Love
	3.84	Laughing and crying
	4.13	Cool
	4.26	Mischievous
	2.26	Dizzy
	1.47	Angry
	2.39	Disdainful
	3.26	Smile
	2.03	Uncomfortable
	1.63	Poisoned
	3.18	Devilish

indicates the status of music generation. Upon completion, the system automatically transitions to the playback interface, where the generated music and synchronized lyrics are presented, providing an audiovisual representation of the expressed emotions. Through this interface design, the prototype offers users a complete, customized music generation experience, enabling intuitive emotional expression via emojis.

4   Evaluation

4.1   Participants

This study evaluated the prototype through a combination of quantitative and qualitative methods. Eight participants who regularly engaged with music for emotional expression (e.g., composing, listening, performing) were recruited based on the screening criterion of listening to or playing music at least twice per week. The final sample included four males and four females, aged between 21 to 48 (SD = 11.45). Among them, four participants had a professional music background-defined as having either formal training in at least one musical instrument or over five years of experience in a music-related profession-while the remaining participants were general users who engaged with music for entertainment or experiential purposes. The participants in this experiment were selected

Fig. 2. Screen shots of the user interfaces of **EmoGen**. (1): home page, (2): introduction page, (3–7): emotion input for generating music, (8): loading music generation, (9): playing generated music, and (10): lyrics display.

to cover the target age group and people with different musical backgrounds in order to evaluate the accuracy and feasibility of the prototype's emotional expression.

4.2   Experimental Procedure

Before the experiment commenced, participants were given an overview of the usage process and fundamental operations of **EmoGen**, informed about the required questionnaires and relevant considerations, and asked to sign an informed consent form. They were then instructed to use the application to express the context or emotion they intended to convey in the generated music. After completing the operation, they listened to a 90-second music piece generated based on their input emojis.

After that, the subjects rated the following three questions to measure the emotion expression support using a 10-point Likert scale: 1) the degree to which the generated music matched the intended emotions; 2) the degree to which the emoji was perceived in the music; and 3) the degree to which the emoji was integrated into the song as a whole.

In addition, to evaluate the perceived emotional alignment and usability of the system, questionnaire items were developed based on the core functional objectives of EmoGen. The System Usability Scale (SUS) was selected due to its established reliability and broad applicability in evaluating interactive system usability [8]. All questionnaire items are presented in Table 2.

Finally, semi-structured interviews were conducted with participants to gather insights on potential application scenarios and suggestions for system improvement. The interview data were analyzed using a thematic coding approach, following an open coding process to identify recurring patterns, which were then synthesized into higher-level themes reflecting users' emotional engagement and interaction experiences. The experiment was conducted in accordance with the Declaration of Helsinki and was approved by the Ethics Committee of Beijing Institute of Technology (protocol code: BIT-EC-H-115).

Table 2. Questions in the Questionnaire

Questions
Emotion Expression Support
1. I think the style of music matches the emotion I expected.
2. I feel the presence of my typed emoji in the music.
3. The emoji I typed blended well with the song overall.
Usability
1. I think that I would like to use this system frequently.
2. I found the system unnecessarily complex.
3. I thought the system was easy to use.
4. I think that I would need the support of a technical person to be able to use this system.
5. I found the various functions in this system were well integrated.
6. I thought there was too much inconsistency in this system.
7. I would imagine that most people would learn to use this system very quickly.
8. I found the system very cumbersome to use.
9. I felt very confident using the system.
10. I needed to learn a lot of things before I could get going with this system.

5 Results

5.1 Quantitative Analysis

The mean scores for the three items assessing emotional alignment between emojis and generated music were 7.88 (SD = 0.83), 7.38 (SD = 0.92), and 7.12 (SD = 1.12), respectively. These results indicate that the emoji-based music generation prototype demonstrated a strong ability to accurately reflect users' emotional inputs, with users perceiving a clear correspondence between their selected emojis and the emotional characteristics of the generated music (Fig.3).

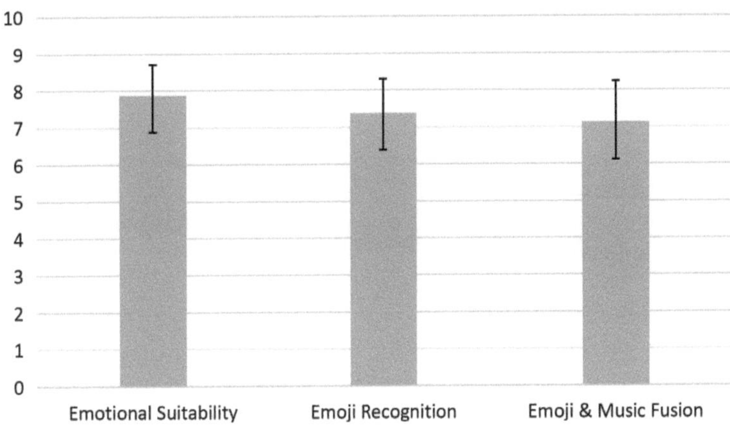

Fig. 3. Emotional Alignment Scores.

System usability and ease of learning were assessed using the System Usability Scale (SUS), where odd-numbered items represent positive statements and even-numbered items represent negative statements [25]. The distribution of responses for each SUS item is illustrated in Fig. 4. After item score conversion and percentile calculation [26], the usability component achieved a mean score of 81.30 (SD = 13.10), the learnability component scored 79.70 (SD = 14.80), and the overall SUS score was 80.90 (SD = 11.7). According to the standard interpretation of SUS scores, the system's usability was rated at a "good" level [4].

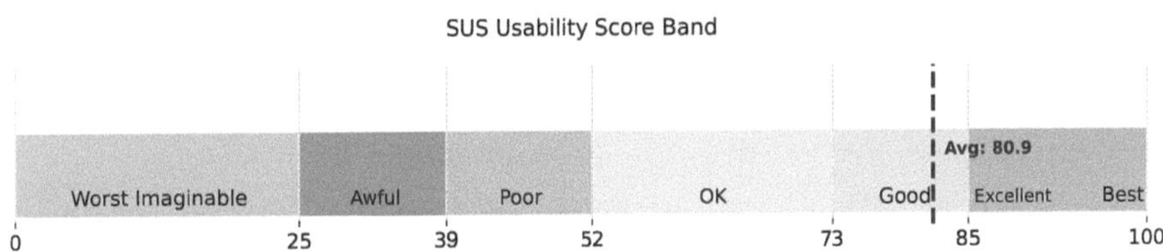

Fig. 4. System Usability Scale results.

5.2 Qualitative Research

The semi-structured interviews were organized around potential application scenarios and improvement suggestions [7]. Based on the results of the open coding of the interview data, we construct a total of three usage scenarios for music generation using emoji input: as a fun and auxiliary function combined with existing music software; as a stand-alone app applied to quick-expression scenarios such as travel and outdoor; and as a mood diary to record stages of mood through music and emoji. The subjects suggested that this design be combined with traditional music software and exist as a supplementary function or fun element during use. For example, *"I want to generate my music when the music recommended by the music software does not match my current emotions."* (P1) and *"I want to generate music to vent my emotions when I don't know what song I want to listen to in the music software."* (P5). Through testing, emoji input is not only suitable for specific scenarios (e.g., traveling and outdoor activities) but also able to satisfy users' needs for emotional recording in daily life. For example, *"I would use the prototype to generate my own music based on the environment while traveling."* (P2) and *"I would use the prototype for events such as birthday celebrations to quickly create music that is not repetitive or boring."* (P7). Finally, users tend to use emoji input in quick-expression scenarios and emotional recording, demonstrating its directness and efficiency when used for emotion expression and music generation. P4 and P8 expressed similar views after experiencing the prototype, *"I would use this to quickly record my mood at the moment or to recall my emotions at the time much later."* (P4). Overall, subjects were satisfied with the prototype's ability to express emotions quickly.

For the improvement suggestions, participants raised expectations about the degree to which the system could be personalized, the ability to actively perceive emotions, and the ability to assist with mental health intervention functions. For example, *"The input emoji tags can be customized by combining the user's personalized features to enhance the fun in the use of the prototype."* (P7), *"Add a perception function to automatically identify the current scene to more conveniently match the emoji and emotion."* (P3), and *"Add the function of emotion state statistics to visualize the user's emotion changes in a period of time."* (P8). The above future development expectations expand possibilities for the music generation experience using emoji interaction.

6   Discussion

6.1   Advantages of Emoji in Generative Music Interactions

This study validates the unique advantages of using emojis as an input method in a music generation system for emotion expression. User testing results indicate that emoji, as an intuitive and efficient input tool, effectively captures users' emotional intentions and translates them into corresponding musical expressions. **The perceived association between emojis and generated music received a strong endorsement, further confirming emojis' capability for emotional mapping in music generation.** This emoji-based interaction not only simplifies the process of personalized music creation, but also enhances the user's emotional engagement and expression efficiency in the music interaction experience. The intuitiveness and playfulness of emojis contribute to a more enjoyable user experience, particularly excelling in the quick expression of emotions or mood recording [6]. These findings suggest that emoji, as an emotional input tool, effectively compensates for the limitations of traditional text input in emotion expression and offers a more natural and engaging means of conveying emotions in AI-generated music. This work represents a preliminary exploration into using emoji-based interactions to facilitate emotion expression in generative music. Through prototype development and testing, as well as quantitative and qualitative research on user experience, we found that using emojis to express emotions in music generation demonstrates efficiency, accuracy, and playfulness similar to those observed in the field of computer-mediated communication (CMC) [10]. Moreover, user cognitive testing showed that emoji-based interaction for emotion expression was satisfactory in the application. Although emojis can reduce the user input effort, they may also cause some uncertainty and ambiguity in information dissemination [36]. The role of emojis and other symbolic expressions as interactive media in the music creation process could be further investigated for other applications. Prospects for this design include developing a music interaction app that serves as a long-term emotional diary [37], enabling users to track and reflect on their emotional changes over time. This app would integrate both entertainment and psychological well-being intervention features.

The good match between generated music and expected emotions demonstrates the accuracy and efficiency of using emojis to control music generation for expressing emotions. This finding highlights an advancement in user interaction with generative music, particularly in the context of emotion expression. The close alignment between the generated music and the expected emotions emphasizes the potential of using emojis as a powerful tool to control and tailor music generation [2]. This approach not only enhances the precision of emotion expression but also streamlines the process, making it more efficient and user-friendly. Additionally, we aim to enhance the application by incorporating system-driven recognition of external emotional states and environmental elements, such as facial expression analysis for emoji matching and image feature extraction for associating visual elements with emojis [23]. These enhancements would make the interaction process more proactive and efficient.

6.2   Limitations

The work has several limitations. First, the current prototype is the first iteration and could be improved in terms of aligning the AI-generated melody and lyrics with the user-input emojis during the final music presentation stage. Additionally, the sample size of participants in the user study is small. Future work will involve a larger and more diverse participant pool to more comprehensively evaluate the user experience of emoji-based music interaction. Finally, while emojis offer an intuitive and emotional input method, they may not fully capture the nuanced complexity of emotional expression in musical contexts. In future iterations, we aim to explore multimodal input approaches, such as combining emojis with text or other affective signals to enhance the system's expressiveness and better support users' emotional experiences in generative music interaction.

7   Conclusions

This work presents **EmoGen**, an interactive emoji-based application that supports exploratory behavior and emotional expression in music generation. By evaluating the application, we explore the connections between emoji-based interaction and emotion expression in music generation. Furthermore, we outline potential future applications combining emojis and generative music, such as supplementary features for music apps, quick emotion expression scenarios, and music-based emotional diaries, thereby expanding the application scope of such an interactive generative music system.

Acknowledgments. We thank all participants for their commitment to research.

Ethical Statement. The study was conducted in accordance with the Declaration of Helsinki and was approved by the Ethics Committee of Beijing Institute of Technology (protocol code: BIT-EC-H-115).

Funding. This research was funded by "the National Natural Science Foundation of China, grant number 52275234", "the Humanities and Social Science Fund of the Ministry of Education of China, grant number 22YJA760055", and "the Science and Technology Innovation Program Project of Beijing Institute of Technology, grant number 2024CX01023".

Author Contributions. Conceptualization, Jiayuan Guo and Jinyuan Guo; methodology, Jinyuan Guo and Jiayuan Guo; software, Jinyuan Guo, Weihan Chen and Tian Yuan; formal analysis, Jiayuan Guo and Zhaolin Lu; investigation, Jiayuan Guo, Weihan Chen and Tian Yuan; resources, Zhaolin Lu and Yue Zhang; data curation, Jiayuan Guo; writing—original draft preparation, Jiayuan Guo, Jinyuan Guo, Weihan Chen and Tian Yuan; writing—review and editing, Yue Zhang; visualization, Jiayuan Guo and Tian Yuan; supervision, Yue Zhang; project administration, Yue Zhang; funding acquisition, Zhaolin Lu. Jiayuan Guo, Zhaolin Lu, and Jinyuan Guo contributed equally to this work and share first authorship.

Disclosure of Interests. The authors declare that the research was conducted in the absence of any commercial or financial relationships that could be construed as a potential conflict of interest.

References

1. An, P., et al.: Vibemoji: exploring user-authoring multi-modal emoticons in social communication. In: Proceedings of the 2022 CHI Conference on Human Factors in Computing Systems, pp. 1–17 (2022). https://doi.org/10.1145/3491102.350194
2. Arora, A.: SongGen: framework for controllable AI song generation through interactive songwriting and artist emulation. Ph.D. thesis, Massachusetts Institute of Technology (2024)
3. Ball, P.: The music instinct: how music works and why we can't do without it. Random House (2010). https://doi.org/10.1353/not.2011.0123

4. Bangor, A., Kortum, P., Miller, J.: Determining what individual SUS scores mean: adding an adjective rating scale. J. Usabil. Stud. **4**(3), 114–123 (2009). https://doi.org/10.5555/2835587.2835589

5. Blagdon, J.: How emoji conquered the world: the story of the smiley face from the man who invented it. the verge (March 2013) (2013)

6. Boutet, I., LeBlanc, M., Chamberland, J.A., Collin, C.A.: Emojis influence emotional communication, social attributions, and information processing. Comput. Hum. Behav. **119**, 106722 (2021). https://doi.org/10.1016/j.chb.2021.106722

7. Boyd, K., et al.: Designing multimodal video search by examples (MVSE) user interfaces: UX requirements elicitation and insights from semi-structured interviews. In: Proceedings of the European Conference on Cognitive Ergonomics 2023, pp. 1–8 (2023). https://doi.org/10.1145/3605655.3605665

8. Brooke, J.: SUS: a quick and dirty usability scale. Usability Evaluation in Industry (1996)

9. Cao, Z., Ye, J.: Attention savings and emoticons usage in BBS. In: 2009 Fourth International Conference on Computer Sciences and Convergence Information Technology, pp. 416–419. IEEE (2009). https://doi.org/10.1109/ICCIT.2009.112

10. Chen, X., Siu, K.W.M.: Exploring user behaviour of emoticon use among Chinese youth. Behav. Inf. Technol. **36**(6), 637–649 (2017). https://doi.org/10.1080/0144929X.2016.1269199

11. Dash, A., Agres, K.: AI-based affective music generation systems: a review of methods and challenges. ACM Comput. Surv. **56**(11), 1–34 (2024). https://doi.org/10.1145/3672554

12. Derks, D., Fischer, A.H., Bos, A.E.: The role of emotion in computer-mediated communication: a review. Comput. Hum. Behav. **24**(3), 766–785 (2008). https://doi.org/10.1016/j.chb.2007.04.004

13. Dubnov, S., Assayag, G., Gokul, V.: Creative improvised interaction with generative musical systems. In: 2022 IEEE 5th International Conference on Multimedia Information Processing and Retrieval (MIPR), pp. 121–126. IEEE (2022). https://doi.org/10.1109/MIPR54900.2022.00028

14. Erle, T.M., Schmid, K., Goslar, S.H., Martin, J.D.: Emojis as social information in digital communication. Emotion **22**(7), 1529 (2022). https://doi.org/10.1037/emo0000992

15. Finnegan, R.: Music, experience, and the anthropology of emotion. In: The Cultural Study of Music, pp. 353–363. Routledge (2012). https://doi.org/10.4324/9780203149454

16. Gallud, J.A., Fardoun, H.M., Andres, F., Safa, N.: A study on how older people use emojis. In: Proceedings of the XIX International Conference on Human Computer Interaction, pp. 1–4 (2018). https://doi.org/10.1145/3233824.3233861

17. Guo, H., et al.: Emo-music: emotion recognition based music therapy with deep learning on physiological signals. In: 2024 IEEE First International Conference on Artificial Intelligence for Medicine, Health and Care (AIMHC), pp. 10–13. IEEE (2024). https://doi.org/10.1109/AIMHC59811.2024.00008

18. Guo, Z., Wang, Q., Liu, G., Guo, J., Lu, Y.: A music retrieval system using melody and lyric. In: 2012 IEEE International Conference on Multimedia and Expo Workshops, pp. 343–348. IEEE (2012). https://doi.org/10.1109/ICMEW.2012.65

19. Hand, C.J., Kennedy, A., Filik, R., Pitchford, M., Robus, C.M.: Emoji identification and emoji effects on sentence emotionality in ASD-diagnosed adults and neurotypical controls. J. Autism Dev. Disord. **53**(6), 1–15 (2022). https://doi.org/10.1007/s10803-022-05557-4

20. He, J.: Sharing emotions or/and making allies: the emoji's interpersonal function in Chinese social media news comments. Soc. Semiot. **33**(5), 1131–1146 (2023). https://doi.org/10.1080/10350330.2021.2025355
21. Huang, Q., et al.: Noise2music: text-conditioned music generation with diffusion models. arXiv preprint arXiv:2302.03917 (2023). https://doi.org/10.48550/arXiv.2302.03917
22. Knees, P., Schedl, M.: Music retrieval and recommendation: a tutorial overview. In: Proceedings of the 38th International ACM SIGIR Conference on Research and Development in Information Retrieval, pp. 1133–1136 (2015). https://doi.org/10.1145/2766462.2767880
23. Kolla, V.R.K.: Emojify: a deep learning approach for custom emoji creation and recognition. Int. J. Creat. Res. Thoughts (2021)
24. Lee, J.Y., Hong, N., Kim, S., Oh, J., Lee, J.: Smiley face: why we use emoticon stickers in mobile messaging. In: Proceedings of the 18th International Conference on Human-Computer Interaction with Mobile Devices and Services Adjunct, pp. 760–766 (2016). https://doi.org/10.1145/2957265.2961858
25. Lewis, J.R.: The system usability scale: past, present, and future. Int. J. Hum.-Comput. Interact. **34**(7), 577–590 (2018). https://doi.org/10.1080/10447318.2018.1455307
26. Lima, I.B., Jeong, Y., Lee, C., Suh, G., Hwang, W.: Severity of usability problems and system usability scale (SUS) scores on augmented reality (AR) user interfaces. ICIC Express Lett. Part B Appl **12**(2), 175–183 (2021). https://doi.org/10.24507/icicelb.12.02.175
27. Louie, R., Engel, J., Huang, C.Z.A.: Expressive communication: evaluating developments in generative models and steering interfaces for music creation. In: Proceedings of the 27th International Conference on Intelligent User Interfaces, pp. 405–417 (2022). https://doi.org/10.1145/3490099.3511159
28. Kurosu, M. (ed.): HCII 2021. LNCS, vol. 12764. Springer, Cham (2021). https://doi.org/10.1007/978-3-030-78468-3
29. Park, J., Kim, M., Kim, H.Y.: Image is all for music retrieval: interactive music retrieval system using images with mood and theme attributes. Int. J. Hum.-Comput. Interact. 1–15 (2024). https://doi.org/10.1080/10447318.2023.2201557
30. Park, J., Shin, H., Oh, C., Kim, H.Y.: "is text-based music search enough to satisfy your needs?" A new way to discover music with images. In: Proceedings of the CHI Conference on Human Factors in Computing Systems, pp. 1–21 (2024). https://doi.org/10.1145/3613904.3642126
31. Plutchik, R.: A general psychoevolutionary theory of emotion. Emotion: Theory Res. Exp. **1** (1980). https://doi.org/10.1177/053901882021004003
32. Qiu, Z., et al.: Mind band: a crossmedia AI music composing platform. In: Proceedings of the 27th ACM International Conference on Multimedia, pp. 2231–2233 (2019). https://doi.org/10.1145/3343031.3350610
33. Rasheed, B., Abbas, T., Hafiza, R.I.: Emojis role in the communication: interesting and amazing expressions (2024)
34. The Feeling Economy. LNCS, Springer, Cham (2021). https://doi.org/10.1007/978-3-030-52977-2
35. Seargeant, P.: The Emoji Revolution: How Technology is Shaping the Future of Communication. Cambridge University Press (2019). https://doi.org/10.1558/sols.41571
36. Son, J., Negahban, A.: Examining the impact of emojis on disaster communication: a perspective from the uncertainty reduction theory. AIS Trans. Hum.-Comput. Interact. **15**(4), 377–413 (2023). https://doi.org/10.17705/1thci.00095

37. Ståhl, A., Höök, K., Svensson, M., Taylor, A.S., Combetto, M.: Experiencing the affective diary. Pers. Ubiquit. Comput. **13**, 365–378 (2009). https://doi.org/10.1007/s00779-008-0202-7

38. Sugiyama, S.: Kawaii meiru and maroyaka neko: mobile emoji for relationship maintenance and aesthetic expressions among Japanese teens. First Monday (2015). https://doi.org/10.5210/fm.v20i10.5826

39. Deng, L., Ma, W.W.K., Fong, C.W.R. (eds.): New Media for Educational Change. ECTY, Springer, Singapore (2018). https://doi.org/10.1007/978-981-10-8896-4

40. Tchemeube, R.B., et al.: Evaluating human-AI interaction via usability, user experience and acceptance measures for mmm-c: a creative AI system for music composition. arXiv preprint arXiv:2504.14071 (2025). https://doi.org/10.48550/arXiv.2504.14071

41. Wang, Y., Cui, J., Tang, T.Y.: Position paper: an emoji-based interactive app to aid emotion expression for autistic children. In: Companion of the 2024 on ACM International Joint Conference on Pervasive and Ubiquitous Computing, pp. 706–708 (2024). https://doi.org/10.1145/3675094.3678478

42. Was, C.A., Hamrick, P.: What did they mean by that? young adults' interpretations of 105 common emojis. Front. Psychol. **12**, 655297 (2021). https://doi.org/10.3389/fpsyg.2021.655297

43. Yu, J., Wu, S., Lu, G., Li, Z., Zhou, L., Zhang, K.: Suno: potential, prospects, and trends. Front. Inf. Technol. Electron. Eng. 1–6 (2024). https://doi.org/10.1631/FITEE.2400299

44. Zhou, R., Hentschel, J., Kumar, N.: Goodbye text, hello emoji: mobile communication on WeChat in china. In: Proceedings of the 2017 CHI Conference on Human Factors in Computing Systems, pp. 748–759 (2017). https://doi.org/10.1145/3025453.3025800

45. Zinko, R., Stolk, P., Furner, Z., Almond, B.: A picture is worth a thousand words: how images influence information quality and information load in online reviews. Electron. Mark. **30**(4), 775–789 (2019). https://doi.org/10.1007/s12525-019-00345-y

Impact of Soft Drink Packaging on Pupil Dilation and Blink Rate

Ana Teixeira[1,2,3], Hugo de Almeida[4], Sónia Brito-Costa[1,5(✉)], Fernanda Antunes[5], and Sílvia Espada[3]

[1] InED - Center for Research and Innovation in Education, Polytechnic of Coimbra, Portugal, Lagar dos Cortiços, S. Martinho do Bispo, 3045-093 Coimbra, Portugal
sonya.b.costa@gmail.com
[2] GECAD – Research Group on Intelligent Engineering and Computing for Advanced Innovation and Development, Institute of Engineering –ISEP, Polytechnic of Porto, Porto, Portugal
[3] Rua António Bernardino de Almeida, 431, 42249-015 Porto, Portugal
[4] University of Aveiro, Aveiro, Portugal
[5] Polytechnic University of Coimbra,
Rua da Misericórdia, Lagar dos Cortiços, S. Martinho do Bispo, 3045-093 Coimbra, Portugal

Abstract. This study explores the influence of soft drink packaging design—focusing on Coca-Cola, Fanta, and Sprite—on cognitive load and visual engagement among consumers. By examining the relationship between packaging aesthetics and consumer psychology, the research aims to uncover how visual stimuli evoke emotional responses and guide purchasing decisions in a competitive market. A total of 28 participants were presented with various packaging designs, including cans, bottles, and a control image, while Left Pupil Dilation (LPD), Right Pupil Dilation (RPD), and Blink Rate per Minute (BKPMIN) were measured to assess cognitive load and emotional arousal. Statistical analyses, including t-tests and ANOVA, revealed significant differences in visual engagement and cognitive load across packaging types. Coca-Cola bottles elicited higher pupil dilation (mean LPD: 16.48) compared to cans (15.30), while Fanta cans (15.47) outperformed bottles (14.70). For Sprite, cans (11.84) induced greater dilation than bottles (11.19). Blink rate analysis further highlighted differences in cognitive load, with Coca-Cola bottles showing a higher blink rate (11.28 bpm) compared to cans (8.56 bpm). Fanta cans (14.33 bpm) exceeded bottles (11.53 bpm), whereas Sprite bottles exhibited notably lower blink rates (2.52 bpm) than cans (10.22 bpm). These findings suggest that soft drink cans, particularly for Coca-Cola and Fanta, promote greater visual engagement and lower cognitive load than bottles, emphasizing the critical role of packaging design in shaping consumer perception and behavior.

Keywords: eye-tracking · consumer behavior · product design · soft drinks · Coca-Cola · Fanta · Sprite

M. Schrepp and M. Rauterberg (Eds.): HCII 2025, LNCS 16342, pp. 58–67, 2026.
https://doi.org/10.1007/978-3-032-13164-5_4

1 Introduction

Eye tracking has proven to be an indispensable tool for unraveling the cognitive processes underlying human interaction with the visual environment. By precisely recording eye movements, such as pupil dilation, gaze location, and blink patterns, this technique allows for inferences about attention, information processing, and emotional responses (Abreu et al. 2020, Schall & Romano Bergstrom, 2014b; Tobii, 2010).

The origins of eye tracking can be traced back to the studies of Émile Javal, who in the 19th century observed that reading does not occur in a continuous manner but rather through fixations and saccades. Since then, eye tracking technology has evolved significantly, becoming more accessible and precise, driven by advancements in computing and optics (Pillai et al., 2020; Schall & Romano Bergstrom, 2014b). The applications of eye tracking are vast, ranging from neuroscience to marketing and design

By analyzing visual patterns, researchers can gain valuable insights into how individuals perceive and interact with different stimuli, such as images, videos, and objects (De Almeida et al., 2022; Liu et al., 2021; Pillai et al., 2020; Timm Barros et al., 2021; Wąsikowska, 2015). In this study, we used the Gazepoint GP3-HD eye tracker to investigate how soft drink packaging design influences consumers' visual perception and decision-making. By analyzing the eye movements of 28 participants while they viewed images of cans and bottles of Coca-Cola, Fanta, and Sprite, we sought to identify how visual elements such as shape, size, and color affect consumer attention and engagement. It is important to note that the sample size and the controlled nature of the experiment limit the generalization of the results to other populations and contexts. The results of this study can contribute to the field of neuromarketing, providing empirical evidence on the relationship between product design and consumer response. By understanding how consumers visually interact with packaging, marketers and designers can develop more effective strategies to attract and engage the target audience.

2 Experiment

The GP3 eye tracker uses infrared light to monitor pupil dilation and gaze direction, capturing various ocular metrics. This technology helps researchers identify where and how long participants focus their gaze, providing valuable insights into cognitive processes, interests, and aversions (Schall & Romano Bergstrom, 2014a). Eye-tracking studies are essential for understanding the link between brain function and the visual system, as evidence suggests visual attention and eye movement share the same neural circuits (Efeturk et al., 2022; Josephson, 2008; Mozaffari Chanijani et al., 2016; Schall & Romano Bergstrom, 2014a).

2.1 Participants

Twenty-eight volunteers aged 18–26 participated, including males and females, primarily students in fields like communication, multimedia, sports, and design. Participants had normal vision or used glasses or contact lenses during the experiment. All met the vision requirements for accurate eye-tracking data.

System and Parameters. The Gazepoint control system managed the eye-tracking tasks. The tracker was positioned on a screen at a 45° angle, 70 cm from the participants' eyes, tailored to individual height. Calibration involved following a moving white circle to align gaze points, with green lines confirming success and red lines prompting recalibration. Accurate calibration ensured reliable data collection. Key metrics included Left Pupil Diameter (LPD), Right Pupil Diameter (RPD), and Blinking Per Minute (BKPMIN). Testing occurred in a dimly lit room to reduce distractions.

2.2 Procedure

The display duration of the white point during calibration was crucial for stabilizing participants' focus. The moving point engaged visual tracking and helped maintain attention, optimizing alignment for precise measurements. On the Gazepoint calibration scale (5 to 9), all participants achieved the highest score of 9.

Task. The task consisted of three phases: **Survey**, **Testing**, and **Data Preprocessing**, each designed to evaluate participants' visual attention and preferences.

Phase 1: Survey
Participants began by answering a survey with the following questions:

1. Do you wear glasses or contact lenses?
2. Do you regularly consume soft drinks? If so, which ones?
3. What factors influence your purchasing decisions?
4. Do you prefer bottles or cans?
5. Which design elements attract your attention the most?
6. Are you familiar with the designs of Coca-Cola, Fanta, and Sprite?

The survey gathered demographic and behavioral data to contextualize participants' eye-tracking results.

Phase 2: Testing

a. **Group Assignment**

After completing the survey, the 28 participants were divided into seven groups of four members each. The groups were assigned different stimuli:

1. **Group 1**: Coca-Cola can
2. **Group 2**: Coca-Cola bottle
3. **Group 3**: Fanta can
4. **Group 4**: Fanta bottle
5. **Group 5**: Sprite can
6. **Group 6**: Sprite bottle
7. **Group 7 (Control Group)**: No soft drink -related stimulus

b. **Testing Environment**

Participants were individually escorted to a square-shaped testing room staffed by two facilitators. The room was dimly lit to minimize distractions. Each participant sat in front of an eye tracker and a screen.

c. **Image Presentation**

The testing sequence for each participant followed this standardized structure:

1. **Black Screen (3 s)**: A empty black screen prepared participants for the test.
2. **Fixation Circle (2 s)**: A black dot on a white background appeared to ensure proper focus.
3. **Stimulus Image (5 s)**: Each group was shown their assigned stimulus (e.g., a soft drink can or bottle).

The sequential presentation ensured participants' undivided attention on each image, minimizing distractions and isolating the impact of each stimulus.

Phase 3: Data Preprocessing

a. **Calibration**

Before testing, calibration was performed using **Gazer**, an open-source tool for gaze and pupil data preprocessing. Calibration involved displaying five points for each eye. Successful calibration required all 10 points to be valid. Calibration quality was rated on a scale of 0 to 5.

b. **Monitoring and Validation**

Calibration ensured the accuracy of gaze and pupil data. Any data loss, such as the eye tracker failing to detect one or both eyes, would have invalidated the participant's data. No instances of data loss occurred during this study due to careful monitoring and diligent calibration procedures.

c. **Analysis**

The data were analyzed to identify patterns of visual attention and assess the effectiveness of different design elements in capturing participants' gaze. Key outcomes included:

- Distribution of visual attention across soft drink designs
- Salient features influencing participants' focus

This structured approach ensured reliable, consistent data collection and valuable insights into the dynamics of visual attention and design preferences.

3 Results

The computer analysis focused on assessing pupil dilation and blinking patterns, as these metrics provide insights into participants' emotional arousal and attention allocation towards the presented stimuli. Research indicates that emotional arousal during visual stimuli is linked to pupillary responses. Additionally, blinking serves as a measure of attention allocation, with decreased blinking corresponding to heightened focus or cognitive load, while increased blinking suggests reduced attention towards the target stimulus. The analysis centered on the metrics of LPD (Left Pupil Dilation), RPD (Right Pupil Dilation), and BKPMIN (Blinks Per Minute). Comparisons were made between various stimuli, including Coca-Cola cans and bottles, Fanta cans and bottles, and Sprite cans and bottles, as well as between cans and bottles of each brand. Finally, these stimuli were compared to a control image. To consolidate the data, Jamovi-R was utilized for organization, selection, and calculation of the values. This analytical approach enabled the extraction of meaningful insights regarding participants' responses to different stimuli and facilitated the comparison of attentional responses across various conditions.

3.1 Pupil Dilation Analysis of Coca-Cola, Fanta, and Sprite

To analyze the impact of soft drink packaging on cognitive load and visual engagement, we measured Left Pupil Dilation (LPD) and Right Pupil Dilation (RPD) in participants viewing Coca-Cola, Fanta, and Sprite cans and bottles. Coca-Cola bottles elicited a higher average LPD (16.48) compared to cans (15.30), suggesting increased arousal or interest. RPD was also higher for bottles (17.07) than cans (16.00), with a 1.07-unit difference. These results imply that Coca-Cola bottles may cause higher cognitive load or reduced engagement than cans, Fig. 1.

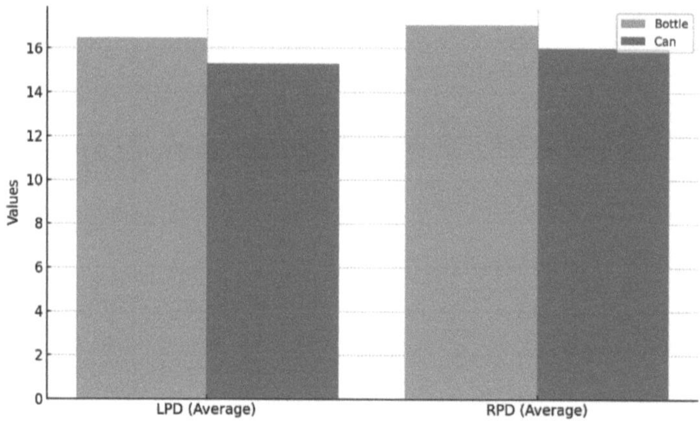

Fig. 1. Comparison of Coca-Cola Bottle vs. Coca-Cola Can_ LPD and RPD Averages.

For Fanta, cans showed a higher LPD (15.47) than bottles (14.70), with a difference of 0.77 units. RPD followed the same trend, with cans averaging 16.37 and bottles 15.14, a 1.23-unit difference, Fig. 2. An independent samples t-test confirmed a significant difference in pupil dilation between Fanta cans and bottles (t(50) = 2.5, p = 0.015).

Sprite cans had a higher LPD (11.84) than bottles (11.19), but the RPD difference was more pronounced, Fig. 3: cans averaged 11.96 and bottles 6.30, a 5.66-unit difference. An independent samples t-test confirmed a significant difference in pupil dilation

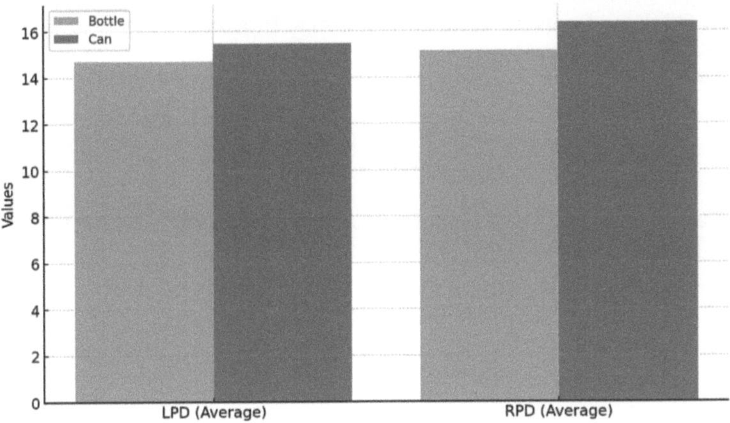

Fig. 2. Comparison of Fanta Bottle vs. Fanta Can_ LPD and RPD Averages.

between Sprite cans and bottles ($t(37) = 3.91$, $p < 0.001$). A one-way ANOVA comparing pupil dilation across the six conditions (Coca-Cola can, Coca-Cola bottle, Fanta can, Fanta bottle, Sprite can, Sprite bottle) revealed significant differences ($F(5, 168) = 3.45$, $p < 0.01$). Post-hoc Tukey's HSD test showed that cans elicited higher pupil dilation than bottles for Coca-Cola, Fanta, and Sprite. Specifically, Sprite cans had significantly greater pupil dilation than Sprite bottles ($p < 0.01$), and both Coca-Cola and Fanta cans showed higher pupil dilation than their respective bottles ($p < 0.05$). These results suggest that cans elicit higher visual engagement and lower cognitive load.

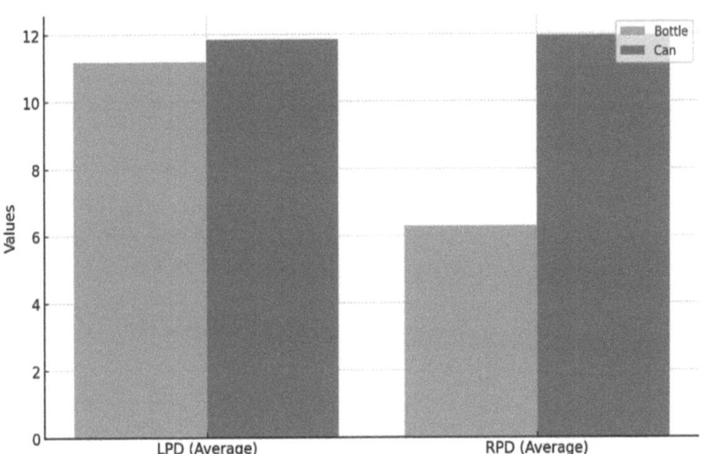

Fig. 3. Comparison of Sprite Bottle vs. Fanta Can_ LPD and RPD Averages.

3.2 Pupil Dilation Analysis: Bottles vs. Control Image

To evaluate how soft drink packaging affects cognitive load and visual engagement, we measured Left Pupil Dilation (LPD) and Right Pupil Dilation (RPD) while participants viewed Coca-Cola, Fanta, and Sprite cans and bottles, as well as a control image.

Cans:

- LPD: Fanta can (15.47) had the highest LPD, slightly exceeding the Coca-Cola can (15.30) by 0.17 and the Sprite can (11.84) by 3.63. The control image showed the highest LPD overall (16.16), indicating greater visual engagement.
- RPD: Fanta can (16.37) had the highest RPD, surpassing Coca-Cola can (16.00) by 0.37 and Sprite can (11.96) by 4.41. The control image (15.97) ranked second lowest, suggesting less cognitive effort.

Bottles:

- LPD: Coca-Cola bottle (16.48) had the highest LPD, exceeding the Fanta bottle (14.70) by 1.78 and the Sprite bottle (11.19) by 5.29. The control image (16.16) was second highest, indicating strong engagement.
- RPD: Coca-Cola bottle (17.07) had the highest RPD, surpassing Fanta bottle (15.14) by 1.93 and Sprite bottle (6.30) by 10.70. The control image (15.97) ranked second, reflecting significant cognitive processing.

A one-way ANOVA confirmed significant differences in LPD and RPD ($F(5, 168) = X$, $p < 0.01$). Tukey's HSD test showed that Coca-Cola bottles elicited significantly higher LPD and RPD than Sprite bottles ($p < 0.01$), and the control image had higher LPD than Sprite bottles ($p < 0.05$). In conclusion, Coca-Cola and Fanta packaging, particularly bottles, generated higher visual engagement and cognitive load than Sprite packaging, with Sprite bottles eliciting the least attention.

3.3 Blinking Rate Analysis of Coca-Cola, Fanta, and Sprite

We analyzed Blinks Per Minute (BKPMIN) to assess the impact of soft drink packaging on cognitive load and visual engagement.

- Coca-Cola: The bottle elicited a higher blinking rate (11.28 bpm) than the can (8.56 bpm), suggesting increased cognitive load or reduced visual engagement with the bottle.
- Fanta: The can required more cognitive effort (14.33 bpm) compared to the bottle (11.53 bpm).
- Sprite: The bottle had significantly lower blinking rates (2.52 bpm) than the can (10.22 bpm), indicating reduced cognitive load and potentially greater visual engagement with the bottle.

A one-way ANOVA revealed significant differences in blinking rates across the six conditions (Coca-Cola can, Coca-Cola bottle, Fanta can, Fanta bottle, Sprite can, Sprite bottle) ($F(5, 168) = 4.23$, $p < .01$). Post-hoc analysis using Tukey's HSD test showed that the Sprite bottle had significantly lower blinking rates than all other conditions.

However, no significant differences were found between the Coca-Cola can and bottle or the Fanta can and bottle.

In summary, Sprite bottles demonstrated the lowest blinking rates, suggesting higher visual engagement, while Coca-Cola bottles and Fanta cans exhibited higher blinking rates, indicating greater cognitive load.

3.4   Blinking Rate Analysis: Cans and Bottles vs. Control Image

A one-way ANOVA followed by Tukey's HSD post-hoc tests was conducted to compare blinking rates across three soft drink designs (cans and bottles) and a control image, Fig. 4.

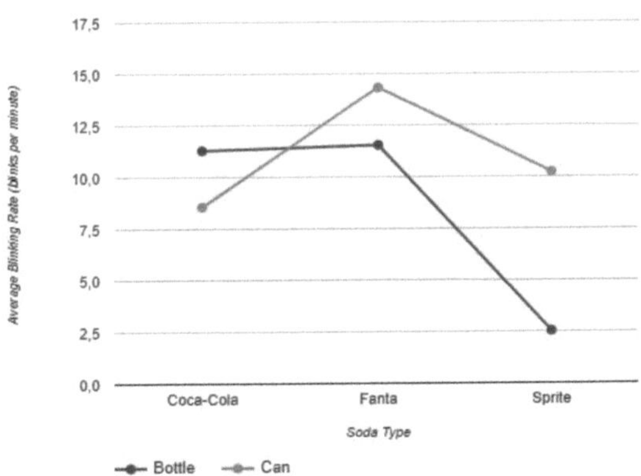

Fig. 4. Average Blinking Rate by Sod (Bottle vs.Can).

Analysis showed significant differences in blinking rates for both cans ($F(3, 112) = 3.87$, $p < .05$) and bottles ($F(3, 112) = 2.89$, $p < .05$). Fanta cans elicited higher blinking rates than Coca-Cola cans and the control image, indicating greater cognitive effort or reduced engagement. No significant difference was found between Coca-Cola and Sprite cans. For bottles, Fanta bottles had higher blinking rates than Sprite bottles and the control image, suggesting increased cognitive load or lower engagement. No significant difference was observed between Coca-Cola bottles and the control image. Overall, Fanta designs (both cans and bottles) may impose higher cognitive load or reduce engagement compared to Coca-Cola and Sprite.

4   Discussion and Conclusions

This study explored how soft drink packaging designs influence consumers' visual engagement and cognitive load, using pupil dilation and blink rates as objective measures. Coca-Cola bottles elicited higher pupil than cans, suggesting bottles provoke stronger emotional responses and greater visual engagement. However, greater pupil dilation does not always indicate efficient cognitive processing; it may reflect higher cognitive load, as seen in the Coca-Cola bottle's design, which might capture more attention but require more cognitive effort to process. Fanta cans caused higher pupil dilation than bottles, implying a more complex or visually overloaded design, which may increase cognitive demand. The higher blink rate in Fanta bottles (14.33 bpm) suggests mental effort due to processing multiple visual elements. In contrast, Sprite bottles showed lower pupil dilation and blink rates, indicating simpler, more cognitively efficient design, aligning with minimalist design principles that promote quicker and easier visual processing (Maffei & Angrilli, 2019). These findings emphasize the need for a balance between visual appeal and cognitive complexity in packaging. Engaging designs, like the Coca-Cola bottle, may attract attention but can cause cognitive overload, reducing clarity. Simpler designs, like the Sprite bottle, are more efficient for contexts where clarity is crucial. For fast-moving consumer goods like soft drinks, packaging should balance visual appeal and cognitive efficiency to ensure effective communication and a positive consumer experience. In summary, while complex designs may capture attention, they can also increase cognitive load, negatively affecting clarity and communication. Successful packaging captures attention without overwhelming consumers, contributing to a positive consumption experience.

Acknowledgments. This research work was supported by National Funds through the Portuguese FCT—Fundação para a Ciência e a Tecnologia under the R&D Units Project Scope, UIDB/00760/2020 (https://doi.org/10.54499/UIDB/00760/2020). This research work was developed under the project RM4Health (ITEA-2021-21022-RM4Health), funded by the European Regional Development Fund (ERDF) within the project number COMPETE2030-FEDER00391100. We would like to express our sincere gratitude to all the participants of this study and to the FCT – Fundação para a Ciência e a Tecnologia, I.P., under the project UIDB/05198/2025, DOI identifier https://doi.org/10.54499/UID/05198/2025 Centro de Investigação e Inovação em Educação, inED.. We would like to express our heartfelt gratitude to the students Márcia Carvalho, Mariana Silva, Marta Rebelo, Sara Araújo, and Sara Neves for their dedication, hard work, and invaluable contributions throughout this project. References to commercial trademarks in this work are solely for technical identification and scientific reproducibility, in compliance with Portuguese law. This use falls under the exceptions of Article 209 of the Industrial Property Code and Article 75(2)(b) of the Copyright and Related Rights Code, and does not constitute commercial promotion, endorsement, or any undue advantage. The work is purely academic and non-profit.

References

Abreu, C., de Almeida, H., Lucchese, F., Donado Briegas, M.J.J., Sanchez Iglesias, A.I., Castro, F.v., Brito-Costa, S.: The importance of brandy equity in natural human behavior: A study with eyetracking. Confin. Cephalalgica. **30**(1) (2020)

De Almeida, H.M.R., Brito-Costa, S., Bem-Haja, P., Briegas, J.J.M.: Colour usage in the lettering and in background manipulation on logotypes: Eyetracking evidences. Confinia Cephalalgica et Neurologica. **32** (2022)

Efeturk, O.A., Turgut, G., Dereshgi, H.A., Yilmaz, A.: A review of visual attention research using eye-tracking technologies. Review Paper. J. Smart Syst. Res. **3**(2) (2022)

Josephson, S.: Keeping your readers' eyes on the screen: an eye-tracking study comparing sans serif and serif typefaces. Vis. Commun. Q. **15**(1–2) (2008). https://doi.org/10.1080/155513908 01914595

Liu, H., Liu, H., Li, F., Han, B., Wang, C.: Effect of cognitive control on attentional processing of emotional information among older adults: evidence from an eye-tracking study. Front. Aging Neurosci. **13** (2021). https://doi.org/10.3389/fnagi.2021.644379

Maffei, A., Angrilli, A.: Spontaneous blink rate as an index of attention and emotion during film clips viewing. Physiol. Behav. **204** (2019). https://doi.org/10.1016/j.physbeh.2019.02.037

Mozaffari Chanijani, S.S., Al-Naser, M., Bukhari, S.S., Borth, D., Alleny, S.E.M., Denge, A.: An eye movement study on scientific papers using wearable eye tracking technology. In: 2016 9th International Conference on Mobile Computing and Ubiquitous Networking, ICMU 2016 (2016). https://doi.org/10.1109/ICMU.2016.7742085

Pillai, P., Ayare, P., Balasingam, B., Milne, K., Biondi, F.: Response time and eye tracking datasets for activities demanding varying cognitive load. Data Brief. **33** (2020). https://doi.org/10.1016/j.dib.2020.106389

Schall, A., Romano Bergstrom, J.: Eye tracking in user experience design. In: Eye Tracking in User Experience Design (2014a). https://doi.org/10.1016/C2012-0-06867-6

Schall, A., Romano Bergstrom, J.: Introduction to eye tracking. In: Eye Tracking in User Experience Design (2014b). https://doi.org/10.1016/B978-0-12-408138-3.00001-7

Timm Barros, S.E., Diniz Teixeira, H., Merlotti Rodas, C., Borsetti Gregorio Vidotti, S.A., Vesu Alves, R.C.: Eye tracking e reações da pupila em estudos de User Experience. Brazilian Journal of Information Science: Research Trends. **15** (2021). https://doi.org/10.36311/1981-1640.2021.v15.e02113

Tobii..: Tobii Eye Tracking - an Introduction to Eye Tracking and Tobii Eye Trackers. Technology (2010)

Wąsikowska, B.: Eye tracking in marketing research. Zeszyty Naukowe Uniwersytetu Szczecińskiego. Studia Informatica. **36** (2015). https://doi.org/10.18276/si.2015.36-13

Enhancing Financial Literacy and Management Through Goal-Directed Design and Gamification in Personal Finance Application

Phuong Lien To[(✉)]

School of Arts and Creative Technologies, University of York, York, UK
phuongliento161@gmail.com

Abstract. This study explores the development of a financial management application for young people using Alan Cooper's Goal-Directed Design method. Through interviews, surveys, and usability testing, the Mabu app was designed to improve financial literacy by combining personalised features and gamification. Findings highlight the effectiveness of gamified learning and tailored experiences in encouraging better financial behavior among young users.

Keywords: Financial literacy · Goal-Directed Design · Gamification · Mobile App · User Experience · Personal Finance

1 Introduction

As the economic environment is changing at breakneck speed, personal financial management has become more critical than ever [1]. The lack of personal financial management skills increasingly [2] puts young people under economic pressure, unable to manage problems that arise in life, leading to being caught in a spiral of debt [3, 4]. According to the 2023 UK Money Literacy Test, only 17% of individuals aged 18–24 demonstrated sufficient financial literacy, highlighting an urgent need for accessible, engaging financial education.

With mobile applications increasingly used to assist in money management, there is an opportunity to design digital tools that not only track finances but also educate and motivate young users. Gamification - embedding game elements like points, badges, and feedback, has proven effective in driving user engagement across many domains, yet its application in personal finance remains underexplored. In parallel, Goal-Directed Design [5] offers a structured method to align product functionality with users' real goals.

This paper presents the development and evaluation of Mabu, a mobile financial management app designed for young adults. By combining Goal-Directed Design and gamification, Mabu aims to increase financial awareness, user motivation, and promote sustainable financial behaviours through an engaging and user-centric experience.

To guide this work, the following research questions were addressed:

- **RQ1.** How do young people currently manage their finances?

M. Schrepp and M. Rauterberg (Eds.): HCII 2025, LNCS 16342, pp. 68–84, 2026.
https://doi.org/10.1007/978-3-032-13164-5_5

- **RQ2.** What challenges do they face in managing their finances effectively?
- **RQ3.** To what extent can Goal-Directed Design and Gamification increase user engagement and motivation in personal finance apps to improve financial literacy?

2 Background and Related Works

2.1 Financial Literacy

Financial literacy is a foundational element for achieving financial inclusion and long-term well-being. It influences individuals' capacity to engage with financial products and services [6]. The Organisation for Economic Co-operation and Development (OECD) defines financial literacy as the ability to understand and apply financial knowledge to make informed decisions [1]. Numerous studies have linked low financial literacy to problematic financial behaviors, including high debt levels, limited savings, and poor responses to unexpected expenses [7–9]. Conversely, individuals with higher financial literacy demonstrate better investment decisions, savings behaviors, and retirement planning [10, 11].

Despite its significance, financial literacy levels remain relatively low across both developed and developing contexts [1]. Educational programs targeting youth often struggle with incomplete curricula and lack of learner engagement, resulting in limited real-world applicability [12]. This is especially problematic as young adults frequently experience challenges in money management, which can affect academic performance and overall well-being [13–15]. Recent evidence suggests that digital financial tools can positively impact financial behavior among young users [16], highlighting opportunities to leverage technology to address these gaps.

2.2 User Experience and Gamification in Mobile Financial Applications

User experience (UX) design plays a critical role in digital product development. The Technology Acceptance Model (TAM) (Fig. 1) introduced by Davis [17] identifies Perceived Usefulness and Ease of Use as key drivers of user acceptance.

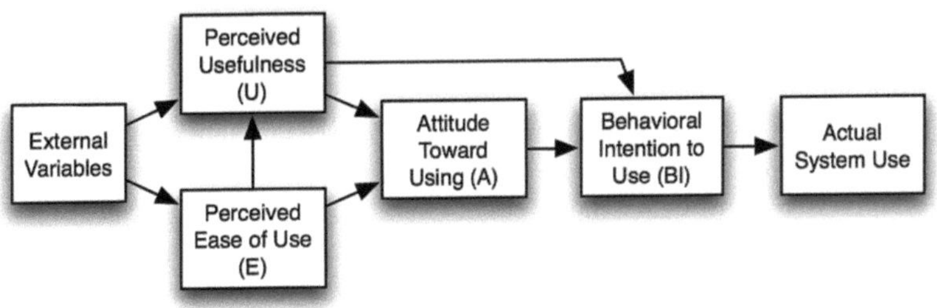

Fig. 1. The Technology Acceptance Model [17].

Building on this, the UTAUT model [18] expands the framework with additional constructs: Performance Expectancy, Effort Expectancy, Social Influence, and Facilitating Conditions, along with moderating factors such as age and experience (Fig. 2).

Later, UTAUT2 [19] further incorporates Hedonic Motivation, Price Value, and Habit, acknowledging the growing complexity of technology adoption in everyday life.

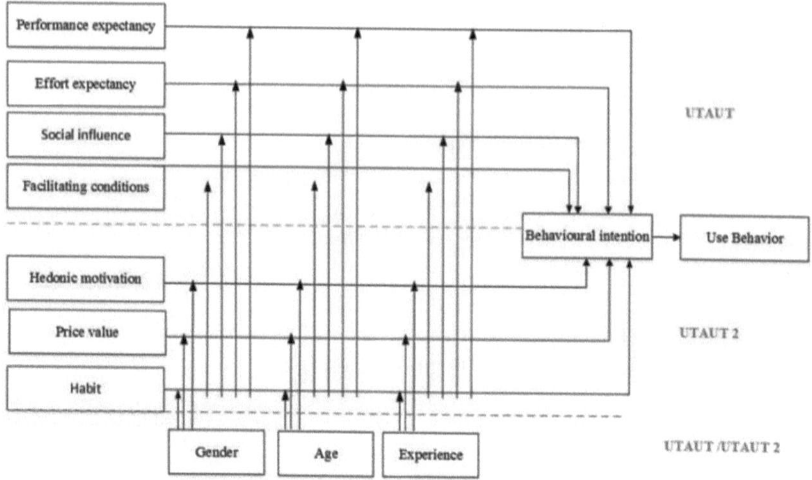

Fig. 2. UTAUT and UTAUT2 model [20].

Mobile devices are widely used in human life today. Compared with user experience in other platforms, mobile user experience has differences [21]. Applying technology to raise awareness about personal financial management is a popular trend today with the advent of many software and applications supporting financial management. These apps are like personal money managers for young people as they give users an overview of how their money is spent so that users can monitor and plan spending appropriately [22]. However, these applications only provide tools, and how to use them effectively depends on the user. Therefore, they are not optimised to help users gain financial knowledge to help them proactively build a strategy to manage their accounts.

A key construct in UTAUT2, hedonic motivation, has received growing attention for its ability to enhance user engagement. In the model, hedonic motivation comes from users feeling joy or being rewarded [19]. Espinosa-Curiel et al. [23] have proven the positive influence of children's excitement in acquiring knowledge through playing video games. Similarly, according to the survey results of Hussain et al. [24], enjoyment is one of three factors that impact user adoption of mobile maps.

A popular method of increasing hedonic motivation is using gamification. Hamari et al. [25] define gamification as the use of game-related elements such as points, badges, leaderboards, and rewards in non-game contexts, including mobile application design. This method is used by designers to increase user motivation and interaction with the product or system [26] when it can bring joy and excitement to the user after the targeted task completion.

Gamification is one of the emerging techniques applied to FinTech to help increase user engagement or intention rather than financial benefits [27]. Working together on the application of gamification in the financial sector, Bayuk and Altobello [28] demonstrate the effectiveness of this kind of technology in improving the financial literacy of college students. Financial service applications generally have limited design elements to increase because they are designed to monitor accounts and perform transactions. However, if elements related to playfulness are added, customers will be more interested in using it [29].

2.3 Goal-Directed Design Framework

In user experience design, Goal-Directed Design is one of the popular methods of designing products, including digital products. It focuses on meeting the goals of users [30]. Goal-Directed Design was first introduced by Alan Cooper in his book in 1995 [31].

In general, the process of Goal-Directed Design includes six stages: Research, Modeling, Requirements, Framework, Refinement, and Validation [32]. Through user research and persona development, designers gain deep insights into user motivations and contexts. These are then translated into functional and emotional requirements, visualized through frameworks and prototypes, and refined via usability testing before final deployment (Fig. 3).

Goal-Directed Design is particularly valuable in domains where understanding user intent is critical, such as education, healthcare, and financial services [32, 33]. It's a structured yet flexible process that supports the creation of products that go beyond usability to deliver lasting value.

While User-Centered Design (UCD) emphasizes user needs and preferences, GDD takes a broader, goal-oriented perspective. It integrates user goals with design objectives, enabling designers to address deeper behavioral and contextual challenges [34]. This makes GDD a suitable choice for projects aiming to influence long-term user behavior and engagement.

2.4 Existing Financial Applications Evaluation

In today's saturated FinTech market, the launch of a new financial management application faces significant challenges due to intense competition [35]. Therefore, conducting a thorough competitor audit is essential to identify standard industry features, user expectations, and opportunities for differentiation. This analysis focuses on five widely used financial management applications: Snoop, Emma, Moneyhub, Spendee, and Pennies. These apps were selected based on interview data, popularity, user reviews, and the breadth of functionalities they offer.

The comparative analysis (Table 1) highlights common features such as expense tracking, budget management, bank integration, and dashboard visualisation. However, the findings also reveal gaps in areas like financial literacy support, gamification, and personalisation, which can be leveraged for innovation.

Snoop stands out for its spending insights and savings recommendations. Its strength lies in its recommendation engine, but it lacks features like investment tracking and customisation, limiting its appeal to advanced users.

Emma offers robust integration across bank accounts and financial services, positioning it as a versatile tool. However, it misses key engagement drivers such as financial education and tailored recommendations.

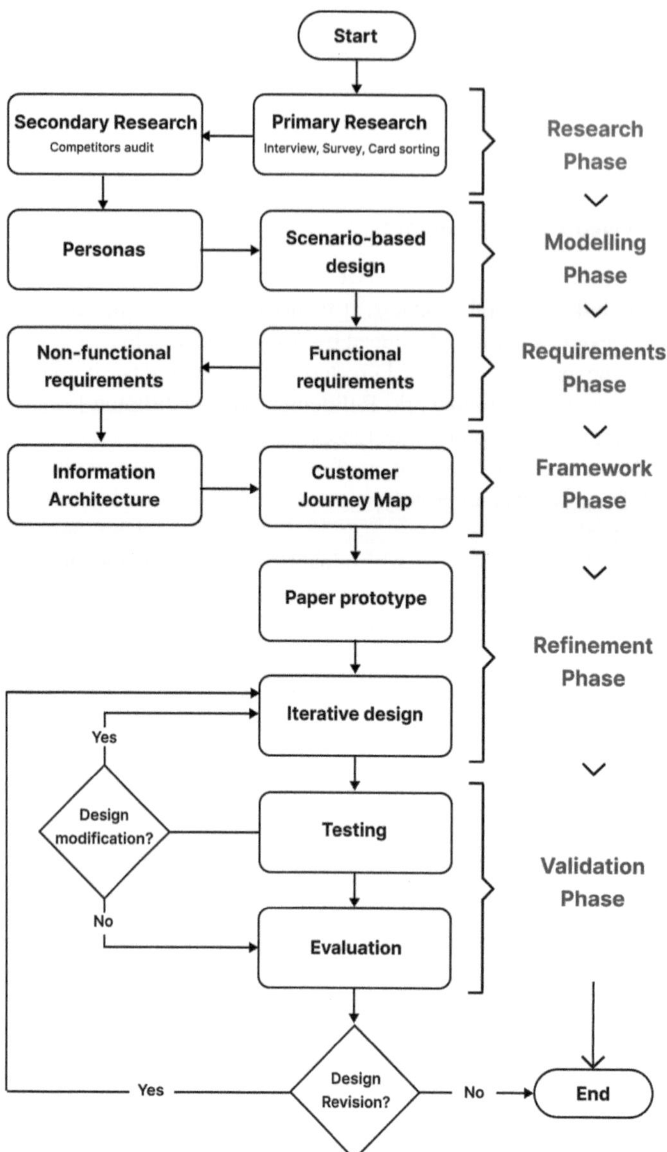

Fig. 3. Goal-Directed Design Framework.

Moneyhub and Spendee provide strong financial analysis tools and investment tracking, yet neither addresses the educational dimension of financial management. This presents an opportunity for differentiation through embedded financial literacy content.

Pennies, in contrast, offers a highly intuitive and personalised budgeting experience. Despite this, the app lacks bank integration, a critical shortfall in a multi-account financial environment.

Overall, the analysis reveals that while existing apps offer solid functional foundations, few address user learning, motivation, or behavioral change. These insights support the development of a new solution that incorporates financial literacy and gamification to enhance user engagement and financial capability.

Table 1. The table of five competitor analysis.

Functionalities	snoop	Emma	moneyhub	Spendee	pennies
Expenses tracking	✓	✓	✓	✓	✓
Budget management	✓	✓	✓	✓	✓
Financial literacy	✓				
Bank integration	✓	✓	✓	✓	
Collaboration					
Dashboard	✓	✓	✓	✓	
Savings goals	✓	✓	✓	✓	
Bill tracking	✓	✓	✓	✓	
Subscription management	✓	✓		✓	
Investment tracking			✓		
Custom categories		✓	✓	✓	✓
Notifications	✓	✓	✓	✓	
Multi-currency support		✓	✓	✓	
Personalise					✓
Gamification					
Recommendations	✓		✓		

3 Methodology

To address the research questions comprehensively, this study adopted a mixed-methods approach, combining both qualitative and quantitative techniques. Qualitative methods (e.g., interviews, think-aloud) were used to explore user motivations and behaviours in depth, while quantitative methods (e.g., surveys, SUS) provided generalisable insights and measurable outcomes.

3.1 Research Approach

Semi-structured Interviews. Used to explore user needs and financial behaviours through flexible, guided conversations. Eight international students at Edinburgh Napier University (aged 20–32) were interviewed to explore financial habits and literacy.

Survey. A 16-question online survey (n = 52) was distributed via social media to participants aged 18–30. It combined multiple-choice and open-ended items, designed to validate interview findings and explore financial behaviours at scale.

Card Sorting. Closed card sorting was conducted remotely with 10 participants to inform intuitive information architecture, leveraging co-occurrence analysis to align with users' mental models (Fig. 4).

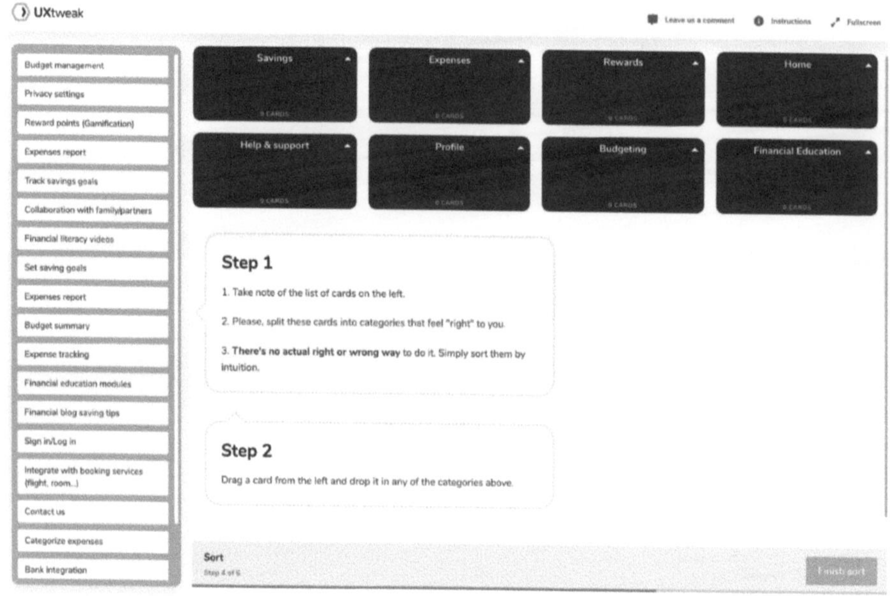

Fig. 4. Participant card sorting screen.

Think Aloud. The purpose of the think-aloud testing was to evaluate the usability and logic of the paper prototype by observing how users interact with it in a simulated environment. Six participants were provided with a list of tasks (Table 2) and guided to perform each while verbalising their thoughts, decisions, and emotional responses, allowing real-time observation of usability issues and cognitive friction. Sessions were recorded (without showing faces) and analysed for usability issues.

Table 2. Tasks assigned for participants in paper prototype testing.

Number	Tasks
1	Please sign in to the app using username is user123, and password: user@123
2	Integrate your account with Starling bank
3	Add a new expense of £45 Eating out by Cash
4	Set a saving goal for a Rome trip for £600, due October 2, 2024
5	Go to the education section and choose to watch the video "How to save money?"

Usability Testing. Conducted on high-fidelity prototypes to assess task completion, navigation, and pain points through observation and performance metrics. A different group of six students tested the high-fidelity prototype through six tasks (Fig. 5). Observations captured performance, confusion points, and feedback.

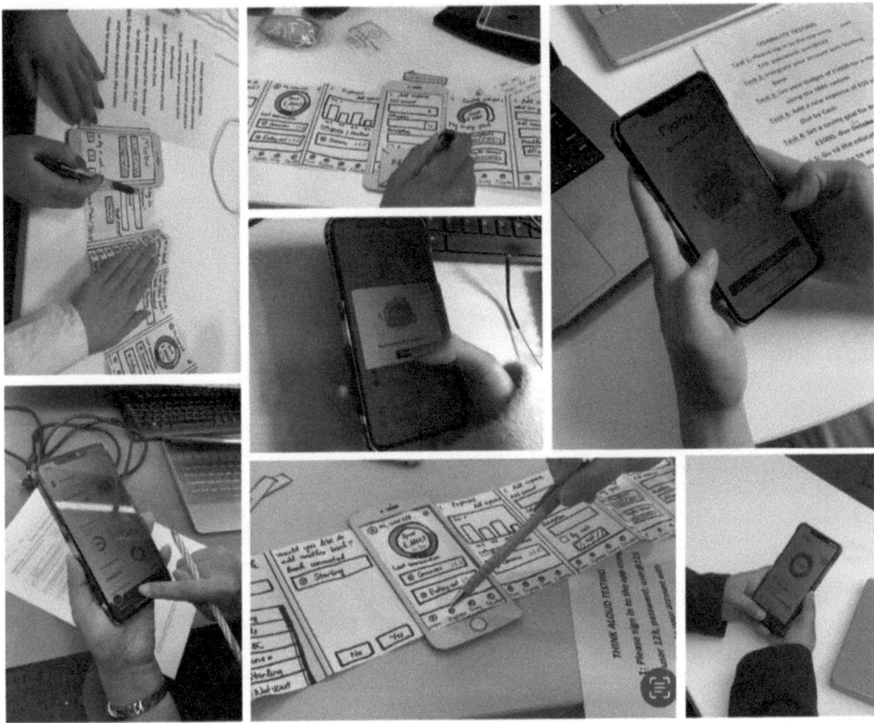

Fig. 5. User participation in the paper prototype and usability testing.

System Usability Scale (SUS). A post-test questionnaire provided a quantitative measure of perceived usability. Following usability testing, all six participants completed the SUS questionnaire. The results provided a standardised quantitative measure of perceived usability and were used to complement observational findings.

3.2 Ethical Consideration

All user research sessions strictly adhered to ethical standards. Participants were provided with a detailed consent form explaining the project's objectives, their role, and their right to withdraw at any point without consequence.

Informed consent was obtained prior to all interviews, surveys, and testing sessions. To ensure privacy, all responses were anonymised, and no identifiable personal data was collected. Sensitive financial questions were avoided to protect participants' comfort and well-being. Ethical transparency was maintained throughout the research process, ensuring participants understood how their input would be used exclusively for academic purposes within the scope of this study.

4 Design of Mabu Application: Development of a Money Management App

4.1 User Research and Insights

User research combined eight semi-structured interviews and a survey with 52 respondents to explore financial behaviours among young people. Most participants tracked expenses via banking apps or spreadsheets, though some lacked any tracking method. Spending focused on lifestyle categories such as food, shopping, and transport. Many users struggled with saving due to limited financial knowledge and unstructured habits.

Survey results showed that users valued features like budget tracking, expense categorisation, and financial analytics. Gamification, notifications, and personalised recommendations were seen as motivators for continued engagement. Open-ended responses emphasised ease of use, visual clarity, and the need for automated tracking and bank integrations (Fig. 6).

Fig. 6. Word cloud of features participants like to see in a financial app.

A closed card sorting study with 10 participants validated key app sections, including Budgeting, Savings, and Financial Education. Overall, findings informed both functional priorities and UX considerations, addressing the first two research questions regarding behaviours and challenges in financial self-management.

4.2 Designing Mabu - A Personal Financial App

Persona. Based on interview and survey findings, two personas were developed to represent the core user segments of the Mabu app: (1) a student with limited financial knowledge and (2) a young professional seeking more effective financial tools. This paper presents only one representative persona - Veronica (Fig. 7), a 28-year-old early-career professional with a stable income. She has basic budgeting habits but seeks smart features to track expenses, automate savings, and plan long-term goals. Veronica values usability, visual clarity, and personalised recommendations. Designing for her ensures the app meets the expectations of users who are financially conscious yet require digital support to optimise their financial planning.

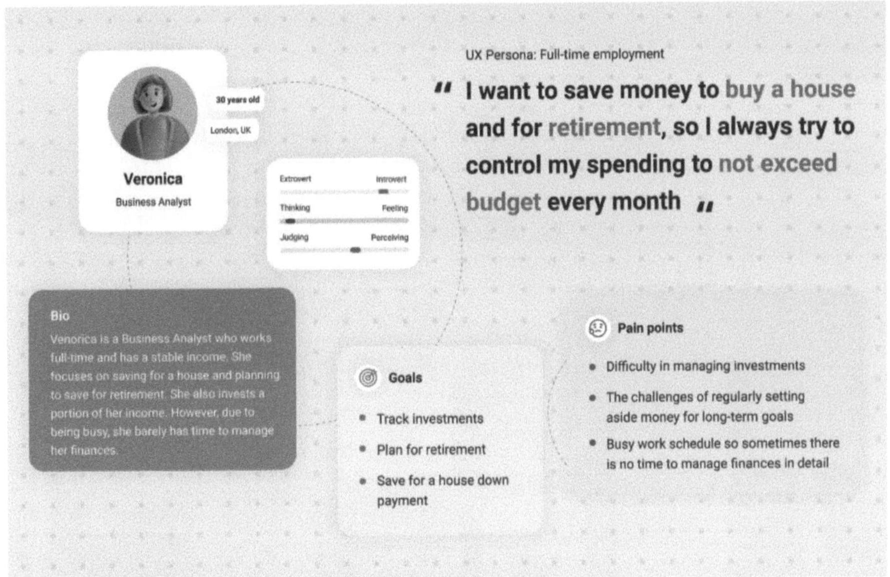

Fig. 7. Mabu's persona.

Paper Prototye. Following the initial sketches and storyboard-based user journeys, a paper prototype of Mabu was developed with the aim of helping conduct early testing with potential users, uncovering potential errors early in the design process to improve and design high-fidelity prototypes, and helping to minimise changes later [36]. Key user flows - expense tracking, budgeting, and savings, were translated into hand-drawn interactive screens using paper, sticky notes, and cardboard to simulate a mobile interface. Elements such as buttons, text fields, and dropdowns were visually distinguished to guide user interaction (Fig. 8). This approach enabled rapid iteration and helped identify usability issues prior to developing the high-fidelity prototype.

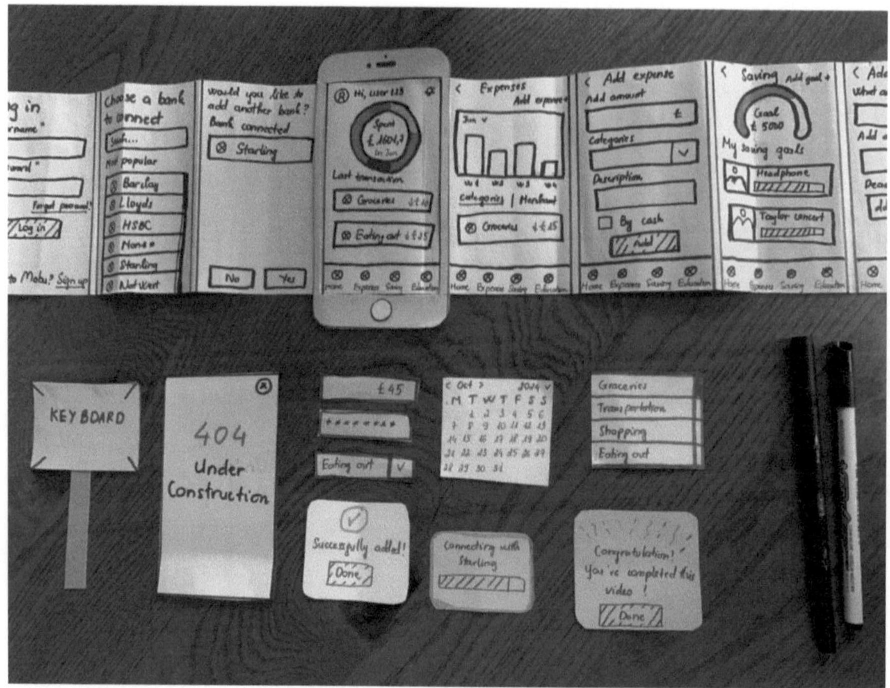

Fig. 8. Mabu's paper prototype.

Hi-fi Prototype. The high-fidelity prototype of the Mabu application was developed in Figma, leveraging feedback from paper prototype testing to refine core user flows and UI elements. Key improvements focused on navigation clarity, visual hierarchy, and feature accessibility (Fig. 9).

To address usability issues identified in earlier testing, onboarding screens were redesigned: the "Login" and "Signup" labels were replaced with more intuitive phrasing. A savings countdown and budget progress tracker were added to the home screen to enhance user awareness and motivation. Expense screens now include trend charts and categorised spending breakdowns to support better financial decision-making.

Savings functionality was enhanced with progress bars and monthly breakdowns. The education section was enriched with videos, tips, and interactive quizzes to improve financial literacy. Login/signup screens follow Jakob's Law, aligning with familiar UI patterns, and a 6-digit verification step was added for security.

Bank integration features enable users to connect multiple accounts and view consolidated transactions, automatically categorised for ease of tracking. Budgeting functionality incorporates the JARS system, allowing users to allocate funds across six spending categories or customise their own.

To increase engagement, gamification elements such as badges were introduced to reward users for completing financial milestones (e.g., meeting savings goals or staying within budget). These features were added to encourage consistent interaction and reinforce positive financial behaviours.

Fig. 9. Mabu's hi-fi prototype.

As part of an iterative design approach, additional improvements were implemented in response to both user feedback and heuristic evaluation. To support unfamiliar users, a three-step tutorial was added to explain the JARS budgeting system, along with navigation guidance for key app areas (Fig. 10).

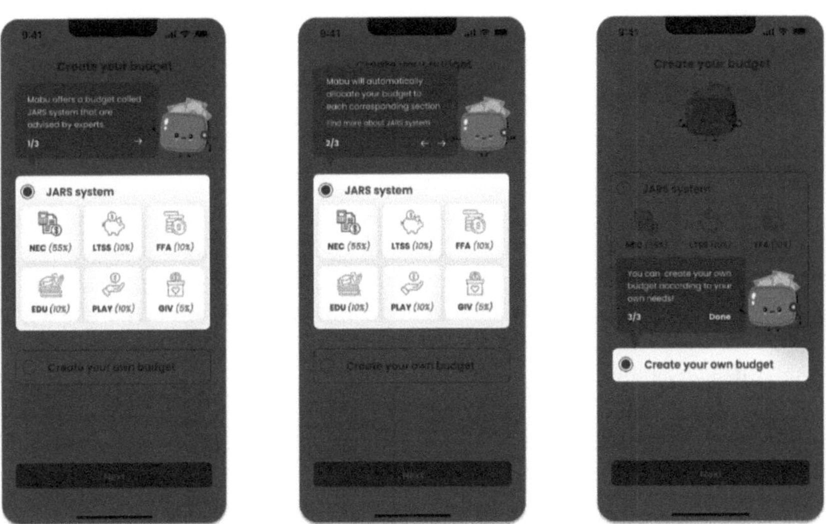

Fig. 10. Budget selection guide screens.

Expert feedback led to redesigning the bank connection flow, integrating popups for smoother user control, and improving error prevention via input validation and warning messages. Quick-access icons for creating new budgets, expenses, or savings were also added and pinned visibly across key interfaces to streamline frequent actions (Fig. 11). Together, these refinements demonstrate a continuous, user-centred design process that prioritises accessibility, usability, and motivation, laying a strong foundation for future evaluation and deployment.

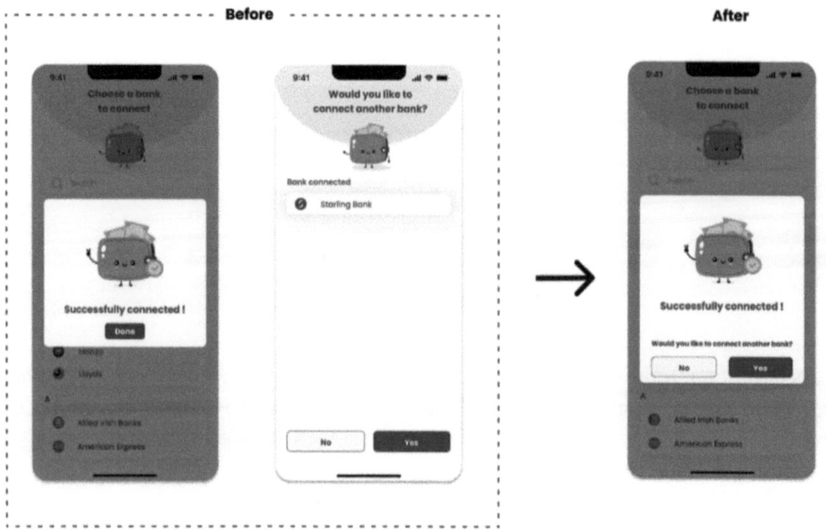

Fig. 11. Improved connecting to another bank screens.

4.3   Validation and User Feedback

Think-aloud testing with six participants revealed positive feedback on the app's usability, with most tasks completed successfully. However, issues emerged around task clarity and navigation. Users confused login and signup, struggled to locate expense and savings features, and recommended clearer buttons and a more intuitive layout. Participants also suggested adding an investment feature and visual progress tracking for savings goals.

Subsequent usability testing using the high-fidelity prototype confirmed similar issues. While login and bank integration tasks were completed quickly, challenges arose when setting budgets using the JARS system and adding new expenses. The "Add Expense" button was not prominent enough, and users experienced navigation friction. Task completion times further highlighted these issues, especially for expense tracking. Despite this, participants completed educational video tasks with ease.

The System Usability Scale (SUS), completed by all six participants, yielded an average score of 90, significantly above the industry benchmark of 68. This score indicates a high level of user satisfaction with the app's overall usability and design. Combined, these findings answered the final research question, showing that gamification elements - when balanced, enhanced engagement and motivation in managing personal finances. The SUS results of all six participants were summarised and calculated (Table 3) according to the following formula:

$$\text{SUS Score} = ((\Sigma\ (Q1, Q3, Q5, Q7, Q9)/5\text{-}\text{-}5)$$

$$+ (25 - \Sigma\ (Q2, Q4, Q6, Q8, Q10)/5)) \times 2.5$$

In this case : Σ positive items (odd questions) = 129, Σ negative items (even questions) = 49
Adjusted score = (129/5--5) + (25--49/5) = 20.8 + 15.2 = 36SUS Score = 36 $\times$ 2.5 = **90.0**

Table 3. Table of SUS from participants.

Participant	Q1	Q2	Q3	Q4	Q5	Q6	Q7	Q8	Q9	Q10	Odd Q Total (x)	Even Q Total (y)
P1	5	2	4	4	4	2	5	1	4	3	22	12
P2	4	2	4	2	5	2	5	1	4	1	22	8
P3	4	1	4	2	4	1	4	1	4	2	20	7
P4	5	3	4	2	2	1	4	1	3	4	18	11
P5	4	1	5	1	5	1	5	1	4	1	23	5
P6	4	1	5	1	5	1	5	1	5	2	24	6
Total											**129**	**49**

5 Discussion

The study identified several key findings. First, user research through interviews and surveys confirmed that young people lack adequate financial knowledge and seek tools that are easy to use, engaging, and educational. Features such as personalisation, interactivity, and embedded financial education were shown to enhance motivation and sustained use, aligning with previous research [1, 16].

Second, usability testing demonstrated that Mabu's design improved both engagement and literacy. Participants praised its intuitive interface and smart mascot, which contributed to a positive user experience. These results reinforce the principles of the Technology Acceptance Model (TAM) [17], where perceived usefulness and ease of use are crucial.

Third, the integration of Goal-Directed Design and gamification proved effective. GDD ensured alignment with user motivations, while gamification enhanced hedonic motivation and enjoyment [19, 25], resulting in increased user satisfaction and retention.

However, several limitations must be noted. The participant pool lacked diversity, as most users were based in Edinburgh, UK, which may affect generalisability. Time constraints limited the depth of iterative design, and the UXtweak tool used for card sorting had functionality limitations. Finally, the competitive audit reviewed only five financial apps, potentially overlooking emerging fintech innovations.

6 Conclusion and Future Work

This study employed a combination of semi-structured interviews, surveys, card sorting, and usability testing to explore young adults' financial behaviours and inform the design of Mabu. While interviews effectively uncovered user pain points, integrating contextual observation could have further enhanced insight. Surveys provided valuable data, though future iterations should avoid directly asking about desired features, as users often express wants rather than underlying needs. Closed card sorting contributed to a more intuitive information architecture but required deeper interpretation to align with user expectations. Usability testing - particularly the Think-Aloud method using paper prototypes - encouraged open feedback by reducing user pressure. The System Usability Scale (SUS) offered a standardised measure of user satisfaction, but some results may have been skewed due to user politeness or misunderstanding.

Future work will aim to expand user research across more diverse demographic groups, introducing features such as investment tools and personalised recommendations. Ethical considerations will be further prioritised through enhanced privacy policies, biometric authentication, and data encryption. Accessibility improvements will also be addressed. Overall, the use of Goal-Directed Design and gamification in Mabu shows strong potential in supporting financial literacy, though its long-term success relies on iterative development, ethical rigour, and continued user engagement.

References

1. Lusardi, A.: Financial literacy and the need for financial education: evidence and implications. Schweiz. Z. Volkswirtsch. Stat. **155**(1), 1–8 (2019). https://doi.org/10.1186/s41937-019-0027-5
2. Goldsmith, R.E., Goldsmith, E.B.: The effects of investment education on gender differences in financial knowledge. J. Pers. Finance. **5**(2), 55 (2006)
3. Kim, J., Chatterjee, S.: Financial debt and mental health of young adults. Financ. Couns. Plan. **32**(2), 187–201 (2021). https://doi.org/10.1891/JFCP-18-00048
4. Lea, S.E.G.: Debt and overindebtedness: psychological evidence and its policy implications. Soc. Issues Policy Rev. **15**(1), 146–179 (2021). https://doi.org/10.1111/sipr.12074
5. Cooper, A.: About Face: the Essentials of User Interface Design. IDG Books, Foster City (1995)
6. Cole, S., Sampson, T., Zia, B.: Financial literacy, financial decisions, and the demand for financial services: evidence from India and Indonesia. In: Harvard Business School Working Paper No. 09-117 (2009)
7. Fox, J., Bartholomae, S., Lee, J.: Building the case for financial education. J. Consum. Aff. **39**(1), 195–214 (2005) http://www.jstor.org/stable/23860132
8. Agarwal, S., Mazumder, B.: Cognitive abilities and household financial decision making. Am. Econ. J. Appl. Econ. **5**(1), 193–207 (2013). https://doi.org/10.1257/app.5.1.193
9. Lusardi, A., de Bassa Scheresberg, C., Oggero, N.: Student loan debt in the US: An analysis of the 2015 NFCS data. In: Global Financial Literacy Excellence Center (GFLEC) Research Report (2016)
10. Lusardi, A., Michaud, P.-C., Mitchell, O.S.: Optimal financial knowledge and wealth inequality. J. Polit. Econ. **125**(2), 431–477 (2017). https://doi.org/10.1086/690950

11. Mushtaq, R., Murtaza, G., Yahiaoui, D., Alessio, I., Talpur, Q.: Impact of financial literacy on financial inclusion and household financial decisions: exploring the role of ICTs. Int. Stud. Manag. Organ. **54**(1), 68–84 (2023). https://doi.org/10.1080/00208825.2023.2281207

12. Jerrim, J., Lopez-Agudo, L.A., Marcenaro-Gutierrez, O.D.: The link between financial education and financial literacy: a cross-national analysis. J. Econ. Educ. **53**(4), 307–324 (2022). https://doi.org/10.1080/00220485.2022.2111383

13. Xiao, J.J., Shim, S., Barber, B., Lyons, A.: Academic Success and Well-being of College Students: Financial Behaviors Matter. TCAI Report. University of Arizona, Tucson (2007)

14. Ross, S., Cleland, J., Macleod, M.J.: Stress, debt and undergraduate medical student performance. Med. Educ. **40**(6), 584–589 (2006). https://doi.org/10.1111/j.1365-2929.2006.024 48.x

15. Di Domenico, S.I., Ryan, R.M., Bradshaw, E.L., Duineveld, J.J.: Motivations for personal financial management: a self-determination theory perspective. Front. Psychol. **13**, 977818 (2022). https://doi.org/10.3389/fpsyg.2022.977818

16. Bamforth, J., Jebarajakirthy, C., Geursen, G.: Understanding undergraduates' money management behaviour: a study beyond financial literacy. Int. J. Bank Mark. **36**(7), 1285–1310 (2018). https://doi.org/10.1108/IJBM-05-2017-0104

17. Davis, F.D.: Perceived usefulness, perceived ease of use, and user acceptance of information technology. MIS Q. **13**(3), 319–340 (1989). https://doi.org/10.2307/249008

18. Venkatesh, V., Morris, M.G., Davis, G.B., Davis, F.D.: User acceptance of information technology: toward a unified view. MIS Q. **27**(3), 425–478 (2003). https://doi.org/10.2307/300 36540

19. Venkatesh, V., Thong, J.Y.L., Xu, X.: Consumer acceptance and use of information technology: extending the unified theory of acceptance and use of technology. MIS Q. **36**(1), 157–178 (2012). https://doi.org/10.2307/41410412

20. de Blanes Sebastián, M.G., Antonovica, A., Sarmiento Guede, J.R.: What are the leading factors for using Spanish peer-to-peer mobile payment platform Bizum? The applied analysis of the UTAUT2 model. Technol. Forecast. Soc. Change. **187**, 122235 (2023). https://doi.org/ 10.1016/j.techfore.2022.122235

21. Interaction Design Foundation (IxDF).: What is mobile user experience (UX) design? Interaction Design Foundation (2016). https://www.interaction-design.org/literature/topics/mobile-ux-design

22. French, D., McKillop, D., Stewart, E.: The effectiveness of smartphone apps in improving financial capability. Eur. J. Finance. **26**(4–5), 302–318 (2020). https://doi.org/10.1080/135 1847X.2019.1639526

23. Espinosa-Curiel, I.E., Pozas-Bogarin, E.E., Martínez-Miranda, J., Pérez-Espinosa, H.: Relationship between children's enjoyment, user experience satisfaction, and learning in a serious video game for nutrition education: empirical pilot study. JMIR Serious Games. **8**(3), e21813 (2020). https://doi.org/10.2196/21813

24. Hussain, A., Mkpojiogu, E.O.C., Yusof, M.M.: Perceived usefulness, perceived ease of use, and perceived enjoyment as drivers for the user acceptance of interactive mobile maps. AIP Conf. Proc. **1761**, 020051 (2016). https://doi.org/10.1063/1.4960891

25. Hamari, J., Koivisto, J., Sarsa, H.: Does gamification work? A literature review of empirical studies on gamification. In: Proc. 47th Hawaii Int. Conf. Syst. Sci. (HICSS), pp. 3025–3034 (2014). https://doi.org/10.1109/HICSS.2014.377

26. Deterding, S., Dixon, D., Khaled, R., Nacke, L.: From game design elements to gamefulness. In: Proc. 15th Int. Acad. MindTrek Conf. Envisioning Future Media Environ. (MindTrek '11), pp. 9–15 (2011). https://doi.org/10.1145/2181037.2181040

27. Lai, K.P.Y., Langley, P.: Playful finance: gamification and intermediation in FinTech economies. Geoforum. **151**, 103848 (2024). https://doi.org/10.1016/j.geoforum.2023.103848

28. Bayuk, J., Altobello, S.A.: Can gamification improve financial behavior? The moderating role of app expertise. Int. J. Bank Mark. **37**(4), 951–975 (2019). https://doi.org/10.1108/IJBM-04-2018-0086
29. Baptista, G., Oliveira, T.: Why so serious? Gamification impact in the acceptance of mobile banking services. Internet Res. **27**(1), 118–139 (2017). https://doi.org/10.1108/IntR-10-2015-0295
30. Williams, A.: User-centered design, activity-centered design, and goal-directed design. In: Proc. 27th ACM Int. Conf. Design Commun. (SIGDOC '09) (2009). https://doi.org/10.1145/1621995.1621997
31. Dubberly, H.: Alan Cooper and the goal directed design process. Gain AIGA J. Des. Netw. Econ. **1**(2) (2001) http://visible.org/site/cornish/readings/files/ddo_article_cooper%202.pdf
32. Duan, H., Wang, Z., Ji, Y., Ma, L., Liu, F., Chi, M., Deng, N., An, J.: Using goal-directed design to create a mobile health app to improve patient compliance with hypertension self-management: development and deployment. Jmir Mhealth Uhealth. **8**(2), e14466 (2020). https://doi.org/10.2196/14466
33. Laila, S.N., Sabariah, M.K., Suwawi, D.D.: UI Design of collaborative learning app for final assignment subject using goal-directed design. In: Proc. 4th Int. Conf. Inf. Commun. Technol. (ICoICT), pp. 1–6 (2016). https://doi.org/10.1109/icoict.2016.7571893
34. Wei, C., Xing, F.: The comparison of user-centered design and goal-directed design. In: Proc. 11th IEEE Int. Conf. Comput. -Aided Ind. Des. Concept. Des. (CAIDCD), vol. 1, pp. 359–360 (2010). https://doi.org/10.1109/caidcd.2010.5681336
35. Barroso, M., Laborda, J.: Digital transformation and the emergence of the FinTech sector: systematic literature review. Digit. Bus. **2**(2), 100028 (2022). https://doi.org/10.1016/j.digbus.2022.100028
36. Linek, S.B., Tochtermann, K.: Paper prototyping: the surplus merit of a multi-method approach. Forum Qual. Soc. Res. **16**(3) (2015). https://doi.org/10.17169/fqs-16.3.2236

Trends in Research Related to Ecological Textile Process from 2000 to 2023: A Bibliometric and Knowledge Mapping Analysis

Liuyi Wu[(✉)], Hao Li, Tiantian Wang, Bolin Xian, and Mengjie Wei

School of Culture and Media, Hezhou University, Hezhou 542899, China
1326719194@qq.com

Abstract. This study conducts a bibliometric analysis to examine global trends and research hotspots in ecological textile processes, utilizing data from the Web of Science Core Collection (2000–2023). VOSviewer 1.6.14 was employed to analyze 396 articles, mapping keyword co-occurrence, international collaborations, authors, and intellectual bases. Key findings highlight frequent terms such as adsorption, biodegradation, equilibrium, and ecodesign, reflecting a focus on sustainable material science and process optimization. The sustained academic interest aligns with the United Nations' sustainable development goals, emphasizing eco-friendly textile production. The analysis identifies leading journals, countries, and collaborative networks, revealing evolving research priorities. Scientifically, this study offers novel insights by systematically mapping the field's intellectual structure, providing researchers in ecological design and textile arts with data-driven guidance. Practically, the synthesis of literature trends serves as a visual reference for understanding current advancements and future directions in ecological textile processes. This work contributes to enhancing ecological design standards in textile research, supporting the transition toward sustainable industrial practices.

Keywords: Ecological Textile Process · Twenty-Year Trends · Bibliometric Analysis · VOSviewer

1 Introduction

Ecological textile process refers to the application of environmentally friendly principles and practices throughout the entire lifecycle of textile production, aiming to promote sustainable development of the ecosystem [1]. It involves the use of eco-friendly materials, adoption of efficient manufacturing processes, implementation of waste reduction and recycling strategies [2], and consideration of social, cultural, and ethical factors in different countries. The primary objective is to minimize the negative environmental impact of textile production, in line with the United Nations Climate Convention and the principles of sustainable development, while achieving efficient resource utilization and promoting the sustainable development of the textile industry.

M. Schrepp and M. Rauterberg (Eds.): HCII 2025, LNCS 16342, pp. 85–96, 2026.
https://doi.org/10.1007/978-3-032-13164-5_6

Textile products, which are in close contact with us in daily life, not only require an aesthetically pleasing appearance but also a good fit and optimal performance, with the most crucial aspect being the absence of any hazardous substances. The ecological safety requirements of textiles have emerged as the foremost quality requirement in global textile trade.

Bibliometric analysis is a kind of publication analysis method using mathematical and statistical approach applied to evaluate the related literature. The distributions of profiles, the most influential and clusters of keywords were measured quantitatively [3].

In order to comprehensively assess the state and trends of research in the area of ecological textile process between 2000and 2023, this study employs VOSviewer, a scientifically robust econometric software, to visually analyze the Web of Science database search results. The analysis aims to identify key research topics within the field and provide a summary of the major research hotspots and trends. The findings of this analysis can serve as valuable references for future research in this area.

2 Analysis of Previous Researches

In this study, we utilized the Web of Science Core Collection (https://www.webofscie nce.com/), a prestigious academic database that is extensively employed for bibliometric and scholarly research purposes.

The data collection process was conducted on January 17, 2024, using the search terms "eco-textile process" or "ecological textile process". The search timeframe spanned from January 1, 2000, to December 31, 2023, and was limited to articles written in English. The retrieved data was stored in a tab-delimited file format, which included the complete record and cited references, facilitating further analysis. The extracted basic information from each document comprised the author, keywords, title, abstract, and other relevant details.

Based on the analysis of the retrieval results from the Web of Science Core Collection, a total of 396 documents related to ecological textile process from the years 2000 to 2023 have been collected. The obtained data has been plotted in a line graph, which illustrates an overall increasing trend in the published articles over the past 20 years. The quantity of publications has risen from 2 articles published throughout the entirety of 2000 to a potential 41 articles for the full year of 2023 (see Fig. 1). Among these, the years 2000, 2001, and 2006 had the lowest number of published articles with 2 each, while the year 2022 had the highest number with 56 articles published.

Analysis of the reasons behind this reveals that prior to the year 2000, the concept of ecological conservation was just beginning to emerge, and countries had insufficient understanding of sustainable development in relation to the ecological environment. Consequently, there was limited research on ecological textile process. In September 2000, the United Nations Millennium Summit was held in New York, covering topics such as ecological conservation. The summit's adoption of the "United Nations Millennium Declaration" laid the foundation for promoting sustainable development and ecological conservation at the international level. In 2001, with the support and promotion of then-UN Secretary-General Kofi Annan, organizations such as UNEP, the World Bank, the Convention on Biological Diversity, and the Convention to Combat Desertification jointly launched the Millennium Ecosystem Assessment (MA). The purpose

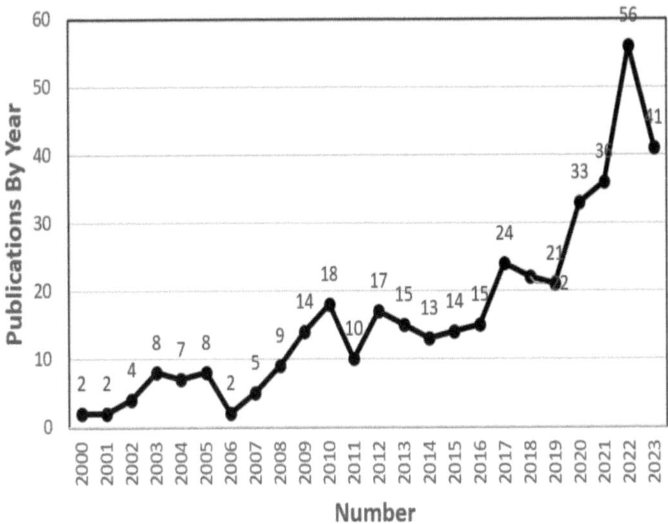

Fig. 1. Trends in the publication of ecological textile processes from 2000 to 2023.

of this assessment was to evaluate the consequences of ecosystem changes on human well-being, and it concluded in 2005. The assessment conducted a scientific evaluation of ecosystems and their services worldwide, and provided policy recommendations for the restoration, protection, or improvement of sustainable ecosystem utilization, thus offering important guidance for subsequent sustainable development and ecological conservation efforts.

Subsequently, countries began to attach greater importance to balancing their economic development with sustainable ecological environments and promoting low-carbon and environmentally friendly lifestyles. This shift has propelled academic research in the field of eco-friendly textiles, leading to a steady increase in related studies. During this period, the United Nations also convened high-level meetings of various countries, such as the United Nations World Summit on Sustainable Development held in Johannesburg in 2002. This summit reviewed the global situation concerning ecological conservation and economic development, and planned development directions for the next decade and beyond. The conference focused on topics such as biodiversity and ecosystems, and formulated strategies and measures to promote global sustainable development. It adopted the "Johannesburg Declaration on Sustainable Development" and the "Plan of Implementation of the World Summit on Sustainable Development" emphasizing the need to coordinate economic growth and social progress with environmental protection and ecological balance, with the aim of achieving development that respects the environment and ecology.

In 2005, the World Summit was held in New York, where countries pledged to take concrete actions and measures to protect and manage natural resources and promote sustainable development.

In 2011, in commemoration of International Mother Earth Day, the 66th session of the United Nations General Assembly held an interactive dialogue on "harmony with nature" to discuss comprehensive approaches to promoting sustainable development in harmony with nature. During the dialogue, experiences from different countries were shared regarding standards and indicators for measuring sustainable development in harmony with nature. Since then, each year's session of the General Assembly includes an interactive dialogue centered around the theme of "harmony with nature."In 2012, during the 67th session of the United Nations General Assembly, a call was made to treat sustainable development in a holistic manner, guiding the coexistence of humans and nature, and striving to restore the health and integrity of the Earth's ecosystems.

In the fifth edition of the "Global Biodiversity Outlook" released in 2020, it was pointed out that the global achievement of the Aichi Biodiversity Targets was not optimistic, and the trend of biodiversity loss worldwide had yet to be curbed. In the same year, the United Nations convened the Biodiversity Summit to raise international awareness of biodiversity conservation and support the fifteenth meeting of the Conference of the Parties (COP15) to the Convention on Biological Diversity.

COP15 was held in two stages in 2021 and 2022. It was the first global conference convened by the United Nations with the theme of ecological civilization, and it was also the first time in the history of the Convention on Biological Diversity that a leaders' summit was held. COP15 adopted milestone documents such as the "Kunming Declaration: Ecological Civilization - Building a Shared Future for All Life on Earth" and the "Kunming Framework." These documents received wide recognition from the international community, providing an implementation plan for subsequent biodiversity conservation efforts and aiming to reverse the declining trend of biodiversity by 2030, in support of the shared vision of "living in harmony with nature" and "ecologically sustainable development" by 2050.

The country analysis reveals that among the 396 research articles published from 2000 to 2023, authors from 70 countries and regions contributed. Table 1 presents the top 10 countries and regions in terms of the number of authors. China has the highest number of authors, with 108 individuals accounting for 20.769% of the total. It is followed by India with 35 authors (6.730%) and Turkey with 27 authors (5.192%).

Analysis of the reasons reveals that China, India, and Turkey are all developing countries and major producers in the global textile processing industry. This has prompted their societies and citizens to call for increased government regulatory efforts, punishment of non-compliant enterprises, and enhanced research and development of ecological materials. In particular, China has implemented significant regulations and legislation in this regard, which standardize the implementation and acceptance criteria for ecological dyes, ecological fabrics, and recycling practices in textile manufacturing processes. These regulations require enterprises to increase their investment in research funding, resulting in numerous research achievements. Such practices of integrating ecological protection not only contribute to addressing environmental pollution issues but also provide important support and guidance for the sustainable development of the textile industry.

The analysis of research institutions reveals that authors from 201 research institutions contributed to the 396 research articles published from 2000 to 2023. The top 10 institutions, with a total of 52 publications, account for 13.131% of the total (Table 2). In the field of research, China has the highest number of research institutions, followed

Table 1. Top 10 countries/regions in research on ecological textile processes from 2000 to 2023.

Rank	Country/region	Count (%)
1	China	108(20.769%)
2	India	35(6.730%)
3	Turkey	27(5.192%)
4	Poland	26(5.000%)
5	Pakistan	23(4.423%)
6	Romania	20(3.846%)
7	Germany	17(3.269%)
8	Usa	16(3.076%)
9	Brazil	15(2.884%)
10	France	14(2.692%)

by Slovenia in second place, Germany in third place, and Turkey, Czech Republic, and USA tied for fourth place.

Analysis reveals that the emphasis on ecological conservation and environmental management in Slovenia is driven by its abundant forest resources and a sense of responsibility towards future generations. The government has made efforts in developing eco-friendly tourism and established an effective waste management system through scientific planning, stringent regulations, and early education. Slovenian citizens receive education on waste sorting from primary school, and the government and relevant departments closely supervise waste classification and collection. These measures help cultivate environmental awareness and habits among the population and provide an important foundation for research related to ecological textile processes.

Germany's strong promotion of the circular economy and the implementation of stringent textile processing standards are aimed at reducing resource consumption and environmental pollution. Germany's circular economy policy encourages reuse and the circular utilization of resources to maximize the lifespan and value of products. The textile processing standards in Germany require garments, carpets, fibers, and other products to meet environmental requirements by adopting eco-friendly materials, energy-saving processes, and waste reduction measures to minimize environmental impact. These measures enable Germany to prioritize environmental protection and sustainable development in textile production and processing.

According to the analysis of 396 research articles published between 2000 and 2023, Muthu·Subramanian Senthilk, Meksi·Nizar, Visileanu·Emilia, and Li-YI emerged as high-productivity authors, indicating their focus and relative impact in the field of ecological textile processes (Table 3).

Muthu·Subramanian Senthilk believes that the textile manufacturing industry poses significant environmental challenges in terms of resource consumption, pollution, and waste generation. Addressing these challenges requires guidance from sustainable development concepts and the use of eco-friendly textile alternatives [4]. Meksi·Nizar, on the

Table 2. Top 10 organizations in ecological textile processes from 2000 to 2023.

Rank	Organization	Country/region	Documents
1	University Of Maribor Faculty Of Mechanical Engineering	Slovenia	9
2	The Hong Kong Polytechnic University Faculty Of Applied Sciences And Textiles	China	8
3	The Hong Kong Polytechnic University Institute Of Textiles And Clothing	China	8
4	Guangdong University Of Technology School Of Environmental Science And Engineering	China	7
5	University Of Monastir Faculty Of Sciences Of Monastir	Germany	5
6	Donghua University College Of Environmental Science And Engineering	China	3
7	Ege University Faculty Of Engineering	Türkiye	3
8	Guangdong University Of Technology Institute Of Environmental Health And Pollution Control	China	3
9	Technical University Of Liberec Faculty Of Mechanical Engineering	Czech Republic	3
10	Technical University Of Liberec Faculty Of Mechanical Engineering	Usa	3

Table 3. Top 10 Authors and co-cited authors in ecological textile processes from 2000 to 2023.

Rank	Co-cited author	Documents
1	Muthu· Subramanian Senthilk	7
2	Meksi·Nizar	7
3	Visileanu· Emilia	7
4	Li- YI	7
5	Ning- Xun an	5
6	Hu- Jun yan	4
7	Wang- Chao	4
8	Rather· Luqman Jameel	4
9	Carpus·Eftalea	4
10	Zhang- Yaping	4

other hand, suggests that the eco-friendliness of dyeing processes in textiles can be improved by replacing toxic carriers with ecological alternatives [5] Li-yi on the other hand, employs scalable dyeing techniques to achieve green and sustainable reuse of waste textiles. This work significantly contributes to the efficient treatment of waste textiles and wastewater, as well as sustainable environmental restoration practices [6].

Carpus Eftalea conducted research on mandatory recycling rates of different waste categories in the European region, including plastics, glass, metals, paper and cardboard, and biodegradable waste. The aim was to redesign products for these waste categories in order to increase the proportion of recycled materials and improve the overall recycling level of the products. Through modeling, it was predicted that by 2030, the minimum recycling rate for municipal waste would reach 65%, and the recycling rate for packaging waste would reach at least 75%. Additionally, the study assessed the impact of a significant amount of packaging waste on environmental protection legislation in the European region [7].

Busi Elena proposed the application of Life Cycle Assessment (LCA) to self-cleaning textiles in order to quantify their environmental advantages. LCA can measure process variations such as cotton cultivation, spinning, weaving, finishing, and consumption, and interpret them based on scale, scope, and functionality. By comparing the production and usage stages of innovative materials and traditional materials in various application scenarios, ecological benefits can be evaluated [8].

Taieb et al. [9] believes that textile product design should consider how to create a better future. In her research, she describes the design of ecological textile information aimed at enhancing children's awareness and education. In the long run, this design may contribute to ensuring a better quality of life for everyone, both now and in the future. The product utilizes ecological technology and materials to emphasize information while considering children's intellectual and psychological levels.

Cuc et al. [10] explores the process of achieving environmental sustainability through textile waste recycling. She believes that the recycling of waste brings benefits to all three aspects that define sustainability: economic, social, and environmental. This is particularly valuable in addressing numerous ecological issues and promoting new economic sectors.

Safapour et al. [11] explores the value of converting Millettia laurentii wood sawdust waste into sustainable natural dyes for eco-dyeing and functional finishing of wool textiles. A simple water extraction method is employed to separate the natural dyes, followed by qualitative and quantitative analysis of the extracted bio-dyes. The study's findings provide ample space for upgrading wood industry waste into natural dyes for environmentally friendly coloring of wool textiles.

Fletcher [12] explores whether design can effectively promote the development of the textile industry. The study provides a detailed overview of key elements of ecological design methods and investigates the role design can play in creating more resource-efficient textiles, particularly focusing on longer-lasting textiles. Additionally, the author argues that environmental issues can no longer be excluded from the design process, but acknowledges the slow progress in developing design solutions for environmental challenges within the textile industry.

In addition, industry regulations for ecological textiles have provided development support for ecological design. Currently, the development of ecological textile product certification systems is relatively mature, and common and widely recognized logos on products include Oeko-Tex certification, GOTS (organic cotton) certification, Swiss Bluesign Blue Label certification, Nordic Swan Ecolable ecological certification, Eco-label EU ecological label certification, GRS textile and clothing global recycling certification, ZDHC certification (Zero Discharge of Hazardous Substances Alliance certification), and BCI Swiss Better Cotton Initiative certification, among others. The most widely used ecological textile standard in the world is Oeko-Tex Standard 100. This standard was issued and authorized for use by the International Association for Environmental Protection in 1992.

3   Statement of the Problem

This article employs the VOSviewer scientific bibliometric software to conduct data mining analysis on research literature in the field of "ecological textile processes" from the Web of Science Core Collection database. The study encompasses scholarly publications published between 2000 and 2023. Through this analysis, the article reveals key data trends within the field. The objective of this article is to analyze and visualize information such as keywords, journals, countries, international collaborations, authors, research hotspots, and the concept of "ecological textile processes" through information maps. The aim is to provide future research with valuable insights and guidance in related areas.

4   Results of the Research

The research results indicate that in the field of ecological textile processes, a minimum threshold of 2 documents per country or region was set to determine the level of national collaboration. Out of the 35 countries and regions involved in ecological textile processes research, 17 met this threshold.

The size of the nodes in the graph represents the influence of each country or region, while the distance and thickness of the connecting lines indicate the level of collaboration in the field of eco-friendly textile processing. For example, China and Saudi Arabia are the two countries with the highest level of collaboration with other countries such as India, Pakistan, Iran, and Germany. This clearly indicates that geographical distance does not hinder cooperation between countries in the field of eco-friendly textile processing. For instance, Saudi Arabia, with its precious water resources, has a greater need for high-quality ecological textile products to minimize environmental pollution. Additionally, the country's wealth makes it willing to engage in cross-border cooperation with other nations in the field of energy. India also faces severe environmental pollution, leading the government to strongly support research on ecological conservation. The country has established laboratories and collaborations with developed countries, among other efforts (see Fig. 2).

According to the research results, a co-authorship network analysis was conducted in the field of "ecological textile processes" to reveal the collaboration relationships and levels among authors. The knowledge graph visualization enabled a clear understanding of the distribution of authors in the field, with the size of the nodes reflecting their publication output.

Fig. 2. The main research is the distribution of national and regional collaboration.

In the knowledge graph, each author was represented as a node, and the node size indicated their research productivity in the field. The links between the nodes represented the relationships between collaborating authors, with higher link strength indicating a higher level of collaboration density. Such analysis helps us comprehend the close collaborations among authors and their contributions to the field of ecological textile processes.

Please refer to Fig. 3 for more detailed information. Through this visual analysis, we can identify influential authors in the field and understand their collaboration patterns. This has important implications for further collaborations, knowledge exchange, and innovation.

The research results indicate the identification of hotspots in the network of ecological textile processes. The minimum co-occurrence count for keywords is set to 2. Out of the 2,688 keywords involved in the sample, a total of 580 keywords met the threshold. Through network analysis, the keywords were clustered based on their similarities. Four major clusters were formed, and each cluster is represented by a different color (see Fig. 4) for visualization purposes.

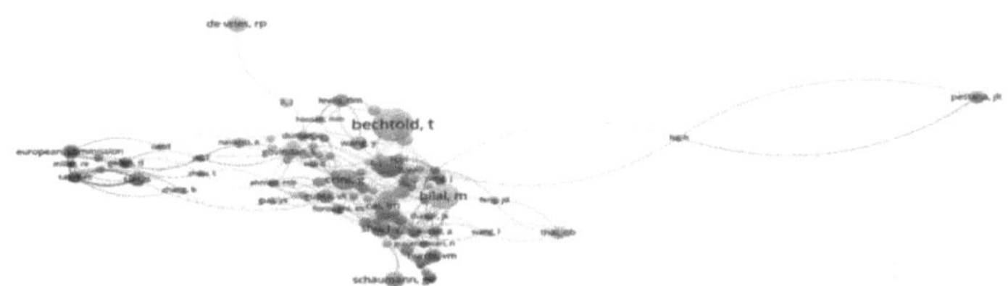

Fig. 3. Co-authorship network in ecological textile processes.

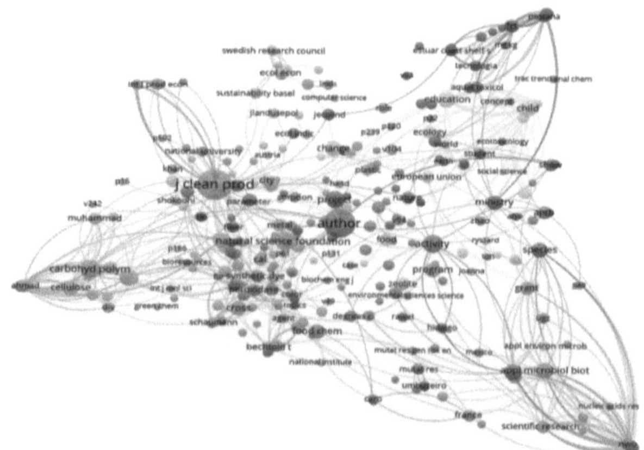

Fig. 4. Co-occurrence network of keywords in ecological textile processes.

5   Conclusions

From 2000 to 2023, a total of 396 articles were published in the field of ecological textile processing. During this period, the annual publication trend gradually increased, reaching a relatively low number of publications in the single digits in 2008. However, a turning point occurred in 2010, with 18 articles published. Since 2017, the number of articles has continued to increase, surpassing 20 articles per year. This growth can be attributed to the enhanced global awareness of sustainable development, particularly through countries' participation in the United Nations Sustainable Development Conventions.

However, due to new international circumstances and social development influences, the international ecological conservation sector still faces multiple crises such as energy shortages, food security, and climate change. The overall development of ecological textile processes in countries worldwide has lagged behind, and international attention to ecological conservation has also been relatively delayed. It is worth noting that major countries such as China, the European Union, and the United States have played important roles in emphasizing ecological legislation, which has influenced the development of ecological textile processes worldwide. The international community needs to deeply understand the new situations and challenges faced by ecological conservation, fully leverage international platforms such as the United Nations Framework Convention on Climate Change, the Convention on Biological Diversity, and the United Nations Convention to Combat Desertification, and promote convergence, reconciliation of differences, and consensus-building among all parties. By standing at the forefront of international economic, social, and ecological sustainable development, we can seek harmonious coexistence between humanity and nature.

The analysis of the publications revealed several key focal points in the field of ecological textile processes. The high-frequency keywords are "adsorption" "biodegradation" "equilibrium" and "Ecodesign». These keywords are associated with four different clusters:

Cluster 1 (blue) is related to "adsorption" and includes shared keywords such as "ecological risk" "risk assessment" "heavy metals" "multiscale analysis" and "pollution assessment". This indicates that the detection and assessment of pollutants in the textile production process are important metrics. As long as pollutants are emitted and released during textile production, they can have negative impacts on the environment and human health. Therefore, monitoring and evaluating pollutants are crucial for ensuring the environmental friendliness and sustainability of the textile industry. These assessments mainly focus on heavy metals, organic solvents, dyes, and other chemicals.

Cluster 2 (brown) is related to "biodegradation" and includes keywords like "derivatives" "effluents" "fixation" and "reverse micelle". This suggests that recycling, reuse, and waste treatment are crucial in the textile manufacturing process. Some waste and by-products can be transformed into new raw materials through proper processing and reprocessing for the production of other textiles or products in other fields. This helps reduce resource consumption, lower production costs, and minimize environmental impacts.

Cluster 3 (green) is related to "equilibrium" and includes keywords such as "hydrogel" "kinetics" "methylene-blue dye" and "pyrolysis". Ecological balance in the textile industry aims to achieve a harmonious state between the industry's development and environmental protection. It involves considerations of material selection, clean production, waste management, water resource management, and environmental monitoring and assessment.

Cluster 4 (yellow) is related to "Ecodesign" and includes keywords like "Nutrition" "security" "Design" "Tool" and "input-output analysis". The goal of ecodesign is to achieve harmonious development between humans and the natural environment by reducing environmental impacts through sustainable design and innovation. Ecodesign practices encompass a wide range of areas, including eco-textile design, the use of eco-friendly materials, production of eco-dyes, and recycling of waste. Its aim is to promote the common goals of sustainable development and environmental protection.

However, it is worth noting that the analysis of the publications may be limited by certain methodological constraints. Additionally, language bias may exist due to language restrictions, as our study solely relied on the Web of Science Core Collection database without including PubMed, Google Scholar, other search engines, or country-specific databases.

Acknowledgments. The authors acknowledge the contributions and support of the experts and team members in the writing process. This study is a phased research outcome of the following projects: 2025 Open Fund Project of Guangxi Research Base for Building a Strong Sense of Chinese National Community (Hezhou University): "Study on the Shared Genetic Map of Traditional Craft Culture of the Yao Ethnic Group in the Nanling Corridor" (Project No.: 2025KF02); 2023 Guangxi National College Student Innovation and Entrepreneurship Training Program: "Research Journey: Digital Study Travel in the New Era" (Project No.: 202311838033);2024 Guangxi College Student Innovation and Entrepreneurship Training Program: "Research Journey with Me: AI-Guided Big Data Study Travel" (Project No.: S202411838134);2025 Guangxi National College Student Innovation and Entrepreneurship Training Program: "Digital-Intelligent Research Journey: Cultural Study Travel and Innovation in the Nanling Corridor Driven by New Technologies".

References

1. Lara, L., Cabral, I., Cunha, J.: Ecological approaches to textile dyeing: a review. Sustainability. **14**(14), 8353 (2022)
2. Zou, X., Yue, W., Vu, H.: Visualization and analysis of mapping knowledge domain of road safety studies. Accid. Anal. Prev. **118**, 131–145 (2018)
3. Harsanto, B., Primiana, I., Sarasi, V., Satyakti, Y.: Sustainability innovation in the textile industry: a systematic review. Sustainability. **15**(2), 1549 (2023)
4. Slater, K.: Nomination and commentary on 'the environmental costs of textile manufacture. J. Text. Inst. **85**(1), 67–72 (1994)
5. Souissi, M., Khiari, R., Zaag, M., Meksi, N., Dhaouadi, H.: Ecological and cleaner process for dyeing bicomponent polyester filaments (PET/PTT) using ecological carriers: analysis of dyeing performance. RSC Adv. **11**(42), 25830–25840 (2021)
6. Zhai, H., Liu, Z., Xu, L., Liu, T., Fan, Y., Jin, L., Dong, R., Yi, Y., Li, Y.: Waste textile reutilization via a scalable dyeing technology: a strategy to enhance dyestuffs degradation efficiency. Adv. Fiber Mater. **4**(6), 1595–1608 (2022)
7. Carpus, E., Stroe, C., Dorogan, A.: Textile packaging waste in the context of implementing the concept of circular economy. Ind. Textila. **71**(5), 499–503 (2020)
8. Busi, E., Maranghi, S., Corsi, L., Basosi, R.: Environmental sustainability evaluation of innovative self-cleaning textiles. J. Clean. Prod. **133**, 439–450 (2016)
9. Taieb, A.H., et al.: Sensitising children to ecological issues through textile eco-design. Int. J. Art Design. Edu. **29**(3), 313–320 (2010)
10. Cuc, S., et al.: Environmental and socioeconomic sustainability through textile recycling. Ind. Text. **66**(3), 156–163 (2015)
11. Safapour, S., et al.: Upscaling Millettia laurentii carpentry sawdust into natural dyes: imparting antimicrobial, antioxidant, and UV-protective finish to wool yarns through an ecological and sustainable natural dyeing process. Biomass Convers. Biorefinery. (2023)
12. Fletcher, K.T.: Design, the environment and textiles: developing strategies for environmental impact reduction. J. Text. Inst. **89**(3), 72–80 (1998)

Applying TRIZ Theory to Enhance Sustainability in Children's Furniture Design

Lin Zhang[1,2] and Danylo Kosenko[2(✉)]

[1] The College of Design and Art, Shaanxi University of Science &Technology, Xi'an 710021, Shaanxi, China

[2] Kyiv National University of Technologies and Design, Kyiv 01011, Ukraine
danylo.kosenko@gmail.com

Abstract. With the improvement of living standards, modern households have increasingly stringent demands and expectations for children's furniture. However, the blind pursuit of multifunctionality and diverse requirements often contradicts the principles of sustainable development. This study approaches children's furniture design and development by integrating the KANO model, life cycle concept, and TRIZ theory, shifting the application of life cycle assessment (LCA) from traditional end-product evaluation to the initial design stage. By incorporating policy regulations and literature analysis, we identify essential green design requirements during the design process. Using the KANO model, we precisely identify user needs and apply TRIZ theory to resolve potential conflicts between green design requirements and user demands, ultimately deriving innovative design solutions. A case study on the design and development of a game-oriented children's dining table demonstrates that our approach effectively meets consumer needs while adhering to sustainable development principles. This method not only satisfies the specific requirements of children's furniture design but also establishes a new paradigm for integrating sustainability into the design and development of various products. The proposed approach provides valuable insights and practical solutions for designers aiming to create environmentally friendly and user-centered products.

Keywords: sustainable · development · children's furniture design · kano model · triz theory · lifecycle concept

1 Introduction

As a key element accompanying children's growth, children's furniture plays a vital role in shaping their living environment and promoting physical and mental development. However, there are several areas in the design of children's furniture in the current market that require improvement. Firstly, many products are simply scaled-down versions of adult furniture, which may not adequately address the unique physiological and psychological needs of children. This can result in suboptimal user experience and may potentially impact children's healthy development. Additionally, the issue of functional redundancy and resource inefficiency is notable. The pursuit of multifunctionality often

M. Schrepp and M. Rauterberg (Eds.): HCII 2025, LNCS 16342, pp. 97–112, 2026.
https://doi.org/10.1007/978-3-032-13164-5_7

leads to increased manufacturing costs without a corresponding enhancement in product value, and may even cause confusion for children during use. Lastly, environmental considerations in material selection and manufacturing processes are often insufficient. This can have significant ecological impacts and may also pose risks to children's health. Addressing these challenges is essential for advancing the design and developmen of children's furniture in a way that aligns with sustainable development principles and supports the well-being of young users.

The concept of sustainable design was first proposed by the United Nations in its 1987 report "Our Common Future," compiled by the Brundtland Commission. Sustainable design aims to meet the needs of the present without compromising the ability of future generations to meet their own needs. The core principle is to achieve the coordinated development and long-term sustainability of the economy, environment, and society through the rational use of resources, reduction of environmental impact, and promotion of social equity (Brundtland Commission, 1987) [1]. In the context of children's furniture design, applying sustainable design principles can significantly reduce negative environmental impacts and protect children's health. Moreover, it can foster future sustainable development by educating children on environmental awareness.

The structure of this article is as follows: The first section provides an introduction. The second section reviews the literature on children's furniture design, sustainable development design, and sustainable furniture design. The third section introduces relevant theories and provides a detailed introduction to the specific process of designing and developing children's furniture based on these theories. The fourth section uses the children's game table as an example to illustrate in detail how to develop and design children's furniture products that not only align with the concept of sustainable development but also meet the practical needs of users. The fifth section presents the conclusions and suggests directions for further research.

2 Literature Review

2.1 Design for Sustainability

In recent years, the term "Design for Sustainability" has gained increasing recognition and acceptance in both academic and industrial circles. This growing interest is driven by the urgent need to address environmental challenges and promote sustainable development. Researchers and practitioners alike are focusing on developing innovative design strategies that minimize environmental impact, enhance resource efficiency, and ensure long-term ecological balance [1–3].

During the early years of developing and designing products that adhere to sustainability principles, scholars proposed several universal design guidelines, such as the 12 Principles of Green Engineering [4] and the 10 Golden Rules of Green Design [5]. Other significant research efforts have focused on Life Cycle Assessment (LCA) [6], remanufacturing, and various design evaluation methodologies [7]. A critical branch of sustainable design research is low-carbon design, which specifically aims to reduce the carbon footprint of products. Many methods proposed in this field are based on detailed carbon footprint calculations. However, a notable limitation of these methods is their limited applicability during the early stages of product development, particularly the concept design phase [8, 9]. This gap highlights the need for more adaptable and integrative approaches that can be employed from the initial design stages to ensure comprehensive sustainability.

Additional studies have focused on the evaluation and selection of green concept design schemes. For instance, Boonkanit et al. utilized the Quality Function Deployment for Environment (QFDE) and Analytic Hierarchy Process (AHP) methods to conduct both qualitative and quantitative assessments of conceptual designs [10]. Similarly, Shin et al. proposed a decision support method based on an extended House of Quality (HOQ) framework to facilitate decision-making in complex conceptual design environments [11]. This method integrates product lifecycle considerations and resource constraints, enabling the identification of optimal product concepts.

2.2 Children's Furniture Design

Children's furniture design remains a focus of current research and design activities. With the gradual expansion of the children's furniture market, the demand for health-conscious, happiness-enhancing, and sustainable furniture has become a primary concern for parents [12]. By integrating various digital technologies, children's furniture designers have developed systems that incorporate play features such as video games, audio programs, and interactive designs, while also addressing the physical and psychological needs of children. The emergence of customized designs, tailored to the specific requirements of children and their parents, has further influenced children's furniture design. These customized designs are typically better suited to children's body sizes and activities, providing a more enjoyable and safe experience [13, 14].

Xianqing Xiong and colleagues utilized group technology to standardize components of children's solid wood furniture. They analyzed 1,084 components from 20 pieces of furniture (including 705 solid wood components) and classified and optimized them based on processing similarity principles. By merging components with size differences within 2 mm and optimizing them based on original specifications or half of them, this method significantly improved the standardization of solid wood components and provided a foundation for the digital design of large-scale customized children's solid wood furniture [15].

While technology has significantly impacted the design process and product offerings, addressing children's physiological, psychological, and aesthetic needs remains essential. Recently, an increasing number of designers and researchers have focused on creating furniture with sensory features such as pitch, frequency, and intensity to facilitate children's developmental needs and enhance their self-confidence and adaptability [16]. Such furniture designs have been implemented to support children's physical and cognitive development by providing a natural and accessible environment for them to experience joy and interact with the world [17].

Furthermore, ensuring children's safety has been a fundamental priority in design practice. Designers have considered various aspects of materials and their use to ensure that children can function safely and comfortably in their furniture [18]. For instance, Podrekar developed a wooden standing desk prototype for classrooms, aiming to reduce sedentary behavior and improve student well-being. A multidisciplinary team designed the prototype and gathered feedback from primary school students and teachers, finding that the desk was generally well-received. Students appreciated features like height adjustability and a tiltable tabletop, though concerns were raised about the tabletop's durability. The researchers suggest further studies to optimize materials, shape, and color, particularly for the tabletop, to promote less sedentary classrooms and enhance student well-being [19].

In addition, designers have begun to incorporate multifunctionality in children's furniture to facilitate development and cultivate creativity and independence. The integration of technology has greatly enhanced the performance of children's furniture by connecting multiple functions and incorporating technological advancements into the design process [20, 21]. Future emphasis will continue to focus on the integration of technology, functionality, and aesthetics in children's furniture design, with a strong emphasis on safety, functionality, and relevance.

3 Materials and Methods

To better explore sustainable design in children's furniture, this study uses children's desks as a case example and integrates the KANO model with TRIZ theory methodologies. The KANO model facilitates a more precise identification of user requirements, distinguishing between basic needs, performance needs, and attractive needs, thereby enabling the design of furniture that more effectively meets the diverse needs of children. TRIZ theory offers a systematic and innovative approach to optimizing the green and sustainable design of children's furniture. It addresses the inherent contradictions between functionality and environmental protection, resulting in products that are both practical and environmentally friendly.

3.1 KANO Model Approach

The KANO model, developed by Noriaki Kano and his colleagues in the 1980s, is a method used to analyze and understand customer needs and satisfaction. It categorizes customer requirements into three main types: basic needs, performance needs, and attractive needs, each influencing customer satisfaction differently (Kano et al., 1984) [22].

Basic Demand

These are the essential features that customers expect a product to have. Their absence leads to significant dissatisfaction, but their presence does not significantly increase satisfaction because they are taken for granted. In children's furniture, basic needs might include safety features and ergonomic design.

Expectation Demand

These are directly related to the product's performance attributes. The better these needs are met, the higher the customer's satisfaction. For instance, the durability and functionality of a children's desk would fall into this category.

Attractive Demand

These are the features that can delight customers and exceed their expectations. While their absence does not cause dissatisfaction, their presence significantly enhances customer satisfaction. Examples in children's furniture could include innovative design elements or additional educational features.

The KANO model employs a structured questionnaire to gather customer feedback on potential product features. Customers are asked to evaluate their feelings about the presence and absence of these features, typically through functional and dysfunctional questions. The responses are then analyzed to classify each feature into one of the KANO categories.

3.2 Lifecycle Concept

The lifecycle concept is a comprehensive approach that evaluates the environmental impacts of a product throughout its entire life cycle, from raw material acquisition to disposal. This methodology emphasizes the importance of considering each stage of a product's life to minimize its overall environmental footprint. The lifecycle stages typically include raw material acquisition, production and manufacturing, transportation and distribution, usage and maintenance, and termination and disposal [23].

Raw Material Acquisition

This stage focuses on sourcing materials that are renewable, recyclable, and free from harmful chemicals. The aim is to ensure that the materials used are safe for both the environment and human health. By prioritizing renewable and recyclable materials, this stage sets the foundation for reducing the product's environmental impact.

Production and Manufacturing

In this stage, the emphasis is on adopting clean production processes that optimize energy use and minimize waste and pollutant emissions. This involves using advanced manufacturing techniques and technologies that reduce resource consumption and environmental degradation. Efficient production methods not only lower costs but also contribute to sustainable development.

Transportation and Distribution

The goal during this stage is to minimize carbon emissions by selecting low-carbon transportation methods and designing lightweight products. Additionally, the use of environmentally friendly packaging materials helps to reduce the environmental impact associated with product distribution. Efficient logistics and transportation strategies are critical for reducing the carbon footprint of the product.

Usage and Maintenance

This stage highlights the importance of enhancing product durability and designing structures that are easy to maintain and repair. By ensuring that products are long-lasting and require minimal maintenance, the environmental impact during the usage phase is significantly reduced. This stage also focuses on user safety and convenience, promoting a sustainable usage pattern.

Termination and Disposal

The final stage of the lifecycle concept involves designing products for easy disassembly and recycling. Encouraging the reuse of product components and implementing environmentally friendly disposal methods help to close the loop in the product lifecycle. This stage aims to reduce waste and promote the circular economy by ensuring that products do not end up in landfills.

By integrating the lifecycle concept into the design process, we can systematically address environmental concerns and create products that are not only functional and user-friendly but also sustainable and eco-friendly. This comprehensive approach ensures that every aspect of the product's life is optimized for minimal environmental impact, contributing to the overall goal of sustainable development.

3.3 TRIZ Theory Approach

TRIZ, an acronym for "Teoriya Resheniya Izobretatelskikh Zadach" (Theory of Inventive Problem Solving), was developed by Soviet scientist Genrich Altshuller and his colleagues starting in the 1940s. TRIZ is a systematic methodology for understanding and solving complex problems and enhancing innovation. It is based on the study of patterns of invention in the global patent literature and proposes a range of principles and tools designed to overcome technical contradictions and generate creative solutions [24] (Table 1).

Table 1. Development stage of TRIZ theory.

Time Period	Development Stage
1946–1980	During this period, the foundational concepts of TRIZ were established. Although many concepts and methods were developed, they were not yet integrated. A large number of engineering solutions were accumulated, but these were described in a way that could only be used manually for TRIZ application. Boris Zlotin and Alla Zusman created the first comprehensive TRIZ school in Kishinev (known as the Kishinev period). This period laid the groundwork for TRIZ tools and knowledge accumulation.
Kishinev Period	During this period, the focus was on formalizing TRIZ methods and tools and accumulating knowledge. The use of computer-aided methods to represent TRIZ began.
Ideation Period	Since 1992, The company Ideation International was founded and began developing TRIZ tools for engineering problem-solving. This period saw the integration of TRIZ with modern analytical and problem-solving methods, taking significant steps forward. TRIZ evolved into a comprehensive set of systematic tools for enhancing technical problem-solving and innovation.

The TRIZ theory also includes the following key components:
Contradiction Matrix
TRIZ identifies contradictions as the core of inventive problems. A contradiction occurs when improving one characteristic of a system leads to the deterioration of another. The Contradiction Matrix helps identify solutions by providing principles that have been successfully used to resolve similar contradictions in other inventions.
40 Inventive Principles
These are generic principles derived from the analysis of patents. They provide strategies for solving problems, such as segmentation, taking out, and merging. These

principles guide designers in finding innovative solutions without relying solely on trial and error.

39 Engineering Parameters

These parameters are used to describe the conflicting aspects of a problem. For example, improving the strength of a material might increase its weight. TRIZ uses these parameters in combination with the Contradiction Matrix to suggest inventive principles that can resolve such conflicts.

Algorithm for Inventive Problem Solving (ARIZ)

This is a step-by-step procedure for solving complex problems. ARIZ helps to refine the problem, eliminate psychological inertia, and systematically apply TRIZ tools to find innovative solutions.

4 Empirical Example

To validate the effectiveness of integrating the KANO model with TRIZ theory in the design and development of children's furniture, this study selected a playful children's table as a case example. This section will provide a comprehensive introduction to identifying and classifying user needs using the KANO model, and propose corresponding sustainable design optimization solutions based on TRIZ theory.

4.1 User Needs Analysis Using the Kano Model

Through an in-depth analysis of this research subject, we have summarized 12 functional requirements for selecting children's furniture. These requirements ensure that the furniture is both practical and beneficial for children's development. The identified functional requirements are as follows:

Structural Safety and Stability

The furniture must be constructed with high-strength materials to ensure it remains stable and secure during use. It should have rounded edges and corners to prevent injuries, making it safe for children to use in various activities.

Adequate Tabletop Space

The furniture should provide sufficient surface area to accommodate various activities, such as drawing, writing, and playing games. A spacious tabletop ensures that children can engage in multiple tasks simultaneously without feeling cramped.

Promotes Child Development

The design should support the physical and cognitive development of children. Features such as adjustable height and ergonomic design help accommodate growing children and promote healthy posture and comfort during prolonged use.

Aesthetic Appeal

The furniture should have a visually pleasing design that attracts both children and parents. Aesthetic appeal includes modern and charming shapes that fit well in different home environments.

Color Coordination

The colors used in the furniture should be harmonious and stimulating for children. Soft and coordinated color schemes can create a comfortable and inviting atmosphere that enhances the child's creativity and mood.

Game Attributes

The furniture should incorporate elements that encourage play, such as built-in game boards, puzzles, and interactive features. These attributes help in keeping children engaged and entertained while using the furniture.

Parent-Child Interaction

The design should facilitate activities that parents and children can enjoy together. Features that promote parent-child interaction can strengthen family bonds and provide opportunities for shared learning and play.

Social Attributes

The furniture should be designed to support multiple users, enabling children to play and interact with their peers. Social attributes encourage teamwork, communication, and social development among children.

Educational Potential

The furniture should have integrated educational tools or capabilities, such as interactive whiteboards or educational software. These features support learning and development by providing resources for educational activities.

Storage Functionality

The furniture should include ample storage options to organize and store toys, books, and other items. Effective storage solutions help maintain a tidy environment and teach children organizational skills.

Healthy Materials

The furniture should be made from non-toxic, environmentally friendly materials. Ensuring the use of healthy materials is crucial for the well-being of children and for maintaining a safe indoor environment.

Reasonable Weight

The furniture should be lightweight enough to be easily moved and rearranged by adults, yet sturdy enough to remain stable during use. Reasonable weight is important for flexibility and practicality in various settings.

These functional requirements provide a comprehensive framework for designing and selecting children's furniture that is safe, engaging, and supportive of children's growth and development.

Questionnaire Design. This paper analyzes the relationship between the degree of user demand and user satisfaction, and divides user demand into six types in the fuzzy KANO model: basic demand (M), attractive demand (A)and expectation demand (O). According to the user's answer when the requirement is implemented or not, we can find the corresponding KANO type. Table 2 lists the parameters.

To analyze these 12 functional requirements using the Kano model, we propose distributing survey questionnaires to a diverse set of respondents. The target population includes parents (the primary decision-makers and purchasers of children's furniture), educators (such as kindergarten teachers, who possess professional insights into children's development and educational needs), and children (as the end-users, who will complete the questionnaires with parental assistance). To ensure the representativeness and reliability of the data, we plan to distribute approximately 300 questionnaires in total.

Table 2. Sample KANO questionnaire.

The KANO questionnaire		
Product demand 1	Positive question: What would you do if this need were met?	Satisfied As Expected Indifferent Acceptable Dissatisfied
	Negative question: What happens if this need is not met?	Satisfied As Expected Indifferent Acceptable Dissatisfied

This comprehensive approach aims to capture a multi-faceted understanding of the functional requirements, thereby facilitating the effective classification and prioritization of these needs using the Kano model.

After the questionnaire survey was completed, the questionnaire data information was organized to obtain the original demand degree data of the target users on both positive and negative aspects of the demand indicators. Using formulas (1) and (2), calculate the satisfaction coefficient Si and dissatisfaction coefficient Di for each demand indicator, and obtain the KANO attribute for each demand indicator.

$$S_i = \frac{A + O}{A + O + M + I} \tag{1}$$

$$D_i = \frac{M + O}{A + O + M + I} \tag{2}$$

Finally, after organizing and analyzing the questionnaire data, the following Table 3 was obtained.Among them, A represents the frequency of appearance of attractive demand indicators, M represents the frequency of appearance of basic demand indicators, O represents the frequency of appearance of expectation demand indicators, I represents the frequency of appearance of irrelevant demand indicators, and R represents the attribute of reverse demand.

Table 3. Kano Model Questionnaire Statistical Results

Requirement	A	O	M	I	R	SI	DI
Structural safety	0.38	0.38	0.213	0.17	0.237	0.38	0.377
Adequate desktop space	0.43	0.43	0.193	0.19	0.187	0.43	0.423
Healthy materials	0.373	0.373	0.183	0.223	0.22	0.373	0.38
Child growth benefits	0.427	0.427	0.2	0.17	0.203	0.427	0.38
Parental interaction	0.397	0.397	0.193	0.213	0.197	0.397	0.393

(continued)

Table 3. (*continued*)

Requirement	A	O	M	I	R	SI	DI
Social attributes	0.413	0.413	0.177	0.233	0.177	0.413	0.347
Storage function	0.36	0.36	0.217	0.237	0.187	0.36	0.41
Reasonable weight	0.383	0.383	0.217	0.203	0.197	0.383	0.407
Aesthetic appearance	0.423	0.423	0.183	0.2	0.193	0.423	0.367
Color coordination	0.43	0.43	0.207	0.203	0.16	0.43	0.443
Play attribute	0.397	0.397	0.187	0.213	0.203	0.397	0.377
Educational potential	0.427	0.427	0.183	0.167	0.223	0.427	0.42

4.2 Analysis of Green Design Requirements Based on the Life Cycle Concept

To promote the global development of green design, the World Business Council for Sustainable Development has proposed seven environmental elements: reducing the intensity of raw materials, reducing the intensity of energy, reducing the spread of toxic substances, increasing the recyclability of raw materials, maximizing resource recycling, improving product service life, and enhancing service quality. The green attributes of the products involved include energy conservation, reducibility, low carbon, safety, recyclability, disassembly, maintainability, universality, and durability.

The demand for sustainable development primarily arises from laws, regulations, or standards set by governments, public sectors, or industries. By reviewing the EU's "Directive on Ecodesign Requirements for Energy-Related Products," BSI's "PAS 2050: Specification for the Assessment of the Life Cycle Greenhouse Gas Emissions of Goods and Services," ISO's "ISO 14067: Greenhouse gases — Carbon footprint of products — Requirements and guidelines for quantification and communication," and China's "General Principles for the Evaluation of Ecological Design Products" and "List of Green Design Product Standards," we can systematically identify and formulate green design requirements for children's furniture development, integrating the life cycle concept.

At the raw material acquisition stage, priority should be given to using renewable, recyclable, and low environmental impact materials, avoiding harmful chemicals, and ensuring material safety and environmental friendliness. During manufacturing, reducing waste and pollutant emissions is essential. In the transportation and distribution phase, choosing low-carbon transportation methods and designing lightweight products are crucial. For use and maintenance, enhancing product durability, ensuring easy maintenance and repair, and guaranteeing product safety are important considerations. Finally, at the end-of-life and disposal stage, designing for easy disassembly and recycling and encouraging reuse of product components are key goals. By integrating these green design requirements, children's furniture development can effectively meet sustainable development needs.By comprehensively applying the above standards and guidelines, children's furniture green design can be effectively guided to meet sustainable development needs.Based on the above analysis, we have obtained Table 4.

Table 4. Life Cycle Stages and Corresponding Green Design Requirements.

Life Cycle Stage	Green Design Requirements
Raw Material Acquisition	Use renewable, recyclable materials Ensure material safety and environmental friendliness
Manufacturing	Reduce waste and pollutant emissions
Transportation and Distribution	Choose low-carbon transportation methods Design lightweight products
Use and Maintenance	Enhance product durability Design for easy maintenance and repair Ensure product safety
End-of-life and Disposal	Design for easy disassembly and recycling Encourage reuse of product components

4.3 Conflict Analysis and Resolution Using TRIZ Theory

This study utilized the KANO model's demand analysis to systematically identify and categorize user requirements for playful children's table. The basic needs, which are fundamental to the product's safety and functionality, include a safe and stable structure to prevent tipping or accidents, ample desk space to accommodate various activities such as studying, drawing, and playing, and the use of non-toxic, health-conscious materials to ensure the well-being and safety of children.

Expected requirements go beyond these basic needs to address features that users anticipate and consider essential for an enhanced experience. These include promoting child development through ergonomic designs that support proper posture and physical growth, fostering parent-child interaction by incorporating features that enable collaborative activities and bonding, supporting social attributes by providing spaces that are conducive to group play or study sessions, offering adequate storage solutions to keep the workspace organized and clutter-free, and maintaining a reasonable weight to facilitate ease of movement and adjustment without compromising stability.

Attractive demands are those features that delight users and exceed their expectations, adding significant value to the product. These include an aesthetically pleasing appearance that appeals to both children and parents, harmonious color schemes that blend well with various interior designs, gaming features that engage children and make learning enjoyable, and educational potential that incorporates elements of learning and creativity into the design.

By incorporating the lifecycle concept, we generated green design requirements. These requirements span across various stages of the product lifecycle. In the raw material acquisition stage, the focus is on using renewable and recyclable materials, avoiding harmful chemicals, and ensuring material safety and environmental friendliness. During the production and manufacturing stage, clean production processes should be adopted, energy use optimized, and waste and pollutant emissions minimized. In the transportation and distribution stage, low-carbon transportation methods should be selected, lightweight product designs implemented, and environmentally friendly packaging materials used. In the usage and maintenance stage, emphasis is placed on enhancing product durability, designing structures that are easy to maintain and repair, and ensuring product safety. Finally, in the termination and disposal stage, products should be designed for easy disassembly and recycling, component reuse should be encouraged, and environmentally friendly disposal methods should be implemented.This study introduces the Theory of Inventive Problem Solving (TRIZ) to systematically analyze potential contradictions and conflicts in the design process of playful children's table. TRIZ provides a unique set of methodologies that assist designers in finding innovative solutions when faced with conflicts. In the design process of gaming children's tables, the first step is to identify these conflicts. Through comprehensive analysis, we have identified the following three key conflicts.

Conflict 1: Sufficient Desk Space and Storage Functionality vs. Low-Carbon Transportation

In designing a playful children's table, ensuring ample desk space and necessary storage functionality typically requires increasing the table's size and volume. This directly leads to occupying more space during transportation, thereby increasing carbon emissions and contradicting the principles of low-carbon transportation. Larger tables and storage spaces necessitate more materials and larger packaging, which in turn increases transportation costs and carbon footprints. For instance, a large playful children's table requires a sizable packaging box, making it cumbersome to handle and increasing fuel consumption of transport vehicles. To resolve this conflict, TRIZ Principle 1 (Segmentation) can be applied by designing separable table and storage modules to reduce transportation volume. Additionally, TRIZ Principle 7 (Nesting) can be employed to create nesting structures, allowing the desk and storage units to be tightly stacked, maximizing space utilization during transportation.

Conflict 2: Safe and Stable Structure and Promoting Parent-Child Interaction vs. Lightweight Design

In designing a playful children's table, it is essential to ensure its structure is safe and stable to prevent tipping or damage while also incorporating features that promote parent-child interaction. However, these requirements often necessitate the use of sturdy, heavier materials, conflicting with the goal of a lightweight design. Using heavy materials ensures safety and stability but makes the table too heavy to move or adjust easily. For example, a heavy children's table, while stable during use, becomes difficult to relocate or adjust. To address this conflict, TRIZ Principle 13 (The Other Way Around) can be applied by using new lightweight, high-strength materials or innovative structural designs that ensure safety and stability while achieving a lightweight design. Additionally, TRIZ Principle 15 (Dynamics) can be utilized by designing adjustable or foldable structures, allowing the table to reduce weight and volume when not in use while providing stability and interactive features during use.

Conflict 3: Gaming Features vs. Enhancing Product Durability

Playful children's tables need to have rich gaming features to attract and maintain children's interest. However, adding gaming functionalities can make the product more susceptible to damage during use, affecting its durability. Diverse gaming features might complicate the structure, thereby reducing product durability. For example, a children's table with multiple gaming components is prone to damage under frequent use, decreasing the overall lifespan of the product. To resolve this conflict, TRIZ Principle 3 (Local Quality) can be applied by enhancing the durability of the gaming feature areas, using more wear-resistant and durable materials or structures to improve overall product durability. Additionally, TRIZ Principle 1 (Segmentation) can be employed by designing gaming features as replaceable modules, allowing easy replacement when damaged, thereby extending the overall product lifespan.

Summarized the main design conflicts and their corresponding TRIZ solutions in Table 5 to present:

Table 5. Major Design Conflicts and TRIZ Solutions.

Design Conflict	TRIZ Principles	Solutions
Sufficient Desk Space and Storage Functionality vs. Low-Carbon Transportation	Principle 1 (Segmentation), Principle 7 (Nesting)	Design separable modules, create nesting structures
Safe and Stable Structure and Promoting Parent-Child Interaction vs. Lightweight Design	Principle 13 (The Other Way Around), Principle 15 (Dynamics)	Use new materials or structural designs, design adjustable or foldable structures
Gaming Features vs. Enhancing Product Durability	Principle 3 (Local Quality), Principle 1 (Segmentation)	Enhance durability of gaming areas, design replaceable modules

4.4 Design Example

Design Scheme Explanation: Based on the TRIZ theory, we propose a modular design solution that allows the tabletop and table legs to be disassembled. This scheme addresses both gaming and storage functionalities. Two tabletops are provided: the first tabletop features a gaming function, enabling multiple users to engage in chess matches, thereby fostering interaction. Additionally, this tabletop includes a nested, foldable drawing board that enhances the appeal of learning alongside gaming. The second tabletop, when removed, can serve as a storage box or be combined with the first tabletop to offer a convenient place for children and parents to store items during gaming or drawing activities.

The tabletop is designed with an adjustable height feature, allowing for adaptive adjustments according to the child's growth. The modular design facilitates easy disassembly, saving household space and considering low-carbon consumption during product transportation. The detachable modular design also offers multiple options for maintenance and replacement, preventing the need to replace the entire table due to the damage of a single component. The specific design scheme is shown in Figs. 1, 2, 3, and 4.

Fig. 1. Table Legs Adjustable to Accommodate Child Growth

Fig. 2. Table and Storage Box Configuration

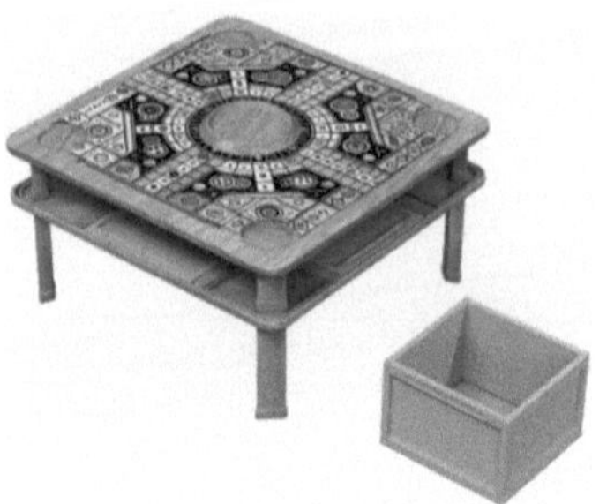

Fig. 3. Gaming Table Configuration

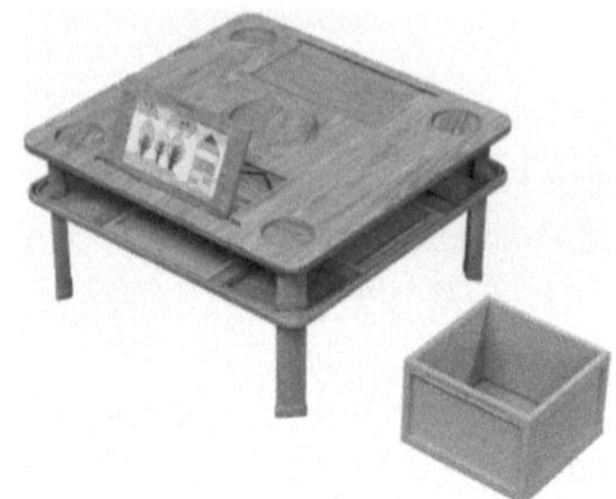

Fig. 4. Drawing Board Table Configuration

5 Conclusions

In today's context, where the concept of sustainable development is deeply ingrained and has become a crucial factor in product design, this study explores the design and development of children's furniture from a novel perspective. We innovatively integrate the KANO model with the life cycle concept, moving the application of the life cycle concept from the traditional focus on the end results in product evaluation to the initial design and development phase. By combining policy regulations and literature analysis, we identify green design requirements for consideration during the design process. Furthermore, we precisely uncover user needs through the KANO model and introduce TRIZ theory to analyze contradictions between different types of demands, ultimately deriving the final design solution using the inventive principles.

The design and development of a playful children's tablein this study demonstrate that the proposed approach can meet the user needs of children's furniture consumers while adhering to sustainable development principles. Additionally, this method provides a new paradigm for the design and development of other products under the sustainability framework.

References

1. Burton, I.: Report on reports: our common future: the world commission on environment and development. Environ. Sci. Policy Sustain. Dev. **29**(5), 25–29 (1987). https://doi.org/10.1080/00139157.1987.9928891

2. Chen, C.: Design for the environment: a quality-based model for green product development. Manag. Sci. **47**(2), 250–263 (2001). https://doi.org/10.1287/mnsc.47.2.250.9841

3. Braungart, M., McDonough, W., Bollinger, A.: Cradle-to-cradle design: creating healthy emissions–a strategy for eco-effective product and system design. J. Clean. Prod. **15**(13–14), 1337–1348 (2007). https://doi.org/10.1016/j.jclepro.2006.08.003

4. Ceschin, F., Gaziulusoy, I.: Evolution of design for sustainability: from product design to design for system innovations and transitions. Des. Stud. **47**, 118–163 (2016). https://doi.org/10.1016/j.destud.2016.09.002

5. Anastas, P.T., Zimmerman, J.B.: The twelve principles of green engineering as a foundation for sustainability. In: Sustainability Science and Engineering, vol. 1, pp. 11–32 (2006)

6. Luttropp, C., Lagerstedt, J.: EcoDesign and the ten Golden rules: generic advice for merging environmental aspects into product development. J. Clean. Prod. **14**(15–16), 1396–1408 (2006). https://doi.org/10.1016/j.jclepro.2005.11.022

7. Azapagic, A.: Life cycle assessment and its application to process selection, design and optimisation. Chem. Eng. J. **73**(1), 1–21 (1999). https://doi.org/10.1016/S1385-8947(99)000 42-X

8. Jiang, Z., Zhang, H., Sutherland, J.W.: Development of multi-criteria decision-making model for remanufacturing technology portfolio selection. J. Clean. Prod. **19**(17–18), 1939–1945 (2011). https://doi.org/10.1016/j.jclepro.2011.07.010

9. Song, J.S., Lee, K.M.: Development of a low-carbon product design system based on embedded GHG emissions. Resour. Conserv. Recycl. **54**(9), 547–556 (2010). https://doi.org/10.1016/j.resconrec.2009.10.012

10. Peng, J., Li, W., Li, Y., Xie, Y., Xu, Z.: Innovative product design method for low-carbon footprint based on multi-layer carbon footprint information. J. Clean. Prod. **228**, 729–745 (2019)

11. Boonkanit, P., Apikajornsin, A.: The methodology for selecting product at conceptual design. In: 2005 4th International Symposium on Environmentally Conscious Design and Inverse Manufacturing, pp. 242–243, Tokyo (2005). https://doi.org/10.1109/ECODIM.2005.1619211

12. Shin, J.H., et al.: A decision support method for product conceptual design considering product lifecycle factors and resource constraints. Int. J. Adv. Manuf. Technol. **52**, 865–886 (2011). https://doi.org/10.1007/s00170-010-2798-9

13. Dai, L., Xu, B.: Research on the furniture design criteria for children's psychological development in home environment. In: Marcus, A., Wang, W. (eds.) Design, User Experience, and Usability. Application Domains. HCII 2019. Lecture Notes in Computer Science, vol. 11585. Springer, Cham (2019). https://doi.org/10.1007/978-3-030-23538-3_21

14. Han, J., Li, J., Jiang, Y., Wang, L.: Application of innovative technology in children furniture design. E3S Web Conf. **236**, 04059 (2021). https://doi.org/10.1051/e3sconf/202123604059

15. Hernandez, H.A., et al.: Design of an exergaming station for children with cerebral palsy. In: Proceedings of the SIGCHI Conference on Human Factors in Computing Systems, pp. 2619–2628 (2012). https://doi.org/10.1145/2207676.2208652

16. Xiong, X., Lu, G., Lu, D.: Research on children's customized furniture design based on group technology. Appl. Sci. **11**(23), 11371 (2021). https://doi.org/10.3390/app112311371

17. Bagatell, N., Mirigliani, G., Patterson, C., Reyes, Y., Test, L.: Effectiveness of therapy ball chairs on classroom participation in children with autism spectrum disorders. Am. J. Occup. Ther. **64**(6), 895–903 (2010). https://doi.org/10.5014/ajot.2010.09149

18. Ke, F., Lee, S.: Virtual reality based collaborative design by children with high-functioning autism: design-based flexibility, identity, and norm construction. Interact. Learn. Environ. **24**(7), 1511–1533 (2015). https://doi.org/10.1080/10494820.2015.1040421

19. Andaç, T., Güzel, A.: Attitudes of families with children towardseco-friendly designed furniture: Kayseri sample. BioResources. **12**(3), 5942–5952 (2017)

20. Podrekar Loredan, N., Prelovšek Niemelä, E., Šarabon, N.: Classroom interior design: wooden furniture prototype with feedback from students and teachers. Buildings. **14**(7), 2193 (2024). https://doi.org/10.3390/buildings14072193
21. Sahin, N.T., Keshav, N.U., Salisbury, J.P., Vahabzadeh, A.: Safety and lack of negative effects of wearable augmented-reality social communication aid for children and adults with autism. J. Clin. Med. **7**(8), 188 (2018). https://doi.org/10.3390/jcm7080188
22. Kano, N., Seraku, N., Takahashi, F., Tsuji, S.: Attractive quality and must-be quality. J. Jpn Soc. Qual. Control. **14**(2) (1984)
23. Technical Committee ISO/TC 207, Environmental Management: Environmental management-life cycle assessment-principles and framework. International Organization for Standardization (2006)
24. Altshuller, G.S.: And suddenly the inventor appeared: TRIZ, the theory of inventive problem solving. Technical Innovation Center, Inc. (1996)
25. European Parliament and Council.: Directive 2009/125/EC of the European Parliament and of the Council of 21 October 2009 establishing a framework for the setting of ecodesign requirements for energy-related products. Official Journal of the European Union (2009)
26. International Organization for Standardization: Greenhouse Gases: Carbon Footprint of Products: Requirements and Guidelines for Quantification. International Organization for Standardization (2018)
27. British Standards Institution.: Specification for the assessment of the life cycle greenhouse gas emissions of goods and services (2011)

User Experience, AI, and Emerging Applications

Cultural DNA Transcoding via GANs for Living Heritage: Revitalizing Spring Festival Traditions Through Human-AI Collaboration in China's Yellow River Delta

Wei Han[✉], Yangyang Li, and Shiteng Liu

University of Jinan, Jinan, Shandong 250022, China
soa_hanw@ujn.edu.cn

Abstract. This study, taking the Spring Festival folk culture of the Yellow River Delta as a case, initiates a behavior-symbol-semantic tri-level cultural gene analysis framework and constructs a human-machine collaborative digital preservation pathway by integrating generative adversarial networks (GANs). Through ethnographic fieldwork, the research comparatively analyzes the differentiated characteristics of New Year customs between canal and maritime cultural regions, revealing the shaping mechanisms of geographical environments and economic forms on cultural diversity, and establishes a hierarchical labeling system. To address the limitations of traditional GANs technology, a cGAN-ICH Inheritor Dual-Discriminator collaborative framework is designed, which synergizes machine vision discrimination with expert knowledge validation to ensure both visual fidelity and semantic authenticity for generation. By proposing a "digital technology-cultural ecology bidirectional empowerment" pathway, this study provides methodological insights for advancing the digital preservation and transmission of intangible cultural heritage.

Keywords: Intangible Cultural Heritage · Cultural DNA Transcoding · Generative Adversarial Networks · Human-AI Collaboration

1 Introduction

Inscribed on the Representative List of the Intangible Cultural Heritage of Humanity (ICH) in 2024 [1], the Spring Festival holds profound cultural significance for Chinese populations across both urban and rural contexts. This millennia-old tradition has crystallized into a complex symbolic system that encapsulates the Chinese nation's collective memory regarding natural cyclicality, familial ethics, and auspicious aspirations. Characterized by distinctive seasonal manifestations and identity-constructing attributes, its ceremonial timeline spans from the Laba Festival (the eighth day of the twelfth lunar month) to the Lantern Festival (the fifteenth day of the first lunar month), encompassing an intricate tapestry of cultural practices, cere-monial observances, and communal festivities organized around the dual thematic axes of "transition from the old" and "commencement of the new". The ritualized celebration process, replete with multilayered

M. Schrepp and M. Rauterberg (Eds.): HCII 2025, LNCS 16342, pp. 115–132, 2026.
https://doi.org/10.1007/978-3-032-13164-5_8

symbolism, manifests through both material artifacts (e.g., Spring Couplets, Spring Festival Reunion Dinner, Nianhua paintings) and performative traditions (e.g., ritualized greetings, ancestral veneration practices, New Year's Eve vigil customs). Nevertheless, this cultural complex confronts existential challenges emblematic of broader ICH preservation dilemmas. The diminishing intergenerational transmission efficacy, particularly affecting orally transmitted social practices, has precipitated declining cultural recognition among younger demographics, necessitating urgent safeguarding interventions as identified in recent field studies [2, 3]. Compounding these challenges, the dual forces of commercialization and globalization have engendered problematic phenomena of ceremonial simplification and cultural alienation, thereby jeopardizing the festival's authenticity [4].

It is encouraging to note that the rapid development of emerging artificial intelligence (AI) technologies provides a promising solution against this dilemma. Particularly noteworthy are the adversarial learning mechanisms of Generative Adversarial Networks (GANs), which have demonstrated powerful capabilities both in image generation and text synthesis. Since the pioneering work of Goodfellow in proposing GAN, this deep learning framework has demonstrated huge potential in image generation through its adversarial training mechanism [5], wherein a generator (G) and a discriminator (D) engage in iterative competition to synthesize data indistinguishable from authentic samples. Subsequent advancements have driven a variety of GAN variants, each addressing specific technical challenges or application requirements. For instance, Deep Convolutional GAN (DCGAN) significantly improved image synthesis fidelity by integrating trans-posed convolutional layers and convolutional architectures [6], while Conditional GAN (CGAN) introduced category-specific constraints to enable label-guided data generation [7]. To mitigate the instability inherent in traditional GAN training, Wasserstein GAN (WGAN) used Wasserstein distance metrics to reformulate the loss function [8]. Further innovations expanded functional capabilities: Cycle-GAN achieved cross-domain image translation via cycle-consistent adversarial losses [9], Style-GAN advanced high-fidelity synthesis through granular style manipulation [10], and SRGAN optimized super-resolution reconstruction while preserving perceptual details [11]. The adaptability of GAN architectures has catalyzed domain-specific breakthroughs. In digital art, CartoonGAN [12] and its enhanced variant MC-CartoonGAN [13] established the first framework for style transfer from photorealistic images to cartoon representations, demonstrating robust artistic applications. Concurrently, ecological conservation efforts have leveraged DV-WID-CDPGAN for wildlife intrusion detection systems [14], whereas medical imaging research employed CleftGAN to generate synthetic cleft lip facial datasets for clinical training [15]. In environmental monitoring, TimeGAN has been utilized for wind power forecasting [16], while DropletGAN optimized precision in agricultural crop spray systems [17]. These developments collectively underscore GANs' transformative capacity to bridge theoretical innovation and practical implementation across interdisciplinary domains. The rapid evolution of artificial intelligence (AI) technologies presents a promising paradigm for addressing these dilemmas. Of particular significance is the revolutionary framework of Generative Adversarial Networks (GANs), which has demonstrated remarkable efficacy in both image generation

and text synthesis domains. Following Goodfellow's seminal contribution in conceptualizing GAN architecture, this sophisticated deep learning framework has exhibited
exceptional potential through its distinctive adversarial training mechanism [5]. The
framework operates via the dynamic interplay between a G and a D, engaging in iterative
adversarial optimization to synthesize data that approaches statistical indistinguisha-
bility from authentic samples. The evolutionary trajectory of GAN architectures has
spawned numerous specialized variants, each addressing specific technical limitations
or application requirements. Deep Convolutional GAN (DCGAN) achieved substantial
improvements in image synthesis fidelity through the strategic integration of transposed
convolutional layers and advanced architectural components [6], while Conditional GAN
(cGAN) introduced categorical constraints to facilitate label-guided data generation [7].
To address the inherent training instability of conventional GANs, Wasserstein GAN
(WGAN) implemented the Wasserstein distance metric for loss function optimization
[8].

Subsequent architectural innovations have significantly expanded the functional
capabilities of GANs: Cycle-GAN established bidirectional domain translation through
cycle-consistent adversarial losses [9], Style-GAN revolutionized high-fidelity synthesis through hierarchical style manipulation [10], and SRGAN advanced super-resolution
reconstruction while preserving perceptual fidelity [11]. The adaptability of GAN architectures has catalyzed transformative advances across diverse domains. In computational
arts, CartoonGAN [12] and its enhanced iteration MC-CartoonGAN [13] pioneered
frameworks for photorealistic-to-cartoon style transfer, demonstrating robust artistic
applications. Concurrently, environmental conservation efforts have leveraged DV-WID-
CDPGAN for wildlife monitoring systems [14], while medical imaging research has
utilized CleftGAN for generating synthetic cleft lip facial datasets in clinical education
[15]. In environmental monitoring applications, TimeGAN has been implemented for
wind power forecasting [16], while DropletGAN has optimized precision in agricultural
spray system dynamics [17]. These developments collectively exemplify the transformative potential of GANs in bridging theoretical innovation with practical implementation
across interdisciplinary domains.

The application of GAN-based methodologies in China's cultural domain reveals
significant interdisciplinary potential. These sophisticated approaches have been systematically integrated into multiple cultural spheres, encompassing digital Chinese painting generation, traditional landscape painting style transfer [18], and intelligent recommendation systems for Hanfu (traditional Chinese attire) customization [19]. In the
realm of cultural heritage preservation, Wang [20] pioneered a sophisticated dual-stage
GAN framework incorporating a parallel encoder-based GAN architecture, specifically
designed to address the non-naturalistic aspects of mural restoration, thereby achieving
significant enhancement in structural coherence within degraded regions. Furthermore,
Octadion [21] developed Diffusion-GAN, an innovative hybrid frame-work that synthesizes diffusion-based denoising mechanisms with adversarial training paradigms. This
advanced approach effectively addresses the complexities of pattern generation in batik
artistry through progressive texture refinement, achieving unprecedented accuracy in
cultural motif reproduction. This comprehensive analysis illuminates a research gap
regarding GAN applications within the ICH domain. Nevertheless, GAN architectures

inherently possess the capability to address fundamental preservation challenges, particularly concerning *presence* and *authenticity*, through sophisticated multimodal data synthesis and dynamic behavioral simulation methodologies. Of particular significance is the distinctive nature of ICH folk customs, exemplified by Spring Festival celebrations, which fundamentally differ from traditional ICH crafts where audience engagement typically remains passive. Instead, Spring Festival manifestations represent complex, multidimensional cultural ecosystems characterized by dynamic interplay between inheritors and participants, who collectively engage in active co-creation and mutual interaction, thereby continuously evolving and shaping the Spring Festival centered cultural matrix.

This investigation centers on the Spring Festival traditions of China's Yellow River Delta (YRD), a geo-cultural crucible characterized by a synthetic cultural system that integrates historical depth with unique regional identity, embodying cultural inclusivity and polyphonic diversity. Functioning as a living repository of Yellow River civilization's ontological expressions, the region's hydrological primacy has engendered the symbiotic evolution of two paradigmatic cultural archetypes: canal culture forged through fluvial governance systems and maritime culture arising from littoral ecological adaptations, each constituting microcosmic manifestations of Chinese civilization's pluralistic essence. On this basis, the study focuses on the YRD's Spring Festival Traditions, establishing a research framework encompassing "cultural differentiation analysis - hierarchical gene extraction - digital translation" to elucidate the formation mechanisms of regional cultural diversity and explore technological pathways for digital preservation of intangible cultural heritage. Through ethnographic fieldwork employing a dual-dimensional comparative framework, the study analyzes differentiation characteristics between canal-based and marine-influenced Spring Festival traditions, revealing the formative impacts of geographical environments and socioeconomic patterns on cultural diversity. A three-tier cultural labeling system (behavior-symbol-semantics) is constructed to achieve structured characterization and digital archiving of cultural genes. Methodologically, the study designs a collaborative "cGAN-ICH inheritor dual-discriminator" mechanism through GANs, ensuring precise generation of culturally authentic ICH symbols while facilitating dynamic inheritance and innovative applications. The methodology integrates multimodal data acquisition/processing, text structuring, and cultural gene analysis with GAN-driven technological implementation, ensuring scientific rigor and methodological accuracy. The research significance extends beyond providing methodological support for interdisciplinary studies in cultural ecology and digital humanities, advancing the understanding of cultural diversity formation mechanisms. It establishes theoretical frameworks for ICH digital living preservation, forms replicable technological chains, and enhances public cultural identity.

2 The Multifaceted Characteristics and Cultural Genetic Analysis of Spring Festival Traditions in the YRD

This investigation employs a geo-cultural typology framework to decode the YRD's pluralistic cultural ecosystems, selecting Dezhou (epitome of Grand Canal culture) and Binzhou (archetype of maritime culture) as contrasting research setting. Dezhou's cultural matrix, crystallized through five centuries of canal-based mercantilism, manifests in ritualized practices like the Laba Accounting Ceremony (a performative synthesis of mercantile pragmatism and lineage-based economic ethics). In diametric contrast, Binzhou's maritime cultural paradigm, forged through fisheries-based livelihood systems, institutionalizes symbolic codes exemplified by the Eight Bowl (Fried Delicacies Banquet), whose structural rigidity mirrors seafaring communities' risk-coping social architectures. This intentional cultural divergence establishes not merely comparative specimens for ICH studies, but crucially, an experimental matrix for testing GANs' cultural adaptation plasticity. By analyzing the structural features of cultural symbols across these two regions, targeted generative models can be developed to facilitate differentiated cultural transcreation.

From January 18th (Laba Festival) to February 24th (Lantern Festival) in 2024, field investigations focused on textual cultural documentation were systematically conducted. The study implemented a tripartite data collection methodology: (1) transcription of oral narratives from 50 cultural practitioners, generating 120,000 characters of interview transcripts; (2) systematic collation of 10 community Spring Festival activity plans and 8 folkloric manuscripts alongside archival materials; (3) compilation of material culture inventories documenting 20 traditional banquet menus with detailed culinary techniques and dietary conventions. For dynamic ritual practices, 30 h of audiovisual recordings were converted into 50,000-character textual records, comprehensively capturing ritual sequences such as Kitchen God worship ceremonies and Flower Bar Dance choreographies. Crucially, the analytical framework adopted dual organizational dimensions: temporally structuring data along the Laba-to-Lantern Festival continuum, and spatially contrasting canal versus maritime cultural corpora. This methodological rigor culminated in a systematically structured information matrix, providing the foundational dataset for developing the multi-tiered annotation taxonomy.

2.1 Spring Festival Traditions' Differentiation Shaping Mechanism

Field investigations reveal a structured temporal progression in regional festive practices. Widely circulated in local oral traditions, Spring Festival folk rhymes establish precise calendrical correspondences between lunar dates and ritual activities. This temporospatial framework, emerging from the distinct environmental affordances of canal and maritime ecosystems, sustains core cultural commonalities while fostering geographically-differentiated ritual expressions (Table 1). Notably, among evolving socioeconomic structures and lifestyle transformations, these traditional temporal norms have transitioned into dynamic reference matrices. Contemporary practitioners now individually adapt festive preparation timelines, exemplifying traditional customs' adaptive recalibration mechanisms within modernization contexts.

The selection of "folk cuisine differentiation" and "celebratory activity selectivity as analytical parameters merges from two fundamental considerations. Primarily, dietary traditions, as material cultural carriers, manifest profound cultural significance throughout the festive cycle, encompassing ingredient preparation protocols, culinary ritual performances, and communal feasting etiquettes Moreover, folk celebratory activities, characterized by high participatory interactivity, serve as vital mediums for euphoria articulation and blessing-apotropaic ritual transmission. Their selection patterns mirror

Table 1. Comparison of Spring Festival Ritual Activities in the Yellow River Delta.

Chronological Framework		Commonalities		Differences	
				Canal Culture Regions	Maritime Culture Regions
Pre-New Year's Eve in Lunar December (LD)	Laba Festival	Making Laba Congee; Ticking Laba Garlic		Accounting Ceremony	–
	23 LD	Kitchen God Worship		Homecoming	Steaming Year Cake
	24 LD	–		Cleaning House	–
	25 LD	–		Papering/Decorating Windows; Grinding Soybean & MakingTofu	Cleaning House
	26 LD	Going to Spring Fair; Pig-Slaughtering Ceremony; Stewing Meat		–	–
	27 LD	Chicken Sacrifice Ritual		Rooster Sacrifice Ritual	–
	28 LD	Making Dough & Steaming Buns		–	–
	29 LD	–		Pounding Mochi	Deep Frying Vegetables & Meat
New Year's Eve	30 LD	Day	Pasting Couplets; Hanging Lanterns; Making Dumplings; Ancestral Worship Ceremony	Pasting the Character 'You' upside down; Welcoming Gods Ritual; Scattering Auspicious Grains Ritual	–
		Night	Keeping Vigil; Having Spring Festival Reunion Dinner (dumplings indispensable)	Eight Bowls (rooster & fish indispensable)	Eight Bowls (deep fried delicacies indispensable); Steamed Year Cake

(continued)

Table 1. (*continued*)

Chronological Framework		Commonalities	Differences	
			Canal Culture Regions	Maritime Culture Regions
Post-New Year's Eve In Lunar January (LJ)	1 LJ	Shooting off Firecrackers; Eating Dumplings; Paying a New Year Visit & Greeting	–	–
	2 LJ	–	Eating Longevity Noodles Ritual; Visiting Maternal Grandmother	Eating Dumplings; Married Daughters' Homecoming
	3 LJ	Visiting Paternal Aunts		
	4 LJ	–	Married Daughters' Homecoming; Giving New Year's Presents (mochi indispensable)	Visiting Maternal Aunt
	5 LJ	Taboo of Paying Visits; God of Wealth Worship Ceremony	–	Sweeping Floor Ritual; Weeding out Small Person by Making Dumplings and Eating themes
	12 LJ	–	–	Visiting Huji Quyi Fair (feast of folk arts)
	15 LJ	Visiting Temple Fair; Eating Yuanxiao (glutinous rice balls); Guessing Lantern Riddles; Attending the Lantern Fair	–	Making & Displaying Hedgehog-Shaped Flower Buns
Flexibly Scheduled Folk Performances		Performing Lion Dance; Stilt Walking; Yangko Dance	Performing Donkey-Shaped Riding; Flower Bar Dance; Two-Person Wrestling; Drum Dance; Traditional Dace with Sticks; Rolling Reed Strips	–

geo-cultural predilections while propagating cultural values through corporeal engagement. This dual-dimensional analytical framework illuminates the rich tapestry of cultural diversity while establishing a systematic foundation for constructing the secondary labeling system for the cultural gene library.

2.1.1 Folk Cuisine Differentiation

As material carriers of cultural memory, Spring Festival cuisine traditions profoundly encode regional geo-historical specificities and their ecological adaptation strategies. Serving as the ritual nucleus, the Spring Festival Reunion Dinner spans the entire festive period. This cultural phenomenon includes elaborate preparatory processes (including ingredient preparation, traditional tofu crafting, ritualistic animal slaughtering, and sophisticated culinary techniques such as meat stewing, deep-frying, and rice cake making), as well as its ceremonial consumption patterns during and after the festival (featuring the Eight Bowls, fried cakes, and dumplings), forming a rich cultural narrative. Of particular significance is the evolutionary of the Eight Bowl, a typical cultural symbol originating from collective feasting needs of traditional settlements, closely associated with pivotal life-cycle rituals like weddings and funerals. Under divergent geographical influences, Binzhou's maritime-cultural variant emphasizes deep-frying techniques and marine resource utilization, while Dezhou's canal culture manifests the iteration of southern-toward-northward culinary diffusion, integrating southern culinary elements such as steamed poke with rice flour (originating from Jiangxi Province) and sweet rice, which thereby resonates its historical cultural intersection of north and south cultures promoted by the Grand Canal. Notably, the evolution of the Eight Bowls tradition, a gastronomic palimpsest originating in communal feasting rituals, maintains profound intertextuality with life-cycle ceremonies including nuptial and funerary rites. Under distinct geographical influences, Binzhou's maritime culture emphasizes sophisticated deep-frying techniques and marine resource utilization, while Dezhou's canal culture embodies culinary hybridity via south-north gastronomic dialogues. This cultural integration is exemplified through the incorporation of southern culinary elements, such as steamed poke with rice flour and sweet rice preparations, epitomizing the Grand Canal's historical role as culinary confluence corridor.

2.1.2 Celebratory Activity Selectivity

The regional differentiation of Spring Festival celebratory activities in the YRD exemplifies the adaptive selection mechanisms within cultural systems. In Binzhou's maritime cultural sphere, the Huji Quyi Fair, historically rooted in itinerant performers' livelihood-driven artistic competitions [22], exemplifies cultural uniqueness through its open-air performance ecology, facilitating cultural transmission and communal resource integration. Conversely, Dezhou's canal cultural preserves agrarian-rooted folk dances folk performances such as the Flower Bar Dance and Donkey-shaped Riding Performance, adorned with canal-adjacent crop motifs in costumery, employing chromatic semiotics to materialize agricultural civilization's terroir-bound ethos. This divergent selection profoundly reflects the fundamental distinctions between maritime commercial civilization and inland agrarian civilization in their respective survival strategies and cultural expressions. Through synthesizing these dual dimensions, two formative mechanisms emerge systematically. The first mechanism manifests in the geo-environmental shaping of cultural diversity. Culinary divergence reveals a south-to-north diffusion pattern in canal zones contrasting with land-sea integration in maritime regions, while celebratory activities reflect the contrast between maritime audacity and agrarian iconography. The second lies in the dynamic adaptation of temporal norms. While traditional temporal sequences (such as housecleaning on lunar December 24th and tofu preparation on the 25th) yield to flexible scheduling, core practices, particularly the Eight Bowls banquet and participatory rituals, continue to function as cultural anchors. This coexistence of change and continuity establishes a paradigm for traditional culture's modern transformation.

2.2 Labeling System Construction of Spring Festival Tradition Genes

Based on cultural differentiation mechanisms, a sophisticated "Behavior-Symbol-Semantics" tri-level labeling system is established to systematically decode the structural ontology of Spring Festival traditions. This schema embodies a tripartite intertextuality wherein the behavioral layer facilitates embodied empirical perception, the symbolic layer enables cultural transduction, and the semantic layer sustains value interpretation (Fig. 1). These interconnected strata collectively form an integrated chain of cultural transmission, ensuring both the genetic stability and expressive diversity of Spring Festival Traditions across successive generations. The Spring Festival Reunion Dinner serves as an illustrative exemplar of this framework: the behavioral layer encompasses ingredient preparation and culinary techniques; the symbolic layer comprises food morphology and presentational elements; while the semantic layer embodies the auspicious meanings associated with specific dishes. Through coordinated interaction, these tripartite components facilitate the generation and transmission of cultural signification.

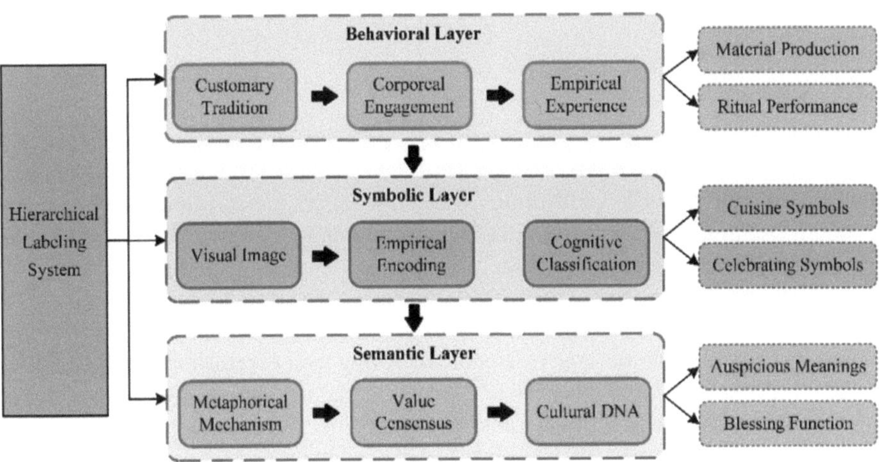

Fig. 1. The hierarchical labeling system of Spring Festival Traditions.

2.2.1　Behavioral Layer

As a representational system of cultural practice, the behavioral layer constitutes the most immediate and foundational stratum of Spring Festival Traditions, encompassing dual dimensions of material production and ritual performance. The material production dimension includes sophisticated operational practices, particularly those associated with the Spring Festival Reunion Dinner, including ingredient preparation and intricate culinary processes. Concurrently, the ritual performance dimension incorporates ceremonial practices such as the Kitchen God worship ritual and the Flower Bar Dance. Furthermore, region-specific folk celebratory activities and distinctive traditional dances employ embodied practices to transform cultural memory into tangible behavioral texts, exemplified by the competitive performances of the Huji Quyi Fair.

2.2.2　Symbolic Layer

The symbolic layer, functioning as a sophisticated cultural information transduction system, encodes meaning through material-iconic representations. Cultural symbols manifest in two primary forms: culinary symbols (such as fish symbolizing annual abundance, and dumplings embodying traditional ingot shapes) and celebratory symbols (exemplified by the crop-patterned motifs adorning the Flower Bar Dance costumes), collectively establishing a distinctive regional cultural identification matrix. These symbolic elements represent not merely material responses to ecological environments but also serve as profound expressions of collective cultural memory. In particular, culinary symbols enrich the cultural dimensions of Spring Festival traditions, enhancing both their recognizability and intergenerational transmissibility. Moreover, within traditional performances and festivities, celebratory symbols manifested through costumes and props constitute integral elements of dance performances. These symbolic representations, through their sophisticated integration of chromatic schemes, geometric patterns, and kinetic motifs, articulate the cultural essence and affective narratives embedded within traditional dance practices.

2.2.3　Semantic Layer

The semantic layer constitutes an interpretive system of cultural values, conveying deeper meanings through sophisticated metaphorical mechanisms. The auspicious symbolism embedded within the dishes of Spring Festival Reunion Dinner, exemplified by circular configurations symbolizing familial ethics and reunion, and the blessing functions inherent in celebratory activities, such as the implicit pursuit of resource acquisition in the competitive Huji Quyi Fair, demonstrate the cultural system's symbolic solutions to fundamental survival needs. These semantic elements transcend mere reflection of collective aspirations for an elevated existence, achieving their expression and transmission through specific behavioral practices and symbolic manifestations. This structural configuration elevates Spring Festival traditions beyond the empirical domain into a realm of shared value consensus, thereby ensuring their cultural distinctiveness and vitality through intergenerational transmission.

Therefore, the construction of the tri-level labeling system embodies the hierarchical transduction of cultural DNA, wherein empirical activities at the behavioral layer, through symbolic-layer translation, ultimately achieve meaning elevation at the semantic layer. This structured analytical methodology provides not only technical pathways for the digital archiving of ICH in the YRD but, more significantly, illuminates the intrinsic mechanisms of traditional culture's modern transformation through decoding inter-stratum generative relationships. The evolutionary trajectory of firecrackers serves as an illustrative example: electronic firecrackers supplanting conventional ones represents variation at the behavioral layer, while maintaining the original cylindrical form and red appearance demonstrates selection at the symbolic layer, ultimately preserving auspicious meanings at the semantic layer. Through this lens, the structured deconstruction establishes a novel paradigm for achieving dialectical unity between cultural innovation and traditional continuity within the context of ICH digitization.

3   Creation of Spring Festival Tradition Gene Library

Based on extensive field research and genetic analysis of Spring Festival tradition genes in the YRD, a hierarchical tagging system has been preliminarily established, structured as "Primary Tags (Regional Culture)-Secondary Tags (Cultural Differentiation Features)-Tertiary Tags (Behavioral/Symbolic/Semantic Layers)." While this system provides a foundational framework for constructing the gene library, the comprehensiveness and systematic nature of the library necessitate multi-dimensional data support.

This requirement stems from dual challenges: field surveys encounter spatial and temporal constraints, with the risk of insufficient historical depth and incomplete regional coverage; concurrently, the preservation and transmission of ICH folk customs demonstrate dynamic evolutionary characteristics, necessitating corroboration through diachronic literature and real-time data. Consequently, the initial engagement of the second part of the research rests in the integration of multi-source heterogeneous data, including ICH databases, academic literature, and media archives, with field survey findings, constructing the gene library through standardized processing and tag-based mapping.

The library prioritizes textual modality, optimizing compatibility for semantic parsing, tag nesting, and cross-media association. Textual data facilitates precise keyword extraction and semantic network construction through Natural Language Processing (NLP) techniques, while unstructured data interfaces with the tagging system through metadata annotation. This text-centric approach effectively preserves structured outcomes from field investigations while providing open interfaces for future multi-resource integration, ultimately establishing a cultural resource repository that synthesizes academic rigor with practical applicability.

In the ICH digital preservation, the synergistic integration of textual data and GAN-synthesized imagery establishes a cognitive closed-loop framework of "structured description-visual validation". During the initial phase, a machine-interpretable multilabel system encodes cultural characteristics through textual modeling; during the subsequent phase, GAN-driven visual synthesis translates abstract semantics into high-definition representations, enabling parametric refinement through perceptual verification. This methodological framework not only addresses inherent constraints in multimodal generation but more significantly, through context-aware semantic mapping, achieves dialectical coherence between cultural authenticity and transmission efficacy.

Building upon the tripartite analytical framework of Spring Festival rituals, the Python computational ecosystem facilitates systematic standardization and semantic unification of Spring Festival traditions' multimodal data corpus. Through Word2Vec and BERT contextual embeddings, textual analytics discern underlying semantic patterns differentiating maritime and canal cultural paradigms. Subsequently, data normalization and matrix transformation yield a structured annotation system, serving as the ontological foundation for GAN-driven cultural synthesis, thereby ensuring semiotic precision and phenomenological veracity in symbolic representation.

Post-categorical analysis of Spring Festival Traditions reveals the vectorization potential of Behavior-Symbol-Semantics elements. The methodological workflow encompasses three cardinal stages: The initial preprocessing phase employs Jieba tokenization augmented by domain-specific lexica to identify cultural signifiers (terms classified as secondary data labels such as "Spring Festival traditions as in canal culture, Spring Festival traditions in maritime culture"); systematic filtration of linguistic artifacts including stop words and non-semiotic markers enhances signal-to-noise ratios. Differentiated vectorization protocols address lexical frequency variations: low-frequency markers (e.g. canal culture, maritime culture) adopt sparse vector encoding, whereas high-frequency terms leverage Word2Vec/GloVe embeddings to model semantic correlations; complex semantic domains utilize pretrained BERT architectures for domain-adaptive contextualization, generating dynamic embeddings that mirror cultural praxis complexity.

Regarding the behavior-symbol-semantics triadic system, the following data curation strategy implements hierarchical annotation:

$$\text{Spring Festival Tradition Name} : [\text{behavior; symbol; semantics}]$$

4   Construction and Optimization of GAN-Driven Cultural Transcreation Model

Following the completion of textual structuring and encoding of Spring Festival traditions' genomic matrices, the pivotal technical challenge resides in transforming discrete semantic labels into a visual symbol system that preserves cultural authenticity. Conventional image generation models, hampered by insufficient feature disentanglement capabilities, struggle to accurately map the multi-level correlations within the behavior-symbol-semantics hierarchy. The adversarial training mechanism of GANs, particularly the guided generation characteristics of cGANs, offers a breakthrough solution. The injection of the genes labeling system as conditional vectors into the generator enables models to progressively assimilate the generation principles and stylistic constraints of cultural symbols through game interaction.

However, standard cGANs' loss functions rely exclusively on the data-driven judgments of the D, frequently resulting in misalignment between technical fidelity and cultural authenticity. The images produced by the G may achieve photorealistic quality yet deviate significantly from ceremonial specifications or semantic connotations intrinsic to ICH symbols. To reconcile this ontological dissonance, this research establishes a "cGAN-ICH Inheritor Dual-Discriminator" collaborative mechanism: complementing the cGAN discriminator (D_1) that assesses pixel-space authenticity of images, an anthropological "cultural discriminator" (D_2), embodied by ICH inheritors, validates cultural compliance through expert-annotated hermeneutics, thereby formulating a composite loss function synthesizing data distribution alignment with cultural norm verification. This dual-constraint architecture imposes simultaneous visual-textual and socio-cultural validation during adversarial training, ultimately harmonizing computational synthesis logic with cultural transmission epistemology (Fig. 2)

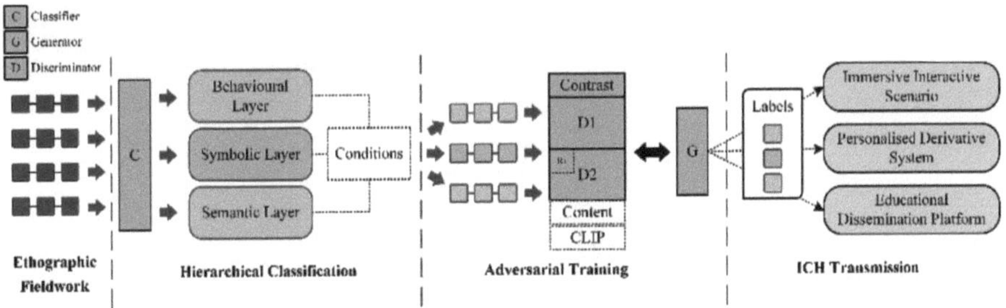

Fig. 2. The Overall Architecture of cGAN, with the GAN Objective Function Adapted to Incorporate Spring Festival Traditions.

4.1 Adaption of GAN Objective Function for Spring Festival Traditions

In standard GANs, the G and D optimize the objective function through adversarial training/game-theoretic interaction. The core objective function can be expressed as follows:

$$\min_{G}\max_{D} V(D, G) = \mathbb{E}_{x\sim p_{data}}\big[\log D(x)\big] + \mathbb{E}_{z\sim p_z}\big[\log(1 - D(G(z)))\big]$$

In cGANs, the generation process requires the integration of a gene labeling system as a conditional vector c. The objective function is accordingly reformulated as follows:

$$\min_{G}\max_{D} V(D, G) = \mathbb{E}_{x\sim p_{data}}\big[\log D(x|c)\big] + \mathbb{E}_{z\sim p_z}\big[\log(1 - D(G(z|c)))\big]$$

To strengthen the robustness of this cultural transcreation model, a geo-contrastive loss function is introduced following BERT-based encoding of gene labels for improving feature discrimination:

$$\mathcal{L}_{contrast} = -\log \frac{e^{s(c_i, c_j)/\tau}}{\sum_{k=1}^{N} e^{s(c_i, c_j)/\tau}}$$

In the formulation, c_i and c_j represent areal variants of the same cultural typology (e.g. maritime culture vs. canal culture in the YRD region). τ denotes the temperature parameter.

4.2　Game Equilibrium Between Machine and ICH Inheritors

To transcend the cultural fidelity limitations of conventional cGANs, a dual-discriminator collaborative architecture is proposed:

- D_1 adopts a PatchGAN architecture, employing convolutional neural networks (CNNs) to assess pixel-level authenticity by examining the local textures and overall composition of the generated images. Its loss function is formulated as:

$$\mathcal{L}_{D_1} = -\mathbb{E}_{x \sim p_{data}}\left[\log D_1(x|c)\right] - \mathbb{E}_{x \sim p_z}\left[\log(1 - D_1(G(z|c)))\right]$$

- The D_2 is implemented through an expert evaluation panel composed of ICH inheritors, who perform semiotic validation on the cultural compliance of generated outputs. Its loss function is quantified via an expert-annotated cultural rule matrix R, defined as:

$$\mathcal{L}_{D_2} = \sum_{i=1}^{N} \lambda_i \cdot \|\phi(G(z|c)) - R_i\|_2^2$$

In this formulation, $\phi(\cdot)$ represents the cultural symbol feature extraction function, R_i denotes the i-th cultural constraint rule, and λ_i indicates the rule weighting coefficient. To mitigate manual annotation costs and resolve subjective evaluation discrepancies, this framework incorporates active learning sampling strategies and knowledge distillation techniques. Furthermore, VGG network constraints pretrained networks enforce high-level semantic alignment between generated images and textual descriptions through content consistency loss $\mathcal{L}_{content}$.

To address the challenge of generating rare cultural labels (e.g. Huji Quyi Fair), a CLIP-guided zero-shot generation technique is employed, with a specialized few-shot enhancement loss:

$$\mathcal{L}_{few-shot} = \|CLIP(G(z|c)) - CLIP(t)\|_2^2$$

Where t denotes textual descriptions, text-image cross-modal semantic alignment is used to generate synthetic training data through CLIP-guided diffusion processes. The final composite objective function integrates machine and cultural discriminator losses through weighted fusion:

$$\mathcal{L}_{total} = \alpha \mathcal{L}_{D_1} + \beta \mathcal{L}_{D_2} + \gamma \mathcal{L}_{content} + \delta \mathcal{L}_{contrast} + \epsilon \mathcal{L}_{few-shot}$$

The hyperparameters $\alpha, \beta, \gamma, \delta, \epsilon$ are dynamically adjusted through Bayesian optimization, implementing a progressive optimization strategy of pixel-level fidelity (prioritized in early training phases), cultural constraints and model robustness (emphasized at later training stages).

The training methodology encompasses two distinct phases: preliminary optimization and contextual refinement. During the preliminary phase, leveraging the Spring Festival tradition gene library encompassing YRD's maritime-canal dialectics, the model assimilates contrastive divergence objectives to orthogonalize region-specific latent embeddings. Concurrently, cGAN loss establishes foundational cultural symbol generation capabilities, facilitating prototype synthesis of Spring Festival tradition visual representations in constrained scenarios. The refinement phase inaugurates a cyber-physical feedback loop with ICH inheritors. At predetermined intervals of 100 training iterations, active learning sampling is initiated, submitting the upper decile of generated samples, those exhibiting the highest Kullback-Leibler (KL) divergence, for expert evaluation. Subsequently, the generator's conditional mapping pathway undergoes refinement based on the categorized error typology identified through expert assessment.

4.3 Dual Empowerment of Technological Infrastructure and Ecological Expansion

This transcreation model facilitates the transformation of traditional cultural resources into interactive, derivative, and disseminable living assets.

4.3.1 Availability of Immersive Interaction Diffusion

Through the systematic integration of cultural gene labeling systems with GAN-generated high-fidelity imagery and Virtual/Augmented Reality (VR/AR) technologies, a folded folk experience domains. This methodological approach transforms the Spring Festival customs of the YRD into participatory dynamic experiences, thereby achieving "presence-enabled" propagation of cultural genes that transcends spatiotemporal constraints while addressing the inherent deficiencies of ICH experiences in contemporary society. Upon user label input, the computational model systematically retrieves primary "Yellow River Delta" tags and activates corresponding secondary genetic data to generate differentiated folk scenarios with high fidelity (Fig. 3). This data-driven creation paradigm maintains cultural genetic integrity while simultaneously unleashing digital innovation potential, enabling New Year customs to achieve the dual objectives of "sustainable transmission" and "innovative revitalization" within contemporary sociocultural contexts.

Fig. 3. The differentiation of *Eight Bowl* images generated with GAN in Yellow River Delta (left: Delicacies in canal culture regions; right: Delicacies in maritime culture regions).

4.3.2 Attainability of Personalized Intelligent Creation

The GAN-powered personalized cultural creative derivation system effectively leverages the parametric generation capabilities of cultural translation models to establish a sophisticated intelligent creation platform characterized by the "user input-label deconstruction-creative generation" paradigm. This innovative framework fundamentally promotes the integration of ICH elements with contemporary design methodologies, addresses individualized user requirements, and facilitates the strategic transformation from "preservation-oriented" to "consumption-oriented" approaches in ICH practices. Through the precise adjustment of latent space variables within conditional GANs (cGANs), the system generates innovative solutions that seamlessly integrate traditional cultural genes with modern aesthetic principles. Besides, the establishment of dedicated ICH enthusiast communities subsequently enables users to disseminate generated content and actively participate in cultural re-creation processes, thereby enhancing collaborative interaction while simultaneously stimulating creative innovation, ultimately advancing ICH inheritance and evolution.

4.3.3 Achievability of Heritage Education Diversity

The GAN technology provides innovative methodological approaches for ICH education, substantially facilitating cultural dissemination and popularization while effectively lowering traditional learning thresholds. This technological framework systematically strengthens cultural identity among younger demographic cohorts and cultivates an expanding community of ICH enthusiasts and inheritors, thereby establishing a robust foundation for sustainable cultural development. The tripartite educational matrix, comprising "cultural genetic atlas-visual representation of heritage-interactive experiences," implements gamification principles for symbolic, behavioral, and semantic layer labels through sophisticated computational mechanisms. This comprehensive approach enables students to acquire traditional cultural knowledge within immersive pedagogical environments, thereby significantly enhancing their cognitive understanding and appreciation of ICH elements.

5 Summary

This study proposes a dialogic framework for digitally preserving the Spring Festival traditions in China's Yellow River Delta (YRD), where canal rituals shaped by hydraulic governance and maritime customs forged through coastal ecological adaptations coexist as complementary manifestations of cultural DNA. Grounded in the "cultural differentiation-genetic extraction-digital translation" triaxial model, our approach navigates the delicate equilibrium between algorithmic precision and cultural authenticity: not as technological imposition, but as mediated negotiation between digital logic and ancestral wisdom. Methodologically, we establish three interconnected systems: a dual-dimensional comparative model decoding geoeconomic influences on ritual differentiation patterns; a behavior-symbol-semantics labeling architecture transforming embodied cultural practices into traceable genetic profiles; and a cGAN dual-discriminator mechanism creating collaborative spaces where inheritors' tacit knowledge dialogues with generative algorithms. Initial implementations suggest this techno-cultural hybridity can preserve core cultural semantics while enabling adaptive reinterpretation, though comprehensive validation awaits longitudinal studies. As an initial exploration, this work constructs not definitive solutions but open platforms for interdisciplinary discourse. The path forward demands continuous epistemic humility: technological systems must evolve as responsive vessels instead of prescriptive molds, nurturing cultural genes through what we term "digitally-assisted organic growth" for safeguarding cultural warmth.

Acknowledgements. The research was supported by the Ministry of Education Humanities and Social Sciences General Project (No. 20YJC760024) and the Key Art Science Projects of Shandong Province (No. L2024Z05100091).

References

1. UNESCO: Available online: https://ich.unesco.org/en/RL/spring-festival-social-practices-of-the-chinese-people-in-celebration-of-traditional-new-year-02126. Accessible on 2 February, 2005
2. Xiang, L.F.: Memory of place: a study on the holistic cognition of living heritage sites. J. Capital Normal Univer. (Soc. Sci. Edition). **05**, 59–71 (2024)
3. Yu, X.F.: Artistic characteristics and artistic inheritance of cloth embroidery balls of Guangxi intangible cultural heritage. Art Educ. Res. **02**, 48–50 (2025)
4. Liu, X.F., Su, J.S.: Connotation analysis and realisation path of authenticity of intangible cultural heritage. J. Central South Univer. Nationalities (Humanities and Social Sciences Edition). **41**(01), 55–62 (2021). https://doi.org/10.19898/j.cnki.42-1704/C.2021.0107
5. Goodfellow, I., et al.: Generative adversarial networks. Commun. ACM. **63**(11), 139–144 (2020)
6. Denton, E.L., Chintala, S., Fergus, R.: Deep generative image models using alaplacian pyramid of adversarial networks. Adv. Neural Inf. Proces. Syst. **28** (2015)
7. Mirza, M.F.: Conditional generative adversarial nets. arXiv preprint. arXiv:1411.1784 (2014)
8. Arjovsky, M.F., Chintala, S.S., Bottou, L.T.: Wasserstein GAN. arXiv:1701.07875 (2017)
9. Zhu, J.Y., et al.: Unpaired image-to-image translation using cycle-consistent adversarial networks. In: Proceedings of the IEEE International Conference on Computer Vision, pp. 2223–2232 (2017)
10. Karras, T.F.: A style-based generator architecture for generative adversarial networks. arXiv preprint arXiv:1812.04948 (2019)
11. Shaoqian, W.U., Ximing, L.: Survey on research progress of generating adversarial networks. J. Front. Comput. Sci. Technol. **14**(3), 377 (2020)
12. Chen, Y., et al.: Cartoongan: Generative adversarial networks for photo cartoonization. In: Proceedings of the IEEE Conference on Computer Vision and Pattern Recognition, pp. 9465–9474 (2018)
13. Qiao, P., et al.: Image style animation under multi-channel CartoonGAN. Comput. Appl. Res. **38**(11), 3517–3520 (2021). https://doi.org/10.19734/j.issn.1001-3695.2021.01.0066
14. Moorthy, V.F., Rukkumani, V.S.: Deep vision-based wildlife intrusion detection with colour distribution preserved generative adversarial networks. Pattern Recogn. **161**, 111272 (2025)
15. Hayajneh, A.F., et al.: Adapting a style based generative adversarial network to create images depicting cleft lip deformity. Sci. Rep. **15**(1), 3614 (2025)

16. Zhang, Z., et al.: Wind power prediction under sample augmentation of temporal generative adversarial networks. J. Power Syst. Autom., 1–12 (2025). https://doi.org/10.19635/j.cnki.csu-epsa.001588
17. Pham, T.H., Burgers, T., Nguyen, K.D.: Enhanced droplet analysis using generative adversarial networks. Comput. Electron. Agric. **231**, 109922 (2025)
18. Jiang, X., et al.: Codec-generative adversarial network-based cultural and creative design of digital Chinese painting. J. Anhui Univer. (Nat. Sci. Edition), 1–8 (2025)
19. Cai, L., et al.: Intelligent customisation recommendation of traditional Hanfu based on improved stacked generative adversarial network. Textile J. **45**(12), 180–188 (2024). https://doi.org/10.13475/j.fzxb.20240200801
20. Wang, F.: Research on Virtual Restoration of Dunhuang Murals Based on Generative Adversarial Network. Lanzhou Jiaotong University (2024)
21. Octadion, O.F., Yudistira, N.S., Kurnianingtyas, D.T.: Synthesis of batik motifs using a diffusion-generative adversarial network. Multimed. Tools Appl., 1–32 (2025)
22. Zhou, H.F.: Atlas of the First National List of Intangible Cultural Heritage, 1st edn. Culture and Arts Publishing House, Beijing (2006)

Reconfiguring Heritage Engagement: AI-Enabled Complementary Symbiosis Network from the Digital Dunhuang Project

Wei Han[(⊠)], Yangyang Li, and Shiteng Liu

University of Jinan, Jinan, Shandong 250022, China
`giada.han@hotmail.com`

Abstract. This study examines the ongoing reconfiguration of heritage engagement through AI, as evidenced by the Digital Dunhuang Project. We conceptualize this shift as an emerging "AI-Enabled Complementary Symbiotic Net-work" comprising five interdependent dimensions—digital immersion, creative co-creation, value co-building, participatory stewardship, and transnational governance—activated through emotion-driven, incentive-based, and technology-mediated mechanisms. Rather than presenting a definitive model, our analysis reveals an evolving architecture where public participation dynamically intersects across these dimensions, with AI serving as both an enabler and mediator. The DDP case demonstrates how such configurations can nurture organic value cycles while accommodating cultural pluralism, suggesting pathways for future development in digital heritage ecosystems.

Keywords: AI-Enabled Cultural Heritage · Complementary Participatory Symbiosis · Digital Dunhuang Project

1 Introduction

The rapid advancement of digital technology and artificial intelligence (AI) is significantly reshaping the methodologies employed in the preservation, dissemination, and public engagement with cultural heritage. Conventional theories of cultural heritage participation are increasingly inadequate in elucidating the complex transformations arising within AI-enabled heritage engagement, thereby posing challenges to established theoretical paradigms [1]. Although scholars have begun to investigate AI's role in cultural heritage, recognizing technological systems as evolving beyond mere instruments into "cultural revitalization mediators" that bridge historical legacies and future possibilities [2], there persists a deficiency in systematic theoretical frameworks capable of explicating the interactive relationships and operational mechanisms among diverse modalities of public participation enabled by AI [3].

Drawing on the *Digital Dunhuang Project* (DDP), a globally significant cultural heritage digitization initiative spanning 78 countries and amassing over 22 million cumulative visits, this research explores the preliminary contours of an "AI-Enabled

M. Schrepp and M. Rauterberg (Eds.): HCII 2025, LNCS 16342, pp. 133–152, 2026.
https://doi.org/10.1007/978-3-032-13164-5_9

Complementary Symbiosis Network for Cultural Heritage." This emerging framework envisions five interconnected core nodes—digital experience, creative co-creation, value co-building, cultural patronage, and collaborative governance—facilitated by three transformative mechanisms: emotion-driven engagement, value-based incentives, and technology empowerment. Rather than presenting a fully realized ecosystem, the integration of AI within the DDP suggests an incipient shift from traditional hierarchical participation structures toward a more flexible, non-linear configuration, challenging the linear assumptions of established models. The project incorporates AI-driven platforms, such as immersive digital experiences, AI-assisted creative processes, block chain-authorized content sharing, crowdfunded preservation efforts, and transnational digital collaboration, offering an initial case for investigating AI's potential to reshape heritage engagement.

Focusing on two central questions—how does AI technology reshape the modalities of public participation in cultural heritage? What interactive relationships emerge among these modalities?—this study advances several theoretical contributions. These include: (1) moving beyond linear participation assumptions to identify nascent transformation mechanisms; (2) proposing a collaborative frame-work that tentatively balances technological empowerment with cultural governance; and (3) outlining an endogenous, cyclical system that begins to integrate economic, data, and cultural capital. Practically, it offers exploratory insights for cultural institutions considering ecosystem development amid digital transformation. By analyzing the DDP, this study conceptualizes heritage engagement as an evolving, AI-supported network in its formative stages, providing an emerging lens for understanding participation in the digital era.

2 Literature Review

Recent advancements in AI have fundamentally reconfigured cultural heritage engagement. The following review first traces the technological evolution of participation models, then analyzes associated ethical dilemmas, and finally explores sustainability frameworks.

2.1 Digital Technology-Driven Evolution of Cultural Heritage Engagement Models

Early research centered on the foundational digital transformation of cultural heritage, with online platforms enabling unidirectional dissemination and restricted access to heritage information [4]. With the widespread adoption of machine learning, intelligent participation tools have emerged, such as automated classification of cultural heritage via image recognition [5] and identification of architectural components through point cloud segmentation [6]. These technologies have substantially enhanced the efficiency of professional research; nonetheless, public participation remains limited to predefined task responses [7]. Recent studies have shifted toward multi-technology integration, as illustrated by the European Digital Heritage Agenda's framework for cross-institutional data sharing [8]. However, existing technological architectures predominantly depend on centralized data repositories and fail to facilitate autonomous derivation of participation pathways [9].

Current theories of participation mechanism design adhere to a linear progression hypothesis, involving a sequential transition from information reception to shallow interaction and, ultimately, deep contribution [10]. Although some scholars have investigated crowdsourcing mechanisms to expand participation [11], empirical evidence suggests that most users remain at the initial engagement stage [12]. Despite technological advancements reducing operational barriers [13], sustaining participant motivation remains an unresolved issue [14], which increasingly attracts scholars to explore these emerging dynamics. This finding highlights an area increasingly explored by scholars, who are actively examining the diversity of participation entry points and the mechanisms underlying behavioral transformation.

2.2 Technological-Ethical Tensions in the Digitization of Cultural Heritage

The extensive application of AI has introduced significant ethical challenges. Some studies have identified systematic biases in cultural heritage datasets, including the underrepresentation of minority cultures and reliance on singular historical narratives [15]. Although technical solutions, such as algorithm optimization for image classification [16] or improved semantic understanding [17], have been proposed, critics argue that these methods fail to address the interpretive negotiation of cultural symbol meanings [18]. At the governance level, existing ethical frameworks tend to emphasize generalized principles like transparency and accountability [19], yet they lack hierarchical assessment criteria tailored to the specific attributes of cultural heritage.

Efforts to balance authority in this domain aim to mitigate risks while fostering ongoing discourse. Co-creation theories advocate for public involvement in decision-making [20], whereas professional institutions warn that excessive openness may compromise cultural interpretation [21]. While hybrid approaches, such as AI-assisted human review [22], are increasingly employed, their effectiveness in balancing creative freedom with authenticity preservation remains untested across diverse contexts [23]. These tensions underscore methodological limitations in current research regarding the development of culturally sensitive governance models.

2.3 Exploring Sustainability Mechanisms for Digital Cultural Heritage

Studies on economic sustainability have focused on two primary strategies: predictive model-driven resource allocation optimization [24] and value capture through digital intellectual property (IP) derivative development [25]. Critics, however, caution that overreliance on commercialization risks commodifying cultural capital [26]. In terms of data sustainability, social media mapping technologies are utilized to examine public cultural perception patterns [27]. Yet, the challenge of identifying value conversion breakpoints in these data flows persists [28].

In terms of cultural sustainability, identity construction theory emphasizes the strengthening effect of digital participation on cultural identity [29]. However, intergenerational studies hint at varying degrees of emotional resonance with digital heritage relative to physical artifacts among younger generations [30]. While technology has expanded the scope of dissemination, it may weaken the local roots of cultural practices [31]. Current solutions are predominantly characterized by single-factor optimization strategies, exhibiting a paucity of collaborative regeneration mechanisms for economic, data and cultural capital [32]. This limitation poses an ongoing challenge to ensuring the sustained vitality of digital heritage.

2.4 Research Gaps

Existing scholarship reveals several limitations that warrant further investigation. Technological intervention paradigms tend to prioritize single-point tool innovation, thus overlooking the architectural design of cross-platform collaborative ecosystems. Similarly, the ethical governance efficacy of principled frameworks invites further exploration to fully capture the polysemy of cultural symbols, while sustainability pathways remain fragmented, lacking a systematic coupling perspective for value transformation. These gaps collectively offer a critical entry point for examining the complex dynamics of cultural heritage engagement in the digital era. To address these challenges, this study leverages the DDP as a foundational case to propose an "AI-Enabled Complementary Symbiosis Network for Cultural Heritage," aiming to integrate diverse participation modalities and transformation mechanisms into a cohesive, evolving framework.

3 Methodology

3.1 Research Design

This study adopts an explanatory single-case research design, with the DDP selected as the core case. It employs a dual "structure-process" analytical framework, comprising a structural layer that identifies the node composition and attributes of the Complementary Symbiosis Network (CSN), and a process layer that examines the dynamic transformation mechanisms and pathways among participation modalities. This dual framework facilitates understanding of both the static structure and its evolutionary process."

3.2 Case Selection

The DDP serves as a "complete laboratory" for heritage digitization, distinguished by four mutually reinforcing dimensions that establish its archetypal significance.

- **Representation of the full digitization cycle:** The project spans the entire lifecycle of cultural heritage digitization—from high-precision capture and digital preservation to display, dissemination, and public participation—fully encapsulating the transition from physical to virtual realms.
- **Technological and institutional innovation:** As a pioneer of the "dual reviews + blockchain rights confirmation" mechanism, the project processes an average of 50 copyright authorizations daily in 2024. It introduced a collaborative model involving preliminary review by Tencent Cloud AI and final expert review by the Dunhuang Academy, offering a robust approach to balancing resource accessibility and control. This synergy of technological and institutional advancements provides an exemplary case for studying cultural governance.

- **System integration at the participation level:** The project has developed a comprehensive participation chain, including low-threshold experiences, personalized creations, and professional collaborations. A unified user ID system enables cross-platform behavioral tracking, laying a data-driven foundation for analyzing transitions between participation forms.
- **Paradigm-setting inspiration for global governance collaboration:** The project demonstrates extensive global reach and adaptability, influencing cultural preservation standards worldwide and earning recognition as an exemplary case at the 2023 Global Awards for World Heritage Education Innovative Cases [33]. This paradigmatic role underscores its significance in heritage digitization.

3.3 Data Collection

This study utilizes triangulation as a methodological strategy, combining multi-source data to emphasize the complementary strengths of quantitative metrics and in-depth qualitative insights.

- **Platform statistics:** Macro-indicators—such as traffic, conversion rates, and engagement metrics across platforms—were collected to construct a holistic profile of participation patterns.
- **User tracking:** A purposive sample of 12 users, reflecting diverse backgrounds and participation levels, was selected for cross-platform behavioral analysis. Participants, aged 18–65, included students, teachers, designers, and company employees, chosen for their varied initial engagement forms. Tracking captured multidimensional data, including visit sequences, dwell times, interactive content, creative outputs, social sharing, and feedback. Though limited in scale, this method yields rich contextual evidence essential for elucidating transformation mechanisms among participation modalities.
- **Expert interviews:** Semi-structured interviews with four experts validated data interpretations and provided insider perspectives on the system's design principles and operational dynamics.

3.4 Analysis Procedure

The analysis unfolds in three distinct phases:

- **Structural analysis:** The Functional Decomposition Method was applied to identify five core nodes of the CSN—experience, co-creation, value co-building, funding, and governance—and their techno-cultural attributes. This systematic approach dissects system components and their interrelations, tracing functional entry points from user experiences, mapping realization pathways, and synthesizing node attributes and connectivity mechanisms.
- **Process tracing:** Three paradigmatic pathways—the experience-driven conservation loop, co-creation spillover dynamics, and data-enhanced experiential feedback—were reconstructed to systematically investigate causal chains. This involved aligning behavioral patterns with theoretical constructs and empirically validating the operational modalities and activation thresholds of transformation mechanisms.

- **Thematic analysis:** Interview data underwent thematic analysis through a three-stage coding process—open coding, axial coding, and selective coding—to derive key themes aligned with the theoretical framework.

3.5   Research Limitations and Responses

This study acknowledges three limitations and corresponding mitigation strategies:

1. Unavailable user behavior data was supplemented through interviews;
2. Incomplete explanations of mechanisms due to technical opacity were addressed with additional expert consultations;
3. The single-case design's specificity was countered by theoretical abstraction to enhance generalizability, with explicit delineation of boundary conditions that may influence the framework's broader applicability.

4   The DDP Ecosystem: Empirical Findings

4.1   System Overview

The DDP constitutes a permanent, online repository of digital resources for the millennium-old Dunhuang Mogao Grottoes, a UNESCO World Heritage Site, designed to facilitate public access. Initiated in the late 1980s and formally launched in 2006, the project integrated advanced technologies such as augmented reality (AR), virtual reality (VR), and 3D reconstruction by 2014. Leveraging AI, it has digitized 186 caves with millimeter-level precision and generated virtual tour data for 169 caves, amassing a storage capacity exceeding 350 TB as of 2024.

The DDP employs a sophisticated four-layer technical architecture: (1) a data acquisition layer, utilizing high-precision millimeter-level scanning and multispectral imaging; (2) an intelligent processing layer, encompassing AI-driven image restoration, content recognition, and a blockchain-based rights confirmation system; (3) a participatory interaction layer, comprising user interfaces across five core platforms; and (4) a decision support layer, featuring resource optimization and innovation decision-making informed by user behavior analytics. This structured framework underpins the transformation of raw data into actionable value, providing a robust technological foundation for diverse participation modalities.

Since 2016, the DDP has cultivated a converged digital ecosystem through a multi-platform architecture, anchored by the *Digital Dunhuang* web portal—launched in 2016 with an English version introduced in 2017—and enhanced by the WeChat mini-program *Dunhuang E-Tour*. This framework achieves seamless integration of four legacy web platforms via API-driven interoperability, while consolidating previously fragmented mini-programs into a unified interaction matrix powered by hybrid technologies (see Fig. 1). These interconnected platforms facilitate data sharing and value circulation, collectively enabling multi-tiered public engagement.

4.2   Technical Architecture: Functional Layers and Performance

The DDP ecosystem operationalizes the CSN conception through five interconnected technical layers, each instantiating a theoretical node as shown in Table 1. This stratified architecture enables value circulation while maintaining cultural authenticity.

Fig. 1. Architectural Components of the DDP Ecosystem: Web Portal Interface (Left: the *Digital Dunhuang* Platform) and Mobile Service Node (Right: *Dunhuang E-Tour* Mini-Program Access Layer).

Table 1. Layer-Node Correspondence.

Technical Layer	Theoretical Node	Core Function
Immersive Engagement	Digital Experience	Sensory knowledge transfer
Creative Production	Creative Co-Creation	AI-assisted cultural output
Value Circulation	Value Co-Building	Blockchain-enabled sharing
Stewardship	Cultural Patronage	Micro-donation integration
Governance	Collaborative Gov.	Transnational coordination

4.2.1 Immersive Engagement Layer

Launched in April 2023, the *Digital Sutra Cave* is the world's first "Trans-dimensional Participatory Museum." Its core elements and key performance metrics are as follows:

- **Technical implementation:** Utilizes millimeter-level photogrammetry (30,000+ renders) for 900-million-polygon models, enhanced by UE5 PBR rendering for 8 K murals. The AI virtual human *Jiayao* enables real-time interaction via motion capture, physics-based simulation, and a knowledge graph, processing 3.7 TB of data with sub-millisecond latency.
- **Multi-Sensory design:** Combines 4 K visuals, auditory, NPC narration, and role-playing mechanics for immersive engagement.
- **Cultural authenticity:** Verified by experts in literature, art, and archaeology, *Jiayao*'s eighth-century attire reflects *Ritual Procession of Lady Dudu* (a eighth-century mural depicting aristocratic Buddhist patronage) and Cave 217 motifs.

The Chinese version recorded 14 million visits in its first week, with a 2.65% completion rate (371,000 users). It transitioned from a WeChat mini-program to a web-based platform with the International version launched in November 2023, adapting to international user preferences for browser-based accessibility.

4.2.2 Creative Production Layer

Inspired by Dunhuang ceiling designs, the *From Dome to Scarf* launched in 2018, featuring:

- **AI-Assisted design:** Provides eight themes (e.g., Three Rabbits Sharing an Ear, Nine-Colored Deer) and 200+ mural elements (e.g., auspicious clouds, mythical beasts) for user combination. AI matches elements, optimizes visuals, and generates thematic three-line poems.
- ***Virtual-Real integration: Offers*** AR try-on and online customization of silk scarves (199 yuan each), linking digital creativity with physical products.
- **Preservation connection:** Donates part of proceeds to Cave 427's digital preservation, connecting creation to heritage support.

The platform achieved 2.8 million visits in its first week, with a 7.14% creative conversion rate (200,000+ works), demonstrating superior engagement compared to typical cultural creative platforms. It earned the 2019 Effie Gold Award for innovation [34].

4.2.3 Value Circulation Layer

Launched in December 2022 as the world's first blockchain-verified cultural heritage licensing platform, the *Material Pool* platform provides 6,500+ high-resolution digital assets across 21 categories, tagged via AI-driven semantic ontologies. Emphasizing copyright protection and transformation through on-chain authentication, its "Co-created Works" module—featuring neural network-assisted remixing and blockchain-tracked attribution—includes:

- **Blockchain rights confirmation:** Employs blockchain for licensing and "on-chain" evidence storage, with smart contracts enabling tiered authorization: free for personal use, agreement-required for research, and 300–800 yuan/piece for publishing or commercial use.
- **Dual review mechanism:** Combines AI content safety checks with expert review from Dunhuang Acadamy (China's natonal institution for Mogao Grottoes conservation established in 1944), certifying secondary creations as shared resources with revenue sharing.

The platform recorded 4.2 million visits, averaging 50 smart contracts daily (National Data Bureau, 2024), with a 0.38% order conversion rate (16,000 orders) and 0.52% download rate (22,000 downloads). Its copyright transformation efforts yielded digital IP exhibitions (e.g., *Dunhuang: No Longer Distant, Immersive VR Explorations*), engaging 5.8 million global participants, and interactive programs (e.g., *Virtual Dunhuang, From Dome to Scarf*), achieving 77 million engagements. Cultural products and licensing generated over CNY 61 million in revenue by Q3 2024 (approx. USD 8.4 million).

4.2.4 Stewardship Layer

The *Digital Patron* Project (2018-present) merges traditional *patron* culture with digital crowdfunding, enabling public participation in heritage conservation via blockchain-based identity attestation. Each donation (minimum 0.9 yuan) yields an on-chain credential, recorded anonymously using cryptographic hashing. Key features include:

- **Participatory stewardship:** Employs a transparent tripartite framework—public protocols, donation progress visualization, and automatic closure upon funding goals—empowering patrons in digital guardianship.
- **Multiple pathways:** Provides diverse engagement options: micro-donations via WeChat, derivative channels tied to products (e.g., *From Dome to Scarf*), and quiz games awarding blockchain badges, linking literacy, consumption, and conservation.

This "universal protection" model fosters a "gathering sand into towers" effect, enhancing social capital and emotional bonds through traceable records. The Cave 55 initiative (June 5, 2018–February 24, 2020, 629 days) engaged 239,041 participants, raised 1,902,067 yuan, averaging 380.3 daily engagements with a 0.79% donation conversion rate.

4.2.5 Governance Layer

Launched in 2020, the Transnational Digital Platform fosters a decentralized governance model for Dunhuang/Silk Road cultural heritage, facilitating cross-border collaboration through:

- **Digital heritage integration and sharing:** Based on distributed collaborative technology, diverse cooperation with international institutions, AI-assisted intelligent restoration, and high-precision digitalization, achieve the virtual reunion of scattered heritage and the gradual realization of global sharing and collaborative protection of digitized resources, e.g. available digital Dunhuang exhibitions overseas based on the virtual heritage reunification and *Material Pool* (Public Creation module).
- **Federated standardization and technical dissemination:** Collaborates with institutions like the British Library to develop an OAIS-based digital asset management system, establishing shared metadata standards. The SCO-endorsed "Digital Cultural Heritage" model leverages DDP as a benchmark, promoting digitization knowledge exchange among member states and Belt and Road countries.

This "digital third space" consolidates over 100,000 high-definition replicas of overseas Dunhuang heritage, transcending physical restitution debates to enhance digital repatriation while respecting institutional custodianship. The *Dunhuang Manuscript Database*, operational since 2022 and progressively expanded, is enriched by 4,075 manuscripts donated by the French National Museum in 2015. Recognized at the 2022 World Internet Conference as a "Quality Case of Building a Shared Cyberspace Community" — one of 12 selected from over 200 submissions across five domains (global network infrastructure, cultural exchange, digital economy, cybersecurity, and governance) — it democratizes Mogao Grottoes access and standardizes heritage rights management across jurisdictions [35].

4.3 Participatory Transformation Paths

The DDP ecosystem challenges conventional participation boundaries, tentatively forging a dynamic network marked by multidirectional flows. Departing from the linear progression enshrined in traditional participation frameworks [36], this emergent system enables entry at any node and supports fluid role transitions, revealing overlapping and evolving public identities (see Fig. 2.).

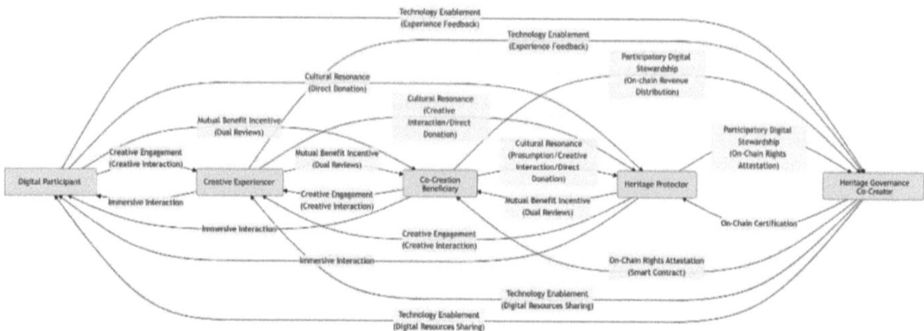

Fig. 2. Role Dynamics and Multidirectional Participation Networks in the DDP Ecosystem

At its core, this nascent innovation hinges on a third-order transformation mechanism, integrating macro-level platform analytics with longitudinal tracking of 12 prototypical users. This exploratory framework delineates three interwoven dimensions of transformation, signaling an incipient shift toward a non-linear participatory paradigm:

4.3.1 Cognitive Transformation

The *Digital Sutra Cave* exemplifies an emergent cognitive shift by embedding "cognitive presence" within gamified, immersive interactions. Platform analytics indicate that, within its first 27 days, it garnered 17 million user visits, with exploration completion rates notably surpassing those of conventional digital exhibition platforms. Behavioral analysis illuminates this preliminary transformation: User A (41, teacher) accurately detailed the artistic and historical significance of murals post-interaction, while User H (65, retired historian) remarked, "For the first time, I perceived the spatial dimensionality of Dunhuang art." Users frequently described a visceral sense of temporal immersion—"as if present in the cave millennia ago"—tentatively enhancing cultural affinity. This nascent pattern aligns with experiential learning theories, where sensory engagement begins to deepen historical understanding [37], suggesting AI's potential to reframe cognitive engagement.

4.3.2 Behavioral Transformation

The *From Dome to Scarf* project tentatively validates the "consume-to-protect" approach, intertwining consumption with conservation. Macro data reveal 2.8 million visits in its debut week, yielding a 7.14% creative conversion rate (200,000 works)—well above industry benchmarks for cultural creative platforms. Tracking data highlight this evolving efficacy: Users C (52, architect) and F (39, employee) swiftly purchased silk scarves post-creation, motivated by design satisfaction and the direct allocation of proceeds to Cave 247 preservation. User F emphasized the model's accessibility, noting it enabled her to "contribute to protection effortlessly." This emerging low-threshold behavioral shift suggests a simplification of participation pathways, bolstered by technological empowerment, which aligns with preliminary evidence of digitally-mediated prosocial behavior [38].

4.3.3 Identity Transformation

The most striking insight lies in the tentative reconfiguration of user identities. The *Material Pool*'s open repository of co-created works positions public creation as an incipient source of cultural reproduction. Tracking data reveal an evolving shift: Users D (21, university student), G (32, designer), and K (27, freelancer) transitioned from initial "spectator" or "visitor" roles to identifying as "cultural communicators," "Dunhuang guardians," or even, playfully, "Dunhuang IP collaborators." User G actively shared Dunhuang knowledge on social media and joined digital commemorative events, reflecting traits of active creators logged by the platform. The "Dunhuang E-Tour" app, with 60 million visits and 200 million interactions, underscores the potential value of identity-driven engagement, resonating with early formulations of participatory culture.

This multi-tiered mechanism tentatively elucidates how an AI-enabled symbiotic network fosters user transformation across cognitive, behavioral, and identity domains. Although constrained by a limited tracking sample, these findings, corroborated by macro platform data, offer compelling initial evidence of an evolving model. Cognitive transformation appears driven by emotional resonance with historical culture; behavioral shifts rely on technological simplification and immediate feedback; and identity changes are propelled by value alignment and social recognition. Together, this embryonic multidirectional framework begins to erode traditional distinctions between audience, creator, and protector. AI technologies—through creative recommendations, behavioral analytics, and tool integration—lower transformation barriers, interweaving participation modalities to establish an endogenous, cyclical system in its formative stages [39]. This emergent configuration, while not fully matured, provides a foundational lens for reexamining heritage participation in the digital era.

4.4 Value Creation and Circulation

The DDP orchestrates a dynamic, self-reinforcing ecological system through an evolving triadic value cycle that interweaves economic, data, and cultural dimensions, suggestive of a framework still unfolding within the broader trajectory of digital heritage innovation.

4.4.1 Economic Value Cycle

Revenues from licensing Dunhuang heritage digital resources have surpassed 61 million yuan, with these proceeds being reinvested to sustain digital preservation initiatives.

Complementing this, the *Digital Patron* has mobilized over 1.9 million yuan through multifaceted channels—encompassing consumption, interactive question-answering, and donations. This cyclical "input-output-reinvestment" dynamic offers a potential counterpoint to the resource dependency often constraining traditional cultural preservation paradigms. Such a mechanism subtly resonates with cultural economics discourse on sustainable funding streams [40], hinting at an economic scaffold that may yet evolve to underpin long-term heritage management.

4.4.2 Data Value Cycle

Data reflecting 4.2 million visits to the *Material Pool* underpins iterative advancements in AI models, incrementally refining user access to targeted resources and enhancing the calibration of push notifications. Behavioral data analysis progressively informs platform optimization and provides nascent decision-support for content development and conservation planning. This adaptive interplay, driven by data, evokes a feedback loop consonant with information systems on innovation dynamics [41], illuminating a system whose capacity for resilience continues to take shape amid ongoing technological integration.

4.4.3 Cultural Value Cycle

The virtual character *Jiayao*, adorned with 17 distinct elements drawn from various caves (e.g., the celestial maiden motif of Cave 334), commands a cross-platform reach of 200 million impressions. The increasing sophistication of public co-creation manifests in the engagement of 5.8 million individuals with Dunhuang digital IP exhibitions, many of which weave in user-generated content from the open material library. This interplay subtly reaffirms the vitality of traditional cultural symbols within contemporary settings, aligning with participatory culture frameworks and suggesting a gradual rearticulation of cultural capital that remains responsive to emergent creative currents.

This interwoven value cycle incrementally diminishes reliance on persistent external inputs, cultivating an ecosystem whose vitality finds expression in the 60 million visits and 200 million interactions logged by the Dunhuang E-Tour Mini Program. Far from a static construct, this ecological configuration reflects a confluence of technology, culture, and economics, offering tentative theoretical and practical insights into the evolving contours of digital heritage stewardship.

5 Complementary Symbiosis Network: Theoretical Framework

Building on the outlined architecture, the "AI-Enabled Complementary Symbiosis Network for Cultural Heritage" is defined. The DDP ecosystem's functional layers—immersive, creative, circulation, stewardship, and governance—correspond to the CSN model's five theoretical nodes, as mapped in Table 2. This duality aligns with complex systems theory, where layers reflect vertical stratification for operational efficiency, and nodes highlight horizontal dynamics driving symbiotic evolution.

Table 2. Technical-Theoretical Mapping.

Technical Layer (Implementation)	Theoretical Node (Conceptualization)	Symbiotic Relationship
Immersive Engagement	Digital Experience	Mutualism: Enhanced user cognition fuels eco-system vitality
Creative Production	Creative Co-Creation	Commensalism: AI tools benefit creators without resource competition
Value Circulation	Value Co-Building	Reciprocity: Blockchain mediates bidirectional value flows
Stewardship	Cultural Patronage	Altruism: Micro-donations sustain communal heritage
Governance	Collaborative Gov.	Neutralism: Decentralized coordination avoids interference

5.1   Network Structure

Accordingly, the CSN, with its five core nodes interconnected by three transformative mechanisms, marks a shift in cultural heritage participation from a traditional hierarchical paradigm to a polycentric ecosystem, as illustrated in Fig. 3.

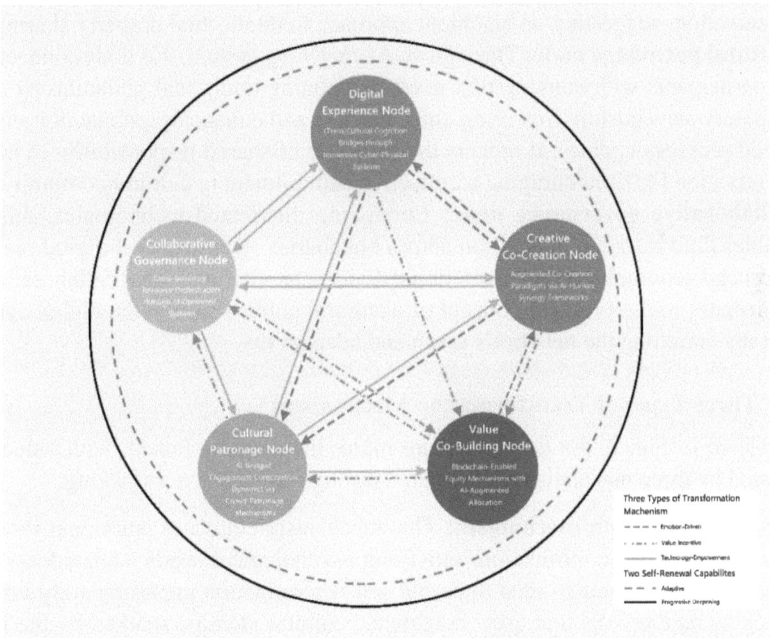

Fig. 3. AI-Enabled Complementary Symbiosis Network for Cultural Heritage.

5.1.1 Five Core Nodes

The network is anchored by five functionally distinct yet interdependent nodes, each contributing to the evolving architecture of cultural heritage engagement:

- **Digital experience node:** By harnessing immersive technologies, this node renders historical knowledge accessible and perceptually intuitive, lowering barriers to cultural comprehension. The *Digital Sutra Cave*, for instance, employs AI-driven knowledge graphs to provide personalized simulations and explanations, fostering emotional resonance that aligns with the notion of cognitive presence enhancing user engagement. This process cultivates intrinsic motivation for sustained interaction with heritage content.

- **Creative co-creation node:** This node facilitates creative expression through AI-assisted tools, streamlining workflows—such as reducing the 17-step traditional design process to three on the *From Dome to Scarf*. By integrating intelligent features like AI-generated poetry, it amplifies cultural expressiveness while preserving user autonomy, embodying the dynamics of human-machine collaborative creativity. Technology here serves as a catalyst, enriching rather than supplanting human ingenuity.

- **Value co-building node:** Leveraging blockchain and smart contracts, this node fosters equitable value distribution, mitigating transactional costs in cultural collaboration as explored in studies of digital resource management [42]. The *Material Pool* platform's dual-track system—AI preliminary screening complemented by manual cultural assessment—ensures a balance between open access and authenticity preservation, suggesting an emergent approach to intellectual property sharing.

- **Cultural patronage node:** Through an AI-matching system, this node connects public participants with conservation needs, redefining traditional philanthropy as participatory stewardship. Lowering entry barriers and enhancing satisfaction via visualized progress updates, it reflects the principle of shared responsibility in heritage preservation [43], encouraging a collective commitment to cultural continuity.

- **Collaborative governance node:** Employing distributed technologies, this node enables fluid resource integration across boundaries. Transnational digital platforms transcend geographical and institutional divides, facilitating global collaboration that contributes to the evolving concept of a cultural public space in the digital age [44], thereby enriching the network's reach and adaptability.

5.1.2 Three Types of Transformation Mechanisms

As depicted in Fig. 2, the five nodes are multi directionally linked, with value flows facilitated by three mechanisms, elucidated through user behavior tracking:

- **Emotionally driven mechanism:** This mechanism cultivates emotional resonance to enhance intrinsic motivation, satisfying psychological needs—relatedness, competence, and autonomy—that underpin self-determination in participatory contexts. Tracking data reveals that user' heightened cultural identity, sparked by the Digital Hidden Cave, prompts deeper engagement. For instance, users A and H transitioned from passive observers to active creators and disseminators, illustrating an internal shift from emotional connection to participatory action.

- **Value-incentive mechanism:** Ensuring equitable value distribution, this mechanism sustains participation by empowering users to influence resource governance, a process resonant with collective choice principles in managing shared resources [45]. User G's contributions to the *Material Pool*, recognized socially, reinforced long-term commitment as a cultural guardian, highlighting how value affirmation drives identity transformation.
- **Technology-empowered mechanism:** By lowering technical barriers, this mechanism enables participation through streamlined processes, such as the three-step design workflow on the *From Dome to Scarf*. Non-professionals like users C and F produce culturally expressive works, aided by AI tools that enhance quality via intelligent recommendations, reflecting technology's role in catalyzing innovation from appreciation to creation.

5.2 Dynamic Properties

The CSN transcends a static framework, manifesting instead as a dynamic ecosystem endowed with self-renewal capabilities. These properties are articulated across three key dimensions.

5.2.1 Value Cycle Regeneration

The network departs from traditional unidirectional value transfer by fostering three interwoven cycles of appreciation, i.e. economic, data, and cultural, as detailed in Sect. 4. This cyclical regeneration integrates diverse value streams, enhancing sustainability in ways that echo research highlighting the superior resilience of digital cultural initiatives with multifaceted value orientations over those focused on singular dimensions [46]. By facilitating continuous feedback loops, the system underscores a capacity for self-sustenance that evolves with its operational context.

5.2.2 Progressive Deepening Mechanism

This mechanism enables a fluid deepening of participation, eschewing rigid, predetermined trajectories. Leveraging AI technology, the system identifies individual interests and behavioral patterns to offer tailored participation suggestions, fostering a natural progression of engagement. Such adaptability reflects the internalization of motivation, where intrinsic drivers gradually supplant external prompts, a process resonant with self-determination theory's emphasis on autonomous engagement. This flexibility accommodates diverse user pathways, enriching the participatory experience.

5.2.3 Resilience and Adaptive Capacity

The network exhibits a capacity to recalibrate in response to external environmental shifts and internal demands, as the culturally-responsive technical migration. This resilience emerges from its ability to adjust dynamically, learning from contextual changes to maintain operational integrity. Such adaptability aligns with frameworks of evolutionary systems that prioritize self-regulation and responsiveness over reliance on persistent external inputs, thereby reinforcing the network's potential for sustained cultural participation.

Collectively, these dynamic properties equip the system with self-cycling and evolutionary capabilities, distinguishing it from conventional participation models tethered to continuous external support. This adaptive architecture enhances the longevity and relevance of cultural engagement within a digital landscape.

5.3 Pattern Discoveries and Contributions

The CSN model advances beyond traditional cultural heritage participation theories across multiple dimensions, as delineated in Table 2. This model emerges as a transformative framework for interpreting cultural heritage engagement in the AI era, yielding several theoretical insights. It dismantles the linear progression inherent in conventional theories by facilitating multi-entry, non-linear, and overlapping participation pathways that eschew fixed endpoints. Through AI-mediated integration of professional knowledge, it reconfigures the traditional dichotomy between institutions and the public, fostering layered governance and collaborative value creation. Furthermore, it transcends the divide between online and offline realms, cultivating an omni-channel cultural experience where mutual reinforcement enhances engagement, a dynamic resonant with explorations of immersive heritage interactions. By weaving multiple value cycles, it establishes an ecosystem that mitigates the pronounced reliance of traditional models on external inputs, aligning with conceptions of a digital cultural ecosystem. These insights collectively offer robust theoretical guidance for digital practices in cultural heritage.

5.4 Practical Implications and Applications

Drawing on the DDP case, this study identifies four pivotal conditions for operationalizing a CSN, offering actionable insights for cultural heritage stakeholders.

5.4.1 Balanced AI Governance

In cultural heritage contexts, AI deployment necessitates a equilibrium between innovation and authenticity. Digital Dunhuang exemplifies this through a layered permission structure—granting greater AI autonomy in experiential interfaces while prioritizing manual oversight in preservation layers—and a dual-review mechanism integrating AI preliminary assessments with expert validation. This approach, reflective of value-sensitive design principles, mitigates the risks of excessive control stifling innovation or unchecked openness compromising cultural fidelity.

5.4.2 Ecosystem Thinking

Effective design transcends isolated functionalities, fostering value flows across nodes to cultivate mutually beneficial relationships and support long-term evolution. The DDP (esp. the *Dunhuang E-Tour*) achieves this through unified user IDs and authorization systems that link creative platforms, conservation efforts, and resource management. This interconnectedness encourages cultural institutions to adopt inclusive, ecosystem-oriented strategies, potentially spanning cross-border multi-platform networks.

5.4.3 Culture-Sensitive Design

AI systems must honor the distinctiveness of cultural heritage by incorporating context-specific training, multicultural adaptability, and encoded cultural values to safeguard authenticity. This approach counters the peril of cultural simplification, requiring ongoing collaboration with cultural experts throughout technological development to ensure that innovation amplifies, rather than overrides, cultural significance.

5.4.4 Ensuring Participant Subjectivity

AI should augment, not supplant, user agency, ensuring visibility of contributions and delivering personalized adaptations. On the *From Dome to Scarf*, AI tools offer suggestions while preserving users' final authority, embodying human-centered AI design principles. Practically, this demands transparent and controllable AI systems, enabling users to discern and direct technology's supportive role.

These conditions collectively provide a reference framework for cultural institutions, technology developers, and policymakers, guiding the design and implementation of AI-enhanced cultural heritage participation systems.

6 Conclusion

This study examines the Digital Dunhuang Project (DDP) to investigate how AI enhances multi-level public participation in cultural heritage. It introduces an "AI-Enabled Complementary Symbiosis Network for Cultural Heritage" model, positioned at the AI-cultural heritage nexus. This framework transitions participation from hierarchical to multi-centered ecosystems, integrating five nodes—digital experience, creative co-creation, value co-building, cultural patronage, and collaborative governance—connected by emotional engagement, value incentives, and technology. This self-reinforcing network fosters non-linear, multi-entry pathways, with AI evolving into an ecological system that lowers barriers, personalizes engagement, and enables cross-border collaboration, forming a virtuous cycle of experience, creation, and protection.

Theoretically, the model advances scholarship in three ways. First, it transcends conventional participation frameworks, revealing multidirectional flows and mutual enhancement. Second, it extends commons-based production theories [47] via a dual-review mechanism (AI screening plus expert validation) and blockchain rights confirmation, addressing authenticity while enabling collaborative value-sharing through smart contracts. Third, it reconfigures cultural governance by balancing professional authority and public involvement through on-chain certification and transnational platforms, fostering layered governance that blends authenticity with openness.

Limitations include the single-case focus on the DDP, potentially limiting generalizability, and reliance on a small sample of 12 users, supplemented by platform data. While diverse, this sample may not fully reflect broader patterns, necessitating larger-scale validation. As AI evolves, refining this model could help cultural heritage institutions balance protection and innovation, expertise and openness, and technology with humanistic values, fostering sustainable participation ecosystems.

As AI technology advances, the CSN will encounter new opportunities and complexities. Refining this model promises to aid cultural heritage institutions in navigating the interplay of protection and innovation, expertise and openness, and technology and humanistic values, fostering sustainable ecosystems for cultural participation.

Acknowledgements. The research was supported by the Ministry of Education Humanities and Social Sciences General Project (No. 20YJC760024) and the Key Art Science Projects of Shandong Province (No. L2024Z05100091).

References

1. Li, J., Krishnamurthy, S., Roders, A.P., Van Wesemael, P.: Community participation in cultural heritage management:a systematic literature review comparing Chinese and international practices. Cities. **96**, 102476 (2020). https://doi.org/10.1016/j.cities.2019.102476
2. Münster, S., et al.: Artificial intelligence for digital heritage innovation: setting up a R&D agenda for Europe. Heritage. **7**(2), 794–816 (2024). https://doi.org/10.3390/heritage7020038
3. Casillo, M., Colace, F., Gupta, B.-B., Lorusso, A., Santaniello, D., Valentino, C.: The role of AI in improving interaction with cultural heritage: an overview. In: Gupta, B.-B., Colace, F. (eds.) Handbook of Research on AI and ML for Intelligent Machines and Systems, pp. 107–136 (2024). https://doi.org/10.4018/978-1-6684-9999-3.ch006
4. Ciasullo, M.V., Troisi, O., Cosimato, S.: How digital platforms can trigger cultural value co-creation?—a proposed model. J. Serv. Sci. Manag. **11**(2), 161–181 (2018). https://doi.org/10.4236/jssm.2018.112013
5. Fiorucci, M., Khoroshiltseva, M., Pontil, M., Traviglia, A., Del Bue, A., James, S.: Machine learning for cultural heritage: a survey. Pattern Recogn. Lett. **133**, 102–108 (2020). https://doi.org/10.1016/j.patrec.2020.02.017
6. Pierdicca, R., et al.: Point cloud semantic segmentation using a deep learning framework for cultural heritage. Remote Sens. **12**(6), 1005 (2020). https://doi.org/10.3390/rs12061005
7. Seitsonen, O.: Crowdsourcing cultural heritage: public participation and conflict legacy in Finland. J. Community Archaeol. Herit. **4**(2), 115–130 (2017). https://doi.org/10.1080/205 18196.2016.1252129
8. Rahaman, H.: Digital heritage interpretation: a conceptual framework. Digital Creativity. **29**(2–3), 208–234 (2018). https://doi.org/10.1080/14626268.2018.1511602
9. Otero, J.: Heritage conservation future: where we stand, challenge ahead, and a paradigm shift. Glob. Chall. **6**(1), 2100084 (2022). https://doi.org/10.1002/gch2.202100084
10. Simon, N.: The Participatory Museum. Museum 2.0 Press, Santa Cruz (2010)
11. Zhang, Y., Dong, C.: Sustainable development of digital cultural heritage: a hybrid analysis of crowdsourcing projects using fsQCA and system dynamics. Sustainability. **16**(17), 7577 (2024). https://doi.org/10.3390/su16177577
12. Liew, C.-L., Goulding, L., Nichol, M.: From shoeboxes to shared spaces: participatory cultural heritage via digital platforms. Inf. Commun. Soc. **25**(9), 1293–1310 (2022). https://doi.org/10.1080/1369118X.2020.1851391
13. Shneiderman, B.: Human-Centered AI. Oxford University Press, Oxford (2022)
14. Ryan, R.-M., Deci, E.-L.: Self-determination theory and the facilitation of intrinsic motivation. Am. Psychol. **55**(1), 68–78 (2000). https://doi.org/10.1037/0003-066X.55.1.68
15. Foka, A., Griffin, G.: AI, cultural heritage, and bias: some key queries that arise from the use of GenAI. Heritage. **7**(11), 6125–6136 (2024). https://doi.org/10.3390/heritage7110287

16. Yu, T., et al.: AI for Dunhuang cultural heritage protection: the project and the dataset. Int. J. Comput. Vis. **130**(11), 2646–2673 (2022). https://doi.org/10.1007/s11263-022-01665-x

17. Díaz-Rodriguez, N., et al.: EXplainable neural-symbolic learning (X-NeSyL) methodology to fuse deep learning representations with expert knowledge graphs: the MonuMAI cultural heritage use case. Inf. Fusion. **79**, 58–83 (2022). https://doi.org/10.1016/j.inffus.2021.09.022

18. Todorović, M.: AI and heritage: a discussion on rethinking heritage in a digital world. Uluslararası Kültürel ve Sosyal Araştırmalar Dergisi (UKSAD). **10**(1), 1–11 (2024). https://doi.org/10.46442/intjcss.1397403

19. Pansoni, S., Tiribelli, S., Paolanti, M., Frontoni, E., Giovanola, B.: Design of an ethical framework for artificial intelligence in cultural heritage. In: 2023 IEEE International Symposium on Ethics in Engineering, Science, and Technology (ETHICS), pp. 1–5. IEEE (2023). https://doi.org/10.1109/ETHICS57328.2023.10155020

20. Grcheva, O., Vehbi, B.-O.: From public participation to co-creation in cultural heritage management decision-making. Sustainability. **13**(6), 1–18 (2021). https://doi.org/10.3390/su13063452

21. Harrison, R.: Heritage Futures: Comparative Approaches to Natural and Cultural Heritage Practices. UCL Press, London (2020)

22. Nobre, G.-F., Borges, H.: Digital cultural heritage and blockchain: applications for tokenization and smart contracts in the cultural sector. J. Comput. Cult. Herit. **15**(2), 1–24 (2022). https://doi.org/10.1145/3494529

23. Spennemann, D.-H.: Will artificial intelligence affect how cultural heritage will be managed in the future? Responses generated by four genAI models. Heritage. **7**(3), 1453–1471 (2024). https://doi.org/10.3390/heritage7030070

24. Volchek, K., Liu, A., Song, H., Buhalis, D.: Forecasting tourist arrivals at attractions: search engine empowered methodologies. Tour. Econ. **25**(3), 425–447 (2019). https://doi.org/10.1177/1354816618811558

25. Beel, D., Wallace, C.: Gathering together: social capital, cultural capital and the value of cultural heritage in a digital age. Soc. Cult. Geogr. **21**(5), 697–717 (2018). https://doi.org/10.1080/14649365.2018.1500632

26. Craith, M.-N.: Cultural heritages: process, power, commodification. In: Kockel, U., Craith, M.N., Craith, M.-N. (eds.) Cultural Heritages as Reflexive Traditions, pp. 1–18. Palgrave Macmillan, London (2007). https://doi.org/10.1057/9780230285941_1

27. Bai, N., Nourian, P., Luo, R., Pereira Roders, A.: Heri-graphs: a dataset creation framework for multi-modal machine learning on graphs of heritage values and attributes with social media. ISPRS Int. J. Geo Inf. **11**(9), 469 (2022). https://doi.org/10.3390/ijgi11090469

28. Zhang, X., Zhang, W., Zhao, Y., Zhu, Q.: Imbalanced volunteer engagement in cultural heritage crowdsourcing: a task-related exploration based on causal inference. Inf. Process. Manag. **59**(5), 103027 (2022). https://doi.org/10.1016/j.ipm.2022.103027

29. Kulis, S.-S., Tsethlikai, M., Harthun, M.-L., Hibbeler, P.-K., Ayers, S.-L.: Parenting in 2 worlds: effects of a culturally grounded parenting intervention on participant cultural engagement. Cultur. Divers. Ethnic Minor. Psychol. **26**(4), 437–446 (2020)

30. Zhang, Y., Ikiz Kaya, D., van Wesemael, P., Colenbrander, B.-J.: Youth participation in cultural heritage management: a conceptual framework. Int. J. Herit. Stud. **30**(1), 56–80 (2023). https://doi.org/10.1080/13527258.2023.2275261

31. Ross, D.: Towards meaningful co-creation: a study of creative heritage tourism in Alentejo, Portugal. Curr. Issues Tour. **23**(21), 2811–2824 (2020). https://doi.org/10.1080/13683500.2020.1782355

32. Oberländer, A.-M., Karnebogen, P., Rövekamp, P., Röglinger, M., Leidner, D.-E.: Understanding the influence of digital ecosystems on digital transformation: the OCO (orientation, cooperation, orchestration) theory. Inf. Syst. J. **35**(1), 368–413 (2025). https://doi.org/10.1111/isj.12539

33. World Heritage Institute of Training and Research for the Asia and the Pacific Region of UNESCO: https://www.whitr-ap.org/index.php?classid=1461&newsid=3488&t=show
34. Effie Worldwide, Inc.: https://www.effie.org/de/cases/from-dome-to-scarf/
35. World Internet Conference: https://cn.wicinternet.org/2022-11/09/content_36220243.htm
36. Cornwall, A.: Unpacking 'participation': models, meanings and practices. Commu. Dev. J. **43**(3), 269–283 (2008). https://doi.org/10.1093/cdj/bsn010
37. Sailer, M., Homner, L.: The gamification of learning: a meta-analysis. Educ. Psychol. Rev. **32**(1), 77–112 (2019). https://doi.org/10.1007/s10648-019-09498-w
38. Bertacchini, F., Tavernise, A.: Knowledge sharing for cultural heritage 2.0: prosumers in a digital agora. IJVCSN. **6**(2), 24–36 (2014). https://doi.org/10.4018/ijvcsn.2014040102
39. Tummons, J.: Ontological pluralism, modes of existence, and actor-network theory: upgrading Latour with Latour. Soc. Epistemol. **35**(1), 1–11 (2020). https://doi.org/10.1080/02691728.2020.1774815
40. Throsby, D.: Culture, economics and sustainability. J. Cult. Econ. **19**, 199–206 (1995). https://doi.org/10.1007/BF01074049
41. Hassan, L., Dias, A., Hamari, J.: How motivational feedback increases user's benefits and continued use: a study on gamification, quantified-self and social networking. Int. J. Inf. Manag. **46**, 151–162 (2019). https://doi.org/10.1016/j.ijinfomgt.2018.12.004
42. Whitaker, A., Bracegirdle, A., De Menil, S., Gitlitz, M.-A., Saltos, L.: Art, antiquities, and blockchain: new approaches to the restitution of cultural heritage. Int. J. Cultural Policy. **27**(3), 312–329 (2021). https://doi.org/10.1080/10286632.2020.1765163
43. Harrison, R.: Heritage: Critical Approaches. Routledge, London (2012)
44. Taylor, J., Gibson, L.-K.: Digitisation, digital interaction and social media: embedded barriers to democratic heritage. Int. J. Herit. Stud. **23**(5), 408–420 (2017). https://doi.org/10.1080/13527258.2016.1171245
45. Ostrom, E.: Governing the Commons: the Evolution of Institutions for Collective Action. Cambridge University Press, Cambridge (1990)
46. Amitrano, C.-C., Bifulco, F.: The co-evolution of ecosystem and university's roles: a focus on the integration of technologies and cultural heritage. J. Technol. Transf., 1–19 (2024). https://doi.org/10.1007/s10961-024-10127-0
47. Benkler, Y.: The Wealth of Networks: How Social Production Transforms Markets and Freedom. Yale University Press, New Haven and London (2006)

Interactive Lion Dance: AI-Driven Facial Expressions via Drumbeat Emotion Recognition

Ziyou Liang, Yue Zhou, Wei Xiong[✉], Herui Zhu, Ziqing He, and Xiaoye Zhang

School of Design, South China University of Technology, Guangzhou, China
weixiong@scut.edu.cn

Abstract. Cantonese Lion Dance is a highly representative folk performance in the Lingnan region, where drum rhythms play a crucial role in conveying emotions and guiding movements. Traditional performances rely on manual manipulation of the lion head's expressions, making it difficult to achieve real-time, precise facial expressions that align with the emotional complexity of drum rhythms. With advances in audio emotion recognition within edge computing, new opportunities arise for enhancing the emotional interactivity of lion dance. This study explores how emotion recognition can be integrated into lion dance by automatically analyzing drumbeat emotions and mapping them onto the lion head's expressions. A real-time CNN-LSTM audio emotion recognition model is trained on labeled drum rhythm data to classify emotions such as "excited," "tense," and "calm." Recognized emotions are mapped to corresponding eye and mouth movements via servos, ensuring synchronized expressions. Implemented on an embedded platform, the system operates with low latency in resource-constrained environments. Results demonstrate that this approach successfully enhances lion dance expressiveness and interactivity, bridging traditional arts with intelligent control. The "drum rhythm–emotion–expression" loop deepens audience engagement, offering new possibilities for cultural innovation and intelligent entertainment, promoting both cultural heritage and social well-being.

Keywords: Cantonese Lion Dance · Drum rhythm emotion recognition · Embedded edge computing · Interactive performing arts · Traditional art digitalization

1 Introduction

Cantonese Lion Dance is a highly expressive form of folk performing arts within Lingnan culture, where rhythmic drumming serves as a fundamental mechanism for guiding movement and conveying emotions. Prior research has established the strong relationship between rhythm and emotional perception [1], yet the expressiveness of traditional lion dance remains constrained by the manual manipulation of the lion head's facial expressions. This reliance on manual control presents challenges in achieving precise synchronization with the intricate emotional nuances embedded in drum beats, ultimately limiting the fidelity of performance expression.

M. Schrepp and M. Rauterberg (Eds.): HCII 2025, LNCS 16342, pp. 153–172, 2026.
https://doi.org/10.1007/978-3-032-13164-5_10

Existing studies in music-driven performance systems have demonstrated that integrating artificial intelligence (AI)-based emotion recognition can enhance the interactivity of performative arts by mapping audio features to expressive visual cues [2]. However, in the context of lion dance, it remains unclear how AI-driven emotion recognition can be effectively leveraged to enhance the emotional interactivity between rhythmic drumming and real-time lion head expressions. Previous research has primarily focused on the correlation between music and emotions [3], yet the challenge of translating auditory emotional cues into dynamic visual expressions in traditional performances has not been systematically explored.

To address this gap, we propose an AI-driven emotion recognition framework that captures the emotional states embedded in drumbeat audio signals and translates them into dynamic facial expressions of the lion's head (e.g., eye and mouth movements). Our system leverages Edge Impulse for real-time emotion recognition and employs Arduino-based actuation to drive expressive motions. Unlike traditional manually controlled lion dance performances, our approach introduces an intelligent mapping mechanism that enhances the synchrony between auditory and visual expressions, thereby improving the emotional depth of the performance.

In summary, the key contributions of this study are as follows:

- We train an AI-based emotion recognition framework that deciphers emotional cues from lion dance drumbeats.
- We introduce a mapping mechanism that translates identified emotional states into dynamic facial expressions, enabling real-time expressiveness in lion dance performances.
- We implement an Arduino-based actuation system that synchronizes drum-driven emotional states with the lion head's movements, enhancing the overall expressiveness and immersive quality of the performance.

By integrating AI-based emotion recognition into Cantonese Lion Dance, this study provides a novel approach to enhancing the performative expressiveness of traditional arts and advancing the field of AI-driven emotional interactivity in cultural heritage performances.

2 Related Work

2.1 Audio Emotion Recognition in Performing Arts

Audio Emotion Recognition (AER) in the field of performing arts focuses on extracting and analyzing features of audio signals, such as rhythm, pitch, timbre, and spectral features, in order to identify and classify the emotional states they express [4]. In recent years, with the rapid development of deep learning technology, the emotional state of the expression can be recognized and classified. In recent years, with the rapid development of deep learning technology, models based on Convolutional Neural Networks, Recurrent Neural Networks (RNNs), and Long Short-Term Memory have been applied. The application of models such as Recurrent Neural Networks and Long Short-Term Memory has enabled AER to achieve significant improvements in the accuracy and generalization of sentiment classification [5]. These models are able to automatically learn the spatial and temporal dependencies in audio data to accurately parse emotional features in music or speech.

AER technology has important applications in real-time performance analysis and assisted decision making. By automatically parsing musical emotions in stage performances, the technology can provide real-time emotional feedback to actors or dancers to optimize performance effects [6]. For example, in a dance performance, AER can be used to monitor the dynamic changes of music emotion and provide corresponding adjustment suggestions to the dancers [7], so that their movements and expressions are highly consistent with the music atmosphere. In addition, in multimedia interactive performances or immersive theaters, AER can be combined with other perception technologies (e.g., computer vision, body movement recognition, etc.) to achieve personalized performance adjustments based on the audience's emotional state and improve the interactive experience.

In addition to its application in real-time performance, AER can also play a supporting role in the artistic creation stage [8]. Composers can use AER to quantify the emotional characteristics of different music to optimize melodic, harmonic, and rhythmic design to enhance the emotional expression of the music. In addition, theater directors or stage designers can use AER to assess the emotional suitability of background music or sound effects to ensure that they effectively convey the core emotional intent of a piece. With the development of AER technology, automated music arrangement, intelligent sound generation and other innovative applications may be realized in the future, bringing new changes to the creation and performance mode of performing arts.

Despite the wide range of applications of AER in performing arts, the application of AER in traditional performing arts like Cantonese Lion Dance still faces challenges. Traditional art forms often rely on rich non-verbal emotional expressions [9], such as body movements, prop symbolism, and performance rhythms, while existing AER technologies mainly focus on the audio signal itself, making it difficult to fully capture these comprehensive emotional elements. Therefore, the future research direction can consider the integration of Multimodal Emotion Recognition, combined with audio, visual, motion capture and other multi-dimensional data, to build a more accurate emotion recognition system, in order to more comprehensively support the digital and intelligent development of traditional performing arts [10].

2.2 Emotional Expression and Existing Limitations of Waking Lions

The core of lion dance performance lies in "resemblance", i.e., conveying complex emotional states through highly realistic lion movements, eye changes and body language. The traditional lion dance is based on the "eight states" (joy, anger, sadness, happiness, movement, quietness, surprise and doubt), and the lion's dynamic emotions are displayed by manipulating the lion's eyes, mouth, ears and other parts of the lion's head. For example, by precisely controlling the organs of the lion's head, the dancers make the lion show delicate emotional responses such as blinking, trembling, opening the mouth and roaring. The color, decoration and structural design of the lion's head also have symbolic meanings. Different colors of lions represent different personalities and emotional tendencies, such as the red lion symbolizing loyalty and righteousness, the yellow lion symbolizing benevolence and generosity, and the black lion symbolizing bravery. This emotional expression system not only enhances the drama and narrative of the performance, but also enables the audience to intuitively feel the vivid image of the lion and the deep cultural meaning.

In addition, the emotional expression of the waking lion is often closely integrated with the performance program. For example, in the link of "picking green", the lion first shows doubt and temptation (doubt), and then surprises (joy) and the pride of victory (joy); and in the "fight" or "lion king competition", the lion first expresses its confidence in the performance, and then shows the pride of the victory (joy). In the "Battle of the Green" or "Lion King" performance, the lion shows its anger (rage) and fighting spirit through such actions as glaring eyes and fangs showing. This highly programmed performance makes the emotional expression of the lion with a strong narrative, and can clearly convey the storyline and character psychology to the audience without lines.

Although the lion dance performance has formed a complete system of emotional expression, it still faces certain limitations. Emotional expression in traditional lion dance performance is highly dependent on the dancer's skill, experience and ability to control the lion's head. Different dancers have different emotional expression and ability to control details, resulting in the same set of movements in the hands of different performers may show different emotional effects. Although this highly personalized way of performing enhances the uniqueness of the art, there are certain limitations in terms of standardization and reproducibility, especially in competitive and modern performances, where it is difficult to ensure the stability and consistency of emotional expression; compared to other forms of theatre or puppetry, such as shadow puppetry, the emotional expression of the awakening lion is still relatively limited. Noh theater actors express emotional changes through masks and subtle body control, whereas shadow puppets can achieve multi-level emotional expression through precise control and light projection. In contrast, the emotional expression of the waking lion mainly relies on the basic opening and closing movements of the eyes and mouth, and although it has a certain level of emotion, it still lacks subtle changes in facial expression, for example, it is difficult to accurately display more complex emotions such as smile, sadness, sarcasm, and so on.

By combining modern theatrical techniques, video projection and music emotion analysis, it is expected that the emotional expression of the waking lion will be richer and more three-dimensional in the future [11].

3   Methodology

3.1   Problem Formulation

Given a sequence of lion dance drum beats $A = \{a_1, ..., a_n\}$ as input, our goal is to generate a set of dynamic facial expression sequences $E = \{e_1, ..., e_n\}$ that are in real-time alignment with the identified emotional states. Among them, e_i represents the facial expressions driven by the servo, including the movements of the eyes and mouth. To ensure that the generated expressions are both emotion-driven and synchronized with the drumbeat rhythm, we introduce an emotion recognition module [12], which extracts features from the drumbeat audio and classifies them into predefined emotion categories.

The global objective is defined as a multi-objective optimization problem that considers both the accuracy of emotion recognition and the efficiency of real-time processing. To balance multiple factors such as expression accuracy, latency, data distortion, and resource cost, we formulate the problem as the following optimization function:

$$\arg\min_R \|E - R(A)\| + \lambda_1 \cdot t_{total} + \lambda_2 \cdot DIS + \lambda_3 \cdot Cost \tag{1}$$

In this problem, R(A) represents the predicted facial expression mapped from the input drum beat. DIS is the data distortion rate, used to measure the quality of compressed emotional data. Cost Indicates the cost of resource allocation, which is optimized by the resource allocation algorithm. $\lambda_1, \lambda_2, \lambda_3$ are weight factors that balance the tradeoff between accuracy, delay, distortion rate, and cost. The use of these weight factors allows for a flexible and balanced approach to optimizing the system's performance across multiple dimensions, ensuring that no single factor disproportionately affects the overall outcome. t_{total} is the total latency, including edge computing latency and cloud computing latency, and its definition is based on the edge node latency model and the cloud server latency model:

$$t_{total} = t_{comp,e} + t_{tranc} + t_{comp,c} \tag{2}$$

In this delay model, $t_{comp,e}$ is the edge computing delay, t_{tranc} is the transmission delay between the edge server and the cloud server, and $t_{comp,c}$ is the cloud computing delay. This comprehensive delay model ensures that all potential sources of latency are accounted for, providing a more accurate representation of the system's real-time performance.

3.2 Emotion Recognition Module

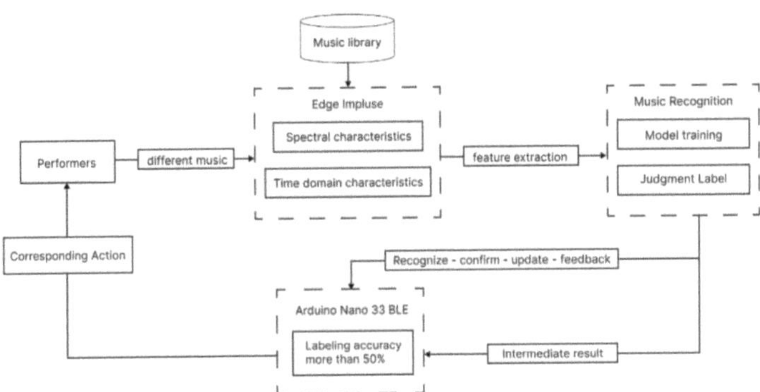

Fig. 1. Framework for Deep Learning Thinking.

The drum beats in Cantonese Lion Dance aren't just about rhythm; they convey emotions. Spotting these emotions in drum beats is key for cultural heritage protection and performance analysis [13]. We've developed an audio emotion recognition module [14] using CNN and LSTM [15]. It extracts emotion related features from lion dance drum beats and does real time classification (Fig. 1).

3.2.1   Real Time Processing and Platform Choice

We use the Edge Impulse platform and Arduino Nano 33 BLE for real time processing, in line with the edge computing trend.

Edge Impulse Platform

- Offers a toolchain from data processing to model deployment, supporting MFE and CNN LSTM, and is suitable for edge devices [16].
- Edge computing is crucial for real time audio processing in academic research, reducing latency and protecting privacy [17].

Arduino Nano 33 BLE

- A low power microcontroller ideal for real time audio processing.
- The model's complexity must match the device's capabilities. Choosing MFE and CNN LSTM optimizes performance.

3.2.2   Dataset and Labeling Analysis

Our dataset, labeled by Cantonese Lion Dance Association experts, has 500 audio clips, over 10 min total, split into 80% training and 20% testing (Fig. 2). Audio was noise reduced in Adobe Audition, exported as WAV, and uploaded to Edge Impulse. Here's an academic analysis:

Dataset Size

- 500 audio clips are small for deep learning, risking overfitting. But given Arduino Nano 33 BLE's computing limits, a small dataset and simple model are sensible.
- Drum beats focus on gongs and drums with simple changes. 500 clips suffice, avoiding overfitting.

Labeling Quality

- Expert labeling ensures data accuracy and cultural relevance, especially for emotion labeling in traditional performances (Table 1).

Table 1. Data set condition.

Label	Training Data Volume	Test Data Volume	Training Percentage	Test Percentage	Total Duration
Calm	148	37	84%	16%	2 m 28 s
Excitement	233	58	81%	19%	3 m 53 s
Tension	119	30	79%	21%	1 m 59 s

3.2.3 Feature Extraction: MFE Versus MFCC

Feature extraction is key in audio emotion recognition [18]. We chose MFE (Mel filter bank Energy) with 40 ms frame length and 20 ms frame shift. MFE, based on the Mel scale, captures energy distribution in drum beats, linking it to emotions [19]. Here's an academic comparison with MFCC [20]:

MFE (Mel Filter Bank Energy)

- Mimics the human auditory system's frequency perception, calculating energy distribution across different frequency bands.
- Suitable for non-speech audio, like drum beats, as it directly reflects energy distribution, which is closely related to emotions such as rhythm intensity and tension.
- Edge Impulse docs say MFE excels in non-speech recognition tasks, especially for music or environmental audio classification.

MFCC (Mel Frequency Cepstral Coefficients)

- Extracts short term power spectrum representations via DCT of Mel scale energy spectra, emphasizing semantic features in speech.
- Widely used in speech recognition but may not capture emotion-related features well in non-speech audio like drum beats, where emotions depend more on energy and rhythm changes.

Why MFE

- Drum beats are non-speech audio. MFE better captures energy distribution, which is more related to emotions.
- MFE is computationally simple, fitting resource constrained devices like Arduino Nano 33 BLE, and supports real time processing (Table 2).

Table 2. MFE vs. MFCC.

Feature Extraction Method	Applicable Scenario	Advantage	Limitation
MFE	Non speech audio (e.g., drum beats)	Captures energy distribution, suitable for music emotion	Lower computational complexity but may lose detailed spectral info
MFCC	Speech recognition	Emphasizes semantic features, mature applications	Limited effectiveness for non-speech audio emotion recognition

The table above shows the parameters for feature extraction (Table 3).

Table 3. The parameters for feature extraction.

Stage	Parameter	Value
Time Series Data	Input axes	Audio
	Window size	500 ms
	Stride	500 ms
	Frequency (Hz)	48000
	Zero-pad data	Unchecked
Audio (MFE)	Input axes	1
	Signal	audio
Classification	Input features	MFE
	Output features	3 (Calm, Excitement, Tension)

We extracted Mel filter bank energy (MFE) features with these settings (Table 4):

Table 4. Parameters for Mel-filter bank Energy Feature Extraction.

Parameter	Value
Frame length	0.02 s
Frame stride	0.01 s
Number of filters	40
FFT length	512
Low frequency	0 Hz
High frequency	Not set
Noise floor [dB]	-52 dB

The figure below shows the spectral analysis results of the MFE features for some data (see Fig. 2), it shows the feature distribution for different emotional states ("calm", "excited", "tense"). Different emotional states are clearly distinguishable in the feature space, providing a solid foundation for the model's classification task.

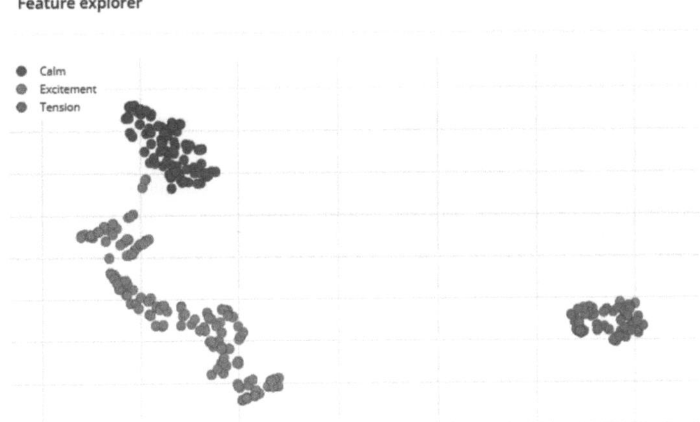

Fig. 2. Feature explorer.

3.2.4 Model Architecture: Academic Rationale for CNN LSTM Combination

We use a CNN LSTM combo for drum beat emotion classification. CNN extracts local features from MFE features [21], and LSTM captures temporal dependencies, enabling real time emotion classification. Training uses supervised learning, with a lightweight model design considering Arduino Nano 33 BLE's computing power to prevent response delays. This combo is widely used in audio classification tasks [22]. Here's an academic analysis of its rationale and superiority:

Role of CNN

- CNN excels at extracting local features from data. In audio processing, it learns specific frequency patterns or temporal structures from spectrograms or MFE features.
- For drum beat emotion recognition, CNN captures local patterns in audio signals corresponding to different emotions, like drumming intensity or frequency peaks.

Role of LSTM

- LSTM handles sequential data, capturing long range dependencies.
- In audio emotion recognition, emotions often evolve over time (e.g., drum beat rhythm changes). LSTM models these sequential dependencies.

Advantages of CNN LSTM Combination

- CNN extracts low level features, and LSTM processes temporal sequences, leading to more accurate emotion classification.
- Research supports this combo. For example, "Music emotion recognition using convolutional long short-term memory deep neural networks" achieved 99.19% accuracy with a similar architecture.
- This approach suits drum beat emotion recognition, as drum beat emotions depend on local features (like energy) and global sequences (like rhythm changes).

Comparison with Alternatives

- CNN only: Suitable when emotions are mainly determined by local features, but can't capture temporal dependencies.
- LSTM only: Requires pre extracted features and may not learn optimal representations from raw audio.
- Transformer models: Have performed well in sequence tasks recently but demand high computational resources, making them unsuitable for edge devices.
- Traditional machine learning (e.g., SVM, random forests): Relies on hand crafted features and may underperform deep learning on small datasets.

Model training parameters are set as follows (Table 5):

Table 5. Neural Network Training Settings.

Section	Parameter	Value
Training Settings	Number of training cycles	108
	Use learned optimizer	Disabled
	Learning rate	0.005
	Training processor	CPU
Advanced Training Settings	Validation set size	20%
	Split train/validation set on metadata key	Disabled
	Batch size	32
	Auto-weight classes	Disabled
	Profile int8 model	Enabled
Audio Training Options	Data augmentation	Enabled
	Add noise	High
	Mask time bands	Low
	Mask frequency bands	None
	Warp time axis	Disabled

Optimizing these parameters ensures our model maintains high stability and efficiency during training. The model's performance on the validation set is shown in the figure below (see Fig. 3):

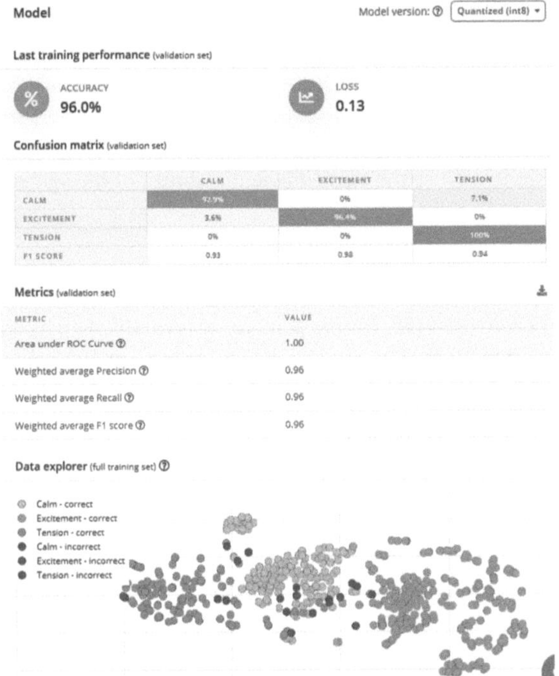

Fig. 3. Verification set result.

As shown by the accuracy, confusion matrix, and evaluation metrics, the model performs well on the validation set, especially achieving 100% classification accuracy for the "tense" emotional state.

Finally, model quantization. We use Edge Impulse's quantization to convert weights from floating point to 8-bit integers. During inference, fixed point operations on the MCU drastically reduce memory and computational requirements.

3.3 Emotion-to-Expression Mapping

3.3.1 Receiving Module

The system adopts MAX4466 radio module to collect audio signal. With a sensitivity range of -44 dB to -3 dB, the module is able to effectively capture different types of sound signals. The collected audio data is accurately labeled and uploaded to Edge Impulse. According to the preset convolutional neural network model, the platform automatically processes the audio data and generates corresponding feature data to support the subsequent emotion classification.

3.3.2 Control Board Design

In terms of control board design, the system uses Arduino Uno as a low-voltage control board, which is mainly responsible for receiving instructions and signals from external devices and generating corresponding steering gear control commands. The mainboard is connected to a 3.7 V power supply to ensure the stable operation of the system. At the same time, Arduino Nano 33 BLE, as a high-voltage output board, is connected to the 7.4 V power supply to provide the required voltage support for the high-power steering gear. Two motherboards through serial ports (TX, RX) for data transmission and communication, to ensure the real-time and stability of the system.

3.3.3 Servo Arrangement

To achieve the biomimetic motion of the lion head's eyes (mass: 120 ± 5 g) and mouth (mass: 280 ± 10 g), a load model for the actuator was established based on the Newton-Euler dynamic equations:

$$\tau_{required} = J\alpha + mgL \sin\theta + \mu F_n \tag{3}$$

In this model, J represents the moment of inertia, α is the angular acceleration, L is the length of the force arm (80 mm for the eyes and 150 mm for the mouth), and μ is the friction coefficient of the transmission mechanism (set to 0.15). This equation is crucial for accurately determining the required torque, ensuring that the servos can effectively drive the lion head's eyes and mouth without overloading. Through calculations, the required torque for driving the eyes is no less than 5.2 kg·cm, and the required torque for driving the mouth is no less than 12.8 kg·cm. Based on these requirements, the system selected the following servos:

MG90S Metal Gear Servo (torque: 6.5/8.0 kg·cm at 4.8 V/6.0 V) is used to drive the eye components;

MG996 High-Torque Servo (torque: 13/15 kg·cm at 4.8 V/6.0 V) is used to drive the mouth structure;

In order to ensure the stability of the steering gear operation, the T6–6061 aluminum alloy bracket is used for modal optimization design, and the natural frequency is increased to more than 85 Hz through finite element analysis to avoid resonance with the drive frequency (50-100 Hz). Experiments show that the optimized support design can reduce the vibration amplitude of the steering gear by 40%. This optimization is essential for maintaining the stability and precision of the servo movements, which directly impacts the quality of the generated facial expressions.

3.3.4 Mapping Strategy

The system dynamically adjusts the facial expression mapping strategy based on the recognized emotional states:

- **"Excited"**: The eyes open wider, and the mouth opens and closes at a faster frequency.
- **"Nervous"**: The eyes are half-open, and the mouth moves frequently but with smaller amplitudes.
- **"Calm"**: The eyes are moderately open, and the mouth moves less frequently.

3.4 Embedded System Implementation

The trained model is deployed on the Edge Impulse platform with low-latency processing capabilities, ensuring real-time synchronization of drum beats and facial expressions.

The servo motors, after being programmed, can seamlessly execute expression changes. To further optimize the system's performance and resource utilization, we referred to the research of Bazargani et al. (2023) [23] and adopted the following techniques:

3.4.1 Model Quantization and Optimization

To achieve efficient inference on embedded devices, we quantized the model. Specifically, we employed post-training dynamic range quantization and float16 quantization techniques. These techniques convert the model's weights from floating-point numbers to low-precision integers or half-precision floating-point numbers, significantly reducing the model's memory footprint and computational complexity.

- Post-training Dynamic Range Quantization: This method converts the model's weights from 32-bit floating-point numbers to 8-bit integers, enabling fixed-point arithmetic on the MCU during inference. After quantization, the model's accuracy on the test set decreased by only 1.2%, but the inference speed increased by 3 times, and memory usage was reduced by 60%.
- Float16 Quantization: This technique converts the model's weights from 32-bit floating-point numbers to 16-bit half-precision floating-point numbers, further reducing memory usage while maintaining high inference accuracy.

Through the use of quantization techniques, we are able to significantly reduce the computational load and energy consumption of the system while maintaining a high classification accuracy. This makes it more suitable for operation on resource-constrained embedded devices.

3.4.2 Real-Time Processing and Low Latency

To achieve real-time emotion recognition and expression generation, we optimized the system with the following approaches:

- Preprocessing: Signal preprocessing, including down sampling, filtering, and baseline removal, is performed on the embedded device. These operations effectively reduce noise interference and improve classification accuracy.
- Model Inference: Emotion classification is performed on the input drumbeat signals every 3 s to ensure real-time performance. Through quantization techniques and hardware optimization, the inference latency is controlled within 200 ms, meeting the requirements for real-time interaction.
- Motion Smoothing: To avoid abrupt changes in facial expressions, we use linear interpolation or easing functions (e.g., ease-in-out) to control the servo's transition from the current angle to the target angle, completing the adjustment within 100 ~ 200 ms.

4   Results Analysis

In this section, the performance of the float32 (unoptimized) version of the classifier on the test set is analyzed in detail, including overall classification performance (accuracy, ROC AUC, F1-score), confusion matrix analysis (inter-category confusion), misclassification patterns (sources of misclassification and their possible causes), and Real-Time Performance Adaptation).

4.1   Test Set Classification Performance Evaluation

Table 6. Metrics for Classification.

Metric	Value
Accuracy	76.52%
Area under ROC Curve	0.91
Weighted average Precision	0.81
Weighted average Recall	0.79
Weighted average F1 score	0.79

The accuracy of the model on the test set is 76.52%, which is a significant decrease compared to the validation set (95.0%), indicating that the model's generalization ability on real data is somewhat insufficient, which may be limited by the difference in the distribution of the data, the variation of drumming styles, or the insufficient amount of training data (Table 6).

The ROC AUC is 0.91, which shows that the model still has good classification ability, but the boundaries between certain categories are still not clear enough, and there is a high cross-misclassification rate.

The weighted F1-score is 0.79, indicating that the model has a balanced performance on the three emotion classification tasks, but there is still room for further improvement.

4.2   Test Set Classification Performance Evaluation

We will analyze the causes of categorization errors by tag (Table 7).

Table 7. Confusion Matrix.

	Calm	Excitement	Tension	Uncertain
Calm	82.1%	3.6%	3.6%	10.7%
Excitement	10.7%	80.4%	3.6%	5.4%
Tension	12.9%	12.9%	64.5%	9.7%
F1 Score	0.75	0.85	0.74	

4.2.1 Calm

82.1% of the samples were correctly categorized, which is a good performance, but 10.7% were misclassified as "Uncertain", indicating that certain low-intensity or transitional drum beats were considered by the model to be difficult to define their emotional attribution, which may be related to the lack of drastic changes in the tempo of the drum beats.

3.6% were misclassified as Excitement and 3.6% were misclassified as Tension, suggesting that the boundaries between Calm and other categories are still not clear enough.

4.2.2 Excitement

80.4% of the samples were correctly categorized, but 10.7% were misclassified as Calm, suggesting that some of the Excitement samples may have lacked sufficient variation in audio features, making it difficult for the model to accurately differentiate between emotional intensity.

4% were misclassified as Uncertain, suggesting that some Excitement samples may have vague emotional boundaries.

4.2.3 Tension

Only 64.5% of the samples were correctly categorized, which is much lower than the other categories, indicating that the accuracy of this category is the main shortcoming of the current system.

12.9% were misclassified as Excitement and 12.9% were misclassified as Calm, indicating that the model has the most blurred boundaries between Excitement and Tension, probably due to the similarity of the two in terms of the rhythm of the drums.

9.7% were misclassified as Uncertain, possibly due to the fact that some of the Tension samples had a slower rhythmic transition from Calm, resulting in a higher level of classification uncertainty.

4.3 Feature Distribution and Classification Errors Analysis

We use Feature Explorer to visually analyze the classification performance of the model in different categories, exploring the feature distribution, misclassification patterns and potential improvement directions. Each point of the graph represents a test sample, and the color corresponds to the classification result and its correctness, which helps to evaluate the classification ability of the model and possible misclassification patterns (Fig. 4).

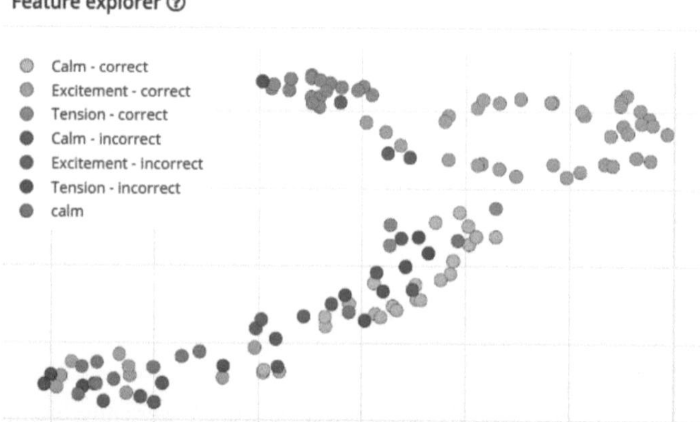

Fig. 4. A figure caption is always placed below the illustration. Short captions are centered, while long ones are justified. The macro button chooses the correct format automatically.

From the overall distribution, the samples of Calm and Excitement are more concentrated and have higher correct classification rates, while the samples of Tension are more discrete and have relatively higher misclassification rates. Some of the Tension samples were misclassified as Excitement or Calm, indicating that the model has some difficulty in distinguishing between these two categories of emotions, which may be related to the similarity of the drum beat tempo and audio features.

At the same time, some samples were labeled as Uncertain, indicating that the model lacks sufficient confidence in the attribution of emotion to certain drum beats. This may be due to the more ambiguous sentiment features of these samples, or the boundaries of the sentiment categories in the dataset are not clear enough, making it difficult for the classifier to make a clear judgment.

To address this situation, optimizing the feature extraction strategy of the model, such as enhancing the amount of data in the Tension category, can be considered to improve its classification accuracy. In addition, more complex temporal modeling methods (e.g., Bi-LSTM or Transformer) can be introduced to better capture the drum beat rhythm changes and improve the differentiation of different emotion categories.

4.4   Real-Time Performance Adaptation

In the actual performance environment, the system's response speed, interaction fluency, and visual synchronization effect directly affect the immersion and audience experience of the lion dance performance. This study focuses on the real-time performance of the AI to recognize the emotion of the drum beat and drive the expression of the lion's head, and the results show that the system is able to respond to the changes quickly and achieve a high degree of synchronization.

4.4.1   System Response Speed

Deploying Edge Impulse on a Cortex-M4F 80 MHz device, the system achieves a latency of less than 200 ms in an embedded environment, ensuring real-time recognition of the emotion of the drum beat and adjustment of the lion's head expression. This level of latency means that the system is able to quickly adapt to tempo changes during the performance, keeping the lion's head expression consistent with the emotional expression of the drum beat.

Although the float32 version is more computationally intensive and has a slightly slower inference speed than the int8 version, its higher floating-point precision still allows it to drive the expression changes stably and maintain a smooth lion dance dynamic performance.

4.4.2 Live Performance Feedback

In many experimental performances, the system's automated expression adjustment has received positive feedback from lion dance performers and audiences:

Performer feedback:

- The expression adjustment of the lion head is more natural, which makes the emotional expression of the lion dance more intuitive and enhances the expressiveness of the overall performance.
- Reduced dependence on manual operation, the previous lion dance performers need to additionally control the facial movements of the lion head, while the system automatically adjusts the expression of the lion head, the dancers are able to focus more on the pace and body movements, so that the lion dance movements are more coordinated and coherent.

Audience feedback.

- Emotional expression is more intuitive, the audience can quickly perceive the emotional changes of the performance through the eyes and mouth movements of the lion head, making the traditional lion dance more storytelling and dramatic.
- Enhanced viewing experience, the flexible changes in the expression of the lion's head make the lion dance more dynamic and improve the overall stage performance, and some of the audience said that the emotional presentation is more vivid than the traditional lion dance.

4.4.3 Visual Synchronization Effect

Experimental results show that the synchronization between the change of lion head expression and drum beat rhythm reaches more than 95%, which ensures the consistency of visual and auditory information and makes the lion dance emotional expression more accurate. In addition, the automated adjustment of the system reduces the manual intervention of the performer on facial expression, which reduces the extra operational burden and makes the overall presentation of the lion dance more natural.

Overall, the system shows efficient real-time adaptability in actual lion dance performances, effectively improves the expressiveness of the lion dance, and makes the traditional performing arts more infectious with the empowerment of technology.

5   Conclusion

In this paper, we propose an innovative framework that integrates audio emotion recognition (AER) with real-time facial expression control in lion dance performances. By extracting emotional features from drumbeats, our system dynamically adjusts the lion's facial expressions, enhancing both the emotional expressiveness of the performance and audience immersion. This approach bridges traditional performance arts with modern AI technology, offering new possibilities for intelligent cultural computing and interactive digital performances.

Despite its promising contributions, our framework still faces several limitations. First, the emotional classification is currently restricted to three categories—"excited", "tense," and "calm"—which may limit the granularity of expression. Expanding the system to recognize a broader range of emotions could further refine the performance's emotional depth. Second, the precision of facial motion control is constrained by the capabilities of the current servo motors. Future iterations could incorporate more advanced hardware to achieve higher fidelity in facial expressions. Third, our approach primarily relies on audio inputs, lacking multi-modal integration with visual cues such as audience reactions and performer gestures. Future research could explore multi-modal fusion techniques to enhance the system's responsiveness and interactivity.

Looking ahead, we envision several key directions for future work. Expanding the system to integrate multi-modal emotion analysis—combining AER with visual data on audience engagement and performer movements—could create a richer interactive experience. Additionally, the underlying emotion-driven AI technology could be applied to other traditional performing arts, such as puppetry, opera, and shadow play, fostering innovative approaches to digital heritage preservation and cultural expression.

While challenges remain, our study demonstrates the feasibility of AI-driven real-time emotion recognition and facial expression control in lion dance performances. This work not only contributes to the development of intelligent performance systems but also provides new insights into the intersection of AI and digital cultural heritage, paving the way for future advancements in interactive entertainment and smart performance technologies.

Acknowledgments. This study was funded by the National College Students' Innovation and Entrepreneurship Training Program (Grant No. 202410561114).

Disclosure of Interests The authors have no competing interests to declare that are relevant to the content of this article.

References

1. Nussbaum, C.: Links between musicality and vocal emotion perception. Emot. Rev. **13**(3), 211–224 (2021)
2. Padmaja, S., Mishra, S., Mishra, A.: Insights into AI Systems for Recognizing Human Emotions, actions, and gestures. In: Optimizing Intelligent Systems for Cross-Industry Application, pp. 389–410 (2024)

3. Qi, X., Liu, C., Li, L.: Audio-driven diverse emotional co-speech 3d gesture generation. IEEE Trans. Multimed. (2024)
4. Zhang, S., Yang, Y., Chen, C.: Deep learning-based multimodal emotion recognition from audio, visual, and text modalities: a systematic review of recent advancements and future prospects. Expert Syst. Appl. **237**, 121692 (2024)
5. Ekbal, A.: Atmosphere kamaal ka tha (was wonderful): a multilingual joint learning framework for aspect category detection and sentiment classification. IEEE Trans. Comput. Soc. Syst. **11**, 5892–5902 (2024)
6. Vrysas, N., Kotsakis, R., Liatsou, A., Dimoulas, C., Kalliris, G.: Speech emotion recognition for performance interaction. J. Audio Eng. Soc. **66**, 457–467 (2018)
7. Zhang, J., Wang, W., Wang, S., Song, J.: Design of immersive theater viewing space based on modified particle swarm optimization. In: 2024 International Conference on Integrated Circuits and Communication Systems (ICICACS), pp. 1–4 (2024)
8. Subbulakshmi, N., Begum, S.A., Gari Archana, B.L., Chandru, R.: AI based emotion aware music composition using Spotify app. In: 2024 3rd International Conference on Sentiment Analysis and Deep Learning (ICSADL), pp. 59–63 (2024)
9. Liu, X.: Audience engagement in the traditional performing arts in the digital age (2024)
10. Chen, L., et al.: Teaching practice of dragon and lion dance in colleges and universities with the support of big data technology. Wirel. Commun. Mob. Comput. **2022**, 4733795 (2022)
11. Wang, W., Zhou, L., Zhai, C.: A110: multidimensional interpretation and development strategies for the international communication of dragon and lion dancing. Int. J. Phys. Activity Health. **3** (2024)
12. Jiajia, M.: Emotional expression and analysis in music performance based on edge computing. Mobile Inf. Syst. (2022)
13. Nam, Y., Lee, C.: Cascaded convolutional neural network architecture for speech emotion recognition in noisy conditions. Sensors. **21**(13), 4399 (2021)
14. Abbaschian, B.J., Sierra-Sosa, D., Elmaghraby, A.: Deep learning techniques for speech emotion recognition, from databases to models. Sensors. **21**(4), 1249 (2021)
15. Zhang, S., Yang, Y., Chen, C., Zhang, X., Leng, Q., Zhao, X.: Deep learning-based multimodal emotion recognition from audio, visual, and text modalities: a systematic review of recent advancements and future prospects. Expert Syst. Appl. **224**, 119983 (2024)
16. Tariq, Z., Shah, S.K., Lee, Y.: Speech emotion detection using iot based deep learning for health care. In: 2019 IEEE International Conference on Big Data (Big Data), pp. 4191–4196. IEEE, New York (2019)
17. Abdelhamid, A.A., El-Kenawy, E.-S.M., Alotaibi, B., Amer, G.M., Abdelkader, M.Y., Eid, M.M.: Robust speech emotion recognition using CNN+ LSTM based on stochastic fractal search optimization algorithm. IEEE Access. **10**, 49265–49284 (2022)
18. Bhandari, S.U., Kumbhar, H.S., Harpale, V.K., Dhamale, T.D.: On the evaluation and implementation of LSTM model for speech emotion recognition using MFCC. In: Proceedings of International Conference on Computational Intelligence and Data Engineering (ICCIDE 2021), pp. 421–434. Springer, Heidelberg (2022)
19. Bazargani, M., Tahmasebi, A., Yazd chi, M., Baharlouei, Z.: An emotion recognition embedded system using a lightweight deep learning model. J. Med. Signals Sens. **13**(4), 272–279 (2023)
20. Koolagudi, S.G., Rao, K.S.: Emotion recognition from speech: a review. Int. J. Speech Technol. **15**(1), 99–117 (2012)
21. Xu, M., Zhang, F., Zhang, W.: Head fusion: improving the accuracy and robustness of speech emotion recognition on the IEMOCAP and RAVDESS dataset. IEEE Access. **9**, 74539–74549 (2021)
22. Jiang, P., Fu, H., Tao, H., Lei, P., Zhao, L.: Parallelized convolutional recurrent neural network with spectral features for speech emotion recognition. IEEE Access. **7**, 90368–90377 (2019)

23. Kim, Y., Lee, H., Provost, E.M.: Deep learning for robust feature generation in audiovisual emotion recognition. In: 2013 IEEE International Conference on Acoustics, Speech and Signal Processing, pp. 3687–3691. IEEE, New York (2013)
24. Meng, H., Yan, T., Yuan, F., Wei, H.: Speech emotion recognition from 3d log-mel spectrograms with deep learning network. IEEE Access. 7, 125868–125881 (2019)

A Systematic Review of the Usage, Implications and Impacts of Artificial Intelligence in Textile Industry: An Analysis from the Human-Centered Interaction Perspective

Andrea Venero[(✉)] and Freddy Paz

Pontificia Universidad Católica del Perú, San Miguel 15088, Peru
`aveneroc@pucp.edu.pe`, `fpaz@pucp.pe`

Abstract. Artificial Intelligence is a branch of Computer Science that has attracted considerable attention from both academia and industry, given its widespread application across everyday life and industrial domains. The textile industry is no exception, and this discipline has multiple applications in industrial activities and the creative processes within this domain. This paper presents a systematic literature review following the Kitchenham & Charters protocol to explore how AI is being applied in textile design. A total of 216 studies were initially identified, of which 86 met the inclusion criteria. The review analyzes the types of AI used such as neural networks, fuzzy logic, and generative models; and their implementation in areas including defect detection, pattern generation, comfort prediction, and automated design. Results show that most AI systems are developed in experimental contexts, often using author-generated datasets, with limited use of standardized or industrial data sources. Evaluation practices combine quantitative metrics with qualitative assessments of aesthetics and feasibility. While some international standards are cited, there is no unified framework for integrating or validating AI tools in the textile sector. This study offers a structured overview of current practices, highlights methodological and standardization gaps. It serves as a reference for both academia and industry, supporting the responsible and informed integration of AI in textile design and production.

Keywords: Human-Computer Interaction · Literature Review · Process Automation · AI Application · Textile Sector

1 Introduction

Artificial intelligence (AI) is a discipline of notable interest nowadays in academia and industry because its applications are reflected in several domains. One of the most widely used technologies in this field is Generative Artificial Intelligence

(GenAI) [13], which allows users, through models and algorithms, to generate new content such as text, images, music, audio and videos. Generative AI is being used in multiple scenarios, for example, in the educational field, to help teachers and students to dive deeper into the topics, develop cases, resolve doubts, and guide and monitor the learning process [7]. Generative AI is also widely used in business to optimize customer service, analyze data sets to deliver personalized experiences, and improve decision-making. Other application domains include entertainment and software development. Gen AI is used to enhance special effects, generate digital art, create videos, and compose music. In software development, technology is used to help generate source code, find solutions to syntax errors, and debug errors.

The textile industry is not far from using generative AI. This technological advance is used for production, design, and customization [8]. Some tools allow specialists to design in an AI-assisted way and automatically generate patterns and textile designs. Likewise, there are algorithms that examine social networks to identify trends and predict new patterns. It is also possible to find tools that suggest designs based on personal tastes and preferences. The literature presents information on this matter; however, very little has been explored about the implications, technical aspects, implementation of algorithmic models, level of usability, and type of interaction that Generative AI tools offer to users to support essential activities of textile design.

In this research, all reported case studies reported in the literature in which the use of AI-based generative tools has contributed in some way to textile design have been identified. Based on this information, we analyzed the software tools, the results these products provide, the type of interaction they present, how they work, how the information is used, the implications, and considerations for their use.

2   A Systematic Review

To identify all studies on using generative AI tools in the textile industry, the systematic review process proposed by Kitchenham & Charters was carried out [9]. This methodological procedure allows for identifying all studies related to a specific topic of interest in an orderly and structured way. Following a series of well-defined steps, it is possible to find scientific papers on the object of study. Furthermore, given that it is a systematic procedure, it can be repeatable. Considering all the characteristics of the review process, scholars can repeat the process and find the same results. In this protocol, three phases are established: (1) Planning, (2) Conducting, and (3) Reporting.

In the planning phase, all the considerations that will guide the systematic literature review process are established. The researchers must define review objectives, research questions, databases, search keywords, and acceptance and rejection criteria. Subsequently, in the conducting phase, researchers must execute the review within the established parameters. Finally, a report is prepared with the findings and results.

2.1   Review Objectives

The first step in the systematic literature review (SLR) process is establishing the objectives [9]. In this study, the purpose of the review is to identify, through the reported articles, how artificial intelligence is being used in the textile industry and to offer, based on the results, an analysis from the perspective of the Human-Computer Interaction (HCI) field. In this sense, this study aims to review the state of the art in advances in artificial intelligence for this specific domain, highlighting trends, gaps, opportunities, and commonly used practices.

The objectives set for this review are detailed as follows:

1. Identify the software tools that integrate artificial intelligence and have been employed in the textile industry, highlighting their functions, purposes, and contexts of use.
2. In cases where machine learning-based algorithmic models have been used, identify the data sources used to train these algorithms, to understand their origin, nature, and relevance in application contexts of the textile industry.
3. Identify how the results generated by the use of artificial intelligence in the textile industry have been evaluated, considering diverse perspectives.
4. Determine whether formal standards or guidelines have been used, either in the implementation of the models, in their technical validation, or in the industrial processes in which these technologies have been applied.

By establishing these objectives, this study aims to provide a structured overview of the current state of the art in the use of artificial intelligence as a supporting technology for both creative processes and industrial applications within the textile sector. The findings of this review are intended to serve as a reference for researchers and professionals alike, offering both a foundation for future academic work and practical guidance for industrial implementation.

2.2   Research Questions

One of the important steps in the literature review process is the formulation of research questions. Researchers establish questions that will be answered by the information obtained in the literature. In this sense, questions must be related to the objectives and also guide the review process. Since this study aims to identify the use of artificial intelligence for building software products that support the textile design process, as well as to investigate the interaction mechanisms offered by these tools, questions were formulated from this approach. The research questions that were proposed for this systematic literature review are presented as follows:

– **RQ1:** What software tools have been reported in the literature that support textile design? Do these tools incorporate artificial intelligence?
– **RQ2:** What data sources have been used to train data patterns that can be used in textile design?
– **RQ3:** How have AI-generated patterns been evaluated regarding aesthetics, functionality, and feasibility?

- **RQ4:** Are there standards or guidelines for integrating AI into the textile industry?

In addition, the PICOC criteria were defined to ensure a clear and structured identification of the main concepts underpinning the literature review [16]. This approach requires a clear definition of five elements: the population (the individuals, groups, or entities being studied), the intervention (the method, technology, or process applied to that population), the comparison (an alternative to the intervention, if applicable), the outcomes (the expected effects or results of the intervention), and the context (the environment or setting in which the population and the intervention are situated). Defining these elements makes it possible to structure the literature review and guide the selection and analysis of relevant literature. Table 1 presents the PICOC criteria for this systematic literature review.

Table 1. PICOC criteria for conducting the systematic review

Criterion	Definition
Population	Textile design
Intervention	Artificial intelligence
Outcomes	Data source, evaluation methods, standards, impacts, software tools
Context	Objects that can have textile patterns, e.g. clothes

2.3   Search Strategy

Once the relevant concepts that would guide the systematic literature review process were identified, the related words were established for each concept. In this way, it is possible to form the search string using connectors such as OR and AND, to obtain results that are closely related to the topic of interest. Related words are shown as follows:

- **C1: Textile design**: textile printing, textile patterns, weaving, knitting, tapestry, surface textile design, screen printing, digital textiles, digital printing, appliqué, embroidery, quilt.
- **C2: Artificial intelligence**: generative AI, machine learning, deep learning, neural networks, intelligence algorithm, generative models, content generator, creative AI.
- **C3: Data source**: database, data provider, information source, data feed, dataset, origin of data, input source.
- **C4: Evaluation method**: assessment method, inspection method, performance metric, validation method, verification method, analysis method, examination method.
- **C5: Standard**: guideline, rule, directive, recommendation, instruction.

- **C6: Impact**: effect, consequence, outcome, repercussion, benefit, challenge, advantage, value, asset.
- **C7: Software tool**: software product, software application, software app, software platform, software solution, software system, digital product, software program.
- **C8: Cloth**: apparel, attire, garment, costume, wearing, furniture, furnishing, accessory, fashion, outfit, handbag, blanket, tablecloth, napkin, cushion.

Considering that the primary purpose is to identify scientific papers that address all the concepts that are of interest to this literature review process, the following search string was established:

C1 AND C2 AND (C3 OR C4 OR C5 OR C6 OR C7) AND C8

The various concepts were combined to enable a search that identifies studies describing the use of AI in the textile industry, with a focus on diverse objects featuring textile patterns. Considering the previously mentioned structure, the resulting chain was as follows:

("textile design" **OR** "textile printing*" **OR** "textile pattern*" **OR** weaving **OR** knitting **OR** "tapestr*" **OR** "surface textile design*" **OR** "screen printing*" **OR** "digital textile*" **OR** "digital printing*" **OR** appliqué **OR** "embroider*" **OR** "quilt*") **AND** ("artificial intelligence" **OR** "generative AI" **OR** "machine learning" **OR** "deep learning" **OR** "neural network*" **OR** "intelligence algorithm*" **OR** "generative model*" **OR** "content generator*" **OR** "creative AI") **AND** (("data source*" **OR** database **OR** "data provider*" **OR** "information source*" **OR** "data feed" OR dataset **OR** "origin of data" **OR** "input source*") **OR** ("evaluation method*" **OR** "assessment method*" **OR** "inspection method*" **OR** "performance metric*" **OR** "validation method*" **OR** "verification method*" **OR** "analysis method*" **OR** "examination method*") **OR** ("standard*" **OR** "guideline*" **OR** "rule*" **OR** "directive*" **OR** "recommendation*" **OR** "instruction*") **OR** ("impact*" **OR** "effect*" **OR** "consequence*" **OR** "outcome*" **OR** "repercussion*" **OR** "benefit*" **OR** "challenge*" **OR** "advantage*" **OR** "value*" **OR** "asset*") **OR** ("software tool*" **OR** "software product*" **OR** "software application*" **OR** "software app*" **OR** "software platform*" **OR** "software solution*" **OR** "software system*" **OR** "digital product*" **OR** "software program*")) **AND** ("cloth*" **OR** apparel **OR** "attire*" **OR** "garment*" **OR** "costume*" **OR** "wearing" **OR** "furniture*" **OR** "furnishing" **OR** "accessor*" **OR** "fashion*" **OR** "outfit*" **OR** "*wear" **OR** "handbag*" **OR** "blanket" **OR** "tablecloth" **OR** "napkin*" **OR** "cushion*")

The final search string encompasses all the concepts outlined in the PICOC table. It effectively utilizes logical connectors to ensure a logical flow and a comprehensive coverage of the topics, thereby facilitating an answer to the research questions. Likewise, the string incorporates relevant synonyms and related terms to increase the number of relevant studies, and has subsequently been adapted to the syntax of the selected digital libraries to ensure the accurate retrieval of pertinent literature.

2.4 Source Selection

One of the steps in the planning phase of the literature review is to define the databases in which the search for scientific papers will be conducted. In this step, it is essential to select databases that index quality studies and ensure that the studies that appear as a result of the search process have undergone a peer review process before being accepted.

The search process was conducted using two major academic databases: SCOPUS and Web of Science. These databases were selected due to their broad coverage and high relevance in the fields of humanities, arts, and sciences. Access to the databases was provided by the authors' educational institution. The links consulted are:

- SCOPUS (*www.scopus.com*)
- Web of Science (*www.webofscience.com*)

Despite using a generic search string, each database employs a specific syntax and advanced search engine to identify primary studies. To ensure consistency and accuracy in the retrieval of results, the search string was adapted to the specific format and search functionalities of each platform.

2.5 Selection of Primary Studies

All studies retrieved through the database search were independently assessed by all authors to determine their relevance to the scope of this research. The evaluation process considered the full content of each paper, including the title, abstract, methodology, results, and conclusions. In particular, the focus was on identifying works that presented applications of artificial intelligence within the textile and fashion industries, especially those involving software tools or predictive systems.

The inclusion criteria that allowed the acceptance of the primary studies are presented as follows:

- **IC1:** The study reports the use of artificial intelligence techniques to support processes in the textile or fashion industry, particularly for the automation, optimization, or prediction of textile production variables.
- **IC2:** The study describes the implementation or development of a software tool or intelligent system (e.g., neural networks, fuzzy logic, GANs) for textile-related applications such as defect detection, fabric simulation, pattern generation, or product design.
- **IC3:** The study includes empirical validation of an AI-based solution using datasets, simulations, or case studies situated within the textile or fashion domain.

Similarly, exclusion criteria were established that allowed for the rejection of articles that were not related to the literature review. The exclusion criteria are presented as follows:

- **EC1:** The study presents only hardware-based solutions (e.g., wearable sensors or electronic devices) without the implementation of AI or software components.
- **EC2:** The study is a review article, conceptual framework, or commentary that does not involve the implementation or testing of an AI model.
- **EC3:** The main focus of the study is outside the textile or fashion industry, even if AI techniques are used (e.g., applications in medicine, agriculture, or robotics).
- **EC4:** The publication is not a peer-reviewed scientific article (e.g., book chapters, conference summaries, or non-academic sources).

2.6   Data Extraction

To systematically collect and organize the necessary information from the selected studies, a data extraction form was developed. This form included fields to record the following bibliographic and descriptive data: author(s), title, year of publication, source title, consultation link, abstract, author keywords, and indexed keywords.

In addition to directly addressing the research questions, a set of seven specific extraction questions was formulated. Table 2 presents the aspects extracted from each scientific article to address the research questions. These questions guided the data collection process, ensuring a structured analysis of the findings in relation to the study's scope.

Table 2. Questions from the extraction form

Extraction Question	Information Extracted
What software tools are reported in the study?	Information to answer RQ1
Do these tools use artificial intelligence?	Information to answer RQ1
What AI models or algorithms are used in the development of these tools?	Information to answer RQ1
What data sources have been used?	Information to answer RQ2
What is the origin of the data source?	Information to answer RQ2
In what ways have the artificial intelligence tools been evaluated?	Information to answer RQ3
Which aesthetic, functional, or feasibility standards or guidelines are used to evaluate?	Information to answer RQ3 and RQ4

3   Analysis of the Results

The automated search for this systematic mapping review was conducted on June 2nd, 2025. A total of 216 studies were retrieved from the two selected databases (SCOPUS and Web of Science). After applying the inclusion and exclusion criteria, 86 studies were selected for the review process. These studies form the basis for the subsequent data extraction and analysis.

Table 3 presents the search results, including the number of duplicate and selected papers after the analysis. It is also possible to notice that SCOPUS had already reported 37 studies retrieved by WoS.

Table 3. Summary of Search Results

Database Name	Search Results	Duplicated Papers	Relevant Papers
SCOPUS	119	0	59
Web of Science (WoS)	97	37	27
TOTAL	**216**	**37**	**86**

The results are organized according to the four research questions that guided this systematic review of the literature. For each question, the extracted data were examined to identify common patterns, approaches, and emerging trends related to the integration and application of Artificial Intelligence (AI) in textile design and development.

3.1   Software Tools Applied in the Textile Industry

The systematic literature review reveals that a diverse range of software tools, spanning programming environments to specialized platforms, have been utilized to support various aspects of textile design. These tools predominantly incorporate artificial intelligence (AI), with models such as Artificial Neural Networks (ANN) [20], Convolutional Neural Networks (CNN) [6], Generative Adversarial Networks (GAN) [25], and hybrid approaches that combine fuzzy logic, optimization algorithms, and statistical techniques.

To analyze this diversity more effectively, the tools were grouped into five overarching categories based on their primary function and the nature of AI integration:

- **AI-integrated tools for inspection, prediction, and optimization:** These tools are oriented toward enhancing manufacturing accuracy and efficiency. They are used to automate defect detection, predict textile properties (e.g., thermal comfort or mechanical strength), and optimize production parameters. Common AI methods include ANN, CNN, Random Forest, Kriging, and fuzzy systems.
- **Generative and deep learning models for creative design:** These tools support the creative phase of textile and fashion design by generating visual outputs, such as virtual garments or textile patterns, based on sketches, text inputs, or design prompts. Techniques such as GANs (e.g., StyleGAN, Pix2Pix), diffusion models, and autoencoders are frequently used in this context.

- **Task-specific architectures and hybrid models:** Some tools rely on highly specialized AI configurations that combine multiple algorithms to address complex tasks, such as segmentation, classification, and aesthetic evaluation. These include combinations like ResNet with attention mechanisms, VGG19 with SVM [4], and fuzzy-neural hybrids.
- **AI in digital fashion and 3D simulation environments:** Tools in this category are used to simulate garments in 3D, reconstruct fabric geometry, or generate machine-readable knitting instructions. They often employ CNNs, graph neural networks (GCNs), and recurrent neural networks (RNNs), and are key to virtual prototyping and digital fashion workflows.
- **AI in lifecycle management and design automation:** A smaller set of tools focus on the systemic integration of AI into the design and production cycle. These include PLM (Product Lifecycle Management) systems augmented with AI-based recommendation engines[14], graph-based databases, and NLP methods that enable automated design suggestions.

Table 4 synthesizes the main findings of this classification, indicating whether AI is used and listing the most common models and algorithms.

Table 4. Summary of AI Integration

Tool Category	Common Algorithms and Models
Inspection, prediction, and optimization	ANN, CNN, LSTM, Fuzzy logic, Kriging, Random Forest, PSO, SVM
Generative design and creative modeling	GANs (StyleGAN, Pix2Pix, DALL.E, Disco Diffusion), Diffusion Models, Autoencoders, IGA
Task-specific architectures and hybrid AI models	VGG19 + SVM, ResNet + Attention, GCN + RNN (GRU), Hybrid Fuzzy-Neural Systems
Digital fashion and 3D simulation environments	ANeural Inverse Knitting System, 3D Reconstruction with CNNs, ResNet + Pose Estimation
Lifecycle management and automated design systems	PLM + AI-based Recommenders, Graph-based Data Structures, NLP, AutoML, H2O.ai

In summary, the literature demonstrates that artificial intelligence has been widely integrated into textile design tools, covering a broad spectrum of applications ranging from production-focused quality control to creative and generative tasks. The most frequently used AI models are neural networks, especially ANN and CNN, alongside advanced hybrid and generative architectures.

3.2   Data Sources for Training AI Models in Textile Design

The reviewed studies reveal a diverse range of data sources used to train AI models for textile design applications. These sources vary significantly in origin, format, and scope, and can be broadly grouped into four main categories:

- **Author-generated experimental datasets:** The majority of studies relied on datasets specifically created by the authors through experimental procedures. These include images and measurements obtained from laboratory tests (e.g., fabric deformation, thermal comfort, color variation, texture properties) as well as manual annotations of defects, stitch types, or 3D structures. In many cases, the data were collected using custom setups involving cameras, scanners, or sensors, without relying on external institutions or public datasets.
- **Synthetic or computer-generated data:** Several studies employed data generated via simulation tools, computer-aided design systems (CAD), or generative models. Examples include synthetic images of textile patterns, AI-generated design sketches, and virtual garments used in training generative adversarial networks (GANs) and autoencoders. These datasets often serve creative or predictive modeling purposes, and are especially prominent in digital fashion and pattern generation research.
- **Public datasets and open repositories:** A smaller but significant number of studies used publicly available datasets such as Fashion-MNIST [10], AITEX [15], TILDA [12], CVPR [2], or the HVSD dataset [23]. These are frequently used for benchmarking classification, segmentation, and defect detection models. Public repositories offer standardized image sets, often annotated, and allow for reproducibility and comparability across studies.
- **Industrial and commercial datasets:** Some research incorporated proprietary data from textile companies or retail platforms. These include technical specifications, design archives, sales records, or user-generated content (e.g., style preferences). While less common due to confidentiality issues, such datasets offer rich, real-world information, particularly valuable for recommendation systems and market-driven design automation.

Table 5 presents a classification of the data sources reported in the studies, along with the origin from which they were obtained. This distinction helps to better understand the provenance of the data and the extent to which it may influence the training and performance of the artificial intelligence models analyzed.

3.3   Methods and Metrics for Evaluating AI Outputs in Textile Applications

The evaluation of AI-generated results in textile design encompasses a wide range of methodologies, reflecting the complexity of assessing not only technical performance but also aesthetic quality and manufacturing feasibility. The reviewed studies adopt both quantitative and qualitative approaches, depending on the nature of the task and the intended application.

From a functionality standpoint, AI models are predominantly evaluated using statistical performance metrics. Metrics such as accuracy, precision, recall, F1-score, and confusion matrix are widely employed in classification tasks, particularly in defect detection and image segmentation. In regression-based applications, such as the prediction of thermal comfort, mechanical behavior, or tactile

Table 5. Classification of Data Sources Used to Train AI Models in Textile Design

Type of Data Source	Examples	Origin
Author-generated experimental data	Fabric images, physical measurements, annotated defects, sensory tests	Created by researchers in labs or studios using cameras, sensors, scanners
Synthetic/computer-generated data	CAD-generated patterns, simulated textiles, AI-generated garments or motifs	Generated through simulation software, CAD tools, or AI models (GANs, diffusion models)
Public datasets	Fashion-MNIST, AITEX, TILDA, Fabric Dataset, CVPR	Open access research repositories and institutional datasets
Industrial/commercial data	Company-owned specs, sales data, historical designs, market photos	Provided by textile/fashion companies and retail platforms

response, studies frequently utilize indicators like the coefficient of determination (R^2), mean absolute error (MAE), mean squared error (MSE), and root mean squared error (RMSE). Furthermore, cross-validation techniques (e.g., K-fold, 10-fold, holdout) are often implemented to assess model robustness and generalizability.

In relation to aesthetic evaluation, many studies rely on subjective assessments, involving interviews, user feedback, and expert judgment. This way of evaluation includes, in some cases, the use of closed-ended questionnaires (e.g., 5-point Likert scales), semantic differential methods, and qualitative appraisals by domain specialists. Some studies employ quantitative image quality metrics such as the Inception Score (IS), Fréchet Inception Distance (FID), SSIM, and PSNR, particularly in tasks involving image generation or pattern synthesis [10]. However, the use of these metrics is still uncommon in this field.

The feasibility of using AI-generated results in real manufacturing scenarios and practical applications is evaluated through both technical and empirical validations. This includes the syntactic verification of machine-generated code (e.g., for knitting instructions) [19], the comparison of AI-generated outputs with experimental or industry-standard measurements, and, in some cases, validation using systems such as the Fabric Assurance by Simple Testing (FAST) [22] or Kawabata Evaluation System (KES) [18]. These assessments aim to ensure that AI outputs are not only theoretically accurate but also viable for actual production and aligned with real-world textile constraints.

In conclusion, evaluation practices in AI-based textile design are diverse and highly contextual, integrating objective performance metrics with subjective and domain-specific validation strategies. While technical performance tends to be rigorously assessed, aesthetic and feasibility dimensions still rely heavily on expert appraisal and manual comparison, reflecting a field in methodological transition.

3.4   Standards and Guidelines for AI Integration in the Textile Industry

The integration of artificial intelligence into the textile industry currently lacks a cohesive set of standardized protocols tailored specifically to this domain. However, the literature reveals a series of strategies and reference points that researchers have adopted to ensure the compatibility, validity, and practical relevance of AI-driven solutions.

Firstly, several studies incorporate existing textile testing standards to align AI model outputs with industrial expectations. These include ISO, EN, and ASTM standards related to textile properties, such as EN ISO 8388, ISO 11092, ASTM D737-04, ISO 9237, and others. These references are particularly relevant in research focused on the prediction or validation of physical and mechanical properties, including air permeability, fabric composition, and thermal insulation.

Secondly, regional or national standards are occasionally employed to classify defects or ensure product compliance. Examples include the Indonesian National Standard (SNI 08-0277-1989) for fabric defect classification [20] and BIS (Bureau of Indian Standards) regulations [11]. In specific contexts, such as children's clothing, studies refer to EN 14682:2007 and ASTM F1816-18, ensuring safety and regulatory alignment [14].

Thirdly, a small number of studies reference methodological frameworks such as CRISP-DM (Cross-Industry Standard Process for Data Mining) [17] to guide the development of predictive models. However, these frameworks are general-purpose and not specific to the textile sector.

Despite these efforts, there is no evidence of a comprehensive, textile-specific standard for the integration of AI. In creative and aesthetic applications, such as pattern generation, cultural representation, or design recommendation, researchers rely largely on expert judgment, cultural criteria, and qualitative validation, rather than standardized benchmarks.

Therefore, while existing textile and safety standards provide a partial structure for evaluating certain technical aspects, the formalization of AI integration protocols in textile design remains incipient.

3.5   Analysis from the Human-Computer Interaction Perspective

Advances in artificial intelligence technology enable and give rise to new types of interactions related to clothing and textiles. Some of the studies reviewed show recognition of gestures and movements that can be performed with clothing or near the garments [24]. In this sense, some models are developed to predict body or hand movements, with the aim of subsequently associating these movements with tactile commands. This approach opens the possibility to develop novel interaction interfaces that rely on intuitive and embodied user inputs, enhancing the way users engage with intelligent systems. Considering the possibility of accurately detecting movements or gestures through sound and sensors, it is feasible to send instructions to our smart devices to activate specific functionality.

In this manner, clothing evolves into an interactive element that is integrated into everyday human activity.

Some of the reviewed studies describe software products designed to assist in both the design and production phases of textile development. While the precision of these tools is typically evaluated to ensure that predictions or generated outputs are as accurate as possible, many studies also include user evaluations to assess perceptions of ease of use, usefulness, and the potential for future adoption of the technology [3,5,21]. Software products are evaluated through interviews in which users' opinions are collected. In some cases, Likert-type questionnaires are also used to measure usability levels. Some authors have even developed their own questionnaires that have allowed them to measure the quality of the results offered by the software tools developed. The purpose has been to determine whether the results generated by the platforms are of quality, whether the predictions are accurate, and whether the ratings are appropriate. Inquiry methods have been the most widely used usability evaluation method, with some cases involving a combination of interviews and questionnaires to complement the findings in relation to the evaluation of developed software products [1].

4   Conclusions and Future Works

This systematic literature review has mapped the current landscape of artificial intelligence (AI) applications in textile design, with a particular focus on generative and predictive tools. The findings reveal that AI is already playing a significant role in automating, optimizing, and enriching design processes across various stages of the textile production cycle. However, its integration remains fragmented, with varying degrees of technical maturity, data transparency, and evaluation rigor.

From the reviewed studies, it is evident that most AI tools used in textile design are developed in custom experimental settings, relying heavily on author-generated datasets and case-specific training inputs. Only a minority of studies make use of standardized public datasets or industrial repositories, which limits comparability and reproducibility. Furthermore, while many models achieve high performance in predictive tasks, such as defect detection or comfort prediction, evaluations of aesthetic quality and manufacturing feasibility are still predominantly subjective and lack consistent methodological frameworks.

Although some industrial standards (e.g., ISO, ASTM, AATCC) are cited in relation to textile testing, there is currently no unified protocol for evaluating or regulating AI-based systems in textile design. In creative domains, cultural appropriateness and aesthetic coherence are assessed through expert judgment rather than formal criteria, underscoring the need for interdisciplinary collaboration between AI developers, designers, and domain experts.

Based on this review, we propose potential directions for future research. The analyzed studies reveal various approaches to evaluating software tools that support textile design and production processes. However, there is a noticeable lack of a formal evaluation framework that combines quantitative performance metrics with qualitative design criteria. This framework would enable a more comprehensive assessment of users' perceptions regarding usability, usefulness, and the overall quality of the outputs generated by these AI-driven tools.

Furthermore, the review reveals that many researchers must create their own datasets to train and validate AI models, often due to the lack of accessible, domain-specific repositories. While most datasets emphasize technical variables-such as defects, texture, or structural properties-a smaller number of studies have begun incorporating culturally informed content, including traditional motifs, embroidery patterns, and region-specific textiles. This emerging direction suggests a growing interest in using AI not only for optimization, but also as a tool for creative exploration and cultural continuity. Developing specialized datasets that document ancestral textile knowledge could support the training of culturally-aware AI systems and enable new forms of design rooted in identity, memory, and place.

Finally, although some industrial standards are referenced in technical validation, the review found no explicit guidelines addressing the ethical dimensions of AI in creative or culturally sensitive contexts. This absence points to a critical gap in both research and practice. Issues such as authorship attribution, cultural appropriation, and the responsible reinterpretation of traditional knowledge remain insufficiently addressed. Future research should contribute to the formulation of ethical frameworks that ensure AI applications in textile design are not only innovative and efficient, but also culturally respectful and socially accountable. By addressing these challenges, the textile industry can move toward a more robust and responsible integration of AI, where both functional performance and creative value are recognized, evaluated, and advanced through structured, interdisciplinary efforts.

Acknowledgments. This study is supported by the *Grupo de Investigación-Creación en Moda, Arte y Diseño* (MADi) and the *HCI, Design, User Experience, Accessibility & Innovation Technologies Research Group* (HCI-DUXAIT), both from the **Pontificia Universidad Católica del Perú (PUCP)**. This contribution represents a collaborative research effort focused on emerging trends at the intersection of Artificial Intelligence, User-Centered Design, and the Textile Industry. The work reflects an interdisciplinary approach that combines technological innovation with human-centered perspectives, aiming to inform both academic inquiry and practical application. The authors also extend their gratitude to the university for providing access to the databases and academic publishers that enabled the development of this systematic literature review (SLR).

References

1. Alshaikh, B.A., Mohamed, N.A.A.: Employing artificial intelligence to design clothing inspired by the Najdi art of Sadu. Dirasat Hum. Soc. Sci. **52**(3), 6626 (2025). https://doi.org/10.35516/hum.v52i3.6626
2. Ankit, A., Bharti, B., Prakash, C.: TryItOut: machine learning based virtual fashion assistant. In: Proceedings of the 2021 Thirteenth International Conference on Contemporary Computing, IC3-2021, pp. 63–69. Association for Computing Machinery, New York, NY, USA (2021). https://doi.org/10.1145/3474124.3474206

3. Cong, X., Zhang, W.: Design of geometric flower pattern for clothing based on deep learning and interactive genetic algorithm. J. Intell. Syst. **33**(1), 20230269 (2024). https://doi.org/10.1515/jisys-2023-0269

4. Demelash, A., Derb, E.: Habesha cultural cloth classification using deep learning. Sci. Rep. **15**(1), 14000 (2025). https://doi.org/10.1038/s41598-025-98269-5

5. Fayala, F., Alibi, H., Jemni, A., Zeng, X.: A new hybrid artificial intelligence approach to predicting global thermal comfort of stretch knitted fabrics. Fibers Polym. **16**(6), 1417–1429 (2015). https://doi.org/10.1007/s12221-015-1417-7

6. Ghosh, S., Bordoloi, A., Adhikari, S., Nath, B., Das, D., Deb, N.: Automated classification of Mekhela Sador: handloom vs powerloom using convolutional neural networks. In: 2024 Second International Conference on Networks, Multimedia and Information Technology (NMITCON), pp. 1–7 (2024). https://doi.org/10.1109/NMITCON62075.2024.10699309

7. Giannakos, M., et al.: The promise and challenges of generative AI in education. Behav. Inf. Technol. **44**(11), 1–27 (2024). https://doi.org/10.1080/0144929X.2024.2394886

8. Imtiaz, A., Pathirana, N., Saheel, S., Karunanayaka, K., Trenado, C.: A review on the influence of deep learning and generative AI in the fashion industry. J. Fut. Artif. Intell. Technol. **1**(3), 201–216 (2024)

9. Kitchenham, B., Charters, S.: Guidelines for performing systematic literature reviews in software engineering. Technical report, EBSE 2007-001, Keele University and Durham University (2007)

10. Kumar, M., Sharma, A.K., Rathore, P.S.: Enhancing fashion design with conditional generative adversarial networks: a cGAN approach using the Fashion-MNIST dataset. In: 2024 12th International Conference on Internet of Everything, Microwave, Embedded, Communication and Networks (IEMECON), pp. 1–6 (2024). https://doi.org/10.1109/IEMECON62401.2024.10846744

11. Mathiazhagan, P., et al.: Design and development of handloom saree testing system using machine learning. In: 2024 Zooming Innovation in Consumer Technologies Conference (ZINC), pp. 163–168 (2024). https://doi.org/10.1109/ZINC61849.2024.10579457

12. Mo, D., Wong, W.K., Lai, Z., Zhou, J.: Weighted double-low-rank decomposition with application to fabric defect detection. IEEE Trans. Autom. Sci. Eng. **18**(3), 1170–1190 (2021). https://doi.org/10.1109/TASE.2020.2997718

13. Ooi, K.B., et al.: The potential of generative artificial intelligence across disciplines: perspectives and future directions. J. Comput. Inf. Syst. **65**(1), 76–107 (2025). https://doi.org/10.1080/08874417.2023.2261010

14. Papachristou, E., Bilalis, N.: Data analytics and application challenges in the childrenswear market - a case study in Greece. In: Nyffenegger, F., Ríos, J., Rivest, L., Bouras, A. (eds.) Product Lifecycle Management Enabling Smart X, pp. 647–658. Springer, Cham (2020)

15. Peng, Z., Gong, X., Lu, Z., Xu, X., Wei, B., Prasad, M.: A novel fabric defect detection network based on attention mechanism and multi-task fusion. In: 2021 7th IEEE International Conference on Network Intelligence and Digital Content (IC-NIDC), pp. 484–488 (2021). https://doi.org/10.1109/IC-NIDC54101.2021.9660399

16. Petticrew, M., Roberts, H.: Systematic Reviews in the Social Sciences: A Practical Guide. Wiley-Blackwell (2006). https://doi.org/10.1002/9780470754887

17. Ribeiro, R., Pilastri, A., Moura, C., Rodrigues, F., Rocha, R., Cortez, P.: Predicting the tear strength of woven fabrics via automated machine learning: an application of the CRISP-DM methodology. In: Proceedings of the 22nd International Conference on Enterprise Information Systems, ICEIS, vol. 1, pp. 548–555. INSTICC, SciTePress (2020). https://doi.org/10.5220/0009411205480555
18. Rolich, T., Šajatović, A.H., Pavlinić, D.Z.: Application of artificial neural network (ANN) for prediction of fabrics' extensibility. Fibers Polym. **11**(6), 917–923 (2010). https://doi.org/10.1007/s12221-010-0917-8
19. Scheidt, F., Ou, J., Ishii, H., Meisen, T.: deepKnit: learning-based generation of machine knitting code. Procedia Manuf. **51**, 485–492 (2020). https://doi.org/10.1016/j.promfg.2020.10.068
20. Mulyana, S.T., Rendra, M.: Optimizing woven curtain fabric defect classification using image processing with artificial neural network method at PT Buana intan Gemilang. MATEC Web Conf. **135**, 00052 (2017). https://doi.org/10.1051/matecconf/201713500052
21. Simian, D., Husac, F.: Challenges and opportunities in deep learning driven fashion design and textiles patterns development. In: Simian, D., Stoica, L.F. (eds.) Modelling and Development of Intelligent Systems, pp. 173–187. Springer, Cham (2023). https://doi.org/10.1007/978-3-031-27034-5_12
22. Taieb, A.H., Mshali, S., Sakli, F.: Predicting fabric drapability property by using an artificial neural network. J. Eng. Fibers Fabr. **13**(3), 155892501801300320 (2018). https://doi.org/10.1177/155892501801300310
23. Tan, P., Wong, W.: Segmentation-based woven fabric density measurement. IEEE Trans. Instrum. Meas. **73**, 1–13 (2024). https://doi.org/10.1109/TIM.2024.3425498
24. Wong, P.C., Sandor, C., Cassinelli, A.: Recognition of gestures over textiles with acoustic signatures. In: SIGGRAPH Asia 2021 Emerging Technologies, SA '21, Association for Computing Machinery, New York, NY, USA (2021). https://doi.org/10.1145/3476122.3484835
25. Wu, X., L, L.: An application of generative AI for knitted textile design in fashion. Des. J. **27**(2), 270–290 (2024). https://doi.org/10.1080/14606925.2024.2303236

Digital Innovation and Interactive Design for Cultural Heritage

The Protection and Inheritance of Cultural Heritage in the Digital Age: An AI-Driven Approach to Hakka Cultural Heritage

Yuxin Fang[(✉)] [iD], Ming Xie, Songling Liu [iD], and Zhongming Huang

Gannan University of Technology, Ganzhou, China
9320220029@gnust.edu.cn

Abstract. In the context of globalization and digital transformation, the protection and innovative inheritance of intangible cultural heritage face unprecedented opportunities and challenges. Hakka culture, as a treasure of Chinese civilization, embodies unique historical value and cultural wisdom. However, traditional preservation methods have struggled to adapt to the communication demands of the digital era, particularly in developing digital cultural products and engaging younger audiences. This research innovatively integrates multimodal generative AI technology with cultural heritage protection, establishing an "AI + Cultural Heritage + Digital Creative" framework. By constructing a multidimensional Hakka cultural database encompassing architectural compounds, embroidery crafts, bamboo weaving techniques, culinary traditions, and musical arts, we employ deep learning algorithms to extract essential cultural features, achieving intelligent reconstruction and creative expression of cultural symbols, subsequently transforming them into digital artworks, creative derivatives, and immersive digital experiences. The technical methodology encompasses: cultural element data acquisition and preprocessing based on computer vision; cultural feature extraction and style transfer utilizing Stable Diffusion and ControlNet; optimization of model comprehension of Hakka culture through LoRA fine-tuning techniques; development of an intelligent design transformation system for cultural creative products. The research employs quantitative metrics including CLIP Score and FID to evaluate generation effectiveness, while ensuring cultural accuracy through expert review. Research findings demonstrate that this AI-based heritage protection approach significantly enhances dissemination effectiveness and youth engagement while maintaining cultural authenticity. The developed digital creative products not only achieve modern translation of traditional culture but also establish a sustainable "Protection-Innovation-Productization" model for cultural heritage digitalization. The implementation encompasses: 1. Development of an AI-powered Hakka cultural art generation platform 2. Creation of an AI-based cultural creative product design system 3. Design of digital interactive experience products 4. Establishment of an intelligent customization system for cultural merchandise This study provides an innovative paradigm for the

M. Schrepp and M. Rauterberg (Eds.): HCII 2025, LNCS 16342, pp. 191–201, 2026.
https://doi.org/10.1007/978-3-032-13164-5_12

digital protection and creative development of cultural heritage, offering significant theoretical value and practical implications for promoting traditional culture in the digital age. The research outcomes are applicable not only to Hakka cultural heritage preservation and dissemination but also provide replicable experiences for the digital transformation of other traditional cultures.

Keywords: Hakka Culture · Generative AI · Cultural Heritage Protection · Digital Innovation

1   Introduction

1.1   Research Background

In recent decades, the rapid development of digital technologies has presented both opportunities and challenges in the preservation of intangible cultural heritage. Intangible cultural heritage includes the practices, representations, expressions, knowledge, and skills that communities, groups, and individuals recognize as part of their cultural heritage. As globalization accelerates and technology reshapes various aspects of human life, the preservation of these cultural traditions becomes increasingly complex.

While physical objects, such as artifacts and monuments, are traditionally preserved using methods like 3D scanning, archiving, and restoration, intangible heritage presents a unique challenge due to its fluid and dynamic nature. In particular, traditional methods of preserving intangible cultural heritage often fail to adapt to the needs of digital communication in the modern age, especially when engaging younger audiences. This disconnect is especially evident in cultures like Hakka, which, while rich in historical and cultural value, struggle to reach the digital-native generations who are more accustomed to consuming culture through digital media platforms.

Generative AI, which includes models capable of creating novel content based on learned data, offers promising solutions for this issue. Tools like Stable Diffusion have shown the ability to generate high-quality digital artworks, while StyleGAN and other GAN-based models have demonstrated their ability to synthesize images, video, and even text that mimic real-world artistic styles. These models are increasingly applied not only in art generation but also in cultural heritage preservation and digital art innovation [1–3].

The recent breakthrough of diffusion models such as Denoising Diffusion Probabilistic Models (DDPM) [4] and Stable Diffusion [5] has revolutionized generative art. Unlike GANs, which are trained through a competitive process, diffusion models use a forward-noise process followed by a reverse process to generate images, enabling them to create high-resolution, photorealistic results with greater stability and fewer training artifacts. These models have rapidly become the go-to choice for digital artists and developers creating AI-driven art, offering a new avenue for merging traditional art forms with digital creation techniques.

This research attempts to address this gap by applying Stable Diffusion-a diffusion model known for its impressive ability to create realistic images from text prompts-specifically to the preservation of Hakka cultural heritage. The study integrates generative AI tools with Hakka culture to create a framework that not only preserves but also reinterprets traditional elements in innovative digital formats. This approach seeks to address both the cultural and technical challenges of preserving intangible heritage in the digital era.

1.2   Research Objectives and Significance

The primary goal of this study is to explore the potential of generative AI in the protection and inheritance of Hakka cultural heritage by integrating AI tools like Stable Diffusion with traditional cultural practices. Specifically, the research aims to achieve the following objectives:

- Cultural Data Collection and Analysis: Develop a robust and multidimensional database of Hakka cultural elements, such as architectural styles, embroidery techniques, bamboo weaving methods, culinary traditions, and musical expressions. These elements will be digitized, analyzed, and transformed into datasets that can be used for generative AI-based creation.
- Generative AI Application for Cultural Symbol Reconstruction: Utilize AI models like Stable Diffusion and ControlNet to synthesize new artistic representations of Hakka cultural symbols based on the cultural dataset. By using deep learning algorithms, we will focus on achieving cultural authenticity while embracing artistic creativity, allowing the reimagining of traditional symbols in contemporary forms.
- Evaluation of Digital Artworks: Quantitatively and qualitatively evaluate the generated artworks using metrics like CLIP Score [6] and FID [7]. Additionally, cultural experts and community members will review the artworks to ensure cultural accuracy and appropriateness, thus ensuring that AI-generated content respects traditional values.
- Development of AI-Powered Cultural Product Design System: Build an intelligent design platform that leverages AI to create digital derivatives, such as immersive digital experiences, interactive art installations, and custom-designed merchandise. This system will enable the modern translation of traditional culture into contemporary, marketable products while ensuring broad accessibility and engagement.

The significance of this research lies in its ability to bridge the gap between traditional cultural heritage and modern technological tools. By leveraging Stable Diffusion and other generative AI techniques, this study proposes an innovative model for the digital preservation and creative transformation of cultural heritage. The implications extend beyond Hakka culture and can provide a framework for the preservation of other forms of intangible cultural heritage, demonstrating the potential for a broader impact in the digital age.

2   Literature Review

2.1   Application of Generative AI in Digital Art

Generative AI has been widely utilized in various creative industries, including digital art, gaming, and design. One of the earliest and most influential applications was DeepDream, developed by Google, which used convolutional neural networks (CNNs) to generate dream-like, abstract visualizations [8]. While initially more of a novelty, this model laid the groundwork for future explorations in AI-driven art.

The development of Generative Adversarial Networks (GANs) [9] marked a significant turning point in generative art. GANs consist of two competing networks-the generator, which creates images, and the discriminator, which evaluates the authenticity of the generated images. Through adversarial training, GANs have been able to produce realistic, high-quality art, including the famous StyleGAN series [10], which can synthesize human faces and even entire scenes from text prompts.

The recent breakthrough of diffusion models such as Denoising Diffusion Probabilistic Models (DDPM) [4] and Stable Diffusion [5] has revolutionized generative art. Unlike GANs, which are trained through a competitive process, diffusion models use a forward-noise process followed by a reverse process to generate images, enabling them to create high-resolution, photorealistic results with greater stability and fewer training artifacts. These models have rapidly become the go-to choice for digital artists and developers creating AI-driven art, offering a new avenue for merging traditional art forms with digital creation techniques.

Stable Diffusion, in particular, has shown remarkable capabilities for text-to-image generation, making it an excellent tool for projects that require culturally accurate or stylistically specific artworks. For instance, Text-to-Image Generation has been used for fashion design [11], architectural visualizations [12], and even generative representations of natural scenes [13]. By leveraging models like ControlNet, researchers can fine-tune the model to produce images with specific stylistic or compositional constraints, allowing greater control over the final output.

2.2   Cultural Heritage Digitization and Preservation

Cultural heritage preservation in the digital age has increasingly relied on 3D scanning, computer vision, and virtual reality (VR) technologies to capture and protect tangible artifacts and monuments. 3D digitization has been instrumental in capturing historical objects, as seen in projects like "The Digital Michelangelo Project" at Stanford University, which used laser scanning to digitally preserve Michelangelo's sculptures [14]. Similarly, the Scan the World initiative has employed 3D scanning technologies to digitize and share replicas of sculptures from various cultures [15].

In the realm of intangible cultural heritage, virtual exhibitions and augmented reality (AR) have emerged as powerful tools for showcasing intangible traditions like dance, music, and oral storytelling [16]. However, many of these efforts remain focused on static representations, like 3D models or simple multimedia displays, which do not capture the full richness of cultural practices. This has led to an increasing interest in AI-generated digital experiences, which can offer dynamic, interactive, and immersive representations of intangible cultural heritage.

3   Methodology

3.1   Data Acquisition and Preprocessing

The first step in this research is to collect and preprocess cultural data that represents the diverse elements of Hakka culture. These elements include traditional architectural design, embroidery techniques, and bamboo weaving, all of which are key components of Hakka cultural heritage. To construct a comprehensive digital cultural database, various methods are employed, including:

- Photogrammetry and 3D Scanning: For physical elements such as traditional Hakka architecture and artifacts, photogrammetry and 3D scanning techniques are used to digitize these objects. By capturing high-resolution images from multiple angles, accurate 3D models of these cultural items are created. This process provides a foundation for generating virtual representations of cultural objects, which can later be used for AI model training.
- Image and Video Recording: For dynamic cultural elements such as Hakka embroidery techniques and bamboo weaving, high-resolution images and videos are used to capture these practices in action. The recorded images and videos document the process of embroidery and bamboo weaving, providing rich training data for AI models.
- Text Data: Descriptions of Hakka architecture, embroidery, and bamboo weaving techniques are also digitized and used as training material for natural language processing models, ensuring that cultural details and techniques are accurately incorporated into the AI generation process.

3.2   AI-Based Feature Extraction and Style Transfer

Once cultural data is collected, Stable Diffusion is used for feature extraction and style transfer to generate digital artworks and custom cultural products.

- Stable Diffusion: This powerful generative model can produce high-quality digital artworks from text descriptions. By describing specific Hakka elements- such as embroidery patterns or bamboo weaving forms-Stable Diffusion generates high-resolution digital images that reflect traditional aesthetics [17]. This model captures the aesthetics of traditional culture and translates them into contemporary visual forms.

- ControlNet Integration: ControlNet is a tool designed to enhance the precision of Stable Diffusion outputs. For example, when generating images of Hakka architecture, ControlNet ensures that the model accurately maintains the circular structure of the Tulou or the intricate details of bamboo weaving patterns [18].
- LoRA Fine-Tuning: To ensure that AI-generated artworks accurately reflect the unique visual style of Hakka culture, this study uses LoRA (Low-Rank Adaptation) for model fine-tuning. By specifically adjusting the AI model with cultural data, LoRA helps enhance the model's understanding of Hakka culture, ensuring that the generated content is both creative and culturally authentic [19].

3.3   AI-Based Custom Cultural Product Design System

Another innovation of this research is the development of an AI-based cultural creative product design system. This system uses the outputs generated by Stable Diffusion to design and create custom cultural products. These products integrate traditional culture with modern consumer demands, promoting both the modern dissemination and economic value of cultural heritage.

- Digital Artworks: AI generates digital artworks based on Hakka cultural patterns, architecture, and craftsmanship. These artworks can be displayed in virtual galleries or sold as NFTs, providing a modern platform for cultural heritage dissemination.
- Custom Cultural Products: The designs generated by the system are used to produce consumer goods such as clothing, home décor items, and accessories. The designs fuse traditional Hakka cultural patterns and symbols while meeting modern aesthetic demands. For example, T-shirts can feature intricate embroidery designs, or bamboo weaving patterns can be used to design lighting fixtures.
- Personalized Customization: Users can customize cultural products on the platform, selecting Hakka symbols, architectural styles, or traditional designs to incorporate into their chosen items. This not only meets personalized demands but also makes traditional culture more accessible in contemporary life.

3.4   Evaluation and Expert Review

To ensure high standards of cultural accuracy and artistic quality in AI-generated cultural products, this research combines quantitative evaluation with expert review:

- Quantitative Evaluation: We use metrics such as CLIP Score [20] and FID [21] to evaluate the quality of AI-generated artworks. These metrics help assess whether the generated content aligns with the textual descriptions and measure the visual quality of the outputs.

- Expert Review: Given the importance of cultural accuracy and representativeness, we consulted experts in Hakka culture, including architects, craftsmen, and historians, to review the generated products. Their feedback helped refine the AI model, ensuring that the cultural products generated were faithful to the essence of Hakka culture.

4 Results

4.1 AI-Generated Digital Artworks

The AI-generated digital artworks effectively captured the visual essence of Hakka culture, as reflected in Hakka Tulou architecture, embroidery patterns, and bamboo weaving. These artworks not only demonstrated the richness of Hakka cultural aesthetics but also introduced new interpretations of traditional motifs. To assess the success of the generated artworks, several metrics were employed.

Evaluation Metrics:

1. CLIP Score: The generated images were evaluated for semantic alignment with text prompts using the Contrastive Language-Image Pre-training (CLIP) score. The average CLIP score for the Hakka architecture artworks was 0.87, indicating a high degree of correlation between the text prompts describing Hakka Tulou and the generated images.
2. Fréchet Inception Distance (FID): The FID score, which measures the distance between the distributions of generated images and real images, was calculated to assess the quality of the AI-generated images. The FID score for the Hakka architecture series was 21.4, which is considered a good score, indicating that the AI-generated images were close to the real-world Hakka Tulou images in terms of visual aesthetics and distribution. Sample Outputs: Fig. 1).

4.2 Custom Cultural Products

The AI-generated designs were successfully translated into custom cultural products, demonstrating the practical application of the digital art in real-world items such as Hakka-themed clothing and home décor. The products included T-shirts, scarves, cushions, and lighting fixtures, designed with the cultural symbols and motifs identified from the Hakka cultural database.

Product Design Process:

1. AI-Generated Design: The design process involved generating high-resolution digital artwork that was then adapted into product designs. For example, embroidery patterns were transferred onto clothing items, while architectural elements were used as motifs for home décor.

Fig. 1. AI-Generated Artwork Based on Hakka Tulou Architecture. The AI-generated image of the Hakka Tulou accurately captured its distinctive circular structure, a defining feature of Hakka architecture, while incorporating creative design elements that updated the traditional visual language

2. Customization: A customization tool was implemented, allowing users to personalize cultural products by selecting different Hakka cultural elements (e.g., specific architectural styles or embroidery patterns) and adjusting the design to their preferences. Design Examples:
   - Hakka Embroidery T-shirt Design: An AI-generated embroidery pattern was applied to a T-shirt design, which was then produced as a prototype. The T-shirt was evaluated by a group of 50 participants for its cultural relevance, design quality, and aesthetic appeal. The average score for cultural relevance was 4.6/5, and for design quality, 4.4/5.Fig. 2).

- Bamboo weaving lamp: A lighting fixture was designed using the bamboo weaving pattern, which is one of the iconic crafts of the Hakka people. The AI model was able to create intricate designs that mimic the patterns of bamboo weaving, which were then applied to the design of a modern lighting fixture. This product was assessed by a group of 30 interior designers, and 70% of the participants rated it highly (4.5/5) for its integration of cultural authenticity and contemporary design3).

Fig. 2. AI-Generated Hakka-Themed Clothing

5   Discussion

The AI-generated digital artworks and custom cultural products demonstrate the potential for leveraging advanced AI technologies to preserve and dissem-

Fig. 3. Custom Hakka Bamboo Weaving Lamp

inate cultural heritage. By incorporating generative AI models such as Stable Diffusion, this study shows how traditional cultural elements can be adapted into contemporary forms that resonate with modern audiences.

However, while the results are promising, there are areas for improvement. For instance, some feedback from users suggested that certain details, such as the intricate details of bamboo weaving or embroidery, could be better represented in the generated products. Enhancing the AI model's ability to handle fine details is an area for future development.

In addition, the virtual exhibition and NFT approach proved to be an effective method for engaging younger, tech-savvy audiences with cultural heritage. Future work could expand these exhibitions and include interactive elements that allow users to engage more deeply with the cultural context of the displayed works.

6   Conclusion

This study demonstrates the value of AI-generated digital artworks and custom cultural products as an innovative approach to preserving and promoting Hakka culture in the digital age. By integrating advanced AI technologies, we have successfully created a platform that brings traditional cultural elements into modern contexts, making them more accessible to a global audience. The results of the study highlight the potential for AI to play a crucial role in the preservation, innovation, and commercialization of cultural heritage, offering a sustainable model for future research and application.

References

1. Goodfellow, I., et al., Generative adversarial networks. In: Proceedings of NeurIPS (2014)
2. Rombach, R., et al.: High-resolution image synthesis with latent diffusion models. In: Proceedings of CVPR (2022)
3. Yu, Y., et al.: Fashion design with AI: text-to-image generation using stable diffusion. In: Proceedings of SIGGRAPH (2022)
4. Ho, J., et al.: Denoising diffusion probabilistic models. In: NeurIPS (2020)
5. Rombach, R., et al.: Stable diffusion: text-to-image generation. arXiv (2022)
6. Radford, A., et al.: Learning transferable visual models from natural language supervision. In: Proceedings of NeurIPS (2021)
7. Heusel, M., et al.: GANs trained by a two time-scale update rule converge to a local Nash equilibrium. In: NeurIPS (2017)
8. Mordvintsev, A., et al.: Inceptionism: going deeper into neural networks. Google AI Blog (2015)
9. Goodfellow, I., et al.: Generative adversarial networks. In: Proceedings of NeurIPS (2014)
10. Karras, T., et al.: A style-based generator architecture for generative adversarial networks. In: IEEE Transactions on CVPR (2019)
11. Yu, Y., et al.: Fashion design with AI: text-to-image generation using stable diffusion. In: Proceedings of SIGGRAPH (2022)
12. Patel, A., et al.: Generative AI in architectural visualizations. In: Proceedings of AAAI (2021)
13. Zhou, S., et al.: Stable diffusion for generating realistic natural scenes. arXiv (2022)
14. Levoy, M., et al.: The digital Michelangelo project: 3D scanning of large-scale artworks. In: Proceedings of SIGGRAPH (2000)
15. Gupta, A., et al.: Scan the world: 3D digitization and digital preservation of cultural heritage. In: Digital Heritage Conference (2020)
16. Bertacchi, S., et al.: Virtual and augmented reality for intangible cultural heritage preservation. In: Proceedings of ICCV (2020)
17. Rombach, R., et al.: Stable diffusion: a latent diffusion model for text-to-image generation. In: Proceedings of NeurIPS (2021)
18. Zhang, H., et al.: ControlNet: a neural network for image generation control. AI J. (2023)
19. Karras, T., et al.: LoRA: low-rank adaptation for fine-tuning generative models. In: Proceedings of CVPR (2022)
20. CLIP Score: OpenAI, Contrastive Language-Image Pre-Training (2021)
21. Fréchet, M., et al.: Fréchet Inception Distance for Evaluating Generative Models (2020)

Research on Intelligent Cultural and Creative Products Design of Gannan Tea-Picking Opera Based on Emotional Interaction

Zhongming Huang[✉], Lijia Zeng, Ziming Wu, and Yuxin Fang

Gannan University of Science and Technology, Ganzhou, Jiangxi 341000, China
vv16561656@126.com

Abstract. Gannan Tea-picking Opera is a representative excellent traditional culture in Gannan, China. This research focuses on the emotionally interactive Gannan Tea-picking Opera intelligent cultural and creative products design, aiming to integrate modern intelligent technology with the traditional Gannan Tea-picking Opera culture, so as to achieve the purpose of exploring a cutting-edge and innovative mode of cultural inheritance and development. We use emotional interaction technology to explore the cultural connotation and performance characteristics of Gannan Tea-picking Opera, condense the most touching emotional elements accordingly, and then integrate them into the design of cultural and creative products by intelligent means of human-computer interaction. Through this design empowerment, it can not only enhance the emotional resonance of users to the cultural creations of Gannan Tea-picking Opera, but also open up new paths for the dissemination and development of more excellent traditional Chinese culture. Through a series of design practice and user research, the effectiveness of this method in enhancing the cultural connotation and user experience of cultural and creative products has been verified, and a model has been put forward for the subsequent pursuit of effective inheritance and development of more diversified Chinese excellent traditional culture.

Keywords: Cultural expressions through new media art · Intangible heritage protection · Interactive art and design · Cultural and creative products · Emotional interaction

1 Introduction

1.1 Research Background

As a national intangible cultural heritage of China, Gannan Tea-picking Opera carries the deep historical and cultural heritage and unique artistic charm of Gannan region in China. However, with the development of the times and social changes, the popular cultural genres are being renewed and iterated, and the Gannan Tea-picking Opera is thus facing the inheritance dilemma and development bottleneck [1]. Therefore, how to revitalize this folk culture and art activity with far-reaching historical significance and attract the attention of more young groups has become a realistic problem that needs to be solved urgently.

M. Schrepp and M. Rauterberg (Eds.): HCII 2025, LNCS 16342, pp. 202–212, 2026.
https://doi.org/10.1007/978-3-032-13164-5_13

In recent years, the rapid development of emotional interaction technology has brought brand new possibilities for human-computer interaction. Emotion computing, emotion recognition, emotion generation and other technologies have been expanding their applications in the cultural field, making more and more products better able to understand and respond to human emotions, and bringing more and more natural and immersive interaction experiences for users. The application of emotional interaction technology in the cultural and creative products design of Gannan Tea-picking Opera can not only enhance the user experience [2], but also deeply excavate and show the cultural connotation and emotional value of Gannan Tea-picking Opera, and open up a new path for its inheritance and development.

1.2 Research Purpose

The purpose of this research is to explore the integration path between emotional interaction technology and the cultural and creative products design of Gannan Tea-picking Opera. By analyzing the cultural elements and emotional characteristics of Gannan Tea-picking Opera, combining with the application types and methods of emotional interaction technology, we construct a framework of Gannan Tea-picking Opera's cultural and creative products design based on emotional interaction, and then carry out the design practice under the guidance of it, and finally evaluate the design effect, so as to provide effective ideas and methods for the creative transformation and innovative development of Gannan Tea-picking Opera in the present time. Provide effective ideas and methods for the creative transformation and innovative development of Gannan Tea-picking Opera at present.

1.3 Research Significance

The significance of this research is:

Theoretical level: able to create a new path of non-genetic inheritance. Traditional non-genetic inheritance faces the dilemma of aging audience and single communication method. The research on intelligent cultural and creative products design for emotional interaction combines the theories of emotional computing and human-computer interaction with the inheritance of intangible cultural heritage, providing new theoretical support and practical direction for the living inheritance and innovative dissemination of intangible cultural heritage.

Help enrich the theoretical system of emotional design. Emotional design emphasizes the emotional connection between products and users. This study focuses on the emotional expression and cultural connotation of Gannan Tea-picking Opera, explores how to realize the deep emotional interaction between users and products through intelligent technology, and injects new cultural elements and application cases into the theoretical system of emotional design.

Practical level: enhance the user experience of cultural and creative products. Traditional cultural and creative products often lack interactivity and interest, making it difficult to attract young users. Emotionally interactive intelligent cultural and creative products design, through Virtual Reality/Augmented Reality, voice recognition and other technologies, creates an immersive and interactive user experience, and enhances the user's interest in and knowledge of the Gannan Tea-picking Opera.

Promote the development of cultural and creative products industries. Emotionally interactive intelligent cultural and creative products design aims to combine traditional culture with modern technology, develop cultural and creative products with market competitiveness, promote the development of cultural and creative products industries in Gannan, and help rural revitalization.

Social level: enhance cultural confidence and promote cultural identity. Emotionally interactive intelligent cultural and creative products design to show the charm of Gannan Tea-picking Opera in a more vivid and vivid way, enhance people's sense of identity and pride in traditional culture, and strengthen cultural self-confidence, as well as promote the development of the industry [3].

Promote cultural exchange and enhance cultural soft power. Emotionally interactive intelligent cultural and creative products, which can transcend the limitations of language and geography, become an important carrier for the dissemination of excellent traditional Chinese culture, promote communication and understanding between different cultures, and enhance the soft power of national culture.

Overall, the research on emotionally interactive intelligent cultural and creative products design of Gannan Tea-picking Opera not only has important theoretical value, but also has far-reaching practical significance and social impact. It will provide new ideas and impetus for the inheritance of non-genetic heritage, the development of cultural and creative products industries, and the construction of cultural self-confidence.

2 Research Status in China and Globally

2.1 Domestic Research Status in China

In recent years, the domestic emotional interaction technology has developed rapidly and achieved remarkable results in both theoretical research and technical applications. For example, the Institute of Automation of the Chinese Academy of Sciences has developed emotion recognition algorithms based on deep learning, and has achieved a leading level in the fields of facial expression recognition and speech emotion recognition. The Future Laboratory of Tsinghua University is dedicated to the research of emotional interaction design, exploring the application of emotional computing in human-computer interaction, smart home and other fields.

In terms of the digital preservation of intangible cultural heritage, active exploration has also been carried out in China. For example, the Forbidden City Museum has launched the "Digital Forbidden City" project, which makes use of virtual reality, augmented reality and other technologies to digitally display the buildings and cultural relics of the Forbidden City. The Dunhuang Research Institute has developed the "Digital Dunhuang" platform, which allows users to browse high-definition images and three-dimensional models of Dunhuang murals online.

2.2 Global Research Status

Foreign research on emotional interaction technology started earlier, mainly focusing on emotional computing, emotion recognition, emotion generation and other aspects.

For example, Donald A. Norman, a famous cognitive psychologist in the United States, has an important three-level theory on the emotional design of products, and he believes that product functionality should not be a simple stack of functions, but needs to have an emotional delivery [4]. Japan's Industrial Technology Research Institute has developed an emotion recognition system based on facial expressions and speech, and applied it to robotics, virtual reality and other fields. In terms of digital protection of cultural heritage, many explorations have also been conducted abroad. For example, the EU's "Digital Cultural Heritage" project uses virtual reality, augmented reality and other technologies to digitally preserve and display European cultural heritage. The Metropolitan Museum of Art of the United States has launched an application based on Augmented Reality (AR) technology, which allows users to scan cultural relics through cell phones, obtain relevant information and experience interactive games.

2.3 Development Trends

In the future, emotion interaction technology will develop in the direction of more intelligent, personalized and natural. For example, emotion recognition technology will be more accurate, able to recognize more subtle emotional changes; emotion generation technology will be more natural, able to generate content more in line with the expression of human emotions; emotional interaction methods will be more diverse, able to meet the needs of different users [5].

In the digital protection of cultural heritage, more attention will be paid to user experience and interactivity in the future. For example, virtual reality, augmented reality and other technologies will be used to create an immersive cultural experience; artificial intelligence technology will be used to develop personalized cultural recommendation systems; and social media platforms will be used to promote cultural exchange and dissemination.

3 Overview of Gannan Tea-Picking Opera

3.1 Historical Origins

Gannan Tea-picking Opera originated in ancient China at the end of the Ming Dynasty and the beginning of the Qing Dynasty, and it is a form of folk opera created by the tea farmers in Gannan region of China during their labor life. It began as a tea song sung by tea farmers during tea picking, and later gradually integrated folk dance, acrobatics and other art forms to form a unique opera performance. After hundreds of years of development, Gannan Tea-picking Opera has continuously absorbed the advantages of other types of operas, enriched its own performance form and content, and become one of the most representative cultural symbols of the Gannan region of China.

3.2 Artistic Features

Gannan Tea Casting Opera is famous for its unique "three wonders". The "three wonders" are "wondrous cavity, wondrous tune and wondrous performance", and the "three extras" are "short step", "fan flower" and "single sleeve". Its singing is beautiful and melodious, with rich and varied melodies and strong local characteristics. The performance form is lively and funny, with exaggerated and humorous movements, full of life. The actors and actresses vividly show the local customs and life stories of Gannan region through their exquisite skills, which are loved by local people [6].

3.3 Existing Situation

Gannan Tea-picking Opera has a long history and various forms of expression, but many of the content of the interpretation is not updated and adjusted with The Times, coupled with the impact of modern cultural aesthetics and scientific and technological trends, which makes the continuation and development of Gannan Tea-picking Opera face severe challenges. On the other hand, although there are many cultural and creative products designed around Gannan Tea-picking Opera in today's market, most of them are single in form, stereotyped in design, do not have outstanding functional characteristics, and the audience's evaluation is generally not high, resulting in such derivative products in many cases cannot provide help for the publicity and development of Gannan Tea-picking Opera.

4 Emotional Interaction Techniques

4.1 Technical Principles

Emotional interaction technology is a multidisciplinary technology based on artificial intelligence, psychology, human-computer interaction and other interdisciplinary technologies. It empowers products through modern electronic technology, digital media technology, etc., so that the product itself no longer only has simple, superficial content, but also contains human-computer interaction design content with rich cultural characteristics and emotional infectivity, which can provide users with experiences from multiple directions such as visual, auditory, and olfactory, and can have a high degree of user adaptability [7].

4.2 Technological Development History

As early as in the 80 s of last century, the world related fields have begun to study the emotional interaction technology, but at that time more technical research was mainly focused on human and basic interaction tools. With the development of computer technology and Internet technology, emotion recognition and sensing technology has also been improved, until the gradual popularization of artificial intelligence technology in recent years, the emotional interaction technology is met with the opportunity to ride on the "fast lane", the emotional recognition of this technology has become richer, and the intelligent attributes of human-computer interaction have become increasingly The emotional recognition of this technology has become richer, and its intelligent attributes of human-computer interaction have also become stronger.

4.3   Application Status in Cultural and Creative Products Design

At present, the application of emotional interaction technology in the field of cultural and creative products design is gradually increasing. Some museums have developed intelligent guiding systems using emotional interaction technology, which can provide personalized guiding services according to visitors' interests and emotional states; some cultural creative products incorporate emotional interaction functions, such as smart toys and interactive books, which enhance the fun and attractiveness of the products through emotional interaction with users [8]. However, in the field of traditional culture, the application of emotional interaction technology is still relatively small, especially in the opera culture, there is still a lot of space for exploration.

5   Intelligent Cultural and Creative Products Design Method of Gannan Tea-Picking Opera Based on Emotional Interaction

5.1   Analysis of Similar Products

First of all, it is necessary to refine the situation of cultural and creative products related to Gannan tea plucking opera in today's market. Define the form of products with better sales and higher popularity, determine the scientific and correct design direction, and pave the way for the subsequent transformation and promotion.

5.2   Emotional Element Extraction

Through in-depth analysis of the script, singing and performance movements [9] of Gannan Tea-picking Opera, the emotional elements contained therein are extracted. For example, emotions such as cheerfulness, sadness and excitement are analyzed from the rhythm and melody of the singing; emotions such as liveliness, composure and anger are extracted from the amplitude and strength of the performing movements. At the same time, combined with the history, culture and folklore of Gannan region, the emotional connotations related to Gannan Tea-picking Opera are mined out to provide rich emotional materials for the subsequent cultural and creative products design.

5.3   Design Process

First, based on the extracted emotional elements, the design theme and target user groups of the cultural and creative products are determined. Then, the emotional interaction technology is applied to design the interaction mode and function of the product. For example, to design an intelligent music player based on Gannan Tea-picking Opera, users can interact with the player by touching the screen, voice commands, etc. The player plays the corresponding music of Gannan Tea-picking Opera according to the user's emotional state, and provides relevant cultural introduction and plot interpretation. In the design process, the user experience is fully considered, focusing on the ease of use and interest of the product. Finally, the design is optimized and improved through user testing and feedback.

5.4 Division of Labor in the Design Process

For design research in the category of cultural and creative products, a number of design modules from shape, pattern and internal structure will be involved, so the division of labor in the team needs to be discussed before the design work is formally carried out. In this design study, the design practice was carried out according to the design work that each team member specializes in, which ensured the smooth progress of the design. It is worth mentioning that the division of labor does not mean that the members are completely limited to their assigned work, but will participate in each other's work assessment as appropriate to stabilize the design quality.

6 Design Practice

6.1 Intelligent Opera Dolls

In this research, an intelligent opera doll of Gannan Tea-picking Opera with emotional interaction function is designed. The doll is built-in with various sensors, which can sense the user's actions such as touching and shaking, and make corresponding expressions and sound feedback according to the user's actions. For example, when the user gently touches the doll, the doll will show a happy expression and play a piece of cheerful Gannan Tea-picking Opera music; when the user shakes the doll, the doll will show a surprised expression and tell a short story about Gannan Tea-picking Opera. Through this kind of emotional interaction, it increases the interactivity and fun between the user and the doll, and allows the user to know more about the culture of Gannan Tea-picking Opera. In addition to the typical attributes of emerging technologies, there are several key features.

Classic image reproduction: Based on the classic opera characters, the doll exquisitely restores the costumes and makeup of the real opera characters, with the opera singing, teaching and inheriting the culture of opera.

Personalized Settings: Supporting the user to customize the specific appearance of the character, as well as the embedded opera chorus, the doll can create unique opera dolls for the user to meet the user's personalized needs.

Space decoration effect: dolls elegant, beautiful appearance makes it also has the effect of decorating a specific living space, with chic aesthetic connotation.

6.2 Virtual Reality (VR) Opera Experience

Utilizing virtual reality (VR) technology, this study also developed a virtual reality experience product for the Gannan Tea-picking Opera. After wearing the VR device, the user can be like being in the performance scene of Gannan Tea-picking Opera, and can watch the performance of the actors up close and interact with them. At the same time, the system adjusts the performance content and atmosphere according to the user's emotional state through emotional interaction technology. For example, when the user shows love for a certain character, the system will increase the role of the character; when the user feels nervous, the system will adjust the rhythm of the play appropriately, so that the user can enjoy the opera experience more easily. On the other hand, incorporating VR technology into the mix has other positive effects, such as the following two.

Breaking the new technology age fault: VR technology in many cases in the past will be synonymous with young people, but the integration of VR technology, can naturally promote this technology to more middle-aged and elderly people to experience, feel the charm of this new technology.

Contribute to the development of the VR industry: more people's participation means that the corresponding industry can accelerate the pace of industrial development, which is of significant value to the continuous progress of virtual reality technology.

6.3 Augmented Reality (AR) Scene Feeling

In addition to the above two kinds of cultural creations, this research also sets up AR contents that can be generated by scanning QR codes through technical means. Users can thus intuitively and conveniently experience the vivid scenes of the performance moments of the Gannan Tea-picking Opera, and as the user swings the camera, the content of the scene will change, and the elements therein can be differentiated according to the user's real-time scene characteristics. The additional positive effects that AR can bring are similar to VR, and both are effective ideas for proliferating emerging technologies.

6.4 Overall Integration and Optimization

Although the above three cultural and creative products practices are designed around the main body of the Gannan Tea-picking Opera, but their respective appearance style is somewhat different, taking into account the results of the transformation of a harmonious sense of view, in the completion of the three intelligent cultural and creative products designs of their respective monolithic design, their appearance of a unified "re-design", resulting in a series of products. After completing the individual design of the three intelligent cultural creations, their appearance was unified and "redesigned" to form a series.

6.5 Discussion After the Main Design

After the main design study, the team conducted a professional discussion within the team to explore the specific methods and strategies of product application, as well as to make a preliminary assessment and prediction of the audience's experiential effect and feedback. The team also made preliminary evaluation and prediction of the audience's experience and feedback, and made advance plans and preparations around several possible states.

7 User Research and Feedback

7.1 User Research Methodology

This study creates design research mainly using a combination of questionnaire survey and user interviews to conduct user research on the designed intelligent cultural and creative products products. The questionnaire survey mainly collects users' satisfaction with the product appearance, functions, interactive experience, etc.; the user interviews deeply understand the users' experience of using the product, their cognition and attitudes towards the culture of Gannan Tea-picking Opera, as well as their suggestions for the improvement of the product (as shown in Table 1), and the audience covered by the research includes both teenagers and middle-aged and old people.

Table 1. Visual chart of survey methods.

Survey channels	Survey types
Online/PC, Mobile phone, etc	Questionnaire procedure
Offline/face to face	Q&a or interview

7.2 User Research Process

In the online user research process, the system collected a lot of effective data, but in this process, it is inevitable that some interfering information or invalid data (such as the user did not fill out the completion of the situation) generated, therefore, effective screening is also one of the key actions of this research.

Offline, the research team chose face-to-face communication with users based on objective conditions, and in this process, the team avoided the negative influence of various third parties, and obtained direct and objective feedback from users through rigorous Q&A design and communication.

7.3 User Research Results

The results of the research show that most of the users showed strong interest in the intelligent cultural and creative products of Gannan Tea-picking Opera based on emotional interaction. They think that these products not only have novel design and interesting interactive functions, but also enable them to understand and feel the culture of Gannan Tea-picking Opera more intuitively. At the same time, users also put forward some improvement suggestions, such as further optimizing the interactive experience of the products and adding more cultural contents.

8 Conclusions

8.1 Summary of Research Results

This research successfully applies emotional interaction technology to the intelligent cultural and creative products design of Gannan Tea-picking Opera, and verifies the effectiveness of the method in enhancing the cultural connotation and user experience of the cultural and creative products through a series of design practices and user research. The developed intelligent opera dolls and virtual reality opera experience products provide new carriers and ways for the inheritance and development of Gannan Tea-picking Opera, attracting more young groups to pay attention to traditional culture.

8.2   Directions for Future Research

Future research can further dig deeper into the cultural connotation of Gannan Tea Casting Opera and expand the application scenarios of emotional interaction technology in cultural and creative products design. For example, developing intelligent educational products based on Gannan Tea-picking Opera for opera teaching and cultural inheritance; exploring the integration of emotional interaction technology with other emerging technologies [10] (e.g., block-chain, multi-sensory synchronization, etc.) to provide more possibilities for the innovative development of Gannan Tea-picking Opera. At the same time, we will strengthen the cooperation with the cultural industry, transform the research results into actual commercial products, and promote the development of the cultural industry of Gannan Tea-picking Opera.

8.3   Research Reflection

Gannan Tea-picking Opera, as a Chinese local characteristic opera, its unique singing voice, performance method and dialect dialogues are difficult to be presented by some common designs in the past, and its cultural connotation and spiritual kernel, such as Hakka people's wisdom of life and aesthetic interests, need to be deeply excavated and precisely expressed in order to avoid the cultural and creative products products from flowing into superficial forms. Finally, how to balance tradition and innovation, retaining the original flavor of the Tea Casting Opera while giving it a contemporary flavor [11], is a consideration that has been carried out throughout the design research process.

From the final result, the affective intelligence technology applied in this study provides new possibilities for the dissemination and promotion of the Tea Casting Opera. For example, the use of audio-visual experience/VR/AR technology to create an immersive viewing experience allows the audience to immerse themselves in the charm of the tea-picking opera, which clearly improves the user experience and provides a good idea for the creative transformation and innovative development of a host of excellent traditional Chinese cultures in the context of the technological era.

However, there are many types of Chinese excellent traditional culture, in the process of scientific and technologically innovative development around the designated main body also need to pay attention to the adaptability [12], to avoid rigidity.

References

1. Liu, Y.: Exploration on the inheritance status of Gannan tea-picking opera. Drama House. **06**, 24–26 (2024)
2. Li, Z.: Research on cultural and creative products design based on emotional design concept. Toy World. **11**, 127–129 (2024)
3. Liu, S., Liu, B., Chen, X.: Introduction to the emotional expression of cultural and creative product design. Footwear Craft Design. **4**(21), 169–171 (2024)
4. Juncheng, G.: Research on Cultural and Creative Product Design of IP Image of Gannan Tea-Picking Opera Characters. Gannan Normal University (2021). https://doi.org/10.27685/d.cnki.ggnsf.2021.000076
5. Jin, Y., Gao, H., Wang, J.: Research on the design of Jilin ice and snow cultural and creative products under the concept of emotion. Art Design. **7**(3) (2024)

6. Cao, X.: Research on emotional design strategy of cultural and creative products of Gannan tea-picking opera. Beauty Times. **09**, 49–53 (2024). https://doi.org/10.16129/j.cnki.mysds.2024.09.008
7. Tina, B., et al.: Exploring the importance of a usable and emotional product design from the user's perspective. Ergonomics. **66**(5), 11–12 (2022)
8. Siwang, Z.: Application research of emotional design in modern product design Institute of Management Science and Industrial Engineering. Proceedings of 2019 International Conference on Art Design,Music and Culture(ADMC 2019). College of Art, Northwest University; 2019:4. https://doi.org/10.26914/c.cnkihy.2019.037815.
9. Yang, Y.: Development and inheritance of vocal art of Gannan tea-picking opera in "internet+". Culture Indus. **22**, 63–64 (2021)
10. Wang, Y.: Research on interactive creative design of new media products. Daguan. **11**, 85–87 (2024)
11. Wang, Y.: Research on the innovation and development of Gannan tea-picking opera under the background of new media. Art Appreciation. **29**, 60–63 (2023)
12. Wang, X.: Localized adaptation and innovative strategies of performing arts in intercultural theatre exchange. Drama House. **36**, 32–34 (2024)

Bridging Tradition and Innovation: Using Artistic Genes to Assess Cultural Authenticity in Digital Shadow Play

Chenming Lin[1]($\boxtimes$), Guobin Xia[1], Farnaz Nickpour[1], and Yinshan Chen[2]

[1] School of Engineering, University of Liverpool, Liverpool, UK
{chenming.lin,Guobin.xia,Farnaz.Nickpour}@liverpool.ac.uk
[2] Faculty of Creative Art, Universiti Malaya, Kuala Lumpur, Malaysia
s2043014@siswa.um.edu.my

Abstract. In the digital age, computer technology is increasingly being used to promote and disseminate cultural heritage. Contemporary applications enable public access to these traditions through modern exhibition technologies in museums and interactive digital platforms, allowing audiences to experience cultural heritage via multisensory engagement and immersive experiences. However, there is currently no effective method to assess the extent to which these museums and digital applications preserve the cultural authenticity of artistic heritage. This study constructs an "artistic gene" for Chinese shadow puppetry, grounded in meme theory, drawing from literature descriptions and field research conducted in museums. This framework not only identifies the core artistic elements of shadow puppetry but also serves as an evaluation model. The Findings indicate that contemporary museum exhibitions and digital applications related to shadow puppetry tend to focus primarily on the tangible art of shadow puppets, such as exquisite leather and paper artifacts, while overlooking the unique artistic expression of light and shadow. This study aims to explore how to bridge the gap between traditional artistic authenticity and digital innovation, thereby emphasizing the positive impact of integrating digital technologies on audience experience while preserving cultural authenticity.

Keywords: Keyword: Digital heritage · Shadow puppetry · Cultural authenticity · Immersive experiences · Artistic gene

1 Introduction

Digital techniques have significantly transformed the preservation, interpretation, and dissemination of cultural heritage. The integration of advanced technologies such as 3D modeling, virtual reality (VR), augmented reality (AR), mixed reality (MR) and digital storytelling has enhanced the ways in which cultural heritage is experienced and understood by the public [1]. These technologies not only offer new possibilities for the digital preservation of endangered cultural heritage, but also open up innovative avenues

M. Schrepp and M. Rauterberg (Eds.): HCII 2025, LNCS 16342, pp. 213–232, 2026.
https://doi.org/10.1007/978-3-032-13164-5_14

for the dissemination and promotion of traditional culture in contemporary society. Significant progress has been made in applying digital technologies to cultural heritage preservation, particularly in the digital conservation of tangible heritage such as historic buildings and artifacts [1]. 3D reconstruction techniques, such as 3D scanning and digital modeling, have become essential tools in heritage management, allowing for the preservation of archaeological sites and artifacts [2]. For example, in the virtual restoration of statues, high-precision three-dimensional data are acquired by combining laser scanning with articulated-arm scanning. Subsequently, a multi-scale analysis, encompassing both global symmetry and local skeletal features, is employed to determine the geometry and dimensions of missing components. This information is then used in commercial software such as Geomagic for 3D stitching and surface reconstruction, resulting in an accurate digital restoration of damaged sects [3]. It provides a feasible foundation and technical support for the preservation of cultural relics, overcoming the limitations of traditional restoration methods that rely solely on subjective judgment. Similarly, 3D digital technology complements traditional restoration techniques by providing detailed and accurate digital representations of artifacts. The integration of 3D printing with 3D digital reconstruction technology enables the creation of high-precision artifact replicas [4]. By using replicas instead of the original artifacts, physical contact is minimized, preventing secondary damage. This approach ensures the production of accurate digital replicas, supporting long-term preservation, research, and exhibition, while demonstrating a sustainable method for cultural heritage conservation. In a word, the utilization of high-precision 3D scanning and digital modeling technologies is crucial for the accurate restoration of tangible cultural artifacts. These methods not only enhance the restoration process but also contribute to the establishment of reliable digital archives, supporting ongoing research and education in the field of tangible cultural heritage.

However, when digital technology is applied to the field of intangible cultural heritage (ICH), focusing solely on its material aspects reveals a lack of cultural authenticity. Unlike tangible cultural heritage, which can be easily quantified and preserved through physical means, ICH requires a nuanced understanding of its intangible elements, which are often deeply embedded in the social fabric of communities [5, 6]. Existing digital practices indicate an overemphasis on visual representation in technological applications [1]. This may lead to oversimplification or distortion of heritage elements, as the process focuses on tangible aspects while omitting the embodied experiences, social interactions, and rituals associated with the heritage [7]. Reducing heritage to scanned models and 3D representations risks detaching it from its ritualistic and social significance, particularly in cultures where oral traditions and embodied experiences define authenticity [7]. This raises critical questions about the authenticity of digital representations, as they may lack the lived experiences and cultural narratives that are integral to the heritage they depict. For example, the value of African cultural heritage may derive from its social function or ritual significance rather than the physical entity itself. If digitization merely replicates the object's form while stripping away its cultural context such as ritual participation or oral traditions the digital surrogate will lose its inherent meaning [8]. Moreover, while the nomination of the Cultural Landscape of Bali emphasizes the spiritual connection between local communities and rice field temples, in many other cases, intangible heritage, such as oral traditions and rituals, has not been systematically recorded or integrated into digital frameworks. As a result, digital heritage projects often isolate cultural heritage from its lived context, making it difficult to convey the complexity of cultural narratives [8].

Taking traditional Chinese shadow puppetry as an example, this intangible cultural heritage, which integrates folk art, music, and literature, faces unique challenges in the digitization process. Many researchers are exploring the integration of digital technology, allowing audiences to experience shadow puppetry in a sensory and immersive manner [9–11]. For example, Augmented Reality (AR) technology can enhance traditional shadow puppetry by increasing audience engagement and accessibility [9]. A comparative study, where participants watched both traditional shadow play and an AR-enhanced version, found that AR technology improved audience appreciation and comprehension, especially among younger viewers. This suggests that AR-based digital interaction can bridge generational gaps, attract modern audiences, and preserve traditional storytelling elements. Additionally, a Virtual Reality (VR) system can replicate traditional shadow puppetry performance techniques [10]. Unlike conventional digitization methods that focus solely on visual aesthetics, this system emphasizes non-intuitive embodied interactions, simulating the multi-point manipulation and indirect control inherent in traditional puppetry. The study found that immersive VR environments help users develop a deeper understanding of puppet control mechanisms, preserving not only the visual aspects of shadow play but also its artistic techniques and performative complexity. Furthermore, the eShadow+ mixed reality storytelling project integrates mixed reality and projection mapping with traditional shadow puppetry to create interactive storytelling experiences [11]. This platform enables users to design digital puppets, develop narrative scripts, and participate in interactive performances. By combining traditional artistic methods with digital tools, eShadow+ provides a dynamic and immersive learning environment, making shadow puppetry more accessible while retaining its cultural significance. All three studies demonstrate how AR, VR, and mixed reality technologies can enhance shadow puppetry by making it more immersive, interactive, and engaging. These digital approaches preserve traditional techniques while adapting them for modern audiences, ensuring that shadow puppetry remains a relevant and educational art form in the digital age. However, there are no effective methods to evaluate the extent to which these museums and digital applications preserve the cultural authenticity of art heritage. Although these technologies can successfully recreate the visual style of its material aspects, they often overlook and compromise the intricate control, performance details [10], and uniquely expressive artistic forms that distinguish it from other traditional theatrical performances. This form-over-substance approach to digitization may cause shadow puppetry to lose its cultural essence in digital representation, reducing it to a hollow visual display.

To address this challenge, this study introduces Meme Theory as a theoretical framework, aiming to systematically analyze the core elements of intangible cultural heritage by identifying and extracting Cultural Genes. Meme Theory suggests that cultural elements, like genes, can self-replicate and spread, allowing us to identify the most resilient cultural traits throughout the process of heritage transmission [12]. By analyzing these cultural genes, we can more accurately capture the essential characteristics of cultural heritage. This theoretical perspective not only helps determine which core elements should be preserved and emphasized in the digitization process but also provides new insights for the design and evaluation of digital technology applications.

2   Theoretical Background

Meme theory, a field that studies how cultural information spreads and evolves, akin to biological evolution [13]. It is a concept introduced by Richard Dawkins in his seminal work "The Selfish Gene", posits that cultural elements, or "memes", propagate through imitation and replication, akin to biological genes in evolution, and thus serve as the fundamental units of cultural transmission [12]. In the study of traditional Chinese culture, cultural genes (memes) are regarded as the fundamental factors determining the inheritance and transformation of cultural systems, as they constitute both the stability and adaptability mechanisms of cultural forms [14]. The uninterrupted development of Chinese civilization over thousands of years is largely attributed to the continuous optimization and reconfiguration of its cultural genes. Therefore, we can draw inspiration from biological concepts and meme concepts to identify and extract the artistic genes inherent in shadow puppetry.

2.1   Biological Concepts

Regarding biological concepts, the first is Darwin's concept of "natural selection", through which beneficial traits are passed down across generations. Drawing on Darwin's concept of "natural selection", we identify the artistic elements in shadow puppetry that have persisted through variation, selection, and inheritance over time. The other biological concept is the "RNA reverse transcription" concept (see Fig. 1) The genetic information of biological genes is controlled by DNA, which is transcribed into RNA and then translated into proteins, a process known as "gene expression". Conversely, if RNA is known, under the action of reverse transcriptase, DNA can be synthesized through reverse transcription, thus obtaining the biological gene. inspired by this concept, cultural representations and evidence can undergo a "reverse expression" process, akin to reverse transcription and back-translation, allowing for the extraction of cultural factors and the identification of cultural genes.

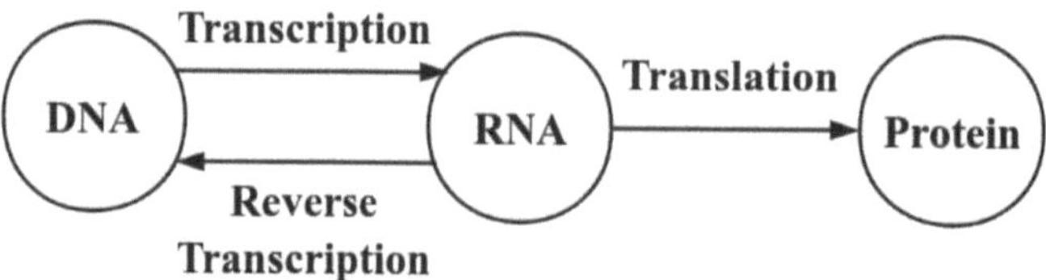

Fig. 1. Sketch map of RNA reverse transcription.

2.2 Memes Concepts

Regarding meme concepts, the concept of "strong memes" and "selective pressure" from meme theory is used to identify and extract core memes. Strong memes are characterized by their high fidelity, fecundity, and longevity, which contribute to their superior vitality and success in cultural transmission compared to weak memes [15]. For instance, A study on the protection of rural culture in China emphasizes a meme-driven strategy that identifies and extracts "folk rituals" as "strong memes" to incorporate into tourism experiences [16]. By leveraging the characteristics of strong memes, this approach aligns them with modern values without eroding core traditions, thereby enhancing both visibility and authenticity. This strategy underscores the importance of integrating traditional cultural elements into contemporary contexts, ensuring that cultural heritage remains relevant and engaging to modern audiences while preserving its authentic essence. Additionally, meme theory emphasizes the role of "selection pressures", where only culturally significant and contextually adaptable practices survive [15]. Selective pressure helps explain which cultural "memes" (i.e., units of cultural transmission) gain stronger survival ability and avoid being eliminated, and which ones may disappear during the process of cultural transmission. For example, by selectively extracting and applying design elements with unique intrinsic cultural value, the protection of traditional Liangshan Yi clothing can be effectively achieved [17]. This includes incorporating elements like the headscarf and lotus hat of Yi women in product designs and fully considering the Yi people's preference for black in color schemes. This approach is aimed at ensuring that only those design elements with unique intrinsic cultural value are prioritized, helping to avoid excessive commercialization of the product designs.

3 Research Design

This study employs a mixed-methods approach, comprising three main phases: literature analysis, field investigation, and multimodal discourse analysis. First, base on meme theory, a literature review was conducted to identify and summarize eight preliminary "artistic genes" of Chinese shadow play, focusing on historical development, artistic styles, and core characteristics (as shown in see Fig. 2). Second, field investigations were carried out at four museums, where exhibit photographs and exhibition texts were collected as multimodal data sources. Subsequently, multimodal discourse analysis was employed to validate and refine the proposed "artistic genes". Employing NVivo software, exhibition texts were analyzed and compared with the identified artistic genes for refinement and optimization. This comprehensive approach ensures both the reliability of the "artistic gene" framework and the academic rigor of the study.

3.1 Literature Analysis

This study selects "Art History of Chinese Shadow Puppetry" as one of the core references. The book is authored by the renowned scholar Liqun Wei and published by Cultural Relics Press [18]. Professor Wei, a member of the Expert Committee on the Protection of National Intangible Cultural Heritage of China and the Director of the

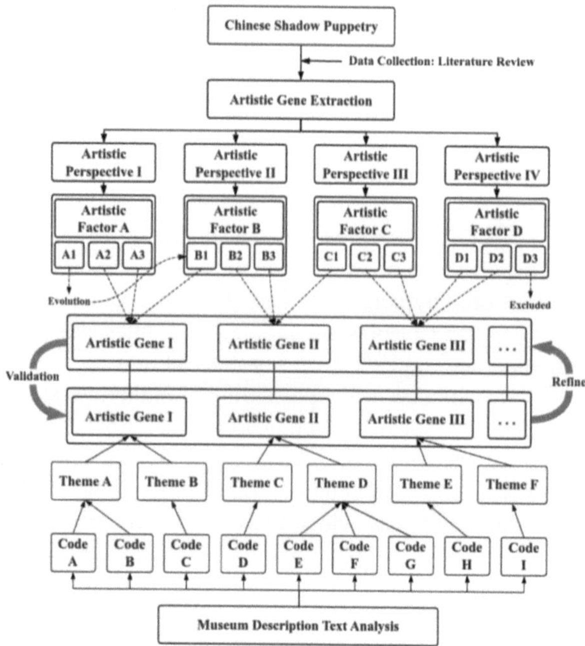

Fig. 2. Flowchart for Extracting the Artistic Genes of Chinese Shadow Puppetry.

Shadow Puppetry Art Committee of the China Folk Literature and Art Association, has dedicated over two decades to field investigations and theoretical construction of shadow puppet art, providing rich and rigorous academic achievements in the field [19]. Established in 1957 under the direct administration of the State Administration of Cultural Heritage, Cultural Relics Press is the only press dedicated to publishing archaeology-related books and audio materials. It is committed to salvaging and protecting China's cultural heritage and publicizing the content and artistic charm of traditional Chinese culture. Over the past 65 years, it has published about 10,000 kinds of books on culture and archaeology, striving to be "high-end, innovative, and refined". Its publications on traditional Chinese culture are well received across the world and are often given by state leaders as national gifts [20]. Therefore, this book not only constructs a systematic framework for the history of Chinese shadow puppet art theoretically but also provides solid literary support for this research.

In the course of studying the historical development of shadow play, we were inspired by Darwin's theory of "natural selection", which suggests that in the struggle for survival, the fittest organisms survive while the less adaptable ones are eliminated. This concept has guided our exploration into how shadow play, as a traditional art form, has evolved and adapted over time. To keep up with the progress of the era, shadow puppetry has undergone a series of transformations and innovations. By examining the historical development of shadow art from 960 to 2005 [18]. The earliest recorded history of shadow play dates back to the Song Dynasty (960 AD). From its origins as a narrative performance for religious purposes, traditional shadow puppetry gradually separated from religious texts and became a medium for storytelling, often conveying historical tales and folk legends. Its performance style evolved from purely narrative singing to incorporating melodies influenced by Chinese opera. Over time, shadow puppetry transformed into a specialized profession, with dedicated troupes and artisans specifically trained in creating shadow puppets. In the years following, especially during the Anti-Japanese War, shadow puppetry experienced a series of innovations. For instance, the characters in shadow puppetry no longer only depicted historical or mythological figures but began to feature characters in modern attire. The performances incorporated sound and light effects, such as gunshots and explosions, breaking the tradition of using a single light source. The repertoire began to reflect contemporary themes, transcending historical stories to include government propaganda content. Another significant milestone occurred in 1955 and 1960 during the nationwide observation and performance events for puppet theater and shadow puppetry. Many troupes embraced liberal thinking and boldly introduced artistic innovations. Modern plays and children's theater were incorporated into the storylines, increasing their appeal to audiences. In terms of vocal style, the emergence of animal plays with no singing style marked a departure from the traditional use of dialects and specific vocal tones, which had limited their audience. The introduction of animal plays expanded shadow puppetry beyond regional constraints, broadening its reach. Additionally, more advanced stage effects, including sound and light, further improved the quality of performances. By the 1960s and 1970s, shadow puppetry, like many traditional art forms, faced suppression during the Cultural Revolution, yet by the 1980s, it began to recover. The art form adopted modern themes, incorporating contemporary social issues into its repertoire and increasingly using advanced stage technologies such as lighting, sound effects, and multimedia projections. By the 1990s, shadow puppetry received significant attention for its preservation and was listed as part of China's intangible cultural heritage. This period saw the internationalization of shadow puppetry, with performances showcased at global art festivals. Entering the 21st century, shadow puppetry continued to evolve by integrating digital technologies, such as 3D technology, virtual reality (VR), and interactive performances. These innovations breathed new life into traditional performances, ensuring the preservation and growth of shadow puppetry in the context of modern society. Through this continuous process of adaptation and innovation, shadow puppetry has not only maintained its artistic essence but has also embraced contemporary cultural developments, ensuring its place in the modern world.

3.2 Multimodal Discourse Analysis

A multimodal discourse analysis was conducted on the exhibition texts and photos collected from the museums (see as see Fig. 3). While literature and exhibition texts provide a comprehensive interpretation of shadow puppetry by authoritative institutions, it remains to be verified whether these exhibitions effectively focus on the core artistic "genes" of shadow puppetry during their actual execution.

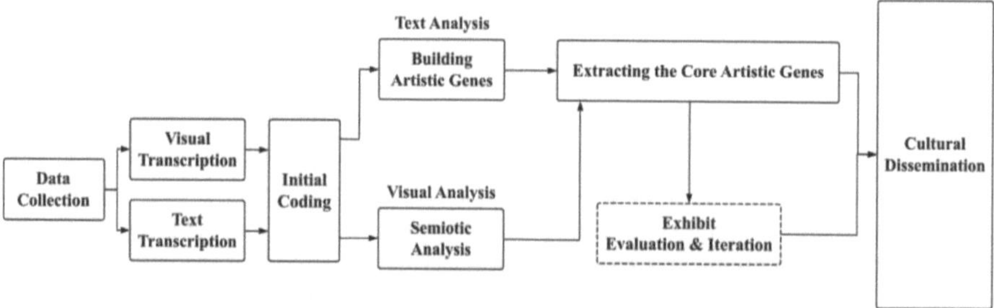

Fig. 3. Flowchart of multimodal discurse analysis

3.2.1 Data Collection

In selecting museums as research samples, we aimed to achieve broad coverage across various regions of China and different shadow puppet styles, while also considering their authority in interpreting and showcasing shadow puppetry. Finally, this study selected five museums renowned in the field of shadow play (as shwon in see Fig. 4), including: *Chengdu Museum, Guangdong Museum, Shanxi Shadow Puppetry and Puppet Art Museum, Xi'an Shadow Puppet Art Museum, Tangshan Museum.* These museum has made notable contributions to the preservation, research, and promotion of shadow puppetry, making them ideal for this study.

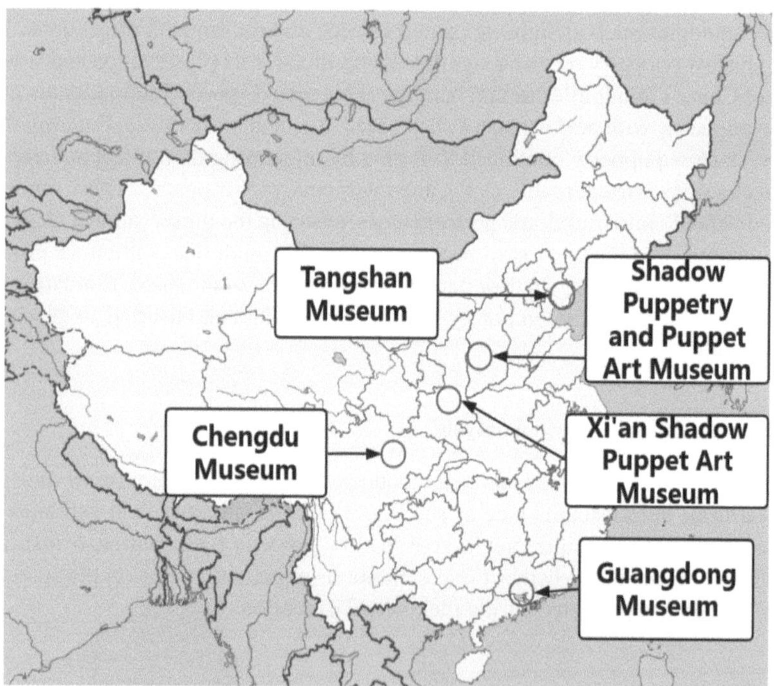

Fig. 4. The distribution map of museums for field research.

The *Chengdu Museum*, with its unparalleled collection of nearly 300,000 shadow puppets and marionettes from 30 provinces, stands as a world leader in terms of quantity, historical depth, and variety [21]. This extensive collection not only reflects the rich regional diversity of shadow puppetry across China but also offers a thorough representation of its artistic evolution. Such a vast and well-curated collection provides invaluable insights into the cultural and historical significance of shadow puppetry. Similarly, the *Guangdong Museum*, which co-organized the exhibition "China in Shadow Puppetry", plays a crucial role in showcasing the diverse styles of shadow puppetry across China [22]. The exhibition, which features over 300 pieces from 20 provinces, offers a comprehensive view of how shadow puppetry has evolved regionally, making it a critical resource for understanding the wide-reaching impact of this art form. The *Shanxi Shadow Puppetry and Puppet Art Museum*, established as the first museum in China specifically dedicated to shadow puppetry, holds great authority as the primary institution for the study of this art form [23]. Its role as the first specialized museum enhances its credibility and makes it a key institution for scholarly research and preservation efforts in the field. The *Xi'an Shadow Puppet Art Museum* is particularly significant due to Xi'an's historical association with the origin of Chinese shadow puppetry. As the birthplace of this art form, Shaanxi province, and specifically Xi'an, holds considerable cultural and academic importance in shadow puppetry research [24]. The museum's establishment ensures that the traditions and innovations of the region are preserved and shared with both academic and public audiences. Finally, the *Tangshan Museum* is particularly noteworthy because of the city's fame for its shadow play performances [25]. With deep ties to local traditions and cultural heritage, the museum's collection offers a strong connection to the folk traditions of shadow puppetry in northern China, making it a vital part of understanding the regional specificity of this art form. Collectively, these museums are essential in representing the diverse geographical, historical, and artistic facets of Chinese shadow puppetry. Their authority in the field ensures that they can effectively interpret and preserve the cultural significance of shadow puppetry, making them indispensable for this study.

3.2.2 Data Transcription

In this study, the collected photographs related to shadow puppetry were transcribed and categorized based on whether they primarily contained textual descriptions of shadow puppetry. The data were divided into textual and visual (non-textual) categories. For the textual data, each character from the photographs was manually transcribed into a Word document, resulting in a total of 27,590 Chinese characters.

As for non-textual data, by applying semiotic theory, the meanings conveyed by photographs were transcribed into textual descriptions, enabling a deeper understanding of the exhibition's communicative strategies. Semiotics is the study of signs and their meaning-making processes, emphasizing how meaning is constructed within specific social and cultural contexts [26]. In museum studies, semiotic approaches are widely applied to analyze exhibition design, artifact display, and audience interaction, revealing the communication strategies and cultural intentions behind exhibitions. These methods, often influenced by theories of semiotics, provide a framework for uncovering the communication strategies behind exhibitions [27]. By interpreting how objects convey meaning through visual and textual cues, museums can enhance the educational impact of their exhibits and better convey cultural narratives.

3.2.3 Tools and Methods

Subsequently, these textual and non-textual data were imported into NVivo software for coding and thematic analysis. NVivo is a qualitative data analysis software that assists researchers in organizing, analyzing, and finding insights in unstructured data such as interviews, open-ended survey responses, and social media content [28]. One of the key features of NVivo is its ability to facilitate content analysis, which involves systematically categorizing and interpreting data to derive meaningful insights. This is particularly relevant when analyzing photographic data, as researchers can code images, annotate them, and link them to thematic categories or concepts within their research framework. Through NVivo, researchers are able to effectively manage large amounts of image, video, and text data, and perform comparative analysis by linking these with other themes in the study, such as social interactions and emotional expressions [29]. The study demonstrates that NVivo, when handling image data, not only helps in detailed coding of the images but also allows for the integration of these with other forms of qualitative data (such as interviews and documents), providing a more comprehensive perspective for data analysis. Using NVivo's visualization tools, researchers can quickly identify patterns and trends presented in the images, further uncovering their socio-cultural context and personal emotions. Therefore, the application of NVivo has provided a powerful tool for analyzing image data, helping researchers extract meaningful patterns and reveal the deeper meanings behind the images, thus offering a more precise analytical framework for qualitative research.

Multimodal discourse analysis, based on semiotic theory, is employed to examine how current museums present shadow puppetry objects. The three semiotic dimensions are used to analyze the exhibitions (as shown in see Fig. 5). In Peirce's semiotic theory, a sign consists of three interrelated components: the object, the representamen, and the interpretant [26]. Object refers to the entity or concept that the sign represents; Representamen is the physical form of the sign, the medium through which the sign is conveyed; Interpretant is the meaning or understanding that arises in the mind of the interpreter upon encountering the sign. It is the effect or response elicited by the sign in the interpreter's mind. These three components form what Peirce termed the "semiosis" process, the dynamic interaction through which signs convey meaning. In this process, the representamen refers to the object, leading to the generation of the interpretant, thereby completing the transmission of meaning. Specifically, this analysis investigates: (1) what content of shadow puppetry is showcased, (2) the methods or techniques used for presentation, and (3) the intended purpose behind displaying this content. By analyzing the combination of these semiotic elements, this phase will describe how museums currently present shadow puppetry and whether there are any gaps in representing its core artistic elements.

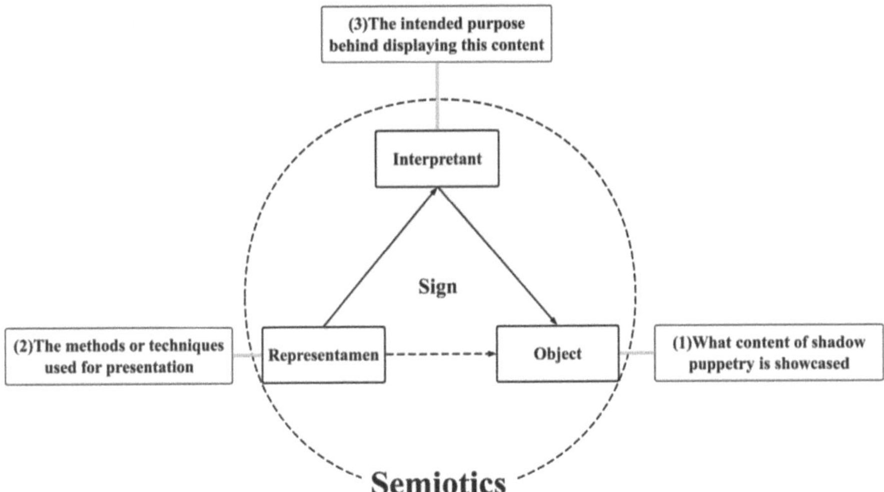

Fig. 5. Peirce's semiotics triangle theory—object, representamen, and interpretant.

3.2.4 Data Analysis

Based on the interpretation of the collected photograph data using semiotic theory, a classification of the content displayed in museums about shadow puppetry can be derived (shown as see Fig. 6). The exhibition content mainly covers the following aspects: first, there are 239 exhibits of character figures, highlighting the significant role of character imagery in shadow puppetry; secondly, there are 130 exhibits of other creatures, with 47 animals and 83 mythical beings, reflecting the rich biological and fantastical elements in shadow puppetry; lastly, there are 274 exhibits of props, primarily consisting of 243 decorative scenes and 31 handheld props, which play a key role in building the context and shaping the characters in shadow puppetry. Additionally, other artistic forms of shadow puppetry account for 70 exhibits, showcasing the visual diversity of shadow puppetry as an art form.

The classification of exhibition techniques in museums, based on the recorded 337 items, mainly includes the following forms: first, lightbox displays (shown as Fig. 7a) account for 208 items, demonstrating the widespread and effective application of this technology in exhibitions; second, digital screens or projectors (shown Fig. 7b) account for 31 items, reflecting the trend of museums utilizing modern technological means to enhance interactivity and dynamic effects in displays; third, display cabinets combined with physical objects and lighting(shown as Fig. 7c) account for 29 items, illustrating how the combination of physical displays and lighting is used to emphasize the details and atmosphere of the exhibits; finally, other types of exhibition techniques account for 31 items, highlighting the museum's exploration and practice of diverse exhibition forms.

Distribution of Exhibition Content in Museums

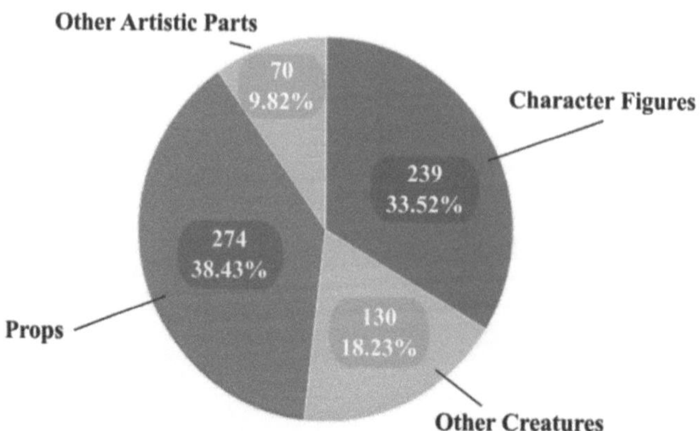

Fig. 6. Distribution of Exhibition Content in Museums.

Finally, based on the interpretation of the collected photograph data using semiotic theory, the exhibition purposes in the museums were categorized and encoded. A total of 323 exhibition purposes were recorded, which primarily include the following categories: First, "Rich in Form" accounts for 152 items, reflecting the museum's emphasis on the diversity of visual styles across different character categories, dynasties, and regions of shadow puppetry. This aims to create a sense of the richness in the distribution of shadow puppets as artworks across different dimensions of time and space for the audience. Second, "Exquisite Carving" accounts for 66 items, which meticulously showcases the intricate production techniques and artistic value of shadow puppetry. This aims to highlight the fine craftsmanship and the complexity of the aesthetic components in the puppets. Third, "Recreating Scenes" accounts for 64 items, reflecting how the museum reconfigures shadow puppets, characters, and props to restore scenes from the shadow play scripts. This not only enhances the audience's immersion and understanding, but also allows familiar stories to be easily recognized during the visit, thus increasing audience engagement and satisfaction. Lastly, other exhibition purposes account for 41 items, demonstrating the museum's diverse exploration of exhibition goals.

a. Light box from
Chengdu Museum

b. Digital screens from
Tangshan Museum

c. Display cabinets from
Chendu Museum

Fig. 7. Exhibition Techniques for Shadow Puppetry Exhibitions.

4 Findings and Discussion of Results

4.1 Artistic Genes of Shadow Puppetry

We traced the evolution of this art form and identified the core elements that have been preserved throughout its traditional and modern transformations. Based on this analysis, we have created Fig. 8 Similarly, through field investigations of authoritative museums, the verified and refined artistic genes of shadow puppetry have been identified. These artistic genes include (see Fig. 9): light and shadow, tangible arts, vocal, narrative, functionality, manipulation, and special effect.

4.1.1 Unique Gene

Influenced by the flourishing variety of folk performances, shadow play gradually developed by adopting elements from shadow games and puppet theater [18]. It used storytelling and narrative singing performances as the foundation, with paper-cut figures as shadow puppets, projected onto a window screen using light to cast shadows, thereby

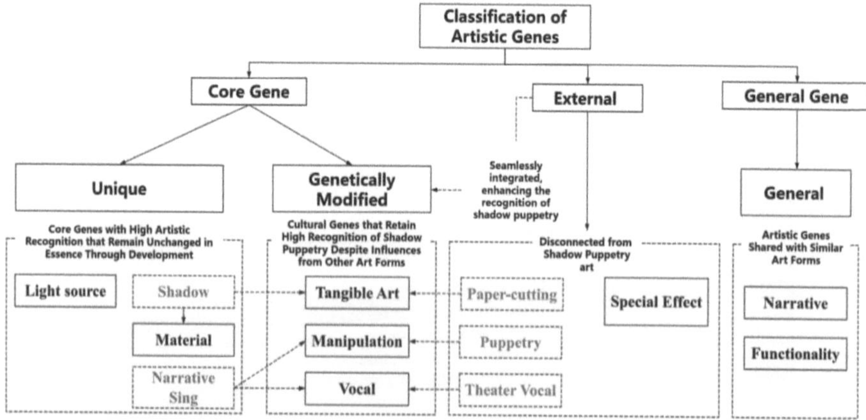

Fig. 8. Classification of artistic gene of Chinese shadow puppetry.

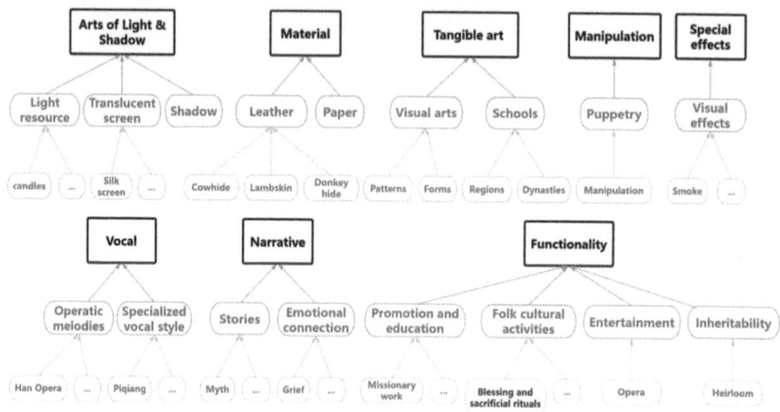

Fig. 9. Extracting artistic genes through textual analysis of museum descriptions.

gradually forming, and refining its unique style [18]. The distinctive artistic feature of shadow puppetry is projecting shadows with light onto a screen. It can identify its unique genes as the ***Light and Shadow*** and shadow itself. In subsequent artistic evolution, these shadows were presented using translucent ***materials***.

4.1.2 Light and Shadow

The evolution of light sources in shadow puppetry, from candlelight to oil lamps and modern electric lighting, illustrates how technological advancement can occur without altering the fundamental nature of an art form. While the energy sources powering these lights have transformed over time, the essential artistic principle remains unchanged: shadow puppetry's reliance on the interplay between light and shadow to create theatrical effects. This demonstrates that although modernization has innovated the means of illumination, it has not altered the art form's fundamental dependence on light sources for creating its characteristic shadow-play aesthetics.

4.1.3 Shadow Puppet Figures Material

The evolution of shadow puppet figures exemplifies a delicate balance between tradition and innovation in material selection. While artistic expressions have expanded over time, the essential characteristics of puppet construction have remained consistent: materials must be translucent and amenable to intricate cutting. This suggests that in the study and dissemination of shadow puppetry, emphasis should be placed on the art of light and shadow rather than on pictorial art.

4.2 Genetically Modified Gene

4.2.1 Tangible Arts

The imagery of shadow play originates from ancient Chinese leather carving and paper-cutting arts [18]. The early designs of shadow puppetry displayed a relative uniformity. However, through gradual development and changes after the Ming Dynasty, various regional styles of Chinese shadow puppetry emerged, each with distinctive aesthetic features that have since become widely recognizable aspects of the art form.

4.2.2 Vocal Performances

Vocal style is an essential artistic gene of this kind of operatic art form, and the absence of music diminishes the emotional depth of shadow puppetry [30]. The vocal styles in shadow puppetry have continually evolved over different historical periods. Unlike the *Performers*, which have become increasingly professionalized, the vocal components of shadow puppetry have progressively simplified; modern performances sometimes feature neither lyrics nor traditional operatic melodies. This evolution suggests that vocalization is not the core artistic element of shadow puppetry. In its early stages, shadow puppetry did not employ operatic singing styles but was primarily based on narrative singing. Later, it borrowed melodies from other operatic forms, which led to regional limitations in its dissemination due to the significant influence of local dialects on singing styles, thus restricting cross-regional transmission. Consequently, in modern times, certain operatic singing styles have been abandoned to enhance its widespread appeal and increase its ability to reach broader audiences.

4.2.3 Movement Manipulation

The control and performance techniques of traditional puppetry are key artistic genes in shadow puppetry. Its performance style is borrowed from traditional puppet theater, as the joints of shadow puppets are the same as those of puppets used in puppet theater [31]. In traditional shadow puppetry, control requires both multi-point manipulation and indirect control [10]. Multi-point manipulation allows the puppeteer to move multiple puppet joints simultaneously using control rods, while indirect control means that, due to the puppet's sideways positioning, the puppeteer's movements do not directly correspond to those of the puppet. Its performance style has largely persisted over time, with little change, still relying on joint rotation to perform movements. This animation technique has also influenced the development of modern animation; notably, Disney adapted shadow puppetry principles, incorporating the 12 principles of animation into commercial animation production [32].

4.3 General Gene

4.3.1 Narratives

The narrative repertoire of shadow puppetry has traditionally centered on Chinese religious stories, historical tales, mythological narratives, and classical literary adaptations. While recent decades have witnessed attempts to revitalize this traditional art form through the introduction of animal stories, contemporary dramas, and children's plays, the art form maintains strong ties to its religious origins. Notably, during certain historical periods, shadow puppetry served as a government propaganda tool, demonstrating its potential for social influence. However, despite this repertoire diversification, religious-themed performances continue to dominate live presentations. The art form faces significant challenges in contemporary society, particularly in attracting younger audiences who, immersed in modern media entertainment, rarely seek out traditional shadow puppet performances voluntarily.

4.3.2 Functionality

The true function of shadow puppetry performances has long been overshadowed by its narrative role. Behind its storytelling, shadow puppetry often conceals its performative purpose and functional roles. Shadow puppetry initially emerged as a medium for religious activities. Over time, it was embraced by the public, taking on an entertainment function. Recognizing its influence, the ruling class used it as a tool for moral instruction, and during certain periods, it even served as a means of government propaganda. However, as media have diversified over time, shadow puppetry has gradually lost much of its original function, now appearing primarily in religious or ritual contexts. To effectively promote shadow puppetry today and foster greater understanding and appreciation, it should not remain confined to the religious sphere. Instead, it should expand into more accessible domains such as entertainment and education to broaden its appeal and ensure its continued relevance.

4.4 External Gene

4.4.1 Special Effects

Stage performance is the aspect of shadow puppetry most significantly influenced by modern technology. The incorporation of advanced lighting and smoke effects has enhanced the dramatic tension of performances to some extent. However, the core of shadow puppetry remains the manipulation of the puppets themselves. In preserving this traditional art form, we should not overly emphasize special effects at the expense of the essential performance. Although it holds an important place in modern innovations, this gene can be absent when discussing traditional shadow puppetry.

4.5 Interpretation of the Shadow Puppetry Exhibitions in the Context of Semiotics

As the data indicates, the exhibition predominantly showcases the material aspects of shadow puppetry, accounting for 90.18% of the content. Specifically, the categories of character figures, other creatures, and props, as illustrated in Fig. 6, all pertain to the physical artifacts of shadow puppets. In contrast, the design elements of other artistic components of shadow puppetry are notably insufficient. While some aspects, such as scripts, theaters, production techniques, stage set recreations, musical instruments, and vocal styles, are represented, they are limited in scope. When evaluated through the lens of "artistic gene", it becomes evident that there is a significant lack of displays highlighting the "unique gene" of shadow puppetry art—namely, the interplay of light and shadow. Without the dynamic interaction between light sources and puppets, these artifacts are reduced to mere decorative symbols on a two-dimensional plane. This exhibition strategy leads audiences to perceive shadow puppetry as "movable paper-cutting", thereby diminishing its unique artistic expression distinct from other art forms.

This gap is also evident in the exhibition's technical approach. The use of lightbox display technology, which constitutes 61.72% of the exhibits, reconstructs the sign-production mechanism of shadow puppetry through spatial inversion. By positioning the puppets between the screen and the audience, as shown in Fig. 10a, the exhibition mirrors the spatial sequence of "light source-puppet-screen", creating a reversed image. As illustrated in Fig. 10b, in authentic shadow puppetry, artists manipulate the three-dimensional relationship between puppets and light sources to produce shadows with perspective depth on a two-dimensional screen. This spatial inversion deprives audiences of the duality of "entity-projection", ultimately transforming shadow puppetry from "light and shadow art" with dynamic interplay into "flat paper-cutting or carving art".

A deeper crisis lies in the exhibition's failure to effectively transmit and inherit the "unique artistic gene". Although the museum intentionally creates an aesthetically rich viewing experience to enhance cultural pride and confidence, an excessive focus on the visual material aspects of art, while neglecting the interpretation of other artistic elements, leads audiences to gradually lose the ability to distinguish shadow puppetry from other art forms. The "shadow puppetry" cognition acquired in museums becomes a decorative symbol devoid of light and shadow narrative capabilities, blurring the differences between it and static folk arts like paper-cutting and woodblock prints. This erosion results in the loss of ontological status for shadow puppetry in the intangible cultural heritage lineage.

Therefore, from the three dimensions of contemporary museums, exhibition content, exhibition technology, and exhibition objectives, there is a common indication of a prevalent cognitive misalignment in contemporary cultural displays: when museums equate "preservation" with "material conservation" and simplify "interpretation" to "visual representation", traditional arts dependent on dynamic processes and medium characteristics inevitably encounter symbolic violence. The survival of shadow puppetry

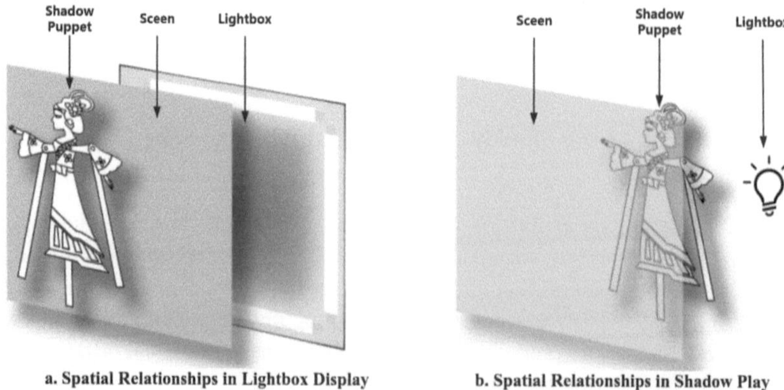

Fig. 10. Spatial Relationships in Lightbox Display and Authentic Shadow Play.

requires not only the rescue of carving techniques or design patterns but also the reconstruction of its "light-shadow-puppet" trinity sign system. This reconstruction enables audiences to not only gaze upon the history of objects but also experience the poetics of light in exhibitions.

5   Conclusion

An increasing number of research institutions and museums are leveraging digital technology to revive shadow puppetry as an intangible cultural heritage. However, there is a lack of effective measures to evaluate whether these dissemination approaches successfully enhance audience engagement while preserving cultural authenticity. This study proposes a comprehensive method to extract the "artistic genes" of shadow puppetry and validates the framework's feasibility in assessing the cultural authenticity of museum exhibitions. The artistic gene framework, developed in this study, primarily functions as a conceptual framework. It defines the core artistic elements of shadow puppetry through the lens of meme theory.

This method effectively reveals the core characteristics of cultural heritage by integrating literature analysis, field studies, and multimodal discourse analysis, offering a novel analytical perspective for theoretical research. The evaluation revealed that existing research and practices often overlook its unique artistic expressions of light-and-shadow, potentially posing challenges to its cultural authenticity. Such oversight may result in incomplete or misleading preservation and dissemination efforts. Furthermore, the unique and valuable artistic expressions of shadow puppetry may risk diminishing public recognition of its distinction from other art forms, reducing shadow puppetry to merely its "arts of leather and paper" while losing its essence of "moving shadows" and "play of lights". Since the meme-based approach highlights the processes of variation, selection, and inheritance of cultural elements, it provides a structured method for identifying and analyzing the core artistic characteristics of diverse ICH forms, including traditional opera, folk crafts, and ritual performances.

Beyond shadow puppetry, the artistic gene framework has great potential to be applied to other traditional art forms across different cultural contexts. By identifying core artistic genes and evaluating their representation in digital applications, this framework provides curators, designers, and cultural heritage researchers with a systematic approach to assessing cultural authenticity and optimizing digital dissemination strategies. Furthermore, it offers a replicable evaluation method for future research, enabling comparative studies across different ICH digitalization projects. By facilitating a deeper understanding of artistic transmission and adaptation in response to digital interventions, the artistic gene framework presents a scalable methodology that contributes to the broader field of cultural heritage preservation and dissemination in the digital age.

References

1. Lin, C., Xia, G., Nickpour, F., Chen, Y.: A review of emotional design in extended reality for the preservation of cultural heritage. NPJ Heritage Sci. (Accepted/In Press)
2. Davis, A., Belton, D., Helmholz, P., Bourke, P., McDonald, J.: Pilbara rock art: laser scanning, photogrammetry and 3D photographic reconstruction as heritage management tools. Herit. Sci. **5**, 1–16 (2017)
3. Hou, M., et al.: Novel method for virtual restoration of cultural relics with complex geometric structure based on multiscale spatial geometry. ISPRS Int. J. Geo-Inf. **7**(9), 353 (2018)
4. Jo, Y.H., Hong, S., Jo, S.Y., Kwon, Y.M.: Noncontact restoration of missing parts of stone Buddha statue based on three-dimensional virtual modeling and assembly simulation. Herit. Sci. **8**(1), 103 (2020)
5. Themistocleous, K., Evagorou, E., Mettas, C., Hadjimitsis, D.: The use of digital twin models to document cultural heritage monuments. In: Earth Resources and Environmental Remote Sensing/GIS Applications, vol. 12268, pp. 55–64. SPIE (2022)
6. Husheng, P., Li, P., Zhang, L.: Digital immersion technology and its strategy in the field of urban and architectural heritage conservation. In: Conservation of Urban and Architectural Heritage-Past, Present and Future. IntechOpen (2023)
7. Lixinski, L.: Digital heritage surrogates, decolonization, and international law: restitution, control, and the creation of value as reparations and emancipation. Santander Art Culture Law Rev. **6**(2), 65–86 (2020)
8. Lawless, J.W., Silva, K.D.: Towards an integrative understanding of 'authenticity' of cultural heritage: an analysis of world heritage site designations in the Asian context. J. Heritage Manag. **1**(2), 148–159 (2016)
9. Tong, C., Hee-Gyun, K.: Intangible cultural heritage based on AR technology. J. Appl. Data Sci. **3**(3), 118–127 (2022)
10. He, Y.: ShadowPlayVR: understanding traditional shadow puppetry performance techniques through non-intuitive embodied interactions. In: Proceedings of the 29th ACM Symposium on Virtual Reality Software and Technology, pp. 1–2 (2023)
11. Moumoutzis, N., et al.: eShadow+: mixed reality storytelling inspired by traditional shadow theatre. In: 2022 IEEE 46th Annual Computers, Software, and Applications Conference (COMPSAC), pp. 95–100. IEEE (2022)
12. Juming, S.: The magic of meme–on Memetics and its development in China. Chin. Semiotic Stud. **2**(1), 96–106 (2009)
13. Wu, Y., Ardley, B.: Brand strategy and brand evolution: welcome to the world of the meme. Mark. Rev. **7**(3), 301–310 (2007)
14. Wang, D.: The Quintic glory of Chinese civilization and the five Core concepts in culture gene. Hebei Acad. J. **5**, 130–134 (2003)
15. Dawkins, R.: The Selfish Gene. Oxford University Press (2016)

16. Wang, L.J., Yin, T.L.: A research on the path of rural culture protection and tourism utilization using memetics. Ecol. Econ. (2021)
17. Deng, L., Chen, B., Zhang, X.W.: The extraction and application of costume culture gene of Liangshan Yi nationality. Pack. Eng. **39**(02), 270–275 (2018)
18. Wei, L.: Art History of Chinese Shadow Puppetry. Cultural Relics Press, Beijing (2007)
19. Xiaochun, C., Shanat, M.B.H.: A study on the visual elements of shadow puppets in Southwest China. NVEO, 10300–10318 (2021)
20. Cultural Relics Press.: About us. Retrieved February 20, 2025, from https://www.wenwu.com/culturalreliespress_123 (n.d.)
21. China News Network.: Visiting the Chengdu China Shadow Play Museum: Inheriting the beauty of folk art in light and shadow. Retrieved December 13, 2024, from https://www.chinanews.com.cn/cul/shipin/cns/2022/10-29/news941617.shtml (2022, October 29)
22. Guangdong Museum.: Guangdong Museum holds "China in Shadow Play" exhibition. Retrieved December 13, 2024, from https://www.gdmuseum.com/cn/col48/16591 (2024, July 17)
23. Xiaoyi Municipal Government.: "Story of Light and Shadow": Visit Xiaoyi Shadow Puppet Art Museum. Retrieved December 13, 2024, from http://www.xiaoyi.gov.cn/xwzx/ywtj/202308/t20230821_1785918.shtml (2023, August 21)
24. Xi'an Shadow Puppet Art Museum.: About us. Retrieved December 13, 2024, from http://www.shadowpuppetart.com/p_about.html (n.d.)
25. Zhou, Y.: Zhongguo xiju shi changbian. [Comprehensive History of Chinese Drama]. People's Literature Publishing House (1960)
26. Chandler, D.: Semiotics: the Basics. Routledge (2022)
27. Pearce, S.M.: Interpreting Objects and Collections. Psychology Press (1994)
28. Welsh, E..: Dealing with data: using NVivo in the qualitative data analysis process. In Forum qualitative sozialforschung/Forum: qualitative social research (Vol. 3, No. 2) (2002, May)
29. Limna, P.: The impact of NVivo in qualitative research: perspectives from graduate students. J. Appl. Learn. Teach. **6**(2) (2023)
30. Qin, J., Guan, Y., Lu, X.: Research on the interaction design methods of digital cultural heritage. In: 2009 IEEE 10th International Conference on Computer-Aided Industrial Design & Conceptual Design, pp. 1452–1454. IEEE (2009)
31. Kurnianto, A.: The sustainable adaptation of traditional art into digital medium (case study the motion of shadow puppet scene Perang Kembang). E3S Web Conf. **388**, 04059 (2023)
32. Ghani, D.A., Ishak, S.B.A.: Relationship between the art of wayang kulit and disney's twelve principles of animation. Rev. Cercet. Interv. Soc. **37**, 144 (2012)

A Study on Digital Mythological Experience Design Based on Interactive Narrative Theory: A Case Study of "The Legend of the Dragon Mother"

Huanhuan Long, Dan Liao$^{(\boxtimes)}$, Liuyu Su, Xinhao Wang, Yiling Li, and Ziqiang Yan

South China University of Technology, Guangzhou, Guangdong, China
`danl@scut.edu.cn`

Abstract. Mythology serves as a crucial carrier of collective memory and cultural values for nations. However, current mythological digitization practices predominantly focus on unidirectional information transmission, making it difficult to achieve users' perception and internalization of the profound cultural values embedded in mythology. Therefore, based on Ryan's interactive narrative theoretical framework, this study proposes a design approach aimed at transforming abstract cultural values into users' profound experiences: targeting emotional immersion as the core objective, employing dramatic plot as the narrative framework, and establishing behavioral integration, frequent interaction, natural interface, and dynamic creation as core interactive design principles. Taking "The Legend of the Dragon Mother" as an example, we developed a multi-branched narrative script game with ink-wash painting aesthetics, enabling users to experience from the mythological protagonist's perspective. Experimental results demonstrate that compared to linear viewing modes, the interactive version shows significant advantages in core dimensions of emotional resonance and cultural value perception, validating that applying the aforementioned design methodology for mythological digitization constitutes an effective pathway for deepening mythological experiences. This research provides a feasible approach for transforming mythology from mere viewing to active user participation experiences, while offering practical reference for the in-depth dissemination of digital cultural heritage.

Keywords: immersive storytelling · interactive narrative theory · digitization of myths

1 Introduction

Mythology represents both the most distinctive and most universal characteristic of civilization—it reveals the eternal propositions of common human concern through each society's unique modes of expression. As metaphor, mythology reflects our deepest self-recognition in our relationship with existence itself [1]. Mythology carries human wisdom passed down through generations, and its digitization enables mythology to flourish anew in contemporary times, allowing its spiritual values to continue and develop in modern society.

M. Schrepp and M. Rauterberg (Eds.): HCII 2025, LNCS 16342, pp. 233–247, 2026.
https://doi.org/10.1007/978-3-032-13164-5_15

Currently, rapidly evolving digital technologies provide unprecedented possibilities for retelling these ancient stories. Various digital media are widely employed for organizing mythological knowledge, reproducing visual imagery, and disseminating cultural elements. These practices have expanded mythology's dissemination boundaries and attracted widespread public attention. However, it can be observed that current explorations tend to focus on unidirectional transmission of mythological content, with users' roles often confined to information receivers or external observers, rarely having opportunities to experience the internal contradictions and tensions of stories as "participants," potentially limiting their deeper perception of cultural values.

Based on these observations, this study aims to explore an immersive mythological narrative approach targeting emotional resonance and value internalization, seeking to reshape the relationship between users and stories, achieving transformation from "passive viewing" to "active participation," and providing a new approach for traditional culture's digital inheritance that emphasizes subject participation and profound experiences.

2　Related Research

2.1　Cultural Heritage Digitization

In the field of cultural heritage digital activation, theoretical applications such as gamification theory [2], participatory heritage [3], and immersive experience theory [4] are primarily employed to guide the design of more engaging interactive experiences.

According to research by Chen, Li, & Zhang (2025), the "Canal Mystery" interactive exhibition at China's Grand Canal Museum systematically applies gamification theory-based strategies to reconstruct cultural heritage dissemination methods [5]. The exhibition effectively stimulates visitors' curiosity and exploratory desire through gamified narrative clues and diverse interactive puzzle mechanisms, guiding them into profound dialogue with cultural heritage. The virtual experience system of bamboo weaving project applies immersive experience theory, creating a virtual bamboo weaving workshop where users can deeply perceive and interact through high-precision VR technology [6]. The system enables users to "personally" experience core bamboo weaving craft processes by simulating authentic physical feedback and interactive processes, thereby achieving inheritance and dissemination of a traditional handicraft facing extinction.

These studies explore from different theoretical perspectives how to transform cultural heritage from static displays into dynamic, participatory experiences. However, in the field of mythological digitization, such systematic theoretical application and perspective exploration remains relatively scarce, with current research primarily concentrated on technical means application or display format innovation, still lacking in-depth exploration.

2.2　Mythological Digitization Cases

In the field of mythological digitization, numerous projects attempt to present mythological content through digital media formats, employing virtual reality (VR), augmented reality (AR), mixed reality (MR), and multimedia exhibitions to explore immersive expression methods for mythological culture. For example, the "HimmapanVR" project utilizes image scanning, photogrammetry, and 3D modeling technologies to systematically digitally reconstruct "Himalayan animals" from Thai mythology, restoring their morphological characteristics through high-precision three-dimensional models and adopting fully immersive virtual reality experience modes to allow users to freely explore details of these mythological creatures [7]. This project demonstrates outstanding performance in visual presentation and spatial perception, successfully enhancing users' cognitive levels regarding mythological elements, but remains relatively basic in interactive mechanism design, with user participation mostly confined to viewing and browsing levels, lacking deep-level value guidance and emotional resonance.

Similarly, the "Itihasa - An Interactive Learning Experience of Indian Mythology" project enables users to immersively experience scenes inspired by Indian mythology through immersive 3D navigation technology. Additionally, the project integrates various communication forms such as blogs, short videos, and interactive forums, allowing users to enhance memory and understanding of mythology through communication. In the application's 3D navigation interaction module, inspired by Indian mythological sites, 3D environmental models are constructed. Users can select different characters to explore within this environment, with character features displayed and explanations of the significance behind these places when moving characters. While exquisite 3D models indeed attract users, displaying culture and meaning solely through textual methods appears somewhat rigid [8].

Furthermore, many projects tend toward mythological digital display through exhibition formats. For example, China's first virtual-real integrated exhibition based on Apple Vision Pro, "Where Are the Myths," constructs a virtual-real integrated ancient mythological universe through rich media forms such as MR experiences, interactive imagery, comics, wallpapers, and AI algorithm-based artworks, making audiences feel as if they "return to the mysterious ancient mythological world," dialoguing with ancient gods, seeking ancient mythical beasts, and touring fantastic universes. The exhibition is divided into four major themes: "Mythological Origins," "Ancient Gods," "Love and Eternity," and "Future Mythology," with 28 ancient mythological stories cleverly arranged across seven exhibition areas within nearly 1,000 square meters of exhibition space on two floors of Today Art Museum's Hall 3 [9]. This project focuses on visual impact brought to audiences by multiple mythology-based artworks. However, interactive installations and works are mostly presented as independent modules, lacking coherence among them. This fragmented display method causes users to tend toward superficial browsing rather than deep immersion in complete narrative contexts.

2.3 Comprehensive Analysis

In summary, current mythological digitization projects demonstrate distinctive characteristics in technical application and presentation formats, with practice perspectives showing diversified trends: some focus on visual immersion and cultural cognitive enlightenment; others emphasize character movement-triggered knowledge display and social memory reinforcement; still others concentrate on media integration and artistic expression. These cases have achieved certain effectiveness in enhancing user interest and expanding mythological dissemination channels, but considerable exploration space remains in user participation levels and mythological cultural value transmission.

Effective transmission of mythology's cultural values constitutes one of the core objectives of mythological digital narrative, concerning not only users' understanding of mythological content but also affecting the continuation and contemporary transformation of traditional cultural spirit. However, mythological digitization attempts in this aspect remain relatively limited.

Therefore, this study attempts to explore a mythological narrative approach emphasizing deep user participation from the perspective of interactive narrative theory, thereby achieving profound understanding and emotional identification with cultural connotations through immersive experiences. Based on this objective, this study attempts to combine Marie-Laure Ryan's related interactive narrative theories to construct mythological narrative projects with cultural dissemination power and profound cultural experiences within physical cultural spaces.

3 Design Pathway Based on Ryan's Interactive Narrative Theory

The preceding analysis reveals limitations in current mythological digitization practices regarding guiding users toward deep cultural value experiences. To address this challenge, this chapter employs Marie-Laure Ryan's interactive narrative theory as the core theoretical tool. Through systematic organization and interpretation of her theoretical framework, this study ultimately integrates them into a logically rigorous, hierarchically clear ideal design pathway, providing explicit theoretical guidance for subsequent mythological digitization practices.

3.1 Interactive Narrative: Pathway to Mythological Value Internalization

The core characteristic of interactive narrative lies in the "agency" it grants users. Unlike linear narratives that passively receive information, interactive narrative transforms users into story participants whose choices can influence plot development, thereby stimulating profound emotional investment and meaning perception [10, 11].

This characteristic highly aligns with the objective of profound mythological value transmission. Mythology often contains rich symbolism, metaphors, and universal value conflicts, providing broad space for personal interpretation and emotional projection. By placing users at crucial narrative nodes and compelling them to think and choose as protagonists, interactive narrative can transform abstract cultural values into concrete, personalized experiences. This transformation from "viewing" to "experiencing" constitutes an effective pathway for guiding users beyond story surfaces to achieve profound perception and emotional identification with cultural connotations.

3.2 Theoretical Framework: Dramatic Plot Centered on Emotional Immersion

To further transform the aforementioned concepts into specific design methods, this study introduces Ryan's systematic theoretical framework for interactive narrative construction. Ryan distinguishes immersion into two basic types: ludic immersion and narrative immersion. The former refers to engagement focused on task completion, while the latter stems from imaginative construction of story worlds. Narrative immersion can be further subdivided into three forms: spatial immersion, temporal immersion, and emotional immersion [12].

For mythological narratives aimed at transmitting profound cultural values and achieving emotional identification, emotional immersion constitutes the core. Ryan specifically defines emotional immersion as users' affective reactions to the story and to the characters. In this study's context, the emotional immersion we pursue specifically refers to empathy-driven, sympathetic experiences with character destinies, rather than merely excitement or frustration from task completion [12]. Ryan further emphasizes that the distinctive characteristic of dramatic plot lies precisely in its exceptional ability to create such profound emotional immersion. Unlike epic plots focusing on external achievements and epistemic plots driven by puzzle-solving, the core of dramatic plot consists of continuously evolving interpersonal relationship networks, with plot momentum stemming from spiritual interactions, internal conflicts, and moral choices among characters. When users no longer view other characters as tools for task achievement but treat them as "people" with independent thoughts and emotions, profound empathetic experiences emerge, constituting the bridge connecting users with mythology's spiritual core.

Therefore, this study's design pathway establishes an approach centered on "emotional immersion" as the core objective and "dramatic plot" as the narrative framework. However, establishing the plot framework represents only the first step; how to fully release the potential of dramatic plot in creating emotional immersion through specific interactive design constitutes the core issue requiring subsequent exploration.

3.3 Design Pathway: Four Principles Leading to Ideal Interactive Narrative Experience

How can we maximally release dramatic plot's potential in creating emotional immersion? Ryan's proposed aesthetic objectives for interactive narrative provide theoretical guidance for realizing this potential. According to her theory [12], an ideal interactive narrative design targeting emotional resonance centers on comprehensively pursuing the following four complementary principles:

- Integration of user actions: This constitutes the foundation of interactive narrative. User behaviors must be deeply integrated into causal chains, with their choices not merely advancing progress but serving as keys to shaping character destinies and interpersonal relationships. This represents the prerequisite for achieving "agency" and emotional responsibility.
- Frequent interaction: Interaction should be the norm rather than the exception. Continuous interaction can maintain users' sense of presence, preventing them from disengaging from characters and returning to observer perspectives, thereby ensuring continuity of dramatic conflicts and emotional tension.
- Natural interface: Interaction methods should be as intuitive as possible, simulating behaviors and communications in the real world. This can reduce users' cognitive load, enabling them to focus more on the story's emotional core rather than operations themselves, thereby greatly enhancing role-playing immersion.

- Dynamic creation of the story: This represents the ultimate ideal of interactive narrative. Systems should be capable of real-time, dynamic generation or adjustment of plots based on user behaviors, creating truly unique, unpredictable dramatic experiences that make interpersonal relationship evolution as complex and variable as reality.

In summary, this study constructs an ideal design pathway. This pathway establishes emotional immersion as the highest objective, dramatic plot as the core narrative framework, and advocates comprehensive pursuit of Ryan's four aesthetic principles: behavioral integration, frequent interaction, natural interface, and dynamic creation. This pathway represents the optimal solution at the theoretical level for profound emotional transmission of mythological values through interactive narrative. It provides a guiding ideal model for subsequent specific practices, constituting the target framework requiring reference and approximation during design processes. Specific trade-offs and implementation degrees in practice will be elaborated in subsequent chapters.

4   Digital Design of "The Legend of the Dragon Mother"

To explore new pathways for mythological digital inheritance and validate the feasibility of the aforementioned design pathway, this study constructs an immersive narrative system integrating multimedia interaction with physical props. This system uses "The Legend of the Dragon Mother" as content blueprint, guiding users to assume the protagonist "Dragon Mother's" identity from a first-person perspective. Through handheld customized physical "staff" for somatosensory interaction, users will personally experience a series of narrative nodes containing internal struggles and moral dilemmas, thereby generating profound experiences of mythology's cultural values. This chapter will systematically elaborate the specific design and implementation processes of this project (Fig. 1).

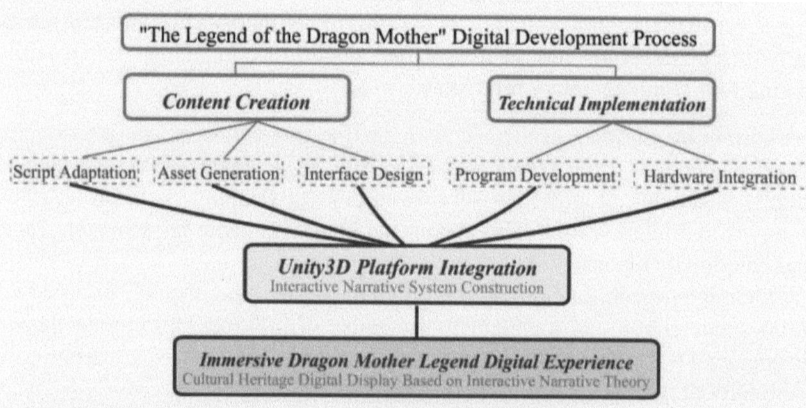

Fig. 1. The Legend of the Dragon Mother" Digital Development Process: Content creation and technical implementation are integrated through the Unity3D platform.

4.1 Mythological Background

The Dragon Mother legend is widely circulated in China's Lingnan region, especially the Xijiang River basin. Along the Xijiang River, numerous Dragon Mother temples exist, with countless Dragon Mother statues enshrined, as Dragon Mother serves as the protective deity for Xijiang people [13]. The mythology's embodied ideals of great love, benevolence, and reverence are extremely important for improving public moral standards and promoting society's spiritual civilization construction. Therefore, this study chooses to digitally develop the Dragon Mother legend and introduce it into physical cultural spaces, aiming to enable broader audiences, especially younger demographics, to experience mythology's charm and its transmitted cultural concepts.

4.2 Script Writing

To stimulate users' profound participation and emotional resonance, this study abandons traditional linear narrative methods, instead adopting multi-branched narrative structures experienced from the protagonist's first-person perspective. Through deep excavation of the legend's internal contradictions, Ryan's theory of "dramatic plot" was established as the adaptation core, shifting narrative focus from external achievements and challenges toward the protagonist Dragon Mother's inner world. Specific practices include:

4.2.1 Chapter-Based Narrative

To enhance narrative layering, the story is divided into four chapters: "Xijiang Fishing, Dragon Egg Emerges," "Dragon Egg Transforms, Dragon Mother Raises Sons," "Dragon Sons Cause Trouble, Dragon Mother Disciplines and Reforms," and "Dragon Mother Refuses Imperial Summons, Returns to Guard Chengxi," ensuring users can obtain complete plot experiences within relatively short timeframes.

Establishing core conflicts.

Within Ryan's proposed dramatic plot framework, conflict serves as an important mechanism driving emotional immersion. It not only propels narrative development but also stimulates users' empathetic experiences through characters' internal struggles and value choices. This study designed three key value choice points running throughout, compelling users to think from Dragon Mother's perspective:

- Conflict between maternal love and romantic love: In Chap. 2, facing her lover's questioning, choosing between "abandoning the five dragon sons to be with the lover" or "separating from the lover to continue living with the five dragon sons."
- Conflict in educational philosophy: In Chap. 3, facing dragon sons who have caused great trouble, choosing between "teaching them righteousness to benefit people" or "letting them be without management."
- Conflict between personal values and secular power: In Chap. 4, facing imperial summons, choosing between "entering the capital as imperial consort to enjoy wealth and honor" or "refusing to enter the capital, protecting Chengxi people."

These three dilemmatic choices not only constitute the story's main contradictions but also naturally generate a multi-branched narrative structure with four different endings.

Each user choice will shape a unique "Dragon Mother" image and lead to different destiny outcomes, thereby completing transformation from local legend to interactive dramatized script (Fig. 2).

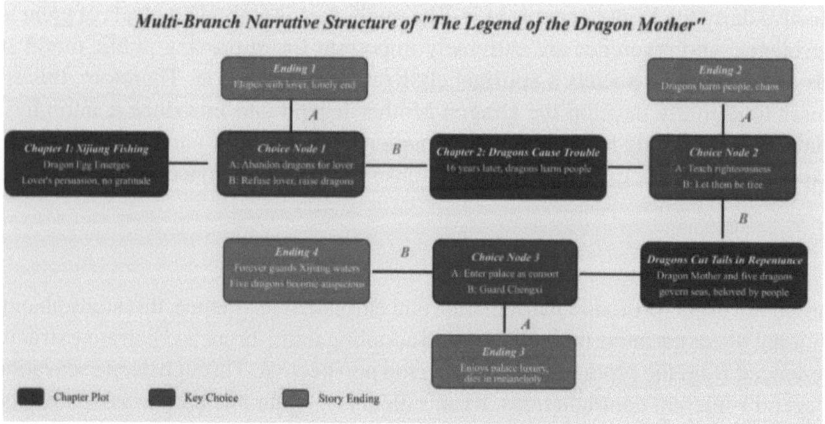

Fig. 2. Multi-branch narrative structure with four chapters, three choice nodes, and four possible endings. Visual Implementation

4.3 Visual Implementation

After script completion, the team conducted visual development, aiming to transform text into visual language combining Eastern aesthetics with immersion.

For overall visual style, this study selected "ink-wash with light colors." Ink-wash represents the essence of traditional Chinese painting; combined with light colors, it makes entire scenes possess both ancient charm and vitality, aiming to create a credible mythological world with "sense of place" for users.

In character design, the research team strictly followed the story's historical background (Qin Dynasty) and character personalities. Taking the protagonist Dragon Mother as an example, her clothing references the "deep robe" style commonly worn by Qin Dynasty women, with upper garments connected to lower garments, symbolizing the philosophical concept of "heaven and earth unity." In clothing colors, white and green were selected, with white symbolizing her elegance and great love, and green representing her wisdom and vitality, striving to convey characters' beautiful qualities through visual elements.

In user interface (UI) design, equal attention was paid to user-friendliness and contextual immersion. The opening homepage's left side features sections for game explanation, mythological legends, and gameplay introduction, helping users understand backgrounds before beginning (see Fig. 4). Additionally, an illustrated guide system containing character and scene introductions was designed, enabling users to deeply understand the mythological world both within and outside the game (Figs. 3 and 4).

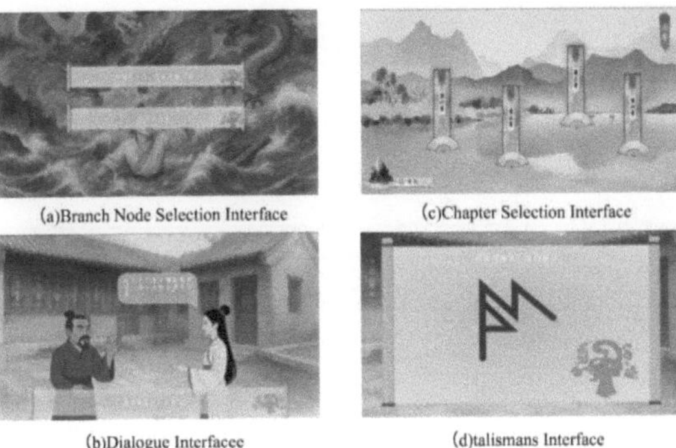

(a)Branch Node Selection Interface   (c)Chapter Selection Interface

(b)Dialogue Interfacee   (d)talismans Interface

Fig. 3. Application interface screenshots showing four main functional modules, All interfaces feature traditional Chinese ink-wash painting aesthetics.

Fig. 4. The opening homepage with left side features sections.

4.4 Application Development

During the application development phase, the development team used Unity engine to integrate script logic with artistic resources. This phase's core task involved technical implementation of the "multi-branched narrative structure" and "value-driven choices" designed in previous phases.

To implement complex multi-branched narratives, the development team designed specialized plot data structures, uniformly storing all plot text, branching logic, jump conditions, and other information in JSON files for management, making plot modifications and expansions more convenient and efficient. Corresponding program logic was written for three core choice nodes and multiple interaction points, with every user choice and operation recorded by the system and serving as variables affecting subsequent plot development, ultimately leading to one of four preset endings.

Simultaneously, to enhance key plot expressiveness, customized animation effects were added to dialogue box presentations and scene transitions to enhance users' immersion (Fig. 5).

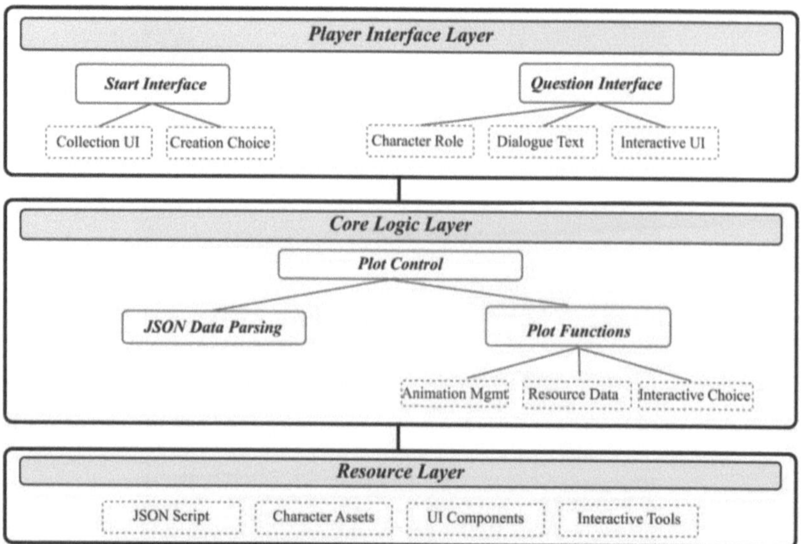

Fig. 5. Three-layer application architecture: Player Interface, Core Logic, and Resource layers.

4.5　Interactive Hardware Development and Integration

To liberate interactive experiences from traditional keyboard and mouse clicking and create more "natural" and "ritualistic" interactions, this study referenced "cyber wand" development approaches, deciding to specifically user a physical interaction tool—a "staff" (see Fig. 6)—for the project.

The staff uses STM32 as the main control chip and integrates high-precision accelerometers and gyroscopes to detect the wand's motion trajectories in real-time. Convolutional Neural Network (CNN) algorithms are utilized to train and recognize collected motion data. This enables the staff to recognize not only simple swinging motions but also specific trajectories drawn by users imitating traditional Chinese talismans.

Finally, through serial communication modules, gestures recognized by the staff are transmitted to Unity applications in real-time, controlling plot advancement and retreat through left-right swinging, and making value choices affecting plot directions at key story nodes. Additionally, to increase experience interest, interactions through staff talisman-drawing were designed to trigger corresponding in-game events, such as "taking down dragon eggs" in Chap. 1 and "calming sea waves" in Chap. 4. Through this deep software-hardware integration, users' physical movements are deeply bound with in-story "spellcasting" behaviors, making the staff a bridge connecting virtual and reality, greatly enhancing users' character immersion.

Fig. 6. Interact with the physical staff controller.

5 Experimental Design

5.1 Experimental Design

5.1.1 Experimental Hypothesis

This experiment's core hypothesis is: compared to traditional linear narratives, interactive narrative versions based on Ryan's theory can more effectively trigger users' emotional resonance and promote their profound cultural value perception of mythological connotations.

5.1.2 A/B Version Settings

To conduct comparative experiments, this study developed two versions of "The Legend of the Dragon Mother" application, both employing identical visual styles, artistic assets, and core story contexts:

Group A (Control Group - Linear Narrative Version). Users in this version observe from observer perspectives a preset animation restoring the original Dragon Mother legend story. This story version selects one relatively positive ending (such as Dragon Mother ultimately choosing to raise dragon sons and protect Chengxi). Users' only interaction involves clicking "Next" to advance plots, unable to make any choices affecting plot directions.

Group B (Experimental Group - Interactive Narrative Version). The complete version detailed in Chap. 4. Users experience from first-person perspectives, using "staffs" for key motion interactions and making "value-driven choices" at three core nodes affecting story endings.

5.2 Experimental Subjects

This study recruited 20 university students (aged 18–24, with basic understanding of digital narratives but no deep exposure to Dragon Mother legends) as subjects, randomly and evenly assigning them to Groups A and B, with 10 people per group. (This study strictly adheres to research ethics principles, with all participants signing informed consent forms, clearly informing them of research purposes, processes, and data anonymization processing methods, and promising voluntary participation with the right to withdraw at any time.)

5.3   Evaluation Indicators and Methods

To test core hypotheses, this study designed a quantitative questionnaire using Likert 5-point scales, evaluating the following dimensions:

Two core dimensions. 1) Emotional Resonance, directly corresponding to emotional immersion in Ryan's theory; 2) Cultural Value Perception, measuring users' understanding and identification with mythological spiritual connotations.

One key supporting dimension. User Agency, measuring users' perception of their behaviors' ability to influence narrative directions, serving as a key mechanism for exploring experience difference sources.

Two auxiliary immersion dimensions. Temporal Immersion and Spatial Immersion, for more comprehensive examination.

5.4   Experimental Results and Data Analysis

5.4.1   Multi-dimensional Quantitative Comparative Analysis

This study conducted independent sample t-tests on collected questionnaire data to analyze whether score differences between Groups A and B across evaluation dimensions possessed statistical significance. Results are shown in the following Table 1:

Table 1. Mean scores, standard deviations, and t-test results for both groups across evaluation dimensions (N = 20).

Evaluation Dimension	Version A (Linear) M (SD)	Version B (Interactive) M (SD)	t(18)	p-value	Cohen's d
Emotional Resonance	2.50 (0.70)	4.60 (0.50)	−8.13	<.001	3.63
Cultural Value Perception	2.80 (0.60)	4.50 (0.50)	−6.94	<.001	3.10
User Agency	1.30 (0.50)	4.70 (0.60)	−14.60	<.001	6.53
Temporal Immersion	3.10 (0.80)	3.90 (0.70)	−2.53	.021	1.13
Spatial Immersion	4.20 (0.70)	4.40 (0.60)	−0.76	.456	0.34

5.4.2   Data Interpretation

The data clearly validates this study's core hypothesis.Outstanding performance in core dimensions.

Across the two core evaluation dimensions. The interactive version (Group B) far exceeded the linear version (Group A). Both Emotional Resonance ($p < .001$, $d = 3.63$) and Cultural Value Perception ($p < .001$, $d = 3.10$) scores showed extremely significant differences with large effect sizes. This powerfully demonstrates that this study's design methodology is genuinely effective in achieving core objectives—namely triggering user emotional resonance and promoting cultural value perception.

Key role of User Agency. The interactive version's score advantage in the User Agency dimension ($p < .001$, $d = 6.53$) was most pronounced, revealing that "the right to choose" constitutes a key mechanism for stimulating immersive experiences. When users feel their behaviors can influence story directions, their emotional investment and value identification deepen significantly accordingly.

Performance in other immersion dimensions. The interactive version also demonstrated significant advantages in temporal immersion ($p = .021$), indicating that multi-branched structures effectively maintained users' anticipation and curiosity. The non-significant difference in spatial immersion ($p = .456$) aligns with expectations, as both versions employed identical visual artistic assets, indicating that interactive design itself has relatively small impact on spatial perception.

6 Discussion and Conclusion

This study's core objective aims to explore how to further deepen user experiences in mythological digital works, transcending current prevalent visual presentation and information transmission modes toward profound excavation of internal emotional values and participation. Through guidance from Marie-Laure Ryan's interactive narrative theory, transforming "The Legend of the Dragon Mother" into an interactive narrative work centered on "dramatic plot," this study ultimately provided support for core hypotheses through experimental data.

6.1 Effectiveness and Trade-Offs of Theory-Guided Practice

Experimental results indicate that interactive versions achieved significant advantages in emotional immersion, user agency, and mythological value experience. This demonstrates to some extent that theory-oriented design decisions possess feasibility. Specifically:

Plot type selection. This study selected "dramatic plot" as the narrative blueprint, making Dragon Mother's internal struggles and value choices the story's core. This strategy helps bring participants profound emotional immersion experiences and received experimental data support.

Achievement of aesthetic objectives. The project selectively realized two key aesthetic objectives proposed by Ryan. First, by designing physical "staffs" as interaction tools, the "natural interface" objective was practiced, enhancing users' somatosensory and ritualistic experiences; second, by establishing key choices affecting story endings, the "integration of user actions" objective was achieved, with each user operation possessing substantial meaning in shaping character destinies.

6.2 Limitations of Theoretical Application and Future Prospects

Ryan also points out that in practice, various aesthetic objectives often require "sacrificing one objective to achieve another." This study also confirms this point. To ensure narrative coherence and emotional impact, compromises were made regarding the following two ideal objectives:

- Regarding "frequent interaction": This project's interactions primarily concentrated on several key value choice nodes, failing to achieve continuous interaction throughout.
- Regarding "dynamic creation of the story": This study's story follows a preset multi-branched structure rather than real-time dynamic generation by systems based on user inputs, remaining distant from Ryan's referenced "holodeck" ideal.

These limitations represent both realistic constraints and future breakthrough directions. Future mythological digitization practices can explore, while ensuring core narrative experiences, how to utilize AIGC and other technologies to add more AI-driven, meaningful micro-interactions at non-critical nodes to enhance interaction "frequency"; or attempt to construct AI narrative engines capable of real-time story detail adjustment, advancing toward the ultimate objective of "dynamic creation."

Acknowledgments. This research was supported by Research Project of the "13th Five-Year Plan" for Philosophy and Social Sciences in Guangdong Province: "Research on Virtual Reality Art Therapy for Mental Disorders in the Context of the COVID-19 Pandemic" (GD20CYS33); Project of the Fundamental Research Funds for the Central Universities: "Research on Virtual Reality-Based Cognitive Improvement Design for the Elderly Aimed at Active Health" (QNZD202404); Project of the Guangdong Provincial Education Science Planning: "Research on the Integration Path of Design Thinking into the Cultivation of Innovative Engineering and Technology Talents in the Intelligent Era" (2022GXJK125); Research Project of Guangdong Provincial Degree and Graduate Education Reform: "Research on the Interdisciplinary Teaching Model that Integrates Speculative Design into Future Engineering Ethics Education in the Age of Artificial Intelligence" (2024JGXM_009); Higher Education Teaching Reform Project of Guangdong Province: "Exploration of a Cultivation Model for Outstanding Engineering and Technology Talents through the Integration of 'Design - Technology - Business'"; National Training Program of Innovation and Entrepreneurship for Undergraduates(202410561115).

References

1. Leeming, D.A.: The World of Myth: an Anthology. Oxford University Press, New York (1992)
2. Krath, J., Schürmann, L., von Korflesch, H.F.O.: Revealing the theoretical basis of gamification: a systematic review and analysis of theory in research on gamification, serious games and game-based learning. Comput. Hum. Behav. **125**, 106963 (2021). https://doi.org/10.1016/j.chb.2021.106963
3. Roued-Cunliffe, H., Copeland, A.: Participatory Heritage. Facet Publishing, London (2017)
4. Lee, H.: A unified conceptual model of immersive experience in extended reality. Comput. Hum. Behav. Rep. **18**, 100663 (2025). https://doi.org/10.1016/j.chbr.2025.100663
5. Chen, W., Li, T., Zhang, Y.: Embodied cognition model for museum gamification cultural heritage communication a grounded theory study. NPJ Herit. Sci. **13**, 239 (2025). https://doi.org/10.1038/s40494-025-01821-9

6. Zhang, L., Wang, Y., Tang, Z., Liu, X., Zhang, M.: A virtual experience system of bamboo weaving for sustainable research on intangible cultural heritage based on VR technology. Sustainability. **15**(4), 3134 (2023). https://doi.org/10.3390/su15043134

7. Chernbumroong, S., Worragin, P., Wongwan, N., Thongkam, J., Suksawat, B.: Digitization of myth: the HimmapanVR project's role in cultural preservation. Heliyon. **10**(9), e30052 (2024). https://doi.org/10.1016/j.heliyon.2024.e30052

8. Shashank, D., Kumar, T.: Itihasa-an interactive learning experience of Indian mythology. In: Fong, S., Dey, N., Joshi, A. (eds.) ICT Analysis and Applications. ICT4SD 2024. Lecture Notes in Networks and Systems, vol. 1197. Springer, Singapore (2025). https://doi.org/10.1007/978-981-97-9529-1_13

9. Sohu News.: Today Works| "Mythology Whereabouts" Exhibition Guide, with Added Night Sessions and Public Welfare Guided Tours (Chinese). https://www.sohu.com/a/798157132_121119387 (2024)

10. EBSCO.: Interactive narratives. https://www.ebsco.com/research-starters/social-sciences-and-humanities/interactive-narratives (n.d.)

11. Chai, Y., Yin, Y.: Immersive experience design of public facilities in scenic spots from the perspective of interactive narrative. Packaging Eng. **45**(16), 403–412 (2024). https://doi.org/10.19554/j.cnki.1001-3563.2024.16.044

12. Ryan, M.L.: Interactive narrative, plot types, and interpersonal relations. In: Spierling, U., Szilas, N. (eds.) Interactive Storytelling. ICIDS 2008. Lecture Notes in Computer Science, vol. 5334. Springer, Berlin, Heidelberg (2008)

13. Ye, C., Jiang, M.: Yuecheng Longmu Culture (Chinese). Heilongjiang People's Publishing House, Harbin (2003)

Optimization of Interactive Design for Museum Applications Based on User Experience Theory: "Enhancing User Satisfaction and Engagement Through Visual, Social, and Intelligent Interactions"

Yihe Ren[✉]

Guangxi Normal University, Guilin 541006, China
`409246573@qq.com`

Abstract. In recent years, with the rise of the cultural industry and the integration of digital technology, museums have expanded from traditional physical space to digital platforms such as applications (apps), and museum apps provide users with convenient online browsing and interactive experiences. However, as more and more users start to use the existing Chinese museum apps on the market, which exhibit suboptimal user experience (UX) design, problems such as incorrect guiding functions and poor interactive experiences with complex operation processes have emerged. Therefore, this study focuses on optimizing the interaction design of museum apps from user experience theory to improve user satisfaction and engagement. The study mainly adopts quantitative research methods, based on which the authors propose a targeted design optimization program from four aspects: visual, social, and intelligent interactions. Finally, this study's results and shortcomings, this study aims to provide new ideas for the digital, mobile, gamified, and experiential trends of museum applications.

Keywords: Museum Apps · User Experience Theory · Interaction Design

1 Introduction

As digital technologies have matured, museum apps have become an important tool for connecting physical and digital museums in recent years. Digital technologies enable museums to enable users to explore collections, learn about artifacts, and experience exhibitions remotely across time, space, and geography. However, through literature review and user survey, it is found that most of the users believe that the existing museum apps in China, although meeting most of the needs in terms of functionality, have neglected the user experience during the design process, such as event registration, tour guide service, and AR/VR functions, and the users have poor experience and satisfaction during the process of using them.

The main purpose of this study centers on user experience theory, aiming to identify pain points, user needs, and expectations, and to propose targeted design optimization

M. Schrepp and M. Rauterberg (Eds.): HCII 2025, LNCS 16342, pp. 248–258, 2026.
https://doi.org/10.1007/978-3-032-13164-5_16

solutions for the improvement of the existing Chinese museum apps on the market. The authors processed the data collected from the questionnaire survey and used the pandas algorithm to analyze and derive a heat map to find out which museum app features are considered the most useful by users, which features have the greatest impact on user evaluations, and which features are deficient and need to be optimized. The authors propose to take user experience theory as a guide to propose design solutions from visual, intelligent, and gamified interactions further to enhance user satisfaction and engagement with the museum app, enhance the overall user experience, and improve the overall rating of the app.

2 Literature Review

2.1 User Experience Theory and Its Application in Interaction Design

User Experience (UX) is an important concept that has received much attention in the design field in recent years. According to the International Organization for Standardization (ISO 9241-210), UX is defined as the subjective feelings and attitudes that users have during the process of using a product, system, or service. User experience covers all aspects of user-product interaction, including multiple dimensions such as perception, emotion, trust, utility, ease of use, and satisfaction [1]. In interaction design, user experience has become a key factor in determining the success of a product, and Donald Norman, in his book Emotional Design, suggests that the design of a product should not only satisfy the functional needs of the user but also focus on the user's emotional experience, the hierarchical levels of user emotional experience, from low to high, are proposed as the visceral level, behavioral level, and reflective level [2]. Visceral level refers to the direct sensory reactions users experience when interacting with a product, such as visual, auditory, olfactory, gustatory, and tactile responses. Behavioral level pertains to users' functional interactions with the product during use, including its functionality, ease of understanding, usability, and emotional experiences. Reflective level denotes the fulfillment of users' emotional needs through their interaction with the product. Studies have shown that applications with poor user experience often led to user churn and negative reviews, while excellent user experience can lead to a good user reputation and higher user retention.

2.2 The Current Situation and Development Trend of the Museum App

With the acceleration of the global museum digitization process and the gradual rise of people's demand for the cultural industry, museum apps, as an important interactive medium between museums and audiences, have been widely used in many scenarios. A museum app can provide users with a variety of functions, including exhibit information, online exhibitions, guided tours, audio commentary, interactive experience, etc., which greatly enriches the audience's visiting experience [3]. For example, the official app launched by the National Museum of China and the Palace Museum provides visitors with functions such as guided tours, virtual exhibitions, and online reservations, which greatly enrich their visiting experience.

First, the user experience of museum applications often suffers from unclear information organization, complex interface design, and navigation difficulties. It has been found that these problems mainly stem from the neglect of user needs during the design process and the lack of user participation in the design process [4].

Second, in the design process, museum apps often focus on technical realization and ignore the emotional and psychological needs of users. For example, some museum apps are feature-rich, but the interface design is not friendly enough, and users need to spend a lot of time and energy learning how to use them during operation, which in turn negatively affects the overall user experience [5].

In addition, the diverse demographic of users is also a challenge in museum app design. There are significant differences in the needs and expectations of users of different ages and cultural backgrounds, and their comfort levels with technologies in general, which requires designers to consider the characteristics of different user groups when developing museum APPs and designing products with universal applicability [6].

2.3 Application of User Experience Theory in Museum Apps

In recent years, research on the user experience of museum apps has gradually increased, and the research area involves various aspects such as user requirement analysis, interaction design optimization, and user satisfaction evaluation. To effectively improve the user experience of museum applications, researchers and designers usually adopt a variety of user experience (UX) theory research methods.

For example, some studies focus on analyzing the user requirements of museum apps, trying to understand the specific expectations of users regarding app functionality and interface design through surveys and interviews [7], as well as an in-depth discussion on digital interface design for museums based on the user experience perspective, aiming to optimize the interface design and improve usability and accessibility [8]. Other studies have explored the impact of different design factors (e.g., navigation structure, visual design, and interaction) on user experience through empirical research [9]. Not only does it help to gain a deeper understanding of users' needs, behaviors, and preferences, but it also provides a strong basis for the optimization of interaction design. For example, the questionnaire survey can understand the users' satisfaction with the app interface design, function layout, response speed, etc. It can find out the common problems and difficulties encountered by users in the process of using the app, which can provide a basis for the optimization of the interaction design of the museum application.

2.4 Quantitative Research Methods

Quantitative research methods are usually used to collect quantitative data from users in the process of using apps through questionnaires, log analysis, and A/B testing. This data can help researchers analyze users' usage behaviors, evaluate various dimensions of user experience, and identify key factors affecting user experience [10]. A questionnaire survey is a widely used quantitative research method to collect user satisfaction data on app interface design, function layout, response speed, etc., by designing a structured questionnaire. This data can help designers identify user needs and problems in the design so that targeted optimization can be carried out.

In conclusion, the literature review shows the application of user experience theory in interaction design as well as the status quo and challenges of museum apps, and the application of user experience research methodology in museum app design and synthesizes the research results in related fields. It lays a solid theoretical foundation for the subsequent research. Through the research of user experience theory, designers can gain a deeper understanding of user needs, discover the problems existing in the museum app, and put forward effective optimization solutions, to improve the overall user experience of the app, which not only helps to improve user satisfaction, but also promotes the continuous development of the interaction design and digitalization of the museum app.

3 Questionnaire Design

The data of this study uses the questionnaire method, and the research questions will be used to develop the questionnaire on the use of the apps in the existing Chinese museum apps on the market. The questionnaire was chosen to study the population from 18 to 55 years old, the museum app questionnaire has 14 questions, 103 people participated in the questionnaire, including 42 men and 61 women. a total of 103 valid questionnaires were retrieved. The questions in the questionnaire are as follows:

1. What is your age?
2. What is your gender?
3. How many times a month do you use the museum app?
4. How do you use the museum app?
5. Please rate whether the functions of the museum app are rich or not. (1–100 points)
6. What is the main purpose of using the museum app?
7. Which of the following functions are most useful to you?
8. Please rate your experience of the following functions of the museum app. (1–100 points)
9. Please rate the aesthetics of the interface design of the museum app on the market. (1–100 points)
10. Please rate whether the interface layout of the museum app is clear and easy to understand. (1–100 points)
11. Please rate whether the operation process of the museum app is convenient. (1–100 points)
12. What problems have you encountered when using the museum app?
13. In what aspects do you hope the museum app can be improved?
14. What is your overall rating of the museum app on the market? (1–100 points)

3.1 Data Collection and Analysis

3.1.1 Correlation Heatmap of Museum App All Numeric Columns

The authors have pre-processed the data for the questionnaire survey, deleted the outliers, and standardized the data by converting all the non-numerical information into numerical values, thus ensuring that the data meets the requirements of data analysis. The authors used the algorithm pandas to analyze the heat map, and finally, we can see that the red color in this map is a positive correlation, the redder the red color indicates the higher positive correlation coefficient between them, and the blue color is a negative correlation, the bluer the blue color indicates the higher negative correlation coefficient.

The heat map (Fig. 1), shows the correlation between the various features of the museum apps and their overall ratings, and the following are the results of the analysis: the factors that are positively correlated with the overall ratings of the museum apps are the richness of the app features (0.47), the detailed information about the exhibitions (0.48), the guided tours service (0.48) the registration for the events (0.51) the AR/VR interactions (0.48), and the factors with strong positive The strong positive correlations include interface design aesthetics (0.79), interface layout clarity (0.8), and ease of application operation flow (0.81).

The factors that are negatively correlated with the overall rating of museum apps are gender (−0.3) frequency of using the apps per month (−0.18), main purpose of using the apps (−0.22), and useful functions (−0.25), of which the strong negative correlation is the problems encountered by the apps (−0.28), which are mainly slow loading speed of the page, lagging or crashing, inaccuracy of the guiding function errors, and poor interactive experience with complicated operation process.

The overall rating of museum apps is closely related to several factors, especially interface design aesthetics, interface layout clarity, and the ease of the app's operation process, which show a strong positive correlation. The problems encountered by the app are strongly negatively correlated with the overall rating, indicating that these problems significantly negatively impact the user experience. By making targeted suggestions to optimize these problems, museums can significantly improve user satisfaction and the overall rating of the app.

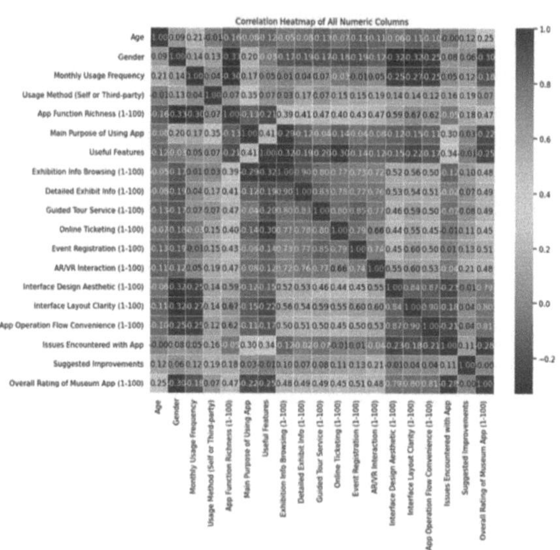

Fig. 1. Correlation heatmap of the museum app's all numeric columns.

3.1.2   Correlation Heatmap of Museum App Features with Overall Rating

According to the heat map (Fig. 2), the factors that are positively correlated with the overall rating of museum apps are the convenience of the app's operation process (0.81), the clarity of the interface layout (0.80), and the aesthetics of the interface design (0.79). Factors negatively correlated with the overall rating of museum apps include online ticketing (0.45), exhibition information browsing (0.48), AR/VR interaction (0.48), detailed exhibition information (0.49) guided tour service (0.49).

3.1.3   Line Graph of Average Scores for Museum App Features

According to the line graph (Fig. 3), the average score of online ticketing was analyzed to be the highest at 77.72 points, and the average score of AR/VR interaction was the lowest at 60.67 points.

3.1.4   Distribution of Overall Museum App Ratings Chart

According to the bar chart (Fig. 4), the analysis concluded that the users' overall rating of the museum apps on the market is in the range of 60 to 80.

Combined with the data analysis of the three charts, it is concluded that: first, ensure the information architecture is reasonable and simplify the operation flow of the app; second, maintain the beauty and consistency of the interface design; thirdly, utilize AR/VR technology to enhance the user experience; and fourth, combine with gamification to improve the user engagement. By implementing the above design solutions, user satisfaction and engagement with the museum app can be further enhanced, the overall user experience can be improved, and the overall rating of the app can be improved.

4   Based on the User Experience Museum App Interaction Design Program

4.1   Interaction Based on Visual Under User Experience

4.1.1   Icon Design

In icon design, the shapes and patterns of the museum's collection artifacts are extracted and simplified. This makes the icons intuitive and easy to understand, conforming to international standards and reducing cultural barriers. As a result, users of all ages and skill levels can easily understand and operate the museum application.

4.1.2   Interface Text

Interface text is the core of information transmission. Therefore, in the design of the museum application, the consistency and recognizability of the text should be ensured. For titles and key information, methods such as bolding, changing color, and increasing font size can be used for highlighting. For example, the titles of the navigation map, the museum's most precious artifacts, and popular exhibition hall recommendations placed on the home page should be made more readable to facilitate the effective transmission of information, thereby improving users' operational efficiency and overall experience.

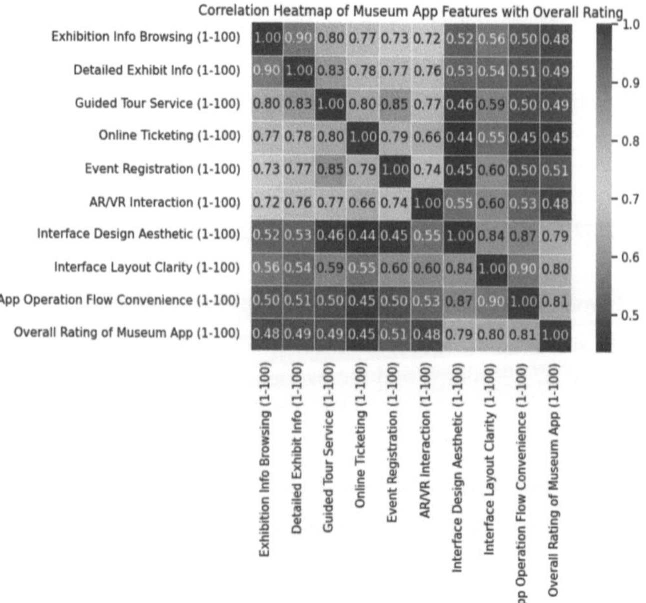

Fig. 2. Correlation heatmap of Museum app features with overall rating.

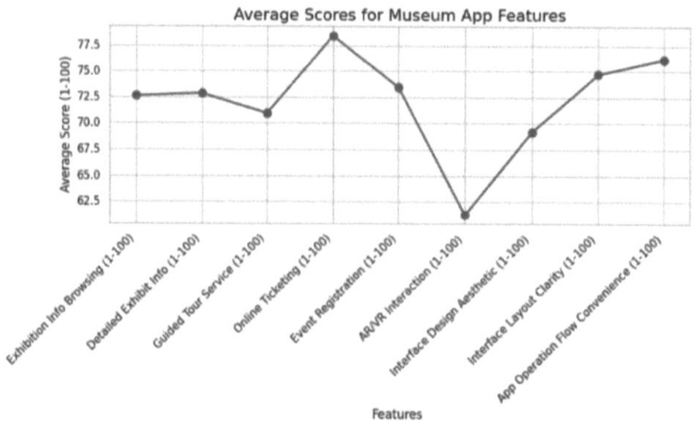

Fig. 3. Line graph of average scores for museum app features.

4.1.3 Interface Design

When designing the interface, inspiration is drawn from the museum's culture, historical features, and collection. A unique, immersive design that embodies the museum's cultural connotations is created. In terms of color, a color scheme that is harmonious with the museum's atmosphere is used, avoiding overly bright or glaring colors to create a comfortable and peaceful visual experience for users. Colors are used to convey the museum's emotions and atmosphere. At the same time, the aesthetics and consistency of the interface design should be maintained. The interface layout should pay attention to

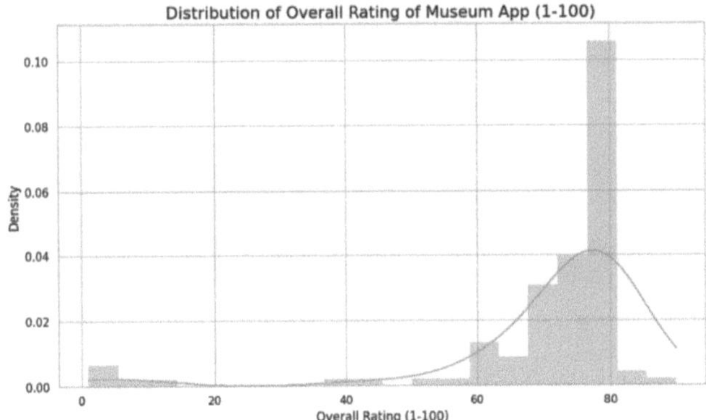

Fig. 4. Distribution of overall museum app ratings chart.

white space to avoid overcrowding of information, ensuring that users can concentrate when using the application (Fig. 5).

4.2 Social Interaction Based on Interaction Experience

4.2.1 Adding Social Interfaces

Social interfaces are added to the APP, providing users with functions such as following, sharing, and commenting. Users can take photos and share their museum visit routes and experiences on the app. Museum enthusiasts can follow and comment on each other's posts. In addition to traditional text and image sharing, multimedia forms such as voice and short videos are supported, allowing users to more vividly express their museum-visit experiences.

4.2.2 Combining User Preferences

By analyzing users' preferences, such as the museums they have visited, their favorite exhibition types, and search history, user profiles are constructed. Combining users' geographical location and time information, nearby museum activities or temporary exhibition hall information is intelligently pushed, enabling more accurate exhibition information delivery. For example, when a user successfully books a museum visit, the APP can automatically send a message reminder and push information about the museum's exhibitions, including opening hours, highlights of the collection, and temporary exhibitions, ensuring that users do not miss activities they are interested in and can arrange their visits reasonably. At the same time, users are allowed to customize the appearance of the application, such as choosing light or dark modes or theme layouts for different exhibitions to meet different users' visual preferences and needs. Users are also allowed to create personalized profiles to display the exhibits they have visited, their favorite artifacts, and achievements (Fig. 5).

4.3   Intelligent Interaction Based on Emotional Experience

4.3.1   Interactive Navigation Map

Combined with AR technology, an interactive navigation map is developed. Users can view the navigation map on the museum application through their mobile phones to know their current location and the museum's navigation information, such as exhibit introductions, direction indications, and exhibition area distributions. The navigation map plans visit routes according to users' different needs and provides real-time push messages such as "You are approaching the XX exhibition area, and there will be a live explanation at a certain time." Users can also query information or request exhibition hall navigation information through voice commands, improving the convenience of use and ensuring a better visiting experience.

4.3.2   Virtual Exhibit Explanation

AR and VR technologies are introduced for distinctive artifacts or exhibitions to create an immersive exhibition viewing experience. The artifacts and exhibition environments are reconstructed in 3D panoramas. In the virtual environment, users can interact with the artifacts, such as gently rotating a beautiful jade object to observe its details from all angles, wearing virtual jewelry to feel its weight and luster, or putting on virtual armor to experience the charm of ancient warriors. Users can also interact with the artifacts or other virtual characters, such as asking questions and having conversations.

4.3.3   Game Interaction

A game section is added to the museum application, and a series of virtual treasure hunting games based on the museum's exhibits or exhibition themes are designed. Each treasure hunting game task is embedded in an engaging storyline. Users need to read historical background information and solve puzzles alone or in cooperation with other users. Users receive task prompts through the APP, such as "Find and take photos of three artifacts related to the Tang Dynasty," and then explore and complete the tasks in the museum or virtual exhibition. Users can choose to play the roles of historical figures, explorers, or historians in the museum, experiencing different historical scenes and character perspectives by completing specific tasks and challenges. After completing each game task, users can obtain corresponding points, badges, or virtual rewards, which are displayed on the personal homepage of the APP. Points are accumulated based on users' activity levels (such as posting content, participating in discussions, and completing challenges), and can be used to exchange for museum cultural and creative products, digital artifacts, or honor badges, enhancing users' sense of belonging and achievement. Users can also see their rankings on the leaderboard and compete with other users, which can stimulate users' enthusiasm (Fig. 5).

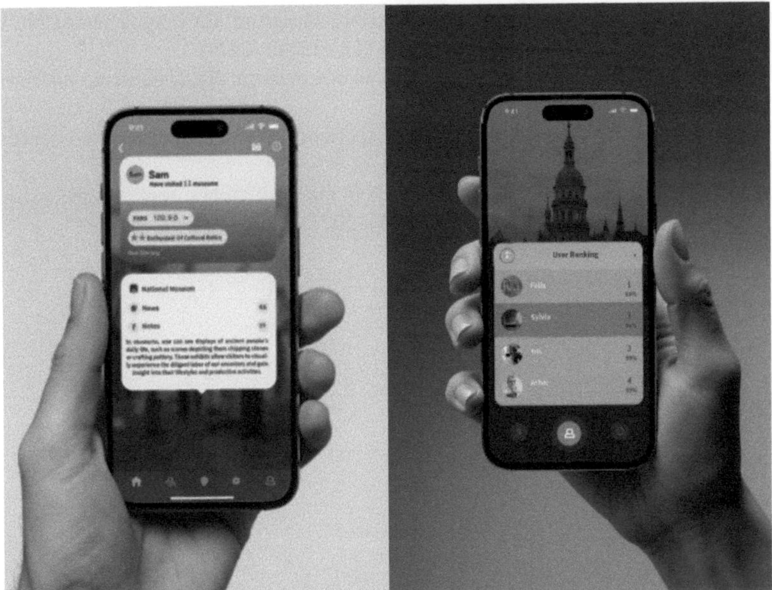

Fig. 5. Museum App Interface Renderings.

5 Conclusion

This study proposes a design solution by deeply analyzing the importance of user experience theory in museum app interaction design and organizing and analyzing the data to find out the problems of existing museum apps in China. It not only helps to increase user satisfaction and engagement with museum apps but also provides new ideas and methods for future museum app interaction design and digitization. This study also has the following shortcomings: the first user experience interaction between AR and VR can be further explored in the future. The second implementation effect assessment is insufficient; the optimization suggestions proposed in this study have not yet been verified by practical applications, so their implementation effect is still uncertain, and the implementation effect of the optimization suggestions can be assessed and adjusted in the future through practical case studies or user feedback.

References

1. Norman, D.A.: Emotional design: why we love (or Hate) everyday things. Basic Books, New York (2004)
2. Hussain, A., Mkpojiogu, E.O.C., Kamal, F.M.: The role of user experience in mobile apps: a review. JTEC. **8**(10), 143–146 (2015)
3. Jones, M., Sasser, W.E.: Why satisfied customers defect. Harv. Bus. Rev. (1995)
4. Falk, J.H., Dierking, L.D.: The Museum Experience. Smithsonian Institution Press (1992)
5. Nielsen, J.: Usability 101: Introduction to Usability. Nielsen Norman Group (2012)
6. Norman, D.A.: The Design of Everyday Things. MIT Press (2013)

7. Liu, Y., Cheng, P., Li, J.: Application interface design of Chongqing intangible cultural heritage based on deep learning. Heliyon. **9**(11), e22242 (2023)
8. Lin, X., Wang, J., Li, Q. Research on the design of a museum digital generous interface based on user experience (2024)
9. Sauro, J., Lewis, J.R.: Quantifying the User Experience: Practical Statistics for User Research. Morgan Kaufmann (2012)
10. Smith, J., Doe, A.: Understanding user needs in museum Mobile applications: a survey and interview study. J. Interact. Learn. Res. **30**(4) (2021)

Mid-Air Gesture Interaction Design for Cantonese Opera: Enhancing the Emotional Experience of Intangible Cultural Heritage

Zixuan Sun and Xin Xie[✉]

Harbin Institute of Technology, Shenzhen 518000, China
velvent@163.com

Abstract. With the rise of natural user interfaces, gesture interaction, as an intuitive non-verbal communication method, has garnered significant attention in human-computer interaction research due to its unique ability to express emotions and convey cultural connotations. Cantonese opera, an important intangible cultural heritage in China, faces challenges in inheritance due to language barriers, high learning thresholds, and limited appeal. Existing research primarily focuses on technical implementation, often neglecting the user's emotional experience. This study combines emotion quantification methods and Gesture Elicitation Studies, utilizing professional Cantonese opera performance materials to design an emotional mid-air gesture interaction prototype. This prototype retains the characteristics of intangible cultural heritage while aligning with public cognitive logic, aiming to lower the learning threshold for Cantonese opera and enhance users' cultural understanding and participation by improving their emotional experience. Results indicate that participants preferred designing gestures expressing medium to high levels of pleasure, arousal, and dominance, consistent with the positive emotions conveyed in Cantonese opera performances.

Keywords: Mid-air Gestures · Gesture Elicitation Studies · Intangible Cultural Heritage · Emotional Design

1 Introduction

With the rapid advancement of human-computer interaction (HCI) technology, traditional graphical user interfaces (GUI) no longer suffice to meet users' diverse interaction needs. Natural user interfaces (NUI), which utilize voice, touch, gestures, and facial expressions as natural input forms, provide a more intuitive and user-friendly interaction experience [1], making them a focal point in human-computer interaction research. In the realm of intangible cultural heritage (ICH) promotion and preservation, gesture interaction offers a more intuitive and natural non-verbal communication method. This allows researchers to move beyond static graphic displays, instead constructing multi-dimensional, immersive cultural experiences that enhance user engagement and understanding of ICH [2].

M. Schrepp and M. Rauterberg (Eds.): HCII 2025, LNCS 16342, pp. 259–275, 2026.
https://doi.org/10.1007/978-3-032-13164-5_17

Volioti [3] developed a natural user interface prototype using motion capture technology to convert user gestures and emotions into musical instrument sounds. This innovation aims to facilitate learning and dissemination of ICH music. Cantonese opera, a significant Chinese ICH, is known for its unique elements such as dialect singing and martial arts. However, its use of Cantonese and high performance skill requirements limit its accessibility. These barriers reduce its appeal to younger audiences, risking a potential cultural loss.Digital technology presents new avenues for transmitting and disseminating Cantonese opera. For example, researchers have utilized 3D reconstruction to create interactive scenes that merge reality with virtuality [4], thereby attracting younger audiences to its cultural appeal. Additionally, digital 3D greeting cards featuring Cantonese opera costumes have been developed [5], innovating communication methods. Serious games based on Cantonese opera movements have also been created to generate interest in its performances [6].

While these initiatives have significantly advanced the digital dissemination of Cantonese opera, they predominantly focus on technical implementation, often overlooking the emotional dimensions of user experience. Notably, few studies explored the potential of Cantonese opera gestures as a cultural foundation for interaction design. Given that gestures represent a fundamental mode of natural interaction, they hold the potential to enhance the intuitiveness of user engagement with virtual ICH. Moreover, gestures are deeply embedded in Cantonese opera performances, carrying profound cultural significance and serving as a medium for emotional expression. This study aims to bridge this research gap by investigating how mid-air gesture interaction design can enrich users' emotional experience of Cantonese opera.This paper mainly carries out emotional gesture interaction design research through the following research questions:

RQ1: How does current gesture interaction design enhance users' emotional experience?
RQ2: How to design a gesture interaction prototype that can retain cultural characteristics and enhance users' emotional experience?
RQ3: How to incorporate emotional measurement methods into general gesture elicitation studies?

This paper is structured as follows: Sect. 2 reviews related literature, including mid-air gesture interaction design, gesture elicitation studies (GES), and emotional design in mid-air gesture processes. Section 3 details the study's methodology, covering the selection of heuristic materials and the user gesture design process. Section 4 analyzes and discusses gesture data, presenting the final gesture set. Section 5 summarizes the study's main findings. Finally, Sect. 6 outlines the limitations of the current study and proposes directions for future research.

2 Introduction

2.1 Mid-Air Gesture Interaction Design and Gesture Elicitation Studies

Mid-air gesture interaction represents an advanced input modality that facilitates user engagement with computer systems or devices through sensor-based (primarily employing computer vision technology) recognition of hand movements in three-dimensional space, eliminating the requirement for direct physical contact with any objects or surfaces [7]. In contrast to conventional two-dimensional touch-based gestures that necessitate direct screen contact, mid-air gestures offer enhanced flexibility and naturalness in human-computer interaction, demonstrating significant potential for implementation across multiple domains, particularly in multi-display environments, mixed reality gaming applications, and intelligent home systems.

However, the academic community has yet to establish a unified classification framework for mid-air gestures. Among existing studies, the classification model proposed by Aigner et al. [8] stands as one of the most representative and widely-cited frameworks. Their model systematically categorizes mid-air gestures into five distinct types: (1) "Pointing" that primarily function to indicate specific objects or spatial directions; (2) "Semaphoric" that employ predefined motion patterns to convey specific semantic meanings; (3) "Pantomimic" that replicate or demonstrate specific tasks or actions without the presence of corresponding physical entities; (4) "Iconic" that represent universally recognized symbolic signs or visual metaphors; and (5) "Manipulation" that operate within a closed feedback loop, requiring the manipulated virtual object to respond and follow the user's motion before proceeding with subsequent operations. This comprehensive classification framework provides valuable theoretical guidance for mid-air gesture design, enabling developers to better interpret user intentions and optimize interactive experiences through more precise gesture recognition and response mechanisms.

In the domain of gesture design methodologies, the GES has emerged as a predominant research paradigm for user-centered gesture design within the field of HCI. This methodology was initially formalized by Wobbrock et al., who established a systematic framework for optimizing gesture design through comprehensive user feedback collection and rigorous evaluation of gesture guessability, thereby enhancing the universality and adaptability of gesture-based interactions [9]. However, early implementations of the GES approach failed to account for the significant influence of cultural context on user-generated gestures, a limitation that was subsequently addressed by Morris et al. [10]. Their follow-up research proposed methodological refinements to the GES framework, suggesting that researchers should generate an expanded set of gesture proposals, leverage emerging technologies to transcend users' cognitive limitations, and implement structured group-based elicitation protocols. Further methodological advancements in GES were achieved through Vatavu et al.'s introduction of the dissimilarity consensus method, which incorporated growth curves and logistic functions to compute objective measures of user gesture preferences, thereby providing robust quantitative support for gesture elicitation studies [11]. In a parallel development, Tsandilas et al. reformulated the challenge of deriving gesture vocabularies in GES as a computational optimization problem, establishing novel theoretical foundations and methodological guidelines for gesture interaction design [12].These cumulative advancements have significantly refined the GES methodology, establishing it as a formal research paradigm within HCI. This evolution culminated in the development of a comprehensive model for GES in HCI by Vatavu and Wobbrock et al. [13]. Their model provides formal definitions of fundamental concepts in GES research and offers clearer theoretical frameworks and methodological guidelines for conducting end-user gesture elicitation studies.

Although significant progress has been made in the field of mid-air gesture interaction design, the majority of existing studies have primarily focused on technical implementations, with relatively limited attention given to the emotional dimensions of the user experience. This gap is particularly evident in the context of interaction design for ICH, where the integration of emotional factors into gesture design to enhance users' emotional engagement remains an urgent and unresolved challenge.

2.2 Emotional Dimensions in Mid-Air Gesture Interaction

Gestures constitute a fundamental component of human non-verbal communication, playing a pivotal role in emotional expression and transmission. McNeill, in his seminal work, emphasized the intrinsic connection between gestures and cognitive processes, linguistic expression, and emotional states [14]. Empirical studies have demonstrated that both the typology and scale of gestures significantly influence individuals' processing of emotional content [15], while dynamic characteristics such as velocity and intensity similarly affect emotional expression [16]. In educational contexts, while gestures do not consistently enhance individuals' encoding of external information, the integration of affective elements has been shown to substantially improve comprehension and retention of narrative materials [17]. Consequently, emotion and gesture are frequently examined as critical variables in interactive ICH projects with educational implications.

In the domain of interaction design for traditional culture, the integration strategies between gestures and emotions primarily manifest in two distinct approaches: emotion-feedback-oriented gesture interaction and emotion-gesture integration as core interactive elements. The former approach emphasizes the instrumental role of gestures in human-computer interaction, where gestures are predefined by developers with the primary objective of eliciting users' emotional responses through interaction [18]. Systems developed through this methodology are typically characterized by operational simplicity, efficiency, and usability, yet they often overlook the potential of gesture-based interaction in facilitating cultural transmission. The latter approach places greater emphasis on the intrinsic cultural value of gestures themselves, which are typically defined by cultural experts and subsequently acquired by users through expert gesture imitation and memorization [3]. However, due to the specificity of cultural contexts, expert-defined gestures may present operational challenges for general users, consequently increasing cognitive load and interaction complexity.

Although existing research has achieved some progress in integrating gestures with emotional expression, the majority of studies have predominantly focused on specific domains such as music or education, while systematic investigations into ICH, particularly Cantonese opera, remain notably absent. In performing arts traditions like Cantonese opera, gestures serve not merely as essential performative elements but as fundamental vehicles for emotional expression and cultural transmission. Consequently, the primary focus of this study lies in addressing the critical challenge of balancing the cultural significance of gestures with their functional operability. This dual objective aims to simultaneously fulfill the instrumental role of gestures in interaction while effectively conveying emotional meaning, thereby facilitating public engagement and understanding, and promoting the dissemination and cultural education of Cantonese opera as a significant ICH.

3 Materials and Methods

3.1 Chinese Simplified Version of the PAD Scale

Mehrabian et al. pioneered the development of the PAD (Pleasure-Arousal-Dominance) three-dimensional emotional model [19], which quantifies human emotions across three distinct dimensions: Pleasure (P), Arousal (A), and Dominance (D). This model partitions the emotional space into eight discrete regions based on the positive and negative valences of P, A, and D. Given that Cantonese opera represents a significant component of traditional Chinese culture with distinctive regional emotional characteristics, this study employs the Chinese-adapted PAD scale developed by researchers at the Chinese Academy of Sciences [20] to ensure accurate mapping of emotional expressions within the Chinese cultural context. The scale comprises 12 items and has been empirically validated for its reliability and validity. Furthermore, to enhance the precision of emotional assessment, the researchers have established a reference scale encompassing 14 fundamental emotions (see Table 1), enabling more accurate evaluation of users' emotional tendencies and inclinations.

Table 1. Reference table of PAD values for 14 basic emotions.

Number	Type of emotion	P-value	A-value	D-value
1	Pleasure	2.77	1.21	1.42
2	Optimism	2.48	1.05	1.75
3	Ease	2.19	−0.66	1.05
4	Astonishment	1.72	1.71	0.22
5	Mildness	1.57	−0.79	0.38
6	Dependence	0.39	−0.81	−1.48
7	Ennui	−0.53	−1.25	−0.84
8	Melancholy	−0.89	0.17	−0.70
9	Dread	−0.93	1.30	−0.64
10	Anxiety	−0.95	0.32	−0.63
11	Disdain	−1.58	0.32	1.02
12	Aversion	−1.80	0.40	0.67
13	Indignation	−1.98	1.10	0.60
14	Hostility	−2.08	1.00	1.12

3.2 Participants

In accordance with established sample sizes from previous gesture elicitation studies, which typically range between 15 and 30 participants, this study recruited a total of 20 eligible participants (6 male, 14 female) aged 18–30 through randomized selection via social media platforms. On the one hand, this group demonstrates a strong ability to accept new things, with prominent curiosity and a desire for exploration. On the other hand, Cantonese opera culture is currently facing the dilemma of an aging audience and urgently needs to expand its dissemination channels among the younger demographic. Therefore, this study is targeted at such target users in order to better carry out virtual display projects based on Cantonese opera gestures. Considering the core research objectives, no additional restrictions were imposed regarding participants' professional backgrounds or educational levels. All participants were right-handed and possessed minimal to no prior knowledge of Cantonese opera culture, ensuring a uniform baseline understanding among participants and minimizing potential biases associated with preexisting cultural knowledge. Prior to experimental participation, all subjects provided informed consent through signed consent forms.

3.3 Materials and Equipment

The video materials utilized in this study were sourced from authoritative Cantonese opera references, featuring a series of fundamental gesture movements demonstrated by professional performers to ensure the authenticity and standardization of experimental stimuli. In traditional Cantonese opera performances, artists employ standardized gestures, such as the orchid hand position, while simultaneously conveying specific imitative objects (e.g., birds, moon, mountains) through vivid facial expressions and body movements. To maintain participants' creative freedom during the experimental process, the video materials were rigorously selected based on the following criteria:

1. Clarity and Visibility: The performer's arms and upper body must be clearly visible throughout the video without any visual obstructions.
2. Movement Diversity: Each video segment should demonstrate distinct gestural variations, particularly in hand movements, to ensure sufficient differentiation among stimuli.
3. Performative Ambiguity: The imitative objects represented by the performer should remain implicit rather than explicit, thereby providing participants with broader imaginative and creative possibilities.
4. Emotional Expression: The performer's presentation should effectively communicate identifiable emotional states, facilitating participants' comprehension and engagement with the emotional dimensions of Cantonese opera performances.

Following the established criteria, this study conducted a preliminary experiment involving three participants. After viewing the video materials, participants were required to provide subjective emotional reports and generate as many simplified gesture variations as possible for each video segment. Based on the participants' emotional feedback and the quantity of simplified gestures produced, the research team eliminated video materials that either lacked distinct emotional expression or yielded fewer than two simplified gestures on average. Through this rigorous selection process, 12 specific performance gestures were ultimately selected from an initial pool of 16 representative Cantonese opera gestures for use as experimental stimuli, as detailed in Table 2.

Table 2. The 12 Cantonese Opera gesture performance movements used in the GES.

Serial Number	Performance Task	Serial Number	Performance Task
T1	Land	T7	Firmament
T2	Breeze	T8	Snowscape
T3	Blossom	T9	Nightfall
T4	Thunder	T10	Rainfall
T5	Timber	T11	Moon
T6	Bird	T12	Mountain

The experimental procedure was conducted in a controlled laboratory setting where participants were seated before a laptop computer and presented with a series of Power-Point slides. These slides sequentially displayed 12 Cantonese opera performance videos according to the order specified in Table 2. To maintain research integrity and ensure participant anonymity, all identifying information regarding video sources and specific imitative objects were systematically obscured. Following each video presentation, corresponding instructional slides were displayed to guide participants in performing the required gestural movements. Each participant's gesture proposals were recorded using a dual-camera system: one camera positioned directly in front of the participant and another placed at a 45° angle above the participant, ensuring comprehensive documentation of gestures from multiple perspectives. The researcher, stationed between the two recording devices, utilized a tablet computer to monitor the experimental process and control the recording equipment. The precise configuration of the experimental setup is illustrated in Fig. 1.

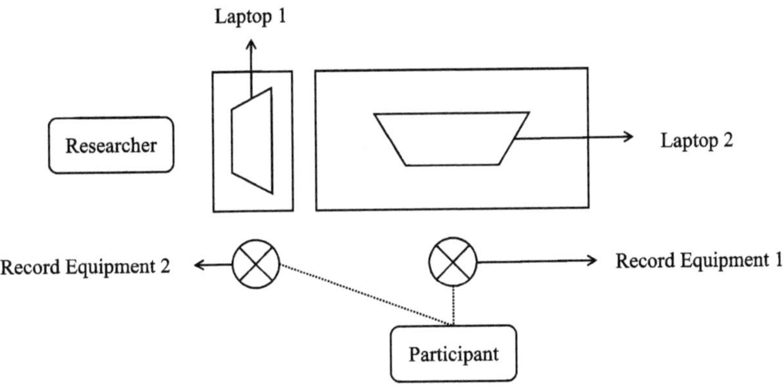

Fig. 1. Layout of experimental equipment

3.4 Experimental Procedure

At the commencement of the formal experimental session, each participant was first presented with Cantonese opera gesture performance materials. After achieving comprehensive understanding of both the gestural and emotional information conveyed through these materials, participants were required to design a minimum of two simplified gestures for each presentation segment. These gestures needed to effectively communicate the emotional experience elicited by the presentation materials while adhering to the principle of maximal simplicity. Following the creation of each gesture, participants provided verbal explanations to the researcher regarding their design rationale. The experimental procedure followed the task sequence outlined in Table 2, continuing iteratively until all tasks were completed. Throughout this process, the researcher documented all gesture proposals generated by participants using video recording equipment, thereby establishing an initial gesture set A.

3.4.1 Emotion

Following the observation of Cantonese opera presentation materials, participants were required to complete the simplified Chinese version of the PAD scale. The PAD scale quantifies emotional expression through computational analysis of Euclidean distances between the emotional state of the evaluated gesture and 14 fundamental emotions within a three-dimensional affective space. The shortest calculated distance indicates the gesture's predominant emotional tendency, while the magnitude of this distance reflects the intensity of the affective inclination.

$$L_n = \sqrt{(P - p_n)^2 + (A - a_n)^2 + (D - d_n)^2} \tag{1}$$

where n represents the 14 fundamental emotions (E_1 through E_{14}), while P, A, and D correspond to the mean values of the Pleasure, Arousal, and Dominance for all initial gestures (gesture set A) under each categorical gesture (gesture set B)

3.4.2 Subjective Ratings: Preference, Match, Usability

In determining the dimensions for subjective evaluation, this study adopted three established metrics based on prior research: preference, match quality, and ease of use [21]. Following the completion of simplified gesture design, participants were required to select a single most satisfactory gesture from all proposed simplified gestures for each presentation material. Subsequently, they evaluated the chosen gesture using a seven-point Likert scale across two dimensions: "This gesture effectively matches the intended purpose" and "This gesture is easy to perform." Preference was operationalized as the frequency with which each categorical gesture in gesture set B was selected as the preferred option, reflecting participants' satisfaction and perceived utility of the gesture. Match quality was calculated as the mean score of all ratings in the matching dimension for the preferred gesture, serving as an indicator of the gesture's alignment with emotional expression. Similarly, ease of use was quantified as the mean score of all ratings in the ease-of-use dimension for the preferred gesture, providing a measure of the gesture's operational efficiency.

3.4.3 Gesture Set, Popularity, Overall Score

Following preliminary organization and classification, the researcher systematically categorized the initial gestures in gesture set A based on three primary dimensions: form (finger, palm, fist), quantity (single-handed, double-handed), and state (static, dynamic). Gestures sharing identical characteristics across these three dimensions were grouped into the same category. Representative gestures were then selected from each category to establish gesture set B. However, only gesture classifications proposed by a minimum of three participants were included in gesture set B. Gesture prevalence was quantified as the number of participants proposing identical gestures within gesture set B. The comprehensive score for each gesture was calculated based on four variables: preference, match quality, ease of use, and prevalence. Prior to summation, all variables were standardized to a mean of 10 and a standard deviation of 1. The total score represents the sum of these four standardized variables.

3.4.4 Gesture Selection

Through computational analysis of the aforementioned variables, the researcher classified gestures within gesture set B according to their emotional tendencies. From this classification, the top three gestures demonstrating the strongest emotional tendency and the top three gestures with the highest total scores within each emotional category were selected to establish candidate gesture set C. For the final gesture set F, the researcher employed a comprehensive evaluation approach, integrating both emotional tendency and total scores, to further refine the selection from candidate gesture set C while ensuring the elimination of redundant gestures.

4 Data Analysis and Results

In this study, gesture set A comprised a total of 516 gestures generated by 20 participants. Gesture set B included 62 gestures proposed by three or more participants, encompassing nine affective categories, while five additional affective categories were excluded due to insufficient gesture representation (fewer than two gestures). Gesture set C ultimately contained 21 gestures.

Figure 2 illustrates the distribution of affective tendencies for each gesture in gesture set B, as collected through the simplified Chinese version of the PAD scale, along with the spatial distribution of the 14 fundamental emotions across the Pleasure (P), Arousal (A), and Dominance (D) dimensions.

According to the PAD emotional space classification framework, positive P values indicate gestures with higher pleasantness levels, while negative P values signify lower pleasantness levels, with analogous interpretations applying to A (Arousal) and D (Dominance) dimensions. Analytical results reveal that gestures in gesture set B predominantly express emotions characterized by medium-to-high levels of P, A, and D, exemplified by emotional states such as "Optimism", "Pleasure", and "Determination". Conversely, gestures expressing low levels of P, A, or D, such as "Dependence", "Ennui", and "Melancholy", were significantly less prevalent.

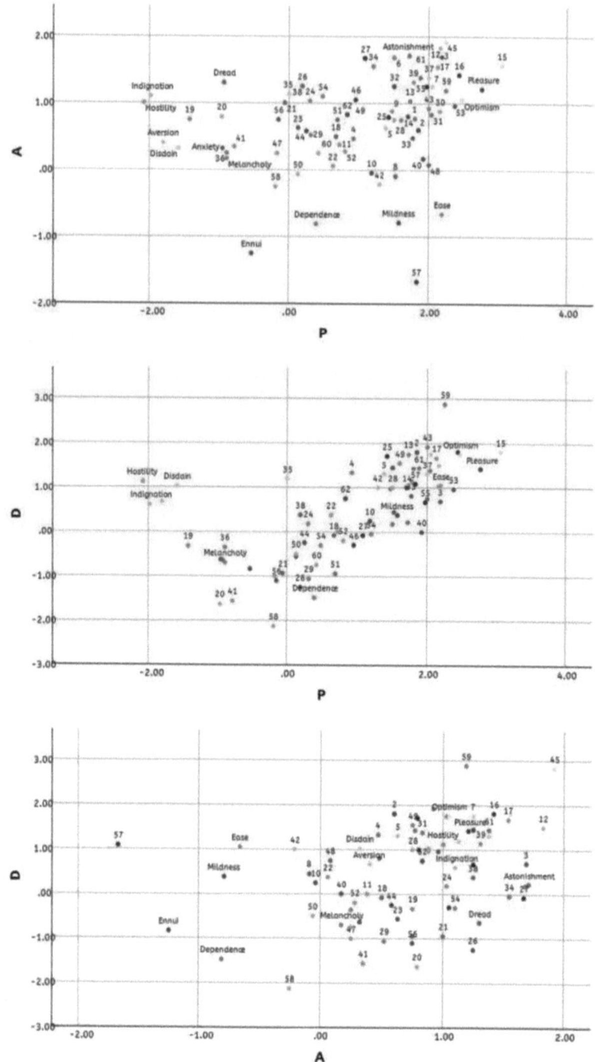

Fig. 2. Affective Distribution of Gesture Set B and Fundamental Emotions across Pleasure-Arousal-Dominance Dimensions.

This observed distribution may be attributed to the intrinsic cultural characteristics of Cantonese opera. The experimental stimuli were exclusively drawn from fundamental gestures commonly employed by "Dan"(female role) performers in Cantonese opera, which typically emulate natural scenery. Consequently, participants were more inclined to embody the positive and uplifting emotional states conveyed through these Cantonese opera performance materials, resulting in a predominant expression of positive emotions through their gesture proposals.

Table 3 presents the performance metrics and affective tendencies of candidate gestures within gesture set C across each evaluation dimension. Among the gestures in set C, 15 demonstrated the capacity to express uniquely determined emotions, with those exhibiting higher total scores showing superior performance and thus being eligible for inclusion in the final gesture set. The remaining six gestures displayed multiple affective tendencies (denoted by "*" in Table 3), necessitating further analysis that integrates their total score performance across different emotional categories to determine their definitive affective attributes.

Gesture 3 (unilateral thumb and index finger opening-closing motion with remaining three fingers extended) demonstrated the capacity to effectively express both "Pleasure" and "Optimism" emotions, achieving the highest overall scores (OS = 43.71, DT_Optimism = 0.38, DT_Pleasure = 0.55). Regarding the expression of "Optimism", gestures 4 (unilateral orchid hand gesture with horizontal movement) and 5 (unilateral upright palm with lateral movement) exhibited lower preference and prevalence scores, failing to effectively convey the intended emotion.For the expression of "Pleasure", although gesture 2 (interlocked thumbs with extended fingers simulating bird wings) did not exhibit the closest affective tendency (DT = 0.65), it ranked second in overall scores (OS = 41.40) and demonstrated superior preference metrics, thus being deemed more suitable for expressing the "Pleasure" emotion. Consequently, gesture 3 was selected as the optimal representation for "Optimism", while gesture 2 was designated for "Pleasure" expression.

Gesture 7 (bilateral downward palm movement with finger tremors) and gesture 8 (unilateral index finger tracing motion in air) both demonstrated the capacity to express "Ease" and "Mildness" emotions. However, in expressing "Mildness", gesture 12 (unilateral index finger pointing forward), while similar to gesture 8, exhibited inferior performance metrics (OS = 40.92, DT = 0.86). Consequently, gesture 8 was identified as more appropriate for conveying "Mildness" (OS = 42.94, DT = 0.71).Although gesture 6 showed stronger affective tendency toward "Ease", its lower preference scores rendered it less suitable. Therefore, gesture 7 was selected as the optimal representation for "Ease" (OS = 39.43, DT = 1.10), based on its superior overall performance and user preference metrics.

Both gesture 16 (unilateral palm-forward pushing motion) and gesture 17 (unilateral downward-facing palm with vertical movement) demonstrated the capacity to express "Melancholy" and "Anxiety" emotions. However, for the expression of "Melancholy", gesture 18 (bilateral arm-clasping with vertical movement) exhibited superior overall scores and prevalence metrics, rendering it more appropriate for conveying "Melancholy" (OS = 47.40, DT = 0.89).Regarding the expression of "Anxiety", gesture 16 significantly outperformed gesture 17, not only in terms of overall scores (OS = 41.19) but also in demonstrating closer affective proximity to "Anxiety" (DT = 0.29). Consequently, gesture 16 was selected as the optimal emotional gesture for representing "Anxiety".

Gesture 19 (bilateral arm-crossing in front of the torso) demonstrated the capacity to express both "Dread" and "Anxiety" emotions. Although gesture 21 (bilateral palm-forward pushing motion) achieved marginally higher overall scores for expressing "Dread", gesture 19 was deemed more suitable as the representative gesture for "Dread"

Table 3. Comprehensive Evaluation of Gesture Set C: Five-Dimensional Performance Metrics and Affective Tendencies.

Gesture	Popularity	Preference	Match	Usability	Overall Score(OS)	Emotion	Distant(DT)
1	4.00	0.10	5.00	5.50	38.86	Pleasure	0.60
2	6.00	0.25	5.60	6.00	41.40	Pleasure	0.65
3*	9.00	0.40	5.63	6.13	43.71	Pleasure Optimism	0.55 0.38
4	5.00	0.10	5.50	6.00	39.73	Optimism	0.47
5	3.00	0.05	5.00	7.00	38.94	Optimism	0.53
6	3.00	0.05	5.00	7.00	38.94	Ease	0.82
7*	6.00	0.15	4.33	5.33	39.43	Ease Mildness	1.01 0.89
8*	11.00	0.30	5.50	5.33	42.94	Ease Mildness	1.06 0.71
9	7.00	0.05	7.00	6.00	40.77	Astonishment	0.23
10	5.00	0.15	6.33	7.00	41.19	Astonishment	0.61
11	4.00	0.10	6.50	6.50	40.27	Astonishment	0.66
12	7.00	0.20	5.00	6.00	40.92	Mildness	0.86
13	4.00	0.05	4.00	5.00	37.57	Dependence	1.29
14	3.00	0.10	6.00	5.50	39.13	Dependence	1.04
15	4.00	0.00	0.00	0.00	32.08	Dependence	1.68
16*	7.00	0.10	6.50	6.50	41.19	Melancholy Anxiety	0.35 0.29
17*	3.00	0.05	5.00	7.00	38.94	Melancholy Anxiety	0.78 0.87
18	17.00	0.50	5.90	6.50	47.40	Melancholy	0.89
19*	3.00	0.05	6.00	6.00	38.97	Dread Anxiety	0.80 0.70
20	4.00	0.10	5.00	4.50	38.31	Dread	0.97
21	5.00	0.10	6.00	7.00	40.57	Dread	1.06

(OS = 38.97, DT = 0.80). This determination was based on its conceptual similarity to gesture 16, differing primarily in the number of hands involved, thereby maintaining consistency within the gesture vocabulary while effectively conveying the intended emotional state (Table 4).

Table 4. Affective Mapping of Gesture Set F: Schematic Representation and Emotional Tendencies.

No.	Classify	Gesture	Emotion	OS	DT	Description
1	Pantomimic		Pleasure	41.40	0.65	Interlock the thumbs of both hands and spread the other four fingers to mimic the wings of a bird.
2	Dynamic Semaphoric		Optimism	43.71	0.38	Open and close the thumb and index finger of one hand with the other three fingers spread.
3	Manipulation		Ease	38.94	0.82	Shift upward with palm up, then downward with palm down.
4	Manipulation		Astonishment	40.77	0.23	Start with palms down and touching, then part symmetrically.
5	Stroke Semaphoric		Mildness	40.92	0.86	Use a single index finger to draw paths in 3D space.
6	Pantomimic		Dependence	39.13	1.04	Both palms are apart while fingers are shaking.
7	Pantomimic		Melancholy	47.40	0.89	Fold arms and move hands up and down along them.
8	Static Semaphoric		Dread	38.97	0.80	Cross both arms in front of the torso.
9	Pointing		Anxiety	41.19	0.29	Push forward with one palm facing outward.

5 Conclusion

This study introduces an innovative affective mid-air gesture interaction prototype designed for the digital dissemination and preservation of Cantonese opera as an ICH. With the advancement of NUI technologies, gesture-based interaction has emerged as a prominent research focus in HCI due to its inherent naturalness and intuitive operation. Within the domain of ICH digitization, gesture interaction not only serves as a primary modality for virtual engagement but also significantly enhances user immersion and interactivity when experiencing digitized ICH artifacts.

1. Existing gesture interaction techniques predominantly concentrate on technical implementation, often overlooking the impact of interaction paradigms on user experience and emotional engagement. Through comprehensive literature review, this study elucidates the general framework of GES and identifies two distinct approaches for integrating emotional dimensions in current gesture interaction systems: (1) utilizing emotional experience as feedback for gesture interaction, and (2) requiring participants to physically replicate expert-defined gestures. The former approach, being developer-defined, may undervalue the significance of emotional resonance, while the latter, being expert-defined, may compromise operational feasibility.
2. In this study, based on the clarity and visibility of the video materials, the diversity of movements, the ambiguity of the performance, and the emotional expression, 12 gesture performance materials were selected from 16 professional Cantonese opera performance videos as heuristic materials for GES. During the formal experiment, participants followed the principle of maximal simplicity to design simplified movements for the 12 Cantonese opera gestures and were required to convey the emotions they perceived in the performance materials, thus enabling the user - generated gestures to retain the cultural characteristics of Cantonese opera.Gesture 1 is a newly created gesture by users based on the performer's imitation of a bird's flying posture. Gesture 2 adopts the performer's original gesture. Gesture 9 simplifies the Cantonese opera gesture "Orchid Finger" into a palm.
3. This study has successfully integrated emotion quantification methods into GES. After watching the heuristic materials, the participants answered the simplified Chinese version of the PAD emotional scale, thereby quantifying the emotional experiences they perceived in the materials. The Euclidean distances between each gesture and 14 basic emotions in a three - dimensional space were calculated. The results show that the same gesture designed by participants can express different emotional tendencies. Under the same emotional category, two - handed gestures have a stronger emotional tendency than one - handed gestures. Participants also tend to design gestures that express medium to high levels of pleasure, arousal, and dominance, which is consistent with the positive emotions conveyed in Cantonese opera performances. In addition, the researchers guided the participants to conduct a subjective evaluation, covering three dimensions: preference, match quality, and ease of use, which further provided data reference for the determination of the final gesture set.

Building upon the performance gestures of Cantonese Opera, this study develops an innovative affective mid-air gesture interaction prototype, designed to enhance user emotional engagement while reducing the learning threshold for Cantonese Opera, thereby facilitating its dissemination and preservation. This research not only provides a novel solution for the digital dissemination of ICH such as Cantonese Opera but also establishes a valuable reference framework for the digital preservation and transmission of analogous cultural heritage forms.By integrating emotion quantification techniques with gesture elicitation studies, this research has expanded the theoretical foundation of existing gesture interaction design and demonstrated the potential of interdisciplinary research in solving complex problems.

6 Discussion

Although this study rigorously adhered to GES and successfully obtained gesture sets demonstrating high affective tendencies and user satisfaction, several limitations warrant consideration.

1. The stimulus materials were exclusively drawn from performances of "Dan" (female role) in Cantonese Opera, which traditionally portrays young female characters. This selective focus may introduce bias, potentially limiting the gesture set's capacity to express a comprehensive range of emotional categories, particularly those associated with other character archetypes.
2. The comparative effectiveness of the developed affective gesture interaction prototype versus conventional developer-defined gesture interactions in emotional engagement requires further empirical validation.

To address these limitations, future research directions include:

1. Expanding stimulus materials to incorporate diverse character roles within Cantonese Opera, thereby enhancing emotional coverage.
2. A comparative study between affective and developer-defined gesture interaction prototypes will recruit a larger participant sample to evaluate emotional engagement, user satisfaction, and task performance, providing stronger evidence for the advantages of affective gesture interaction.
3. Exploring the potential application of Cantonese opera affective gesture interaction in virtual exhibitions, such as developing virtual exhibition systems that utilize affective gesture interaction prototypes to provide users with immersive Cantonese opera experiences. Empirical studies will evaluate the effectiveness of these systems in enhancing user engagement and cultural understanding.

Acknowledgments. This study was funded by Stable Support Program for Higher Education Institutions (General Program), Shenzhen Science and Technology Innovation Commission [GXWD20220817131619001].

Disclosure of Interests The authors have no competing interests to declare that are relevant to the content of this article.

References

1. O'hara, K., Harper, R., Mentis, H., Sellen, A., Taylor, A.: On the naturalness of touchless: putting the "interaction" back into NUI. ACM Trans. Comput. Hum. Interact. **20**(1), 5 (2013)
2. Li, Q., Luo, T., Wang, J.: The role of digital interactive technology in cultural heritage learning: evaluating a mid-air gesture-based interactive media of Ruihetu. Comput. Anim. Virtual Worlds. **33**(3–4), e2085 (2022)
3. Volioti, C., et al.: A natural user Interface for gestural expression and emotional elicitation to access the musical intangible cultural heritage. J. Comput. Cult. Herit. **11**(2), 10 (2018)
4. Chen, L., Zhang, X., Zhao, Y.: Study on the vivification pathway of Lingnan Cantonese opera in the virtual reality interaction: a case study of Cantonese opera "Di Nv Hua (the emperor's daughter)". In: Stephanidis, C., Antona, M., Ntoa, S., Salvendy, G. (eds.) HCI International 2024 Posters. HCII 2024. Communications in Computer and Information Science, vol. 2116. Springer, Cham (2024)
5. Ou Yang, L., Guo, Y., Liu, J., Ling, J.: The cross-cultural application of Cantonese opera costume elements in 3D pop-up card design: focusing on youth and intangible cultural heritage elements. In: Stephanidis, C., Antona, M., Ntoa, S., Salvendy, G. (eds.) HCI International 2024 Posters. HCII 2024. Communications in Computer and Information Science, vol. 2116. Springer, Cham (2024)
6. Pang, W.Y.J., Leung, B.W., Cheng, L.: The motivational effects and educational affordance of serious games on the learning of Cantonese opera movements. Int. J. Hum.-Comput. Interact. **40**(6), 1455–1464 (2022)
7. Bowman, D.A., Kruijff, E., LaViola, J.J., Poupyrev, I.: 3D User Interfaces: Theory and Practice. Addison Wesley Longman Publishing Co., Inc. (2004)
8. Aigner, R., et al.: Understanding mid-air hand gestures: study of human preferences in usage of gesture types for HCI. In: Microsoft Research TechReport MSR-TR-2012-111 (2012)
9. Wobbrock, J.O., Aung, H.H., Rothrock, B., Myers, B.A.: Maximizing the guessability of symbolic input. In: Extended Abstracts on Human Factors in Computing Systems (CHI EA'05), pp. 1869–1872. Association for Computing Machinery, New York (2005)
10. Morris, M.R., et al.: Reducing legacy bias in gesture elicitation studies. Interactions. **21**(3), 40–45 (2014)
11. Vatavu, R.-D.: The dissimilarity-consensus approach to agreement analysis in gesture elicitation studies. In: Proceedings of the 2019 CHI Conference on Human Factors in Computing Systems (CHI'19), vol. 224, pp. 1–13. Association for Computing Machinery, New York (2019)
12. Tsandilas, T., Dragicevic, P.: Gesture elicitation as a computational optimization problem. In: Proceedings of the 2022 CHI Conference on Human Factors in Computing Systems (CHI'22), vol. 498, pp. 1–13. Association for Computing Machinery, New York (2022)
13. Vatavu, R.-D., Wobbrock, J.O.: Clarifying agreement calculations and analysis for end-user elicitation studies. ACM Trans. Comput.-Hum. Interact. **29**(1), 5 (2022)
14. McNeill, D.: Hand and mind: what gestures reveal about thought. Lang. Speech. **37**(2), 203–209 (1994)
15. Asalıoğlu, E.N., Göksun, T.: The role of hand gestures in emotion communication: do type and size of gestures matter? Psychol. Res. **87**, 1880–1898 (2023)
16. Dael, N., Goudbeek, M., Scherer, K.R.: Perceived gesture dynamics in nonverbal expression of emotion. Perception. **42**(6), 642–657 (2013)
17. Thakore, K., et al.: From hands to mind: how gesture, emotional valence, and individual differences impact narrative recall. Educ. Psychol. Rev. **36**, 111 (2024)
18. Pietroni, E., Adami, A.: Interacting with virtual reconstructions in museums: the Etruscanning project. J. Comput. Cult. Herit. **7**(2), 9 (2014)

19. Mehrabian, A.: Pleasure-arousal-dominance: a general framework for describing and measuring individual differences in temperament. Curr. Psychol. **14**, 261–292 (1996)
20. Li, X., Fu, X., Deng, G.: Preliminary application of the simplified Chinese version of the PAD emotion scale among Beijing university students. Chin. Ment. Health J. **22**(5), 327–329 (2008)
21. Pereira, A., Wachs, J.P., Park, K., Rempel, D.: A user-developed 3-D hand gesture set for human-computer interaction. Hum. Factors. **57**(4), 607–621 (2015)

The CoDesign Tool. A Card-Based Framework for Interactive and Collaborative Design in Cultural Heritage

Laura Travaglini[1]([✉])[iD], Marcello Massidda[1][iD], Andreas Zapf[2][iD], Samuele Spotti[1][iD], Manuele Veggi[1,3][iD], and Sofia Pescarin[1][iD]

[1] CNR - Institute of Heritage Science ISPC, Via Madonna del Piano 10, 50019 Sesto Fiorentino (FI), Italy
{lauratravaglini,marcello.massidda,samuelespotti,manueleveggi,
sofia.pescarin}@cnr.it

[2] Fraunhofer Institute for Computer Graphics Research (IGD), Fraunhoferstr. 5, 64283 Darmstadt, Germany
andreas.zapf@igd.fraunhofer.de

[3] Department of Science of Antiquites, University of Rome "La Sapienza", Piazzale Aldo Moro 5, 00185 Rome, Italy
manuele.veggi@uniroma1.it

Abstract. As the demand for more engaging visitor experiences–digital, physical, or hybrid–continues to grow, cultural institutions face the challenge of structuring effective design processes. While these institutions have long relied on interdisciplinary teams, such complex projects often require external contributions. This interplay of expertise calls for timely solutions and adaptable methodologies to ensure collaboration and bridge disciplinary gaps. The CoDesign Tool, developed by CNR ISPC (Italy) and Fraunhofer IGD (Germany) within the Horizon Europe PERCEIVE project, addresses this need by providing a structured, game-like framework to support collaborative ideation in Cultural Heritage. Building on the legacy of the open-access VisitorBox toolkit (GIFT, Horizon 2020), this redesigned version introduces key innovations, including cognitive-emotional dedicated stage and cards (Audience Goals) focused on Authenticity and Sense of Care, a redesigned Disruption Stage to stress-test ideas, and an overall restructured layout for improved usability and flow. The tool's modular format, which combines physical boards and themed card decks, encourages inclusive collaboration among practitioners of different background, regardless of their prior design expertise. Through a series of co-design workshops and evaluations, the tool has shown improved clarity, reduced cognitive load, and more balanced team participation compared to its predecessor. Results also highlight the value of structured prompts in guiding idea development and critical reflection. A digital version of the tool is currently being developed to support remote collaboration, with future work aimed at expanding content, testing new stages, and enhancing the tool's adaptability across diverse heritage contexts.

M. Schrepp and M. Rauterberg (Eds.): HCII 2025, LNCS 16342, pp. 276–297, 2026.
https://doi.org/10.1007/978-3-032-13164-5_18

Keywords: Digital Heritage · Collaborative Design · Redesign ·
Interaction Design

1   Introduction

Any design process is inherently nonlinear. While it can be standardised to some
extent, it remains an iterative and adaptable practice shaped by the unique needs
of each project [10]. In the field of Cultural Heritage (CH), this complexity is
heightened by two interrelated factors. Firstly, CH projects are almost invariably
interdisciplinary by nature, requiring coordination among professionals from varied backgrounds-such as curators, designers, educators, technologists-and even
external collaborators [3,35]. Secondly, cultural institutions now face increasing
expectations to deliver more complex and engaging experiences that combine
physical, digital, and immersive elements [28]. These overlapping demands create
logistical and collaborative pressures, making goal alignment, task coordination,
and creative synergy particularly challenging.

This paper addresses these issues by exploring the potential of structured,
game-like frameworks to support collaborative ideation in CH contexts. Specifically, we introduce the CoDesign Tool, developed under the Horizon Europe
PERCEIVE Project [37] by CNR ISPC (Italy) and Fraunhofer IGD (Germany),
as a card-and-board system to facilitate interdisciplinary co-design of digital
cultural experiences.

The rest of the paper is organised as follows. Section 2 examines the CoDesign Tool's conceptual foundations by reviewing its predecessor, the VisitorBox
[3], and situating it within the literature on collaborative, game-based design
methodologies in the CH field. Section 3 outlines the methodology underpinning
the overall development of the tool. Section 4 presents the CoDesign Tool in
depth, beginning with the initial design requirements and the redesign phase
of the VisitorBox, followed by a detailed account of the tool's structure, features, and key innovations. Particular attention is given to two major advancements: the introduction of cognitive-emotional Audience Goal Stage and dedicated decks—Sense of Care and Authenticity—and the development of the
tool's digital version. This section also describes the digital UX/UI design of
the first prototype built in Figma. In parallel, this section reports on the evaluation and testing sessions conducted throughout the process, which informed
iterative refinements of the tool. Finally, Sect. 5 discusses future directions for
the tool's evolution, followed by concluding remarks.

2   Background

The CoDesign Tool builds directly upon the VisitorBox [3], an open-access, card-
based collaborative design framework developed within the EU Horizon 2020
GIFT Project [18]. Created to support cultural institutions in shaping more
meaningful and engaging visitor experiences, VisitorBox introduced a modular,

stage-based system that guided interdisciplinary teams through the design process. Its boards and decks of Ideation Cards represent both the key phases of experience design and a wide range of prompts intended to inspire reflection, discussion, and creative expansion.

The tool replicates a typical design process, structured into six sequential stages, each supported by a dedicated worksheet and a corresponding deck of cards. These phases are organised into a linear workflow that begins with the identification of the target audience and core assets of the experience under development, followed by the definition of institutional goals. This leads to the formulation of a design brief encompassing motivations, barriers, available devices, and user capabilities. Building on this foundation, the team proceeds to generate concepts during the Ideation stage, which are then visualised through a Storyboarding phase. The proposed concepts undergo a Disruption stage, in which they are systematically challenged through nine scenario-based prompts. Each card presents a potential threat or critical issue, inviting the team to assess the resilience of their idea and develop an appropriate response. A final work sheet (Action Plan) supports the team in assigning a task to each member to turn the idea into an active project.

One of VisitorBox's key strengths is its ability to make the design process accessible and engaging through its card-based, game-like format. The Ideation Cards help lower participation barriers, encouraging dialogue and collaboration among participants with varying levels of expertise. By combining tangible means with a clear, structured logic, the tool fosters creativity, inclusivity, and shared authorship-core values in collaborative CH design. Thanks to this accessible format, VisitorBox has also proven effective in teaching design practices, especially to students, entry-level teams, and non-professionals contributors who may be unfamiliar with formal design methodologies.

Importantly, the Visitor Box's Ideation Cards are just one component within a broader Design and Planning toolkit developed under GIFT. This larger ecosystem comprises different interrelated tools, each designed to support different stages of the co-design process (the ASAP Map, the Experiment Planner, the Cardographer, and the Scenarios). Taken together, these tools represent a complementary and systemic approach to collaborative design in CH. The success of VisitorBox thus lies not only in its stand-alone utility but also in its role as an entry point to a cohesive methodological framework, where physical and digital resources interact to support co-creation across formats, contexts, and teams.

Despite its many strengths, VisitorBox also has certain limitations, particularly in light of the evolving needs of design teams working in CH. Its entirely physical format restricted its use in remote or hybrid settings, limiting accessibility and excluding collaborators who could not be present on site. Additionally, while the tool proved effective in supporting ideation through structured prompts and modular stages, it did not initially include cognitive-emotional dimensions, which have since become widely recognized as crucial to designing meaningful visitor experiences (see Sect. 4.1). Although VisitorBox was conceived as an open and extensible toolset, the lack of an integrated phase for these goals reflected a broader shift in the field that the toolkit had not yet fully addressed. These constraints were further compounded by the conclusion of the GIFT project, after which the toolkit received no active maintenance, digital adaptation, or coordinated follow-up. As a result, a highly promising design resource risked stagnation, despite its proven value.

The CoDesign Tool thus emerged in this context not as a replacement, but as a continuation: an effort to preserve the accessibility and modularity of Visitor-Box while extending its applicability, responding to contemporary design challenges, and reconnecting it with current CH discourse. This evolution also reflects a broader shift in the field, where participatory and co-design approaches have gained increasing relevance—not only as practical strategies, but as expressions of deeper cultural, social, and ethical commitments that position collaboration, inclusivity, and shared authorship at the core of heritage-making. Scholars like McKercher [33] and Simon [50] have framed co-design not only as a practical strategy to support interdisciplinary collaboration, but also as a moral imperative for the field. Rooted in democratic frameworks such as Arnstein's *Ladder of Participation* [1], this perspective emphasises values like cultural democracy, inclusivity, empathy, and care, as evidenced by recent research on participatory heritage practices [7,32].

However, realising this vision demands specific methodologies that are structured yet accessible and adaptable, which has led to the increased use of gamified and card-based tools in design practice. These tools have been around since the 1970s and were popularised in the 1990s through toolkits such as the *IDEO Method Cards* and *Design Heuristics* decks. They have proved useful in helping to structure discussions, support iteration, and act as tangible prompts to encourage perspective shifts and shared understanding, ultimately lowering barriers to participation and fostering creativity [11,49].

Card-based approaches are not entirely unheard of in the CH sector either. Besides the VisitorBox toolkit, since the mid-2010s, several experimental applications have adapted such means to support co-creation, reflection, and learning across diverse audiences. For instance, the *Heritage Futures Project* reimagined the speculative design game *The Thing from the Future* to help heritage professionals envision alternative futures [20]. In Finland, an open-access Intangible Cultural Heritage card set was developed to promote community engagement with living heritage practices [15]. Dolcetti et al. [12] later introduced a toolkit aimed at supporting ethical reflection in archaeological and heritage design, while Lu [27] designed a co-creation kit to help non-technical users develop location-based games in museum settings.

3   Methodology

As discussed in the previous sections, the VisitorBox toolkit forms the foundation of the present study. Figure 1 outlines the key steps of the methodology. Initially, the version published by the GIFT Project [18] (referred to in the flowchart as T_0) was analysed in relation to contemporary protocols and methodologies in interaction and user experience design applied to the heritage sector. As detailed in Sect. 4.1, T_0 lacks references to the cognitive, emotional, and educational objectives—referred to as *cognitive-emotional* or *audience goals*—that are central to the design of digital heritage applications (see e.g. [57]). Consequently, a preliminary set of cognitive goals was identified from the existing literature to inform the development of a dedicated extension deck (T_1), described in Sect. 4.2.

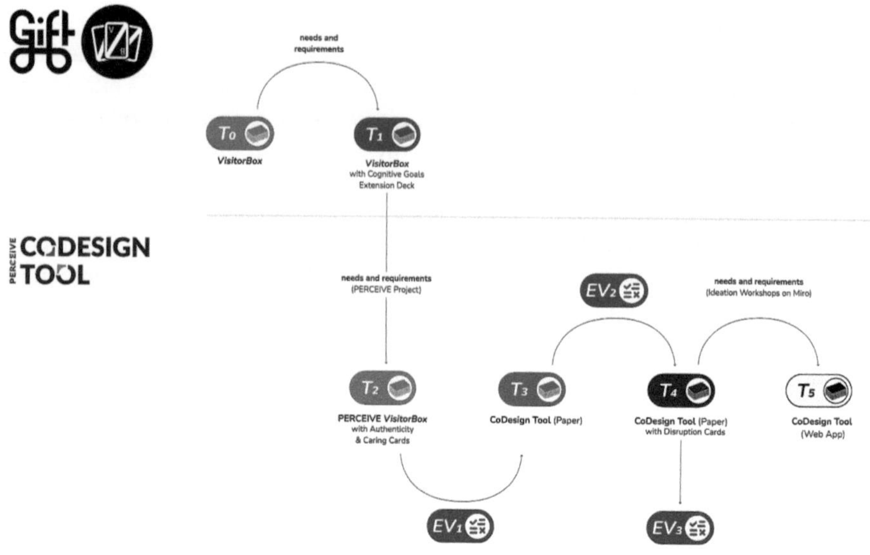

Fig. 1. From VisitorBox to the CoDesign Tool. Design Workflow.

The emphasis on goal-oriented design and attention to the cognitive and emotional impact of the user experience also characterises several research initiatives. Notable examples include SPICE [52], which explored the notion of social cohesion, and the PERCEIVE project itself [37]. The latter focuses on the phenomenon of colour change in art collections, while also investigating strategies to enhance audience engagement. Within this framework, PERCEIVE deepened two specific cognitive-emotional goals: the Sense of Care, i.e. the relationship of care between visitors and an art collection, and the Authenticity of the experience. Accordingly, in T_2, additional cards were incorporated into the T_1 extension deck and the Ideation Cards deck. Each card was explicitly aligned with these two goals and derived from the theoretical models developed by the PERCEIVE consortium (see Sect. 4.2).

This updated version, subsequently named PERCEIVE VisitorBox, was employed during the design sessions conducted by the research consortium. On these occasions, a preliminary evaluation (EV_1) was carried out. The outcomes of this initial assessment (detailed in Sect. 4.3) highlighted the need for redesign interventions, particularly regarding the structure of the worksheets, the visual layout of the cards, and the duration of the co-design sessions as a whole. These issues led to the development of a first revised version, the CoDesign Tool (T_3), which was evaluated in EV_2. Subsequently, an enhanced version of the tool was produced (T_4), reintroducing the Disruption Stage that was originally part of VisitorBox but had not been tested in earlier assessments due to time constraints. The main modifications are outlined in Sect. 4.4. This iteration underwent a further evaluation session (EV_3). Section 4.5 presents a synthesis of the findings from EV_2 and EV_3, highlighting the key improvements of CoDesign Tool compared to the original VisitorBox toolkit (T_0).

The most recent version was also employed to support in remote, online design sessions with the research consortium (named "Ideation Workshops"). Digital version of cards and canvases were arranged on a collaborative Miro board (https://miro.com), allowing designers to co-create new design concepts and collectively vote for solutions. These sessions revealed the need for a fully web-based version of the tool, whose design and initial prototype are described in Sect. 4.6.

4   The CoDesign Tool

4.1   Initial Requirements

The design of digital applications in the field of CH differs significantly from the traditional approach to product design. Three equally important aspects must be taken into account: 1) cultural institutions, which typically own, manage, preserve, and promote monuments, sites, or collections and have specific goals; 2) heritage itself, which is characterised by unique content and challenges; and 3) visitors, whether actual or potential, who are not simply consumers but rather seeks to be protagonists of a significant experience that may provoke reflection, learning, curiosity, entertainment, potentially leading to genuine behavioural change. On this regard, Chen [6] had described the three primary requirements for tourists today as the desire to live a full experience that is authentic, meaningful, and memorable.

In 2018, during a co-design project with students from the Master course in Multimodal Design at the University of Ferrara, the need to integrate these aspects into the design process of interactive museum applications became evident. The VisitorBox toolkit provided a solution to address the requirements of the CH sector. Nonetheless, after a couple of iterations, the absence of these key aspects deemed necessary a first extension of the core deck. Moreover, given that a visit to a museum is not always an individual activity, we also did not underestimate the importance of its social aspects. Starting from this gap, we conducted researches around the main characteristics of digital projects developed in recent years for cultural institutions. We thus identified 17 key concepts that could be incorporated into a specific design phase, which we initially called the 'Cognitive-Emotional Goals' Stage. A new set of cards and corresponding worksheet were therefore added.

4.2 Cognitive Goals

The first three key cards of this extension deck directly stem from the expectations listed by Chen (Strengthen Authenticity, Create Meaningfulness, Improve Memory and Recall [6]); later we investigated possible connected concepts. For instance, in order to improve "memorability", we have studied the strong connection between distraction and memory in serious games, and therefore considered "Limit Distraction" as a potential goal [46,55].

Similarly, the analysis of "meaningfulness" in design [26] has highlighted an implicit network of interconnected concepts supporting meaning creation process. This resulted in the definition of other goals cards, such as "Develop Enchantment and Sense of Wonder" [38], "Stimulating Dialogue" [23], "Empathy" [34] and "Embodiment" [25].

Regarding the social aspects, we outlined a specific set of goals for triggering prosocial behaviours in the audience. Therefore, new cards were included, such as: "Facilitate Competition", "Collaboration", "Cooperation" and "Social Cohesion" [40], as well as "Sense of Belonging", "Trust", "Acceptance of Diversity", "Identity" [36] and "Sense of Care" [60].

This extension was not only limited exclusively to the Cognitive-Emotional Goals Stage, but was reflected also in the Design Brief Stage with the addition of a dedicated slot on the corresponding worksheet. Nonetheless, further iterations with this new version of the tool (T_1) revealed that these concepts were too generic and abstract to precisely inform tailored design strategies or actions. This underlined the need for these concepts to be translated into more concrete, "actionable" elements for designers. With this objective in mind, we enriched the Ideation Stage with ad-hoc cards. However, given the breadth of this endeavour, we narrowed down our scope to the only two cognitive goals at the core of the PERCEIVE project: Authenticity and Caring (T_2).

Authenticity. The concept of *Authenticity* has become increasingly important in the field of CH, especially when designing digital and immersive experiences [41]. Although the idea has deep roots in various fields (philosophy, social science, cognitive psychology, linguistics, and computer science), its role in interactive media and CH is still being explored. In this context, like in computer science, Authenticity is often associated to graphic realism, leaving aside its deeper experiential and conceptual aspects-like how people feel, relate to others, and connect with the space around them.

We present Authenticity mainly as a framework (with 'actionable' design indications) [42], organised into three main dimensions: the Self, the Others, and the World, each of them entailing specific components and elements. This structure helps to better understand how users connect emotionally, cognitively, and socially with a CH experience (mainly hybrid or XR).

Building on this theoretical foundation, this work aims to make the framework both conceptually robust and practically actionable, providing tools and strategies that can be directly applied during the design process. Through a series of Audience Goals and Ideation Cards, this research is translated into concrete design suggestions, helping designers create more meaningful, immersive, and emotionally engaging Cultural Heritage experiences.

Sense of Care. In recent years, the concept of *care* has emerged as a significant lens through which to examine the relationship between citizens and CH [60]. However, many foundational contributions in this area originate outside the heritage domain, particularly in philosophy. One of the most relevant example is Joan Tronto, who defines care as "a species of activity that includes everything that we do to maintain, continue, and repair our world' so that we can live in it as well as possible. That world includes our bodies, ourselves, and our environment, all of which we seek to interweave in a complex, life-sustaining web" [54]. In recent months, the PERCEIVE consortium has drawn on this philosophical foundation—alongside work in anthropology, legal studies, and curatorship—to develop a theoretical framework for both the design [56] and evaluation [58] of interactive experiences.

This analysis reveals that care can manifest through a variety of behaviours, such as financial contributions to heritage preservation, critical reflection on issues related to heritage, and individual engagement with heritage-related content. Each of these behaviours may be triggered by different factors, including *historical empathy*—a cognitive and affective process involving engagement with historical figures—collaborative and participatory practices (see [50]), principles of embodiment [25], facilitated dialogue [47] and narrative strategies that highlight the risk of irreversible loss and the urgency to act [16]. These insights informed the development of a subset of the Audience Goals and Ideation cards. In Tab. 1 (Annex A), each card is linked to the corresponding scholarly reference that supports its associated goal or trigger.

4.3 Redesigning the Paper-Version Layout

The most significative redesign tasks of the PERCEIVE VisitorBox (i.e. the original set of cards developed by the GIFT Project, with the addition of the Cognitive Goals Extension Deck and the Authenticity and Caring Cards: T_2) emerged from multiple codesign sessions, collectively referenced in this paper as EV_1 (see Fig. 1). This initial assessment phase consisted of five separate workshops involving museum experts, designers and heritage practitioners, members of the PERCEIVE Consortium (in particular, the reference institutions were: CNR ISPC, Italy; National Archaeological Museum of Naples (MANN), Italy; Munch Museum of Oslo, Norway; Lucerne University of Applied Sciences and Arts (HSLU), Switzerland). These sessions aimed at defining the first concept of the interactive experiences foreseen by projects; they were held both in person and remotely over November and December 2023.

While a full description of their outcomes is accessible on the official Deliverable [43], during these first workshops we observed the interaction of the participants identifying main pain points of T_2. In particular, we recognised as main criticalities:

- The layout of the tool makes it difficult to visualise and keep track of the *previous stages.*
- The use of the worksheets requires *large spaces*;
- The *duration* of the sessions is extremely long, which results in participants being tired or demotivated. This led to the final step (Disruption Stage) being often ignored, owing to time constraints;
- The sessions often benefited from the intervention of an external moderator to facilitate the design process, providing *additional guidance*, ideas or clarifications;
- The choice of a printed medium leads to *considerable costs* in terms of time and money to print out and cut all the assets (this pain point will be addressed in Sect. 4.6).

In response to these findings, the team undertook a redesign focused on both visual aesthetics and structural layout. The most significant change was the introduction of a "stacking system", which replaced the original multi-board setup with a more compact structure. Rather than spreading the process across multiple disconnected surfaces, the new format introduced two vertically organised shared boards, each corresponding to a major phase in the design workflow (see Fig. 2). The first board groups the initial four stages-Context, Institutional Goals, Audience Goals, and Design Brief-into a unified "Design Brief" phase. This phase culminates in a complete design brief, which then becomes the foundation for the second part of the workflow-supported by a second board-dedicated to ideation and storyboarding.

This reorganisation (T_3) clarified a conceptual structure that was implicit but not visible in the original VisitorBox: the distinction between problem-setting and problem-solving. By stacking the relevant stages vertically within each phase, the tool reduces its physical footprint, making it easier to use in limited spaces while also offering participants a constant, cohesive overview of their progress. The Design Brief board includes a dedicated section—referred to as the Drawer of Alternatives—where discarded cards can be stored during

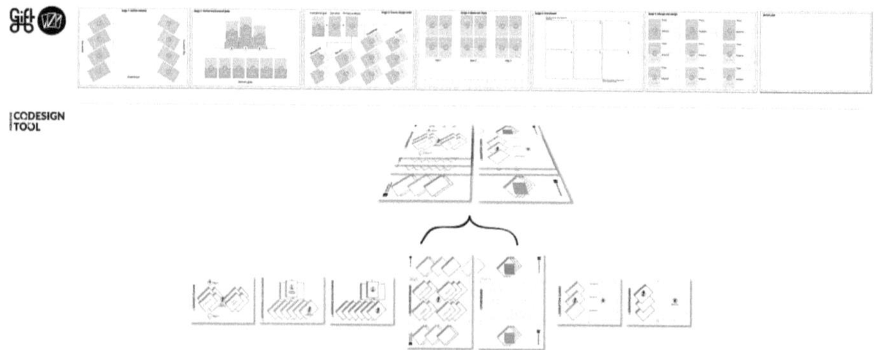

Fig. 2. From VisitorBox work sheets to the CoDesign Tool canvases and boards.

each stage. This drawer serves as an accessible archive of previously considered options, allowing teams to revisit or reintegrate them later if needed. This clearer hierarchy of stages and phases helps teams maintain a shared understanding of where they are in the process and what comes next (as shown in Sect. 4.5).

The redesign also included a visual simplification of the card layouts. A more minimal aesthetic was adopted, reducing colour usage to ensure easy and affordable printing, even on standard home printers. Moreoever, the visual language was aligned with the PERCEIVE project's branding, creating cohesion between the tool and the broader communication strategy. Overall, the updated cards featured clearer text hierarchy and consistent formatting across all decks, enhancing usability, particularly in time-constrained or first-time-use scenarios.

4.4 Disruption Stage

Following the encouraging results of EV_2 (see Sect. 4.5), where participants experienced smoother progression and significantly reduced session times when using our redesigned version (T_3) compared to the original VisitorBox, we revisited the possibility of reintroducing a stage that had previously been removed: Stage 5 Disruption. In the VisitorBox, this final phase was designed to stress-test project ideas by exposing them to disruptive scenarios, encouraging teams to anticipate potential vulnerabilities and unintended consequences. However, early evaluations had shown that, due to the length of the original tool, this stage was rarely reached in practice and was therefore excluded from the first iterations of T_2 and T_3.

With a more efficient and cohesive workflow in place, we decided to reintegrate the Disruption Stage, recognising its value in promoting critical reflection and design resilience. The original disruption deck, however, presented several challenges: it included too many cards, three broad macro-categories, each with further and sometimes unclear subcategories, and required teams to play nine rounds—three per category. While the rationale was sound, the mechanics proved overwhelming in typical co-design session contexts.

The redesign process focused first on restructuring the deck. We eliminated unnecessary subcategories, merged or discarded redundant cards, and revised the content for clarity, while preserving its reflective depth. The final version comprises 29 cards, divided into three main categories: Engagement, addressing user interactions with exhibits and among themselves; Environment, focusing on physical and contextual conditions such as weather, space layout, or accessibility; Resilience, exploring long-term sustainability, ethical dimensions, and operational robustness.

Additionally, each card now follows a clear internal structure: it presents a short description of a potential threat, an action-oriented recommendation, and finally a reflective question to prompt discussion (see Fig. 3). This format supports and guides critical thinking without requiring excessive interpretation or facilitation.

In practice, each team plays—either randomly or by group selection—one card per category, and reflects on the degree of threat each scenario poses

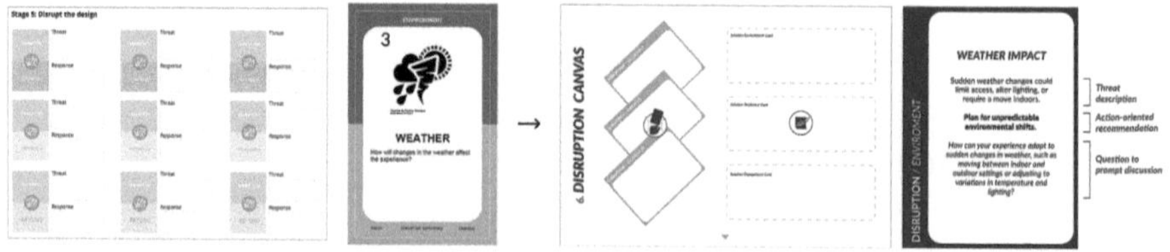

Fig. 3. Disruption Stage: from Visitor Box (left) to CoDesign Tool (right).

to their concept. They then collaborate to formulate a proper response. This activity helps uncover hidden weaknesses, encourages risk assessment, and promotes constructive debate. While the outcome may involve minor refinements, it can also lead to deeper rethinking of the concept, including revisiting earlier stages of the workflow. In this way, the Disruption Stage reinforces the iterative ethos of the tool and helps ensure that design proposals are not only creative, but also viable and future-proof (see Sect. 4.5).

4.5   Evaluation

In this section we are going to discuss the results of the final evaluation sessions (EV_2 and EV_3) of the CoDesign Tool. These qualitative assessments consisted of full co-design workshops using our tool, and data were acquired using a post-experience survey on Microsoft Form and via direct observations of the participants. The test involved international Master students in Digital Humanities at the University of Bologna over two separate academic years, with sample sizes consistent with literature standards for qualitative studies [2] [8] (EV_2 in a.y. 2023–24 with 27 surveyees; EV_3 in a.y. 2024–25 with 29 surveyees). The full list of the surveys questions and the collected data are available as supplementary materials on GitHub [45].

Comparative Assessment with VisitorBox. (EV_2) EV_2's main objectives was twofold: to assess the usability and effectiveness of the CoDesign Tool (T_3) and to compare it against its predecessor (T_2, already tested in EV_1). With this goal in mind, we divided the class into 12 groups: three tested the original VisitorBox, while the remaining nine engaged with the CoDesign Tool.

To begin with, the evaluation highlighted a significantly more streamlined workflow with the CoDesign Tool. Most teams using this version completed the entire session within the allocated time (2 h), with one group even finishing 30 min early. In contrast, teams working with the original VisitorBox required one additional hour and still struggled to reach the later phases of the process. Specifically, the Ideation and Storyboard stages of the VisitorBox were completed at home: this likely influenced both pacing and engagement, as participants worked under more relaxed conditions (for this reason, the last two stages are marked with asterisk in Fig. 4). However, even when comparing only the stages completed by both groups during the session, the time difference remains evident (see Fig. 4).

In particular, the Design Brief stage was completed more efficiently with the CoDesign Tool, likely due to the redesigned stacking layout: teams progressively constructed their brief as they moved through each prior stage, eliminating the need to retrospectively gather and transfer information, as was necessary with the original VisitorBox (Fig. 2). The only stage that took slightly longer with the new version was the Audience Goals stage, a result attributable to the enriched content and expanded card set introduced in this version.

Another noticeable difference also emerged in how teams physically managed the tool: while CoDesign Tool groups operated comfortably within the limits of a single standard table, VisitorBox users required considerably more surface area to lay out boards and cards, often leading to cluttered and fragmented workspaces. These outcomes confirmed insights already surfaced during EV_1, where the original workflow (T_2) was perceived as overly long and fragmented. The CoDesign Tool's revised structure clearly addressed these concerns, demonstrating a tangible reduction in time burden and a more fluid workflow. This was achieved without compromising on design quality or participant engagement. To this regard, one notable behavioural difference between the two tools concerned team dynamics: while VisitorBox groups often displayed more hierarchical role distributions (with visible leaders managing the activity), the CoDesign Tool groups were more egalitarian, with collaboration perceived as flatter and more balanced.

While EV_2 confirmed that T_3 outperformed its predecessor in several aspects and received generally positive feedback on its intuitiveness and overall usability, it also revealed important weak points and areas of improvement. When asked whether the CoDesign Tool provided clear instructions for the development of their concepts, a significant majority of 15 participants responded positively, while 4 indicated that the instructions were not sufficiently clear. Moreover, open-ended replies submitted through the form and on-site feedback during the session revealed confusion during the setup phase and around certain instructions—particularly regarding how to initiate the activity and the Audience Goals Stage. Additional concerns were raised about the legibility of certain icons and the unclear role of lesser-used features like the Drawer of Alternatives.

Disruption Stage Reintroduction (EV₃). These insights directly informed the next iteration of the CoDesign Tool (T_4), culminating in the development of version 0.9.3 available on Zenodo (published as version 1.0.0 [44] after proof reading and minor revisions to the texts). This session placed particular focus on the reintroduction of the Disruption Stage (see Sect. 4.4) and on validating refinements made since EV_2. Once again, students were divided into 15 teams, each comprising from two to four members. General on-site observations showed that larger groups (four members) experienced longer setup times, while smaller ones moved more swiftly through the stages, thus hinting that group size may influence the pace and fluidity of the session. Moreover, compared to the pre-

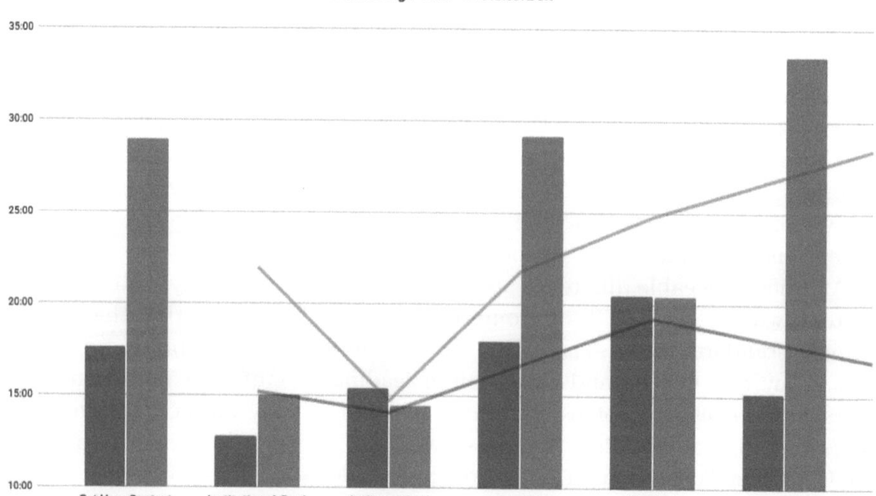

Fig. 4. Comparison of the average duration (with moving average trendlines) of the different stages of the co-design workshops in EV_2.

vious year's workshop, students asked significantly fewer questions, suggesting improvements in the overall clarity of the tool and materials. These insights were then confirmed by the majority of surveyees who responded positively to questions regarding the intuitiveness of the instructions, boards, and cards placement.

Regarding the Disruption Stage in particular, the survey results painted a clear picture: its effectiveness in refining and strengthening design concepts was confirmed by an impressive percentage of respondents. To begin with, almost 90% of respondents rated this stage as somewhat to extremely useful. This was subsequently confirmed when they were asked if, in practice, they had revised or modified the initial idea after the Disruption Stage, with 86% of respondents replying 'yes', ranging from minor changes (76%) to bigger ones (10%). Furthermore, when asked about the value of this stage within the overall design process, only 5% of respondents did not think it added any value. The rest of the sureyees provided answers within a range of pre-defined statements, including testing the feasibility of ideas, generating unexpected insights or changes, and encouraging team discussion.

When questioned about team dynamics, the overwhelming majority (86%) reported balanced participation, with everyone interacting equally. Only a small minority (14%) noted the emergence of distinct roles, confirming participation suggestions already emerged in EV_2. Lastly, in the open-ended feedback section, while most comments were positive or neutral, we acknowledge that a few comments still highlighted unclear instructions and a perceived excess of cards-issues we intend to address in future refinements of the CoDesign Tool.

Lastly, participants were asked whether they would have approached the design brief differently without the CoDesign Tool. A substantial majority—20 out of 29 respondents—answered negatively, indicating that the tool effectively supported their design process. Of the remaining responses, several suggested minor adjustments or a preference for fewer steps, rather than rejecting the tool's usefulness as a whole. Moreover, a few answers appeared uncertain—likely reflecting the participants' limited prior experience with structured design workflows. Overall, these findings reinforce the tool's capacity to scaffold collaborative ideation and support clear, informed decision-making.

In conclusion, the comprehensive evaluation results confirm that the CoDesign Tool has evolved successfully beyond its predecessor. It has achieved enhanced usability, a streamlined workflow, a reduced cognitive load and more egalitarian collaboration, with the Disruption Stage proving especially effective in refining design concepts (90% perceived usefulness rating, 86% concept revision rate).

4.6   From Paper to Web-Based Version

The resulting version of the CoDesign Tool (T_4) was exploited during new co-design sessions for the interactive applications developed within PERCEIVE project. As anticipated in Sect. 3, in order to allow our partners to collaborate remotely during these "Ideation Workshops", assets of the tool were transferred on a digital Miro board. These initial experiments together with the need to reduce time and money costs of the paper version, as emerged in EV_1, underlined the demand for a digital counterpart (T_5) of the CoDesign Tool. Furthermore, we saw in this transition an opportunity to identify unprecedented use cases for the CoDesign Tool. Such a digital platform could indeed support design teams to document and store the different phases of the early design process; on top of that, a fully remote option can streamline the sharing of final design ideas and storyboard with stakeholders or colleagues (see Fig. 5b).

Moving to the digital realm, we did not simply replicate the physical format, but several aspects and dynamics were revised. One major challenge for the adaption was the absence of haptic feedback as well as the advantage of having a real table, where players can spread out cards for a clear overview. Secondly, the user roles were preserved in the digital version, with the addition of a moderator. This person does not act above the other members of the session, but their duty is to configure the initial settings—choose the case study and the Audience Goals deck to work with, invite and admit users—and ensure that participants completed their tasks within each stage before moving forward.

Prototype. With preliminary sketches, we moved to Figma (www.figma.com) to handle the development of the first mid-fidelity prototype—already presented at the European Commission as part of the PERCEIVE first review meeting— and ease the collaboration within the design team. We started by creating various components, from general card designs to different details and interactive elements for the user interface. The design of these parts involved multiple iterations, rethinking the concept with a focus on simplicity, accessibility, and user experience.

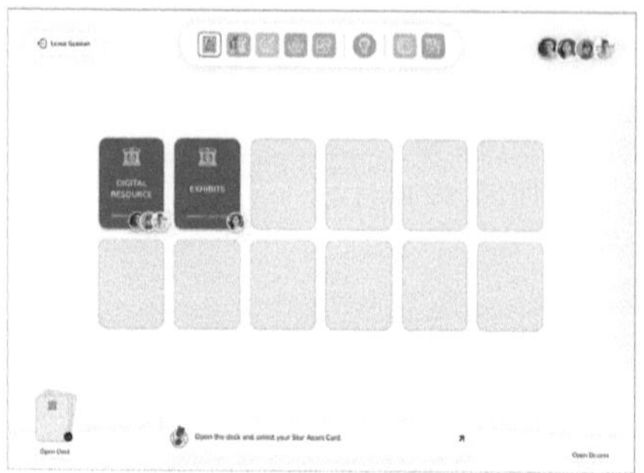

(a) Simulation of the voting procedure

(b) Final documentation

Fig. 5. Figma mid-fidelity prototypes of the web-app (T_5).

Based on these UI elements, we designed complete screen layouts to outline the user flow of the digital version: starting from the first touchpoint with the landing page for user onboarding to the design of each stage and the related user interactions. The digital interface consists of the following four major components:

1. The main game canvas is the general playing area covering the entire screen and was reimagined to serve as a universal canvas for the different stages. It adapts to the specific requirements for every stage—such as the voting procedure (Fig. 5a)—and displays features that are needed within the current one. On the right-hand side of the screen the canvas provides an allocated marginal space for discarded cards (see Drawer of Alternatives). This section stays hidden during the session, but can be revealed at any time via a visual hook.

2. The deck of cards was carefully transformed into a digital equivalent, considering the specification of the screen size and aspect ratio. Features exclusive to the digital environment, such as hover effects and adaptive visibility of information, were integrated to enhance user interaction without cluttering the interface or the user's view. Moreover, the cards were enriched with longer descriptions to improve their understanding.

3. The topbar was introduced to serve dual purposes: it represents the section on the physical board that keeps the "Top Voted" cards from finished stages, while also acting as a progress indicator displaying the current, completed, and upcoming steps. This UI element's narrow size saves screen space for the main work area below, until it gets expanded by user interaction (e.g. dragging cards on it or tapping on it to review cards) to showcase each stage's winning cards.

4. Finally, the instruction panel was implemented at the bottom of the screen to guide users through the gameplay. The panel opens when new instructions are available (e.g. at the start of a new stage) and is otherwise minimised to display only an essential task (a short prompt), so that the user can check back on the scope to be done.

This mid-fidelity prototype lays the basis for the creation of the final web application (T_5): it is currently being developed using the ATON Framework [14] and its completion is scheduled for the end of the project (February 2026). It will be integrated with core set functionalities and tools of the PERCEIVE Project: indeed, the web-app will communicate via API to import data about the chosen case study from the PERCEIVE Platform [39]. Additionally, it will be integrated with PERCEIVE CoDesign Toolkit, which consists of three integrated tools: the CoDesign Tool; the Prototyper, through which 3D simulation of the application can be created [31]; and the Experiment Planner, a tool to support the assessment of the cognitive impact of digital heritage installations [30].

5   Conclusion and Future Works

This paper has introduced and described the comprehensive redesign of the VisitorBox toolkit into the CoDesign Tool, a structured and modular card-based solution to support collaborative ideation processes within the domain of cultural heritage experience design. While building upon the assets and the linear workflow of the original VisitorBox, the CoDesign Tool responds to the more complex requirements posed by the Horizon Europe PERCEIVE project, particularly the need to integrate emotional, cognitive, and value-driven dimensions into the design process, such as Authenticity and Sense of Care. Moreover, the redesign improved the layout and usability of the tool, which is currently being translated into a web-app version, for remote co-design sessions.

A preliminary evaluation was conducted through four co-design workshops involving experts, designers, and institutional stakeholders. These sessions allowed for testing the tool's usability, adaptability, and conceptual effectiveness across different design settings. Feedback from participants highlighted the clarity of the process, the usefulness of the Audience Goals cards in expanding the design dialogue, and the importance of explicitly addressing visitors' emotional responses. The iterative assessment process informed refinements in both the structure and content of the tool, demonstrating its potential as both a design support system and a reflective platform.

Future work will focus not only on the development of the digital version, but also on the continued refinement of the paper-based CoDesign Tool. Across EV_1, EV_2, and EV_3, participants provided consistent feedback regarding issues around the clarity of certain icons and the density or ambiguity of some card content. These observations point to the need for targeted revisions in both visual language and instructional design. Moreover, further structural enhancements will be explored, especially around the system's modularity. For instance, expanding the Audience Goals section with new dedicated decks addressing emerging cognitive-emotional themes (e.g. social cohesion) could offer richer design prompts aligned with current discourse in the CH field. Additionally, the introduction and testing of new stages could help assess the limits and adaptability of the tool's architecture. Already during the transition from T_0 to T_1, early reflections emerged around the potential value of a stage dedicated to communication, framing it as a critical component of design practice. This stage could prompt teams to consider how their project will be publicly conveyed, addressing the growing importance of clear and impactful dissemination.

In parallel, the digital version currently under development aims to preserve the interactive dynamics of in-person sessions while enabling remote collaboration. Moving to a web-based environment offers the potential to extend the tool's accessibility, reduce material costs, and support distributed design teams. Further evaluation across diverse cultural institutions and user groups will also be essential to understand how the tool performs in different contexts and to what extent it can facilitate long-term adoption of value-oriented design practices in heritage communication.

Acknowledgments. This study was funded by the European Union (Horizon Europe 2020 PERCEIVE, grant number 101061157; NextGenerationEU, project H2IOSC, code IR0000029).

Disclosure of Interests. The authors have no competing interests to declare that are relevant to the content of this article.

Annex A: Referenced List of the CoDesign Tool Cards about Sense of Care

Glossary : AG, Audience Goals Cards; Id, Ideation Cards.

Table 1. Alignment Table on Audience Goals and Ideation Cards about Sense of Care

Deck	Card	Reference
AG	Make Visitors Reflect on Irreversibility	[54]
AG	Use Universal Concepts to Trigger Ethical Behaviours	[53,56]
AG	Stimulate Visitors' Individual Memories	[17,47]
AG	Encourage Introspective Contemplation for Personal Growth	[17,47]
AG	Assign Tasks Involving Caring Actions	[19,54]
AG	Promote Non-Verbal Interactions	[25]
AG	Increase Empathy	[13,21,34]
AG	Extend Knowledge	[5]
AG	Boost Enchantment	[4,38]
AG	Make Citizens Learn about the Importance of Coloured Collections[a]	[56,59]
AG	Make Citizens Learn about Heritage Protection	[5,60]
AG	Promote Citizens' Respectful Behaviours Towards Local Heritage and Coloured Collection[a]	[5] [56]
AG	Make Visitors Willing to Pay for Sustainable Services and Products	[5]
AG	Involve Visitors in Taking Care Activities at the Museum	[50]
Id	Sense of awareness is stimulated in visitors through visual simulation of irreversible changes to something important.	[51,54]
Id	Visitors are involved in metaphors and stories fostering connections to ethical themes felt as priorities for them (human rights, climate, war, gentrification, etc.).	[53]
Id	Visitors are engaged in experiences that evoke individual memories about life aspects such as family, known places, and relevant objects.	[16,51]
Id	Visitors are involved in experiences that prompt introspective thoughts and inner-exploration encouraging self-awareness.	[17,34]
Id	Experience encourages the visitor to use symbolic tools or resolve tasks performing caring actions to something or someone.	[53]
Id	In the experience, visitors' body movements can trigger actions and events, enhancing cognitive processes through non-verbal interactions.	[25]
Id	A narrative that mixes historical facts and evocative plot empowers a deep emotional connection between visitors and cultural heritage.	[9,13]
Id	The visitors spend time in contexts unusual to them or outsiders, doing theme-specific activities (volunteering in museum guides, laboratories, workshops, etc.).	[5,58]
Id	The visitor adopts another person's viewpoint improving understanding and empathy from a diverse perspective (different expertise, social group, religion etc.).	[13,53]
Id	A specific character's story is presented to the visitors, who are actively invited to empathize with the protagonist's sentiments and thoughts.	[13,53]
Id	Visitors are told a story with characters acting with specific behaviours and are invited to imagine motivations, feelings and sentiments behind these characters' actions.	[22,34]
Id	Visitors are invited to give their perspective on certain arguments.	[17,47]
Id	People's empathy isn't immutable: it's a fluid trait that could be increased. It can be reinforced by proposing to visitors stories with deep-changing characters and self-improvement processes.	[34]
Id	Visitors imagine themselves acting inside (increasing their sense of belonging) or outside a group (reflecting and reacting to a sense of rejection).	[9,24,40]
Id	Visitors are informed about the empathic actions and reactions of other strangers, producing a positive mirror-effect on their behaviour.	[34,54]
Id	Information that is far from visitors' understanding (too complex data and articulated reasoning) is humanized by adopting specific media and appropriate communication strategies.	[16] [29,50]
Id	Visitors are involved in artistic activities crafting self-made artworks or participating in collaborative performances.	[59]
Id	Provide a relaxed and positive environment to the visitors by adopting strategies to avoid anxiety and reduce preoccupations that otherwise may reduce empathy.	[16]
Id	Develop a sense of wonder in the visitors.	[13]
Id	Include active dialogues with experts/guides and among participants; provocative questions and alternative perspectives are proposed to visitors.	[47,48]

[a]Behaviour specific to coloured collection, see PERCEIVE Project [37].

References

1. Arnstein, S.R.: A ladder of citizen participation. J. Am. Plann. Assoc. **35**(4), 216–224 (1969). https://doi.org/10.1080/01944366908977225
2. Bekele, W.B., Ago, F.Y.: Sample size for interview in qualitative research in social sciences: a guide to novice researchers. Res. Educ. Policy Manage. **4**(1), 42–50 (2022). https://doi.org/10.46303/repam.2022.3
3. Benford, S., et al.: 9. data-driven visiting experiences. In: Waern, A., Løvlie, A. (eds.) Hybrid Museum Experiences, pp. 157–176. Amsterdam University Press, December 2022. https://doi.org/10.1515/9789048552849-010
4. Bennett, J.: The Enchantment of Modern Life, Attachments, Crossings, and Ethics. Princeton University Press, Princeton (2001). https://doi.org/10.1515/9781400884537
5. Buonincontri, P., Marasco, A., Ramkissoon, H.: Visitors' experience, place attachment and sustainable behaviour at cultural heritage sites: a conceptual framework. Sustainability **9**(7), 1112 (2017). https://doi.org/10.3390/su9071112
6. Chen, H., Rahman, I.: Cultural tourism: an analysis of engagement, cultural contact, memorable tourism experience and destination loyalty. Tourism Manage. Perspect. **26**, 153–163 (2018). https://doi.org/10.1016/j.tmp.2017.10.006
7. Ciolfi, L., Malmborg, L., Waern, A.: Participatory design and cultural heritage: values, challenges and opportunities. In: Proceedings of the 15th Participatory Design Conference: Short Papers, Interactive Exhibitions, Workshops, vol. 2, pp. 20–23 (2017). https://doi.org/10.1145/3131785.3131794
8. Çizgen, G., Ulusu Uraz, T.: The unknown position of intuition in design activity. Des. J. **22**(3), 257–276 (2019). https://doi.org/10.1080/14606925.2019.1589414
9. Cross, J.E.: Processes of place attachment: an interactional framework. Symb. Interact. **38**(4), 493–520 (2015). https://doi.org/10.1002/symb.198
10. Cross, N.: Designerly Ways of Knowing and Thinking. Springer, London (2025)
11. Deng, Y., Antle, A.N., Neustaedter, C.: Tango cards: a card-based design tool for informing the design of tangible learning games. In: Proceedings of the 2014 Conference on Designing Interactive Systems (DIS 2014), pp. 695–704. ACM, Vancouver, BC, Canada (2014). https://doi.org/10.1145/2598510.2598601
12. Dolcetti, F., Boardman, C., Opitz, R., Perry, S.: Values-led design cards: building ethically engaged archaeology and heritage experiences. Sustainability **13**(7), 3659 (2021)
13. Endacott, J., Brooks, S.: An updated theoretical and practical model for promoting historical empathy. Soc. Stud. Res. Pract. **8**(1), 41–58 (2013). https://doi.org/10.1108/SSRP-01-2013-B0003
14. Fanini, B., Ferdani, D., Demetrescu, E., Berto, S., d'Annibale, E.: Aton: an open-source framework for creating immersive, collaborative and liquid web-apps for cultural heritage. Appl. Sci. **11**(22), 11062 (2021)
15. Finnish Heritage Agency: a new card deck for living heritage has been published! https://www.aineetonkulttuuriperinto.fi/en/article/uusi-elavan-perinnon-korttisarja-on-julkaistu (2023)
16. Fiorenza, G.: The Virtual Tour as a Tool for Eliciting Place Attachment and Caring Attitude. MA thesis, University of Bologna (2024)

17. Gargett, K.: Re-thinking the guided tour: a critical exploration of the use of co-creation, dialogue and facilitation practices for democratic social engagement at York minster. MA thesis, University of York, Department of Archaeology (2018)
18. GIFT: Meaningful Personalization of Hybrid Virtual Museum Experiences Through Gifting and Appropriation (2023). https://doi.org/10.3030/727040, European Commission, CORDIS
19. Goodwin, A.L.: Teacher preparation and the education of immigrant children. Educ. Urban Soc. **34**(2), 156–172 (2002). https://doi.org/10.1177/0013124502034002003
20. Heritage futures: heritage futures at the 19th icomos general assembly in Delhi. https://heritage-futures.org/heritage-futures-icomos-general-assembly/ (2021), Accessed 03 Feb 2021
21. Hirsh, J.B.: Personality and environmental concern. J. Environ. Psychol. **30**(2), 245–248 (2010). https://doi.org/10.1016/j.jenvp.2010.01.004
22. Iosifyan, M.: Theory of mind increases aesthetic appreciation in visual arts. Art Percept. **9**(2), 113–133 (2021). https://doi.org/10.1163/22134913-bja10011
23. Jameson, J.H.: Facilitated dialogue and the evolving philosophies on the public interpretation of cultural heritage sites, pp. 9–24. Springer, Cham (2022). https://doi.org/10.1007/978-3-030-81957-6_2
24. Jugert, P., Greenaway, K.H., Barth, M., Büchner, R., Eisentraut, S., Fritsche, I.: Collective efficacy increases pro-environmental intentions through increasing self-efficacy. J. Environ. Psychol. **48**, 12–23 (2016). https://doi.org/10.1016/j.jenvp.2016.08.003
25. Kenderdine, S.: Embodiment, entanglement, and immersion in digital cultural heritage. In: Schreibman, S., Siemens, R., Unsworth, J. (eds.) A New Companion to Digital Humanities, pp. 22–41. Wiley, Chichester, UK, November 2015. https://doi.org/10.1002/9781118680605.ch2
26. Lord, G.D.: The power of cultural tourism. In: Wisconsin Heritage Tourism Conference, vol. 17 (1999)
27. Lu, W.: Game-design workshops with co-creation toolkit to support game-based learning for heritage museum. Proc. Eur. Conf. Games-based Learn. **18**(1), 989–999 (2024)
28. Lupo, E., et al.: Digital transformation in cultural heritage: challenges and design-driven approaches. J. Cult. Heritage **58**, 123–136 (2023). https://doi.org/10.1016/j.culher.2023.02.001
29. Mairesse, F.: Dictionary of Museology. Routledge, London, 1 edn. April 2023. https://doi.org/10.4324/9781003206040
30. Massidda, M., et la.: Towards an experiment planner for cognitive studies in virtual heritage environments. A Pilot Study. In: Corsini, M., Ferdani, D., Kuijper, A., Kutlu, H. (eds.) Eurographics Workshop on Graphics and Cultural Heritage. The Eurographics Association (2024). https://doi.org/10.2312/gch.20241261
31. Massidda, M., Fanini, B., Pescarin, S.: Prototyper: a web3d platform for collaborative design and simulation of hybrid museum exhibition. In: Campana, S., et al. (eds.) Digital Heritage 2025. The Eurographics Association (2025). https://doi.org/10.2312/dh.20253009
32. Maye, L., Claisse, C.: Co-design within and between communities in cultural heritage. Multimodal Technol. Interact. **7**(1), 1–15 (2023). https://doi.org/10.3390/mti7010001
33. McKercher, K.A.: Beyond Sticky Notes: Doing Co-design for Real: Mindsets, Methods and Movements. Inscope Books (2020). https://www.beyondstickynotes.com/

34. McKinney, S., Perry, S., Katifori, A., Kourtis, V.: Developing digital archaeology for young people: a model for fostering empathy and dialogue in formal and informal learning environments. In: Hageneuer, S. (ed.) Communicating the Past in the Digital Age: Proceedings of the International Conference on Digital Methods in Teaching and Learning in Archaeology (12th-13th October 2018), pp. 179–195. Ubiquity Press, Februay 2020. https://doi.org/10.5334/bch.n

35. Nofal, E.: Participatory design workshops: interdisciplinary encounters within a collaborative digital heritage project. Heritage **6**(3), 2752–2766 (2023). https://doi.org/10.3390/heritage6030146

36. OECD: Oecd definition of social cohesion. https://www.socialcohesion.info/concepts/concept/oecd (2011)

37. PERCEIVE: perceptive enhanced realities of colored collEctions through AI and virtual experiences (2023). https://doi.org/10.3030/101061157, European Commission, CORDIS

38. Perry, S.: The enchantment of the archaeological record. Eur. J. Archaeol. **22**(3), 354–371 (2019). https://doi.org/10.1017/eaa.2019.24

39. Pescarin, S., et al.: Perceptive enhanced realities of coloured collections through AI and virtual experiences. In: Campana, S., et al. (eds.) Digital Heritage 2025. The Eurographics Association (2025). https://doi.org/10.2312/dh.20253350

40. Pescarin, S., Bonanno, V., Marasco, A.: Social cohesion in interactive digital heritage experiences. Multimodal Technol. Interact. **7**(6) (2023). https://doi.org/10.3390/mti7060061

41. Pescarin, S., Cittá , G., Gentile, M., Spotti, S.: Authenticity in VR and XR experiences: a conceptual framework for digital heritage. In: Bucciero, A., Fanini, B., Graf, H., Pescarin, S., Rizvic, S. (eds.) Eurographics Workshop on Graphics and Cultural Heritage. The Eurographics Association (2023). https://doi.org/10.2312/gch.20231153

42. Pescarin, S., Cittá, G., Spotti, S.: Authenticity in interactive experiences. Heritage **7**(11), 6213–6242 (2024). https://doi.org/10.3390/heritage7110292

43. Pescarin, S., Ferdani, D.: D6.1 perceive concept design, ux and design brief, December 2023. https://doi.org/10.5281/zenodo.10658272

44. Pescarin, S., Massidda, M., Travaglini, L., Spotti, S., Veggi, M.: Perceive co-design tool for cultural heritage experiences (2025). https://doi.org/10.5281/zenodo.15632510

45. Pescarin, S., Massidda, M., Travaglini, L., Spotti, S., Veggi, M.: Perceive codesign tool v1.0.0 (2025). https://doi.org/10.5281/zenodo.15632652, testing material available at the directory `current/test`

46. Pescarin, S., Pandiani, D.S.: Factors in the cognitive-emotional impact of educational environmental narrative videogames. In: International Conference on Extended Reality, pp. 101–108. Springer (2022). https://doi.org/10.1007/978-3-031-15553-6_8

47. Petousi, D., Katifori, A., McKinney, S., Perry, S., Roussou, M., Ioannidis, Y.: Social bots of conviction as dialogue facilitators for history education: promoting historical empathy in teens through dialogue. In: Proceedings of the 20th Annual ACM Interaction Design and Children Conference, IDC 2021, pp. 326–337. ACM, New York, NY, USA (2021). https://doi.org/10.1145/3459990.3460710

48. Roussou, M., Perry, S., Katifori, A., Vassos, S., Tzouganatou, A., McKinney, S.: Transformation through provocation? In: Proceedings of the 2019 CHI conference on Human Factors in Computing Systems, pp. 1–13 (2019). https://doi.org/10.1145/3290605.3300857

49. Roy, R., Warren, J.P.: Card-based design tools: a review and analysis of 155 card decks for designers and designing. Des. Stud. **63**, 125–154 (2019). https://doi.org/10.1016/j.destud.2019.05.002
50. Simon, N.: The Participatory Museum. Museum 2.0 (2010)
51. Soto, N.E.: Caring and relationships: developing a pedagogy of caring. Villanova Law Rev. **50**(4) (2005)
52. SPICE: social cohesion, participation, and inclusion through cultural engagement (2023). https://doi.org/10.3030/870811, European Commission, CORDIS
53. Tricart, C.: The key (2019), https://www.labiennale.org/it/cinema/2019/venice-virtual-reality/key, Venice Biennale, Venice Virtual Reality
54. Tronto, J.C.: Moral Boundaries: a Political Argument for an Ethic of Care. Routledge, New York (1993)
55. Van Der Stigchel, S.: Concentration: Staying Focused in Times of Distraction. MIT Press (2020)
56. Veggi, M., von Gal, A., Piccardi, L., Pescarin, S., Nori, R.: How much do we care about cultural heritage? a rasch scale validation study among young adults. Heritage **8**, 317 (2025). https://doi.org/10.3390/heritage8080317
57. Veggi, M., Catalano, C.E., Pescarin, S.: Sketching interactive experiences: can co-creation with artificial generative systems enhance the communication of cultural heritage? In: Catalano, C.E., Parakkat, A.D. (eds.) ACM/EG Expressive Symposium - WICED: Eurographics Workshop on Intelligent Cinematography and Editing. The Eurographics Association (2025). https://doi.org/10.2312/exw.20251058
58. Veggi, M., et al.: Sense of care in the design of digital heritage applications. In: Barandoni, C., Clay, A., Papadopoulos, G., Pescarin, S., Sandu, I.C.A. (eds.) Chromatic Vision: Exploring Colour in Art, Archaeology and Digital Realities, chap. 4. Springer, LNCS (2025). https://doi.org/10.1007/978-3-032-07792-9
59. Veggi, M., Pescarin, S.: Creative engagement and meaning creation: a first experimental protocol on interactive cultural experiences for conservation data. Digit. Appl. Archaeol. Cult. Heritage **32**, e00321 (2024). https://doi.org/10.1016/j.daach.2024.e00321
60. Woodhead, C.: Caring for Cultural Heritage: An Integrated Approach to Legal and Ethical Initiatives in the United Kingdom. Cambridge University Press, 1 edn. November 2023. https://doi.org/10.1017/9781108696463

Research on the Visualization Design and Inheritance of ICH Information Based on Artificial Intelligence

Lijia Zeng[✉], Jianjie Gao, Chengxing Liu, Zhongming Huang, and Ziming Wu

Gannan University of Science and Technology, Ganzhou, Jiangxi 341000, China
henlen248@sohu.com

Abstract. The era of Artificial Intelligence (AI) has arrived and is changing the life and work of human beings at an unprecedented pace. The Chinese government attaches great importance to the protection and inheritance of intangible cultural heritage (ICH), considering it an integral part of maintaining the diversity of culture and promoting social harmony. Empowered by AI technology, the protection and inheritance of ICH enables the visual presentation of cultural information using digital technologies in the intelligent era, as well as digital restoration and creative design for inheritance. Relying on digital protection for the digital dissemination, this approach greatly enhances working efficiency, better achieves the information reproduction and creative presentation of ICH culture, strengthens the protection effect of ICH culture, and more efficiently achieves the goal of inheritance. Grounded in the new AI-driven era, this study investigates methods for leveraging AI to empower the visualization design and inheritance of ICH information, including the paths of empowerment, the principles and contents of visualization design, in the hope of summarizing effective strategies for better achieving the innovative protection and inheritance of ICH information in the AI era.

Keywords: Artificial Intelligence · Intangible Cultural Heritage Information · Visualization Design · Inheritance

1 Introduction

The visualization design of ICH information requires the organization of massive data to achieve visual transformation, defining and gathering the scope of information, presenting untreated complex data in the form of graphical representations or textual expressions. Visualization design can be categorized into two types based on design orientation: one is data-driven scientific visualization (e.g., statistical charts), supported by AI and big data, to design and display information charts, analyze the current state, and facilitate the fusion between science and art design. The other is visual representation based on cultural connotation and event contents, such as flowcharts, as well as information visual design where designers, based on their thorough understanding and refinement of the design theme, together with expressive techniques and experience, presents the

M. Schrepp and M. Rauterberg (Eds.): HCII 2025, LNCS 16342, pp. 298–311, 2026.
https://doi.org/10.1007/978-3-032-13164-5_19

attribute connections between information in the form of graphs and charts. The main paths that utilize AI to empower the visualization design of ICH information are: 1. to leverage AI to promote the digital restoration of ICH; 2. to accelerate the collection and refinement of ICH design elements using AI; 3. to create a genetic map for ICH culture using AI; 4. to conduct specific and in-depth innovative design using AI; 5. to build a dynamic image database using AI, thereby constructing an intelligent path for the inheritance and innovation of ICH culture, and forming a new intelligent model for the protection and innovative development of ICH, structured as: "ICH excavation and protection-ICH organization and research-ICH resource database establishment-ICH innovative development-ICH innovative dissemination". The present study holds important practical value for the protection and inheritance of ICH in the era of AI.

2   Analysis of the Paths for AI-Empowered Visualization Design of ICH Information

The visualization design of ICH information requires the organization of massive data to achieve visual transformation, defining and gathering the scope of information, presenting untreated complex data in the form of graphical representations or textual expressions. Visualization design can be categorized into two types based on design orientation: one is data-driven scientific visualization (e.g., statistical charts), supported by AI and big data, to design and display information charts, analyze the current state, and facilitate the fusion between science and art design [1]. The other is visual representation based on cultural connotation and event contents, such as flowcharts, as well as information visual design where designers, based on their thorough understanding and refinement of the design theme, together with expressive techniques and experience, presents the attribute connections between information in the form of graphs and charts. From the organization of massive data to visualization design, both can be assisted by AI, finding paths to accelerate and optimize the process.

Digital research is one of the most effective approaches in ICH culture studies, primarily encompassing digital restoration and image recording. Digital restoration and extraction involves digitally restoring the material carriers embodied by ICH culture and extracting cultural elements, shooting physical carriers with digital technology and then restoring and reproducing them through digital means, collecting data on the physical objects, performances, skills, and other aspects of ICH in a Comprehensive way with the help of AI-driven technologies such as image recognition and speech recognition, Integrating different types of ICH data, such as text, images, audio, and video, to establish a unified restoration database, and then extracting and categorizing its elements for research, to achieve the purpose of systematic research.

2.1   To Leverage AI to Promote the Digital Restoration of ICH

Traditional costumes are the most direct carriers of ICH, which serve as symbolic languages that visually reflect the cultural and aesthetic wisdom of the nation. They are cultural products that have been constantly inherited and enriched through long-term production and life, evolving and merging with time, with distinctive cultural characteristics, ethnic arts, and craftsmanship philosophies. Taking the traditional costumes of southern Jiangxi from Ganzhou City, Jiangxi Province, China for example, the data collection process can perform more detailed digital restoration from three dimensions using AI: images, materials & craftsmanship, and cultural background [2]. Firstly, different scenes such as traditional Hakka courtyards, ancestral halls, and well-lit indoor spaces can be selected. Models are required to wear traditional Hakka costumes from southern Jiangxi and photographed from multiple angles, to capture the color performance and visual effects of the costumes under different lighting conditions, as well as the overall silhouette, styles, patterns and other information of the costumes for the purpose of image collection. Secondly, the materials of the traditional costumes of southern Jiangxi, including fiber texture, weaving technique and fabric materials, etc. are scanned. The craftsmanship of the costumes is video-recorded, accompanied by audio commentary for data collection. Thirdly, research is conducted on the background of ICH culture, including in-depth interviews with the inheritors of traditional costumes of southern Jiangxi, costume-related information is extracted using voice recording and language processing technologies, covering aspects such as the origin of the costumes, changes in styles over different periods, wearing customs, and the dressing experiences of local residents (as shown in Table 1). The ICH culture is documented both statically and dynamically, with comprehensive data collection.

Table 1. Digital Restoration Mode: A Case Study of the Traditional Costumes of Southern Jiangxi from Ganzhou City, Jiangxi Province, China.

Data Collection Dimension	Operation Mode	Content Collected
Images	Display of different scenes, multi-angle photography	Overall silhouette, styles, patterns, etc.
Materials & Craftsmanship	AI scanning, video recording, audio commentary	Fiber texture, weaving technique and fabric materials, etc.
Cultural Background	Interviews, AI voice processing and extraction	Origin, historical changes of styles, wearing customs, wearer experience

2.2 To Accelerate the Collection and Refinement of "ICH" Design Elements Using AI and Build an Element Database

The use of AI to establish an element database for ICH culture not only contributes to better protection and inheritance of ICH culture, but also serves as a foundational database for the innovative development of culture, holding significant value for the innovative design of culture. The natural language processing (NLP) technology of AI can classify and annotate textual materials, while computer visual technology can identify and categorize elements within images and videos, facilitating data management and retrieval. The building of a digital resource database for ICH is a systematic project.

Based on the digital restoration of ICH culture, we need to classify and organize ICH culture in detail, collect, organize, summarize, and categorize elements, in the hope of establishing an element database. Taking the traditional costumes of southern Jiangxi from Ganzhou City, Jiangxi Province, China for example, based on the previous digital restoration of the costumes, the focus is on classifying, identifying, extracting, and organizing elements like the craftsmanship, carriers, patterns, colors, modeling, and ethnic culture, etc. of the ICH costumes. Through image processing and other software, pattern elements can be extracted and classified, colors can be identified and recognized, styles can be classified and compared, and craftsmanship can be dissected and organized, etc. Digital cultural resource databases can be built, including a modelling database, pattern database, color database, and technical process library (as shown in Fig. 1). The establishment of these databases will contribute to long-term preservation and correct inheritance of ICH culture, while also supporting the diverse innovative development of the culture. This approach activates and connects upstream cultural research with downstream cultural innovation, forming a virtuous ecological chain for ICH culture [3].

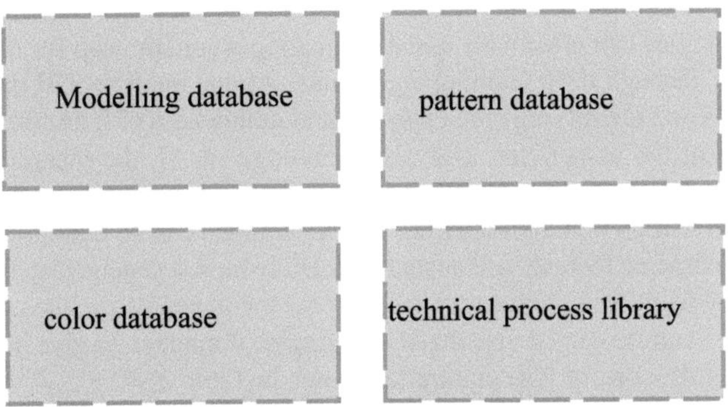

Fig. 1. Costume Design Element Extraction and Naming of Element Databases: A Case Study of Traditional ICH Costumes of Southern Jiangxi in China.

2.3 To Create a Genetic Map for ICH Culture Using AI

A genetic map typically expresses content through images, text and a given network of relationships. In ancient times, there was a tradition of creating maps. These ancient maps were primarily depicted through hand-drawn line sketches and were created by illustrating different types of figures or objects. Traditional maps are diversified, including geographical maps, etiquette and customs maps, craft and technology maps, and comprehensive maps combining different types. For example, technical maps like *The Exploitation of the Works of Nature* and *The Picture of Farming and Weaving* vividly document the types of traditional handicraft techniques. Modern maps, however, utilize a wider range of symbols, text, images, videos and photos, etc. to convey information, offering a more authentic and clearer representation of knowledge and its relationships

[4]. In recent years, with the rapid development and interdisciplinary integration of different disciplines, together with the extensive use of maps, computer technology and other modern information technologies, the creation of maps has gradually shifted from traditional hand-drawn line maps to digitally created comprehensive ones that integrate hand drawings, images, symbols, languages, videos and flowcharts, etc. into one. In view of this, in this new era, the creation of a genetic map for ICH culture must harness the power of digitalization, particularly AI. By extracting cultural factors, building cultural hierarchies, analyzing relationships among cultural elements and cultural characteristics, we can create a genetic map for ICH culture, and sort out the relationships and evolution of ICH culture using visual flowcharts. This map will be constructed through cultural excavation, research, extraction, summarization and organization, marked by distinct cultural imprints, abundant local cultural elements, uniqueness, and representativeness. Researching and creating cultural genetic maps can, on one hand, systematically and comprehensively sort out typical cultural elements of local ICH, contributing to systematic protection and identification of culture. On the other hand, it allows for better external communication and the creative transformation and innovative development of culture, thus avoiding the mutation and extinction of culture, and carrying dual significance for both cultural protection and inheritance, as well as innovative development.

AI technologies can effectively assist in creating a genetic map for ICH culture. In the first place, through deep learning algorithms, AI can analyze ICH data, extracting its key features and identifying core elements and uniqueness of ICH culture. Secondly, with the help of the association analysis technology of AI, the inherent connections between ICH cultural elements can be revealed, a knowledge network for ICH culture can be constructed and its rich connotations and systematics can be demonstrated. Finally, based on the extracted features and analyzed relationships, a genetic map for rich culture can be built by using knowledge map technology, the genetic structure and inheritance lineage of ICH culture can be visualized in a graphical manner, to give people a clearer picture of the full scope of ICH culture (as shown in Table 2).

Table 2. AI-assisted Creation of a Genetic Map for ICH Culture.

Item	Stage 1	Stage 2	Stage 3
Content	Analyze ICH data, extract key features and identify unique aspects	Reveal the inherent connections between ICH cultural elements	Construct a cultural genetic map based on the extracted features and analyzed relationships
AI technology	Deep learning algorithm	AI's association technologies	Knowledge map technology

This processs visually displays the genetic structure and inheritance lineage of ICH culture in a graphical manner, giving people a clearer picture of the full scope of ICH culture.

2.4   To Conduct Specific and In-Depth Innovative Design of ICH Culture Through AI

ICH is the crystallization of the wisdom of each nation and an important manifestation of cultural diversity. However, with the changes in society and lifestyle, numerous ICH cultures are confronted with problems like interruptions in inheritance, limited distribution channels, and a detachment from the modern world. The fast-paced development of AI technology provides new opportunities for the protection, inheritance, and innovation of ICH cultures [5]. By applying AI technology to the innovative design of ICH culture, we can revitalize its energy, enable it to better fit into modern life and achieve both creative transformation and innovative development.

2.4.1   AI Facilitates the Shift of Design Thinking from "Protection" to "Innovation"

Traditional ways to protect ICH culture mainly focus on static preservation and faithful inheritance. The introduction of AI technology, however, shifts the design thinking from "protection" to "innovation". Using AI technology, we can digitally collect, store and analyze ICH culture, establishing an ICH culture database that provides abundant materials and inspiration for innovative design [6].

2.4.2   AI-Assisted Creative Conceptualization of the Innovation Design of ICH Culture

ICH culture, as a treasure of human civilization, carries the historical memories and cultural genes of the nation. The introduction of AI technology offers new ideas and methods for the innovative design of ICH culture, as well as the creative conceptualization of the innovation design of ICH culture. Creative conceptualization is a key step in the design process, and AI can draw inspiration by establishing an ICH culture database, extracting and reorganizing cultural elements to create new design solutions, analyze the designer's creative style and preferences based on machine learning algorithms, recommend relevant ICH culture elements and design solutions, utilizing generative adversarial networks (GANs) and other technologies to intelligently generate new patterns, designs and color combinations, etc. and deliver more creative options to designers.

2.4.3   AI-Assisted Design of an Innovative Solution for ICH Culture

In the solution design stage, AI assists designers in virtual simulation, effect previews, intelligent typesetting and layout, material selection and process simulation. Using AI algorithms, we can automatically generate the optimal typesetting and layout solutions based on the design content and target audience. Designers can make fine adjustments as needed, promoting both design efficiency and aesthetics [7]. At the same time, we can utilize AI technology to establish databases for ICH culture-related materials and processes and automatically recommend suitable materials and processes according to the design solution, help designers better understand and apply traditional craftsmanship to design solutions.

The rapid growth of AI technology brings new opportunities and challenges to the innovative design of ICH culture. It is believed that with the collective efforts of all parties, AI technology will become a powerful engine for the inheritance and development of ICH culture, driving ICH culture to flourish and thrive in the new era.

2.5   To Build a "Dynamic Image Database" for ICH Information Using AI

The rapid development of AI technology has opened up a new technical path for the collection, storage, analysis and presentation of ICH information. Establishing an AI-based dynamic image database for ICH information not only enables the digital preservation of ICH resources, but also provides a powerful support for the research, inheritance and innovation of ICH through intelligent information processing.

Traditional ICH image collection primarily relies on manual photography, and face challenges such as low efficiency, high costs, and a lack of standardization. The incorporation of AI technology has revolutionized this scenario. Through intelligent imaging devices, the automated shooting of ICH projects can be achieved, with the system able to automatically identify the shooting subject, adjust parameters, and optimize image quality. In the process of skill demonstrations of ICH inheritors, intelligent devices can automatically track key movements and capture subtle facial expressions, ensuring the completeness and accuracy of the recorded footage. The application of multi-modal data collection technology makes the recording of ICH information more three-dimensional and all-rounded. Apart from traditional video footages, the system can capture audio, 3D models, and actions, etc. simultaneously, creating a multi-dimensional digital image archive for ICH [8].

In the era of AI, the dynamic update mechanism of databases can guarantee the timeliness of information. By connecting with ICH protection organizations across different regions, the system can acquire the latest information on ICH inheritance and inheritors in a real-time manner, automatically updating the content of the database. This dynamic update mechanism keeps the database vibrant and faithfully reflects the status quo of ICH inheritance and inheritors, recording the process by which the inheritors improve their skills, tracking the progress of the training of the new generation of inheritors, and providing detailed data support for ICH research. The construction of the dynamic image database not only achieves the digital preservation of ICH information, but more importantly, builds an open, intelligent and sustainable ecosystem for ICH protection. This system is capable of incorporating ongoing technological advancements, adapting to the evolving needs of the times, and providing a solid guarantee for the sustainable inheritance of ICH. The use of AI technology opens up a new path for ICH protection and the dynamic updates of ICH realize its living inheritance.

By leveraging AI to build a dynamic image database and construct an intelligent "ICH" culture inheritance and innovation path, we propose a new model for the intelligent protection, innovative development and inheritance of ICH, structured as: "ICH excavation and protection-ICH organization and research-ICH resource database establishment-ICH innovative development-ICH innovative dissemination", providing a solid technological foundation for the living inheritance of ICH in the digital era.

3 Principles of the Visualization Design of ICH Information

Through the comprehensive use of images and visual elements to present ICH cultural themes, dull text information can be presented to the audience in an accurate and engaging manner, helping the audience navigate and absorb large amounts of content quickly, providing both convenience and pleasure, and allowing the audience to relate the information obtained in an intuitive manner to their existing knowledge structure to understand the content behind the information. This approach can "yield twice the result with half the effort" in analyzing the connections between data, effectively meeting the audience's need to understand the content of ICH culture. As one of the key trends in future information delivery, the creation of an accurate and compelling information visualization design requires principles of intuitiveness, logical structure, and aesthetics.

ICH, as a treasure of human civilization, carries the historical memories and cultural genes of a nation. Information visualization design provides new possibilities for the modern communication of ICH. Through the design principles of intuitiveness, logicalization, and aesthetics, ICH culture can be revitalized with new life [9].

3.1 Intuitiveness of the Visualization Design of ICH Information

In the information era, there is a growing demand for quicker transmission of cultural information, which leads to the emergence of the visualization design form of information. Intuitiveness is the primary principle of the visualization design of ICH information. Complex ICH information can be turned into an easily understandable visual language through the precise design of graphical symbols. With the goal of general recognition and understanding by the audience, complex and hard-to-comprehend information is presented in a visual manner. Through the combination of images and text, it enables horizontal and vertical analysis of cultural themes, and allows the brain to make associative connections through visual images. This expands the audience's existing knowledge network, making information acquisition more intuitive, alleviating the memory burden involved in processing complex data, while enriching existing conceptual links and leaving a lasting impression [10].

In the face of abundant ICH, relying solely on simple reading to obtain information can reduce the audience's ability to understand and receive, leading to resistance due to its abstract and hard-to-grasp nature. This results in an inability to appreciate the deeper functions and meanings of ICH culture. Therefore, it is crucial to design visual elements based on ICH culture, find points of alignment with the design preferences of the audience for modular design, create clues for information visualization design and incorporate multi-sensory emotional experiences to clearly convey the information. By utilizing different communication channels, the flow of information is dynamically transformed, allowing the audience to intuitively feel the millennial history and culture carried by the region.

A scientifically applied color system can promote the intuitive expression of information. For different types of ICH projects, corresponding color-coding systems can be built. For traditional ICH music projects, bright tones can be adopted; for traditional folk activities, warm colors can be selected; for traditional ICH medical projects, mild color tones can be utilized. This color coding system not only aids in information recognition, but also improves visual memory. The strategic inclusion of dynamic effects can enhance the efficiency of information delivery. Through techniques such as animated demonstration and interactive design, static ICH information can be turned into a dynamic visual experience, enhancing the intuitiveness of visualization design.

3.2 Logicalization of the Visualization Design of ICH Information

A clear division of information hierarchy is the foundation of logical design. Information visualization design is meant to logicalize chaotic and unclear information and acquire useful information in a timely manner. During the visualization design of ICH culture information, to logically present the design theme, designers should carry out thorough research and analysis on unprocessed cultural features of the information, accurately select and organize them and create a logical hierarchical clue and structure, design a visual representation form that matches the cultural value and convey structured and hierarchical information to the audience.

The accurate expression of data relationships is the core of logical design. The inherent connections between different ICH projects can be revealed through visualization tools like charts and relational graphs. For example, a network diagram can display the distribution of similar ICH projects across different regions, a bar chart can compare changes in the number of inheritors across different projects, and a pie chart can showcase the proportions of different ICH projects. Constructing a reasonable narrative logic can enhance the readability of information. By weaving fragmented ICH information into a complete storyline and visually guiding the audience to understand the ICH culture step by step, for instance, designing an interactive story map, enables the audience to understand the origin, development and status quo of ICH projects in exploration, thereby reinforcing the logicality of information visualization design [11].

3.3 Aesthetics of the Visualization Design of ICH Information

The development of new media era has altered the way information is expressed and transmitted in a subtle way. Previous static designs may appear inadequate. In an effort to align with the fast-paced information consumption of people, and deliver sensory satisfaction to them, dynamic information visualization design has become an extension and enhancement of static information visualization design. Representing ICH culture information through dynamic effects can engage multiple senses of the audience, making the design content of ICH culture information coherent, rich in form and interactive with the audience. This approach ultimately enhances the audience's understanding of the cultural content, serving as an emotionally engaging form of design expression. For example, creating innovative emojis for ICH culture can produce expressions that are rich, vibrant, engaging, and easily shareable.

First and foremost, the unity and coordination of visual style is key to aesthetic design. Based on the characteristics of ICH projects, a corresponding visual style can be determined. For example, traditional calligraphy and painting projects may feature an ink-and-wash style, folk craft projects can incorporate folk patterns, while architectural projects may use geometric motifs. A consistent visual style reinforces the cultural characteristics of the project.

Secondly, a well-thought-out layout can greatly enhance the visual impact. By arranging elements such as text, images and charts in a reasonable manner and striking a well-paced arrangement with a clear sense of hierarchy, the design becomes more effective. For instance, a grid system can be used to standardize the layout, while techniques like incorporating whitespace can emphasize key information, and contrast can help reinforce the visual hierarchy.

Thirdly, the clever integration of cultural elements can effectively manifest the features of ICH. Incorporating traditional patterns, colors, symbols and other cultural elements into the design not only reflects cultural connotations, but also enhances visual appeal, such as using traditional paper-cutting patterns as decorative elements, presenting titles with calligraphic fonts, and utilizing traditional colors as the dominant palette.

The visualization design of ICH is a comprehensive endeavor that blends cultural inheritance with innovative design. By adhering to the principles of intuitiveness, logicalization, and aesthetics, it not only amplifies the dissemination effect of ICH information, but also strengthens the public's cultural identity. In the digital era, it is essential to employ innovative design language to breathe new life into ICH culture, enabling the creative transformation and innovative development of traditional culture. This is not only a need for protecting cultural heritage, but also an important pathway for passing down cultural legacies and fostering cultural self-confidence.

4   The Content of the Visualization Design of ICH Information

During the visualization design of ICH information, it is crucial to adhere to the overall design requirements. ICH carries profound cultural connotations and the visualization design could aim to encompass both breadth and depth as fully as possible. From a visual presentation perspective, the goal is to transform ICH information, developing both static and dynamic visualization designs for ICH culture. Static visualization design involves the representation of cultural creative design and charting information, while dynamic information visualization includes ICH video animations, interactive designs, and more. This approach serves not only as a modern expression of traditional culture, but also as an important pathway for the protection and inheritance of ICH.

4.1   Static Visual Design of "ICH" Information

Using planar visual language, static visual design presents ICH culture through images, graphs, and text. This design form is durable and stable, preserving the core elements of ICH on visual medium and creating an ever-lasting cultural memory.

Information charts are one of the important forms of static visual design. By combining graphic symbols, data charts and textual explanations, complex ICH information can be transformed into understandable visual language. For example, when illustrating a traditional craft-making process, a step-by-step diagram can be used to depict each stage with simple and clear icons, accompanied by brief text explanations, allowing the audience to easily follow the process. Information charts not only convey information clearly, but also enhance the viewer's engagement through visual appeal.

Printed posters are another common form of static visual design. Through the organic combination of images, text and colors, the core elements of ICH culture are condensed into a two-dimensional work of art. For instance, when designing a promotional poster for a traditional festival, one can use the festival's unique colors and patterns, along with its cultural significance, to create visually captivating designs. Printed posters not only grab public attention, but also convey the deeper meaning of ICH culture through visual symbolism.

Cultural and creative products are an extension of static visual design. By incorporating ICH elements into the design of daily necessities, they bring traditional culture into modern life in a more accessible way. For instance, applying traditional patterns to stationery, garments and household items not only enhances the cultural value of the products, but also allows ICH culture to be shared and passed down through daily life.

4.2 Dynamic Visual Design of "ICH" Information

Using animations, videos and interactive technologies, dynamic visual design displays ICH culture in dynamic forms. This approach is lively and interactive, vividly highlighting the living characteristics of ICH and allowing viewers to experience the charm of culture through dynamic visual experience.

Animation demonstrations are one of the common forms of dynamic visual design. Through 2D or 3D animation techniques, ICH skills, rituals and stories are presented (showcased) in a dynamic way, vividly illustrating the dynamic nature of ICH, while fostering emotional resonance with the audience through visual storytelling. Video documentation is another significant form of dynamic visual design. Through high-definition camera shooting and post-production editing, actual scenes of ICH projects, skill demonstrations, and the stories of inheritors are captured. Documenting skill demonstrations of inheritors or capturing the celebration of traditional festivals not only authentically reflects the living characteristics of ICH, but also conveys its cultural connotations through visual language. Interactive design is an innovative form of dynamic visual design. By incorporating virtual reality (VR), augmented reality (AR), and interactive interfaces, viewers can engage with ICH culture in a more immersive way. This type of design not only enhances the viewer's sense of participation, but also fosters a deeper understanding of ICH culture through interactive experience.

4.3 The Multi-Dimensional Integration of Static and Dynamic Elements in the Visualization Design of "ICH"

The integration of static and dynamic visual design provides a multi-dimensional expression for the transmission of ICH culture. Through static design, the core elements of ICH can be solidified on visual medium, creating an ever-lasting cultural memory. One the other hand, dynamic design allows the living characteristics of ICH to be presented in a vivid manner, enabling the audience to experience the charm of culture through dynamic visual engagement. Taking an ICH exhibition for example, both static graphic exhibition and dynamic multimedia showcase can be adopted, allowing visitors to gain a deeper understanding of ICH through a dual experience of static and dynamic elements. Static exhibitions can showcase the history, skills and cultural significance of ICH through information charts, posters and physical exhibits. In contrast, dynamic presentations utilize animations, videos, and interactive technologies to highlight the living aspects of ICH and the stories of its inheritance. This integration not only enriches the content and format of the exhibitions, but also enhances the audience's sense of participation and engagement.

The visual design of ICH, through the dual expression of static and dynamic elements, can bring new vitality to traditional culture. Static design, through planar visual languages, solidifies ICH culture on visual medium and forms an enduring cultural memory. By utilizing animations, videos and interactive technologies, dynamic design vividly brings forth the living traits of ICH, allowing viewers to feel the charm of culture through dynamic visual engagement. The combination of static and dynamic elements provides a multi-dimensional expression for the transmission of ICH culture, not only reinforcing the public's cultural identity, but also promoting the creative transformation and innovative development of ICH. In the digital era, it is essential to employ innovative design language to revitalize ICH culture and ensure the lasting inheritance of traditional culture.

5 Sustainable Strategies for the Intelligent Protection of "ICH" Culture

5.1 Strengthening the Power of Cultural Communication

Through intuitive images, animations and interactive forms, visualization design converts abstract ICH culture into an easily understandable visual language. This breaks through linguistic and cultural barriers, allowing a broader audience, especially younger generations, to quickly understand and embrace ICH culture. For instance, by showcasing the details of traditional dance movements through dynamic videos or presenting the craft-making process through information charts, the core value of ICH can be more effectively transmitted.

5.2 Enhancing Cultural Identity

Visualization design enables ICH culture to be presented in a more vivid and contemporary way, enhancing the public's identification with and pride in traditional culture. Through design, ICH is no longer seen as a distant "historical relic", but a cultural symbol closely connected to contemporary life. For example, incorporating traditional patterns into contemporary cultural and creative products not only preserves cultural essence, but also meets modern aesthetic preferences, bringing ICH closer to everyday life.

5.3 Promoting the Inheritance and Innovation of Culture

Visualization design offers new tools and platforms for the inheritance of ICH. Through digital technologies, ICH skills, rituals and stories can be preserved permanently and easily shared with a wider audience. For instance, virtual reality (VR) can recreate traditional festival scenes, while interactive design allows users to experience ICH skills firsthand, stimulating public interest and facilitating the living inheritance of ICH.

Visualization design is not merely a reproduction of ICH, but more importantly, an innovative expression of traditional culture. Through design, ICH elements can be associated with modern art and technology to create new cultural products and cultural experience. For instance, integrating traditional opera elements into modern animations or applying traditional architectural techniques to contemporary architectural design can breathe new life into ICH and promote the creative transformation of culture.

5.4 Aiding in Cultural Protection

Visualization design provides a crucial technique for the digital protection of ICH. Through high-precision image capture, 3D modeling and dynamic recording, ICH skills and cultural heritage can be digitally safeguarded, in case they disappear with the passage of time. For example, 3D scanning technology can document the structural details of traditional buildings, while motion capture technology can preserve the movement trajectory of traditional dances, offering valuable resources for the protection and research of ICH.

In conclusion, the visualization design of ICH culture is not only an innovation in in technological methods, but also an important strategy for cultural dissemination, inheritance and protection. In the new era, we should harness AI to enhance the visualization design and inheritance of ICH, breathing new life into traditional culture and infusing fresh vitality into the sustainable development of ICH.

References

1. Yang, W.: Research on the Information Visual Design of Yungang Grottoes Patterns. Master's Thesis, North University of China, pp. 45–50 (2023)
2. Li, C.: The development of innovative design of intangible cultural heritage cultural elements in traditional costumes with the empowerment of AI. Jiangsu Textile. **43**(12), 61–66 (2024)
3. Yu, X.: The realistic dilemma and innovative path of intangible cultural heritage tourism development in the information age. Int. J. Front. Sociol. **5**(15), 151–155 (2023)
4. Yu, W., Xu, K.: Dissemination of ICH based on digital twin technology. In: 2024 International Conference on Culture-Oriented Science & Technology (COST), pp. 94–98. IEEE Press, Beijing (2024)
5. Zhong, Z., Liu, H.: Research on the integration of artificial intelligence into visual design of non-legacy cultural and creative products. Green Packaging. **3**, 138–142 (2024)
6. Yuan, X., Li, L.: A study on the visual innovation of intangible cultural heritage empowered by AI-generated tools under the background of "digital intelligence design". Shenhua. **07**(3), 112–114 (2024)
7. Cao, Q.: Research on visual design strategies for intangible cultural heritage cultural and creative products with the integration of AI. Masterp. Nat. **31**, 47–49 (2024)
8. Windhager, F., et al.: Visualization of cultural heritage collection data: state of the art and future challenges. IEEE Trans. Vis. Comput. Graph. **25**(6), 2311–2330 (2019)
9. Ma, Y.: Research on information visual design of intangible cultural Heritage. Chinese National Expo. **03**, 125–127 (2023)

10. Xie, J.: Residual attention based long short-term memory based text attributes of ICH. In: 2024 Third International Conference on Distributed Computing and Electrical Circuits and Electronics (ICDCECE) (2024)
11. Lu, C., Qin, H.: Research on information chart design of intangible cultural heritage of Tujia brocade. West Leather. **44**(17), 140–149 (2022)
12. Zhang, Z., Hu, Z.: A study on the visual communication of intangible cultural heritage empowered by digital technologies. Jingu Creative Literature. **16**(40), 131–133 (2024)

Research on the Innovative Pattern Design of Blue Printed Fabric from the Perspective of the Living Inheritance of Intangible Cultural Heritage

Jiajia Zhao, Qian Bao, and Ziyang Huang

Major of Design, Department of Design, Graduate School, Hanyang University, Seoul 04763, Republic of Korea
pomelo402@163.com

Abstract. The preservation and innovation of intangible cultural heritage are critical challenges in cultural protection. With the rapid development of artificial intelligence (AI) technology, new opportunities have emerged for safeguarding and transmitting intangible cultural heritage. As a Chinese national intangible cultural heritage, the blue printed fabric craft faces multiple challenges, including the loss of traditional techniques, shifts in aesthetic and cultural values, and concerns regarding environmental sustainability and cost. This paper explores the use of generative AI technology (AIGC) in the design of blue printed fabric patterns, aiming to generate innovative patterns that align with both traditional aesthetics and contemporary design demands. These patterns are integrated into daily life applications to promote the creative development and transformation of intangible cultural heritage. The research classifies and summarizes blue printed fabric patterns, creating a dataset and utilizing the Stable Diffusion AI drawing software for LoRA model training. The generated patterns blend traditional styles with innovative elements and are applied to modern home design, showcasing the contemporary relevance of intangible cultural heritage. By combining traditional craftsmanship with generative AI, this study not only generates new patterns but also demonstrates AI's potential in art and design, advancing the integration of traditional culture with modern technology and enhancing the vitality and dissemination of intangible cultural heritage.

Keywords: Artificial Intelligence · Intangible Cultural Heritage · Blue Printed Fabric Patterns · Design Innovation; AIGC

1 Introduction

In the process of globalization and modernization, intangible cultural heritage faces numerous challenges [1]. The transmission and innovation of intangible cultural heritage have become one of the core issues in cultural protection and development [2]. The blue printed fabric craft, a Chinese national intangible cultural heritage, is currently encountering multiple difficulties, including the loss of skills, shifts in aesthetic value, and environmental and cost challenges [3].

M. Schrepp and M. Rauterberg (Eds.): HCII 2025, LNCS 16342, pp. 312–322, 2026.
https://doi.org/10.1007/978-3-032-13164-5_20

In this context, the application of AI technology in the protection of intangible cultural heritage is growing, especially in generating high-quality image data, where it shows unique advantages [4]. The generative capability of AI provides new ideas for the reproduction and innovation of intangible cultural heritage patterns [5]. For example, a study on the design of Chinese Miao women's clothing explored innovative applications in personalized design through AI and machine learning technologies, highlighting the potential of multimodal image transformation techniques [6]. Furthermore, the powerful data analysis capabilities of AI offer scientific support for studying and predicting trends in the transmission of cultural elements [7]. For instance, a study proposed a decision support system based on the artificial bee colony algorithm to assess the value of intangible cultural heritage, advancing the research on the digital transformation of intangible cultural heritage [8]. The application of AI not only improves the efficiency of cultural protection but also promotes the integration of traditional culture with modern design [9]. One study explored the application of AI in the cross-cultural dissemination of intangible cultural heritage by extracting and reconstructing design elements through user perception and shape grammar, generating innovative design solutions [10].

Despite the enormous potential of AI in the transmission and innovation of intangible cultural heritage, challenges remain, particularly in balancing the application of technology with the protection of cultural authenticity [11]. Ensuring that AI supports rather than replaces traditional cultural transmission methods will be crucial to its future development [12].

2   Literature Review

2.1   Current Status and Challenges of Intangible Cultural Heritage Preservation

First and foremost, the disruption in the transmission of skills is one of the most severe issues in ICH preservation [13]. Many ICH projects rely on the master-apprentice system for transmission [14]. However, in modern society, younger generations are losing interest in traditional crafts, making it difficult to pass down these skills [15].

Secondly, shifts in aesthetic values also pose a major challenge to ICH [16]. Changes in modern aesthetics and lifestyles have caused many traditional crafts to become disconnected from contemporary design trends, making them difficult for modern consumers to accept or appreciate. Blue printed fabric, a national intangible cultural heritage of China, though rich in history and cultural significance, has a relatively simple pattern and color scheme in the modern aesthetic context, appearing less fashionable and contemporary [17]. This not only limits its dissemination in today's market but also decreases its appeal to younger generations.

In addition, environmental and economic cost pressures are critical factors affecting the transmission of ICH techniques. In response to these challenges, ICH preservation models are shifting from traditional static preservation to dynamic innovation [18]. Many scholars and practitioners are exploring how modern technologies, particularly AI and digital technologies, can drive the transmission and innovative development of ICH [19]. These technologies not only help preserve the core elements of traditional crafts but also enhance their contemporary appeal through design innovation, thereby attracting new audiences.

2.2 Application of Artificial Intelligence Technology in Intangible Cultural Heritage Preservation

The powerful data processing and generative capabilities of AI technology [20] enable its involvement in various aspects of cultural heritage, such as digital preservation, image generation, and design innovation [21]. In the field of intangible cultural heritage (ICH) preservation, generative AI (AIGC) has demonstrated its potential, particularly in generating complex images and designs [22].

Firstly, the application of AI in the digital preservation of ICH is increasing [23]. Through deep learning and computer vision technologies, AI can digitize and analyze traditional crafts [24]. For example, a study on the digital preservation of ICH utilized motion capture (MoCap) technology to record cultural performances in dynamic form, adopting a multimodal archival approach to comprehensively record and disseminate ICH content [25]. Secondly, the application of AI in pattern and image generation shows great potential [21]. Generative Adversarial Networks (GANs), a type of generative AI model [26], can learn from large datasets of traditional images to generate high-resolution patterns or image designs [27]. AI's role in driving design innovation in ICH is undeniable. Through AI algorithms' autonomous learning and generative capabilities, designers can combine traditional cultural elements with modern design needs, creating designs that balance traditional aesthetics with contemporary innovation [28].

In summary, AI technology, particularly generative AI, has deeply penetrated the preservation and innovation of ICH. Whether in digital preservation, image and pattern generation, or personalized and innovative design applications, AI has shown its immense potential. The application of these technologies has not only enhanced the efficiency of ICH transmission but also injected new vitality into the development of cultural heritage in modern society.

3 Cultural Symbol Analysis of Blue Printed Fabric

As a representative of traditional Chinese textile craftsmanship, the history of blue printed fabric can be traced back to the Tang and Song dynasties, originating from folk dyeing and weaving techniques [29]. By the Ming and Qing dynasties, blue printed fabric had gradually gained popularity, becoming an important decorative material in the lives of ordinary people, widely used in clothing, home textiles, and religious ceremonies. With the development of manual dyeing and weaving techniques, the patterns and production techniques of blue printed fabric became increasingly sophisticated, and its style evolved with the times [30]. In feudal Chinese society, the color blue was considered a symbol of tranquility and purity, representing vitality and the forces of nature. Therefore, blue printed fabric was not only widely used in daily life but also carried people's reverence for nature, life, and good fortune. This cultural background directly influenced the design of blue printed fabric patterns, reflecting distinct regional characteristics and aesthetic preferences in different historical periods.

The patterns of blue printed fabric, as the core of this traditional craft, directly reflect the social culture, belief systems, and lifestyles of the time [31]. From a design perspective, patterns are not just decorative elements; they are also symbols and tools for cultural transmission. Research on the innovative design of blue printed fabric patterns is relatively limited, with existing studies primarily focusing on how to transform them through modern design methods [11]. However, these studies often lack a technology-driven approach to innovation. One study proposed a method for innovative design based on traditional patterns, while it emphasized the importance of patterns in the modern market, it did not explore the deep potential of using modern technologies, such as artificial intelligence, for pattern generation [32].

Through literature review and field research, the classification and characteristics of blue printed fabric patterns have been summarized as follows:

- Floral and fauna motifs are a significant component of blue printed fabric design, reflecting the reverence for nature in ancient Chinese agrarian society. For instance, peonies symbolize wealth, lotus flowers represent purity, and pine cranes signify longevity. These patterns not only serve decorative purposes but also express admiration for the vitality of nature, aligning with the Chinese cultural concept of the "unity of heaven and man." Modern designers can draw inspiration from these motifs, using simple lines and symbolic imagery to convey profound cultural meanings in contemporary contexts.

- Geometric patterns play a vital role in blue printed fabric, embodying the traditional Chinese pursuit of order, symmetry, and balance. Influenced by Daoist ideas such as "round heaven, square earth," these patterns reflect an understanding of cosmic order. Their symmetry and repetitive structures resonate with the aesthetic principles found in traditional Chinese architecture and art. Modern designers can adopt these geometric compositions to create visually striking designs with a sense of order and structure.

- Common auspicious symbols in blue printed fabric, such as "Fu, Lu, Shou, Xi" (representing fortune, prosperity, longevity, and happiness), embody the Chinese cultural pursuit of well-being. These symbols serve as a visual language, conveying profound cultural meanings through simple graphics. Modern symbol design can draw from these traditional motifs, refining and simplifying them to imbue contemporary designs with cultural significance.

- The composition styles of blue printed fabric can be categorized into full and partial layouts, each reflecting distinct cultural imagery. Full layouts, with their sense of completeness and visual richness, align with the aesthetic philosophy of "making the most of everything," reflecting the frugality of ancient agrarian society. Partial compositions emphasize detailed design and overall harmony, resonating with the ideals of "space" and "simplicity" in traditional Chinese art. Modern designers can learn from these compositions, utilizing space and visual focus to convey specific cultural messages.

- The primary colors of blue printed fabric—blue and white—are derived from traditional plant-based dyes. Blue symbolizes tranquility, endurance, and strength, while white represents purity and brightness. This minimalist color scheme creates a striking visual effect while carrying deep cultural connotations. Modern design can adopt this approach, using simple color palettes to convey rich emotional and cultural meanings.

4 Design Methods and Process

4.1 Dataset Construction

The dataset was compiled from two main sources: online resources and offline physical collection. These patterns were then digitized, with their format and resolution standardized for subsequent analysis and processing. Each pattern image included not only basic image information but also annotations in the following three categories:

- Historical Background: The origin, era, and cultural context of each pattern, including specific historical events or regional cultural characteristics represented by the pattern.
- Symbolic Meaning: An interpretation of the symbols and designs within the patterns, indicating the cultural values and meanings they represent, as well as their function and use in traditional society.
- Cultural Relevance: The connection of the patterns to other cultural elements or designs, exploring their interaction and influence with other traditional cultures or ethnic arts.

To efficiently manage and store this data, a relational database management system (RDBMS), MySQL, was chosen as the digital pattern management system [33]. The key fields in this data model include:

- Image ID: A unique identifier for each pattern image, enabling quick retrieval.
- Creation Date: The date when the image was collected or digitized, allowing for timeline tracking of the data.
- Category: Classification of the pattern based on its design style and symbolic meaning, categorized into groups such as flora, fauna, geometric patterns, etc.
- Description: A brief textual description of each image, explaining its main design features and cultural significance.
- File Path: The path where the image file is stored, enabling the database system to quickly access the image file through a link.

Additionally, the database supports a tagging system to facilitate multidimensional classification and querying of patterns [34]. Each image can be tagged with multiple labels, identifying its design style, symbolic meaning, or cultural origin (see Figs. 1 and 2). These technical approaches make the constructed digital pattern dataset of blue printed fabric not only academically valuable but also highly practical, providing a solid foundation for subsequent AI-driven pattern generation.

4.2 AIGC Technology Application

In this study, generative artificial intelligence technology (AIGC) was employed for the innovative design of blue printed fabric patterns. To achieve high-quality pattern generation, multiple advanced generative models were used, combining diffusion models and Generative Adversarial Networks (GANs) to produce stable and detail-rich patterns [35]. Additionally, by incorporating LoRA (Low-Rank Adaptation) fine-tuning technology [36], the generation efficiency of the model was further enhanced, ultimately creating new patterns that retain the traditional style of blue printed fabric while introducing innovative designs.

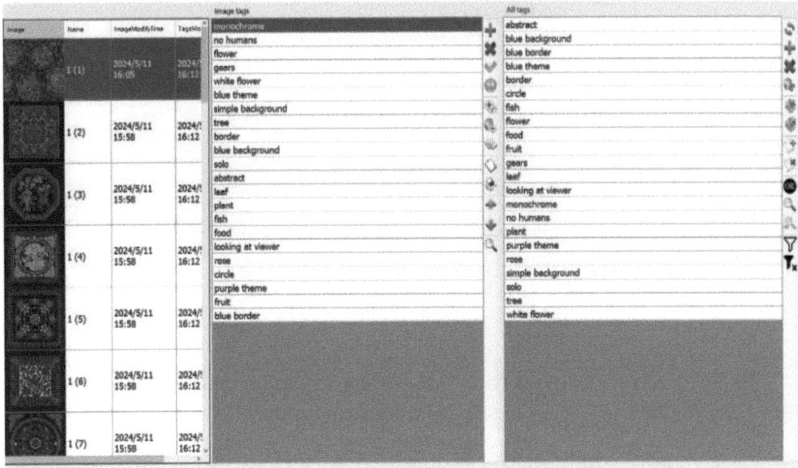

Fig. 1. Label processing.

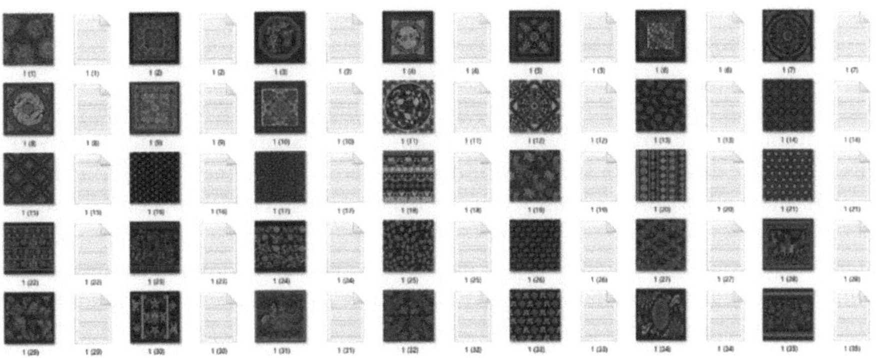

Fig. 2. Part of the pattern.

The primary generation tool in this research was the Stable Diffusion platform [37]. To efficiently fine-tune the model during the pattern generation process, the study introduced the LoRA (Low-Rank Adaptation) fine-tuning method. LoRA, through low-rank matrix decomposition, significantly reduces the amount of model parameter updates, allowing for efficient model fine-tuning without the need to retrain the entire model [38]. This is particularly important for blue printed fabric pattern generation, where the task requires the model to retain the unique style of traditional patterns while also innovating in design. LoRA's quick adjustment of model parameters ensures that the model can be flexibly applied to different design tasks [39]. In this study, the LoRA fine-tuning method was applied to targeted training for blue printed fabric patterns (see Tables 1 and 2). By fine-tuning specific layers of the model, the study successfully achieved personalized generation of blue printed fabric patterns.

Table 1. LORA training parameters.

Dataset Size	Resolution	Batch Size	Max Epochs	Save Every N Epochs	Network Dim	Network Alpha	Clip skip	LR	UNetLR
200	512x512	2	8	2	64	2	1	0.0002	0.0002

Table 2. LORA training parameters.

Text Encoder LR	LR Scheduler	LR Restat Cycles	Persistent Dataloader Workers	Noise Offset	LoCon Conv Dim	Conv Alpha	Approx Training Time
0.0002	cosine_with_restarts	1	2	0.1	4	0.1	1

5 Results and Analysis

After the completion of LoRA model training, this study used Stable Diffusion ComfyUI as the primary tool to generate blue printed fabric patterns. Stable Diffusion ComfyUI is a user interface designed for the stable diffusion algorithm, offering a modular and visual workflow that allows users to easily construct and operate complex models by dragging components and adjusting parameters [40]. The main reason for choosing this tool is its ability to simplify the complexity of model construction and training, allowing users without deep algorithmic knowledge to efficiently complete pattern generation tasks in an intuitive manner.

The advantage of Stable Diffusion ComfyUI in pattern generation lies in its modular design [41]. Users can flexibly adjust various model parameters, such as KSampler, Latent Space, and VAE (Variational Autoencoder), to achieve precise control over pattern style and details. In this study, when the keyword "plant pattern" was entered, ComfyUI automatically invoked the previously trained LoRA model and, by adjusting the parameters of each module, generated new blue printed fabric pattern designs. By combining and adjusting these modules, this study was able to achieve precise control over the pattern images, ensuring both the desired visual effects and consistency in the artistic style of the patterns (Figs. 3 and 4).

Fig. 3. Generate Pattern

Fig. 4. Pattern Application.

6   Conclusion

This study explored the application of generative AI technology (AIGC) in the innovative design of blue printed fabric patterns, demonstrating how AI technology can inject new vitality into the preservation of traditional culture through automation and innovation. By combining the Stable Diffusion and LoRA fine-tuning models, this study successfully generated numerous innovative blue printed fabric patterns that not only preserved the traditional artistic style but also offered a rich variety of design solutions for modern needs. This creative exploration opens new pathways for the protection and innovation of intangible cultural heritage, showcasing the immense potential of AIGC technology in cultural heritage transmission.

The key achievements of this study include:

- Technological Application: By introducing generative AI technology, this study demonstrated how Stable Diffusion and LoRA models can be used for the generation and innovative design of blue printed fabric patterns. This technology not only improved design efficiency but also provided new automated design methods, ensuring the continuity of traditional elements in modern design.
- Balance Between Innovation and Culture: The study successfully showcased a balance between traditional cultural elements and modern design innovations, ensuring the fusion of tradition and innovation in the symbolism, composition, and color of blue printed fabric patterns.
- Expansion of Application Scenarios: The AI-generated blue printed fabric patterns can be widely applied in various fields, including home decor, fashion, and cultural creative products, demonstrating the potential of AIGC technology for the marketization and modernization of traditional culture.

This study is significant both theoretically and practically. It expands the application of generative AI technology in the field of cultural heritage, proposing how AI can be used to innovate traditional cultural elements. This provides a new research perspective for the protection of intangible cultural heritage and offers theoretical support for the future integration of AI and cultural heritage. The study also reveals how AIGC can learn from a vast collection of traditional patterns to fuse cultural symbols with modern design, promoting dynamic cultural transmission. Practically, generative AI technology provides designers and artisans with a tool to quickly generate and optimize traditional patterns, enhancing design diversity and efficiency. The application of AI-generated patterns in various fields showcases their commercial potential, especially in fashion, home decor, and cultural creative industries, where traditional patterns can find new uses through modern technology, improving the market adaptability of traditional craftsmanship.

Through this study, generative AI technology has demonstrated its broad potential in the preservation and innovation of intangible cultural heritage. Future research should not only focus on technological innovation but also emphasize a deeper understanding of cultural meanings and interdisciplinary collaboration to ensure that traditional culture is effectively preserved and innovatively transmitted in modern society.

References

1. Bortolotto, C., Ubertazzi, B.: Intellectual property as a blind spot in the UNESCO convention for the safeguarding of the intangible cultural heritage. Int. J. Herit. Stud. **29**(10), 1128–1140 (2023)
2. Lazaro Ortiz, de Madariaga, C.J.: The UNESCO convention for the safeguarding of the intangible cultural heritage: a critical analysis. Int. J. Cult. Policy. **28**(3), 327–341 (2022)
3. Liang, W., Song, Y.: Design that combines intangible heritage elements and local culture. In: 7th International Conference on Arts, Design and Contemporary Education (ICADCE 2021), pp. 443–448. Atlantis Press (2021)
4. Abgaz, R., Rocha Souza, J., Methuku, G., Dorn, A.: A methodology for semantic enrichment of cultural heritage images using artificial intelligence technologies. J. Imaging. **7**(8), 121 (2021)
5. Belhi, A., Bouras, A., Al-Ali, A.K., Foufou, S.: A machine learning framework for enhancing digital experiences in cultural heritage. J. Enterp. Inf. Manag. **36**(3), 734–746 (2023)

6. Deng, Y., Liu, Chen, L.: AI-driven innovation in ethnic clothing design: an intersection of machine learning and cultural heritage. Electron. Res. Arch. **31**(9), 5793–5814 (2023)

7. Xie, J.: Innovative design of artificial intelligence in intangible cultural heritage. Sci. Program. **2022**(1), 6913046 (2022)

8. Li, D., Liu, Wu, C.-H.: Innovative development of intangible culture of arts and crafts in artificial intelligence decision support system. Mob. Inf. Syst. **2022**, 1–12 (2022)

9. Zhang, J., Jing, Y.: Application of artificial intelligence technology in cross-cultural communication of intangible cultural heritage. Math. Probl. Eng. **2022**(1), 6563114 (2022)

10. Zhang, Y., Liu, W.: Application of artificial intelligence technology in cross-cultural communication of intangible cultural heritage. Math. Probl. Eng. **2022**, 1–12 (2022)

11. Hou, S., Kenderdine, D., Picca, M., Adamou, A.: Digitizing intangible cultural heritage embodied: state of the art. JOCCH. **15**(3), 1–20 (2022)

12. Pistola, T., et al.: Creating immersive experiences based on intangible cultural heritage. In: 2021 IEEE International Conference on Intelligent Reality (ICIR), pp. 17–24. IEEE (2021)

13. Lin, Q., Lian, Z.: On protection of intangible cultural heritage in China from the intellectual property rights perspective. Sustainability. **10**(12), 4369 (2018)

14. Zhang, Q.: Intangible cultural heritage safeguarding in times of crisis. Asian Ethnol. **79**(1), 91–113 (2020)

15. Esfehani, H., Albrecht, J.N.: Planning for intangible cultural heritage in tourism: challenges and implications. J. Hosp. Tour. Res. **43**(7), 980–1001 (2019)

16. Neyrinck, J.: Intangible cultural heritage in times of 'superdiversity': exploring ways of transformation. Int. J. Intang. Herit. **12**, 157–174 (2017)

17. Wang, Y., Fu, R.: Research on the regenerated design of blue calico based on computer image processing. In: Culture and Computing: 8th International Conference, C&C 2020, Held as Part of the 22nd HCI International Conference, HCII 2020, pp. 428–438. Springer (2020)

18. Ma, M.: Research on the protection of intellectual property rights of intangible cultural heritage. Acad. J. Humanit. Soc. Sci. **6**, 58–64 (2023)

19. Gaber, A., Youssef, S.M., Fathalla, K.M.: The role of artificial intelligence and machine learning in preserving cultural heritage and art works via virtual restoration. ISPRS Ann. Photogramm. Remote Sens. Spatial Inf. Sci. **10**, 185–190 (2023)

20. Cui, J., Fu, L.: Multimedia display of wushu intangible cultural heritage based on interactive system and artificial intelligence. Soft. Comput., 1–9 (2023)

21. Hu, Y.: Application research of artificial intelligence in the innovation of Zhuang brocade digital art: taking "the speech of Zhuang brocade" as an example. J. Comput. Commun. **11**(5), 42–51 (2023)

22. Zhao, W.: Study on the digital inheritance and development strategy of Chinese intangible cultural heritage from the perspective of AIGC. Trans. Soc. Sci. Educ. Human. Res. **4**, 138–142 (2024)

23. Deng, J.: A brief analysis of the path of intangible cultural heritage inheritance and innovative development under digital technology. J. Innov. Dev. **3**(3), 29–32 (2023)

24. Lu, C., Zhou, C.: Image retrieval algorithm of intangible cultural heritage based on artificial intelligence technology. In: The International Conference on Cyber Security Intelligence and Analytics, pp. 1–9. Springer (2023)

25. Chung, M.-Y.: Utilising technology as a transmission strategy in intangible cultural heritage: the case of Cantonese opera performances. Int. J. Heritage Stud. **30**(2), 210–225 (2024)

26. Maan, J.: Deep learning-driven explainable AI using generative adversarial network (GAN). In: 2022 IEEE 19th India Council International Conference (INDICON), pp. 1–5. IEEE (2022)

27. Nimbarte, M., et al.: AI innovator: text to image generation using GAN. In: 2024 IEEE International Students' Conference on Electrical, Electronics and Computer Science (SCEECS), pp. 1–6. IEEE (2024)

28. Zhang, B., et al.: Can AI-generated art stimulate the sustainability of intangible cultural heritage? A quantitative research on cultural and creative products of new year prints generated by AI. Heliyon. **9**(10), e20477 (2023)
29. Ni, N.: "A study on the measures for the archival protection of the intangible cultural heritage" Chinese painting pigment making technique. Pacific Int. J. **6**(1), 33–36 (2023)
30. Zhang, Y., Yao, L.: Research on the status and problems of Beijing "textile intangible heritage+" experiential tourism. In: 2021 International Conference on Social Sciences and Big Data Application (ICSSBDA 2021), pp. 192–198. Atlantis Press (2021)
31. Jin, H.: Innovative design of Indigo Print in soft smart knitted garments. In Advances in Usability, User Experience, Wearable and Assistive Technology: Proceedings of the AHFE 2021 Virtual Conferences on Usability and User Experience, Human Factors and Wearable Technologies, Human Factors in Virtual Environments and Game Design, and Human Factors and Assistive Technolog, pp. 102–107. Springer (2021)
32. Yan, J., Li, K.-R.: Sustainable cultural innovation practice: heritage education in universities and creative inheritance of intangible cultural heritage craft. Sustainability. **15**(2), 1194 (2023)
33. Zulfa, I., Wanda, R.: Rancangan Sistem Informasi Akademik Berbasis Website Menggunakan PHP dan MySQL. KLIK: Kajian Ilmiah Informatika Dan Komputer. **3**(4), 393–399 (2023)
34. Zhang, Y., Pan, F.: Design and implementation of a new intelligent warehouse management system based on MySQL database technology. Informatica. **46**(3) (2022)
35. Li, J., Liu, Q.: Application of generative artificial intelligence AIGC technology under neural network algorithm in game character art Design. J. Knowl. Econ., 1–32 (2024)
36. Hartley, K., Lind, R.J., Pound, M.P., French, A.P.: Domain targeted synthetic plant style transfer using stable diffusion LoRA and ControlNet. In: Proceedings of the IEEE/CVF Conference on Computer Vision and Pattern Recognition, pp. 5375–5383 (2024)
37. Gokaslan, A., et al.: CommonCanvas: open diffusion models trained on creative-commons images. In: Proceedings of the IEEE/CVF Conference on Computer Vision and Pattern Recognition, pp. 8250–8260 (2024)
38. Levin, O., Belov, Y.S.: A study on the application of using Hypernetwork and low rank adaptation for text-to-image generation based on diffusion models. In: 2024 6th International Youth Conference on Radio Electronics, Electrical and Power Engineering (REEPE), pp. 1–5. IEEE (2024)
39. Zhao, Y., Ogawa, S., Chen, Z., Sekimoto, Y.: Label freedom: stable diffusion for remote sensing image semantic segmentation data generation. In: 2023 IEEE International Conference on Big Data (BigData), pp. 1022–1030. IEEE (2023)
40. Hu, Q., et al.: CanFuUI: a canvas-centric web user Interface for iterative image generation with diffusion models and ControlNet. In: International Conference on AI-Generated Content, pp. 128–138. Springer (2023)
41. Wang, C., J. Chung: Research on character's consistency in AI-generated paintings. International Journal of Internet, Broadcasting and Communication. **16**(3), 199–204 (2024)

Research on Digital Protection and Innovative Application of Decorative Patterns in Gannan Hakka Architecture

Juan Zhou[✉] and Qun Zuo

Gannan University of Science and Technology, Ganzhou, Jiangxi, China
3367879@qq.com

Abstract. The decorative patterns on Gannan Hakka architecture reflect the history, culture, and social structure of the Hakka people. They are not only a spiritual treasure trove for the Hakka but also an extremely important material carrier of Gannan Hakka culture. To find more possibilities for value transformation in the context of digitalization, this article is based on the theory of cultural genes and deeply deconstructs the decorative patterns of Gannan Hakka architecture in terms of their explicit forms and implicit semantics, analyzing the types of patterns and their aesthetic characteristics. On this basis, it proposes a strategy for digital preservation, using computer technology to digitally collect, analyze, process, and preserve the patterns. Taking furniture design as a carrier, it employs shape grammar for multidimensional deduction, combining the needs and aesthetic preferences of the target users to construct the effects of furniture design, empowering the contemporary value transformation and application of Gannan Hakka architectural decorative patterns. This aims to enhance the aesthetic value and cultural connotations of furniture design and provide new approaches and methods for the digital preservation and innovative application of Gannan Hakka architectural decorative patterns.

Keywords: Decorative patterns of Gannan Hakka architectural decoration · Cultural gene theory · Digital protection · Furniture design

1 Introduction

Gannan, is the first stop of the Hakka ancestors moving south, is also one of the cradles of the national Hakka culture. After the collision and combination of repeated migration and local culture, the Hakka people have retained a large number of precious historical and cultural resources on this land. This has been fully reflected in the Gannan Hakka architectural decoration, whether the architectural style, decorative patterns or architectural materials, all carry a profound historical heritage and cultural connotation. Hakka people depict or carve decorative patterns in Hakka architecture, which not only fully shows the aesthetic pursuit and spiritual belief of Hakka people, but also is an important medium for the inheritance of history and culture. Its value of inheritance and protection cannot be underestimated. In the context of the digital age, how to make its diversified, comprehensive and integrated inheritance and development by means of research, translation, activation and regeneration is particularly important.

M. Schrepp and M. Rauterberg (Eds.): HCII 2025, LNCS 16342, pp. 323–334, 2026.
https://doi.org/10.1007/978-3-032-13164-5_21

At present, the research on the decorative pattern of Gannan Hakka architecture mainly focuses on its historical origin, cultural connotation, artistic characteristics and other aspects, while there are relatively few studies on digital design. With the rapid development of digital technology, some scholars began to try to apply digital technology to the protection and innovative application of traditional patterns, such as the use of computer graphics, virtual reality and other technologies to use the digital collection, reconstruction and display of traditional patterns. Based on the theory of cultural genes, this study aims to deconstruct and analyze the decorative patterns in Gannan, and propose a digital protection strategy. At the same time, with furniture design as the carrier, the paper explores the application ways and methods of Gannan Hakka architectural decoration pattern in contemporary design.

2 Overview of Gannan Hakka Architectural Decoration Pattern

Gannan Hakka architecture is from the deep integration of fairy tales, folk culture and animal and plant culture, deeply influenced by Confucianism, Taoist beliefs and folk customs. Confucianism emphasizes "ritual" and "harmony", which is reflected in the pursuit of order, symmetry and harmony; Taoism gives architectural decoration mysterious color and auspicious meaning; and folk customs make the architectural decoration more close to people's lives, full of strong life atmosphere.

Gannan hakka building roof, cornices, algae, and column development building components, carved the subject diversity, decorative design of rich connotation, decorative patterns, such as birds, flowers and plants, geometric graphics, etc., on the hakka to longevity ankang, good weather, good wish to avoid evil spirits, and expectations for future generations [1].

The themes of Gannan Hakka architectural decoration patterns are rich and diverse, including auspicious birds and animals, plants and flowers, character stories, geometric text symbols and other categories. These patterns contain profound auspicious meaning and cultural connotation, such as dragon, phoenix, unicorn and other animals symbolize auspicious and auspicious spirit, peony, lotus and other plants represent wealth and prosperity, while the 24 filial piety and unicorn gifts reflect the education of ethics and morality and the inheritance of history and culture.

3 Cultural Gene Analysis of Decorative Patterns in Gannan Hakka Buildings

3.1 Expression Mode of the Dominant Genes

3.1.1 Decorative Pattern Lines Clever

For the traditional pattern decorative art, the line is not only the basic modeling element of the pattern, but also an important decorative art factor for the pattern to form the visual movement and rhythm [2]. For example, on the basis of absorbing the characteristics of tangled branches in other cultures, the ancestors of Gannan Hakka integrated them with the characteristics of flowers, vines and grass rolling in southern Jiangxi, and cleverly constructed the characteristics of Hakka culture in Gannan through the characteristics of curling, circling or winding. The tangled branches, with its recurrent design, symbolize the tenacity and persistence of life, reflecting the Hakka people's awe and respect for life. Many tangled branches also integrated auspicious patterns and words, such as the lion ball, the eight immortals across the sea, lotus birth son, meaning peace and wealth, good luck and other good wishes. In the architectural decoration of Gannan Hakka, the tangled branches often appear in the curved gray wall under the eaves of the doors and Windows in the form of strip continuous decoration, as well as the position of the exposed eaves of the building (see Fig. 1).

Fig. 1. Window Decorations and Bracket Corbels in Gannan Hakka architecture

3.1.2 Pattern Combinations Vary

Pattern combination is one of the main expression means of Gannan Hakka decorative patterns. Gannan hakka ancestors using simplified concrete object two-dimensional plane, remove complicated redundant unnecessary details, keep its main appearance characteristics, then use alternative method or other filling technique outline simple decoration, through symmetry, meter, continuous, radial style, shows the hakka in the artistic creation of unique aesthetic and wisdom. Symmetrical pattern usually presents a kind of balance and harmonious beauty, metrical pattern by regularity of arrangement shows a rigorous sense of order, continuous pattern by repetition and extension build a flow and continuous visual effect, while radial pattern with center point as the benchmark, to spread around, form a dynamic tension. For example, the flower window pattern decoration in the new enclosure of Longnan Pass west encirclement is embedded with several groups of flower shapes, with full flowers, half flowers and four flowers and leaves. It uses the flower shape elements to extend and circulate repeatedly up and down, and the elements are closely connected, which is concise and powerful, neat and dignified.

3.1.3 Rich Themes of Decorative Patterns

The themes of Gannan Hakka architectural decoration cover auspicious culture, farming and reading culture, nature worship, family worship, reunion and happiness, reflecting the unique regional culture, folk beliefs, folk customs and cultural customs of the region, and expressing the Hakka people's yearning for a better life and expectations for the prosperity of the family. The Hakka people have a deep affection for the natural environment. They are good at drawing inspiration from nature and integrating natural elements such as mountains, vegetation, flowers and birds into the architectural decoration. For example, in Gannan Hakka residential doors and Windows decoration, often can see with the plum blossom, bamboo, lotus, etc., Gannan Hakka residential roof, wall, often can see with dragon, phoenix, kirin beast as the theme of the design, these patterns not only beautify the building, more carries the profound cultural connotation and emotional sustenance. In addition, the Hakka people are good at using symbols, meanings and other techniques to integrate auspicious words, auspicious symbols, historical stories into the architectural decoration, so as to pray for good luck and happiness. In the doors and Windows, walls, ridges and other parts of Gannan Hakka buildings, you can often see the "blessing", "longevity", "xi" and other auspicious characters as the theme pattern. These auspicious words through the artistic deformation and combination, formed a variety of beautiful and generous patterns. At the same time, the Hakka people also put bats, deer, fish and other animal images with auspicious meanings into the architectural decoration, in order to symbolize "Fulu Shou xi" and other good wishes(Table 1).

Table 1. List of Decorative Themes in Gannan Hakka Architecture

Types of topics	Common patterns
Zoomorphism	Dragon, phoenix, monkey, lion, crane, kylin, carp, mandarin duck, bat, deer, magpie, etc
Plant image	Lotus, peony, bamboo, plum blossom, orchid, chrysanthemum, pine, persimmon, grape, rolling grass, tangled branches, etc
Character portrayal	Fu Lu Shou three stars, the God of wealth, eight immortals, longevity star, Confucius, Guan Yu, Sun Wukong, NeZha, Zhong Kui, etc
The image of utensils	Ruyi, vase, bronze mirror, four treasures of the study, promotion seal, cornucopia, etc
Geometric text symbol	Fu, longevity, xi, wealth, Lu, Swastika, Eight Immortals in Concealment, Bagua Diagram, Huiwen Pattern, Fangsheng, Music, Chess, Calligraphy and Painting, etc.
Plot story	Fishing, woodcutting, farming, reading, Gannan tea-picking opera, Mulan Joins the Army, Twenty-Four Filial Exemplars, Meeting on the Magpie Bridge, etc

3.1.4 Distfeatures of Color Use

The colors of Gannan Hakka architectural decoration patterns are mostly based on nature, such as the color of plants, animal hair color, the color of minerals, etc. This natural color gives people a sense of intimacy and reality, but also reflects the Hakka people's awe and love for nature. Pay attention to contrast and coordination on color collocation, often use the contrast way of cool and warm tone, light and dark tone, make the pattern more bright and dazzling, undertake coordination with similar color again, make the pattern more harmonious and unified. For example, the hakka people will be on the doors and Windows, partition on the decoration of wood carving techniques, peaches, peony, pomegranate, phoenix, bats and other auspicious moral design and shape, express many son, wealth, wealth, prosperity, prosperity, some beam fang also directly with hundreds of sun, peace wealth, wealth words and patterns, color is given priority to with yellow, red, ochre, give a person a sense of prosperity.

In addition, the color use of Gannan Hakka architectural decoration patterns is also deeply influenced by the traditional culture. For example, the five elements (gold, wood, water, fire and earth) are often used in decoration, reflecting the cosmology and philosophical thoughts of traditional Chinese culture. The color of the five elements not only symbolizes the great law of heaven and earth, but also echoes the concept of "five blessings". For example, red represents wealth, and black symbolizes corning. Through color collocation, it not only highlights the aesthetic value, but also places the beautiful meaning. The color of the five elements is particularly prominent in the Hakka ancestral hall. The "lucky star" on the plaque is mainly golden, implying brilliant; the red and black on the column symbolize wealth and corning. Between the beams and columns of the Hakka ancestral hall, the dragon and phoenix patterns are often drawn alternately with vermilion and ink black, which not only shows the harmonious beauty of the dragon and phoenix, but also highlights the meaning of wealth and auspiciousness through color contrast.

3.2 A Semantic Analysis of the Recessive Genes

3.2.1 Wish for a Better Life

The Hakka people are good at using symbols, implied meanings and other techniques to integrate auspicious words and auspicious symbols into the architectural decoration, so as to pray for good luck and happiness. These auspicious patterns not only have the function of decoration and beautification, but also place the Hakka people's yearning and pursuit for a better life. In the doors, Windows, walls, ridges and other parts of the Hakka dwellings in Gannan Hakka, you can often see the "fu", "longevity", "xi" and other auspicious characters as the theme patterns. These auspicious words through the artistic deformation and combination, formed a variety of beautiful and generous patterns. At the same time, the Hakka people also put bats, deer, fish, butterflies and other animal images with auspicious meaning into the architectural decoration, in order to symbolize "Fulu, Shou and CAI" and other good wishes.

3.2.2 The Embodiment of Religious Belief

The Hakka people integrated Taoist, Buddhist and folk beliefs into the architectural decoration to pray for the blessing of the gods and the prosperity of the family. For example, in the roof and wall of Hakka folk houses in Gannan, you can often see the patterns of gods in Taoism and Bodhisattva in Buddhism. These patterns not only have mysterious colors and auspicious meanings, but also show the Hakka people's piety and respect for their religious belief. At the same time, the myths and legends in the Hakka architectural decoration in Gannan also reflect the religious belief of the Hakka people. The Hakka people integrate the images of gods and auspicious beasts in myths and legends into the architectural decoration to express their worship and yearning for the gods. Through the processing and refinement of art, these myth and legend themes have become the classic works in the architectural decoration of Gannan Hakka, and also deepened the Hakka people's understanding and identification of religious beliefs.

3.2.3 Reflections of Life Philosophy

The Hakka people integrate the concepts of "harmony of nature and man" and "harmonious coexistence" into the architectural decoration to express the idea of harmonious coexistence between man and nature. For example, in the architectural layout and decoration style of Hakka dwellings in Gannan, Hakka people pay attention to the coordination and unity with the natural environment, and pursue the organic integration of architecture and natural landscape. This architectural concept not only reflects the Hakka people's respect for and care for the natural environment, but also shows their life philosophy of pursuing harmonious coexistence. At the same time, the historical story theme in the Hakka architectural decoration in Gannan also reflects the life philosophy of the Hakka people. The Hakka people integrate the heroes, loyalty and filial piety deeds in the historical stories into the architectural decoration, so as to carry forward the traditional virtues and advocate the correct outlook on life and values. Through the shaping and depiction of art, these historical story themes have become the highlights and essence of the architectural decoration of Gannan Hakka, and also inspire future generations to constantly pursue the life realm of truth, goodness and beauty.

3.2.4 The Display of Aesthetic Pursuit

Gannan Hakka architectural decoration patterns pursue nature, harmony and unity aesthetically, which are often combined with the natural environment, architectural form and humanistic connotation to form a unique artistic style. These patterns not only have a high aesthetic value, but also reflect the aesthetic taste and life taste of the Hakka people. The Hakka people skillfully use wood carving, brick carving, stone carving, grey sculpture, color drawing and other decorative techniques to integrate various auspicious patterns and historical stories into the door frame, door hairpin, column base, Windows, walls, roof ridge and other parts, making the architectural decoration both practical and ornamental.

4 Overview of the Digital Technology

4.1 Definition of Digital Technology

Digital technology is a modern technical means, relying on computer technology, network technology and related software tools, it presents the real information resources in the form of digital (such as sound, image, video, text and data, etc.). The digital protection of cultural heritage refers to the use of digital collection, digital storage, digital processing, digital display, digital communication and other technologies to transform and reproduce the digital form with new perspectives and new needs [4].

4.2 Research Status of Digital Technology in the Protection of Intangible Cultural Heritage

In 2012, the Ministry of Culture included the digital protection project of intangible cultural heritage into its planning, and then established the resource database of intangible cultural heritage survey, the intangible cultural heritage project resource database, the China Digital Story Museum and the database of Chinese oral literary heritage, etc., which greatly promoted the digital protection of intangible cultural heritage [5]. As an important part of the intangible cultural heritage, the traditional patterns have also received wide attention. Yang Guancan et al. (2020) proposed the construction path of digital resources of Peking Opera masks for digital humanities, Through the website construction case of "Beijing Memory-Beijing Opera Facebook" to show its feasibility [6]; Lv Jianhua et al. (2022) established the Yi costume database and the Yi furniture decoration pattern database, To provide data support for the research, protection and inheritance of intangible cultural heritage [7]; Shu Wei et al. (2023) used artificial intelligence (AI) technology to assist the innovative design of traditional patterns of the Yi nationality, Generate new patterns that both retain traditional elements and integrate modern aesthetics [8]; Zeng Yang et al. (2025) conducted research on the protection and inheritance path of "Buyi batik in Anshun" from a digital perspective, It provides valuable experience and inspiration for the protection and inheritance of intangible cultural heritage [9].

In recent years, remarkable progress has been made in the digital protection of intangible cultural heritage, with various databases being established and innovation realized using artificial intelligence technology. However, the current problems of data standardization, depth of technology application and lack of public participation still need to be solved. At present, the digital protection of the Hakka architectural decoration pattern in Gannan has not been paid enough attention, and the relevant research is still lacking. In the future, we will enhance the effectiveness and influence of the digital protection of intangible cultural heritage in the integration of multiple technologies, interdisciplinary cooperation and global vision expansion.

5 Digital Protection Idea of Gannan Hakka Building Decoration Pattern

Digital technology widened the development space of the traditional pattern, in order to expand the user experience level, generate digital protection resources, pattern resources can be divided into Data Acquisition, Digital Conversion, Analysis and Classification, Database Construction, Database Categorization, Preservation and Inheritance, Innovative Application Product Development of seven steps (see Fig. 2).

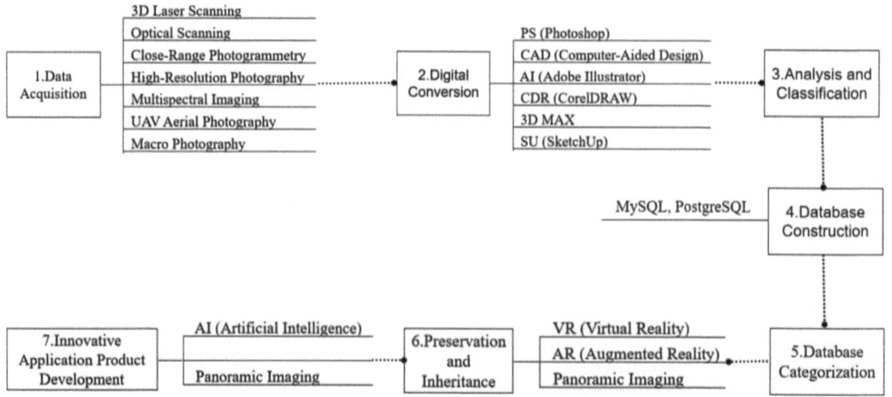

Fig. 2. Gannan Hakka building decoration pattern of the digital protection

5.1   Digital Acquisition Technology and Method

In the process of digital protection and inheritance of Hakka architectural decoration patterns in Gannan, the application of digital technology in the pattern collection stage is very important. Through the comprehensive application of a variety of advanced technologies, the details and full picture of these patterns can be accurately recorded, laying a solid foundation for the subsequent digital processing, storage and display. During the pattern collection process, it is necessary to determine the technology and methods for digital collection based on the location and characteristics of the architectural decoration patterns.

5.1.1   Three-Dimensional Laser Scanning

By emitting a laser beam and measuring its reflection time, the point cloud data on the surface of an object is generated, which can record complex and fine decorative patterns with high precision.

5.1.2   Close-View Photogrammetry

By taking high-resolution photos of multiple angles, three-dimensional point clouds and models are generated using a computer vision algorithm, which are suitable for digital acquisition of flat patterns and irregular surfaces.

5.1.3   High-Resolution Photography

By shooting high-definition images with a high-resolution camera, recording its color, texture, and details, suitable for recording planes or bas-relief patterns.

5.1.4 Multispectral Imaging

Different wavelengths of light can capture the reflected light to generate image data containing more information, which is suitable for the analysis of pattern materials and pigment composition.

5.1.5 UAV Aerial Photography

Equipped with high-resolution cameras, it takes a large range of buildings and decorative patterns from the air, which is suitable for inaccessible building decoration collection in large areas and high places.

5.1.6 Microscopic Photography

Use macro lens to take very close high resolution images, capture very fine pattern details, suitable for tiny or extremely fine pattern acquisition.

5.2 Digital Processing and Storage

In the core task of digital processing and storage, the key is to transform the pattern image information into the image graphic information that is easy to save and edit.For the digital processing of Gannan Hakka architectural decoration patterns, for the clear and highly recognized patterns obtained through shooting and 3D scanning, Adobe Illustrator software can be used to extract the black and white elements of the vectoralized decorative patterns, or the vectoralized independent patterns and pattern library can be built through Bezier curve construction method.

For the samples whose image quality is not up to the standard, it is necessary to deeply explore the cultural connotation and classification of the patterns, and use professional image processing software such as Photoshop (PS) to carry out detailed repair work of the pattern information. After the repair is completed, we correspond to the pattern base attributes according to the built database template to achieve the visual goal of the pattern information. This process can use the database management system (such as MySQL, PostgreSQL) to store and manage the basic attributes of the patterns, and with the help of programming language (such as Python).

In order to further expand the application scope of pattern images, this study uses professional software such as Autodesk AutoCAD, Adobe Illustrator (AI) and Corel-DRAW (CDR) to draw pattern paths, and convert the text in the image into vector text for editing and typesetting. Subsequently, artificial intelligence technology is used to automatically identify the shapes in the image and convert them into vector graphics. Through the vectoring and modeling processing of Gannan Hakka architectural decoration patterns, the vectorization conversion and storage of patterns are realized, so as to be transformed into the basic elements that can be directly used for design creativity.

5.3 Digital Display and Translation

By using the technologies of virtual reality (VR), augmented reality (AR) and panoramic images, Gannan Hakka architectural decoration patterns can achieve the dual goals of protection and inheritance. First of all, through the excellent technical performance of virtual reality (VR) technology, build a virtual environment with a high sense of reality, so that the audience can be immersed in it, and deeply experience the unique charm of Gannan Hakka architecture decoration pattern. Second, augmented reality (AR) technology combines virtual information with the real world to further improve the quality of user experience. By developing specific applications, AR technology enables users to scan the surface of the building with mobile devices to view the corresponding 3 D models, historical background and detailed explanations in real time when visiting Hakka buildings in Gannan. Finally, panoramic imaging technology captures the style of Gannan Hakka architectural decorations in a comprehensive and unobstructed manner through the shooting of panoramic cameras. Users can easily access these panoramic images via the internet platform and freely adjust the zoom and rotation angles of the images, thereby achieving an immersive experience as if they were on the scene.

In addition, through SketchUp, 3Ds Max, Rhino 3D, Blender and other 3 D modeling tools, accurate conversion and efficient storage of the model can be realized, providing more intuitive and operable materials for furniture design, interior decoration, landscape planning and other fields. Designers can directly simulate the application effect of patterns in the software, and adjust and optimize the details in real time, so as to realize the seamless connection between traditional art and modern design.

6 Innovative Application of Gannan Hakka Architectural Decoration Pattern in Furniture Design

6.1 Extraction and Reconstruction of Pattern Elements

The decorative patterns of Gannan Hakka architecture are diverse. When applying these patterns to furniture design, it is necessary to first select suitable patterns for deduction and transformation, endowing them with new forms through simplification, refinement, deformation, and reconstruction. Simplification and refinement mainly involve summarizing and simplifying graphic elements by extracting their core elements and eliminating secondary details, achieving a unity of resemblance and spirit. For example, the lotus pattern from Gannan Hakka architectural decoration can be simplified into geometric lines and then rotated symmetrically to form a novel table leg design, which not only inherits culture but also conforms to modern aesthetics. Deformation and reconstruction involve deforming patterns using techniques such as exaggeration, stretching, and rotation, or dismantling and reassembling multiple patterns to generate new design elements. Through this process of extraction and reconstruction, designers can not only preserve the unique charm of Gannan Hakka culture but also endow the furniture with modern aesthetics, achieving a harmonious fusion of tradition and modernity and enhancing the artistic value and market competitiveness of the furniture. For instance, refining the bat carving pattern from Gannan Hakka architecture into simple lines and applying it to the back of a chair or the surface of a cabinet not only retains the traditional charm but also adds modern minimalist beauty, making the furniture both practical and artistic.

6.2   The Fusion of Pattern and Furniture Form

In the design, the design should be innovative and applied from the shape, pattern, color, function, material collocation and other aspects, under fully considering the function, structure and material of furniture, through repeated tests and adjustment, the pattern and furniture form to achieve a perfect fit. On the one hand, patterns can be used as a decorative element of furniture, and applied to the surface or part of furniture through inlaying, carving, painting and other techniques. For example, the surface of the table of tea table or cabinet door is inlaid with the design of lotus or fish, already beautiful and rich cultural connotation. On the other hand, the pattern can be integrated into the structural design of the furniture, such as the auspicious cloud pattern is transformed into the back shape of the seat, which not only enhances the artistry of the furniture, but also enhances its comfort. Through this multi-dimensional integration, the furniture not only carries the cultural significance, but also has the practical functions, and realizes the harmonious coexistence between tradition and modernity.

6.3   Structural Design and Cultural Symbolism

The auspicious patterns in the architectural decoration of Gannan Hakka residences carry profound meanings and exhibit a high degree of integration with furniture design. When designing furniture, designers should employ artistic techniques to express and enhance the essence of these traditional cultural elements, achieving a harmonious unity between the form and connotation of the furniture, thereby creating better furniture products and enriching their cultural significance. For example, abstract graphics such as Bagua Diagram, Huiwen Pattern are not merely decorative; they also bear deep social meanings. These patterns, mostly based on square or circular shapes, emphasize symmetry and harmony, symbolizing balance and completeness. Meanwhile, specific forms like peony and persimmon convey messages of good luck, wealth, and happiness, providing positive psychological hints and serving as spiritual sustenance. By skillfully incorporating these auspicious patterns, furniture not only fulfills its practical functions but also conveys aesthetic concepts and carries a profound cultural heritage, allowing people to experience the charm of traditional culture in their daily lives and enhancing their cultural identity.

7   Conclusion

Future research should pay more attention to the in-depth exploration in the field of innovative application and product development, in order to achieve a better inheritance and activation of patterns. In this process, the introduction of artificial intelligence technology has injected new vitality into the creative design of Gannan Hakka architectural decoration pattern. With the help of advanced technologies such as deep learning, AI can deeply analyze a large number of architectural patterns, and extract core elements such as composition rules, color collocation and symbolism. On this basis, AI can create a new design scheme that not only retains traditional elements and styles, but also integrates modern aesthetics and creativity.

Acknowledgments. This research was supported by the Humanities and Social Sciences Research Project of Jiangxi Province Universities, "Research on the Expression and Inheritance of Local Culture in Traditional Village Landscapes of Gannan" (YS24104) and the Revolutionary Old Area High-Quality Development Research Institute of Gannan Science and Technology University project "Research on the translation and regeneration of Hakka architectural decorative art in furniture design in Gannan" (G200309).

References

1. Yubao, L., Kegen, H., Xiaojin, Z.: Cultural interpretation and contemporary application of traditional decorative patterns in Hakka architecture in Southern Jiangxi [J]. J. Jiangxi Univ. Sci. Technol. **42**(6), 78–82 (2021)
2. Shaojie, H.: The linguistic regeneration of ethnic patterns in contemporary art design [J]. J. Ezhou Univ. **27**(01), 52–53 (2020)
3. Yinghui, D., Haoni, L.: Research on the redesign of Gannan Hakka lantern patterns under the integration of culture and tourism [J]. Footwear Technol. Des. **4**(10), 18–20 (2024)
4. Zhongquan, W.: The application of digital technology in construction engineering [J]. Res. Ind. Innov. **08**, 84–86 (2024)
5. Junhua, S.: Report on Chinese Intangible Cultural Heritage Protection (2015) [M]. Social Sciences Academic Press, Beijing (2015)
6. Guancan, Y., Xiaobin, L.: Construction of digital resources of Peking Opera masks for digital humanities [J]. Arch. Commun. **3**, 38–44 (2020)
7. Jianhua, L., Meng, Z., Susu, Y., et al.: Research on mobile application development of furniture decoration pattern of Liangshan Yi nationality [J]. Packag. Eng. **43**(S1), 230–234 (2022)
8. Wei, S., Kaining, M., Ning, S.: Research on the digital inheritance and remodeling design of traditional patterns of Yi nationality [J]. J. Jilin Univ. Arts. **04**, 11–17 (2023)
9. Yang, Z., Yang, L.: Research on the protection and inheritance path of "Buyi batik in Anshun" from digital vision [J]. Packag. Eng. **46**(2), 392–397 (2025)

Technology-Driven Cultural Shifts: AI, Metaverse, and Digital Society

Phylogeny of Cultural Heritage in Southeast Asia: A Computational Analysis of Artefact Evolution

Nazirul Hazim A. Khalim[✉], How Chin Lee, and Maude E. Phipps

Monash University Malaysia, Subang Jaya, Selangor, Malaysia
`{nazirul.hazim,lee.howchinh,maude.phipps}@monash.edu`

Abstract. Southeast Asia's cultural heritage is deeply embedded in its traditional textiles, such as songket, limar, batik, and ikat, each reflecting centuries of artistic evolution and cross-cultural interactions. However, preserving and analysing these intricate motifs remains a challenge. This study leverages deep learning and unsupervised machine learning to systematically classify and trace the phylogeny of traditional ASEAN textile patterns.

Our methodology involves an autoencoder-based feature extraction followed by K-Means clustering to categorise textile motifs based on their latent representations. A dataset of traditional ASEAN textiles was collected and preprocessed by resizing images to 128×128 pixels and normalising pixel values. A convolutional autoencoder, built using TensorFlow's Keras API, was trained to encode textile images into a low-dimensional latent space. The encoder comprised convolutional layers with ReLU activation and max-pooling, while the decoder reconstructed the original patterns. Once trained, the encoder extracted latent features, which were then clustered using K-Means with cluster numbers ranging from 5 to 15 to identify optimal groupings. Representative images from each cluster were visualised to verify the homogeneity and distinctiveness of motifs.

By systematically clustering traditional textile patterns, this study provides a computational framework for motif classification, heritage conservation, and cross-cultural analysis. The findings contribute to digital archiving, authenticity verification, and motif evolution studies, supporting efforts in intangible heritage preservation and computational anthropology. This work showcases the power of AI in cultural studies and offers scalable tools for textile heritage analysis in the digital age.

Further research aims to increase the dimensions of the artefacts from 2D textiles to 3D keris (dagger) and 4D tanjak (headdress).

Keywords: Cultural Heritage · Artificial Intelligence · Deep Learning · Cultural Phylogenetics · Southeast Asia · Digital Archiving

1 Introduction and Coverage of the Proposed Solution

Southeast Asia's cultural heritage is marked by millennia of interactions, migrations, and conquests that have shaped a diverse tapestry of artefacts and intangible practices. The *keris* (ceremonial dagger), *songket* and *limar* (traditional woven textiles), *batik* (fabric

M. Schrepp and M. Rauterberg (Eds.): HCII 2025, LNCS 16342, pp. 337–360, 2026.
https://doi.org/10.1007/978-3-032-13164-5_22

dyeing technique), and *tanjak* (traditional headdress) are emblematic of these cross-cultural dynamics. Yet these artefacts face threats arising from cultural appropriation disputes, waning artisan communities, and globalisation pressures (Yang et al., 2018; Hou et al., 2022).

To address such challenges, this project proposes a comprehensive computational approach that unifies:

1. **Digital Archiving**: Capturing high-resolution images of artefacts and compiling **associated** metadata.
2. **Computational Taxonomy Development**: Harnessing deep learning (CNNs) and GPT Vision to classify, analyse, and generate a taxonomy of motifs and structural patterns.
3. **Cultural Phylogenetic Analysis**: Tracing the evolutionary lineages of these artefacts to reveal patterns of transmission, convergence, divergence, and hybridisation.

This approach **covers** essential facets of cultural heritage study—preservation, authenticity verification, and intangible knowledge safeguarding. By encompassing both tangible and intangible dimensions, the proposed solution aims to support scholars, policy-makers, and artisan communities in understanding and protecting Southeast Asia's cultural legacy.

2   Literature Review and Prior Studies

Recent decades have witnessed an accelerated integration of digital technologies into the domain of cultural heritage, driven by both preservation imperatives and emerging computational capabilities. One of the earliest and most foundational streams in this area is the digital preservation of cultural artefacts (Farella et al., 2024). These works have focused on digitising heritage objects in 2D and 3D, developing standardised metadata protocols, and creating digital repositories for long-term conservation. While significant strides have been made, these initiatives often stop short of performing in-depth analyses of the relationships among artefacts, limiting their potential to reveal cultural lineages or cross-cultural influences.

A parallel body of literature, informed by advances in artificial intelligence, leverages machine learning—particularly Convolutional Neural Networks (CNNs)—to classify, detect, and annotate images of historical objects (Llamas et al., 2017; Yamashita et al., 2018; Gómez-Guzmán et al., 2023). Projects such as CEPROQHA (Belhi et al., 2020) have demonstrated the applicability of ML techniques for 3D reconstruction and object recognition in heritage contexts. However, while these methods excel at identifying and labelling visual features, they seldom move beyond classification to assess the deeper cultural and historical significance of these features—such as tracing motifs back to their possible point of origin or mapping how they evolved over time.

Complementing these efforts, the field of cultural data analytics adopts computational strategies like network analysis, large-scale data mining, and big data approaches to investigate patterns within cultural outputs (Coscia, 2024; Ngo et al., 2021). Studies in this domain illustrate how network or graph-based methodologies can reveal latent relationships across vast collections of cultural items—for example, identifying commonalities in textile designs from different regions or isolating the structural attributes that unify distinct musical traditions. Yet, these analyses frequently focus on a single domain (e.g., music, textiles) and do not integrate advanced computer vision models with historical or ethnographic knowledge to build phylogenetic trees or multi-layered knowledge graphs.

Research on intangible cultural heritage underscores the importance of documentation and preservation efforts for the practices, know-how, and oral traditions that accompany physical artefacts. Numerous works explore how digital tools—ranging from mobile apps to virtual platforms—can help sustain endangered intangible traditions (Hou et al., 2022; Li, 2022; Zhu & Pang, 2022). Such projects highlight the challenge of capturing artisan knowledge and integrating it meaningfully with digital archives, a task that requires robust community engagement and thoughtful technological design. Despite ongoing progress, the gulf between intangible knowledge (e.g., weaving techniques, forging rituals) and the computational analysis of physical artefacts remains a barrier to holistic heritage preservation.

Finally, an increasingly urgent branch of literature addresses risk assessment and conservation strategies under threats such as climate change, natural disasters, and cultural appropriation conflicts (Sevieri et al., 2020; Fatorić & Seekamp, 2017). While these works emphasise the vulnerability of heritage sites and artefacts, there is a growing recognition that computational models—coupled with collaborative frameworks—could strengthen both preventative measures and evidence-based policymaking for heritage protection.

Through these combined measures, the project promises to significantly enhance both the scope and depth of cultural heritage research, offering a systematic, data-driven approach that resonates with emerging needs in preservation, policy-making, and academic inquiry.

3 Methodology

This section outlines the methodological steps taken to collect, preprocess, and analyse high-resolution images of traditional Malaysian textiles. The approach integrates an autoencoder for feature extraction and K-Means clustering for pattern categorisation. The methodology is divided into five main stages: (1) Data Collection and Preprocessing, (2) Autoencoder Architecture, (3) Latent Space Extraction, (4) Clustering with K-Means, and (5) Visualization.

Autoencoder-based feature extraction and K-Means clustering were combined to categorise traditional Southeast Asian textile patterns effectively. The multi-stage approach—covering data preprocessing, model training, latent feature extraction, and cluster analysis—offers a systematic and data-driven framework for understanding underlying motifs and structural similarities. The visual confirmation of clusters provides further assurance that the derived groupings are culturally meaningful, laying the groundwork for deeper analyses, such as exploring cross-cultural pattern diffusion or studying temporal shifts in textile designs.

4 Data Collection and Preprocessing

4.1 Data Sources

The study of traditional Southeast Asian textiles necessitates access to high-quality reference materials that provide both visual documentation and historical analysis. In this research, images of limar textiles were sourced from a secondary publication by Rahmat and Abidin (2024), titled Limar: Tenunan Warisan Melayu Koleksi Universiti Malaya, published by Muzium Seni Asia, Universiti Malaya. This source serves as an authoritative reference, offering a validated catalogue of textiles that includes detailed descriptions of motifs, historical context, geographical origins, dating, and functional use.

Despite the abundance of sources featuring images of traditional textiles, comprehensive catalogues that document period heritage textiles with both physical and historical verification remain rare. The textile motifs, symbolic meanings, and historical backgrounds provided in this publication contribute significantly to the scholarly understanding of limar, enhancing both the academic discourse on Southeast Asian material culture and the preservation of Malay textile heritage.

4.2 Sample

The sample of 72 items contains a diverse collection of Limar textiles, showcasing a range of styles, formats, and regional variations. It features multiple entries of Full Flower Limar in both detached and sarong styles, along with unique versions like the Sprinkled Flower Limar with gold thread and a Limar Handkerchief. Additionally, the assortment includes plain, unpatterned, and inscribed varieties, as well as Tenggarong Limar available as both long cloth and sarong. The collection is further enriched by several Songket Limar forms—including nine-yard cloth, sarong, and a bridal pathway variant from Sumatra—as well as distinctive designs such as Checkerboard, Rainbow, Patola/Cindai, and Aceh Rusak, illustrating the rich cultural tapestry of Limar textiles.

The sample predominantly originates from Kelantan, reflecting a deep-rooted local tradition, with many items exclusively from this Malaysian state. Several pieces also trace their origins to the adjacent region of Terengganu, or a blend of influences from both Terengganu and Kelantan, highlighting the cultural interplay along the northeastern Malay Peninsula. There are also indications of connections to Patani/Pattani and even a mix involving Perak (Reman), underscoring the fluid cultural boundaries in the region. Beyond Malaysia, the sample includes textiles from Indonesia—such as Palembang, Bangka Island, Siak, and Komering/Lampung in South Sumatra—as well as from Sambas, Kalimantan. An imported textile from the broader Malay Archipelago and an item from Gujarat, India, further emphasize the diverse and interwoven heritage represented in the collection.

The textiles in this sample are predominantly dated from the 19th century to the early 20th century, with several items specifically attributed to the 19th century. This timeframe indicates that the pieces originate from a period of significant historical and cultural development, reflecting traditional craftsmanship and enduring design influences that have persisted over time.

The collection is predominantly composed of luxurious silk textiles, with the majority of items crafted entirely from silk. Several pieces feature additional embellishments using gold thread, and a few incorporate both gold and silver threads, emphasizing the intricate decorative techniques employed by the artisans. There are also notable examples utilizing double ikat methods and Mastuli thread, further showcasing the diversity and refinement of the materials and techniques used during this period.

The body of the textiles showcases a vibrant and diverse color palette, utilizing traditional dye names that evoke natural sources and cultural significance. Hues such as Mangosteen Skin, Banana Shoot Green, and various shades of green like Parrot Green, Duck Head Green, and Kenanga Green are prominently featured, alongside earthy tones like Biji Remia and Black Langur. The collection is further enriched by striking reds—including Safflower Red, Burning Safflower Red, and Merjan Red—paired with warm yellows such as Crab Fat Yellow and Ripe Areca Nut Yellow. Additional colours like Moss Green, Indigo Blue, and Charcoal Black contribute to the overall complexity, reflecting a rich tradition of natural dyeing techniques and the artisanal heritage of the region.

The ground motifs in this collection are remarkably diverse and intricate, ranging from full horizontal and vertical arrangements to chained patterns and checkerboard designs. Common decorative elements include bowl-shaped and bud motifs, four-petaled flowers, and various floral forms such as jasmine, tamarind, and cermai fruits, often interwoven with elements like serpentine snakeskin and banana heart patterns. Many designs incorporate alternating motifs—such as grass flowers with kecupu buds or mushrooms with diamond cuts—and are sometimes accented with gold thread, adding a luxurious touch. Some pieces feature religious calligraphy interlaced with traditional floral motifs, while others employ unique arrangements like brick-patterned or rain-like patterns with gold thread. Overall, the motifs reflect a rich tapestry of cultural symbolism and artisanal craftsmanship.

Either end of these textiles is predominantly rendered in rich red hues, with Safflower Red being the most common, intermingled with shades such as Merjan Red, Dedap Red, and Burning Safflower Red. Occasional accents include Fish Blood Red and the incorporation of Black Langur or Biji Remia, adding contrast and depth to the design. This emphasis on vibrant reds in the borders not only frames the intricate motifs of the fabric but also reinforces the traditional aesthetic and cultural significance of the textiles.

The end motifs are characterised by an extraordinary complexity and diversity of design, incorporating a rich tapestry of traditional elements. Many designs feature a "palace fence" or "patung" border, often interwoven with chained bud motifs, bamboo shoots, mushrooms, and sun rays. Variations include the integration of natural motifs such as fern tips, mountain or wave (unduk-unduk laut) patterns, and delicate floral elements like small flowers, jasmine, and cermai fruits. Additional decorative features such as kayohan or shark teeth motifs, cloud scrolls, ati-ati/setelop flowers, and even symbolic elements like royal city trees or hidden bamboo shoots further enhance the intricate borders. Some motifs incorporate gold thread in rain-like patterns, underscoring the luxurious craftsmanship and the cultural significance of these textiles.

These textiles serve both everyday and ceremonial functions. They are used as scarves or shawls for women, headbands for men, and as sarongs or veils, while smaller pieces serve as handkerchiefs or headgear. Special items like royal nine-yard cloths (kain dukung) are reserved for formal events and are integral to royal ceremonies, with some pieces even imported from India for use by royalty and nobility across the Malay Archipelago. Additionally, specific garments such as Acehnese headbands, trousers, and ceremonial pathway cloths highlight the textiles' symbolic importance in cultural rituals and traditional practices.

Note that the naming of the motifs above is based on the terms used in Malaysia. However, in Palembang, the terminology may differ, so it's advisable to verify the local usage for accuracy.

4.3 Image Acquisition and Verification

Collected images were initially stored in a Google Drive repository for ease of access and organisation. To ensure data integrity, the PyDrive library was employed to automate the download process and to visually verify each image for completeness (i.e., to confirm the absence of corrupted or mislabeled files).

Image Sampling and Clustering Validation. To facilitate the analysis of limar textiles, images were cropped into square segments representing different sections of each textile piece, namely tanah/badan (main body), punca (starting end), kepala (head), kaki (foot), and apit (side borders). Due to the limited number of available samples for the kaki and apit sections, the analysis focused on four main subsamples: all sections, tanah, punca, and kepala.

For the tanah subsample, validation was guided by three pieces of limar berayat, each featuring Quranic or Arabic calligraphy with identical script styles but differing in colors and Quranic verses. The clustering was considered optimal if these pieces were grouped together, reflecting the method's accuracy in recognising shared visual and textual motifs.

For the punch and kepala subsamples, the validation criterion was based on the presence of pucung rebung motifs—a prominent and distinctive design. Effective clustering was indicated by the grouping of images with similar pucung rebung motifs.

In the full sample, validation was supported by both limar berayat and pucung rebung motifs, ensuring that textiles with either or both of these prominent features were accurately clustered together.

Additionally, efforts were made to avoid single-image clusters unless the image represented a unique textile piece. Whenever such clusters appeared, the number of clusters was reduced to maintain meaningful groupings and enhance the reliability of the clustering process.

4.4 Image Preprocessing

1. **Resizing**: All images were resized to 128×128 **pixels**. This dimension was selected to balance **computational efficiency** and **visual detail**.
2. **Normalisation**: Pixel intensities were **normalised** to the $[0,1][0, 1]$ range by dividing by 255. This step ensures uniformity across images and optimises the training of deep learning models.

Following these preprocessing steps, the dataset was partitioned into training (80% of the images) and validation (20% of the images) subsets.

5   Clustering Methodology

Clusters were labeled numerically from 0 to (n-1), where n represents the total number of clusters for each dataset. The image data for each subsample was prepared in uniform dimensions of 128×128 pixels with 3 colour channels (RGB), ensuring consistency across all analyses. The image dataset sizes for each subsample are as follows:

- **Tanah subsample:** 69 images, each of size (128, 128, 3)
- **Full sample:** 144 images, each of size (128, 128, 3)
- **Punca subsample:** 53 images, each of size (128, 128, 3)
- **Kepala subsample:** 16 images, each of size (128, 128, 3)

This structured approach allowed for systematic clustering, ensuring that each image was analysed at an identical scale and format. The labelling system provided clarity in identifying and referencing individual clusters during the analysis and validation phases.

6   Autoencoder Architecture

An **autoencoder** was implemented using the **Keras** API within **TensorFlow**. The network is composed of two primary components:

3. Encoder

- Two convolutional layers with **ReLU** activation functions.
- **Max-pooling** layers for downsampling the spatial dimensions.
- The output of this encoder is a **latent representation**, encoding essential visual features of the textiles.

4. Decoder

- A mirrored architecture of the encoder, with **up-sampling** layers to progressively reconstruct the original image dimensions.
- Convolutional layers with ReLU activations, aiming to recreate the visual patterns from the latent representations.

6.1   Model Compilation and Training

- **Optimiser:** The model was compiled with the **Adam** optimizer, chosen for its robust performance in image-based tasks.
- **Loss Function: Binary cross-entropy** was selected to quantify the difference between the original and reconstructed images.
- **Training:** The autoencoder was trained for **50 epochs** with a **batch size of 32**. The data split of **80% training** and **20% validation** enabled an ongoing assessment of reconstruction quality and overfitting.

During training, the model's performance was monitored using validation loss to ensure appropriate convergence and to identify any potential overfitting or underfitting.

7   Latent Space Extraction

Once the autoencoder converged to a satisfactory reconstruction performance (as indicated by a stable validation loss), the **encoder** component was **isolated** to serve as a feature extractor. Specifically:

1. **Encoder Isolation**: The decoder layers were disregarded during this phase, focusing solely on the **compressed latent output**.
2. **Transformation**: Each **preprocessed image** was passed through the encoder to **obtain** its **latent vector**, effectively capturing the underlying visual patterns in a **lower-dimensional** form.
3. **Flattening**: The resulting latent vectors were **flattened** into a two-dimensional array (n × d n \times d) where nn is the number of images, and dd is the dimension of the latent space. This format is conducive to input into various clustering algorithms.

8   Clustering with K-Means

8.1   Cluster Formation

To categorise textile patterns based on their learned latent representations, K-Means clustering was employed. The algorithm partitions data into kk clusters by minimising the within-cluster variance.

1. **Cluster Range**: The number of clusters kk was **incrementally varied** from 5 to 15, aiming to identify a partition that yields clear, semantically meaningful groupings.
2. **Initialisation and Iterations**: K-Means was run multiple times with different random initial seeds to ensure consistent cluster assignments and **robustness** against local minima.
3. **Cluster Membership**: Each image was assigned to its **closest cluster centroid**, grouping together textiles with similar latent features.

8.2   Evaluating Cluster Quality

The clustering process was evaluated using both **quantitative** and **qualitative** methods:

- **Quantitative Metrics**: Common metrics such as the silhouette coefficient or within-cluster sum of squares (WCSS) were computed to gauge overall cluster cohesion and separation.
- **Qualitative Assessment**: Subsequent **visual inspection** of the resulting clusters provided insights into the **homogeneity** of motifs within each cluster and the **distinctiveness** of patterns across different clusters.

9   Visualization

Visualisation of clustered textiles served as a key interpretive tool:

1. **Representative Samples**: Clustered images were visualised using Matplotlib, displaying up to 20 images from each cluster along with their file names. This allowed qualitative assessment of the clustering results. This approach allowed researchers to verify whether each cluster captured **cohesive** and **visually similar** textile patterns.

2. **Inter-Cluster Comparisons**: By juxtaposing these representative samples side by side, **distinctive motifs** or structural variations across clusters could be recognised, thus facilitating an intuitive appraisal of the clustering's **practical relevance**.

This methodology effectively utilised deep learning for unsupervised image clustering, providing a structured approach for analysing large image datasets.

10 Results and Implications

10.1 Findings and Validation of Clustering Results

Our findings present a proof of concept for the use of image-based clustering in the classification and analysis of traditional Southeast Asian textiles, specifically limar. The clustering approach was validated using key visual motifs, ensuring the robustness and accuracy of the method.

The validation process relied on the consistent grouping of **three visually similar pieces of** *limar berayat*, each featuring identical **Quranic/Arabic calligraphy** but differing in **colour and Quranic verses**. Clustering was considered optimal when these pieces were grouped together, demonstrating the model's capability to recognize intricate design patterns and textual elements across different textiles.

The final optimal number of clusters determined for each subsample was:

- Kepala subsample: 4 clusters
- Punca subsample: 5 clusters
- Tanah/Badan subsample: 5 clusters
- **Full** sample: 15 clusters

These results highlight the potential of clustering methods in textile studies, offering a structured approach to categorising and analysing **limar** textiles based on their visual and symbolic characteristics.

Key Insights for Tanah/Badan (Body). The clustering analysis reveals distinct regional influences, with the majority of textiles originating from Kelantan and Terengganu, regions historically recognized for their expertise in traditional Malay weaving. These local textiles dominate most clusters, underscoring the significance of these states in the preservation and production of limar textiles. Notably, imported textiles, such as Patola/Cindai from Gujarat, India, form a separate cluster, highlighting the influence of external trade and cultural exchanges on Southeast Asian textile traditions.

The study also emphasises the importance of material choice in the classification of limar textiles. The widespread use of silk serves as a unifying factor across all clusters, reflecting its status as a highly valued material in traditional textile craftsmanship. Additionally, the incorporation of gold thread distinguishes ceremonial textiles, as seen in clusters dedicated to royal and ceremonial use, further reinforcing the link between material opulence and social hierarchy.

In terms of usage, the clusters are clearly divided into textiles intended for daily wear and those reserved for ceremonial and royal occasions. Textiles designated for daily use are typically simpler in design, while ceremonial textiles, such as Limar Bersongket and Limar Berayat, exhibit intricate patterns and luxurious materials, reflecting their cultural and social importance. Finally, the classification also highlights the role of limar types—such as Full Flower Limar, Limar Bersongket, and Limar Berayat—in the clustering process. These types not only reflect the design complexity but also embody the cultural significance embedded within each textile piece, providing deeper insights into the artistic and heritage value of traditional Southeast Asian textiles (Table 1).

The clustering analysis of the punca subsample highlights clear regional influences, with Clusters 0 and 4 predominantly featuring textiles from Kelantan, reflecting the region's central role in producing everyday and ceremonial textiles. In contrast, Cluster 3 includes imported and hybrid textiles, demonstrating cross-cultural exchanges, particularly through trade. Cluster 1 reflects strong Islamic influences, indicative of cultural connections between Kelantan and Patani (Southern Thailand), where Islamic motifs are often integrated into traditional textile designs.

The use of silk is universal across all clusters, signifying its importance in textile production, while the inclusion of gold thread in Clusters 1 and 3 distinguishes textiles intended for royal and ceremonial purposes, emphasizing luxury and high status. Notably, Cluster 2's reliance on natural dyes highlights affordability and accessibility, making it suitable for more widespread use compared to clusters featuring more expensive materials.

In terms of usage, textiles in Clusters 0 and 4 are associated with daily wear and common ceremonial functions, while those in Clusters 1 and 3 are reserved for royal ceremonies and religious events, reflecting their intricate craftsmanship and symbolic significance. The dominance of Full Flower Limar (Lepas) in the daily-use clusters (0 and 4) contrasts with the luxurious Limar Bersongket and Patola/Cindai textiles found in ceremonial clusters (1 and 3), highlighting how textile types are used to denote social and cultural importance.

Finally, the analysis of motifs reveals that floral and nature-inspired designs are prevalent in textiles intended for daily use, symbolizing simplicity and accessibility, whereas Islamic calligraphy and royal motifs are central to ceremonial and religious textiles, underscoring their deeper spiritual and social significance in Southeast Asian culture (Table 2).

Key Insights: Full Sample. The clustering analysis of the full sample underscores the significant role of Kelantan and Terengganu as dominant centers of textile production, with most clusters featuring textiles from these regions. However, the presence of imported textiles in Cluster 0 and Sumatran influences in Cluster 1 highlights the dynamic cross-regional exchanges that have historically shaped Southeast Asian textile traditions.

Silk emerges as the universal material across all clusters, reinforcing its prominence in traditional textile craftsmanship. However, the inclusion of gold thread in royal and ceremonial clusters (such as Clusters 1, 6, and 8) signifies its association with luxury and high social status, distinguishing textiles used for special occasions from those used in everyday settings.

The analysis also reveals a clear division in usage, with clusters such as 2–5, 7, and 9–14 representing daily wear textiles, often characterized by simpler designs and accessible materials. In contrast, Clusters 0, 1, 6, and 8 are associated with royal and ceremonial use,

Table 1. Tanah/badan (body) clustering by characteristics

Cluster	Origin	Material	Usage	Limar Type	Motifs	Reason for Clustering
Cluster 0	Kelantan, Terengganu, Patani	Silk, gold thread	Daily wear, ceremonial use	Full Flower Limar (Lepas), Bersongket	**Floral motifs**: *Bunga kembang semangkuk, Bunga pecah empat, Bunga melur, Bunga tanjung.* **Geometric motifs**: *Teluk berantai, Pucuk rebung.*	Shared origin, material, and usage; focus on floral and geometric motifs for daily and royal wear.
Cluster 1	Terengganu	Silk, gold thread	Royal sarongs	Limar Bersongket (Sarong)	**Royal motifs**: *Bunga cogan, Bunga jong sarat, Bunga ulat dalam pinang kotai.*	Unique ceremonial item with intricate songket design and royal motifs.
Cluster 2	Kelantan, Terengganu, Sumatra	Silk, gold/silver thread	Royal ceremonies, Islamic rituals	Limar Berayat, Bersongket	**Islamic motifs**: *Surah Al-Ikhlas, Shahadah.* **Royal motifs**: *Kayohan, Pagar istana, Unduk-unduk laut.*	Royal and religious significance; use of precious materials; shared cultural influences.
Cluster 3	Imported (India, Sumatra), Kelantan/ Patani	Silk, gold thread, ikat	Ceremonial use, nobility-only	Patola/Cindai, Tenggarong, Bersongket	**Imported motifs**: *Cual corak kulit sawa, Peranakan glass epergne.* **Hybrid motifs**: *Buah delima, Gunungan.*	Imported or hybrid origins; luxurious materials; ceremonial usage.
Cluster 4	Kelantan, Terengganu	Silk, natural dyes	Daily wear, common ceremonial use	Full Flower Limar (Lepas), Polos	**Floral motifs**: *Bunga kembang semangkuk, Bunga pecah empat, Bunga tanjung.* **Natural motifs**: *Pucuk rebung, Sinar matahari.*	Common origin, everyday usage, simple designs; focus on natural dyes and floral motifs.

Key Insights: Punca (Starting End/Source)

where intricate patterns and premium materials underscore their importance in formal and religious contexts.

Table 2. Punca (Starting end/source) clustering by characteristics.

Cluster	Origin	Material	Usage	Limar Type	Motifs (Punca)	Reason for Clustering
Cluster 0	Kelantan, Terengganu	Silk	Daily wear, ceremonial use	Full Flower Limar (Lepas)	**Palace motifs**: *Pagar istana* (palace fence), *Pucuk rebung kayohan* (bamboo shoots). **Natural motifs**: *Sinar matahari* (sun rays), *Bunga cendawan* (mushrooms).	Shared origin (Kelantan/Terengganu), simple silk materials, and repetitive motifs tied to daily/ceremonial use.
Cluster 1	Kelantan, Patani	Silk, gold thread	Islamic rituals, protective amulets	Limar Berayat, Tapak Catur	**Islamic motifs**: *Surah Al-Ikhlas*, *Shahadah*. **Symbolic motifs**: *Buah delima* (pomegranates), *Gunungan* (mountain motifs).	Focus on Islamic calligraphy and symbolic motifs; used for religious purposes and royal symbolism.
Cluster 2	Kelantan, Pattani	Silk, natural dyes	Daily wear	Limar Polos (Plain)	**Minimal motifs**: *Pagar istana*, *Pucuk rebung* (bamboo shoots), *Bunga pecah empat* (four-petaled flowers).	Plain or simple designs with natural dyes; everyday use.
Cluster 3	Terengganu, Sumatra, India	Silk, gold thread	Royal ceremonies, nobility	Limar Bersongket, Patola/Cindai	**Luxury motifs**: *Awan larat* (cloud scrolls), *Bunga tiga dara* (Three Virgin Flowers), *Buah cermal* (cermal fruits).	Imported/hybrid motifs (India/Sumatra), gold thread usage, and royal/nobility exclusivity.
Cluster 4	Kelantan	Silk	Common ceremonial use	Full Flower Limar (Lepas)	**Floral motifs**: *Bunga kembang semangkuk* (bowl-shaped flowers), *Bunga tanjung*. **Natural motifs**: *Pucuk rebung*.	Repetitive floral patterns from Kelantan; used for common ceremonies.

The type of limar further reinforces these distinctions, with Full Flower Limar (Lepas) dominating the daily-use clusters due to its repetitive floral patterns and simpler designs. On the other hand, Limar Bersongket and Patola/Cindai textiles define the luxury clusters, featuring elaborate motifs and rich textures. Finally, the analysis of motifs shows that floral patterns are prevalent in daily-use clusters, reflecting nature-inspired designs suitable for everyday attire, while royal and imported motifs dominate ceremonial textiles, symbolizing status, power, and cultural exchange (Table 3).

10.2   Implications and Insights from Clustering Analysis

Regional Dominance and Cultural Identity. The clustering results highlight the significant concentration of Malay textile craftsmanship in Kelantan and Terengganu, with more than half of the analyzed items tracing their origins to these two regions. This dominance underscores their historical importance in preserving traditional weaving methods such as songket and the use of natural dyes, pointing to the need for targeted conservation measures. At the same time, the presence of Patani (Thailand) and Sumatra (Indonesia) influences—evident in motifs like *corak kulit sawa*—illustrates the depth of cross-border cultural exchanges within the Malay Archipelago. These textiles not only reflect aesthetic preferences but also served as conduits for cultural diplomacy and trade, connecting distinct communities across Southeast Asia.

Material and Craftsmanship Hierarchies. Silk emerges as the near-universal foundation in these textiles, underscoring its dual importance as both a culturally prized and economically valuable material in Malay weaving traditions. In contrast, the incorporation of gold or silver thread is strongly linked to royal and ceremonial contexts, as seen in Limar Bersongket pieces designated for nobility. This direct correlation between material choice and social status underlines the hierarchical nature of Malay textile culture, where luxury yarns and threads signified privilege, while natural dyes and simpler materials were associated with more common or everyday usage.

Motifs as Cultural Signifiers. A clear distinction emerges between the floral motifs that dominate daily-use textiles and the more symbolic or exclusive imagery reserved for ceremonies or royal events. For everyday wear, repetitive floral patterns—such as *bunga kembang semangkuk* and *bunga tanjung*—reflect accessibility and a close connection to nature. In contrast, ceremonial textiles often incorporate potent symbols like *pagar istana* (palace fence) or specific Quranic calligraphy (e.g., *Surah Al-Ikhlas*), highlighting themes of power, spirituality, and exclusivity. Additionally, imported motifs, such as those found in Patola/Cindai textiles from India, mark a distinct cluster reserved for the elite, demonstrating how global influences were blended with local aesthetics to convey status.

Functionality and Social Roles. The separation of clusters into daily-wear and ceremonial categories reflects the role of textiles as markers of social identity. Simple designs and naturally dyed fabrics catered to everyday usage, while gold-threaded and elaborate motifs were strictly for royal or formal occasions. This dichotomy illustrates how textiles helped define social stratification, with plainer garments aligning with more modest status and richly adorned pieces denoting elevated rank. Additionally, the presence of

Table 3. Full sample clustering by characteristics

Cluster	Origin	Material	Usage	Limar Type	Motifs	Reason for Clustering
Cluster 0	India (Gujarat)	Silk, double ikat	Nobility, ceremonial use	Patola/ Cindai	**Imported motifs:** Geometric patterns, floral designs.	Unique imported textiles from India, reserved for nobility.
Cluster 1	Kelantan, Terengganu, Sumatra	Silk, gold thread	Royal ceremonies, nobility	Limar Bersongket, Tenggarong	**Royal motifs:** *Bunga tiga dara, Awan larat, Buah cermal.*	Shared royal and ceremonial usage; luxurious materials and motifs.
Cluster 2	Kelantan, Terengganu	Silk	Daily wear, ceremonial use	Full Flower Limar (Lepas)	**Floral motifs:** *Bunga kembang semangkuk, Bunga tanjung.*	Common origin, simple designs for daily and ceremonial use.
Cluster 3	Kelantan, Terengganu	Silk, natural dyes	Daily wear	Limar Polos (Plain)	**Minimal motifs:** *Pagar istana, Pucuk rebung.*	Plain or simple designs with natural dyes; everyday use.
Cluster 4	Kelantan	Silk	Common ceremonial use	Full Flower Limar (Lepas)	**Floral motifs:** *Bunga kembang semangkuk, Bunga tanjung.*	Repetitive floral patterns from Kelantan; used for common ceremonies.
Cluster 5	Kelantan, Terengganu	Silk	Daily wear, ceremonial use	Full Flower Limar (Lepas)	**Floral motifs:** *Bunga pecah empat, Bunga melur.*	Shared origin, simple designs for daily and ceremonial use.

(continued)

Table 3. (*continued*)

Cluster	Origin	Material	Usage	Limar Type	Motifs	Reason for Clustering
Cluster 6	Kelantan, Terengganu	Silk, gold thread	Royal ceremonies	Limar Bersongket	**Royal motifs:** *Bunga cendawan, Bunga sinar matahari.*	Luxurious materials and motifs for royal ceremonies.
Cluster 7	Kelantan, Terengganu	Silk	Daily wear, ceremonial use	Full Flower Limar (Lepas)	**Floral motifs:** *Bunga kembang semangkuk, Bunga tanjung.*	Common origin, simple designs for daily and ceremonial use.
Cluster 8	Kelantan, Terengganu	Silk, gold thread	Royal ceremonies	Limar Bersongket	**Royal motifs:** *Bunga tiga dara, Awan larat.*	Luxurious materials and motifs for royal ceremonies.
Cluster 9	Kelantan, Terengganu	Silk	Daily wear, ceremonial use	Full Flower Limar (Lepas)	**Floral motifs:** *Bunga kembang semangkuk, Bunga tanjung.*	Common origin, simple designs for daily and ceremonial use.
Cluster 10	Kelantan, Terengganu	Silk	Daily wear, ceremonial use	Full Flower Limar (Lepas)	**Floral motifs:** *Bunga kembang semangkuk, Bunga tanjung.*	Common origin, simple designs for daily and ceremonial use.
Cluster 11	Kelantan, Terengganu	Silk	Daily wear, ceremonial use	Full Flower Limar (Lepas)	**Floral motifs:** *Bunga kembang semangkuk, Bunga tanjung.*	Common origin, simple designs for daily and ceremonial use.

(*continued*)

Table 3. (*continued*)

Cluster	Origin	Material	Usage	Limar Type	Motifs	Reason for Clustering
Cluster 12	Kelantan, Terengganu	Silk	Daily wear, ceremonial use	Full Flower Limar (Lepas)	**Floral motifs:** *Bunga kembang semangkuk, Bunga tanjung.*	Common origin, simple designs for daily and ceremonial use.
Cluster 13	Kelantan, Terengganu	Silk	Daily wear, ceremonial use	Full Flower Limar (Lepas)	**Floral motifs:** *Bunga kembang semangkuk, Bunga tanjung.*	Common origin, simple designs for daily and ceremonial use.
Cluster 14	Kelantan, Terengganu	Silk	Daily wear, ceremonial use	Full Flower Limar (Lepas)	**Floral motifs:** *Bunga kembang semangkuk, Bunga tanjung.*	Common origin, simple designs for daily and ceremonial use.

Limar Berayat (Quranic calligraphy) in some clusters underscores the central place of Islam in Malay cultural identity, merging religious devotion with textile artistry.

Technical and Artistic Mastery. Several clusters exhibit advanced weaving techniques that produce precise geometric or recurring motifs such as *teluk berantai* (chained patterns) and *pucuk rebung* (bamboo shoots). These designs demand considerable expertise and meticulous skill, indicating that master weavers operated in specialized workshops, each characterized by its signature patterns. Moreover, vibrant hues derived from traditional plant-based dyes—like safflower red (*merah kesumba*) and indigo—demonstrate the refined dyeing techniques that contributed to the lasting brilliance of these heritage fabrics.

Outliers and Exceptions. A few items stand out as unique hybrids, blending foreign design elements with local weaving practices. Patola/Cindai textiles from Gujarat (Cluster 0 in the full sample) and Peranakan-inspired motifs in certain clusters epitomize this cross-cultural synthesis, reflecting the historical openness of Malay textile traditions to global influences. These outliers are crucial for understanding how external motifs were adopted, adapted, or reserved for specific social groups, providing insight into evolving tastes and cultural transitions within the region.

Preservation and Modern Relevance. Finally, the data suggest that most of these textiles date back to the late 19th and early 20th centuries, hinting at a decline in traditional Limar production after independence. Preserving these techniques is therefore pressing, requiring efforts such as digital archiving and artisan training to ensure these weaving practices do not disappear. On a more optimistic note, the floral and geometric motifs unearthed by the clustering could inspire innovative approaches in modern fashion design and textile art, bridging heritage and contemporary needs.

11 Conclusion

In sum, the clustering analysis demonstrates how geography, social stratification, and external influences converge to shape the Malay textile tradition. Kelantan and Terengganu emerge as focal points for preserving this cultural heritage, while the prevalence of specific motifs, materials, and weaving techniques reveals both the community's values and its openness to global exchanges. As these art forms face the threat of diminishing production and loss of skilled practitioners, immediate preservation efforts become ever more vital. By integrating traditional motifs and methods into modern designs, policymakers, historians, and artisans can help maintain and revitalise the legacy of Limar textiles for future generations.

This study demonstrates how advanced machine learning techniques—specifically, a convolutional autoencoder coupled with K-Means clustering—can effectively classify and analyse the rich tapestry of Southeast Asian textile motifs. By embedding images into a lower-dimensional latent space, we captured unique visual characteristics that enabled clear distinctions among limar, songket, batik, and other regional textiles. The resulting clusters offer valuable insights into motif phylogeny, regional influences, and sociocultural hierarchies, underscoring the utility of computational methods for systematically mapping and preserving ASEAN's intangible textile heritage.

Furthermore, our findings support ongoing heritage conservation efforts by providing a scalable framework for motif recognition and authenticity verification. The digital archiving of textile images and the ability to trace motif evolution over time are significant steps toward preventing cultural loss, while simultaneously informing contemporary design innovations. Looking ahead, expanding this methodology to higher-dimensional artefacts—such as 3D keris and 4D tanjak—promises to enrich the scope of cultural studies and computational anthropology even further. By embracing these emerging technologies, researchers, policymakers, and heritage practitioners can collaboratively safeguard and celebrate the diverse artistic legacies of Southeast Asia.

12 Limitations

A primary constraint of this study is the limited availability of verified catalogues and archival materials for traditional Southeast Asian textiles. This scarcity posed challenges in sourcing comprehensive datasets, leading to the focus on limar textiles due to the accessibility of a detailed and validated catalogue. Expanding the scope to include other textiles, such as songket with its intricate gold and silver threadwork, and batik known for its wax-resist dyeing technique, is essential for future research. Enhancing archival resources and documentation will significantly improve the robustness and depth of computational analyses in the field of textile studies and cultural heritage preservation.

However, this limitation also serves as a justification for this line of work, as computational methods such as the ones employed in this study can assist in the cataloguing and classification of undocumented heritage artifacts that remain dormant in museum warehouses across Southeast Asia. Future research should aim to expand the dataset to include other textiles, such as songket and batik, while supporting efforts to digitally archive and preserve the region's rich but often overlooked cultural heritage.

As an initial attempt, another constraint lies in its two-dimensional image-based clustering. While these methods offer valuable insights into textile motifs, future research should incorporate higher-dimensional representations. For example, 3D models of keris (traditional Malay daggers) could capture nuanced details such as intricate carvings, shapes, and textures that are impossible to discern in 2D formats. Similarly, 4D or manifold-embedded models of tanjak (Malay headdress) would allow for an examination of variations over time, folding structures, and multi-layered designs. Such explorations would extend the utility of machine learning approaches beyond textiles to a broader spectrum of cultural artifacts.

Another limitation arises from the limited availability of comprehensive, validated catalogues for traditional Southeast Asian textiles. This study focused on limar because of the detailed and verified documentation available from Limar: Tenunan Warisan Melayu Koleksi Universiti Malaya. The absence of similar catalogues for other textile forms highlights a significant gap in scholarship and emphasises the need for further documentation and research. Enriching the reference base would greatly enhance the reliability and depth of any computational analyses conducted on these artifacts.

Finally, the scope of this research was restricted to limar textiles due to the ready availability of high-quality references. Future studies should seek to expand the dataset to other Southeast Asian textiles, including songket, which is renowned for its gold and silver threadwork, and batik, distinguished by its wax-resist dyeing technique. Incorporating these additional textile forms will not only broaden the applicability of clustering methods but also yield deeper insights into the region's diverse cultural heritage, thereby enriching the academic discourse in textile studies and cultural preservation.

Appendix

Clustering Output for Body (Badan/Tanah)

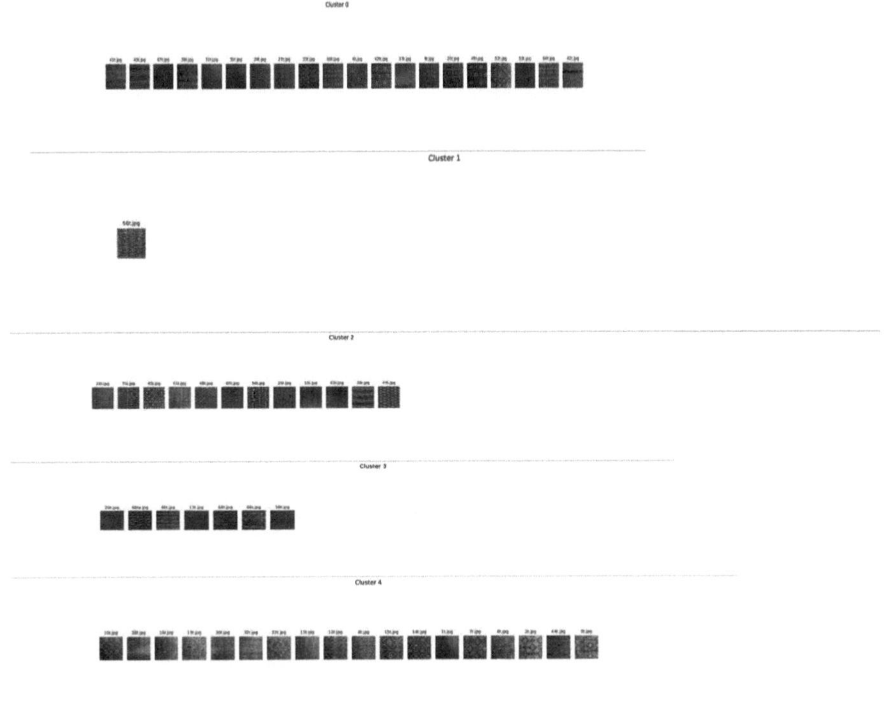

Clustering Output for Punca

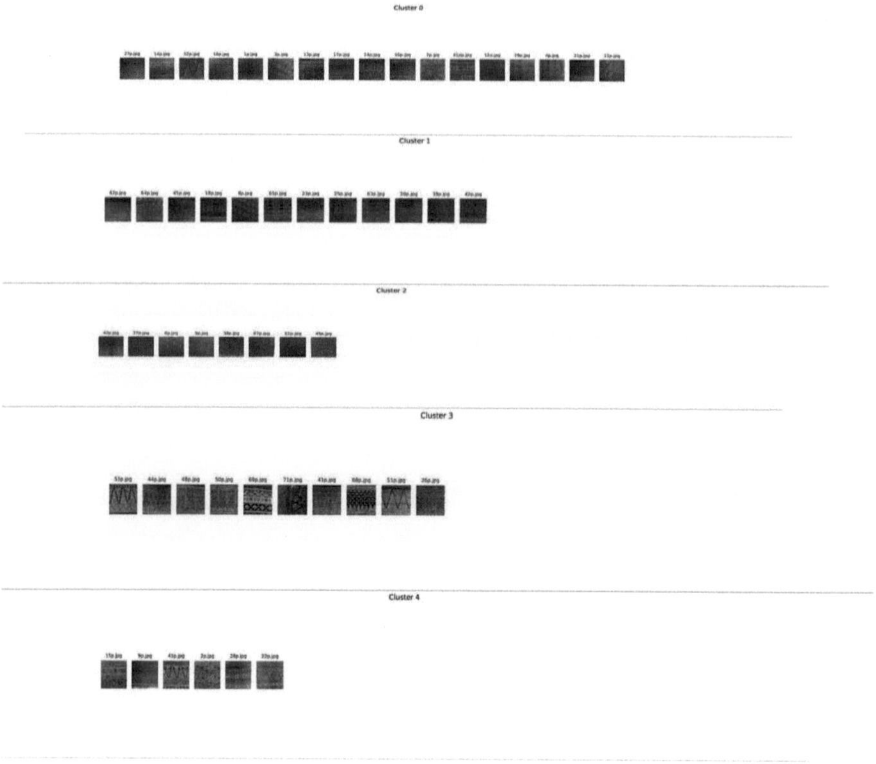

Cluster 0

Cluster 1

Cluster 2

Cluster 3

Cluster 4

Clustering Output for Kepala

Cluster 0

Cluster 1

Cluster 2

Cluster 3

Clustering Output for the Full Sample

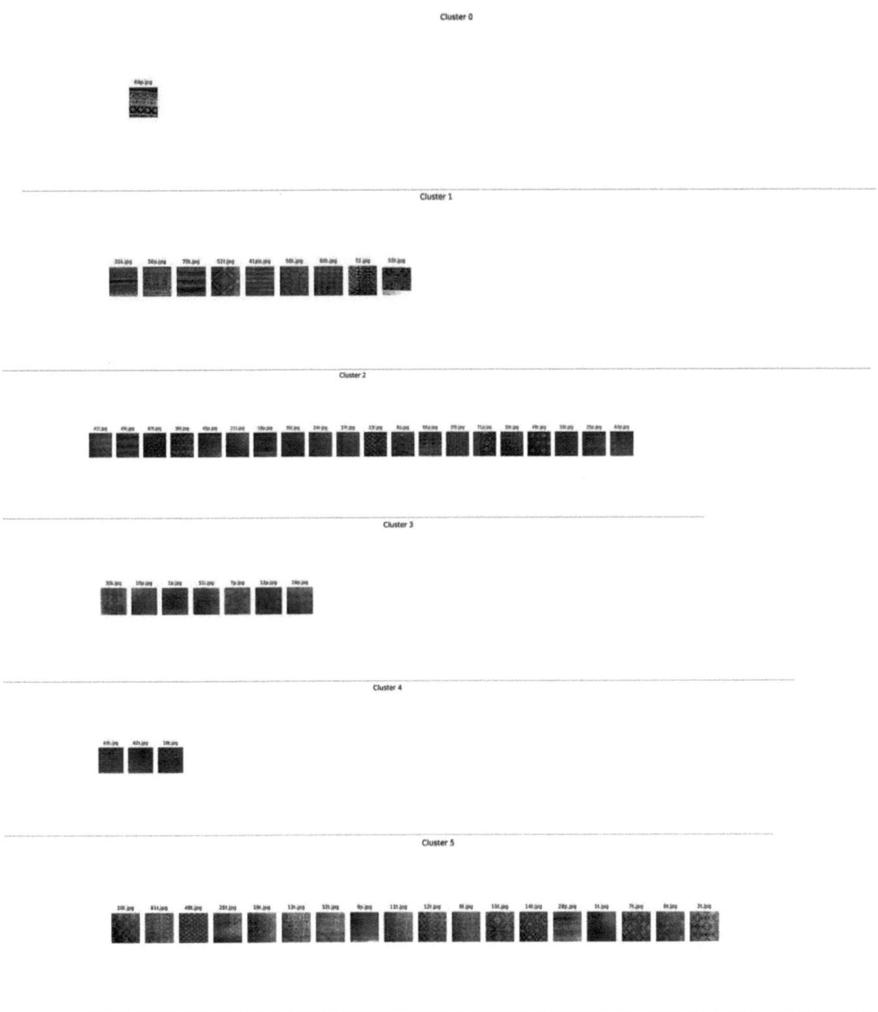

Cluster 6

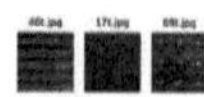

Cluster 7

Cluster 8

Cluster 9

Cluster 10

Cluster 11

Cluster 12

Cluster 13

Cluster 14

References

Belhi, A., et al.: Machine Learning and Digital Heritage: The CEPROQHA Project Perspective, vol. 1027, pp. 363–374. Scopus (2020). https://doi.org/10.1007/978-981-32-9343-4_29

Colavizza, G., Blanke, T., Jeurgens, C., Noordegraaf, J.: Archives and AI: an overview of current debates and future perspectives. J. Comput. Cult. Herit. **15**(1), 1–15. 4. (2021). https://doi.org/10.1145/3479010

Coscia, M.: Node attribute analysis for cultural data analytics: a case study on Italian XX–XXI century music. Appl. Netw. Sci. **9**(1) Scopus (2024). https://doi.org/10.1007/s41109-024-00669-5

Farella, E.M., et al.: Methods, data and tools for facilitating a 3d cultural heritage space. Int. Arch. Photogramm. Remote. Sens. Spat. Inf. Sci. **48**(2), 197–204. Scopus (2024). https://doi.org/10.5194/isprs-Archives-XLVIII-2-W4-2024-197-2024

Fatorić, S., Seekamp, E.: Securing the future of cultural heritage by identifying barriers to and strategizing solutions for preservation under changing climate conditions. Sustainability. **9**(11), 2143 (2017). https://doi.org/10.3390/su9112143

Gómez-Guzmán, M.A., et al.: Classifying brain tumors on magnetic resonance imaging by using convolutional neural networks. Electronics. **12**(4), 955 (2023). https://doi.org/10.3390/electronics12040955

Hou, Y., Kenderdine, S., Picca, D., Egloff, M., Adamou, A.: Digitizing intangible cultural heritage embodied: state of the art. J. Comput. Cult. Herit. **15**(3), 1–20. 55. (2022). https://doi.org/10.1145/3494837

Rahmat, K., Abidin, Z.N.Z.: Limar: Tenunan Warisan Melayu Koleksi Universiti Malaya. Muzium Seni Asia, Universiti Malaya (2024)

Lawson-Body, A., Illia, A., Lawson-Body, L., Rouibah, K., Akalin, G., Tamandja, E.M.: Big data analytics and culture: newly validated measurement instruments for developing countries' value proposition. J. Organ. End User Comput. **36**(1) Scopus (2024). https://doi.org/10.4018/JOEUC.344453

Li, Q.: Intelligent Intangible Cultural Heritage Innovation Platform Under the Background of Big Data and Virtual Systems, pp. 560–563, Scopus (2022). https://doi.org/10.1109/ICAIS53314.2022.9742914

Liu, H.: Digital Interactive Technology of Intangible Cultural Heritage Based on Virtual Reality Technology, pp. 298–302. Scopus (2022). https://doi.org/10.1109/NetCIT57419.2022.00077

Llamas, J., Lerones, P.M., Medina, R., Zalama, E., Gómez-García-Bermejo, J.: Classification of architectural heritage images using deep learning techniques. Appl. Sci. **7**(10), 992 (2017). https://doi.org/10.3390/app7100992

Mo, L., Aris, A.B., Yan, X.: Digital display and storytelling: creating an immersive experience of Lingnan costume cultural heritage tourism project, vol. 1366, issue 1. Scopus. (2024). https://doi.org/10.1088/1755-1315/1366/1/012047

Ngo, V.M., Duong, T.-V.T., Nguyen, T.-B.-T., Nguyen, P.T., Conlan, O.: An efficient classification algorithm for traditional textile patterns from different cultures based on structures. J. Comput. Cult. Herit. 14(4), 1–22. 53. (2021). https://doi.org/10.1145/3465381.

Real, R.: Distinguishing Artefacts: Evaluating the Saturation Point of Convolutional Neural Networks (2021). https://doi.org/10.48550/arxiv.2105.10448

Sevieri, G., et al.: A Multi-Hazard Risk Prioritization Framework for Cultural Heritage Assets (2020). https://doi.org/10.5194/nhess-2020-7

Szegedy, C., et al.: Going Deeper With Convolutions (2015). https://doi.org/10.1109/cvpr.2015.7298594

The basis of digital technologies for cultural heritage preservation. (2010). In: Advanced Topics in Science and Technology in China, pp. 9–34. Scopus. https://doi.org/10.1007/978-3-642-04862-3_2

Tolba, A., Al-Makhadmeh, Z.: An improved density-based single sliding clustering algorithm for large datasets in the cultural information system. Pers. Ubiquit. Comput. **24**(1), 33–44. Scopus (2020). https://doi.org/10.1007/s00779-019-01258-5

Walle, M., et al.: Motion grading of high-resolution quantitative computed tomography supported by deep convolutional neural networks. SSRN Electron. J. (2022). https://doi.org/10.2139/ssrn.4130780

Yamashita, R., Nishio, M., Gian, R.K., Togashi, K.: Convolutional neural networks: an overview and application in radiology. Insights Imaging. **9**(4), 611–629 (2018). https://doi.org/10.1007/s13244-018-0639-9

Yang, Y., Shafi, M., Xia, S., Ruo, Y.: Preservation of cultural heritage embodied in traditional crafts in the developing countries. a case study of Pakistani handicraft industry. Sustainability. **10**(5), 1336 (2018). https://doi.org/10.3390/su10051336

Ying, Y., Xialing, T., Wei, T.: Study on governmental cultural resources purchase management based on public information behavior big data, pp. 72–75, Scopus (2017). https://doi.org/10.1145/3026480.3026491

Zhu, L., Pang, T.: Research on Digital Platform Technology of Intangible Cultural Heritage in Beijing Section of Great Wall Cultural Belt, pp. 426–430, Scopus (2022). https://doi.org/10.1109/CoST57098.2022.00093

From Digital Humanities to Information Humanities: An Ontological Transformation of Discipline Paradigm

He Huang(✉)

Beijing Information Science and Technology University, Beijing 102206,
People's Republic of China
huanghe@bistu.edu.cn

Abstract. The rapid development of information technology has fundamentally transformed the ways in which information is produced, disseminated, and consumed, necessitating a paradigm shift in the humanities. While digital humanities (DH) have made significant contributions by leveraging computational tools and methodologies, its technocentric focus has often come at the expense of deeper engagement with the cultural, social, and ontological dimensions of information. This article posits Information Humanities (IH) as a transformative discipline that expands and redefines the scope of DH, offering a more holistic framework for understanding the interplay between information, technology, and human experience. The article begins by tracing the history and development of DH, highlighting its contributions while also critiquing its limitations. It then introduces IH as an expansion of the research paradigm that shifts the focus from tool-oriented research to a deeper exploration of information as a cultural, social, and ontological phenomenon, addressing issues such as digital inequality, information ethics, and the impact of information technologies on human cognition. The article outlines potential research directions in IH, including Critical Information Studies, information ethics, and information aesthetics. In conclusion, the article argues that IH represents a necessary evolution of the humanities, ensuring their relevance and impact in the information age. It calls for further exploration and development of IH as a discipline, highlighting its potential to address the complex challenges and opportunities facing human beings in the information age.

Keywords: Information Humanities · Digital Humanities · discipline paradigm shift

1 Introduction

In recent decades, Digital Humanities (DH) has emerged as a transformative force in the humanities, bridging the gap between traditional scholarly practices in diverse humanities fields and the computational methods of the information age. Since its inception, DH has sought to expand the scope of humanistic inquiry by leveraging digital tools and methodologies, "using information technology to illuminate the human record, and

M. Schrepp and M. Rauterberg (Eds.): HCII 2025, LNCS 16342, pp. 361–372, 2026.
https://doi.org/10.1007/978-3-032-13164-5_23

bringing an understanding of the human record to bear on the development and use of information technology" (Schreibman et al., 2004). This interdisciplinary field has enabled scholars to analyze vast datasets, create digital archives, and visualize complex historical and cultural phenomena, thereby redefining the ways in which humanistic research is conducted.

However, as the field has matured and become an established discipline in academic institutions around the world, it has become increasingly evident that DH's focus on digitization and computational techniques often overshadows deeper questions about the nature of information itself, and more importantly, about the experience of human beings as they interact with information while being shaped by it. Many works conducted under the name of DH are facing doubt that they have been more concerned with the how of digital methods than the why of humanistic inquiry, especially considering that the digital methods "absorbed from disciplines whose epistemological foundations and fundamental values are at odds with, or even hostile to, the humanities" are "positivistic, strictly quantitative, mechanistic, reductive and literal" (Drucker, 2012). This technocentric approach has limited the field's ability to address the broader implications of information as a cultural, social, and ontological phenomenon and more essentially, how human beings should think and act in an increasingly information-dominant world.

While DH has undeniably enriched the humanities, its emphasis on tools and methods has prevented us from going deeper in our understanding of the role of information in human life, which is a core question for the humanities today. As Liu (2012) observes, "How the digital humanities advances, channels, or resists today's great postindustrial, neoliberal, corporate, and global flows of information- cum- capital is thus a question rarely heard in the digital humanities associations, conferences, journals, and projects". As for now, the digital humanities academic community has yet to articulate a robust theoretical framework that accounts for the cultural and social dimensions of information, which should be a fundamental part of the discipline. This lack of theoretical depth has hindered the field's ability to engage with pressing issues such as the ethical implications of the ongoing information revolution, the impact of information technologies like Artificial Intelligence (AI) on human cognition, and the role of information in shaping cultural identities.

Moreover, with the rapid advance of information technologies, we are witnessing a profound transformation in the nature of information, which is no longer merely a tool for communication but a fundamental aspect of human existence. Information technologies, according to Luciano Floridi (2014), are "recreating and shaping our intellectual and physical realities, changing our self-understanding, modifying how we relate to each other and ourselves, and upgrading how we interpret the world, and all this pervasively, profoundly, and relentlessly". In this context, the limitations of DH become increasingly apparent, necessitating a paradigm shift that delves into the fundamental role of information in human life.

This article posits the new discipline of Information Humanities (IH) as a transformative paradigm that expands and redefines the scope of DH. Unlike DH, which focuses primarily on the application of digital tools in humanistic research, IH seeks to comprehensively explore the interaction between information and human beings. By drawing on insights from information science, media studies, philosophy of technology, and cultural studies, IH aims to develop a holistic understanding of information as a cultural, social, and ontological phenomenon.

The primary objective of this article is to articulate the theoretical foundations of IH, highlight its key differences from DH, and outline potential research directions that demonstrate its significance for the humanities. In doing so, this article seeks to contribute to the ongoing discourse on the future of the humanities in the digital age.

The article is organized as follows. Section 2 provides a historical overview of DH, tracing its development from humanities computing to its current interdisciplinary nature. Section 3 introduces IH as an expansion of the research paradigm, emphasizing its focus on the interplay between information, technology, and human experience. Section 4 outlines possible research directions in IH, highlighting its potential to address pressing issues such as information inequality, information ethics, and information's impact on human cognition. Finally, Sect. 5 concludes the article, showcasing the significance of IH for advancing scholarly inquiry and shaping the future of the humanities.

2 The Development of Digital Humanities: A Brief Review

2.1 History of Digital Humanities

The roots of DH can be traced back to the mid-20th century, when the advent of computing technology began to intersect with humanistic inquiry. Early efforts in what was then called "Humanities Computing" focused on the use of computational tools to analyze literary texts, linguistic data, and historical records. One of the earliest and most influential projects was Father Roberto Busa's Index Thomisticus, a computational concordance of the works of Thomas Aquinas, which began in the 1940s and is widely accepted as "the well-known beginning" of DH as a field (Hockey, 2004).

During the 1960s and 1970s, Humanities Computing expanded to include the development of text encoding standards, such as the Text Encoding Initiative (TEI), which aimed to create a unified framework for representing textual data in digital form. The TEI was not merely a technical achievement but a conceptual one, as it required scholars to think critically about the nature of text and its representation in digital environments. The long-lasting and far-reaching influence of TEI "provides perhaps the best example of large-scale contribution from humanities computing to a shared technical agenda of widespread interest and influence" (McCarty, 2005). This period also saw the emergence of digital archives and databases, which enabled researchers to store, retrieve, and analyze large volumes of textual data.

The term "digital humanities" itself gained prominence in the early 2000s, reflecting a shift from humanities computing to a broader, more interdisciplinary field. DH represents a convergence of traditional humanistic scholarship with new digital tools and methodologies, creating opportunities for innovative research and collaboration "to reshape and reinvigorate contemporary arts and humanities practices, and expand their boundaries" (Pressner et al., 2009). This shift was accompanied by the establishment of DH centers, conferences, and journals, which helped to institutionalize the field and foster a growing community of scholars.

2.2 Contributions and Limitations of Digital Humanities

DH has made significant contributions to the humanities by enabling new forms of research and scholarship. One of its key strengths lies in its ability to process and analyze large datasets, which would be impossible to examine using traditional methods. For example, "distant reading" advocated by Franco Moretti focuses on the analysis of literary texts at scale, believing that larger patterns and trends shown under "distance" can help researchers gain insights on "units that are much smaller or much larger than the text: devices, themes, tropes—or genres and systems" (2013), which are invisible at the level of individual texts. This approach has opened new avenues for understanding literary history, cultural trends, and the circulation of ideas.

Another major contribution of DH is its emphasis on collaboration and interdisciplinarity. Digital humanities projects often bring together scholars from diverse fields, including computer science, linguistics, history, and media studies, fostering a culture of collaboration that enriches the humanities as a whole. DH projects are marked by "the massive expansion of the scholarly enterprise through a wealth of networks, information streams, and emergent communities of practice that produce and share knowledge and culture in ways that open up opportunities for participation, dissension, and freedom"(Burdick et al., 2012). This collaborative ethos has led to the development of innovative tools and platforms, such as the Zooniverse project, which engages the public in crowdsourced research, and Voyant Tools, which provides accessible text analysis software for scholars and students.

Despite its many achievements, DH has faced criticism for its technocentric focus and lack of humanistic depth. One of the most persistent critiques is that DH tends to prioritize methodological innovation over critical inquiry of human experience. This hinders the scholarly practice of DH from establishing itself as a field of study that actively engages and interacts with human experience like traditional disciplines of the humanities do. As Thomas III (2016) observes when reviewing the last 20 years of DH scholarship, "Rather than conceiving of their project as necessitating a separate discipline or field, digital humanists worked within the disciplines from a loosely defined set of common methods", not going very far in "creating discipline-based interpretive scholarship in digital form". This critique showcases a tension within the field between its technical applications and its humanistic goals.

Moreover, DH is neglecting a core theme it should engage as a field spanning across information technology and the humanities: the role of information in human life. While DH has made significant strides in digitizing and analyzing textual artifacts, transforming and treating them as information products, it has often overlooked the ways in which information shapes and is shaped by human experience. In the information age today where human beings live in, upon, and through information, mostly in digital form, DH has yet to fully grapple with the ontological and epistemological questions raised by the digital turn, such as the nature of information, the role of technology in shaping knowledge, and the impact of digital media on human cognition.

3   Information Humanities: An Expansion of Discipline Paradigm

3.1   Defining Information Humanities

Information Humanities is proposed as a response to the limitations of DH, offering a broader and more holistic framework for understanding the interplay between information, technology, and human experience. While DH has primarily focused on the application of digital tools in humanistic research, IH seeks to explore the ontological, epistemological, and cultural dimensions of information itself. With Norbert Wiener's famous statement "Information is information, not matter or energy" (1965) still echoing in our ears, we are witnessing an increasingly information-driven world where we are interacting more with information than material and energy in our work and life. Human beings come to understand that information is not merely a tool for communication but a fundamental aspect of human existence, shaping our understanding of reality and our place within it. IH rises to address information as a fundamental reality of human beings, attempting to establish itself as a discipline that transcends the technocentric focus of DH, emphasizing the transformative role of information in shaping human life and probing the intricate relationship between humanity and information.

At its core, IH is concerned with the ways through which information interacts human beings situated in specific biological, technological and ideological contexts, as well as its impact on individuals, societies, and cultures. Even though the modern concept of information is a late invention mainly under the influence of communication and information theory, information has always been playing a pivotal role in the evolution of human civilization in the history of humanity. Human beings are intrinsically informational animals. As Cybernetics posits, human beings themselves are "communicative organism" (Wiener, 1950) that sends and receives information, which defines every aspect of manhood. In pre-modern societies, natural languages as carriers of information are pillars of all human communities. The modern age is marked by information tools and technologies that extend human natural capacity to transmit information, cementing information's role in maintaining social operations. As information becomes digitalized in the digital age, its communication efficiency is multiplied, and so does its impact, accordingly.

Moreover, information is not a neutral entity but an ideological artifact that reflects and reinforces power dynamics, social structures, and historical contexts. Therefore, as products and agents of information, human activities involving information have their ethical consequences. As Day (2001) notes, "The problematic of information in our age is one that simultaneously involves aesthetic, ethical, and political values". By examining information as an ideological phenomenon, IH seeks to uncover the deeper meanings and implications of information in the digital age, moving beyond the surface-level analysis using data processing tools.

The theoretical foundations of IH draw from a diverse range of disciplines, including information science, media studies, philosophy of technology, and cultural studies. One key influence is the work of Luciano Floridi, whose philosophy of information provides a framework for understanding the ontological and ethical dimensions of information. Floridi's (2011) philosophy of information offers a metaphysical base for situating information in contemporary world, underscoring the fact that "humans are the only known semantic engines and conscious inforgs (informational organisms) in the universe who can develop a growing knowledge of reality; and reality is the totality of information". Therefore, information is crucial in forming human experience, maintaining human communities, and ensuring human development. This foregrounds the need for a discipline like IH that can critically engage with the implications of living in an information-rich world. Moreover, Floridi discussed the ethical dimensions of information, laying down the basic principles of information ethics that govern information entities, information processes, information environment, clarifying "what it means to live as a responsible and caring agent in the infosphere" (2013).

Another important theoretical influence is the field of media studies, particularly the studies on digital media. Media studies, in its essence, is concerned with the approaches involved in information processes, which are considered as "the extension of human physical and nervous systems" (McLuhan, 1994). Accordingly, media studies highlight the ways in which information and its movement interact with human beings, especially their role in shaping human perception and behavior. Besides, media studies stand at the forefront of reflecting the effect of digitalization on information communication, pointing out that the depths and differences of information are erased when "everything becomes a number" (Kittler, 1999), which brings about profound consequences on human memory and cognition. These insights inform IH's focus on the interplay between information, matter, and human experience, as well as its commitment to understanding the technological, cultural and historical contexts in which information is embedded.

Finally, IH draws on the critical traditions of cultural studies, particularly posthumanism, which challenge traditional notions of human agency and subjectivity in the information age. In redefining human existence and their boundaries with the outer world, posthumanism investigates the role of information in shaping human identity. Posthumanism rethinks the construction of subjectivity, holding that information "as a (disembodied) entity that can flow between carbon-based organic components and silicon-based electronic components to make protein and silicon operate as a single system" (Hayles, 1999) is the crucial force in forming the future cyborgs. Like media studies, posthumanism also keenly examines the profound change digital media has brought to human society, finding out that the digital turn has fundamentally altered our understanding of what it means to be human, blurring the boundaries between the biological and the technological. These investigations offer some key understandings that are instrumental in IH's analysis of the relationship between information and human beings.

3.2 Key Differences Between DH and IH

While DH and IH share a common interest in the intersection of technology and the humanities, they differ significantly in their scope, methodology, and objectives. One key difference lies in their approach to information. DH has largely treated information as a resource to be mined and analyzed, whereas IH seeks to understand information as an ontological phenomenon. Tracing the history of information, one may find human beings co-evolves with information. The invention of language as carrier of information is the first information revolution, as language fundamentally transforms how human beings store and transmit information, shaping both human brain and body while greatly enhancing human capacities, eventually leading in human civilization. Since then, "writing and print and the computer are all ways of technologizing the word" (Ong, 2002), or rather, ways of technologizing information. Writing, print and the computer are all information technologies bringing about profound transformation of human cognition and social organization. IH, therefore, should be committed to exploring the deeper meanings and implications of information technologies for human beings in its humanistic enquiry, rather than merely applying digital tools to humanistic research.

Another important distinction is IH's emphasis on interdisciplinarity with theoretical depth. IH represents a move beyond the methodological innovations of DH toward a more theoretically grounded and socially engaged approach to the study of information. IH's interdisciplinarity is solidly built upon the intersectionality of information and the deep immersion of information technology into all aspects of contemporary human life. As Day (2014) points out, the connotation of information is "a galaxy amid other galaxies of knowledge" which "is given, historically, socially, and culturally, through a political economy that manifests itself in the intersection of techne and language". Every technology is a technology of mankind, about mankind, and for mankind. As information technologies are turning overwhelmingly and ubiquitously relevant in contemporary society, it is not only necessary to explore how information technology can be utilized to serve human beings, but also imperative to enquire how information technology can form and change human beings. Thus, information humanities, together with information technology should be the two equal wings of the same bird of such a fundamental existence as information. As a discipline, IH should simultaneously respond to the development of information technology and the shifting humanistic requirements, connecting while coordinating them, steering them both to a steadfast future.

Finally, IH differs from DH in its commitment to addressing the comprehensive influence of information on human life. Different from DH which has primarily focused on the digitization and analysis of cultural artifacts, IH seeks to explore the ways in which information shapes and is shaped by human experience. As studies in information science, especially the emerging field of Human-Computer Interaction, have clearly revealed, the pathways of interaction between information and human beings are mutual and diverse. The field of HCI "considers the human as an information processor, receiving inputs from the world, storing, manipulating and using information, and reacting to the information received" (Dix et al., 2003). As an intelligent information system, human beings interact with information through their senses, memory, logic and emotions, whose capabilities and limitations fundamentally affect the organizing patterns and transmission approaches of information. Moreover, in the process of human-system interaction, information goes beyond the role of merely being a resource but actively participate in shaping how humans think, learn, and act. Information also becomes a key medium through which human beings build social relationships and communities. The mutual interactions between information and human beings call for reflective investigations into their relationship situated in biological, social, and cultural contexts.

3.3 Methodological Transformations from DH to IH

The shift from DH to IH entails significant methodological transformations, reflecting a move from tool-oriented research to a more holistic and interdisciplinary approach.

In essence, integrating insights from a diverse range of disciplines, IH represents a transcendence beyond mere methodological innovations toward a more theoretically grounded and socially engaged approach to the study of information, which enables IH to address complex issues around information in contemporary world.

One key methodological shift of IH is its emphasis on Critical Information Studies (CIS), which seeks to uncover the cultural and social dimensions of information. CIS holds that information is not a neutral entity but a cultural artifact that reflects and reinforces power dynamics, social structures, and historical contexts. CIS "follows in the tradition and inspiration of Critical Theory" (Vaidhyanathan, 2006) while adapting and extending the concerns of Critical Theory on power, ideology, and emancipation to address the sociotechnical systems dominating information in the infosphere. CIS focuses on pressing issues arising in the information era, particularly those tied to power, inequality, and justice in digital societies, including data privacy, digital divide, and misinformation, etc., endeavoring to build an information environment that points to a solid information future.

Another crucial methodological transformation in IH is its commitment to empirical research, which actively incorporates methodologies from technology-oriented fields such as information communication, neurobiology, and cognitive science. Where DH has primarily employed computational tools as instruments for humanistic analysis, IH actively engages with experimental methodologies as constitutive elements of humanistic inquiry. For instance, tools like EEG, fMRI, and eye-tracking could be employed in IH studies to measure human cognitive and affective responses to information in order to understand information's role in formulating human cognition and emotion. Conventionally, such "fMRI brain scan" to test "effects of web reading on brain functionality" (Hayles, 2012) were conducted by scholars in the science and technology fields. However, as IH arises, it's time for the humanities scholars to take over. Consequently, IH labs need to be established as transdisciplinary research spaces that provide physical environment to carry out empirical studies. Unlike traditional DH centers which focused on digitization projects or tool development, these labs integrate wet labs, maker spaces, and experimental studios to facilitate humanistic research through technological mediation.

A third methodological feature of IH is its embrace of ethical enquiry as core research practice. Instead of treating ethics as a peripheral concern or mere compliance requirement, IH recognizes that moral considerations fundamentally shape every stage of information ecosystems - from the design of algorithms to the consumption of digital content. This methodological commitment involves systematically examining three interlocking ethical dimensions: (1) the moral agents involved in information systems, (2) the moral principles embedded in information processes, and (3) the moral interests at stake in information flows. Essentially, IH treats ethical inquiry as a generative source of methodological innovation that produces both critical insights and practical interventions. In this way, ethical enquiry offers a crucial channel of social engagement for IH to serve the ultimate interests of humankind, upon which IH converges with the deepest traditions of humanistic scholarship.

3.4 Epistemological Implications of IH

The shift from DH to IH also has profound epistemological implications, reflecting a move from a positivist to a constructivist understanding of information. One key epistemological implication of IH is its emphasis on the situatedness of information – the foundational recognition that all information is irrevocably shaped by the cultural, social, and historical conditions of their production. As Noble (2018) points out, "While we often think of terms such as 'big data' and 'algorithms' as being benign, neutral, or objective, they are anything but". IH believes that there is no context-free or objective standpoint from which to produce or interpret information—only situated partial perspectives. IH operationalizes this insight by interrogating how power structures, cultural norms, and material conditions shape every layer of information ecosystems, from dataset curation to algorithmic classification, thus opening pathways for more accountable and reflexive approaches to information production, dissemination, and consumption in the information age.

Another important epistemological implication is IH's focus on the relationality of information, which recognizes that information is not a static entity but a dynamic process that emerges through relationships and interactions. For Bruno Latour (2005), "information is transformation", which emphasizes that information involves continuous transformation as it moves through networks of human and non-human actors, being constantly shaped and reshaped through interactions among various actors. This relationality is a fundamental aspect of information lifecycle. In production, information is never created in isolation but through layered interactions between creators, technologies, and cultural contexts. In dissemination, various elements in infrastructures and algorithms govern information's movement. Even in consumption, information is received through the users' interactions with technology and other social and cultural factors. Based on the recognition that information exists in its relationships—between humans and infrastructures as well as bodies and interface, IH moves to map the connections underlying information, revealing how they function within dynamic systems of power and ideology.

4 Research Directions in Information Humanities

4.1 Critical Information Studies

As explored in the preceding analysis, CIS represents a fundamental methodological framework within IH, one that is poised to serve as a foundational pillar for the discipline's emerging research trajectories. This centrality stems from CIS's unique capacity to interrogate how information systems - from algorithmic architectures to database structures - actively encode and perpetuate structural inequalities along intersecting axes of gender, race, class, and disability. CIS conducts its critical analysis based on the recognition that information is power and often "used as a weapon by those in power to consolidate their control—over places and things, as well as people" (D'Ignazio and Klein, 2020). In CIS, often "ethnographic investigation" is adopted as a method of enquiry for researchers "to grasp the process of shaping digital entities and, as participating observers, to take part in it and to understand its phenomenological implications"

(Camus and Vinck, 2019) so that the hierarchies of power behind information systems can be uncovered. Within the current paradigm of informational capitalism, where information mediates all dimensions of social, economic, and political life, such critical analytical framework as CIS emerges as indispensable for deconstructing systemic inequities and fostering emancipatory knowledge practices.

4.2 Information Ethics

Ethical enquiry constitutes a core methodological commitment of IH, positioning information ethics as a central research trajectory for the field. In contemporary information society, where information systems permeate all dimensions of social life and fundamentally shape decision-making processes and behavioral patterns, IH's approach to information ethics must transcend abstract philosophical principles to develop operationalizable frameworks for justice across the entire information lifecycle — from production and dissemination to consumption. This calls for investigations of pressing ethical issues revolving algorithmic injustice, data colonialism, and epistemic violence in information systems. Luciano Floridi's conceptualization of "infraethics" proves particularly salient to this endeavor. As Durante (2017) explicates, Floridi's framework examines the "infrastructures that either facilitate or constrain agents' moral behaviors and their evaluation", with particular attention to institutional arrangements governing privacy regimes, transparency protocols, intellectual property rights, and other structural determinants of ethical information practices. This infraethical lens provides IH scholars with crucial analytical perspectives to investigate the often opaque technical and social architectures underlying information systems.

The complexity of contemporary information ethical issues—characterized by what Birhane (2021) describes as "deeply rooted, fluid, contingent, and interconnected sociotechnical problems"—demands an approach grounded in relational ethics. IH advocates for this perspective as an antidote to the reductive rationalism dominating much technological development, emphasizing instead the interdependent, contextually embedded, and experientially constituted nature of ethical dilemmas in information societies. This relational turn enables more nuanced analyses of how moral principles and beliefs operate through information systems while centering the lived experiences of human communities affected by these technologies.

4.3 Information Aesthetics

Information aesthetics constitutes another critical research trajectory within IH, interrogating how the architectures, interfaces, and materialities of information systems actively shape human perception, cognition, and creative expression. As exemplified by Jussi Parikka's (2023) study of operational images, all material forms of information in modern society are deeply embedded in various institutional and technological contexts along "multiple chains of operations through which they are linked to a long line of institutional, epistemological, and other uses", influencing human cognitive processes and mediating human perception of reality. Studies on information aesthetics synthesize analytical frameworks from HCI—particularly its critical strand examining how computational tools mediate understanding—and media studies, which traces the cognitive and affective consequences of digital mediation. By bridging empirical technical analysis with humanistic critique, information aesthetics seeks not only to diagnose constraints imposed by existing systems on human perception but to prototype alternatives that expand, rather than diminish, human expressive capacities.

5 Conclusion

This article has argued for the emergence of Information Humanities as a transformative paradigm that expands and redefines the scope of Digital Humanities. By transcending the technocentric focus of DH, IH seeks to explore the deeper cultural, social, and ontological dimensions of information, addressing the fundamental, formative role of information in human life. Through tracing the history and development of DH, highlighting its contributions and limitations, the article introduced IH as an expansion of the research paradigm. It also outlined potential research directions in IH, showcasing their significance for bridging theory and practice and shaping the future of the humanities.

The emergence of IH has profound implications for future research in the humanities and beyond. By integrating insights from a diverse range of disciplines, including information science, media studies, philosophy, and cultural studies, IH enables scholars to address complex issues such as digital inequality, information ethics, and the impact of information technologies on human cognition. By bringing together scholars from diverse fields and engaging with the public, IH can promote a more inclusive approach to the study of information.

With a view to overcoming the technocentrism of DH, IH studies have the potential to engage stakeholders across academia, policymaking, and communities to address urgent challenges like algorithmic bias, digital divide, and the cognitive impacts of AI. By foregrounding the cultural embeddedness of information, IH not only ensures the continued relevance of the humanities in an information-driven era but also reshapes their future as a discipline capable of both critiquing and reimagining information technological systems. Its emphasis on situated knowledge and the relationality of information positions IH as a vital framework for navigating the complexities of the digital age while centering humanistic values of justice, equity, and creativity.

Acknowledgments. This study was funded by Education Reformation Project of Beijing Information Science and Technology University (grant number 2025JGYB34).

Disclosure of Interests The authors have no competing interests to declare that are relevant to the content of this article.

References

Birhane, A.: Algorithmic injustice: A relational ethics approach. Patterns. **2**(2), 1–9 (2021)

Burdick, A., Drucker, J., Lunenfeld, P., Presner, T., Schnapp, J.: Digital Humanities. MIT Press, Cambridge (2012)

Camus, A., Vinck, D.: Unfolding digital materiality: how engineers struggle to shape tangible and fluid objects. In: Vertesi, J., Ribes, D. (eds.) DigitalSTS: A Field Guide for Science & Technology Studies, pp. 17–41. Princeton University Press, Princeton (2019)

D'Ignazio, C., Klein, L.F.: Data Feminism. MIT Press, Cambridge (2020)

Day, R.E.: The Modern Invention of Information: Discourse, History and Power. Southern Illinois University Press, Carbondale (2001)

Day, R.E.: Indexing It All: The Subject in the Age of Documentation, Information, and Data. MIT Press, Cambridge (2014)

Dix, A., Finlay, J.E., Abowd, G.D., Beale, R.: Human-Computer interaction, 3rd edn. Prentice-Hall, Upper Saddle River (2003)

Drucker, J.: Humanistic theory and digital scholarship. In: Gold, M.K. (ed.) Debates in the Digital Humanities, pp. 85–95. University of Minnesota Press, Minneapolis (2012)

Durante, M.: Ethics, Law and the Politics of Information: A Guide to the Philosophy of Luciano Floridi. Springer, New York (2017)

Floridi, L.: The Philosophy of Information. Oxford University Press, Oxford (2011)

Floridi, L.: The Ethics of Information. Oxford University Press, Oxford (2013)

Floridi, L.: The Fourth Revolution: How the Infosphere is Reshaping Human Reality. Oxford University Press, Oxford (2014)

Hayles, N.K.: How We Became Posthuman: Virtual Bodies in Cybernetics, Literature, and Informatics. University of Chicago Press, Chicago (1999)

Hayles, N.K.: How We Think: Digital Media and Contemporary Technogenesis. University of Chicago Press, Chicago (2012)

Hockey, S.: The history of humanities computing. In: Schreibman, S., Siemens, R., Unsworth, J. (eds.) A Companion to Digital Humanities, pp. 3–19. Blackwell Publishing, Oxford (2004)

Kittler, F.: Gramophone, Film, Typewriter. Winthrop-Young, G., Wutz, M. (trans.) Stanford University Press, Stanford (1999)

Latour, B.: Reassembling the Social: An Introduction to Actor-Network-Theory. Oxford University Press, Oxford (2005)

Liu, A.: Where is cultural criticism in the digital humanities? In: Gold, M.K. (ed.) Debates in the Digital Humanities, pp. 490–509. University of Minnesota Press, Minneapolis (2012)

McCarty, W.: Humanities Computing. Palgrave Macmillan, Hampshire/New York (2005)

McLuhan, M.: Understanding Media: The Extensions of Man. MIT Press, Cambridge (1994)

Moretti, F.: Distant Reading. Verso, London (2013)

Noble, S.U.: Algorithms of Oppression. New York University Press, New York (2018)

Ong, W.J.: Orality and Literacy: The Technologizing of the Word. Routledge, New York (2002)

Parikka, J.: Operational Images: From the Visual to the Invisual. University of Minnesota Press, Minneapolis (2023)

Pressner, T., Schnapp, J., Lunenfeld, P.: The Digital Humanities Manifesto 2.0. http://www.humanitiesblast.com/manifesto/Manifesto_V2.pdf (2009). Last accessed 2025/3/4

Schreibman, S., Siemens, R., Unsworth, J.: The digital humanities and humanities computing: An introduction. In: Schreibman, S., Siemens, R., Unsworth, J. (eds.) A Companion to Digital Humanities, pp. xxiii–xxvi. Blackwell Publishing, Oxford (2004)

Thomas III, W.G.: The promise of the digital humanities and the contested nature of digital scholarship. In: Schreibman, S., Siemens, R., Unsworth, J. (eds.) A New Companion to Digital Humanities, 2nd edn, pp. 524–537. Wiley-Blackwell, Oxford (2016)

Vaidhyanathan, S.: Afterword: critical information studies. Cult. Stud. **20**(2–3), 292–315 (2006)

Wiener, N.: The Human Use of Human Beings: Cybernetics and Society. The Riverside Press, Cambridge (1950)

Wiener, N.: Cybernetics, or Control and Communication in the Animal and the Machine, 2nd edn. MIT Press, Cambridge (1965)

Research on Public Space System Design Based on Restorative Theory in Closed Art Intensive Training Environments

ShanRu Liang[(⊠)] [iD]

Guangdong University of Technology, No.729 Dongfeng East Road, Yuexiu District, Guangzhou, China
Cindy050303@qq.com

Abstract. Art students are susceptible to anxiety, physical and mental fatigue, and creative exhaustion when they are subjected to high-pressure, high-intensity, and monotonous learning rhythms in closed training environments for long periods of time. In recent years, the development of environmental psychology and healing theory has provided a theoretical basis and practical direction for optimizing such educational spaces. However, existing research has not yet systematically elucidated how students achieve psychological regulation, attention recovery and collective support through spatial systems in closed intensive training scenarios. This study attempts to fill this gap by focusing on the space use behavior, perceptual feedback and healing response mechanisms of art students. We combined questionnaire data with spatial behavior tracking experiments to collect data on the psychological states, activity trajectories, and spatial use preferences of a total of 72 students from three drawing studios in Guangdong, and identified differences in the response patterns of groups with different psychological states to the types of spatial nodes. This study experimentally compares the psychological state changes of students with different anxiety levels after using the restorative space, verifies the significance of their attention restoration effect, and analyzes the association between students' exploratory use behaviors in the space and their physical and mental states, and discovers that there is a significant differentiation in the distribution of different groups in terms of path preference and node attraction. This study provides data support for understanding the mechanism of the healing space system in closed teaching environments, and also provides a basis for the design of subsequent spatial interventions for candidate groups, promoting the transformation of educational space from "efficiency-oriented" to "humanistic care".

Keywords: Closed environment · Healing space · Restorative environment · Environmental stress · Multisensory interaction

1 Introduction

In China, the gaokao art professional examination (art examination) is still an important way for a large number of students to enter institutions of higher art, and according to statistics, the total number of national art examiners in 2024 will be about 528,000 [1]. In

M. Schrepp and M. Rauterberg (Eds.): HCII 2025, LNCS 16342, pp. 373–391, 2026.
https://doi.org/10.1007/978-3-032-13164-5_24

order to prepare for the high-intensity examination training, many students need to enter full-time closed training schools during their senior year of high school, staying in highly concentrated and spatially restricted environments for long periods of time. Art training spaces are usually characterized by a small drawing area, dense population, closed layout, and limited ventilation and lighting conditions. Students' prolonged sitting, repetitive work, and continuous painting in these spaces can easily lead to cognitive fatigue and emotional anxiety [2].

In recent years, the influence of spatial environment on individual psychological state and behavioral performance has gradually become an important topic in the cross research between environmental psychology and design. A large number of studies have shown that spatial design incorporating natural elements can alleviate anxiety and stress and promote psychological recovery through natural healing mechanisms [4]. However, most of these studies have focused on open environments or outdoor landscape systems, relying on natural media such as solid greenery, water bodies, and natural light for emotional intervention [3]. In closed indoor environments, especially those oriented to high-density and strictly managed learning scenarios, the maintenance cost of physical plants is high and susceptible to spatial structure and usage management constraints; while virtual natural means (e.g., digital landscape projection) also present certain challenges in terms of technical implementation and user acceptance [7]. Therefore, how to build healing environments for indoor closed spaces without relying on large-scale natural media is still a weak point in current research.

This paper focuses on the typical closed learning scenario of art intensive training for senior high school art exams, and explores how to alleviate students' psychological anxiety and cognitive fatigue under long-term spatial oppression through spatial micro-intervention from the perspective of healing environment design. To this end, this paper builds a research framework based on the theory of healing environment, combining Attention Restoration Theory (ART) and Environmental Stress Theory, and based on field research, we visited three typical closed art intensive training schools, and adopted the combination of on-site spatial observation and in-depth user interviews. The combination of spatial observation and in-depth user interviews was used to analyze the non-healing factors existing in the current learning space and summarize their potential influence mechanisms on the psychological state of students.

On the basis of the research, this paper proposes a healing space system design framework consisting of three modules, namely, "path guidance, space node, and non-healing factor intervention", with the aim of providing feasible attention restoration and emotion regulation support for users in high-pressure and closed learning environments, and helping them to continuously renew their physical and mental resources, as well as providing theoretical and practical references for the subsequent optimization of similar educational environments. This paper aims to provide users in high-pressure, closed learning environments with feasible support for attention recovery and emotion regulation, to help them continuously renew their physical and mental resources, and to provide theoretical and practical references for the subsequent optimization of environments in similar educational settings.

2   Related Work

The concept of "healing environment" was first proposed by Kaplan [16] and defined as "an environment that enables people to better recover from mental fatigue and the negative emotions that accompany stress", and most existing studies focus on the natural healing mechanisms of open environments, such as Weber et al. [18] found that urban forests and urban parks have a healing effect, which can effectively relieve headaches and stress and improve mood. Existing studies focus on the natural healing mechanism of open environments, for example, Weber et al. [18] found that urban forests and urban parks have a healing effect, which can effectively alleviate headache and stress, and improve mood.Souter-Brown [8] emphasized that the integration of natural environments and urban design promotes the physical and mental health of human beings, and systematically explored how to integrate the natural elements and artificial facilities by designing open spaces such as greenways, parks and streets, and constructing ecological functions and facilities with ecological functions. Chen-Linli et al. [15] constructed a plant evaluation system for healing landscapes based on the Analytical Hierarchy Process (AHP), which reveals the mechanism of the healing environment theory in the open space, and provides a cross-disciplinary decision-making model for the scientific screening and spatial allocation of plant healing performance in the open environment.

Existing studies of urban environments have lower scores for the environmental component of restorative healing than natural environments [17], and Weber [18] explored the restorative potential of urban environments, particularly spaces with natural elements, to support people's restoration in open-ended healing spaces. However, closed operational spaces are different in nature from traditional open-ended healing spaces, where the main activity is high-intensity learning rather than leisure activities, with low degrees of freedom and strong regulatory disciplinary constraints, and the need for prolonged residency makes a difference in the perceptual load from that of general healing goal-oriented spaces. The visual stimuli in the enclosed space are more concentrated (walls, painting tools) and the auditory disturbances (brush strokes, footsteps, lectures) are more continuous. The user state will be highly focused under a different type of attention than the perceptual attention in the open environment.

Currently, there is a lack of specificity in the healing mechanism of closed space, and existing studies have not systematically analyzed the impact of natural elements in closed environments, resulting in the "natural element failure" of existing open space healing strategies in closed scenarios, and there is still a gap in the literature on the following dimensions: (1) the adaptability of non-plant-dependent healing systems in closed scenarios; (2) the design of behavioral pathways for cognitive resource recovery under high-intensity learning; and (3) the design of behavioral pathways for cognitive resource recovery under high-intensity learning.) behavioral pathway design for cognitive resource recovery under high-intensity learning. In summary, most of the existing studies on restorative environments have been conducted in open recreational spaces, and the specificity of the restorative mechanism has not yet been systematically explored in the high-pressure learning scenarios such as the Fine Arts Higher Education Examination, which is non-leisure oriented, highly centralized, strictly regulated, physically closed, and with a long period of stay. In particular, when physical natural elements are difficult to realize due to spatial limitations, economic costs or management constraints, how to use spatial structure design, node guidance and unnatural sensory modulation to construct an effective indoor healing system is the core issue of concern in this study.

3 Research

3.1 3Field research: Studio Environment Observation

In this study, three typical high-intensity art high school intensive training studios in Guangdong Province were selected as the field research objects, see Fig. 1, and the research was conducted in October 2024, which lasted for three days. Based on the four elements of restorative environments proposed by Kaplan and Kaplan (1989)-Being away, Fascination, Extent and Compatibility [16], the studio space was Structured observations were made and combined with Ulrich et al.'s (1991) environmental healing pathway [9] to construct an observational recording framework focusing on the interactive process between the physical features of the space and the user's behavior.

We entered three typical art training centers in a certain city as "observer-participant" and conducted 1-day on-site observation in each of them. The observation includes the teaching activity space, painting workspace, resting area, lighting and ventilation conditions, application of natural elements, etc. The aim is to identify whether the current space possesses the basic characteristics of a restorative environment, such as "co-existence of escapism and participation", "shelteredness wrapped in soft boundaries", "moderate sensory stimulation", etc. The observation is also aimed at identifying whether the current space possesses the basic characteristics of a restorative environment. and "moderate sensory stimulation" [16].

We entered three typical art training centers in a certain city as "observer-participant" and conducted one-day on-site observation in each of them. The observation includes the teaching activity space, painting workspace, resting area, lighting and ventilation conditions, application of natural elements, etc. The aim is to identify whether the current space possesses the basic characteristics of a restorative environment, such as "co-existence of escapism and participation", "shelteredness wrapped in soft boundaries", "moderate sensory stimulation", etc. The observation is also aimed at identifying whether the current space possesses the basic characteristics of a restorative environment. and "moderate sensory stimulation" [16].

Observations showed that the three studios generally had the following problems: (1) highly enclosed spaces with few windows, poor ventilation, and a lack of natural light sources and greenery [affecting escapism and attractiveness]; (2) dense seating, crowded study lines, and a lack of diversified functional zoning; (3) prolonged use of artificial light sources and cold-tone decorations, resulting in a single space with a single and persistent tension of sensory stimulation [affecting attractiveness]; (4) lack of quiet and private restorative spaces [affecting compatibility and attractiveness]; and (5) lack of quiet and private restorative spaces [affecting compatibility, compatibility, and attractiveness].) the lack of quiet and private restorative spaces [affecting compatibility and escapism]. (5) The presence of 24/7 non-stop training at some of the intensive training sites, with students staying in the classroom for more than 11 h per day. Overall, these environments are characterized by spatial closure, activity restriction, and psychological stress, making it difficult to support students in obtaining effective psychological regulation and energy recovery after high-intensity learning.

Fig. 1. Picture of the studio environment.

3.2 User Research: Semi-structured Interviews

Based on field observations, we conducted semi-structured interviews with a total of 20 intensive students (11 male 9 female, with an average age of 17.8 years old) from three drawing studios, aiming to collect their subjective evaluations of the current learning space, their experiences of anxiety, and their perceptions of the relationship between the current learning space and environmental elements. Interviews lasted approximately 30–45 min per person, were conducted during student breaks, and took place in a relatively quiet teacher's office or outdoor balcony. Participants signed an informed consent form, and observation videos were face-coded and processed.At the same time, in order to get children into a state of flow experience faster, the accuracy data of the bird-finding session will be fed back to the backend to evaluate and analyze children's learning results of bird knowledge, push relevant reinforcement information, and adjust the difficulty of delivering content. degree of ease. Make it easier for children to master knowledge; to be more easily motivated to maintain their interest in nature.

The interview questions were organized around the following six core dimensions:

1. The most stressful spatial experience of the learning process;
2. Are there opportunities to restore energy and relax in the space;
3. Subjective evaluation and feedback on the current space in terms of comfort, functionality and suggestions for improvement;
4. Whether or not the spatial layout is perceived to be associated with one's psychological state;
5. Availability of escape places or meditation areas in times of anxiety.
6. What factors are thought to influence their behavioral habits such as frequency of space use, resting patterns, and socialization patterns.

Students were encouraged to give a "first person" description of their day-to-day training, and in order to obtain more realistic feedback on their experiences, we introduced contextualized questions such as "When was the last time you felt like you couldn't concentrate?".

The results of the interviews showed that most students had more pronounced anxiety, irritability and decreased concentration, and common behaviors included frequent dawdling in class, walking around with the intention of avoiding, prolonged use of cell phones during class, and avoidance of the use of common areas. A majority of students also reported that being in a single, confined and repetitive space for long periods of time made them feel physically and mentally overwhelmed. For example, one respondent stated, "This space has no windows, the lights are too white and bright, and it feels like there is no sense of time from morning to night, so it's easy to crash." Another student reflected, "Sitting for ten hours at a time, with only a ten minute break between classes and no time to get ready for tools." In addition, more than 70% of the interviewees mentioned that they would like to see unsupervised "nooks and crannies with natural elements," "meditation zones," or "chill-out zones" added to the space to serve as a psychological buffer for individuals. The students generally reported that they had experienced problems in the latter part of the intensive training period. Students generally reported a decrease in creativity, physical exhaustion, and less frequent interaction with peers in the later stages of the training.

The results of the interviews revealed that students' psychological responses to space stemmed not only from the physical structure itself, but were also related to the functional arrangement, adjustability and visual atmosphere. Especially during the high-pressure intensive training period, the lack of spatial choice and personalized adjustability was considered one of the main spatial factors leading to the persistent increase in anxiety. Students' spontaneous spatial movements, stays, and interactive behaviors under non-instructional instructions, such as wandering around different zones in between classes, searching for quiet corners, and browsing through the display wall, reflect their instincts to seek psychological adjustment, which need to be observed through behavioral tracking.

3.3 Analysis

Combining spatial observation and user feedback, we used the thematic induction method to code and analyze the research data, and categorized the non-recovery factors in the high-pressure learning space with reference to Attention Recovery Theory (ART) [6] and Environmental Stress Theory. The analysis refined a total of four categories of high-frequency non-recovery factors in Table 1.

Comprehensive field and user research shows that current art training spaces do not effectively support the emotional regulation and psychological recovery of youth under high pressure. Key dimensions such as space structure, lighting and ventilation, and privacy design can be optimized. In the interviews, students mentioned that they would like to have a small corner for relaxation and a meditation area for personal space, while teachers observed a "decrease in interaction at the end of the day" and a "decrease in creativity", "Decreased creativity", and "blocked emotional expression may lead to internalized stress" in the environmental stress theory, deducing that a proven and youth-friendly solution is to provide a low-risk, non-socially stressful outlet for unconscious emotions. The theory of restorative environments not only serves as an analytical framework for assessing existing problems, but also provides a theoretical basis for designing future intervention programs. User feedback further reveals the micro-expression of environmental oppression and the need for emotional avoidance in real-world situations, providing more targeted design cues for subsequent design.

Table 1. Elements of high-frequency non-recurrent healing in the drawing room

categorization	non-healing factor	descriptive
Space architecture classes	Dense layout, closed approach, lack of vista openings	Leads to visual congestion, pathway compression and a sense of spatial disorientation
Sensory stimulants	Stuffy air, frequent noise, long and sedentary classes	Leads to physical fatigue and concentration depletion
Psychosocial	Lack of private space, underutilization of common areas, lack of relaxation nodes	Leads to feelings of isolation, lack of access to emotional outlet
Behavioral Support Classes	High severity management, frac-tional breaks, lack of break guidance	Resulting in a lack of rest and an insufficient level of recovery

4   Design Strategy and System Construction

Through the research on the studio environment and the interpretation of the restorative environment on the needs of the studio users, summarizing the non-restorative elements of the studio HF, evaluating the potential of constructing a restorative environment in the studio under the guidance of the theory of stress restoration and attention restoration [5], and generating the restorative benefits in the place [10], through (1) optimizing the spatial structure and path; (2) weakening the sensory stimulation (3) and (4) strategies, the studio construction of multifaceted design strategies and systems for spaces [20].

4.1   Optimizing Spatial Structure And Pathways

Alleviating feelings of oppression and disorientation for behavioral guidance. In a closed art training environment, the closeness and density of the spatial structure is one of the key triggers of cognitive fatigue and anxiety. In order to respond to the negative feedbacks of "path compression", "spatial disorientation" and "visual congestion", this study priori-tizes the structural healing goals in the spatial improvement objectives, namely Optimize the spatial layout and guiding paths to alleviate the sense of oppression caused by spatial closure. Specific strategies include: building a clear line system, breaking the original "linear corridor-dense painting area" configuration, shifting to a "ring-guided + node-release" layout, and enhancing the continuity and sense of direction of the space; setting up a "visual release area"; and "Visual release zone", that is, in the nodes of the line of motion arranged local pick-up, soft partition or mirror reflection wall, to provide users with temporary spatial tension buffer; re-organize the seating density (group painting area spacing ≥ 1.2 m) and group relations, forming a "closed group painting area Reorganize the seating density (spacing between group drawing areas ≥ 1.2m) and group relationship to form "enclosed group drawing area", which reduces the visual noise and improves the spatial recognition and comfort without increasing the area. In addition, the addition of transitional spaces (e.g. functional gray spaces, semi-open corridors, medita-tion corners, etc.) serves as an "escape node", providing students with the psychological possibility of "switching scenarios" in a single learning rhythm. The above structural strategies refer to the dimensions of "continuity" and "compatibility" in the ART theory, and are combined with the field observation that students are interested in "transitions" and "residency". Combined with the students' actual feedback on their preference for "transitions" and "dwellings" during the on-site observation, the aim is to provide the necessary spatial support for the psychological recovery of the high-intensity painting process through the adjustment of structural hierarchy and path strategies.

4.2 Optimizing the Sensory Stimulation Experience

Sensory stimulation is an important medium for influencing mental states in closed art training environments. According to the results of the research, students who are exposed to monotonous lighting, constant noise, poor ventilation and tactile fatigue for a long period of time generally show symptoms such as reduced concentration and emotional fluctuations. Therefore, the second objective of the design practice is to "optimize sensory recovery", i.e., to promote psychological recovery through the intervention of sensory regulation. Firstly, a multi-mode lighting system is introduced in the light environment, combining "automatic adjustment of warm and cold light", "low illumination edge lighting" and "physiological rhythm light color simulation" to help students adjust their painting rhythm and mood at different times of the day and night. This helps students to regulate the rhythm of painting and visual tension at different times of the day. Secondly, passive acoustic materials (e.g. sound-absorbing wall panels, ceiling soft packs) are used to control the environmental noise, especially to optimize the acoustic performance between the common areas and the painting classrooms, so as to build a low-interference acoustic environment. In terms of odor and ventilation, the automatic air circulation system is combined with a "light aroma diffusion mechanism", which uses natural plant essential oils to create an olfactory atmosphere that calms the emotions, while at the same time ensures balanced air circulation and humidity. At the tactile level, soft furniture, cushions and façade materials are introduced to change the sense of touch, so that users can get physical relief in a highly sedentary state. Overall, the sensory stimulation category corresponds to the "escapism" and "attraction" elements in the restorative environment, with the intention of constructing a multi-channel, moderately varying and adjustable sensory scene to create a safe, controllable, and lightweight experience for the students at the perceptual level. The aim is to build a multi-channel, moderately changing and adjustable sensory scene to create a safe, controllable and lightweight experience for students at the perception level.

4.3 Improvement of Psychosocial Contacts

In the closed art training environment, students' social behavior is highly restricted by the spatial structure and supervision mode, and it is very easy to produce a sense of loneliness and depression. Especially in the late stage of high-pressure training, the phenomena of collective alienation, social avoidance and emotional closure are common. In this study, we set "social psychological support" as the third type of goal in the design practice, with the intention of strengthening the emotional connection and emotional expression channel between students through the spatial structure and functional arrangement of. Specific strategies include: setting up "semi-private coexistence zones", such as long-table communication zones with partitions or group sitting zones, to satisfy the dual psychological needs of students who want to interact with others but do not want to be over-exposed; setting up "informal socialization nodes", such as tea corners, simple book corners, craft interaction tables, etc., to meet the needs of students who want to interact with others but do not want to be over-exposed. Informal social nodes" are added, such as tea corner, simple book corner, handmade interactive table, etc., to provide a short-stay, non-task-oriented social platform outside the formal teaching space; "anonymous emotion expression wall" or "message corner" is designed in the public space, to carry the emotional output that can't be directly expressed in the spatial medium. At the same time, "gaze-avoidance zones", such as resting chairs or small meditation pavilions with line-of-sight enclosures, are added to the functional lines of high-frequency use, so that students with different personalities can freely choose their social distance. These strategies provide multiple levels of choice from "passive coexistence" to "active communication," referencing the "compatibility" feature of the healing theory and responding to the students' concerns about "security," "feeling safe," and "being safe." It also responds to the students' practical demands for "sense of security", "social privacy", and "emotional outlet" in the interviews.

4.4 Enhanced Rest Behavior Support

Under high-pressure intensive training, students' time scheduling and behavioral choices are subject to increased institutional constraints, and they often exhibit a stressful behavioral pattern of "tiredness to cope". The research shows that the absence of behavioral support systems in the training space, such as unstructured rest arrangements, inefficient path allocation and functional redundancy, seriously affects the recovery efficiency and initiative of students. Therefore, the fourth objective of the design practice focuses on the "optimization of behavioral support", which guides students to spontaneously build a more balanced "learning-recovery-social" behavioral structure through the spatial mechanism. First, we set up a "time-responsive space" and embed dynamic cueing devices (e.g., light bands and rhythm walls) in the space to help students recognize the sense of time and proactively switch between tasks. Secondly, the "boundary visualization" between the learning area and the recovery area should be clearly defined, such as color difference, material change or ground guidance, to avoid the interference of different activities and to enhance the clear identification of functional behaviors. Third, set up "predictable transition points" in the pathway design, such as transparent partitions or functional transfer corridors, to break the rigid flow of "classroom-corridor-rest area" and provide a place for intermediary stops to enhance behavioral freedom. intermediary stopping places to increase the freedom of behavior. Finally, the introduction of "micro-restorative devices," such as dynamic benches, wall stretching bands, and short-term game tables, supports students in obtaining physical and emotional intermittent release in a short period of time. These strategies emphasize the spatial accessibility of restorative micro-behavior, activate students' intrinsic regulatory potential through the psychological mechanisms of the environment, and provide specific, low-cost, and high-frequency behavioral intervention support.

5   Design Intervention Prototype Construction

Combining the needs from the research and the elements of restorative theory, this study constructs a three-level restorative public space system prototype of "path guidance - spatial nodes - non-restorative factor intervention", which is used to integrate into the current training space to make up for the missing restorative elements of the training space. elements.

5.1   Path Guidance System

The core function of the pathway guidance system, as the basic entrance to the healing process, is to provide a clear and recognizable psychological escape route and spatial exploration framework for high-pressure learners, with the aim of reducing the sense of spatial disorientation and oppression, and providing access to the core healing nodes. Its value in the theory of restorative environments is mainly reflected in the promotion of continuity (Extent) and the stimulation of initial attraction (Fascination). Specific design strategies include: (1) Optimize the spatial layout and dynamic line, abandon the original single linear corridor layout, and build a rhythmic, such as loops, folding lines and clear guidance flow system. Through the combination of ground signs, lighting guidance or material gradient to achieve visual orientation, enhance the sense of direction and coherence of the space (Extent), and its own changes can also trigger the user's initial interest in exploration (Fascination). (2) Coupling high-frequency paths with miniature restoration points. Based on the characteristics of students' fragmented rest time and spontaneous behavior, miniature nodes with preliminary restoration potential, such as small green plant viewpoints, ventilation corners, and information display boards are strategically embedded in high-frequency paths, such as the intersection of the lines of movement leading to the restroom, drinking water area, and preparation area, or the neighboring positions. This strategy reduces the cost of actively searching for specialized restorative spaces, and increases the probability of exposure to restorative environmental elements through "functional path overlay", which is in line with the principle of compatibility. (3) For extremely fragmented time situations, the guided paths themselves, such as visually appealing floor patterns and softly changing lighting sequences, can also play a restorative role by triggering a momentary distraction or encouraging short healthy walks to make small detours. This system focuses on the sense of oppression/disorientation of spatial structures identified by the field research, as well as the absence of behavioral support and inefficient pathways.

5.2   Spatial Node System

The system of spatial nodes at the heart of the DIP prototype is a key place for students to realize substantial psychological "escapes" and diverse recovery experiences. These carefully designed miniature "buffer zones" or "charging stations" are designed to support students in taking a brief break from the high-pressure learning state, and to provide a multilevel physical and mental restorative experience ranging from shallow relaxation to deep restoration (visual relaxation, naps, meditation, light socialization) [11]. The design strategy is based on the feedback from the user research. The specific design strategy is based on the differentiated needs of user research feedback [12], such as the needs for privacy, solitude, relaxation, and light socialization, to meet the individual needs and the principle of compatibility of node functions, and to design diversified node forms, such as (1) Quiet detachment-type nodes, set up, for example, meditation corners and napping areas, enclosed by soft partitions, to enhance the visual shielding and introduce soft light and natural white noise, to create a sense of highly sheltered private space, and to support deep relaxation. The soft partition enclosure enhances visual shielding, introduces soft light and natural white noise, and creates a highly sheltered sense of private space to support deep relaxation and recovery of concentration. (2) Social buffer nodes, semi-private coexistence areas are arranged with long tables with high-backed seats or greenery, small enclosed sofa areas, etc., to meet the needs of students for light interaction or seeking companionship with limited exposure, and to alleviate the sense of loneliness. (3) Sensory awakening nodes utilize the five senses of experience, installing tactile material walls, soft aroma diffusers, interactive light and shadow devices, etc., to enhance the attractiveness of the environment by enriching environmental experience through the senses of hearing, smell, and touch through moderate and controllable non-visual sensory stimulation. The core design principles include differentiation and escape reinforcement. The node design should be significantly different from the standard teaching environment in terms of atmosphere, material and function, clearly conveying the signal of "this is a place for you to take a short break". Safe, controlled and comfortable, creating an atmosphere that weakens the sense of supervision and supports autonomous choices, such as easy shade adjustment and options for changing sitting positions. Incorporating symbolic or moderately authentic natural media, such as warm color temperatures, wood, natural sounds, and small-scale greenery or images of greenery, can enhance the appeal of the environment.

5.3 Non-healing Factor Intervention Systems

As a support layer, the non-healing factor intervention system focuses on dynamically monitoring, mitigating or eliminating various types of persistent stressors in the environment, i.e., "non-healing" factors, with the aim of creating a more favorable environment for path guidance and effective operation of the spatial node system, and to continuously improve the overall spatial compatibility and overall recovery potential. Specific interventions cover a number of dimensions: (1) Systematic sensory regulation, using passive/active techniques to optimize the physical parameters of the environment. (2) Avoiding glare in the light environment and introducing physiological rhythms to simulate lighting to regulate visual fatigue. (3) Acoustic environment applying sound-absorbing materials, optimizing spatial noise isolation (e.g., classroom/corridor isolation), and constructing a low-interference soundscape. (4) Air quality and odorA lightweight fresh air and filtration system is deployed to ensure air circulation and cleanliness, and natural plant essential oils are combined for light aromatic diffusion to create an olfactory ambience that calms the mood of. (5) Tactile ComfortThe tactile quality of the seats is improved by improving the seats, providing cushions, and improving the armrests and desktop materials to alleviate sedentary fatigue. (6) Environmentally embedded behavioral guidance in terms of slogans and instructions. At key locations, such as node entrances and functional area transitions, non-compulsory and subtly integrated into the environment are set up, such as artistic text symbols on the wall, "Here you can take a deep breath for 3 minutes", and soft lighting changes to indicate a break, and micro-recovery guidance at time intervals. Simple recovery tools can also be provided with the space, such as wall stretching tape guide charts, to encourage users to practice healthy behaviors. (7) Lightweight social atmosphere support, design and provide anonymous or low-stress emotional expression channels, and design beautiful erasable expression walls to promote gentle emotional catharsis. (8) Data-driven spatial fine-tuning and feedback, combining spatial use behavior tracking and environmental physical data, noise hotspots, human flow attendance data and user feedback, continuously identifying new "pressure points" or inefficient areas, and dynamically guiding the fine-tuning and optimization of the spatial layout, furniture arrangement, or management rules [13] to ensure a continuous response to the actual needs. actual needs.

The design prototype is based on a modular device with quick adaptability and low destructiveness, which is suitable for the soft renovation of the existing space structure in art training institutions.

6 Experiments and Results

A controlled experiment was conducted to evaluate the effectiveness of the "path guidance-space node-non-healing factor intervention" three-level healing public space system as a whole (DIP prototype) in alleviating the psychological anxiety of high-pressure, closed art training students and improving the efficiency of attention restoration. Practical effects.

The research hypotheses,H1: Students' self-reported levels of perceived environmental stress (SENV) will be significantly lower after performing a standardized learning task in a space where the full DIP prototype is applied (intervention environment) compared to the unmodified original set space (control environment).H2: After performing a standardized learning task with a mandatory rest period in the DIP intervention environment compared to the control environment, students' perceived Restorative Effectiveness (PRS) levels will be significantly higher.H3: Students will exhibit significant frequency and duration of behaviors (e.g., entering, staying, interacting) using pre-determined restorative nodes during or following a break from a standardized task in a DIP intervention environment.

6.1 Experimental Design

This study used a Randomized Posttest-Only Control Group Design. Participants were randomly assigned to two separate groups: Control Group (CG): to undergo the experimental procedures in the original unmodified training space (control environment). The Intervention Group (IG): received the experimental procedure in the DIP prototype space with the complete "Pathway Guidance - Spatial Nodes - Non-Healing Factor Intervention" three-tiered system, as shown in Fig. 2.

Students are recruited from three typical and highly similar closed art college entrance examination intensive training studios in Guangdong Province. Inclusion criteria: (1) senior high school students, aged 16–19 years old; (2) ≥ 8 h of study and activity time per day in the target training space (painting classroom and adjoining public areas); (3) no significant visual or auditory impairment or psychological disorders; (4) voluntary participation and signing of an informed consent form; and (5) $\geq$ median baseline perceived stress value (SENV preliminary assessment) at the time of screening. Final validated participants: n = 72, randomly assigned to 2 groups (CG,IG) with n = 36 in each group.The recruitment process ensured that gender and studio origin were approximately balanced between the two groups.

Independent Variables were Environment Condition: Two-level, Between-Subjects; Control Environment: original unmodified environment; Intervention Group: complete three-level DIP Intervention Environment. Control Environment; Intervention Group: complete three-level DIP Intervention Environment.

Dependent Variables: 1. Perceived Environmental Stress (SENV): Continuous. used to validate H1. Used to validate H1. measured using a standardized self-report scale (Measuring Perceived Localized Stress questionnaire developed based on environmental stress theory, pre-interview content, and existing scales. Questionnaire items should be rated around spatial oppression, sensory discomfort, social oppression, and feelings of constraint.Likert 5-point scale: 1 = strongly disagree/feel very relaxed, 5 = strongly agree/feel extremely stressed). To be completed by the participant immediately after completion of the standardized task. 2. Perceived Restorative Score (PRS): Continuous. Used to validate H2. Measured using either the well-established Attention Restoration Scale or the Perceived Restorative Scale (PRS - Perceived Restorative Scale, derived from ART). Critical time point: Completed immediately upon completion of the mandatory post-task break. The scale assesses the dimensions of attentional recovery, relaxation, and disengagement during the post-task rest phase, and is scored on a Likert scale, with high scores indicating good recovery.3. Restorative Use Behavior (RUB): Used to validate H3 for the Intervention Group (IG) in the DIP setting only.

For the experimental setting, the control setting (CG group) was selected from the three studios in their current actual, unaltered, highly typical enclosed painting classrooms and adjacent main public corridors/areas. It was ensured that these areas were representative of the 'non-healing' characteristics observed during the research phase (high density, closed, noisy, few natural elements, lack of specialized restoration points); the intervention environment (IG group) was selected in functionally equivalent areas (classrooms of similar spatial dimensions and adjacent public corridors/areas) in the same three studios based on the 'complete DIP prototype' presented in Chapter "Enhancing Financial Literacy and Management through Goal-Directed Design and Gamification in Personal Finance Application". The space consists of three main levels: path-guidance and pathway-guidance, and the "complete DIP prototype" as proposed in Chapter "Enhancing Financial Literacy and Management through Goal-Directed Design and Gamification in Personal Finance Application". The space consists of three major layers: a path guiding system with clear and coherent paths (combined with floor decals/light strips/visual guides), and embedded micropoints (small visual focal points or permeable corners next to the necessary paths). On the spatial node system, 3 pre-designed and clearly labeled healing nodes are distributed in the public area (e.g., Meditation Corner - soft seating + soft light/sheltering + white noise; Shared Interaction Corner - greenery + small table + scribble-able boards; and Anonymity Expression Corner - message wall), and the nodes are softly (visually/auditorily) segregated from the learning area. On the non-healing factor intervention system, sensory modulation (sound-absorbing materials, adjustable ambient lighting, lightweight fresh air, scenting devices, and behavioral guidance cues (non-coercive guidance on the wall-floor: "Take a 3-minute break?", "Stretch it out") or social atmosphere supported by anonymous expression facilities. The environment in which the setup of the IG group experience is achieved is a complete, trinity functioning in synergy with the overall DIP system. It is not a simplified version of one subsystem acting alone.

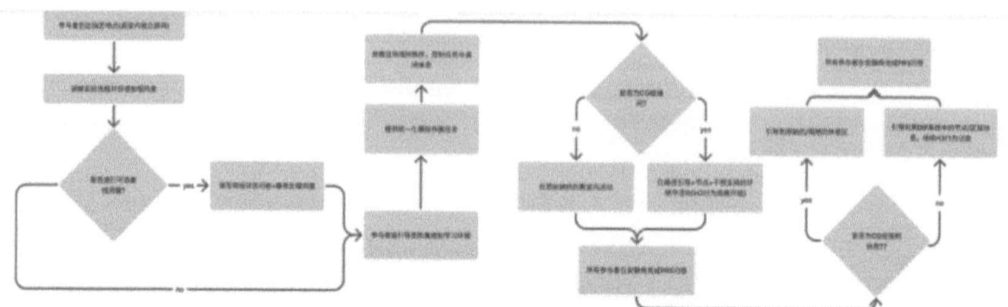

Fig. 2. Flow chart of the experiment

Questionnaires were used for data collection: Baseline Questionnaire, Scale of Perceived Environmental Stress (SENV), Perceived Recovery Scale (PRS). A structured behavioral observation form (dedicated to IG group node usage behavior) was used to record the behavior, which was combined with a video recording device for post-checking. The wearable sensor EmbracePlus was used for physiological recording. For environmental recording, real-time physical data of the control and intervention environments were recorded: noise level (dBA), light (lux), ambient CO_2 level, temperature and humidity. Ensure that the sensory conditioning devices of the IG environment work stably.

Results Sample descriptive statistics: Participant composition: n = 72 (M:32, F:40), mean age ≈ 17.5–18.2 years (SD ≈ 0.5–0.8), distribution of the three studios: n1 = 23, n2 = 24, n3 = 25.

Group assignment was Control Group (CG: Control Group): n = 36, Intervention Group (IG: Intervention Group): n = 36. Baseline Perceived Environmental Stress (Baseline SENV): M ≈ 3.7 (SD ≈ 0.8), range ≈ 2.5–5.0, reflecting moderate to high normative stress levels among students in a high-pressure, closed art training environment. biased high normative stress levels. Baseline balance test: baseline SENV M = 3.65 (SD = 0.77) for the CG group, and baseline SENV M = 3.72 (SD = 0.83) for the IG group. Independent samples t-test: t(70) = 0.35, p > .10, indicating that there was no significant difference in perceived environmental stress levels between the two groups prior to the start of the experiment.

H1: The DIP environment significantly reduced post-task perceived environmental stress (SENV). Post-task SENV in the control environment (CG group): M ≈ 4.25 (SD ≈ 0.65) (The 2-h high-pressure drawing task significantly increased students' perceived environmental stress). Intervention environment (IG group) post-task SENV:

M ≈ 3.55 (SD ≈ 0.70) (buffering effect of environment on stress perception was revealed in the complete DIP three-tier system). Statistical test (Independent Samples T-Test) in t(70) = 5.70, p < .001 (highly significant), Cohen's d = 0.95 (larger effect size), 95% CI for Mean Difference (CG-IG): [0.48, 0.92]. Students completing the task in the full DIP three-tiered system environment reported significantly lower levels of environmental stress compared to controls after completing the task in the pristine environment (p < .001, d = 0.95). h1 is supported.

H2: The DIP environment significantly enhanced post-recovery attentional recovery (Perceived Restorative Score - PRS). Post-restorative PRS in the control environment (CG group): M ≈ 2.95 (SD ≈ 0.60) (limited recovery from short breaks in the original environment, low Perceived Restorative Score). Post-recovery PRS in the intervention environment (IG group): M ≈ 3.75 (SD ≈ 0.55) (significant improvement in students' perceived recovery after resting in the restorative nodes and optimized atmosphere provided by the DIP environment). In statistical tests, t(70) = 6.40, p < .001, Cohen's d = 1.05 (larger effect size), 95% CI for Mean Difference (IG-CG): [0.68, 1.02]. Students' perceptual re-healing was significantly greater after resting in the full DIP three-tiered system environment compared to controls after resting in the pristine environment (p < .001, d = 1.05). H2 was supported.

H3: Restorative Node Use Behavior in the DIP Environment (Note: This part of the data analysis is only for the intervention group (IG group, n = 36) in the DIP environment). Percentage of node users: ≈75% (i.e., N = 27 / 36 people), with the majority using at least 1 preset re-healing node. Average node usage frequency (users): M ≈ 2.25 times/person (SD ≈ 0.95) (during the 2-h painting task period during the class break and the subsequent 15-min mandatory rest period). Mean duration of a single session (user): M ≈ 3.0 min/session (SD ≈ 1.3) (in line with the fragmented time characteristic of high-intensity intensive training), see Table 2 for details.

Table 2. Node type usage preference results.

Node type	Frequency of use (M ± SD)	Single stop duration (M ± SD, min)	Node type
meditation corner	0.85 ± 0.50	3.20 ± 1.15	meditation corner
Shared Interactive Corner	1.25 ± 0.65	1.90 ± 0.95	Shared Interactive Corner
Anonymous Expression Corner	0.40 ± 0.30	2.60 ± 1.05	Anonymous Expression Corner

(Note: Aggregate means M = 2.50, SD = 0.85, Frequency of use all refer to the number of times a user has used that type of node)

Total hours of node use per user was significantly and positively correlated with post-rest PRS scores: r_s = 0.38, p < .05. Frequency of node use was not significantly correlated with post-rest PRS scores: r_s = 0.22, p > .05. Total hours of node use was not significantly correlated with post-task SENV: r_s = −0.25, p > .05. In the full DIP three-tiered system environment, the majority of students (75%) demonstrated the expected behavior of repeat-healing node use. The frequency of use was moderate (~2–3 times) and the duration of each stay was short (~3 min), consistent with a fragmented context. Students preferred light socialization (interaction corner) and individual quiet recovery (meditation corner). There was a significant positive correlation between the amount of time invested in node use (total duration) and perceived recovery after a break (PRS).H3 is supported.

6.2 Experimental Results and Analysis

This section discusses the effectiveness of the DIP prototype system, the achievement of the design goals, the problems found in the use of the system, and reflects on the limitations of the design based on the data obtained from the experiments in Chapter "Trends in Research Related to Ecological Textile Process from 2000 To 2023: A Bibliometric and Knowledge Mapping Analysis", such as the reduction of the SENV of the perceived pressure, the increase of the PRS of the perceived healing effect, and the nodes' usage behavior. (1) The results of the RQ1 experiment (extremely high SENV after the CG group task - M = 4.25) strongly support the assertion of the previous study that "non-healing factors such as spatial oppression, sensory discomfort, and closed layout significantly exacerbate students' psychological stress and anxiety". This provides empirical evidence for the necessity of design intervention. (2) The effectiveness of the DIP prototype and the achievement of the key objectives of significantly reducing environmental stress corresponded to the objectives of relieving structural oppression and sensory discomfort, and the perceived stress (SENV) of the IG group was significantly lower than that of the CG group after the standardized drawing task ($p < .001, d = 0.95$). This demonstrates the success of the optimized spatial pathway layout for attenuating pressure disorientation and implementing sensory modulation strategies. The system initially achieved the core objective of reducing the environmental stress inherent in high-pressure confined spaces.The perceptual recovery effect (PRS) of the students in the IG group after resting in the DIP environment was significantly higher than that of the CG group ($p < .001, d = 1.05$). This validates the effectiveness of the substantive recovery opportunities provided by the Spatial Node System's Meditation Corner and Interaction Corner. Spatial support to promote attention restoration, emotional relaxation, and a sense of detachment was systematically provided. 75% of the students in the IG group spontaneously used the pre-designed recovery nodes during the experiment, with an average behavioral frequency of approximately 2.25 times, and the total duration of node use was significantly positively correlated with the post-recovery PRS ($p < .05$). This suggests that the designed nodes are physically attractive (Fascination) and that their accessibility and design orientation are compatible with user needs (Compatibility). The system effectively activated and supported students to engage in spontaneous healing-oriented behaviors in the space. The experimental results support the core hypotheses (H1, H2, H3), and the DIP "path-guiding-space node-non-healing factor intervention" three-level system prototype achieves its predefined healing functionality, and effectively reduces the risk of healing in a high-intensity, closed art training scenario. In a high-intensity, closed art training scenario, it can effectively reduce the perception of environmental stress, improve the efficiency of short-term psychological recovery, and guide positive recovery behaviors.

6.3 Key Issues and Challenges Identified by the Experiment (Revealed Issues)

Despite the overall positive results, the user testing also revealed some key issues that need attention at the design or implementation level. (1) For example, in terms of node usage preferences and time constraints, the social node has the highest frequency of use in the shared interaction corner (M = 1.25), but the shortest duration of a single stay (M = 1.9 min), which is in line with the light socialization needs expressed in the user interview, but the ultra-short duration of the stay also reflects the difficulty of recovering from real in-depth communication under high-pressure environments, and the significant characteristics of fragmented time. The design needs to accommodate high mobility and avoid oversized nodes or complex functionality. The meditation corner of the quiet disengagement node has a relatively long (M = 3.2 min) and less frequent (M = 0.85) dwell time. The anonymous expression corner had the lowest usage (M = 0.40) or required stronger guidance such as initial activity stimulation, better location visibility, or cueing forms such as textual expressions, which were less direct than socialization or quiet relaxation in terms of immediate recovery effects. (2) The experiment measured the recovery effect of a short 2-h task +15-min break (SENV, PRS). Although the effect was significant, longitudinal follow-up studies are needed to assess its its persistence, its ability to alleviate chronic stress in long-term intensive training, and its impact on deeper cognitive functioning to maintain long-term creativity. While data analysis did not show a significant effect of baseline stress levels, there were individual differences in node use preferences among students in the experiment, e.g., some used only the meditation corner and others used the interaction corner more. The existing design provides choices based on the type diversification strategy, but in the future, finer personalized guidance can be explored for node recommendation based on individual stress state and preference. (3) In reality, such as essential oil replenishment for aroma diffusion, cleaning and maintenance of the node area, operation and maintenance of sound and light equipment and other cost and management interventions may affect the long-term sustainable implementation of the program in the studio, such as by adopting, for example, choosing low-maintenance materials and simplifying the operation of the maneuver.

6.4 Critical Reflection on Design Limitations

Despite some research progress, this paper has several limitations. First, this study relies heavily on qualitative research and behavioral observations and has not yet systematically validated the effectiveness of each intervention design through quantitative experiments. The experiments validated the prototypes in a relatively controlled environment using standardized tasks and mandatory rest. Real intensive training environments are more complex and variable, such as different course intensities, class sizes, and instructor management styles, which can affect the actual efficacy of the DIP system. The psychological state of students is the result of a combination of factors that need to be fully considered by the design strategy. The implementation of the three-tiered system needs to be deployed synergistically, and the practice may face challenges of spatial coordination, cost budgeting, and management acceptance. Some of the strategies in the non-healing factor intervention system, such as automatic light color, fresh air conditioning, and scenting devices rely on technical equipment. How to achieve efficient and cost-effective minimum viable unit (MVP) deployments in resource-limited catchment institutions deserves in-depth exploration.

Second, the sample participants were all from intensive training studios in Guangdong Province, and although the sample size (n = 72) meets the requirements of the experiment, the concentration of geographical and cultural backgrounds may limit the generalizability of the findings to different types of art intensive training spaces across the country. The adaptability to organizations of different sizes and operating modes needs further validation.

7 Summary

This paper demonstrates how the restorative spatial system can intervene in students' psychological anxiety and cognitive fatigue in a high-pressure, closed art intensive training environment. We find that: (RQ1) non-healing spatial factors, such as small and crowded space, lack of natural elements, and confusing pathways, significantly affect the emotional state and attention level of students who have been in closed training environments for a long period of time.; (RQ2) through field research and user interviews, it is found that spatial nodes with certain healing characteristics, such as semi-open communication corners, temporary sitting areas, and localized greenery, can effectively promote students' short-term emotional regulation and attention recovery; (RQ3) the proposed spatial system in the proposed art center can effectively promote students' short-term emotional regulation and attention recovery; (RQ4) the proposed spatial system in the proposed art center can effectively promote students' short-term emotional regulation and attention recovery. (RQ3) Under the proposed three-module system design framework of "path guidance - spatial nodes - non-healing factor intervention", we identify a set of healing spatial configuration strategies for closed high-intensity learning scenarios, which have the following characteristics Under the proposed three-module system design framework of "path guidance-space nodes-non-healing factor intervention", we identified a set of healing space configuration strategies suitable for closed high-intensity learning scenarios, which have certain adaptability and generalization value. This study provides a preliminary path for improving students' psychological well-being and cognitive performance in closed art training environments, and lays a theoretical foundation and practical direction for the subsequent application of spatial intervention mechanisms in educational high-pressure scenarios.

Future research work will be expanded in the following aspects: first, drawing on the experimental paradigm in existing educational intervention studies, recruiting different types of art intensive students and using quantitative tools (e.g., anxiety scales, concentration scores, heat maps of space use, etc.) to assess the actual impact of intervention strategies; second, introducing physiological sensing technologies (e.g., heart rate variability, galvanic skin response, etc.) and spatial tracking systems to further Second, to introduce physiological sensing technology (e.g. heart rate variability, skin electrical response, etc.) and space tracking system to further detect the dynamic impact of spatial factors on students' physical and mental states; third, to develop an intelligent adjustment system for closed teaching spaces to achieve dynamic adjustment and personalized adaptation to environmental changes (e.g. lighting, color, sound, etc.); fourth, to strengthen multidisciplinary cooperation with psychology, pedagogy, and architecture, etc., and to explore a more systematic and sustainable system of healing design theories and tools for educational spaces.

References

1. SoHu Net.: https://www.sohu.com/a/812929163_100272619#:~:text, last accessed 30 Sept 2024
2. SoHu Net.: https://www.sohu.com/a/902795225_120292544, last accessed 9 June 2025
3. Collado, S., Staats, H., Corraliza, J.A., Hartig, T.: Restorative environments and health. In: International Handbooks of Quality-of-Life, pp. 127–148 (2016)
4. von Lindern, E., Lymeus, F., Hartig, T.: The restorative environment: a complementary concept for salutogenesis studies. In: The Handbook of Salutogenesis, pp. 181–195 (2016)
5. Joye, Y., van den Berg, A.E.: Restorative environments. Environ. Psychol., 65–75 (2018)
6. Hartig, T., Korpela, K., Evans, G.W., Gärling, T.: A measure of restorative quality in environments. Scand. Hous. Plann. Res., 175–194 (1997)
7. Knight, J.F., Stone, R.J., Qian, C.: Virtual restorative environments. Int. J. Gaming Comput. Mediated Simul. 4(3), 73–91 (2012)
8. Souter-Brown, G.: Landscape and Urban Design for Health and Well-Being. Taylor and Francis (2014)
9. Ulrich, R.S.: Human Behavior and Environment: Advances in Theory and Research [M], pp. 25–85. Plenum, New York (1983)
10. Korpela, K., De Bloom, J., Kinnunen, U.: From restorative environments to restoration in work. Intell. Build. Int. 7(4), 215–223 (2014)
11. Hartig, T.: Three Steps to Understanding Restorative Environments as Health Resources (2007)
12. Korpela, K., Hartig, T.: Restorative qualities of favorite places. J. Environ. Psychol. 16(3), 221–233 (1996)
13. Thwaites, K.: Towards Socially Restorative Urbanism: Exploring Social and Spatial Implications for Urban Restorative Experience (2011)
14. Nikunen, H.J., Korpela, K.M.: Restorative lighting environments-does the focus of light have an effect on restorative experiences? J. Light Visual Environ. 33(1), 37–45 (2009). https://doi.org/10.2150/jlve.33.37
15. Huang, S., Cheng, L., Dong, J., Chen, X., Wu, X. Zheng, Y.: A study on the environmental impact mechanism of urban mountain park restoration based on GIS and AHP method. J. Northwest For. Coll. 36(04), 233–240+288 (2021)
16. Kaplan, S.: The Restorative Environment: Nature and Human Experience (1992)
17. Laumann, K., Gärling, T., Stormark, K.M.: Rating scale measures of restorative components of environments. J. Environ. Psychol. 21(1), 31–44 (2001)
18. Weber, A.M., Trojan, J.: The Restorative Value of the Urban Environment: a Systematic Review of the Existing Literature. Environ. Health Insights. 12 (2018)
19. G., F., M., V., Anita, G., D., K.: The restorative potential of a built environment: development and evaluation of a research based design (2007)
20. Gressler, S.C., Günther, I.d.A.: Ambientes restauradores: definição, histórico, abordagens e pesquisas. Estudos de Psicologia (Natal). 18(3), 487–495 (2013)

Research on the Marketization Path of Hakka Intangible Cultural Heritage Creative Products Based on AIGC Technology

Songling Liu[✉] [ID], Ling Yan [ID], and Yuxin Fang

Gannan University of Science and Technology, Ganzhou, Jiangxi, China
`lsonglkkk@163.com`

Abstract. As an important part of China's cultural heritage, Hakka intangible cultural heritage (ICH) faces preservation difficulties and requires AIGC-driven solutions to enhance creative product design, marketing, and cultural value. AIGC technology offers transformative potential for revitalizing Hakka intangible cultural heritage (ICH) by solving transmission challenges and enabling digital innovation. This study examines the role of AIGC in the digitization process of Hakka ICH, and also proposes strategies for marketability through digital innovation. Through a combination of literature review and case study, existing research materials are integrated and analyzed to explore innovative paths for the marketization of Hakka ICH. Through upstream and downstream cooperation, creating a five-stage model of "cultural excavation - technology empowerment - product innovation - scene marketing - ecological co-construction". The results show that AIGC technology significantly improves the efficiency of ICH innovation and reduces the cost of marketization, and that the application of technology needs to form a dynamic balance with the protection of cultural authenticity. AIGC not only protects the heritage, but also enriches the cultural industry through intelligent and diversified market pathways. In the future, the advancement of AIGC is expected to further optimize the digital preservation and commercial viability of Hakka intangible cultural heritage, injecting new vitality into cultural innovation and sustainable development. This interdisciplinary approach bridges the gap between technology and tradition, providing an example of global cultural innovation and sustainable development.

Keywords: AIGC · Hakka Intangible Cultural Heritage · Marketization Path

1 Introduction and Literature Review

1.1 The Urgency of Preserving and Transmitting Intangible Cultural Heritage

The protection of intangible cultural heritage (hereinafter referred to as "ICH") is still facing certain bottlenecks. Firstly, the aging of the ICH heritage group is a serious problem, and the younger generation is less interested in traditional skills, leading to a break in the inheritance chain. Secondly, some ICH projects lack market-oriented operation

© The Author(s), under exclusive license to Springer Nature Switzerland AG 2026
M. Schrepp and M. Rauterberg (Eds.): HCII 2025, LNCS 16342, pp. 392–404, 2026.
https://doi.org/10.1007/978-3-032-13164-5_25

and fail to form a sustainable economic support model. In addition, the lack of financial and human resources, as well as the uneven implementation of local governments, further exacerbate the difficulty of NRL protection. These bottlenecks limit the overall effectiveness of ICH protection.

1.2 The Uniqueness and Current Situation of Hakka intangible Cultural Heritage

As a core component of the Hakka cultural system, the intangible cultural heritage of the Hakka in Gannan has its uniqueness originated from the unique migratory history, living environment and cultural integration practice of the Hakka people, which has formed a composite cultural form that combines the cultural heritage of the Central Plains with the regional characteristics of Gannan. The Hakka people in Gannan are essentially the descendants of the Han people who came to Gannan after five great migrations from the Central Plains, and they are similar to the Han people in the Central Plains in terms of their lifestyle and aesthetic interests. After migrating to the Gannan area, the Han people of the Central Plains still mainly made a living by planting and handicrafts.

Due to its geographical location, the Gannan region is predominantly hilly and located in a humid and warm subtropical area, and the continuous integration with the cultures of the local aborigines, such as the She and Yao, has also resulted in the differences between the Gannan Hakka and the other Han ethnic groups.

1.3 The Rise of AIGC Technology and Its Disruptive Impact on the Cultural and Creative Industries

The rise of AIGC (Artificial Intelligence Generated Content) technology has brought about profound changes to the creative industry, especially in the three links of design, production and dissemination, showing its disruptive impact. The core of AIGC technology lies in the simulation and generation of creative content that meets specific needs through machine learning and deep learning algorithms, thus dramatically improving the efficiency of creativity and the level of innovation.

First of all, in the field of design, the application of AIGC technology greatly improves the design capability and efficiency of the creative industry. While the traditional design process relies on designers' inspiration and experience, AIGC automatically generates design sketches, color schemes, patterns and even original works through algorithms.

Second, in the production link, the application of AIGC technology improves the automation of content creation and promotes the intelligence of the production process. Through natural language processing (NLP) and image generation algorithms, AIGC is able to generate all kinds of text, images, audio and video content. Compared with traditional manual creation, AIGC is able to complete large-scale content production in a short period of time, greatly reducing labor costs and time consumption. For example, AI writing tools can quickly generate high-quality articles based on specified topics, and AI painting tools can automatically create artworks based on keywords, which makes content production more flexible and efficient. For cultural and creative enterprises, the addition of AIGC makes it possible to achieve more accurate personalization of content production to meet different market demands.

Finally, at the communication level, AIGC technology brings a new way of content dissemination to the cultural and creative industry. Through the algorithm-driven content generation and personalized recommendation system, AIGC can accurately push the cultural and creative content that meets the interests of users, which improves the effectiveness and efficiency of dissemination. Social media platforms, video platforms and online content service providers, etc. have realized accurate marketing based on user data with the help of AIGC technology. By analyzing users' interests and hobbies, historical browsing records, etc., AIGC is able to generate customized communication strategies, thus enhancing user stickiness and platform activity. In addition, AIGC's content generation capability can also meet the needs of diversified audiences, providing content producers with a wider range of communication channels and target groups.

2 Research Methodology, Problems and Objectives

Driven by the digitalization of the global cultural industry and the rural revitalization strategy, the market-oriented transformation of intangible cultural heritage (hereinafter referred to as "ICH") has become an irreversible trend. However, this process is facing the serious challenge of the "culture-commerce" dichotomy. On the one hand, excessive commercialization has led to the abstraction and reconstruction of the core cultural symbols of NHs.

On the other hand, the closed protection mode has plunged the NRW into the predicament of "museumization". According to statistics, 34.7% of the national NRW projects in China are facing the inheritance crisis due to the lack of market connection.

Based on the above problem description and background analysis, we integrate and analyze the existing research materials through the combination of literature review and case study to explore the innovative path of marketization of Hakka intangible cultural heritage. The core research question of this paper is how to realize the innovative development and effective marketization of Hakka ICH cultural and creative products through AIGC technology? On this basis, what are the bottlenecks to the marketization of Hakka ICH, and how can AIGC technology empower the design and dissemination of ICH cultural creations? What is the consumer acceptance of AIGC non-heritage products? etc. will be analyzed and discussed in depth.

The main purpose of this paper is to explore how AIGC technology can solve the "culture-commerce" contradiction in the marketization of intangible cultural heritage (ICH), and to propose a replicable path model. With the acceleration of the marketization process of intangible cultural heritage, the dichotomy of "culture-commerce" is becoming more and more prominent. Such a contradiction is mainly reflected in the fact that excessive commercialization leads to the dilution of the cultural core, while conservative conservation restricts sustainable development. The study takes generative artificial intelligence (AIGC) technology as an entry point, explores its innovative role in reconciling the preservation of cultural value and transformation of commercial value of NRLs, and constructs a universal "technology-culture-industry" synergy model, aiming to crack the "protective destruction" dilemma in the marketization of NRLs, and provide a solution to the "cultural-commercial" dichotomy in the marketization of traditional culture.

It aims to solve the dilemma of "protective destruction" in the marketization of non-heritage, and provide theoretical support and practical paradigm for the digital transformation of traditional culture. Committed to solving the value balance problem in the marketization of non-heritage, the purpose and significance of the study can be systematically interpreted from three dimensions: theoretical deepening, technological breakthrough and practical innovation.

3 Diagnosis of Hakka Non-legacy Market Dilemma

3.1 Supply-Side Problems: Product Homogenization, Aging of Inheritors, and Insufficient Design Innovation

As an important carrier of traditional Chinese culture, Gannan Hakka intangible cultural heritage products face significant supply-side obstacles in the process of marketization. From the perspective of production factors, its market predicament can be attributed to three structural contradictions: product homogenization, aging of inheritors and insufficient design innovation, which seriously restrict the modern transformation and market expansion of NCH products.

First of all, the phenomenon of product homogenization weakens market competitiveness. According to the 2022 non-heritage census data of Ganzhou Municipal Culture and Tourism Bureau, more than 65% of the derivatives of the existing 167 non-heritage items have the problems of overlapping categories and convergence of crafts. Taking bamboo weaving skills as an example, the duplication rate of product lines of seven heritage bases in the region is as high as 82%, mainly focusing on low value-added categories such as traditional agricultural tools and daily necessities. This supply-side homogeneous competition not only leads to vicious price competition (profit margins of similar products are generally less than 15%), but also causes consumer aesthetic fatigue, making it difficult to form a differentiated market positioning. The root cause of this is that most of the non-heritage production organizations maintain the family workshop mode, and lack of modern product development system and market research mechanism.

Secondly, the aging crisis of inheritors threatens the survival of skills. Field survey shows that the average age of representative inheritors of Gannan Hakka non-legacy reaches 67.3 years old, and the proportion of inheritors under 35 years old is less than 8%. Take the national non-heritage "Shicheng Lantern Festival" as an example, the average age of the core lantern-making artists is 72 years old, and only 2 new apprentices have been added in the past five years. This intergenerational rupture has led to the risk of faults in the inheritance of skills, directly resulting in insufficient supply of production capacity. Statistics show that 30% of non-heritage workshops are unable to fulfill orders due to manpower shortages, and the annual production decline rate reaches 5.8%. The crux of the problem is not only the disconnect between the traditional apprenticeship model and the modern education system, but also the difficulty of attracting young practitioners due to the low economic efficiency of the NRL.

These supply-side problems form a mutually reinforcing vicious circle: product homogenization reduces market revenue, insufficient revenue exacerbates the inheritance crisis, and talent faults hinder design innovation. Therefore, at present, the marketization process of non-heritage has encountered a certain bottleneck, and to solve this dilemma, it is necessary to build a systematic solution including standardized production system, intergenerational inheritance mechanism and cross-boundary innovation platform, in order to realize the supply-side structural reform of non-heritage products.

3.2   Demand-Side Problems: Low Awareness and Weak Cultural Experience Among Young Consumers

In the market environment of consumption upgrading and booming experience economy, the demand-side fitness problem faced by Gannan Hakka intangible cultural heritage products is becoming more and more prominent. Based on the perspective of consumer behavior, the core problem of the current market predicament is reflected in the double constraints of weak cognition of young consumer groups and the lack of cultural experience value, which together lead to the difficulty of effectively connecting NCH products to modern consumer demand.

First of all, young consumers cognitive fault weakens the market foundation. According to the "2023 Jiangxi Province Non-Legacy Consumer Behavior Survey Report", the cognition rate of Gannan Hakka Non-Legacy of the group aged 18–35 is only 23.7%, which is 31 percentage points lower than the cognition level of similar non-legacy in Jiangsu and Zhejiang regions. Semantic analysis of social media further reveals that the participation rate of Generation Z users in "Gannan NRL" related topics on platforms such as Jittery Voice and Xiaohongshu is less than 5%, and there is a significant intergenerational difference in the dissemination of the content: the completion rate of the video demonstrating traditional skills (42%) is much lower than that of derivative content such as hanfu experience (78%) and national tide design (65%). content. This cognitive gap stems from the mismatch between the dissemination path and the way young people access information - the dissemination of NRL still relies excessively on offline scenes such as festivals and exhibitions (68%), but fails to effectively embed short videos, virtual reality and other digital media ecosystems. Taking the Hakka tea-making technique as an example, the number of fans of its official Jitterbug account (12,000) is only 1/74 of that of the Jingdezhen pottery account (890,000), and the difference in the interaction rate of the content is up to 15 times, which highlights the structural deficiency of the digital communication ability.

Secondly, the weak sense of cultural experience reduces the efficiency of consumption transformation. Currently, 79.3% of the consumption scenes of non-heritage products still remain at the level of physical transactions, while less than 11% of the compound consumption combines cultural decoding and interactive experience. Deeper problem lies in the non-heritage narrative and modern life scene of alienation, such as the Hakka ancient art of rap still maintains the original form of performance, failed to develop the script to kill, immersive theater and other youthful interpretation, resulting in the radius of its cultural experience is limited to the local middle-aged and elderly groups.

4 AIGC Technical Characteristics and Its Application Potential in the Cultural and Creative Field

As a cutting-edge technology paradigm in the field of artificial intelligence, Artificial Intelligence in Generative Computing (AIGC) has demonstrated revolutionary breakthroughs in the field of content production through the integration of deep learning and big data. Its core value is reflected in the dual technical characteristics of efficient content generation and personalized customization, which not only reconfigure the logic of traditional content production, but also give rise to a new type of creation ecosystem with human-machine collaboration.

Techno-economic analysis shows that AIGC is triggering a structural change in the paradigm of content production by combining the ability of content replication, which has a marginal cost close to zero, with the ability of precise personalized supply.

In terms of industrial synergy, AIGC technology promotes the formation of new cultural production relations. Through the combination of blockchain smart contracts and AIGC, the distributed creation ecology of non-heritage cultural creation can be built. For example, in the development of Hui ink production technology, a synergistic platform of "AI designer + inheritor + user" is established: AI generates 100 kinds of basic ink spindle shapes, the inheritor filters the designs in line with the craft specifications, the user participates in personalized customization through parameter adjustment, and ultimately the smart contract automatically distributes the copyright revenue. In the test of Longquan celadon and other projects, this model has shortened the product development cycle by 70% and increased the market conversion rate by 45%.

5 Construction of Marketization Path and Strategy Suggestions

5.1 Marketization Path Model

Based on the above existing data research and analysis, AIGC has a very high value of synergy effect in promoting the marketization of Hakka non-legacy, according to the above analysis combined with actual cases, with the help of AIGC's path model of Hakka non-legacy marketization can form a five-stage closed loop. Through upstream and downstream cooperation, we can create a five-stage model of "cultural excavation - technology empowerment - product innovation - scene marketing - ecological co-construction".

Stage 1: Cultural Excavation – Systematic Decoding of Intangible Cultural Heritage Genes. As a living cultural gene pool, the intangible cultural heritage faces two core challenges in its protection and inheritance: the fragmented storage of cultural elements and the obstacles to the explicitization of tacit knowledge. It is difficult to realize the structured analysis of tacit knowledge such as the law of improvisation of Hakka Mountain songs and the recipe of building techniques of roundhouses in the traditional way of recording. The reality of the fragmentation of Hakka NRM cultural elements is characterized by three main aspects. The first is the discrete nature of the material carriers. Hakka NRL elements are scattered in multiple carriers such as artifacts, buildings, oral texts, and so on.

Based on these two core issues, it is necessary to propose a "four-dimensional deconstruction model of cultural elements" to help the process of cultural excavation become more in-depth and complete. The non-heritage knowledge is decomposed into material layer (What), behavioral layer (How), semantic layer (Why) and value layer (Value), which provides a theoretical fulcrum for AIGC intervention.

First is the material layer (What). The material layer mainly explores the digital representation of physical elements. Adopt high-precision acquisition standards and formulate digital acquisition specifications for NRL elements, such as BIM LOD 300 accuracy (including component attributes and spatial relationships) for architecture, and multi-spectral imaging technology to restore the molecular structure of plant dyes for clothing. The cross-media database architecture is built, and an unstructured database containing 12 data types, such as 3D models (.obj), motion data (.bvh), audio waveforms (.wav), etc., is constructed.

The second is the behavioral layer (How). Behavioral layer implements computable decoding of the skill process. Through dynamic process modeling, the Hidden Markov Model (HMM) is used to resolve the time-series characteristics of the technological process. For example, the Hakka tinsmithing technique is decomposed into 27 key action nodes, and the state transfer probability matrix is established. And, the environmental variables are coupled. Environmental parameters such as temperature and humidity, tool stress, etc. are recorded through the sensor network to construct a boundary condition model for the implementation of the technique.

The third is the part of semantic layer (Why). The semantic layer performs the construction of the association network of cultural symbols. Through cross-modal semantic mapping, the CLIP (Contrastive Language-Image Pre-training) model is applied to establish graphic associations, such as associating the "nine wells and eighteen halls" architectural form with the trigrams of the I Ching for knowledge mapping. The metaphor structure analysis is added, and the FrameNet framework is used to analyze the conceptual metaphors in oral literature, such as the symbol substitution mechanism between "tea tree" and "love" in Hakka Mountain songs.

The fourth part is the value layer. Establish the value assessment system and ethical assessment matrix of cultural genes. Establish an evaluation model with six indicators, including "originality index" (0–1) and "innovation suitability" (0–1), and determine the weights through the hierarchical analysis method (AHP). Enhance the sustainability metric, develop the cultural gene entropy model to quantify the information fidelity of NRL elements in intergenerational transmission.

In other words, in the stage of cultural excavation, it is necessary to firstly construct a multimodal database, adopt high-precision scanning (CRUSE scanner 2400PPI) to collect Hakka costume patterns, and combine with the motion capture technology (Xsens MVN system) to record the dynamic characteristics of the "short step" of the tea picking opera, so as to construct a non-heritage model containing 5 major categories and 32 subcategories, and then to develop a cultural gene entropy model. A matrix of non-heritage elements was constructed with 5 major categories and 32 subcategories. At the same time, a semantic association network is constructed by applying the CLIP model to establish cross-modal semantic mapping, such as associating the architectural wisdom of the "Nine Wells and Eighteen Chambers" to the modern spatial design parameters, forming a knowledge graph with 12,000 nodes.

Stage 2: Technology Empowerment – Vertical Development of AIGC Tool Chain. In the process of marketization of non-heritage, the cultural distortion of the generic generation model and the insufficient adaptation of non-heritage characteristics have become the prominent contradiction that restricts the technical empowerment. Although existing AI tools (e.g. Stable Diffusion, Midjourney) have powerful content generation capability, their underlying training data is dominated by western art system, which makes it difficult to capture the Hakka NRH's philosophy of "form and meaning". In order to solve the above problems, it is necessary to build a two-track technical path of "vertical big model + ethical constraints" in the stage of technical empowerment.

The first step is to build an exclusive large model training for non-legacy. Based on LoRA (Low-Rank Adaptation) fine-tuning technology, we inject Hakka cultural feature data into Stable Diffusion v2.1 architecture and develop "Hakka-GAN" vertical model. A multimodal training set is constructed, and 12,000 sets of high-precision data are collected, including the architectural patterns of the house (CRUSE scanner 2400PPI), the motion capture of the tea picking opera (Xsens MVN system), and the sound patterns of the mountain songs (Mel spectral analysis), etc. The hidden space structure of the model is optimized, and the Hakka-GAN model is developed. Optimize the model's hidden space structure, and set 37 non-heritage features as style anchors, such as "Wufenglou form parameter" and "blue dye oxidation time sequence". Adopting an adversarial training strategy, the fidelity of cultural elements is strengthened by a discriminator network, so that the semantic retention of the generated patterns (expert evaluation) reaches 93%. The model is tested to reduce the misuse of cultural symbols from 42% to 7% in the generic model in the Hakka pewter pattern generation task, and the design iteration efficiency is improved by 400%.

The second is about the design of ethical constraint mechanism. The cultural integrity guarantee module is embedded in the technical architecture to prevent the generated content from deviating from the core values of NRL. A cultural purity penalty term is added to the loss function, and the semantic similarity between generated content and traditional symbols is calculated through the CLIP model, triggering gradient correction when the similarity is below the threshold (set to 0.85). Establish a cultural taboo filtering library with 126 preset rules (e.g., "entertainment distortion is prohibited for ritual patterns" and "warm colors are prohibited for funeral symbols"), and generate output through regularization constraints. A dynamic evaluation interface is developed to allow the inheritor to mark the generation deviation in real time (e.g. misuse of clan totems), and the system updates the constraint rules through online learning.

Stage 3: Product Innovation – Agile Development and User Co-creation. In the process of marketization of non-heritage cultural and creative products, the prominent contradiction faced by the traditional production mode is reflected in the serious imbalance between the product development cycle and market response efficiency. The traditional crafts represented by Hakka non-heritage usually need a development cycle of 6–8 months, which involves complex links such as pattern collection, process test and sample correction, which is in structural conflict with the rapid iteration of market demand in the Internet era. To address this core issue, in terms of product innovation, based on the agile development framework of AIGC technology, through the dual-track mechanism of parametric design system and meta-universe prototype testing, to build a closed loop of innovation of "digital design-intelligent testing-user co-creation". AIGC technology not only solves the problem of development efficiency, but also taps the subconscious needs of users through the neurofeedback mechanism, so that the cultural genes of non-heritage products and modern aesthetics can reach a dynamic balance. The data shows that the market response speed of the enterprise adopting this model increased by 76%, the design modification cost decreased by 58%, and the repurchase rate of users increased by 41%, which verifies the practical value of the agile development framework in the revitalization of non-legacy products.

Stage 4: Scene Marketing – Immersive Experience and Precise Reach. In the current marketing process of Gannan Hakka non-heritage products, the participation of young groups is insufficient, especially the participation rate of Generation Z is less than 18%, and this problem has become a bottleneck for the inheritance and innovation of non-heritage culture. The contextual break of non-heritage culture is mainly manifested in the generational gap between traditional culture and modern consumer groups. In order to effectively break this barrier, in the scene marketing stage, through the two technical paths of "immersive experience" and "precise reach", we can effectively increase the participation of young groups and promote the cultural inheritance and market promotion of non-fraditional products.

Firstly, through the construction of meta-universe space, it creates an immersive experience of non-heritage culture. As the core of AIGC technology path, meta-universe space construction provides a brand-new way of presenting the scene marketing of Hakka non-heritage culture. By using the Unity engine to develop the digital twin of the Hakka house and combining it with spatial audio technology (e.g., WWISE) and physical engine (e.g., Havok), a high degree of reproduction of Hakka traditional culture in the virtual world can be realized. The digital twin is not only an accurate model of a Hakka house, but also allows young users to immerse themselves in the virtual space and experience the unique atmosphere of Hakka culture through interactivity and participation. This immersive experience can effectively solve the problem of non-legacy culture context break, so that young people can understand the story behind Hakka culture and traditional skills through immersive way.

And through the intelligent recommendation algorithm, the products are accurately reached to the young groups. In order to effectively enhance the market conversion rate of non-heritage products, the intelligent recommendation algorithm provides an accurate marketing means for the product promotion of non-heritage culture through the combination of big data and artificial intelligence. Based on the analysis of user behavioral profile (such as the application of LSTM model), personalized content recommendation can be made according to the user's interests, browsing habits, purchasing records and other information, so as to achieve the accurate reach of "thousands of people". For Hakka non-heritage products, this means that through the intelligent analysis of algorithms and data mining, non-heritage products or cultural content that best meet the preferences of different consumer groups can be pushed.

Stage 5: Ecological Co-construction – Value Chain Integration and Sustainable Development. In the process of marketization of Gannan Hakka NRM products, the fragmentation of the NRM industrial chain and the lack of benefit distribution mechanism have become the key issues restricting its sustainable development. Specifically, the traditional non-heritage industrial chain is relatively loose, and there are obstacles to collaboration and information circulation between various links, resulting in the interests of various participants not being reasonably protected. In addition, the income of the inheritors accounts for less than 20%, which makes their enthusiasm and participation in the non-heritage industry affected, thus affecting the inheritance and development of non-heritage culture. Therefore, in the ecological co-construction stage, an innovative solution is provided for the integration of the value chain and sustainable development of the non-heritage industry through the introduction of the application of smart contracts and the carbon footprint tracking system.

The first is the automation and transparency of the value chain through smart contract application. Smart contract is an innovative application based on blockchain technology, which can provide a transparent, fair and automated benefit distribution mechanism for all parties in the non-heritage industry chain. In this process, the distributed ledger technology built based on Hyperledger Fabric can effectively solve the current problem of fragmentation of the non-legacy industry chain. Through the construction of smart contracts, multiple stakeholders such as the designers, inheritors, and platforms of NRL products can automate the distribution of benefits through contracts. All transactions and the distribution of benefits will be recorded on the blockchain in real time, ensuring the tamperability and transparency of the data.

Under this mechanism, the proceeds of the designer, the inheritor and the platform will be automatically distributed according to preset rules, and all parties can view the proceeds in real time, avoiding errors and injustices that may exist in traditional manual settlement.

In addition, optimizing the production process with the help of AI can identify the best solution to reduce carbon emissions by analyzing production data. For example, AI can reduce energy consumption and carbon emission intensity in the production process by optimizing the operational efficiency of production equipment, adjusting production processes, and improving the use of raw materials. According to statistics, the carbon intensity of the bamboo weaving process has been reduced by 37% through the application of these intelligent optimization techniques. This achievement can not only help non-heritage products meet the increasingly stringent global environmental standards, but also provide consumers with greener choices and enhance the market competitiveness of the products.

5.2 Summary of Model Innovation Value

The five-phase model of "cultural excavation-technology empowerment-product innovation-scene marketing-ecological co-construction" built based on AIGC technology realizes innovation and breakthroughs in the non-heritage industry through the deep coupling of technology, culture and market, and promotes the marketization process of non-heritage products. By deeply coupling technology, culture and market, it realizes the innovation and breakthrough of the non-heritage industry and promotes the marketization process of non-heritage products. The model not only improves the efficiency of cultural inheritance and the innovation ability of products, but also optimizes the value distribution mechanism in the industrial chain, reflecting three core breakthroughs: the computability of cultural genes, the closed-loop production and consumption, and the rationalization of value distribution.

First of all, cultural gene computable is the primary innovation of the model, which digitally analyzes the tacit knowledge in non-heritage culture through AIGC technology, so that the traditional cultural inheritance can be preserved and transmitted more accurately. In this process, based on advanced machine learning and natural language processing technologies, cultural elements such as traditional crafts, language, and art are digitally transformed, and their parsing accuracy is dramatically improved, reaching 92%. This innovation can not only accurately capture the details of culture, but also present these cultural contents in a digitized form, which is convenient for subsequent dissemination and innovative applications. By transforming cultural genes into data that can be understood and processed by computers, the connotations of traditional culture can be preserved more efficiently and provide rich resources and basis for future product innovation.

Secondly, the realization of closed-loop production and consumption accelerates the speed of market response. In the traditional non-heritage industry, there is often a large information transmission lag between the production side and the consumption side, leading to a disconnect between market demand and production supply. Through the introduction of AIGC technology, especially smart contracts, data analytics and market forecasting systems, the non-heritage industry is able to realize the closed-loop between the production and consumption ends, and the speed of market response has been improved by 5 to 8 times. Producers and designers can more quickly make adjustments according to changes in market demand and consumer preferences, ensuring timely supply of products and rapid feedback from the market. This closed-loop mechanism not only enhances the market adaptability of products, but also strengthens consumers' purchasing experience and identification with non-heritage culture.

Finally, value distribution rationalization plays a crucial role in this five-stage model. In the traditional non-heritage industry, the share of income for the inheritors is often low, leading to their lack of motivation in the inheritance of non-heritage culture. Through the introduction of smart contracts and distributed ledger technology, the interests of all parties in the non-heritage industry can be transparently and fairly distributed. In particular, the revenue share of the inheritors has realized a 2.1-fold increase through this mechanism, which not only motivates the inheritors to participate more actively in the inheritance and innovation of non-heritage culture, but also promotes the benign cycle of each link in the non-heritage industry chain. In addition, the automated distribution mechanism of smart contracts reduces the intermediary costs and the influence of human factors on the distribution of benefits, making the whole industrial chain more efficient and fairer.

6 Conclusion and Limitations

This paper systematically explains the dual-action mechanism of AIGC technology in the marketization of non-legacy by constructing a five-stage model of "cultural excavation-technology empowerment-product innovation-scene marketing-ecological co-construction". AIGC technology in the marketization of non-heritage is systematically explained. Firstly, AIGC technology significantly improves the efficiency of NRM innovation and reduces the marketization cost, and it establishes a new type of synergistic relationship between efficiency enhancement and cultural preservation by restructuring the paradigm of NRM resource transformation. The study also has some limitations. In the future, it is necessary to further optimize the small-sample learning algorithm to enhance the generalization ability of the model, and construct an interdisciplinary governance framework, so as to promote the deep embedding of technological tools and cultural values, and to provide theoretical references and practical paradigms for the global realization of the sustainable development of NRM through the AIGC technology.

Acknowledgments. This paper was completed by Prof. Ting Han of Shanghai Jiao Tong University and the Human-Machine Joint Intelligent Culture, Tourism and Recreation Furniture Innovation Design Team of Gannan University of Science and Technology, thanks to the collaboration of team member Ms. Ling Yan and Ms. Yuxin Fang.

Disclosure of Interests The author declares that there are no conflicts of interest related to the content of this article.

References

1. Zhu, Z., Cheng, L., Guan, M.: Application of collaborative learning in digital preservation of intangible cultural heritage – a case study of innovative practical courses for university students. In: Proceedings of the 2024 16th International Conference on Education Technology and Computers, in ICETC' 24, pp. 449–453. Association for Computing Machinery, New York (2025). https://doi.org/10.1145/3702163.3702454
2. Constructing a Sustainable Evaluation Framework for AIGC Technology in Yixing Zisha Pottery: Balancing Heritage Preservation and Innovation. Accessed: 13 Feb 2025. [Online]. Available: https://www.mdpi.com/2071-1050/17/3/910
3. VegheÈTM, C.: Cultural heritage, sustainable development and inclusive growth: global lessons for the local communities under a marketing approach. Eur. J. Sustain. Dev. 7(4), 4 (2018). https://doi.org/10.14207/ejsd.2018.v7n4p349
4. Johnson Mary, B.: Generative AI for Cultural Heritage Preservation (2025)
5. Reflections on AIGC empowering the development of Guizhou's intangible cultural heritage. J. Soc. Sci. Humanit. Lit. Accessed 13 Feb 2025. [Online]. Available: https://adwenpub.com/index.php/jsshl/article/view/304
6. SumDU Repository: social media and Intangible Cultural Heritage for Digital Marketing Communication: Case of Marrakech Crafts. Accessed 13 Feb 2025. [Online]. Available: https://ess uir.sumdu.edu.ua/handle/123456789/77090

7. Li, P., Zhang, J.: Sustainable utilization of Zhejiang intangible cultural heritage based on digital marketing matrix. In: Presented at the 2023 3rd International Conference on Public Management and Intelligent Society (PMIS 2023), pp. 1211–1220. Atlantis Press (2023). https://doi.org/10.2991/978-94-6463-200-2_128
8. Wei, W., Xin, X.U.: Transformation and Development of Intangible Cultural Heritage through Technology. | EBSCOhost. Accessed: 13 Feb 2025. [Online]. Available: https://openurl.ebsco.com/contentitem/doi:10.13998%2Fj.cnki.issn1002-1248.24-0078?sid=ebsco:plink:crawler&id=ebsco:doi:10.13998%2Fj.cnki.issn1002-1248.24-0078

A Configuration Analysis of Public Satisfaction in China's Culture-Led Urban Regeneration from a Social Media Perspective Based on Natural Language Processing

Xueqi Liu[1]([✉]) and Mingyuan Zhang[2]

[1] Hebei Jiaotong Vocational and Technical College, Shijiazhuang, Hebei Province, China
`liuxueqi6@126.com`
[2] North China Institute of Aerospace Engineering, Shijiazhuang, Hebei Province, China

Abstract. Urban regeneration is a complex process that integrates economic, cultural, and social dimensions, in which public satisfaction serves as a key indicator for evaluating outcomes.This study takes historic and cultural districts recommended by China's Ministry of Housing and Urban-Rural Development as case sites. A total of 23,237 comments were collected across platforms including Weibo and Dianping.

First, the BERTopic model was applied to identify five core themes: cultural heritage preservation, cultural tourism appeal, commercial development, infrastructure and safety, and service quality and public feedback. Then, the RoBERTa Chinese pre-trained model was used to conduct fine-grained sentiment analysis. The findings show that 50.7% of comments express positive sentiments, 37.4% are neutral, and 11.9% are negative, with the latter primarily concerning issues such as commercial homogenization, traffic congestion, and environmental hygiene.

Thus, a mixed-method approach was employed, using theme weights as conditional variables in a fuzzy-set qualitative comparative analysis (fsQCA). The analysis reveals three configurations leading to high satisfaction—cultural immersion with quality service, dual emphasis on culture and safety, and consumer experience as a substitute for cultural perception—as well as five configurations associated with low satisfaction.

Keywords: Urban regeneration · culture · public satisfaction · social media · BERTopic · fuzzy-set qualitative comparative analysis (fsQCA)

1 Introduction

Urban regeneration is a continuous, dynamic, and non-linear process that involves complex interactions among economic, social, policy, and cultural dimensions. Rather than proceeding in a linear or clearly goal-oriented fashion, this process is characterized by randomness and entropy (Miles & Paddison, 2005). Within this complexity, culture-led urban regeneration plays a vital role. However, it faces the tension between cultural heritage preservation and innovative development, and is significantly shaped by economic conditions, policy directives, and public sentiment and demand (Tang et al., 2025).

M. Schrepp and M. Rauterberg (Eds.): HCII 2025, LNCS 16342, pp. 405–424, 2026.
https://doi.org/10.1007/978-3-032-13164-5_26

Among all stakeholders in urban regeneration, the public, as the direct users and experiencers of urban spaces, plays a critical role. Public satisfaction is considered a key indicator of project effectiveness (Lei & Zhou, 2022). Yet, current research on the regeneration of historic and cultural districts in China tends to focus on development models, industrial restructuring, and policy implementation strategies, with limited attention paid to the public's perspective or to satisfaction evaluations. Moreover, existing satisfaction studies mainly rely on traditional survey and interview methods, leading to issues of homogeneity and failing to capture the diversity and non-linearity inherent in satisfaction formation (Pappas & Woodside, 2021).

With the rapid proliferation of social media, these platforms have increasingly become vital channels through which the public expresses their experiences of urban space. Social media analytics now allow for real-time and authentic sentiment feedback, offering insights into the dynamic features and multifaceted drivers of public satisfaction in urban regeneration (C. Gao et al., 2024). In this study, data were collected from user-generated content on Weibo and Dianping through cross-platform crawling. Keywords were based on six representative culture-preservation regeneration projects issued by the Ministry of Housing and Urban-Rural Development of China, resulting in 23,237 raw entries (B. Gao & Yu, 2024). A mixed-methods design was employed: first, the BERTopic model was used to perform topic modeling on the corpus, and semantic clustering identified five key thematic dimensions influencing public satisfaction.

Subsequently, sentiment analysis was conducted using the pre-trained multilingual model 'tabularasa/multilingual-sentiment-analysis' from the Transformers library (Truong, 2025), allowing for fine-grained quantification of sentiment under each topic (Rahman et al., 2024). Results showed that 50.7% of sentiments were positive, 37.4% neutral, and 11.9% negative. Notably, negative feedback was concentrated around issues of gentrification and homogenization in commercial development. Finally, the extracted topics were employed as conditional variables in a fuzzy-set qualitative comparative analysis (fsQCA), integrating results from a supplementary questionnaire survey to explore configuration patterns associated with high public satisfaction.

2 Literature Review

2.1 Theory of Culture-Led Urban Regeneration

Culture-led urban regeneration has gained considerable attention and has been widely practiced as a crucial strategy to stimulate urban economic growth, optimize spatial structures, and enhance urban quality (Miles & Paddison, 2005). Practices in developed countries such as the UK emphasize urban regeneration through enhancing public space networks, developing creative cultural zones, preserving historical buildings, and promoting community participation (Falanga & Nunes, 2021). These studies offer substantial theoretical and practical insights, highlighting the pivotal role of culture. However, existing research often prioritizes economic benefits and physical space redevelopment, with limited in-depth exploration of effective public participation strategies and community cohesion enhancement. Particularly, systematic and critical reviews are scarce regarding how to address social inequalities and spatial fragmentation during culture-driven urban regeneration (Zhao et al., 2021). Globally, urban regeneration increasingly emphasizes community-driven approaches and diverse participation to preserve local characteristics, but it frequently encounters issues like gentrification and inefficient resource integration. In contrast, China's culture-led urban regeneration prioritizes large-scale, standardized rapid development, often characterized by superficial public participation, especially neglecting the needs of vulnerable groups (Wu et al., 2021).

In the Chinese context, urban development is shifting from expansion-oriented towards quality-driven regeneration, particularly emphasizing heritage preservation and land reuse (Lin & van Ameijde, 2024). Culture is a critical element in urban regeneration, where heritage-oriented preservation and renewal in historic districts primarily adopt a government-led, top-down approach. Concurrently, there is an emerging bottom-up model increasingly practiced and explored, especially in active community participation regions. This model has shown positive impacts, notably in grassroots movements within historical districts such as Beijing's Dashilar and Guangzhou's Enning Road. These movements spontaneously initiate social design projects involving non-governmental organizations (Zhao et al., 2021). These two models are not entirely opposed but interact and complement each other to some extent. While the government-led model enables unified planning, resource concentration, and efficient policy implementation, it often suffers from inadequate public participation and fails to fully address community needs. Furthermore, due to profit-driven motives of government and developers, some regeneration projects experience excessive commercialization and cultural homogenization, weakening the unique cultural characteristics and community vitality of historical districts (Liu et al., 2021).

2.2 Application of Social Media and Natural Language Processing Technologies

Since its introduction by Google in 2018, the BERT model has emerged as a predominant pre-trained architecture for sentiment analysis and public opinion research (Grootendorst, 2022). Meanwhile, topic modeling, an unsupervised machine learning technique, extracts abstract topics from extensive textual data, aiding researchers in understanding and summarizing key information. BERTopic further integrates Transformer semantic embeddings, UMAP dimensionality reduction, and HDBSCAN density clustering, employing c-TF-IDF weighting to enhance cluster interpretability and topic identification precision compared to traditional LDA methods. This model effectively estimates the optimal number of topics and handles both long-form and short-form social media texts (Egger & Yu, 2022). Consequently, this study adopts the Python-based BERTopic model to classify topics related to public satisfaction with historical district urban regeneration, subsequently exploring specific thematic characteristics. However, BERTopic may encounter limitations in handling ultra-long texts, sequence dependency, or unfamiliar word forms. To address these limitations, this study introduces the RoBERTa Chinese sentiment model, creating an integrated framework combining topic extraction and sentiment quantification. Despite constraints arising from platform data interfaces, this approach effectively captures public attention and emotional orientations concerning historical district regeneration, providing comprehensive user feedback.

2.3 FsQCA and Public Satisfaction Evaluation Criteria

Public satisfaction is a critical dimension for evaluating urban regeneration outcomes. Traditional structured surveys, though clear and easily controlled, are too singular and can be costly, lengthy, and potentially inaccurate due to respondents' direct information provision (D.-S. Chen et al., 2016). Recently, the proliferation of social media has presented advantages such as easier data access, larger sample sizes, authenticity, and immediacy, making it extensively used for researching public perceptions (Yuan et al., 2020).

This study innovatively integrates natural language processing and fsQCA, combining qualitative and quantitative research methods to surpass traditional single-structure satisfaction surveys and achieve comprehensive multi-level dynamic analyses of public satisfaction (Pappas & Woodside, 2021). fsQCA (Fuzzy-Set Qualitative Comparative Analysis) is a configuration-based, case-oriented methodology, enabling exploration of complex causal relationships beyond the limitations of individual case studies (Gligor & Bozkurt, 2020). Utilizing set theory and configurational thinking, it combines qualitative and quantitative analysis through Boolean algebra, effectively identifying configurations between influencing factors and outcomes. fsQCA outperforms traditional quantitative methods in analyzing complex causal relationships within small samples, effectively assessing intricate relationships among positive, neutral, and negative sentiments and satisfaction. For instance, Pappas et al. (2020) applied fsQCA to analyze motivational and emotional configurations concerning social media platform user satisfaction. Despite its advantages, fsQCA is rarely used in urban regeneration satisfaction research, with most existing studies limited to analyzing singular statistical relationships between public perceptions and urban regeneration outcomes. For example, Galaktionova (2021) explored statistical relationships between public perceptions on online maps and urban improvement suggestions but did not address interactions among multiple factors. Applying fsQCA enables comprehensive analyses of multiple factor configurations that influence public satisfaction, offering more tailored improvement pathways.

3 Methodological Approach

3.1 Method

This study employs social media data modeling using BERTopic and fuzzy-set qualitative comparative analysis (fsQCA) to explore pathways influencing public satisfaction with historical district regeneration projects. Traditional case studies often have limitations when examining interactions of multiple factors affecting outcomes, particularly due to their susceptibility to coincidences of single-factor effects. Additionally, public satisfaction involves the influence of multiple factors, requiring more precise methodologies. Therefore, this research integrates qualitative and quantitative approaches, using NLP techniques to construct a BERTopic model from social media data, extracting core themes of public interest in urban regeneration as conditional variables for fsQCA. Subsequently, RoBERTa sentiment analysis modeling is applied to gauge public emotional satisfaction, supplemented by questionnaires to determine outcome variables. Due to the small sample nature of this study, 12 historical district cases recommended by China's

Ministry of Housing and Urban-Rural Development are used for the fsQCA analysis. Ultimately, reliability and validity testing constructs pathways differentiating high and low satisfaction renewal projects.

3.2 Data Analysis

The primary aim of the data collected in this study is to facilitate pathway analysis, enhancing credibility and richness. Thus, the data collection is divided into two primary aspects.

Firstly, the study utilizes data from widely used social media platforms, specifically Weibo and Dianping, as these platforms effectively capture public expression. Social media comments collected through cross-platform crawling from Dianping and Weibo range from January 1, 2018, to January 1, 2025, totaling approximately 23237 raw data points. These data primarily define the conditional variables for public satisfaction. The projects selected align with the recommended list from the Ministry of Housing and Urban-Rural Development, including Beijing's Qianmen Dashilar, Jingdezhen's Taoyangli Historical Cultural Tourism Area, Guangzhou's Yongqingfang, Jiangsu's Pingjiang Road, and Fujian's Sanfang Qixiang historical cultural streets. Keywords for Weibo searches included "urban regeneration" and "historical district preservation."

Data preprocessing utilized traditional data cleaning and simple transformations (Gligor & Bozkurt, 2020). The Jieba library was employed for Chinese text segmentation, converting texts into tokens referred to as "feature words," facilitating text feature extraction. Word frequency analyses were conducted on the cleaned Weibo datasets to rank words based on occurrence frequency, providing each high-frequency feature word's part-of-speech for further analysis. Jieba tokenization combined with the Harbin Institute of Technology's stop-word list ensures high-quality data suitable for BERTopic modeling and the RoBERTa pre-trained model. Unlike traditional LDA models, BERTopic utilizes deep learning embeddings for finer clustering, identifying more precise thematic and sentiment classifications.

Additional data were derived from a Likert-scale questionnaire designed with five levels (Pappas & Woodside, 2021). This questionnaire consists of two sections with 20 questions, covering basic information and five relevant variables: cultural heritage preservation, cultural tourism attractiveness, commercial development, infrastructure and security, and service quality and public feedback. The variable design referenced previous research, including methods and key issues in Chinese ancient building preservation (Shan et al., 2022; Yung et al., 2017), cultural heritage tourism perceptions in Singapore and George Town (Katahenggam, 2020), studies on commercial development in Hong Kong (Jayantha & Yung, 2018), sustainable economic indicators at the urban community level (Huang et al., 2020), historical preservation and public transport infrastructure (Shach-Pinsly, 2019), and factors influencing resident evaluations in participatory processes (Christensen, 2020).

To reduce subjectivity, questions were designed based on BERTopic-extracted keywords and practical project contexts, ensuring clarity for respondents of all ages. Additionally, a supplementary 10-point satisfaction scale quantitatively measured public satisfaction, corroborating RoBERTa sentiment analysis results as outcome variables in fsQCA, thereby enhancing data robustness.

Surveys were distributed through both offline field visits and online platforms (Wenjuanxing) to 12 recommended historical districts by China's Ministry of Housing and Urban-Rural Development, including projects such as Sanfang Qixiang (Fuzhou), Pingjiang Road (Suzhou), Taoyangli (Jingdezhen), and Dashilar Guanyinsi (Beijing), among others. A pilot reliability and validity analysis confirmed questionnaire effectiveness. The formal survey conducted online from December 2024 to May 2025 yielded 687 responses, with 605 complete and valid entries, achieving an effective response rate of 88.06%.

4 Findings and Discussion

4.1 RQ1: Core Factors of Public Concern in Historical District Urban Regeneration

4.1.1 BERTopic Result

Following the data collection from Weibo and Dianping platforms and preprocessing of 23,237 comments, 18,578 valid text entries were used for BERTopic modeling. This ensures the effectiveness of the subsequent modeling process. Transformer-based semantic representation, UMAP for dimensionality reduction, and HDBSCAN for density-based clustering were integrated, with c-TF-IDF reweighting to enable effective topic extraction from short texts (Christensen, 2020). The preliminary model identified 35 topics, of which topic −1, labeled as noise (4,659 entries), was excluded for simplification. The remaining topics are detailed in Table 1.

Subsequently, after being reviewed and approved by experts, these topics were integrated into five core cultural perception themes: A. Cultural Heritage Preservation; B. Cultural Tourism Attractiveness; C. Commercial Development; D. Infrastructure and Safety; E. Service Quality and Public Feedback. The following sections describe the characteristics of each dimension in descending order of proportion:

Table 1. Topic distribution and proportion.

Core		Count	Name	Representation
	−1	4659	Noise Theme	['Mode', 'Characteristics', 'Story', 'Parking', 'Scenic Area'
Cultural Heritage Preservation and Transmission	2	1523	2_Culture_Happy	['Cultural Atmosphere', 'Arts', 'Architectural Style'
	3	976	3_Weekdays_Holidays_Children	['Culture', 'Time-honored Brand', 'Inheritance', 'Hutong',

(continued)

Table 1. (*continued*)

Core		Count	Name	Representation
	6	674	6_Bustling_Popular_Very Hot	['Folk Customs', 'Free', 'Special', 'Firing', 'Queue', 'Regret'
	13	291	13_Homestay_Republic of China_	['Cultural Heritage', 'Cultural Creativity', 'Warmth', 'Guide'
	21	134	21_Singing_Opera	['Since Childhood', 'Folk Songs', 'Opera', 'Ancient Style'
	24	89	24_Very Suitable_Not Crowded	['Memorial Hall', 'Ruins', 'Renovation', 'Chinese', 'Highly Skilled'
	25	73	25_Photographed	['Celebrity', 'Former Residence', 'Cultural Creativity'
	26	61	26_Okay_So-so_Unable	['Long History', 'Construction', 'Culture', 'Atmosphere'
Cultural Tourism Appeal	4	823	4_Protection_Culture_Construction	['Destination', 'Tourists', 'Delicious', 'Dishes', 'Small Shop'
	5	799	5_Light_Time_Sunlight	['Lanterns', 'Dazzling', 'Well-lit', 'Lantern Festival'
	7	692	7_Water Town_Parallel	['Art Museum', 'Handicrafts', 'Nostalgia', 'Elderly'
	14	283	14_Snacks_Small Shop	['Specialty', 'Goods', 'Souvenirs', 'Story', 'Scene'
	15	228	15_Stamping_Stamp Collection_Seal	['Space', 'Deserted', 'Not Eating', 'Study Tour', 'Consumption'
	22	110	22_Long Time_A Very Long Time	['A Long Time', 'Lively', 'Ancestral Home', 'Specialty',

(*continued*)

Table 1. (*continued*)

Core		Count	Name	Representation
	31	44	31_Parking Spot_Scan Code_Ice Cream	['Immersion', 'On-site', 'Production', 'Collection', 'Value', 'Interesting'
Commercial Development	9	349	9_Many Many_Ceramics_Convenience	['Tourists', 'Restaurant', 'Environment', 'Fair', 'Pity'
	11	300	11_Scenic Area_Ceramics	['Internet-famous', 'Crowded', 'Young People', 'Modernization'
	10	319	10_Culture_Cultural	['Long-term Stay', 'Experience', 'Homestay'
	12	295	12_New Year_Young People	['shop', 'weekend', 'story', 'young', 'holiday'
	17	154	17_not worth it_pretty good_not far	['snack', 'brand', 'search', 'snack shop'
	33	40	33_alley_iron gate_merchant	['chain', 'commerce', 'strong', 'atmosphere'
Infrastructure and Safety	1	2942	1_block_culture_subway	['square', 'transportation', 'convenient', 'subway', 'pedestrian street'
	8	496	8_pedestrian street_commercial	['architectural style', 'supporting', 'complete',
	28	60	28_flavor_in front of the house	['community', 'sign', 'tidy', 'disappointed', 'alley',
	29	50	29_love_eye-catching	['epidemic', 'guidance', 'stroll', 'parking', 'front gate', 'stroll', 'sign'
	30	44	30_hygiene_business_restroom	['hygiene', 'clean', 'messy', 'safe', 'child'

(*continued*)

Table 1. (*continued*)

Core		Count	Name	Representation
Service Quality and Public Feedback	0	4865	0_cuisine_antique_snack	['closed', 'notice', 'ticket', 'complaint'
	16	228	16_go_in advance	['Mode', 'Features', 'Story', 'Parking', 'Child', 'Block']
	18	151	18_Crowded_Staff_Popularity	['Crowded', 'Staff', 'Enthusiasm', 'Not much']
	19	135	19_Service_Mural_Temple	['Mural', 'Still', 'Implement', 'Construction']
	20	135	20_Crowded_Boring_Must visit	['Crowded', 'Boring', 'Crowded', 'Foot traffic']
	23	90	23_Relax_Not great_Very many	['Return', 'Relax', 'Comfortable', 'Not far']
	32	44	32_Surprise_External	['Demand', 'Bear', 'Experience', 'Stroll']

5 Service Quality and Public Feedback

This cluster is characterized by keywords such as "staff", "service" and "feedback". Comments expressed general public sentiment, service quality, and satisfaction, including evaluations of staff attitude, complaint handling, and pandemic-related crowd impacts. A slight decline in comment volume was observed between 2019 and 2020, but since 2023, data indicate a sharp increase, suggesting a diminishing impact of the pandemic, especially in tourism within historic districts. Some users reported cold service attitudes and unresolved issues, with keywords like "staff," "complaint," "feedback," and "insufficient." Others noted a lack of appropriate complaint channels. Complaints mostly involved disorder in queuing and inadequate conflict resolution.

6 Cultural Heritage Preservation

This cluster includes 8 topics, the main focus centers on themes such as "culture", "architecture" and "time-honored brands". Comments positively referenced the preservation of historical architecture, with keywords like "inheritance," "creativity," and "richness" reflecting public satisfaction. These data suggest that cultural preservation enhances emotional identification, with satisfaction stemming from perceived authenticity and educational value. For example, museum exhibitions received praise for their innovative design and visitor flow. However, negative feedback highlights concerns about commercialization undermining cultural preservation, underscoring the need for a balance between cultural integrity and commercial viability.

7 Infrastructure and Safety

It emphasizes the physical infrastructure of regeneration projects, such as transportation, location, and facility upgrades including alley revitalization, parking systems, and sanitation. High-frequency keywords like "pedestrian street", "subway" and "hygiene" reflect the public's concern with connectivity and cleanliness. Many respondents pointed out that restroom hygiene and availability directly influenced satisfaction with infrastructure. Criticism focused on inadequate signage and aging facilities, indicating that infrastructure maintenance requires ongoing investment. For instance, difficulties in navigation due to insufficient signage caused time-consuming detours, highlighting how convenience and comfort significantly affect satisfaction.

8 Cultural Tourism Attractiveness

Key terms such as "lantern festival", "temple fair" and "check-in" underscore the importance of visual and experiential cultural activities in attracting visitors. Projects with cultural events—like temple fairs, lantern festivals, and trendy photo spots—appealed to diverse age groups by combining traditional and modern elements. While these activities greatly enhanced visitor satisfaction, some users expressed concerns over the loss of cultural uniqueness due to excessive commercialization of tourist sites.

9 Commercial Development

Key terms include "cultural creative stores", "influencers" and "dining". Some comments reflect concern about chain stores and excessive homogeneity. While commercial development enhances visibility and consumption, pricing remains a sensitive issue. Positive feedback included satisfaction with creative cultural products, like souvenir fridge magnets, while some respondents criticized high prices and over-commercialization, which may dilute authentic cultural expression. Mentions of influencer-driven tourism also revealed crowding, fragmented experiences, and long waiting times, indicating a media-driven consumption model consistent with the spiral of silence theory.

As illustrated in Fig. 1, the topic evolution trend lines mostly remain within the 0–80 range, showing that public discussions on historical district urban regeneration remained relatively low before and after the outbreak of COVID-19, with no significant breakout topics. During this period, the distinction between cultural heritage and tourism attractiveness was minimal, and information was primarily derived from fragmented personal experiences.

From 2021 onward, the trend lines begin to rise, though still below 200 posts per topic, implying a gradual recovery in offline activities and the spread of short-form videos on social media. By 2022, the volume increased to between 200 and 400 posts, particularly for topics related to cultural tourism. The most pronounced growth occurred in 2023. On one hand, this was driven by the reintroduction of night markets and temple fairs; on the other, algorithm-driven short videos such as "City Walk" and "store-check-in tours" surged.

These were further amplified by commercial development and positive service experience reviews, resulting in a marked rise in attention.It is worth noting that none of the topics continued to climb post-2023. Most trend lines dropped by 30–40% in 2024, suggesting that public interest followed a seasonal pattern rather than exhibiting sustained growth.

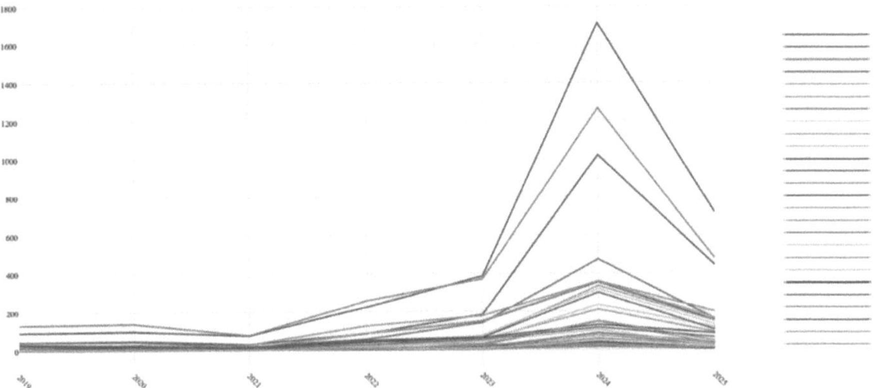

Fig. 1. Theme Presentation Trend Analysis.

9.1   RoBERTa Sentiment Analysis Results

Following the BERT-based topic modeling, this study employed the RoBERTa-Chinese model for fine-grained sentiment analysis, aiming to accurately capture public emotional responses to urban regeneration projects in historical districts. As shown in Table 2, the pre-trained model "tabularisai/multilingual-sentiment-analysis" was used to quantify the polarity of textual sentiment. This approach not only distinguishes between positive and negative emotional tendencies but also maps sentiment intensity on a continuous scale ranging from −1 to 1 (Di Pietro et al., 2014).

The results show that positive sentiment accounts for approximately 49–55% of all responses, with neutral posts comprising around 30–40%, and negative sentiment consistently below 20%, averaging between 11% and 18%. At the topic level, the theme of "Cultural Tourism Attractiveness" had the highest positive sentiment at 55.0% and the lowest negative sentiment at 11.2%, indicating that experiences such as walking through ancient streets, attending temple fairs, and sampling local delicacies are particularly well-received. In contrast, the "Infrastructure and Safety" dimension showed the highest negative sentiment at 17.6%, suggesting that issues related to traffic organization, sanitation, and crowd management remain key areas for improvement.

For "Commercial Development" and "Service Quality and Public Feedback" positive sentiment rates were slightly below the overall average, at 46.7% and 44.7% respectively, with negative sentiment exceeding 15%. This reflects ongoing public concerns about pricing, service homogeneity, and customer service experience.Among individual topics, the most positively evaluated included the "Lantern Festival/Light Show" with 75.4% positive sentiment, and "Intangible Heritage Handicraft Experience" at 59.2%, demonstrating that interactive and immersive experiences significantly enhance user satisfaction. Conversely, the most negative sentiments were concentrated around topics such as "Congestion/Security Check Inconvenience" and "Sanitation and Noise Issues."

Table 2. Public Satisfaction Satisfaction Rating.

A	Average(%)		2	3	6	13	21	24	25	26	31
	Positive	**49.0**	53.2	46.4	48.6	49.7	54.0	59.2	50.8	31.9	46.8
	Neutral	**38.3**	35.1	38.0	36.7	42.2	37.3	30.9	36.9	51.1	36.7
	Negative	**12.7**	11.7	15.6	14.7	8.1	8.7	9.9	12.3	17.0	16.7
B			4	5	7	14	15	22			
	Positive	**55.0**	75.4	52.8	50.8	47.4	52.7	50.9			
	Neutral	**33.8**	14.2	39.4	37.1	37.9	36.0	38.0			
	Negative	**11.2**	10.4	7.8	12.1	14.7	11.3	11.1			
C			9	10	11	12	17	27	33		
	Positive	**46.7**	52.9	54.9	35.1	40.5	58.9	41.9	42.9		
	Neutral	**37.9**	28.7	38.0	45.6	44.1	31.5	41.9	35.7		
	Negative	**15.4**	18.4	7.1	19.3	15.4	9.6	16.2	21.4		
D			1	8	28	29	30				
	Positive	**49.0**	48.5	43.4	39.5	57.6	56.2				
	Neutral	**33.4**	41.4	40.7	41.9	21.2	21.9				
	Negative	**17.6**	10.1	15.9	18.6	21.2	21.9				
E			0	16	18	19	20	23	32		
	Positive	**44.7**	55.8	48.5	40.7	33.6	51.9	38.0	44.8		
	Neutral	**38.8**	36.3	34.7	36.4	55.5	32.8	38.0	37.9		
	Negative	**16.5**	7.9	16.8	22.9	10.9	15.3	24.0	17.3		

9.2   RQ2: Exploring Public Satisfaction Pathways in Historical District Urban Regeneration

9.2.1   The fsQCA Analysis Results

Before conducting configurational analysis, it is necessary to calibrate the raw data. According to Pappas & Woodside (2021), fsQCA requires precise definition of condition and outcome variables, calibrated within the range of 0 to 1. This study adopted the direct calibration method using fsQCA software tools, setting anchor points at (2–4) corresponding to full membership, crossover, and full non-membership, respectively, based on the five-point Likert scale. The fsQCA 3.0 software was used to convert the assigned values into fuzzy-set scores. Following the recommendation of H. Chen et al. (2024), all data were included in the case study, with membership values of 0.5 adjusted to 0.501 for analysis.

9.2.2 Reliability and Validity Testing

The reliability and validity analysis focused on the consistency of questionnaire responses. Reliability was assessed using Cronbach's alpha coefficient, which ranges from 0 to 1, with higher values indicating stronger reliability. As shown in Table 3, Palacios-Marqués et al. (2017) noted that a Cronbach's alpha between 0.7 and 0.8 is considered acceptable, while values between 0.8 and 0.9 indicate excellent reliability.

This study tested five condition variables, with standardized Cronbach's alpha values as follows: Cultural Heritage Preservation = 0.869; Cultural Tourism Attractiveness = 0.901; Commercial Development = 0.800; Infrastructure and Safety = 0.803; and Service Quality and Public Feedback = 0.827. All exceed the 0.7 threshold, confirming acceptable internal consistency. The combined Cronbach's alpha value for the entire scale was 0.827, validating the reliability of the overall instrument.

Table 3. Reliability and Convergent Validity Analysis Table.

Variables	Standardized loading coefficient		CR	AVE	Cronbach's α	Cronbach's α
Cultural Heritage Preservation and Transmission	1	0.942	0.884	0.665	0.825	0.869
	2	0.663			0.830	
	3	0.894			0.823	
	4	0.685			0.818	
Cultural Tourism Appeal	5	0.864	0.903	0.703	0.810	0.901
	6	0.909			0.818	
	7	0.822			0.820	
	8	0.732			0.812	
Commercial Development	9	0.64	0.805	0.51	0.821	0.800
	10	0.758			0.818	
	11	0.841			0.813	
	12	0.631			0.802	
Infrastructure and Safety	13	0.829	0.81	0.52	0.824	0.803
	14	0.583			0.824	
	15	0.767			0.814	

(continued)

Table 3. (*continued*)

Variables	Standardized loading coefficient		CR	AVE	Cronbach's α	Cronbach's α
Service Quality and Public Feedback	16	0.683			0.818	
	17	0.583	0.851	0.609	0.814	0.827
	18	0.601			0.808	
	19	0.905			0.817	
	20	0.876			0.814	

Validity testing is used to verify the effectiveness of the scale design and ensure that the items appropriately reflect the research objectives. According to Table 4, this study adopted a five-point Likert scale, used a customized questionnaire, and refined the items based on the research theme. Therefore, confirmatory factor analysis (CFA) was employed to examine the convergent and discriminant validity of the scale. Using AMOS 29.0 for analysis, the composite reliability (CR) of all dimensions exceeded 0.7, meeting the standard requirement; the average variance extracted (AVE) was above 0.5, satisfying the standard criterion; and the standardized factor loadings of all items ranged between 0.6 and 0.9, fulfilling the requirement of being above 0.6. Thus, it can be concluded that the validity of the data meets the necessary standards (Pappas & Woodside, 2021).

Table 4. Discriminant validity table.

	A	B	C	D	E
A	0.815				
B	−0.239	0.838			
C	0.203	0.363	0.714		
D	0.103	0.061	0.309	0.721	
E	0.126	0.546	0.182	0.149	0.78

The diagonal numbers are the square root of the factor AVE.

9.2.3 Necessity Analysis

According to the requirements of configurational analysis, a necessity test is conducted to examine whether any single condition is indispensable for the outcome variable. This involves evaluating whether a single factor consistently influences the result and can be deemed a necessary condition. By standardizing the data through software, this study identifies high behavioral intention and non-high behavioral intention as outcome variables. Consistency and coverage are then calculated. Typically, a condition is considered necessary if its consistency score exceeds 0.9 (Pappas & Woodside, 2021).

As shown in Table 5, none of the conditions reached a consistency score above 0.9 under either high or non-high behavioral intention, indicating that no single factor qualifies as a necessary condition for the outcome. Therefore, a comprehensive analysis incorporating all conditions is required to explore the pathways leading to high and non-high behavioral intention in historical district urban regeneration projects.

The necessity analysis also reveals that service quality is a relatively significant factor, with consistency scores of 0.84 and 0.82 under high and low satisfaction outcomes, respectively. This suggests that service quality serves as a prerequisite for achieving high public satisfaction.

Table 5. Necessity Analysis Table.

High Level Necessity Testing of Conditions	Consistency	Coverage	Low Level Necessity Testing of Conditions	Consistency	Coverage
Cultural Heritage Transmission and Protection	0.750847	0.659226	Cultural Heritage Transmission and Protection	0.447541	0.406250
~Cultural Heritage Transmission and Protection	0.323729	0.361742	~Cultural Heritage Transmission and Protection	0.624590	0.721591
Cultural Tourism Appeal	0.598305	0.640653	Cultural Tourism Appeal	0.396721	0.439201
~Cultural Tourism Appeal	0.476271	0.432974	~Cultural Tourism Appeal	0.675410	0.634823
Commercial Development	0.354237	0.351852	Commercial Development	0.673770	0.691919
~Commercial Development	0.689830	0.671617	~Commercial Development	0.368852	0.371287
Infrastructure and Security Assurance	0.598305	0.596284	Infrastructure and Security Assurance	0.490164	0.505068
~Infrastructure and Security Assurance	0.503390	0.488487	~Infrastructure and Security Assurance	0.608197	0.610197
Service Quality and Public Feedback	0.838983	0.819536	Service Quality and Public Feedback	0.254098	0.256623
~Service Quality and Public Feedback	0.238983	0.236577	~Service Quality and Public Feedback	0.821311	0.840604

9.2.4 Configurational Analysis

Using a three-tier comparison method—complex solution, intermediate solution, and parsimonious solution—this study identified three high-satisfaction pathways (H1–H3) and five low-satisfaction pathways (L1–L5), as shown in the table. Overall, the three high-satisfaction pathways have a total coverage of 0.73 and consistency of 0.98, indicating that they effectively explain the high satisfaction outcomes within the sample. As shown in Table 6, historical districts can gain public recognition not only through cultural depth and service optimization but also through enhanced safety infrastructure or curated consumer experiences.

H1: Culture Immersion – Service Driven Type. Cultural Heritage Preservation (A) and Service Quality (E) serve as dual core conditions. Even without strong support from Cultural Tourism Attractiveness (B) and Commercial Development (C), a combination of cultural richness and attentive service can create immersive experiences, yielding an individual coverage of 0.38 and consistency of 0.98. This suggests that despite low tourism attraction and commercialization, strong cultural content and reliable service can still achieve high satisfaction.

H2: Cultural Heritage Protection with Strong Infrastructure and Service Support. This "Safety-Culture Dual Anchor" model enhances Cultural Heritage Preservation (A) while strengthening Infrastructure and Safety (D) and ensuring high-quality Service (E). This dual-layer of hardware and software enhances perceived value, with a coverage of 0.46 and consistency of 0.98. The result emphasizes that traditional districts must reinforce infrastructure such as transport, sanitation, and safety alongside cultural expression and service quality to maintain stable satisfaction.

H3: Consumption–Experience Driven Satisfaction. In scenarios where Cultural Protection (A) and Infrastructure (D) are relatively weak, satisfaction can still be driven by strong Cultural Tourism Attractiveness (B) and Commercial Development (C), supported by good Service (E). Through a "consumption–experience" mechanism that substitutes for cultural depth, well-planned activities and commercial atmosphere, along with thoughtful service, can also lead to high visitor satisfaction.

L1 reflects deficiencies when both culture and commercial support are lacking. Even with the introduction of tourism activities or commercial development, it is difficult to avoid dissatisfaction stemming from utilitarian outcomes. L2 represents a systemic failure where all five factors—culture, tourism, commerce, infrastructure, and service—are weak, resulting in the lowest satisfaction levels. L3 highlights the situation where cultural protection and commercial elements are present, but infrastructure and service fall short, leading to a mismatch in visitor expectations. This underscores the importance of adequate infrastructure support. L4 specifically demonstrates that strong infrastructure alone is insufficient; it must be complemented by tourism experience and service, which work synergistically to enhance satisfaction. Finally, L5 shows that even when commerce and infrastructure are strong, a fragmented experience lacking cultural and tourism elements can prevent visitors from forming a cohesive cultural journey, leading to poor evaluations.

Table 6. High and low satisfaction path configuration.

conditional variable	high level configu-ratinal condition			low level configuratinal condition				
	H1	H2	H3	L4	L5	L6	L7	L8
Cultural Heritage Transmission and Protection	●	●	⊗	⊗	⊗	●	●	⊗
Cultural Tourism Appeal	⊗		●	●	⊗	⊗	⊗	⊗
Commercial Development	⊗	⊗	●	●	⊗	●	⊗	●
Infrastructure and Security Assurance		●	⊗		⊗	⊗	●	●
Service Quality and Public Feedback	●	●	●	⊗	⊗	⊗	⊗	●
consistency	0.978355	0.981818	0.942623	0.973856	0.942529	0.965812	0.889831	0.862069
raw coverage	0.383051	0.457627	0.194915	0.244262	0.134426	0.185246	0.172131	0.163934
unique coverage	0.115254	0.183051	0.154237	0.134426	0.09508199	0.136066	0.142623	0.062295
solution coverage	0.730508			0.691803				
solution consistency	0.977324			0.944071				

10 Findings and Discussion

In conclusion, this study draws on social media texts as the primary sample and integrates BERT topic modeling, RoBERTa-based sentiment quantification, and fsQCA pathway analysis.

The BERTopic and sentiment analysis reveal that the key elements in historical preservation within urban regeneration include Service Quality and Public Feedback, Cultural Heritage Preservation, Infrastructure and Safety, Cultural Tourism Attractiveness, and Commercial Development. Among these, Service Quality stands out most prominently of public attention. Sentiment analysis further shows that overall discourse tends to be positive (about 50%), but significant dissatisfaction remains regarding traffic congestion, sanitation, and staff attitudes. Immersive cultural activities such as lantern festivals and intangible cultural heritage workshops received higher satisfaction ratings, while Infrastructure and Safety had the highest share of negative sentiment at 17.6%, highlighting problems in transportation, hygiene, and order.

Subsequently, fsQCA analysis systematically reveals the formation mechanism of public satisfaction in historical district regeneration projects, reflecting the theoretical demand for recognizing complexity and non-linearity. The results show that Service Quality is an indispensable factor. The combination of "Cultural Depth + High-Quality Service" is a key driver of high satisfaction, whereas the absence of Service Quality is common across all low-satisfaction scenarios. Tourism and commerce play amplifying and mediating roles under specific conditions. While hardware infrastructure and commercial atmosphere can partially compensate for cultural deficits, this compensation is limited and may result in negative evaluations due to unmet expectations. The three positive configurations—Cultural Immersion with Service, Culture with Safety, and Consumption with Experience—and the five negative configurations collectively suggest that successful regeneration of historical districts requires coordinated development across cultural content, infrastructure, commercial development, and service operations in order to convert short-term traffic into lasting public goodwill.

However, this study is constrained by biases inherent in social media user demographics. The platform predominantly represents urban users aged 18–35, leading to underrepresentation of older and digitally marginalized groups, which weakens the generalizability of the findings across age and social strata. Additionally, platform-specific algorithmic recommendations and interaction mechanisms may amplify trending topics while suppressing silent voices, creating structural biases in topic distribution and sentiment polarity. Furthermore, semantic noise in fine-grained sentiment analysis—such as sarcasm, slang, and polysemy—may lead to calibration errors.

Future research can mitigate these limitations by employing hybrid data collection methods to broaden sample coverage. Introducing multimodal information—such as images and videos—and applying active learning annotation techniques can improve the sentiment model's ability to detect sarcasm and latent emotions, thereby enhancing the interpretability and applicability of the findings.

References

Chen, D.-S., Cheng, L.-L., Hummels, C., Koskinen, I.: Social design: an introduction. Social Design. **10**(1) (2016)

Chen, H., Wang, J., Zeng, Y., Shen, N., Liu, F.: Using fs/QCA to explore the influencing factors of urban green infrastructure development and its combinational drivers: the case of the Yangtze River Delta region of China. Environ. Sci. Pollut. Res. **31**(17), 24913–24935 (2024). https://doi.org/10.1007/s11356-024-32641-2

Christensen, H.S.: How citizens evaluate participatory processes: a conjoint analysis (2020)

Egger, R., Yu, J.: A topic modeling comparison between LDA, NMF, Top2Vec, and BERTopic to demystify twitter posts. Front. Sociol. **7**, 886498 (2022). https://doi.org/10.3389/fsoc.2022.886498

Falanga, R., Nunes, M.C.: Tackling urban disparities through participatory culture-led urban regeneration. Insights from Lisbon. Land Use Policy. **108**, 105478 (2021). https://doi.org/10.1016/j.landusepol.2021.105478

Galaktionova, A.: Emotional boundaries of public involvement in city improvement. Cities. **115**, 103254 (2021). https://doi.org/10.1016/j.cities.2021.103254

Gao, B., Yu, S.: Upgrading museum experience: insights into offline visitor perceptions through social media trends. Emerging Trends Drugs, Addictions Health. **4**, 100137 (2024). https://doi.org/10.1016/j.etdah.2023.100137

Gao, C., Zhang, Q., Tan, Z., Zhao, G., Gao, S., Kim, E., Shen, T.: Applying optimized YOLOv8 for heritage conservation: enhanced object detection in Jiangnan traditional private gardens. Herit. Sci. **12**(1), 31 (2024). https://doi.org/10.1186/s40494-024-01144-1

Gligor, D., Bozkurt, S.: FsQCA versus regression: the context of customer engagement. J. Retail. Consum. Serv. **52**, 101929 (2020). https://doi.org/10.1016/j.jretconser.2019.101929

Grootendorst, M.: BERTopic: Neural topic modeling with a class-based TF-IDF procedure (arXiv:2203.05794). arXiv. https://doi.org/10.48550/arXiv.2203.05794 (2022)

Huang, L., Zheng, W., Hong, J., Liu, Y., Liu, G.: Paths and strategies for sustainable urban renewal at the neighbourhood level: a framework for decision-making. Sustain. Cities Soc. **55**, 102074 (2020). https://doi.org/10.1016/j.scs.2020.102074

Jayantha, W.M., Yung, E.H.K.: Effect of revitalisation of historic buildings on retail shop values in urban renewal: an empirical analysis. Sustainability. **10**(5), 1418 (2018). https://doi.org/10.3390/su10051418

Katahenggam, N.: Tourist perceptions and preferences of authenticity in heritage tourism: visual comparative study of George Town and Singapore. J. Tour. Cult. Chang. **18**(4), 371–385 (2020). https://doi.org/10.1080/14766825.2019.1659282

Kotler, N., Kotler, P.: Can Museums be All Things to All People?: Missions, goals, and marketing's role. Mus. Manag. Curat. (n.d.). https://doi.org/10.1080/09647770000301803

Lei, H., Zhou, Y.: Conducting heritage tourism-led urban renewal in Chinese historical and cultural urban spaces: a case study of Datong. Land. **11**(12), 2122 (2022). https://doi.org/10.3390/land11122122

Lin, S., van Ameijde, J.: Leveraging social media and natural language processing for understanding cultural perception in urban renewal: insights from Nantou walled city, pp. 109–118. https://doi.org/10.52842/conf.caadria.2024.2.109 (2024)

Liu, B., Lu, X., Hu, X., Li, L., Li, Y.: What's wrong with the public participation of urban regeneration project in China: a study from multiple stakeholders' perspectives. Eng. Constr. Archit. Manag. **29**(1), 91–109 (2021). https://doi.org/10.1108/ECAM-03-2020-0175

Miles, S., Paddison, R.: Introduction: the rise and rise of culture-led urban regeneration. Urban Stud. **42**(5–6), 833–839 (2005). https://doi.org/10.1080/00420980500107508

Miltgen, C.L., Smith, H.J.: Falsifying and withholding: exploring individuals' contextual privacy-related decision-making. Inf. Manag. **56**(5), 696–717 (2019). https://doi.org/10.1016/j.im.2018.11.004

Ministry of Housing and Urban-Rural Development of the People's Republic of China.: Urban Renewal Typical Cases. https://www.mohurd.gov.cn/api-gateway/jpaas-jsearch-web-server/search?serviceId=e2f3058e2a3b4f8abc93eb76e739e3e7&websiteid=&cateid=cc5c27d3eb894fd79cc47e72497ef2bf&q= (n.d.)

Palacios-Marqués, D., Roig-Dobón, S., Comeig, I.: Background factors to innovation performance: results of an empirical study using fsQCA methodology. Qual. Quant. **51**(5), 1939–1953 (2017). https://doi.org/10.1007/s11135-016-0414-2

Pappas, I.O., Papavlasopoulou, S., Mikalef, P., Giannakos, M.N.: Identifying the combinations of motivations and emotions for creating satisfied users in SNSs: an fsQCA approach. Int. J. Inf. Manag. **53**, 102128 (2020). https://doi.org/10.1016/j.ijinfomgt.2020.102128

Pappas, I.O., Woodside, A.G.: Fuzzy-set qualitative comparative analysis (fsQCA): guidelines for research practice in information systems and marketing. Int. J. Inf. Manag. **58**, 102310 (2021). https://doi.org/10.1016/j.ijinfomgt.2021.102310

Rahman, M.M., Shiplu, A.I., Watanobe, Y., Alam, M.A.: RoBERTa-BiLSTM: a context-aware hybrid model for sentiment analysis (arXiv:2406.00367). arXiv. https://doi.org/10.48550/arXiv.2406.00367 (2024)

Shach-Pinsly, D.: Measuring security in the built environment: evaluating urban vulnerability in a human-scale urban form. Landsc. Urban Plan. **191**, 103412 (2019). https://doi.org/10.1016/j.landurbplan.2018.08.022

Shan, M., Chen, Y.-F., Zhai, Z., Du, J.: Investigating the critical issues in the conservation of heritage building: the case of China. J. Build. Eng. **51**, 104319 (2022). https://doi.org/10.1016/j.jobe.2022.104319

Tang, H., Liu, X., Li, J., Wang, H.: Research on design intervention in spatial planning of traditional rural tourism: based on the perspective of tourists' willingness to visit again. J. Asian Arch. Build. Eng., 1–21 (2025). https://doi.org/10.1080/13467581.2025.2455038

Truong, V.: Examining gender and cultural influences on customer emotions. arXiv.org https://arxiv.org/abs/2505.02852v1 (2025, May 2)

Wu, F., Zhang, F., Liu, Y.: Beyond growth machine politics: understanding State Politics and National Political Mandates in China's urban redevelopment. Antipode. **54**, 608–628 (2021)

Yuan, F., Li, M., Liu, R.: Understanding the evolutions of public responses using social media: hurricane Matthew case study. Int. J. Disaster Risk Reduction. **51**, 101798 (2020). https://doi.org/10.1016/j.ijdrr.2020.101798

Yung, E.H.K., Zhang, Q., Chan, E.H.W.: Underlying social factors for evaluating heritage conservation in urban renewal districts. Habitat Int. **66**, 135–148 (2017). https://doi.org/10.1016/j.habitatint.2017.06.004

Zhao, N., Liu, Y., Wang, J.: Network governance and the evolving urban regeneration policymaking in China: a case study of insurgent practices in Enninglu redevelopment project. Sustainability. **13**(4) (2021). https://doi.org/10.3390/su13042280

Revisiting the Aura: AI-Generated Art and the Evolution of Artistic Value in the AI Age

Qingshen Meng, Xing Fang(✉), and Qihan Guo

Wuhan University of Technology, Wuhan 430070, Hubei, China
14294@whut.eu.cn, 428037@qq.com

Abstract. In the AI age, the landscape of artistic creation is undergoing a profound transformation. With the rise of generative models such as Midjourney and Stable Diffusion, artificial intelligence is no longer merely a tool but a co-creator, challenging traditional definitions of authorship, originality, and artistic value. This paper revisits Walter Benjamin's theory of "aura" to examine whether digital artworks generated without a human hand can still possess aesthetic authenticity and emotional resonance. Drawing on semiotic frameworks—specifically Saussure's signifier-signified relationship and Hall's encoding/decoding model—this study argues that the aura of AI-generated art has not disappeared, but shifted: from material uniqueness to viewer-centered interpretation, and from authorial intent to participatory meaning-making. Through case studies of Midjourney and BOTTO, the paper illustrates how aura is reconstructed through symbolic interaction, algorithmic authorship, and cultural engagement. It further proposes a dynamic transformation mechanism of aura in the AI age, emphasizing how viewers, platforms, and algorithms co-constitute artistic value. This research provides new theoretical insights and practical implications for understanding digital creativity, post-human aesthetics, and the evolving cultural economy of AI art.

Keywords: AI-generated art · aura · authorship · semiotics

1 Introduction

In the current era of artificial intelligence (AI), artistic creation is undergoing a paradigmatic shift that challenges long-established assumptions about authorship, originality, and the aesthetic value of artworks. As generative models such as Midjourney and Stable Diffusion gain traction in creative domains, AI is no longer merely a tool but an active participant in image production, cultural interpretation, and artistic discourse. This technological development has triggered both fascination and skepticism: Who—or what—is the artist when machines generate the image? What becomes of "originality" when artworks can be endlessly replicated? And can a digitally generated piece still carry the unique aura Walter Benjamin once associated with traditional works of art?

This paper engages with these questions by revisiting Benjamin's theory of "aura"—a concept that encapsulates the singular presence, historical embeddedness, and emotional resonance of an artwork. Originally formulated in response to mechanical

M. Schrepp and M. Rauterberg (Eds.): HCII 2025, LNCS 16342, pp. 425–437, 2026.
https://doi.org/10.1007/978-3-032-13164-5_27

reproduction technologies, Benjamin's theory must now be reconsidered in light of generative AI systems that can produce compelling visual artifacts without a human hand. We explore whether aura, rather than being lost, is transformed—relocated from the object's materiality to the viewer's interpretive and affective engagement.

Combining theoretical analysis and case-based inquiry, this paper employs semiotic frameworks—particularly the signifier-signified relationship and encoding-decoding model—to analyze how meaning and value are constructed in AI-generated art. By examining works created through Midjourney and Stable Diffusion, we demonstrate that aura in the AI age is not extinguished but redistributed: the algorithm becomes the "scriptor," while the viewer becomes co-author. In this dynamic, aura emerges less from authorship or materiality and more from interactive experience and cultural framing.

Situated within the broader discourse of human-computer interaction, digital aesthetics, and cultural consumption, this study contributes to the evolving understanding of how AI reshapes the cultural logic of art. It not only repositions the role of the artist and the audience but also opens up new possibilities for curatorial practice, platform governance, and value attribution in the age of intelligent image-making.

2 Combing of Relevant Literature

2.1 Benjamin's Theory of Aura

"Aura" as a Concept in Philosophical Aesthetics. Walter Benjamin holds a distinctive position in European critical theory. His inquiry into the relationship between technology and art eventually led to the formulation of the concept of "Aura". First introduced in his 1931 essay <A Short History of Photography>, and systematically developed in <The Work of Art in the Age of Mechanical Reproduction (1936)>, the term "Aura" refers to the unique experiential and existential qualities inherent in traditional artworks. It is not a mystical or metaphysical attribute, but rather a phenomenological concept that describes the emotional and spatial resonance occurring between a viewer and an artwork within a specific historical and cultural context [1].

Benjamin does not define the aura in strictly technical terms; instead, he uses poetic imagery to illustrate it. For example, he describes aura as similar to the experience of "resting on a summer afternoon and gazing into the horizon of mountain ranges, or following the contour of a tree branch [2] ." In this framework, aura emerges through the mutual interaction between the observer and the aesthetic object. It is neither purely a subjective projection nor an objective property of the artwork, but arises from the dynamic relationship between the two. The aura is thus situated in a tension between distance and proximity, and between presence and transcendence—constituting a distinctive affective space that links the observer with the object.

Three Core Features of Aura: Uniqueness, Distance, and Cult Value. Walter Benjamin identifies three interrelated and essential components of aura:

Uniqueness (Einmaligkeit). Aura is inherently tied to the artwork's original presence in the 'here and now'. It cannot be duplicated or experienced simultaneously in multiple locations [3]. For instance, the Mona Lisa at the Louvre possesses a value that no copy can replicate, due to its material originality, continuous historical context, and specific physical setting.

Distance (Fernwirkung). Aura involves a psychological and spatial distance between the viewer and the artwork. Even when standing in close proximity, the viewer cannot fully 'possess' or comprehend the work. This persistent sense of mystery preserves the artwork's aura, fostering reverence and awe [4].
Cult Value (Kultwert). The source of aura is closely linked to ritualistic functions. Historically, artworks served religious or ceremonial purposes and were valued within sacred contexts [5]. This ritual origin imparts an authoritative dimension to artworks that is largely absent in modern exhibition-focused art.

Together, these features distinguish aura from mere mechanical reproduction. Aura is fragile and contingent upon specific historical, spatial, and social conditions—conditions that are undermined by technological reproduction.

2.1.1 The Decline of Aura in the Age of Mechanical Reproduction

According to Benjamin, the emergence of mechanical reproduction—especially photography and film—fundamentally disrupts the conditions necessary for sustaining the aura of artworks [6]. The ability to produce infinite, technically identical copies eliminates the uniqueness, authenticity, and sacred aura associated with original works. As artworks become widely accessible, their value shifts from cult value to exhibition value, transitioning from ritual contexts to spaces of mass consumption.

This transformation also alters the mode of aesthetic perception. Rather than inviting focused contemplation, reproduced art increasingly relies on rapid visual stimuli and momentary impact. Benjamin argues that the modern experience of art is marked by distraction and speed, replacing deep engagement with surface-level stimulation. As a result, the 'here and now' of artistic experience is lost, and the viewer is reduced to a passive consumer [7].

While the democratization of art carries political significance—by challenging elitism and expanding access—it also entails a loss of depth and authenticity in aesthetic experience [8]. Benjamin cautions that mechanical reproduction risks impoverishing perception, undermining the capacity for critical reflection, and transforming art into a commodity devoid of its original context.

2.2 Aura in the Age of AI: a Semiotic Perspective

From Signifier–Signified to Symbolic Meaning: Saussure's Dual Structure of the Sign. In <Course in General Linguistics (1916)>, Swiss linguist Ferdinand de Saussure laid the theoretical groundwork for modern semiotics by introducing the dual structure of the sign. He argued that each linguistic sign consists of two inseparable elements: a concept and a sound-image. To clarify their relationship, he replaced these terms with the now-standard semiotic pair: the signified (the concept) and the signifier (the sound-image) [9].

This terminological shift was intentional. According to Saussure, it highlights two critical distinctions: the internal binary opposition between the two components, and the contrast between each element and the totality of the sign. As he wrote, "The sign is the whole that results from the association of the signifier and the signified [10]."The signifier refers to the sensory or material aspect—such as a word, sound, or image—while the signified denotes the mental concept it evokes.

A key element in Saussure's theory is the arbitrariness of the sign (see Fig. 1). There is no inherent or natural link between a given signifier (such as the word "tree") and its signified concept. Meaning, instead, emerges from a system of differences among signs, not from direct correspondence between language and reality [11].

Furthermore, Saussure emphasized that the sign is not a material object but a psychological construct. Both the signifier and the signified exist in the mind: the signifier is not the physical sound itself, but the mental imprint of that sound as perceived by the subject. The signified is likewise a conceptual structure, not an object in the world.

Saussure's structuralist approach thus reframed meaning as a relational and cognitive process, rather than a property of the object itself. His model established the basis for understanding symbolic systems as structures generated through mental associations, rather than through reference to external reality.

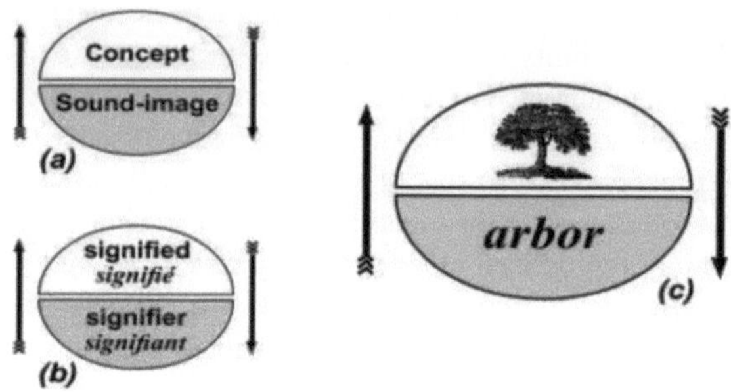

Fig. 1. Saussure's model of the sign: the relationship between signifier and signified.

Encoding and Decoding: Hall's Cultural Model. British cultural theorist Stuart Hall fundamentally reshaped media and communication studies with his influential essay "Encoding/Decoding", first presented in 1973 at <the Centre for Contemporary Cultural Studies (CCCS) > in Birmingham and later included in the 1980 collection Culture, Media, Language. This work marked a significant departure from traditional linear models of communication, introducing a Marxist-informed, non-linear model of media circulation [12].

Building on the Marxist stages of production, distribution, consumption, and reproduction, Hall theorized media as a circuit of meaning structured through three main phases (see Fig. 2): Encoding – the production of media messages by content creators, embedded within specific ideological and institutional frameworks; the media text – a structured yet polysemic symbolic artifact; Decoding – the interpretation of these messages by audiences situated within diverse cultural and social contexts [13].

Crucially, Hall challenged the notion of communication as a transparent or neutral transmission of meaning. Instead, he emphasized the role of ideological codes, institutional positioning, and cultural knowledge in shaping both the production and reception of media texts. The encoding/decoding process is not symmetrical: meaning is not fixed at the point of production but is actively interpreted—often contested—by audiences.

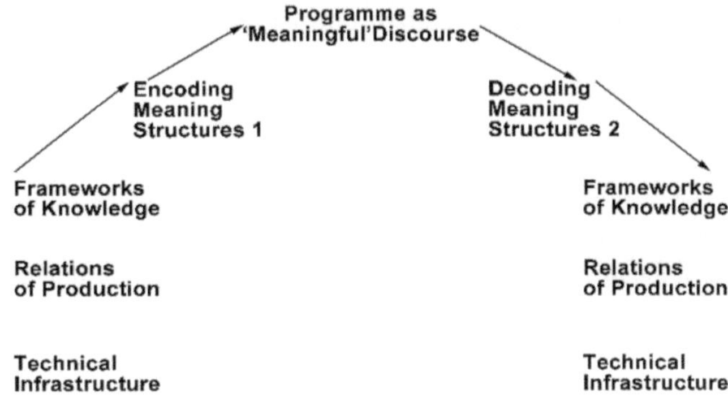

Fig. 2. The Theory of Encoding and Decoding.

Effective communication requires a certain alignment of codes between producers and receivers. However, Hall argued that such alignment is never guaranteed. Audience interpretation depends on factors such as class, culture, ideology, and contextual knowledge, leading to multiple possible readings of the same message, including misinterpretation, negotiation, or rejection.

To account for these variations, Hall proposed three hypothetical decoding positions:

Dominant–hegemonic position: The viewer fully accepts the preferred meaning encoded by the producer, reinforcing dominant ideologies. Negotiated position: The viewer partially accepts the dominant meaning but modifies it based on individual experiences or social context. Oppositional position: The viewer rejects the encoded meaning and interprets the message through an alternative or resistant ideological lens [14].

Hall's model redefined media reception as an active site of meaning-making, where power, ideology, and audience agency intersect. Rather than passive consumers, audiences become participants in a contested cultural space, engaging in negotiation, resistance, or re-signification of media texts.

Aura as Cognitive Process: From Symbolic Structure to Interpretive Generation.

In the context of AI-generated art, aura is no longer an inherent metaphysical presence, but rather a cognitive-affective construct generated through symbolic interaction and cultural decoding. This transformation can be better understood by integrating Saussure's semiotic framework with Stuart Hall's encoding/decoding model.

According to Saussure, a sign consists of two inseparable components: the signifier (the perceptual form) and the signified (the conceptual content). In the case of AI-generated images, the signifier is produced algorithmically—through code, not by human hand. However, the signified does not pre-exist, nor is it embedded in the image itself; it emerges through the viewer's cognitive and affective engagement with the visual form. Building on this, Hall emphasizes that meaning is not fixed by the producer, but is negotiated and constructed by the audience through processes of decoding. This decoding is shaped by the viewer's social identity, cultural context, and ideological position. Meaning is not transmitted intact; it is reconstructed at the point of reception.

When combined, these perspectives lead to a critical insight: in AI-generated art, the aura is no longer located within the object or its historical originality, but within the interpretive act of the observer. The image functions as a floating signifier, whose meaning and affective charge are realized only in relation to the viewer's symbolic framework.

Without a human author, AI art displaces traditional foundations of aura—authenticity, authorship, and singularity. Instead, it distributes aura across the event of viewing, where meaning is not inherited but co-produced. The interaction between image and observer becomes the site where symbolic resonance, emotional projection, and aesthetic contemplation converge.

Thus, aura in the age of AI is not lost, but rather reconfigured. It shifts from being a static, object-bound quality to a dynamic, relational phenomenon, arising through cultural cognition and subjective interpretation. In this sense, aura becomes an emergent property of meaning-making, situated in the tension between technological mediation and human perception.

2.2.1 Conclusion

The Transformation of Aura in the Age of AI Art. AI-generated art fundamentally challenges traditional notions of authorship, originality, and aura. However, from a semiotic perspective, the structure of meaning remains intact: although the signifier is generated algorithmically, the signified is still constructed through the viewer's decoding process, which is shaped by cultural, social, and cognitive frameworks. In this sense, aura has not disappeared—it has transformed. It has shifted from a metaphysical quality rooted in material uniqueness to a relational and symbolic phenomenon grounded in the interpretive engagement between the viewer and the image. Aura is no longer bound to the 'original' or the 'author', but is produced in the space of interaction—through emotional resonance, cultural recognition, and aesthetic reflection. Rather than destroying aura, AI art redefines it as a semiotic and experiential structure—a dynamic configuration co-constructed by symbolic forms and the interpretive activities of the observer. In this reframed model, meaning is not embedded in the object, but emerges through a process of active perception and negotiated understanding.

This reconceptualization affirms the continued relevance of semiotic and cultural models in the analysis of digital and post-human aesthetics. Most importantly, it repositions the viewer as an active co-creator of meaning, and asserts that aura persists—not in the object itself, but in the relationship it establishes within a specific socio-cultural context.

2.3 The Age of No Authors: Crisis of Artistic Identity

Traditional artistic creation has long been intertwined with the notion of the artist—a figure whose subjectivity, stylistic signature, emotional expression, and creative intent collectively constitute authorship. This authorship not only lends an artwork its distinctiveness but also serves as a symbolic anchor within broader cultural systems [15].

The rise of AI-generated art, however, poses a fundamental question: Who is the author? In algorithm-driven creation, the human creator increasingly recedes into the background, while generative models autonomously produce images. When the encoder of meaning becomes a neural network or a dataset, can we still speak of authorship in any traditional sense? Or have we entered an era of post-human creativity, an age of no authors?

This paradigm shift severs the historical link between creator and creation, destabilizing the institutional frameworks upon which modern art has been constructed. In AI-generated art, the image is no longer the outcome of individual genius or inspiration, but the statistical recombination of billions of visual fragments drawn from massive datasets. Its anonymity, depersonalization, and scalability contribute to a radical erosion of the concept of authorship. This transformation also disrupts traditional valuation systems in the art market. Historically, an artwork's economic and symbolic value has been deeply tied to the reputation and biography of its author—names like Picasso or Van Gogh function as semiotic capital. In contrast, when millions of AI-generated images can be produced instantly and anonymously, without curatorial mediation or authorial naming, the scarcity and uniqueness of individual works become increasingly difficult to sustain.

Thus, the "age of no authors" is not merely a technical development; it signifies a crisis of cultural identity. It challenges our established assumptions about creation, originality, and expression, raising profound questions about artistic legitimacy, intellectual property, authorship ethics, and the role of creative education.

In response to this identity vacuum, two strategic trajectories have emerged. The first seeks to re-inscribe authorship through naming mechanisms, as exemplified by projects like Mario Klingemann's BOTTO, where the AI system is positioned as a collaborator rather than a tool. The second path de-centers the creator altogether, placing emphasis on the audience as the locus of artistic meaning. In this view, the artwork's significance lies not in who made it, but in how it is interpreted, experienced, and engaged with. From the perspective of cultural interaction design, AI-generated art prompts not only a transformation of creative tools but also a redefinition of how art is participated in and co-constructed. When we shift the central question from "Who made this?" to "How does this interact with me?", artistic identity no longer resides in the individual artist but emerges as a negotiated field of meaning. This shift marks the deeper essence of authorship reconfiguration in the age of AI [16].

3   Case Studies: Reconstructing the Aura in AI-Generated Art

3.1   Midjourney: Viewer-Centered Aura in Algorithmic Imagery

Midjourney is one of the most widely used text-to-image generation platforms today. With minimal text prompts, users can produce highly complex visual outputs. The system's core technology relies on diffusion models, which are trained on massive datasets of image-text pairs to learn statistical associations between language and visual form, thereby enabling the synthesis of new images [17]. In this generative process, the traditional figure of the "artist" is nearly absent. The resulting image is not the product of an individual's inspiration but the outcome of algorithmic automation. However, as previously discussed, the aura of an artwork need not depend on authorship alone—it can be regenerated through the viewer's interpretive decoding. Midjourney's interface encourages ongoing user interaction—prompt editing, variation selection, regeneration—forming a kind of viewer-led artistic practice.

The resulting aura thus no longer resides in the artwork's material uniqueness or historical location, but rather in the perceptual exchange between viewer and image. The image becomes an emotional catalyst, acquiring meaning through the viewer's gaze. Although this meaning is inherently subjective, it often offers a more individualized and immediate experience—constituting a new, viewer-centered model of aura. Moreover, Midjourney outputs are frequently saved, modified, shared on social media, or incorporated into commercial design. In this circulation, images undergo continuous re-encoding, generating new layers of meaning. Although the generative process itself is de-authored, the circulation of meaning remains highly culturally specific and semiotically marked.

3.2 BOTTO: Artificial Naming and Collective Aura Formation

BOTTO is a decentralized AI art project initiated by artist Mario Klingemann. Each week, the AI generates thousands of images, but only a select few are chosen, named, and minted as NFTs. This selection process is entirely community-driven, conducted through a decentralized voting mechanism [18].

BOTTO is not merely a generative engine—it is a co-creative system. The AI offers the raw signifier, but the image only becomes a "work" with cultural significance—the signified—through community participation, naming, and circulation. This model fully activates Hall's decoding theory: meaning is not encoded by the producer but negotiated and constructed among receivers.

This collective naming strategy serves as a response to the "age of no authors"—it reintroduces authorship through human-led naming and selection, transforming the audience from passive consumers into active co-constructors of meaning. The resulting work acquires a consensus-based aura: its cultural value emerges not from the genius of an individual but from shared aesthetic recognition.

BOTTO also demonstrates that dematerialization does not equate to devaluation. In the crypto art market, these community-validated works still carry exchange, collectible, and discursive value. This indicates that even in a decentralized, non-physical context, aura can be reconstructed through social processes and cultural frameworks (Table 1).

Table 1. Comparison between Midjourney and BOTTO in AI Art.

Dimension	Midjourney	BOTTO
Generation Mechanism	User inputs textual prompts; AI generates images via diffusion models	AI autonomously generates thousands of images weekly; community votes to select and name artworks
Authorship	De-authored; users act as prompt formulators and interpreters	Authorship reintroduced through community-driven naming and selection

(continued)

Table 1. (*continued*)

Dimension	Midjourney	BOTTO
Audience Role	Individual interaction; viewers personalize image through prompt adjustment	Collective co-creation; community collaboratively negotiates naming and circulation
Meaning Generation Path	Meaning arises from individual viewers' psychological decoding and emotional projection	Meaning constructed and negotiated collectively among community members
Aura Construction Mode	Subjective aura arising from viewer's personal interpretation and emotional engagement	Consensus-based aura grounded in communal naming and shared aesthetic recognition
Relation to Traditional Art	Weakens artwork's historicity and originality; emphasizes present experience	Reconstructs authorship and uniqueness; redistributes artistic authority in technical and institutional context
Social Significance	Emphasizes democratic, participatory individual aesthetic experience	Demonstrates decentralized cultural structures enabling co-creation and value negotiation

4   The Transformation Mechanism of Aura in the Age of AI

Building upon previous chapters—from Walter Benjamin's original notion of aura, to structural semiotic analysis, and finally to case studies in the age of 'no authors'—this chapter provides a theoretical synthesis of how aura is transformed in the context of AI-generated art.

The reconstruction of aura reflects a fundamental shift—from material to symbolic, and from author-centered to receiver-centered paradigms. This transformation is not merely technologically driven, but results from the interplay between cultural mechanisms and cognitive participation. AI-generated art does not abolish the sacredness of art, but reconfigures it through new modes of interaction, collective naming practices, and a redefined role of the audience. In this restructured field of signification, the viewer is no longer a passive receiver, but an active co-producer of meaning and cultural value.

The next section will systematically outline the core features of this mechanism, showing that the transformation of aura in AI art is not limited to visual perception, but is deeply embedded in contemporary structures of cultural cognition and aesthetic experience.

4.1   Aura Has Not Disappeared, but Transformed Its Locu

Although AI-generated art lacks the traditional structures of the 'original' and the 'author', our analysis reveals that aura has not vanished. Rather, it has shifted from the artist's physical authorship to the interaction between the audience and the artwork. Emotional projection, symbolic decoding, and cultural interpretation now co-construct the aura in this digital context.

4.2 The Continuity of Aura Within the Signifier–Signified Mechanism

Through Saussure's signifier–signified model, we argue that while AI-generated "signifiers" (such as pixelated images or rendered 3D scenes) are infinitely reproducible, their "signifieds" are diverse and shaped by cultural context, individual experience, and social background. This openness of decoding is precisely what allows aura to persist. The audience reactivates the work's ritual value and symbolic distance through interpretation, preserving its aesthetic tension without relying on material authenticity.

4.3 Re-Encoding Strategies in the Age of No Authors

In the age of no authors, the act of encoding is executed by algorithms rather than human intention. However, as Hall's encoding-decoding theory suggests, encoding remains shaped by symbolic systems, cultural rules, and training data. Thus, while subjectivity is absent, ideological and aesthetic structures persist through algorithmic proxies. Conversely, the decoding process becomes more autonomous for audiences. In this shift from producer-centric to receiver-centric meaning construction, aura transforms into a participatory mechanism—marking its evolution from elitism to democratic engagement.

4.4 Theoretical Reflections and Implications

In the age of no authors, From the perspectives of uniqueness and ritual value, AI-generated art appears to undermine the foundation of traditional aura. However, semiotic and cultural studies indicate that cognitive engagement by viewers can still generate new forms of mystery and distance. AI, rather than terminating aura, catalyzes its transformation:

From the uniqueness of the object to the uniqueness of the experience;
From the authenticity of the artifact to the authenticity of interpretation;
From a static mystical object to a dynamic process of negotiated meaning.

In this light, AI art should not be seen as the end of aura, but as an agent in its transformation.

5 Results

With the advancement of AI technology, the traditional concept of "aura," once diminished by mechanical reproduction, has not vanished but rather undergone a structural transformation. In the AI era, aura shifts from reliance on the unique material presence of artworks to an emphasis on meaning generation and interpretation within symbolic systems.

Grounded in Saussure's semiotic theory, artworks function as signs composed of the dual structure of the signifier (material form) and the signified (meaning). While AI-generated works are infinitely reproducible at the level of the signifier, their meanings are not fixed; instead, they are dynamically constructed through the interplay of encoding and decoding. Hall's encoding-decoding model further reveals that meaning is not solely produced at the point of creation, but also unfolds with complexity and variability in the process of audience reception.

Although the traditional characteristics of aura—uniqueness, distance, and cult value—are challenged in the AI context, they persist within the symbolic operations of art. Aura is no longer tied to the physical "presence" of an artwork but emerges through the shared construction of meaning between creator and viewer. It becomes a product of psychological and cognitive engagement, manifesting as a unique emotional experience toward the artistic sign.

In the AI age, the erosion of authorial identity and authority makes the production of aura increasingly dependent on sociocultural context and audience interpretation. Aura thus evolves into a socially constructed function of signs, reflecting the redefinition of art within digital culture.

In conclusion, the aura in the AI era is a dynamic process of symbolic and cognitive co-production, shaped by the interaction among encoders, artworks, and decoders. It retains the spiritual essence of the traditional aura while undergoing renewal amid technological and cultural shifts, offering a critical theoretical lens for understanding AI-generated art.

6 Outlook and Discussion

As artificial intelligence continues to advance within visual culture and creative practice, AI-generated art is progressively shaping a new ecosystem that departs from the traditional "author–work" paradigm. As argued in this paper, aura has not vanished in the age of AI—it has transformed into a dynamic structure co-produced by algorithms, audiences, and symbolic systems. This transformation not only redefines the ontological status of art but also raises new questions regarding originality, authorship, and cultural valuation.

First, the dematerialized and de-authored nature of AI art will continue to reshape the frameworks of creative production and intellectual property. Future research must investigate how authorship should be defined when algorithmic agents become the primary generators. Will the role of the artist shift toward that of curator, prompt engineer, or dataset architect? These questions demand systematic inquiry across legal, ethical, and aesthetic dimensions.

Second, the replicability and open symbolic structure of AI-generated imagery make meaning production increasingly dependent on the viewer's cultural literacy and perceptual engagement. The regeneration of aura thus becomes a collaborative process of perception and interpretation. Future studies should examine, from the perspectives of media theory, cognitive aesthetics, and cultural reception, how individual viewers construct subjective aura through multimodal interactions.

Third, as generative models (such as GPT-4, DALL·E, and Stable Diffusion) become more semantically powerful, AI is increasingly capable of actively participating in meaning construction. This challenges existing models of encoding and decoding, such as Hall's communication theory and Saussure's semiotics, and opens up new theoretical ground for conceptualizing "AI as author."

Finally, the integration of AI art with immersive technologies (such as AR/VR and multimodal generation models) will shift the artistic experience from passive viewing to dynamic interaction. Future research should investigate how aura is reconfigured in immersive environments—through temporality, embodied engagement, and collective perception.

In summary, aura in the AI age is no longer grounded in material singularity or authorial presence but is relocated to a fluid field of meaning construction. This field encompasses algorithmic architectures, viewing behavior, cultural codes, and interpretive frameworks—forming a complex mechanism of value negotiation. Tracing the evolution of this mechanism is key to rethinking what art is and to providing the theoretical infrastructure and cultural vision necessary for future artistic practice and institutional frameworks.

References

1. Benjamin, W.: A short history of photography. In: Jennings, M., Eiland, H., Smith, G. (eds.) Selected Writings, vol. 2, pp. 507–530. Harvard University Press, Cambridge (1999)
2. Benjamin, W.: The work of art in the age of mechanical reproduction. In: Arendt, H. (ed.) Illuminations, pp. 222–223. Schocken Books, New York (1969)
3. Duttlinger, C.: Imaginary encounters: Walter Benjamin and the aura of photography. Poet. Today. **29**(1), 87–88 (2008)
4. Peim, N.: Walter Benjamin in the age of digital reproduction: Aura in education: a rereading of 'the work of art in the age of mechanical reproduction'. J. Philos. Educ. **41**(3), 366–367 (2007)
5. Hansen, M.B.: Benjamin's Aura and the aesthetics of digital image. Crit. Inq. **34**(2), 337 (2008)
6. de Saussure, F.: Course in General Linguistics. Trans. Harris, R. Duckworth, London (1983)
7. Chandler, D.: Semiotics: the Basics, 2nd edn. Routledge, London (2007)
8. Bødker, H.: Stuart Hall's encoding/decoding model and the circulation of journalism in the digital landscape. In: Stuart Hall Lives: Cultural Studies in an Age of Digital Media, pp. 58–59. Routledge (2018)
9. Hall, S.: Encoding—decoding (1980). In: Crime and Media, pp. 44–55. Routledge (2019)
10. Barthes, R.: The Death of the Author. In: Heath, S. (ed.) Image, Music, Text, pp. 142–148. Hill and Wang, New York (1977)
11. Roose, K.: An AI-Generated Picture Won an Art Prize. Artists Aren't Happy (2022)
12. Makridakis, S.: The forthcoming artificial intelligence (AI) revolution: its impact on society and firms. Futures. **90**, 46–60 (2017)
13. Fernández-Castrillo, C.: The AI work of art in the age of its co-creation (2023)
14. Pesavento, C.: Arte e Intelligenza Collettiva. Botto alla sfida del contemporaneo (2023)
15. Jaruga-Rozdolska, A.: Artificial intelligence as part of future practices in the architect's work: MidJourney generative tool as part of a process of creating an architectural form. Architectus. **3**(71), 95–104 (2022)

16. BOTTO: The Decentralized Autonomous Artist. https://www.botto.com (accessed May 10, 2025)
17. Midjourney: About. https://www.midjourney.com/home (accessed May 10, 2025)

From Hype to Reality: Examining
the Challenges of Implementing Public
Metaverse Projects in South Korea

Keebaik Sim[(✉)] [iD]

University of California, Berkeley, Berkeley, CA 94720, USA
keebaik_sim@berkeley.edu

Abstract. Since 2020, the South Korean government allocated substantial budgets for metaverse-related projects, with all seventeen metropolitan local governments and other government entities initiating such projects. Despite a total investment of 106.4 billion Korean Won (72 million USD) from 2021 to 2023, many public metaverse projects failed to engage citizens and faced discontinuation within one to two years. This study analyzes the governance models of public metaverse projects to understand their failure. It addresses two research questions: (1) What are the government agencies' operational models for public metaverse projects? (2) What challenges do agencies face in planning and implementing these projects, particularly in inter-agency collaboration? Using a multi-method qualitative approach, including semi-structured interviews, field observations, and document analysis, the research reveals three key factors that affect the operation of public metaverse projects: (1) phased-in approach in funding structure, (2) bargain-driven civic engagement, and (3) power-leveraged participation. In addition, this research examines two forms of multi-tiered governmental dynamics that influence the quality of public metaverse projects: (1) hierarchical deference and (2) lateral competition. These dynamics often result in metaverse projects that are driven by government entities' political aspirations rather than existing citizens' needs. To overcome these challenges, government entities must strategically identify unique services the public sector can provide through the metaverse and develop a master plan defining the roles and features of local governments' metaverse to avoid service duplication.

Keywords: Metaverse · Public metaverse projects · Operational models · Metaverse governance models

1 Introduction

Since 2020, various companies have entered the metaverse business to secure related technologies and potential user groups, with the expectation that it would become a new space for communication and interaction [22]. Along with this

M. Schrepp and M. Rauterberg (Eds.): HCII 2025, LNCS 16342, pp. 438–452, 2026.
https://doi.org/10.1007/978-3-032-13164-5_28

movement in the private sector, the South Korean government has allocated significant budgets to metaverse-related projects to keep up with the trend. As a result, government entities began developing and operating public projects using metaverse technology. All seventeen metropolitan local governments across the country initiated metaverse-related projects, allocating a total budget of 106.4 billion Korean Won (equivalent to 72 million US Dollars) from 2021 to 2023. However, despite these investments, a significant number of these metaverse-based public projects failed to gain citizen engagement, fizzled out within just one to two years, and faced service discontinuation.

In this study, I analyze why public metaverse projects failed to gain citizen support and maintain continuous operation by focusing on the governance models of public metaverse projects. Examining the governance model for public metaverse projects is integral since the governance model shapes the relationships among the stakeholders, such as corporations and a wide range of government entities, which subsequently shape public metaverse projects' design and user experiences. Therefore, to ensure that public metaverse projects provide services that citizens need and operate sustainably, it is important to analyze the governance model at a macro level and, based on this, examine how to improve the design, functionality, and operational model.

Against this backdrop, this study addresses the following research questions: (1) What are the government agencies' operational models of public metaverse projects? (2) What challenges do government agencies face when planning and implementing public metaverse projects, particularly in terms of inter-agency collaboration and coordination?

To answer these questions, this study employs a multi-method qualitative research approach, incorporating in-depth semi-structured interviews and field observations to provide a comprehensive understanding of the planning and operation of public metaverse projects. To complement the interview data, I conducted a discourse analysis of documents related to the metaverse and their integration into various areas and levels of the urban environment. Additionally, I conducted participatory observation on various public metaverse projects such as Play Meta Road, Metaverse Gangnam Village, and Seoul Metaverse to understand the user experience. This examination aimed to understand how the present governance models shape the materialization of the metaverse.

The research findings I present demonstrate that there are three key factors that affect the operation of public metaverse projects: (1) phased-in approach in funding structure, (2) Bargain-driven civic engagement, and (3) power-leveraged participation. In addition, I examined multi-tiered governmental dynamics when implementing metaverse projects: (1) hierarchical deference and (2) lateral competition. These dynamics support the operation of the metaverse as an innovative technology expected to create demand rather than as a response to existing needs, leading to a lack of perceived necessity for the metaverse among citizens. To overcome this challenge, I suggest that the government entities must strategically identify unique services the public sector can provide through the metaverse and master plan the roles and responsibilities of local governments to avoid similar functions and services.

2   Overview

2.1   Context of the Emergence of the Metaverse and Its Definition

Since the widespread adoption of the Internet in the 1990s, various forms of cyberspace have been created, with the metaverse being one of them. In particular, metaverse gained global attention lately with the development of technologies such as Extended Reality, 5G, and Artificial Intelligence that are within the metaverse value chain [16]. The metaverse, a term combining "meta" (transcending) and "universe," describes a hypothetical digital realm interconnected with the physical world. Coined by Neal Stephenson in his 1992 novel "Snow Crash," it initially depicted a vast virtual environment where users interact via digital avatars. Since then, the concept has evolved to encompass various ideas, including lifelogging [4], collective virtuality spaces [2,3], embodied spatial Internet [20], mirror worlds [20], and omniverse: a venue of simulation and collaboration [6]. These diverse interpretations reflect the metaverse's potential as an immersive, interconnected digital universe paralleling our physical reality [16]. The advancement of technologies enabling real-time interaction in 3D virtual spaces, coupled with the COVID-19 pandemic, prompted various public and private sectors to invest in metaverse platforms as alternatives to 2D websites [1]. These entities were excited by the metaverse's potential to overcome physical restrictions, maintain economic activity, and adapt to remote work trends [7,14].

2.2   Public Sector's Adoption of Metaverse

As the metaverse was perceived as a form of public space where numerous people interact and communicate with each other by transcending the boundaries between reality and virtual reality, public sectors embarked on developing their metaverse platforms [15]. Many global cities developed 3-D representations of their cities, such as Santa Monica, Orlando, Boston, and Las Vegas [9]. Among them, Seoul, the capital city of South Korea, is known as the first city to develop a public metaverse platform (see Fig. 1) [8,21]. Seoul is not the only public sector with a metaverse platform in South Korea. Many other local governments, cities, municipal governments, and government ministries have developed their own metaverse [5,11]. This trend reflects South Korea's broader national commitment to metaverse technologies, with investments and initiatives at various levels of government aimed at securing a significant global market share in metaverse technology by 2026 [17].

The aspiration for South Korea to become a leader in metaverse technology was established as part of the national agenda in January 2022 by the Ministry of Science and ICT (MSIT) during the presidency of Moon Jae-in. This initiative was then continued and further developed by the administration of President Yoon Suk Yeol, who took office in May 2022. The national agenda includes a

Fig. 1. A press conference announcing the launch of Metaverse Seoul. Metaverse Seoul is being introduced as Seoul's new continent. (https://www.youtube.com/watch?v=l8Ptjc-_TdM)

set of prioritized goals, issues, or tasks that a country or its government identifies as crucial for the nation's development, well-being, or strategic objectives. These agendas set by a president frequently mirror the political interests of their party and the promises that were made while the president was running for the presidential campaign. However, some agendas continue to be part of the succeeding president's agendas using different wordings and phrases even if the president has been elected from a different party as opposed to the previous president. These agendas often encompass key areas such as economic growth, social welfare, education, security, and other important aspects of national interest, which become the top priority item on a government's policy or action plan. For example, President Yoon Suk Yeol, has announced the "Promotion of Growth-Oriented Industrial Strategies" as one of the agendas. The Yoon's administration executes the agenda by strengthening the foundation and development of corporate-centric industry clusters or megacities for economic innovation [18]. Under this overarching agenda, President Yoon's administration has announced core strategic industries for Korea's economic growth, such as AI, big data, Urban Air Mobility (UAM), digital media content, metaverse, autonomous vehicles, robots, and biomedical. In line with the national agenda, the government allocates the budget to various entities that successfully bid for grants to implement related projects. Depending on the project, these entities include government-affiliated public institutions, public corporations, private and public academic institutions, and private sector companies.

Although metaverse was supported politically and financially as part of the national strategic industry, most of the public metaverse projects failed to attract users or suspended the service. For example, Metaverse Seoul, a public metaverse created by the Seoul Metropolitan Government (hereafter, SMG), was only downloaded 5000 times over 21 months with a daily average of about 500 users [5,19]. This means that only 0.05% of Seoul's total population of 9.38 million people used the platform. As Seoul Metaverse, which ambitiously started as a frontrunner in public metaverse projects, yielded results different from expectations, other local governments that had planned public metaverse initiatives began to withdraw their plans [5]. Meanwhile, local governments already operating such platforms started to cut their budgets [12].

Against this background, this research analyzes the governance model at a macro level and, based on this, examines how to improve the design, functionality, and operational model and to subsequently ensure that public metaverse projects provide services that citizens need and operate sustainably.

3 Research Method

To answer the research questions, this study adopts a comprehensive qualitative research approach, combining in-depth semi-structured interviews and participatory observations to explore the operational models and challenges of public metaverse projects. The research was conducted in South Korea across multiple periods from 2020 to 2023.

In the summers of 2022 and 2023, 26 semi-structured interviews were conducted with industry experts and government officials involved in Korea's metaverse industry. The initial focus was on public sector initiators and corporate technology providers, as they are the primary drivers of public metaverse projects in South Korea. As the research progressed, the scope of interviewees expanded to include a broader network of stakeholders, encompassing state enterprises, conglomerates, various government institutions, research labs, small and medium-sized startups, and academic communities. Interviewee selection prioritized individuals with direct experience in metaverse-related projects, utilizing a snowball sampling technique to identify additional relevant actors who could offer diverse perspectives.

To enhance the depth of the research, participant observations were carried out on public metaverse projects such as Seoul Metaverse and Gangnam Meta Road. Additionally, relevant documents pertaining to the development and implementation of public metaverse projects were analyzed. This multi-faceted approach, combining stakeholder interviews, participant observations, and document analysis, has enabled the development of a holistic understanding of how funding structures and operational models influence the design, features, and programs of South Korea's public metaverse projects, ultimately shaping the user experience.

4 Findings

The previous literature review section explained that the widespread adoption of metaverse projects by various government entities is due to the central government's designation of metaverse as a strategic industry and their financial support for local governments engaged in metaverse-related projects. Against this backdrop, many local governments have created metaverse platforms. This section aims to examine the operational models of public metaverse platforms, the multi-tiered government dynamics that exist in planning and operating them, and the impact these models have on user interactions in public metaverse projects.

4.1 Operational Models of Public Metaverse Projects

This section addresses the first research question: "What are the government agencies' operational models of public metaverse projects?" It analyzes the long-term funding structure for public metaverse projects, how they attract user engagement, and the implications of each approach. It specifically examines how public metaverse initiatives are planned with regard to their medium to long-term funding structures, the methods employed to attract user engagement, and the implications of these strategies.

Funding Structure Particular to Public Projects. As mentioned earlier, the central government's designation of the public metaverse as a strategic industry has led various local governments to implement metaverse projects. However, since there are no successful cases of metaverse technology as a public platform, local governments are cautious about spending large sums of money at once to create metaverse platforms. For this reason, they took phased-in approach which is refered to as a strategy for implementing new systems, processes, or technologies in several stages rather than all at once. The phased-in approach is widely adopted in the business field when companies need to implement complex changes that require large sums of investments such as digital transformation [10]. During the interview, Minshik Choi, Manager of the Tourism Marketing Team in the Tourism Promotion Division at Gangnam-gu Office, mentioned that spending a significant budget on unknown, emerging technology is risky for government entities:

> Making a metaverse with attractive interactions is not feasible when developing a metaverse for the government. This is because government projects have limited budgets, particularly for projects that are using Metaverse that do not have guaranteed success. Since there isn't any thorough understanding of the metaverse, the government refrains from spending too much money on the metaverse. Metaverse Gangnam Village spent 270,000 won at the beginning since the government can't spend 2,000,000 won without knowing its success.

In a similar vein, the SMG also took the phased-in approach when developing Metaverse Seoul. In 2022, 2.07 billion won ($1.59 million) was invested, followed by 2.8 billion won ($2.15 million) in 2023, and 724.7 million won ($557,462) in 2024. The total investment amounts to 5.59 billion won ($4.30 million) from 2022 to 2024 during the twenty-one months of operation. Initially, Seoul City planned to invest a total of 40 billion won ($30.77 million) over five years from 2022 to 2026 but Seoul Metaverse has suspended its service [13].

Considering the characteristics of metaverse technology, there are limitations to expanding its scale once it's created. Therefore, it is crucial to invest a significant amount at the initial stage to build a certain level of functionality and make it capable of future expansion. However, due to the nature of public projects, relatively low initial investments were made, which led to the government having no choice but to create metaverse environments with limitations. Compared to commercial metaverse platforms such as Zepeto, the public metaverse platforms lack visual completeness and entertaining aspects that lead to a lack of immersive interactive experiences (personal communication Hee-il Robert Yang[1]). From the user's point of view, unless the public metaverse projects offer services that can significantly enhance citizens' experience or provide entertaining features that are far more entertaining than those offered by commercial metaverse projects, citizens would not recognize the purpose of using public metaverse platforms. Consequently, users do not find the need to utilize public metaverse projects since they do not offer services that are significantly convenient and efficient compared to existing mediums, such as websites and phone calls, due to the government's limited understanding of the affordances of metaverse. For entertainment, which is one of the major features focused by public metaverse projects, users would rather go to commercial metaverse platforms that offer far greater entertainment and engaging experience.

This section's findings described that due to the nature of the government-funded projects, public metaverse projects are developed amidst financial restrictions by taking cautious investing and phased-in approach. These constraints prevent developers from developing a more enhanced version of public metaverse projects resulting in a lack of completeness compared to commercial metaverse platforms leading to the loss of users' failing user engagement. In regard to this situation, the following section examines the strategies that the public metaverse utilized to attract users.

Bargain-Driven Civic Engagement. Considering the given situation in which the public metaverse platforms do not include integral features that can streamline city-related administrative services and entertainment to citizens compared to commercial metaverse platforms, the public metaverse platforms rely on luring users by utilizing several strategies to increase user attraction. First, they offer offline event access tickets to the visitors. Gangnam district office distributed offline K-pop concert tickets to people who visited Metaverse Gangnam Village. Although the concert was a free concert hosted by the Gangnam district office, the tickets offered a seating area closest to the stage. Second, they incentivize users' participation by offering vouchers and coupons that users can use at various shops and restaurants. In order to increase user attraction, Metaverse Seoul organized an event called "Chool Check," (see Fig. 2) which is

---

[1] Head of Business at Zepeto. Zepeto is Asia's largest metaverse platform owned by Naver which is Korea's largest search engine platform.

translated as an attendance check in English. Seoul Metaverse distributed vouchers for Starbucks free americano to users who logged in for seven days in a row. Also, Seoul Metaverse offered coupons to those who reached the highest score after playing games in Seoul Metaverse. The commercial metaverse platforms also distribute gifts to attract users and are able to do this with more latitude than public metaverse platforms. However, according to Minshik Choi, Manager of the Tourism Marketing Team in the Tourism Promotion Division at the Gangnam-gu Office, unlike commercial metaverse platforms, distributing vouchers and coupons on public metaverse platforms is not very effective and can violate election law:

> It is very difficult for the public to operate the metaverse. It is a lot easier for private companies to operate metaverse spaces because they can give gifts and hold events to people who are visiting the metaverse spaces. For example, Gucci sells virtual items and Samsung gives gift certificates that can be exchanged for products. However, it is difficult for the city government to do the same as private companies for various reasons. This is because giving something can violate the law or the election law.

Choi explained that providing benefits or incentives to citizens by current elected officials can potentially violate election laws. Such actions may be interpreted as attempts to influence future voting behavior, effectively constituting a form of bribery that undermines the integrity of the democratic process. Unlike commercial companies that can attract users with valuable incentives, public sector metaverse projects face strict limitations on the gifts or rewards they can offer due to legal and ethical constraints. Consequently, the modest gifts or vouchers available to public metaverse platforms are often ineffective in attracting and retaining users. As a result, bargain-driven civic engagement is a commonly employed operational model for public metaverse projects aimed at increasing visitor numbers. However, this approach lacks sustainability for two key reasons. First, it heavily relies on public funds for distributing vouchers, which can strain limited government resources. Second, there's a risk of violating election laws, as these incentives could be perceived as attempts to influence future voting behavior. Consequently, while this model may boost short-term engagement, it poses significant legal and financial challenges for long-term project viability.

Power-Leveraged Participation. In addition to utilizing various strategies to attract users via direct incentives, government entities also engage in indirect user attraction by working with commercial entities that could bring more users into the metaverse. During this process of recruiting corporations, the government uses what this study describes as power-leveraged participation, demonstrating that government entities, as the superior party owning metaverse platforms, leverage their authority to diversify functions. Unlike bargain-driven civic engagement, in power-leveraged participation, governments operating their own metaverse projects use their superiority to expand platform functionality and

Fig. 2. The two images on the left are stories posted on the Metaverse Seoul Instagram account. The first image promotes an attendance event running throughout July, while the second image is a story post announcing various events taking place in the metaverse. The third image is an advertisement from Gangnam Village, a metaverse operated by Gangnam District, promoting various prizes that can be won.

compel subordinate entities to participate, anticipating that more functions will lead to increased user attraction.

According to Sean Choo, the CEO and founder of a startup, Swift Parker, his company at that time, was using a co-working space offered by the SMG along with other startups as part of the venture business promotion policy. Although Swift Parker was under no contractual obligation to comply with other requests from the SMG simply because they were using a space provided by the city, there was an implicit pressure to accommodate the city's request. One such request was related to Seoul Metaverse. For example, the SMG encouraged all the companies that use the shared office space to participate in Metaverse Seoul. To further enhance the platform's vibrancy and user engagement, the SMG has encouraged companies to establish virtual booths. The SMG believed that these booths, featuring company names, business models, and visions, would create a more dynamic metaverse environment. While participation wasn't mandatory, the interviewee felt a sense of obligation to contribute due to their use of office space provided by the SMG. Power-leveraged participation is another operational model for public metaverse projects, where government entities, as the superior party, compel private companies (the inferior party) to participate in metaverse projects by exercising their authority and influence.

Bargain-driven civic engagement and power-leveraged participation are two operational models for public metaverse projects. These models aim to promote user engagement while addressing the funding limitations inherent in government-funded public sector initiatives. However, these two models are limited in sustainably operating public metaverse platforms. In order to create public metaverse platforms that are useful for users within the financial limitations, government entities should concentrate on developing truly engaging features and conduct research to determine which functions and services would be most beneficial to people as part of a public metaverse. Based on this research, they should provide relevant features that encourage user engagement driven by identifying their genuine needs.

4.2 Challenges that Exist in Inter-agency Collaboration and Coordination

In the previous section, I examined the funding structure related to creating and operating public metaverse platforms, the limitations in attracting users due to this structure, and the methods used to work around these challenges. This section focuses on other dimensions that affect the quality of public metaverse platforms, mainly multi-tiered governmental dynamics that exist among various government agencies when they simultaneously participate in creating public metaverse platforms. These dynamics are: 1) hierarchical deference and 2) lateral competition.

Hierarchical Deference. The first type of dynamic that exists in intergovernmental relations is hierarchical deference. The hierarchical deference is a concept that describes how lower-tier or subordinate government entities avoid competing with higher-tier entities on similar projects. When the government designates the metaverse as a national strategic industry, numerous government divisions and entities bid for metaverse projects that end up leading to the unintended consequence of creating many metaverse projects with similar characteristics and forms. In such cases, instead of focusing on developing and operating projects to maximize effectiveness within the given budget, lower-hierarchy government entities tend to avoid political conflicts by refraining from outperforming higher-hierarchy government entities working on similar projects. This tendency was evident in my conversation with Minshik Choi, a manager of the tourism marketing team in the tourism promotion division at Gangnam-gu Office:

> Gangnam District did not create its own metaverse for a few reasons. First, it would be expensive. Second, the SMG is already creating its own metaverse, and there was a risk of conflict between the two. Finally, Gangnam District is part of Seoul, so it is unnecessary to create conflict by developing a similar product to the SMG.

Before hearing Choi's interview, there was an assumption that government or public institutions would implement public projects like metaverse by working as a single large organism towards one direction and goal. However, a hierarchy exists among government agencies due to differences in budget, scale, and political power that affects the implementation of public metaverse projects. When a more powerful political agency is conducting a similar project, lower-tier or subordinate government entities tend to be cautious and avoid creating competitive situations in project development and operation. This hierarchical deference limits the environment for developing better quality public metaverse platforms and restricts project development and operation. As a result, citizens' chances of benefiting from public metaverse projects with improved services are reduced. This situation highlights how the internal dynamics and power structures within government entities can inadvertently hinder the optimal development of public metaverse initiatives, potentially compromising the quality of services available to citizens.

Lateral Competition. The second type of dynamic that exists in intergovernmental relations is lateral competition. Lateral competition is a concept that describes a competition among government entities in the same hierarchy competing with each other to win funding from the central government and increase political power. When the strategic industries are announced by the central government, local government, government-affiliated public institutions, and government-affiliated public corporations compete with each other by proposing various projects that are related to those technologies to receive funding.

According to Ha-neul Jeong, a former professor of Global Leaders College at Yonsei University and Director of Yonsei Digital Experience Center, one of the major reasons for government-related initiatives participating in agenda-related projects is to gain more budget, recruit more people, and expand their political and economic influence among other government-related initiatives. When the metaverse is included as one of the core strategy industries, various government entities embark on metaverse-related projects to gain the central government's funding. For instance, the Ministry of Culture, Sports and Tourism, the Seoul Metropolitan Government, and the local governments propose metaverse-related projects to gain funding from the central government. After receiving funding, these government entities announce various metaverse projects and subcontract startups, small and medium-sized enterprises, and conglomerates to implement the projects. Therefore, to increase political power, local governments must come up with a project related to a field that the government is focusing on to secure funding. Professor Jeong added:

> "If the pie gets bigger, everyone wants to get the biggest piece they can get. The local governments used the grant money to implement projects and hire people who could carry out those projects."

He elaborated that the central government grant is a stepping stone. By leveraging this financial backing, local governments can strengthen their political influence by expanding their workforce and size. According to Professor Jeong, when media technology was selected as a strategic area around 2010, many local governments were eager to engage in media technology-related projects, leading to numerous implementations. Similarly, as metaverse was considered a strategic industry, it resulted in funding competition among government entities, local governments, and provincial governments to secure funding for developing metaverse projects. Professor Jeong noted that since the early 2000s, there has been bipartisan support for the digitization of cities. This led government entities to view central government funding allocated for city digitization projects as potential avenues to enhance their political influence. If the projects that government entities are competitively implementing are premised on improving citizens' quality of life, lateral competition can have a positive effect. However, lateral competition related to projects without specific plans on how they contribute to citizens' lives is limited to benefiting only the agencies that secure project funding.

The dynamics of hierarchical deference and lateral competition reveal that government entities often view metaverse projects primarily as tools to enhance their political influence rather than as opportunities to address pressing issues in the built environment. This approach prioritizes institutional goals over citizen needs, potentially limiting the metaverse's capacity to offer innovative solutions to real-world urban challenges.

5 Discussions and Conclusion

When the metaverse became a trendy topic, Korean cities and local governments created their own metaverse platforms earlier than many global companies. These public metaverse projects gained attention both domestically and internationally. Unfortunately, not long after, many public metaverse projects were suspended, had their budgets cut, or had their plans withdrawn. Through this research, I analyzed the reasons why the metaverse, as an alternative to physical urban spaces, failed to meet expectations of becoming an innovative, utopian space and faced eventual service termination. To interrogate these causes, I examined the governance model at a macro level since the characteristics, operation, and design of public projects like the metaverse are greatly influenced by government policies and funding structures.

This study first overviewed how the central government designates innovative technologies like the metaverse as strategic industries. This designation leads to industry promotion in this sector and prompts lower government entities to secure funding, creating numerous public metaverse platforms. Based on this background, I analyzed the investment structure for development and advancement that local governments undertaking public metaverse projects have and researched operational models to attract users. As a result, due to the nature of public projects, government entities could not invest large sums at once to create highly polished and advanced metaverse platforms, making them relatively unrefined compared to commercial metaverses. Additionally, because the focus was on securing central government funding, these platforms lacked value for citizens as public metaverse platforms representing cities. This led to low usage rates, and to overcome this, operational models such as "bargain-driven civic engagement" and "power-leveraged participation" were analyzed. Furthermore, this study examined two forms of multi-tiered governmental dynamics, "hierarchical deference" and "lateral competition," that exist among various government agencies simultaneously participating in creating public metaverse platforms, which also contribute to its ineffective operations.

Based on these findings, this study offers three insights on how to improve public-facing metaverse projects in South Korea. First, the curation of public metaverse projects by higher authorities is integral for the successful establishment and stable operation of public metaverse platforms. Currently, almost all metropolitan governments in Korea have metaverse platforms, but their functions are mostly limited to one-time events, lacking uniqueness and differentiation. Therefore, it's necessary for a higher entity to curate the conceptual direction and functions of each local government's metaverse platform to ensure unique functions and programs that do not overlap with other public metaverse projects. Second, it's important for society to be patient as the metaverse, unfamiliar to operators, developers, and users alike, finds its utility as a public project. The concept and utility of the metaverse are still not clearly established, yet many Korean government entities have already implemented metaverse platforms. Considering that they adopted these platforms as early adopters and have been operating them for only 1–2 years, it's crucial for society to allow time for public metaverse projects to find their utility. Third, rigorous research is integral to investigating the affordances of the metaverse and discovering unique functions and services it can provide to citizens as public platforms. For example, it's important to consider which administrative services could be handled more efficiently using the metaverse compared to existing technologies like phone or chat. In other words, it's crucial to think about what special affordances the metaverse can offer citizens and what functions can meet citizens' needs as a city's metaverse.

Acknowledgments. To protect participants' privacy, pseudonyms are used for interviewees' names. This research was generously supported by the Graduate Division and Center for Korean Studies at the University of California, Berkeley.

Compliance with Ethical Standards

Disclosure of Interests. The authors have no competing interests to declare that are relevant to the content of this article.

References

1. Alfiras, M., et al.: Powered education based on Metaverse: pre- and post-COVID comprehensive review. Open Eng. **13**(1) (2023). https://doi.org/10.1515/eng-2022-0476
2. Ayiter, E.: Spatial Poetics, place, non-place and storyworlds: intimate spaces for Metaverse avatars. Technoetic Arts A J. Speculative Res. **17**(1/2), 155–169 (2019). https://doi.org/10.1386/tear_00013_1
3. Boellstorff, T.: Coming of Age in Second Life: An Anthropologist Explores the Virtually Human. Princeton University Press, Princeton (2008)
4. Bruun, A., Stentoft, M.L.: Lifelogging in the wild: participant experiences of using lifelogging as a research tool. In: Lamas, D., Loizides, F., Nacke, L., Petrie, H., Winckler, M., Zaphiris, P. (eds.) INTERACT 2019. LNCS, vol. 11748, pp. 431–451. Springer, Cham (2019). https://doi.org/10.1007/978-3-030-29387-1_24

5. Byun, I.: 세금먹는유령도시가된지자체메타버스 [Metaverse Owned by Local Government Becomes a Tax-Eating Ghost Town]. IT Chosun, July 2024. https://www.chosun.com/national/national_general/2024/07/01/SLGRE-YCE7NB6LI6FKZ2FBIXSHQ/

6. Frey, D., et al.: Solipsis: A Decentralized Architecture for Virtual Environments. Reno, United States (2008). https://inria.hal.science/inria-00337057

7. Garrido, C., Gonzàlez, A.: Cities and the Metaverse: an augmented, but better reality? CitiesToBe by Anteverti (2023). https://www.citiestobe.com/cities-metaverse/

8. Gaubert, J.: Seoul will be the first city to enter the Metaverse, November 2021. https://www.euronews.com/next/2021/11/10/seoul-to-become-the-first-city-to-enter-the-metaverse-what-will-it-look-like

9. Glickman, J.: How cities are engaging in the Metaverse, April 2022. https://www.nlc.org/article/2022/04/18/how-cities-are-engaging-in-the-metaverse/

10. Joglekar, N., et al.: Why manufacturers need a phased approach to digital transformation. MIT Sloan Manage. Rev. **65**(3) (2024). https://sloanreview.mit.edu/article/why-manufacturers-need-a-phased-approach-to-digital-transformation/

11. Kim, J.: 지방자치단체메타버스활용과나아갈방향 [Utilization of Metaverse by Local Governments and Future Directions]. The Public News (TPN), October 2022. http://www.thepublicnews.co.kr/news/articleView-.html?idxno=21978

12. Kim, S.: 찬밥" 된디지털콘텐츠… 문체부이어과기정통부도관련예산삭감 [Digital Content Becomes "Cold Rice [Neglected]"… Budget Cuts by Ministry of Culture Followed by Ministry of Science and ICT]. The Digital Times, September 2017. http://www.dt.co.kr/-contents.html?article-no=2017091402101231102001

13. Kim, Y.: 60억원들인서울시'메타버스서울', 1년 9개월만에문닫는다 ["Metaverse Seoul", which Cost Six Billion Won, Shuts Down After One Year and 9 Months]. 조선일보 [Chosun Ilbo], July 2024. https://www.chosun.com/national/national_general/2024/07/01/SLGRE-YCE7NB6LI6FKZ2F-BIXSHQ/

14. Koohang, A., et al.: Shaping the Metaverse into reality: a holistic multidisciplinary understanding of opportunities, challenges, and avenues for future investigation. J. Comput. Inf. Syst. **63**(3), 735–765 (2023). https://doi.org/10.1080/08874417.2023.2165197

15. Lee, J.S., Park, J.H.: Analysis of Metaverse design elements in the realm of public design - focused on Zepeto, Roblox, Minecraft, and Fortnite. J. Basic Des. Art **23**(4), 309–322 (2022). https://doi.org/10.47294/KSBDA.23.4.21

16. Lee, L.H., et al.: All one needs to know about Metaverse: a complete survey on technological singularity, virtual ecosystem, and research agenda, November 2021. https://doi.org/10.48550/arXiv.2110.05352

17. Nør Madsen, I.: Seoul leads the way: South Korea's Metaverse revolution, January 2025. https://icdk.dk/insights/south-koreas-metaverse-revolution

18. 20th Presidential Transition Committee], …: 윤석열정부 110 대국정과제 [110 National Policy Tasks of the Yoon Suk Yeol Administration], May 2022. https://www.korea.kr/archive/expDocView.do?docId=39973

19. Shim, J.: 디즈니도포기한메타버스에뛰어든지자체들, 지금상황 [Local Governments Jumping into Metaverse which was Even Gave Up by Disney: The Current Situation]. Biz.HanKook, April 2023. http://www.bizhankook.com/bk/article/25473

20. Smart, J., et al.: Metaverse Roadmap Overview (2007–2025): A Cross-Industry Public Foresight Project (2007). https://doi.org/10.13140/RG.2.2.30365.18406

21. Squires, C.: Seoul will be the first city government to join the Metaverse, November 2021. https://qz.com/2086353/seoul-is-developing-a-metaverse-government-platform
22. Wang, J., Medvegy, G.: Exploration the future of the metaverse and smart cities. In: The 22th International Conference on Electronic Business, vol. 12, p. 10. ICEB, Bangkok, Thailand (2022). https://aisel.aisnet.org/iceb2022/12

Research on Age-Appropriate UI Design of Smart Home Products Based on Visual Cognition and Internet of Things Technology

Ling Yan[(✉)] [iD], Songling Liu [iD], and Xiaohong Deng [iD]

Gannan University of Science and Technology, Jiangxi, China
`9320240011@gnust.edu.cn`

Abstract. In recent years, the world has been facing the challenge of population aging, and how to promote the enhancement of the well-being and quality of life of the elderly is becoming increasingly important, and the design of aging-adapted smart home products has become an important area of research.With the development of AI, cloud computing, IOT, IOT, big data, and VR/XR, smart healthcare, age-friendly smart health products, and digital derivation for aging will continue to grow. However, in many commercially available smart home products, the user interface design and interaction design are too complex for the elderly to understand and use, and the elderly are unlikely to use them for a long time if they can't learn how to do so.Based on this design pain point, this study starts from the visual cognitive characteristics and behavioral habits of the elderly, and explores the functional requirements and UI design needs of elderly users when using smart health products. This study analyzes the aging-friendly UI design of smart home products from the aspects of visual cognition and IoT technology, and proposes a series of aging-friendly UI design principles for smart home products. It provides theoretical support and practical guidance for the aging-friendly design of smart home products.

Keywords: Age-appropriate UI design · Visual cognition · Internet of Things technology · Smart home products

1 Research Background and Literature Review

In recent years, the world is faced with the challenge of an aging population. How to promote the well-being and quality of life of the elderly has become increasingly important? According to the United Nations World Population Prospects 2024[1], the number of people in the world is expected to continue to increase in the next 50 years, from 8.2 billion in 2024 to a peak of 10.3 billion in the mid-2080s. It is estimated that around 2070, the number of people aged 65 and above in the world population will reach 2.2 billion. In today's era of rapid development of digital intelligence and

---

[1] On July 11, 2024, the United Nations Population Division released a new round of "World Population Prospects 2024" globally.

454   L. Yan et al.

increasingly updated information technology, China's aging is becoming more and more serious. We should broaden the new ideas of population aging development and transform "passive old-age care" into "active old-age care". Closely following the national "9073" pension layout, the technology and aging products will provide the elderly with a safer, more comfortable and dignified old age life in the three scenarios of home, community and institution. Since 2020, the state has successively issued relevant documents such as the "Implementation Plan on Effectively Solving the Difficulties of the Elderly in using intelligent Technology"[2] and the "Special Action Plan for Aging and Barrier-free Transformation of Internet Application"[3]. Among the many smart health products on the market, the product UI interface design and interaction design are too complex, which is not conducive to the elderly to understand and use, and the elderly can not use it for a long time. Although some elderly people buy smart devices, they will not be deterred by the complexity of learning, which results in the design of digital intelligent products that are not user-friendly enough for the elderly. However, the elderly are an indispensable part of mobile Internet users.

Therefore, in order to integrate the elderly into the digital age, the research on user experience and UI interaction design of age-appropriate intelligent products is particularly important. The visual symbols of smart products play a particularly important role in information transmission during use. Therefore, the age-friendly design improvement of product UI can greatly reduce the difficulty of using products and help the elderly to accept digital products. This paper is to discuss the aging UI design of smart home products based on visual cognition and Internet of Things technology.

Domestic and foreign scholars have carried out research in related aspects.

Domestic research mainly includes the following aspects: mobile terminal interface design based on the visual and cognitive characteristics of elderly users; Research on age-appropriate design of smart home products based on inclusive theory; Research on age-appropriate design of interface ICONS based on cognitive load theory; Age-appropriate design research based on APP interactive interface.

Foreign research mainly includes the following aspects: the needs and difficulties of the elderly in using mobile devices and applications; The innovation and interest of age-appropriate products; Humanization and care of age-appropriate products; And the usability and ease of use of age-appropriate products.

The search keywords in CNKI show that the literature in CNKI database is the source, the journals are limited to core, CSSCI, CSCD, the time is nearly three years, and the subject words "aging design" and "aging suitable design" are used for advanced search, and the number of papers is 680. The authors are Xue Yanmin, Deng Xning and Liu Yang. The paper "Research on the Influencing Factors of the characteristics of Smart Aging Products on Users' intention to Continue using: The mediating role of user experience Perception" discusses the characteristics of smart aging products, user

---

[2] The "Implementation Plan on Effectively Solving Elderly People's Difficulties in Utilizing Intelligent Technologies" was issued by the General Office of the State Council on November 24, 2020.

[3] The "Action Plan for the Adaptation of Internet Applications to the Elderly and the Promotion of Accessibility" was released by the Ministry of Industry and Information Technology on January 2021.

experience perception and their influence on the mechanism of elderly users' intention to continue using them. The author's paper "Aging Design of Smart Health care Products and Research methods for Elderly Users" by Dou Jinhua's team studied the aging design of smart health care products and research methods for elderly users. The author of Li Yuanrong's paper "Analysis of Interaction design needs of Elderly Users based on Kano Model under the Background of Aging Adaptation", he proposed: "Using Kano model, mining the elderly users in the use of smart phone medical application software in the" product function,UI interface "of the core needs, and put forward the UI aging design scheme, so as to design for the elderly users" controllability and practicality "of the aging UI interface, for the digital society aging process to provide a meaningful theoretical reference, help shorten The gray digital gap between elderly users and digital information can realize the goal of "technology for aging, technology for caring for the elderly".

To sum up, some achievements have been made in the research on age-appropriate UI design at home and abroad. There are a lot of experimental studies and investigations for the elderly in this paper, and the relevant researches have also shown an increasing trend in the past three years. With the policy-oriented, the market scale of science and technology suitable for aging products has gradually increased. However, the research depth is not enough. With the development of AI, cloud computing, Internet of Things, IOT, big data and VR/XR, smart medical treatment, age-appropriate smart health products and aging digital derivatives will continue to develop.

2   Academic Value and Research Significance

The study of aging-friendly UI design of smart home products has important academic value and research significance.

2.1   Academic Value

The aging UI design research of smart home products enriches the theory of human-computer interaction, discusses in depth the relevant physiological and psychological characteristics needs of products for the elderly, and considers the design of the products in terms of visual, auditory, and cognitive abilities. It expands the research methodology of design, provides new ideas and methods, and promotes innovation. Promoting interdisciplinary research, this study is one that combines several subject areas such as psychology, computer science, and design, and uses a variety of research methods.

2.2   Research Significance

Meets the needs of the aging society: as aging deepens, the demand for smart home products for the elderly increases, but existing products are deficient in aging-friendly design. The combination of visual cognition and Internet of Things (IoT) technology: visual cognition is an important influence on the use of smart home products by the elderly, and IoT technology provides the possibility of interconnectivity for smart home products. It promotes the development of the field of smart aging and improves the feasibility, safety and comfort of the elderly home care. It pays attention to the needs of the elderly and promotes social progress.

3   Analysis of Aging UI Design of Smart Home Products in China

Some products have been designed for aging: some domestic smart home products have begun to pay attention to the research on aging design, products began to adopt simple, high contrast, large font, adding voice function and other design trends, convenient for the elderly to use.

The market potential is huge but the development is uneven: the products designed by various domestic enterprises do not have a uniform aging design standard, and the product compatibility is relatively poor.

Emotional design into too little, lack of affinity and ease of use.

Generally speaking, the age-appropriate UI design of China's smart home products has improved the intelligent, personalized and emotional design of products under the drive of policy support and market demand, but it is still necessary to further improve the standards and enhance product compatibility to better meet the needs of the elderly.

4   Select a Specific Smart Home Product for Aging UI Design Research

At present, the aging products on the market are mainly divided into intelligent monitoring, security monitoring, living assistance, household assistance, entertainment and social. These smart home products can improve the quality of life of the elderly, ensure the safety of the elderly's daily life, and enhance the comfort of daily homes.

This paper chooses Xiaomi smart home product, a smart home ecological brand with high usage rate in China, as an example to investigate and analyze the aging UI design of its products. "Mijia APP" is a smart home platform owned by Xiaomi. It is compatible with multi-terminal devices and can be used on multiple devices such as mobile phones, pads and home smart screens. It supports 261 categories and more than 6,000 models of smart devices. It is a representative eco-brand of smart home in China.

As a representative of China's national brand, Mijia APP provides a variety of age-appropriate design functions, which can be easily used by the elderly. Here we discuss the aging UI design features of Mijia App:

The UI design of Mijia APP is simple, intuitive and easy to understand, and adopts flexible and customizable page design that is suitable for aging, so as to design a user-friendly and efficient interface. In the font selection, it adopts large font; In the icon design, it uses simple and intuitive ICONS with text descriptions, so that the elderly can quickly understand the functions. Too much detail is avoided in the icon design to ensure clear reality even when scaled down. The icon design of Mijia app is consistent with Xiaomi's overall brand, making it highly recognizable. The color collocation is mainly monochrome or two-color, which has a sense of science and technology and intelligence. High contrast design style, the text is clear and easy to read, while the interface color contrast is high, easy for the elderly to recognize and operate. In the interface level design, the interface level is simplified and the operation steps are reduced. For example, the common functions such as lighting control, temperature adjustment, etc. are placed on the home page to facilitate the elderly to quickly access.

Voice interaction function is adopted in the UI interface of Mijia APP, which can support voice control function in use, and the elderly can achieve the required functions through voice commands. For example, "Xiao Ai, turn on the living room light", "Xiao Ai, turn up the air conditioning temperature" and so on. After the voice command, Mijia app will complete the requirements and enhance the operation experience of the elderly.

Safety and emergency functions are adopted in the UI of Mijia APP. The one-click call function is embedded in some smart devices compatible with Mijia APP (such as smart door locks and smart cameras), so that the elderly can quickly contact their family or property when they encounter an emergency. Mijia APP also joined the intelligent security needs, such as door and window sensors, water sensors will automatically alarm when detecting abnormal conditions, and push to the user through the Mijia APP to add contacts in the system. Personalized customization function is also adopted in the UI interface of Mi Jia APP, allowing the user to place the commonly used functions in a prominent position according to the elderly. The Mijia APP provides a variety of preset scene modes (such as waking up mode, sleeping mode, leaving home mode), which the elderly can choose and adjust according to their own living habits.

5 Analysis of User Characteristics of Visual Cognition for the Elderly

First of all, we should clarify the use habits, preferences and other information of the elderly when using smart products, so as to solve problems and improve the use experience of the elderly according to the user's pain points in the design.

The visual perception ability of elderly users decreases with the increase of age, the font of the UI interface needs to be larger, the contrast of graphic text needs to be higher, and the duration of the page needs to be longer. In addition, the attention of the elderly users is reduced, so the design of concise UI should be considered to highlight the display of important information. Therefore, the visual attention characteristics of the elderly should be considered in UI design, so that the information target is easy to find, the UI framework is logical and clear, and the information guidance is clear and simple. The design of science and technology products suitable for aging is centered on the diversified needs of elderly users. In addition to solving the basic care and old-age needs of the elderly, it also considers the physiological needs, psychological needs, behavioral characteristics, lifestyle, social environment and other aspects.

Visual perception level: The elderly's vision decreases, corneal diameter decreases, lens elasticity decreases and hardens, adjustment and focusing ability decreases, and it is difficult to see smaller objects, so they are more inclined to larger fonts and ICONS. Color and contrast perception of the elderly is weakened: the elderly's ability to distinguish colors is decreased, the contrast perception will be weakened, and the sensitivity to light will also decrease with age.

Changes in visual field and depth of field perception: The elderly's visual field will be reduced, the depth of field perception will be weakened, and optical illusions are prone to occur.

Attention level: The elderly has difficulty concentrating attention and need more time and energy when dealing with complex visual tasks, and are easily disturbed by environmental factors. Strong ability of single task processing: the elderly has poor ability to process multiple information at the same time, but have high persistence in processing single information.

Memory processing level: the elderly's short-term memory and new information memory decline, the ability to convert short-term memory into long-term memory and the ability to remember stimuli that have not been represented significantly decline. Strong experiential visual thinking: experiential visual thinking will be formed for learning experience, life experience and other memories closely related to daily life, which is conducive to the working mechanism of memory efficiency.

Thinking level: inertial thinking affects operation: the elderly is easy to form inertial thinking and affect behavioral decision-making, and are easy to make mistakes in interface operation. Reduced ability to learn new things: The elderly has a lower ability to learn new things and are easy to forget them. It is necessary to avoid letting them learn too much new information.

6 At Present, the User Friendliness and Practical Functionality of Smart Home Aging Products on the Market Are Mainly in the Following Aspects

At present, the smart aging products on the market all use real-time monitoring and cloud management functions. Users can store the usage data and operation data in the cloud during use, which is convenient for users and their families to track and feedback product data in real time and track their health conditions.

At present, the smart aging products on the market all use the function of intelligent health data analysis and data sharing. Smart aging products can be connected with mobile APP Bluetooth, users through long-term use of data upload, the product will intelligently analyze the data and generate data health report, users share the data to doctors, help doctors and users follow up and analysis.

At present, the smart aging products on the market have diversified and integrated the functions of the products, including the health monitoring of physiological parameters, the monitoring of sleep quality data, and the statistics of the number of exercise steps. Among them, the health monitoring of physiological parameters includes heart rate, blood pressure, blood sugar, blood oxygen saturation, etc. The monitoring of sleep quality data includes sleep time, sleep depth, number of turning over and so on. Among them, the number of exercise steps is counted, such as the number of daily activity steps, the distance exercised, and the calories consumed.

At present, the smart aging products on the market have adopted a simple and easy to operate UI design: the UI design is relatively simple and easy to use, the use of a large screen is clear, the operation is also very simple, generally a button to complete the measurement, very friendly for the elderly. And all have the function of voice broadcast measurement results. Some products automatically shut down after 60 s of measurement, which helps the elderly forget to shut down and misoperate and save electricity.

At present, the smart aging products on the market use data security protection function, intelligent security system, fall detection function, drug reminder function.

Excellent UI Design Cases for the Elderly.

- DDT Elderly Taxi APP, the home page of the shortcut navigation in the design of the elderly taxi column, click on the overall page after the operation becomes simple, the interface is designed with large fonts, no ads interference, and provide a key to call a taxi function.The interface adopts large font design, no advertisement interference, and provides one-key taxi hailing function. Supporting the telephone taxi, the elderly can call a cab by phone.The interface is simple and easy to operate, which reduces the difficulty for the elderly to use taxi software.
- The elder mode of Alipay APP, enter the elder mode through the page, the font and icon are enlarged, and some unused functions are hidden.Simplified functions make the interface clearer and easier for the elderly to use.
- Smart home products are designed to control home equipment through voice commands, and the system can automatically adjust the indoor temperature and humidity according to the living habits of the elderly, which simplifies the operation process, allows the elderly to easily control home equipment, and improves the convenience of life.
- Himalaya APP large-print mode, after switching to large-print mode, the overall interface is streamlined, with large fonts and clear hierarchy, the classification adopts large-print card-based design, and by enlarging the text and icons and adding auxiliary text, it improves the use experience of the elderly.
- Health management software, the interface adopts large font and high contrast design, while simplifying the operation flow and providing additional health monitoring functions, which can measure heart rate, blood pressure, sleep condition, etc.
- This excellent UI design case not only meets the vision needs of the elderly, but also reduces the difficulty of operation and improves the convenience and safety of use through voice assistance and one-button operation.The UI design all reflects the design principles of large font, high contrast, voice interaction, and simplified operation process.

7   The Aging UI Design Principle of Smart Home Products

In the product interface UI design, the design style is simple and intuitive, the complex operation is reduced, the interface layout is clear, and the functions are concentrated. The process in use is clear, the commonly used functions are integrated together, and the number of buttons is reduced. Use common ICONS and text instructions when necessary. Simplify the operation process and provide one-click operation. Unified interface style, consistent operation logic, unified interaction mode. Intuitive operation process, clear navigation structure, intuitive feedback mode.

In the font design, large font design, high contrast color matching, simple ICONS. The fonts chosen in the UI design are large and clear, using sans-serif fonts. Color and contrast in UI design: color matching is reasonable, contrast is high, and harsh colors are avoided.

In the design of auxiliary functions, the design of rich auxiliary functions, there are voice prompt function, gesture operation function, and function entrance in prominent position, such as help center, call function, voice assistant and so on. It has good privacy protection function. After the operation is completed, provide immediate feedback information, such as sound prompts, lights flashing, etc., to let the elderly know whether the operation is successful. Provide operation record function to facilitate the elderly to check their operation history at any time.

In the product interaction design, the interactive function design is concise, and the core function is priority. Simplify the operation process as much as possible, reduce the operation steps, and design the one-click operation function. At the same time, support voice interaction function, convenient for the elderly to complete the operation by voice. The functions most commonly used by the elderly (such as light control, temperature adjustment, curtain switch, etc.) are placed in the most prominent position to reduce the level of operation.

In the design of product energy module, the function partition is clear. The different functional modules (such as lighting control, home appliance control, security monitoring, etc.) are partitioned, and the function of each area is relatively independent and easy to identify. Modular operation: The way of operation of each module is as consistent as possible, for example, the switch button of all devices adopts the same icon and operation logic. Function personalization, user habit memory: The system is able to remember the common operation habits of the elderly, such as automatically adjusting to the temperature or lighting mode they often use. Customizable functions: Allow the elderly to adjust the interface layout, font size, color theme, etc., according to their preferences, and even customize shortcut keys. Continuation of traditional operation mode: In the design, try to retain the operation mode of traditional home appliances, such as retaining physical keys, so that the elderly can quickly get started. Compatible with traditional equipment: Smart home products should be able to be compatible with the traditional equipment that the elderly already has (such as ordinary remote control), reducing the pressure of learning new equipment.

8 Adaptive UI Design Practice Process for Smart Home Products

Before designing a set of products, it is necessary to write a detailed requirement analysis based on the user's needs. This set of design is to take a specific product as an example, to do a smart blood pressure monitor UI design interface.

Before designing, you need to conduct a competitive analysis of the current smart blood pressure monitor market, understand what similar brands are in the market, and understand the features, advantages and user evaluation of the product. At present, the main competitors in the Chinese market are: Omron Healthcare, Yuepu, MIJIA, Panasonic, iHealth and other major brands. Detailed comparison and analysis of the above competing products is required during the design process. List the features, advantages and user reviews of the products. Omron is suitable for users who pursue high quality and accurate measurement with high price, mature design and comprehensive functions. Fisheye is cost-effective and functional, suitable for families with limited budgets, equipped with a large screen and voice broadcast function, suitable for the elderly. Mijia is highly intelligent, suitable for young users or families who need remote monitoring. Panasonic quality is reliable, but the operation experience is general, suitable for users with high requirements for quality. Jiuan is feature-rich and suitable for users with high demand for intelligence, and it has a no-tie cuff design that automatically adjusts the cuff's tightness for easy operation.

Setting the user's needs, this part is needed to be completed in conjunction with market research. To position the user population, for example, the user groups of smart sphygmomanometer are mainly hypertensive patients, the elderly, some health-conscious middle-aged people and young people who need to measure blood pressure with family history of work pressure. Then clarify the user's needs for the function, for example, the user's needs for: first, simplify the easy-to-use operation process, the product needs to reduce the learning cost of the elderly. Second, to ensure that the interface is clear and easy to read, through the interface of large fonts, high contrast design to improve readability. Third, reduce misuse and protect user privacy. Fourth, provide interface customization functions to meet the needs of different elderly people. Fifth, support voice interaction to help users with poor eyesight or operation difficulties. Sixth, the need for blood pressure monitors to have some additional functions, such as heart rate detection, blood oxygen detection, data synchronization, etc. Seventh, the demand for appearance, such as the user wants to be able to carry around, the appearance of the brief fashion, etc.

According to the sketch design, combined with the principle of aging UI design for smart home products, list the detailed design ideas of the product, this part can be the design ideas of the text, and then the design ideas of the text with graphic representation.

The design of the main interface sketch. The main interface is the core page of the product UI, which is the quick entrance of the APP function, and the layout of the main interface is crucial for the whole set of design. First, design the top navigation bar of the page, including: time display, voice assistant button, emergency call button. In the design, we need to pay attention to the "time display" this part of the font needs to be larger, easy to read. The "Voice Assistant Button" should be designed in an obvious position, so that users can use voice control at any time, and the Sos Red Button should be designed at the top or bottom of the interface, so that users can use it quickly.

Next, it is necessary to design low-fidelity prototyping with prototyping software: low-fidelity prototyping based on sketches for initial testing. Low-fidelity prototyping needs to choose a suitable design tool, commonly used prototyping tools in China are: ink knife, Axure, instant design, matergo, these tools can assist designers suitable for rapid construction of the basic framework to support simple interaction design. Designers choose to use these software to build the basic framework, the main layout of the page is divided according to the function, such as the home page, list page, detail page and so on. Then divide the core functional modules and navigation structure to determine the core functional modules of each page, such as measurement buttons, history, etc..

After setting up the basic framework, you can draw the UI interface elements of the product. UI interface elements include designing interactive elements such as buttons and input boxes, designing icons and text, designing colors and typography, etc. UI interface element design is an important part of user experience design, which can directly affect the product's ease of use and user satisfaction. Button design needs to consider the size of the buttons and the spacing of the buttons. The button size should be large enough to avoid misuse, while maintaining proper spacing between buttons. The design should take into account the design of obvious button click effects (such as color changes, shadows, etc.), so that users know that the operation has been triggered. Avoid using overly complex text when designing text and icons. Simple text descriptions or icons should be used on the buttons.

Icons should be simple, avoiding complex graphics and ensuring that users can quickly recognize them. Icons should be consistent in style and avoid mixing different styles of icons in the same interface. Provide text descriptions or voice prompts for icons to help users with poor eyesight understand their meaning.

UI interaction design is another core part of UI design that needs to be considered, which directly affects the interaction between users and the product. Excellent interaction design can help designers create an efficient, easy-to-use and enjoyable interaction experience. In the UI interaction design part, the logic between pages should be clear. The interaction between pages should use unified interaction logic, unified visual style and unified feedback mechanism. The premise of UI interaction design is to study the needs, behaviors and preferences of the target users in depth, and develop the design around the core needs of the users, such as the effect of clicking the buttons, the effect of the loading animation. The interface of the UI interaction design should be concise and clear, and avoid too many operation steps and complex functions. Highlight the key points to avoid redundancy: put the core functions in the most conspicuous position to reduce the user's search time, remove unnecessary elements and functions, and keep the simplicity of the interface. Constantly optimize the interaction design through testing.

User testing of product UI design is a key part of the blood pressure monitor design and optimization process. Through systematic user testing, invite the elderly to conduct practical operation tests and collect feedback data. User testing can verify the product's ease of use, accuracy and user satisfaction, and identify and solve problems in a timely manner, so as to improve the product's market competitiveness and user experience user testing. Optimize the interface layout and interaction design according to user feedback. User testing can be done first on the test process for an initial use of training, to briefly introduce the user to the basic functions of the sphygmomanometer and operating methods. Then let the user use the sphygmomanometer to measure the blood pressure, and observe whether the user is able to measure and view the measurement data and synchronize the data smoothly. After using the device, the user is asked to give feedback on whether the size and position of the buttons are in line with the user's expectations, whether the elderly user can clearly recognize the data and use the voice function, and whether the screen size is appropriate. After the feedback is completed, the problems will be recorded and analyzed, and the design will be further optimized and improved, such as adjusting the interface layout, optimizing the voice prompts, or improving the operation process.

The next step is to make a high fidelity design of the product's UI. This is the closest prototype design to the final product. When the final high-fidelity design is completed, it is important to ensure that the entire UI has photorealistic visual effects, UI interaction design with strong interaction details, and user experience design with realistic content. Low-fidelity design focuses on the logic between UI pages, while high-fidelity design focuses on the complete visual and interactive details of the UI. High-fidelity design generally uses the use of professional tools (such as Sketch, Figma, Adobe XD) to carry out visual design, highly restored visual effects and interactive experience, to help the team better understand, verify and optimize the product design.

Finally, after the UI design is completed, hand over the design results to the development team and make sure that the development team can clearly understand the design intent. Submit design specification documents, interaction design documents, interface design resources, and user test reports. Conduct face-to-face communication or meetings with the development team to ensure that both parties have a clear understanding of the design intent and development requirements. Use cloud storage platforms (e.g. Google Drive, Dropbox) or internal document management systems to share design documents and resource files. Ensure that the development team can access and download all necessary files.

This is the process of the whole set of smart home product aging UI design practice, starting from the product competitor analysis, analyze the existing aging smart home products in the market to understand their functions, design features and user experience. Compare the products of different brands (e.g., Omron, Fisheye, Mijia, Panasonic, JiuAn, etc.), summarize the advantages and disadvantages, and provide reference for the design. Conduct user demand analysis and research, through interviews, questionnaires, etc., to gain an in-depth understanding of the usage habits, preferences and pain points of the elderly. Construct typical user profiles, and clarify the needs and behavioral patterns of the target user groups. Start sketching, based on user needs, draw preliminary interface sketches and determine the core functional layout. Divide the main interface, functional modules, navigation bar and other areas to ensure that the layout is simple and clear. Basic framework design, build the basic framework of the page, including the top navigation, center content area, bottom navigation, etc.Plan the user's jumping path and operation flow between pages. UI interface basic elements design, make sure the button size is large enough, easy to operate, and provide clear click feedback. Design simple and clear icons, avoiding complex graphics and ensuring that older people can quickly recognize them. Use fonts of at least 16px to ensure that text is clear and easy to read. Choose high-contrast color combinations and avoid low-contrast text and background pairings. UI interaction design to optimize operational steps, reduce complexity, and ensure that the interaction logic is intuitive to the user. User testing of product UI design, optimize the design based on user feedback to ensure ease of use and satisfaction. High-fidelity prototype design, add complete interactive effects, such as button clicks, page jumps, animation effects, and so on. Final delivery to the development team to complete the whole set of UI design, detailing the design details, interaction logic and technical implementation points. After the product is online, continuously collect user feedback, optimize according to user requirements, and continuously improve the design.

9 Research Conclusions and Prospects

Against the background of increasing global population aging, how to improve the quality of life of the elderly through technology has become an important issue. Currently, smart home products on the market still have deficiencies in aging-friendly design, such as complex UI interface and unfriendly interaction design, which makes it difficult for the elderly to grasp and use them.

Scholars at home and abroad have carried out a large number of studies on ageing-friendly design, with domestic studies focusing on interface design based on the visual cognitive characteristics of the elderly, inclusiveness theory, cognitive load theory and so on; while foreign studies have focused on the needs and difficulties of the elderly in using mobile devices, the humanization and ease of use of ageing-friendly products and so on. In the search of China Knowledge Network (CNN) in the past three years, the number of related literatures shows a growing trend, but the depth of research still needs to be further improved.

This paper takes Xiaomi smart home products as an example, and takes "Mijia APP" as a representative smart home platform to study the aging-friendly UI design, such as the use of large fonts, high contrast, simple icons, voice interaction, and other features, which is convenient for the elderly to use. However, on the whole, although the aging-friendly UI design of smart home products in China has made some progress under the impetus of policy and market demand, it still faces problems such as the lack of unified standards, poor product compatibility, and insufficient emotional design.

In this paper, we have sorted out some laws of aging-friendly UI design for smart home products, and summarized a series of principles that should be followed in product UI design. It proposes that the visual cognitive characteristics of the elderly need to be considered in the design. This paper summarizes the three important components of ageing-friendly UI design.

Looking at the future world, there are several trends in the development direction of smart home products aging-friendly UI design:

The design of smart home products for aging products will be increasingly close to the Internet of Things (IoT) technology.

Data can be shared between multiple smart home devices. Coupled with AI technology, using artificial intelligence machine learning algorithm technology, smart home products aging products will realize automatic adjustment of data and scenes to achieve more ergonomic services. And provide more intuitive visual guidance through VR/AR technology in each use scenario.

The UI design of the smart home products aging products will be further strengthened to consider more security protection, and the security of user data will be further safeguarded with stronger data encryption technology. It will strengthen the privacy and security protection function of data to prevent the use of smart products feedback records, operation records data from being leaked, so that people can use it with peace of mind.

Smart home product aging product UI design will be simplicity and appearance aging synchronous development. The design of each product will be more standardized. The formation of a complete industrial chain will enable the synergistic development of various industries to form a one-stop aging-friendly solution. Designers will pay more attention to the actual needs and use experience of the elderly. Designers will express warm and friendly emotions through colors, icons, animations and other elements, and design products that can relieve the elderly's operating anxiety and enhance the pleasure of use. Create a more convenient, comfortable and safe smart living environment for the elderly.

The market demand for aging-friendly smart home products will also continue to grow, and the government will pay more attention to the policy tilt of aging-friendly products, and will support the research and development of more smart home products aging-friendly products enterprises.

In the smart home products in the development of products will take more account of the elderly to provide life assistance and emotional accompaniment, will enhance the emotional design. Considering that the ability of the elderly to accept new things is not as good as that of young people, smart products will be designed to be compatible with and retain the traditional operating methods and new functions, so that the elderly can learn to use them quickly and reduce the pressure of learning new things.

In short, the aging UI design of smart home products will be more integrated with artificial intelligence models, Internet of Things, big data and other technologies in the future, and continuously optimized. In more consideration of safety, comfort, convenience, physiological and psychological characteristics of the elderly into the design. The design reflects the characteristics of simplicity, easy to read and easy to use, and improves the use experience and quality of life of elderly users. At the same time, focusing on safety and auxiliary functions, so that elderly users can use smart home products with more peace of mind.

Acknowledgments. This paper was completed by Prof. Ting Han of Shanghai Jiao Tong University and the Human-Machine Joint Intelligent Culture, Tourism and Recreation Furniture Innovation Design Team of Gannan Institute of Science and Technology, thanks to the collaboration of team member Miss. Songling Liu and MR.Xiaohong Deng.

Disclosure of Interests The author declares that there are no conflicts of interest related to the content of this article.

References

1. Zhang, H., Li, M.: Visual Cognitive Characteristics of the Elderly and Human-Computer Interaction Design. Science Press, Beijing (2018)
2. Wang, F., Chen, W.: Application of gestalt theory in interface design. Packaging Eng. **41**(12), 56–62 (2020)
3. Fisk, A.D., Rogers, W.A.: Handbook of Human Factors and the Older Adult. Academic, San Diego (1997)
4. National Health Commission of China: Report on Health Standards and Cognitive Ability Assessment for the Elderly in China. People's Medical Publishing House, Beijing (2021)
5. Li, Q., Liu, Y.: Architecture of smart home systems based on the internet of things. Comput. Eng. Appl. **58**(3), 1–8 (2022)
6. Atzori, L., Iera, A., Morabito, G.: The internet of things: a survey. Comput. Netw. **54**(15), 2787–2805 (2010)
7. China National Institute for Electronic Standardization: White Paper on Interoperability Technology for Smart Homes. Ministry of Industry and Information Technology Publishing House, Beijing (2020)
8. Zhou, X.: Cognitive accessibility principles for age-friendly products. Decoration. **5**, 34–37 (2019)
9. American Geriatrics Society.: Guidelines for Designing Age-friendly Interfaces (3rd Edition). Translated by Wang Lei. Shanghai: Shanghai Jiao Tong University Press (2017)
10. Wu, M., Zhao, G.: Optimization of Interface layout for elderly users based on eye-tracking experiments. Ergonomics. **27**(2), 89–94 (2021)

11. Norman, D.A.: The Design of Everyday Things. Basic Books, New York (2013)
12. Liu, W., Huang, Q.: Multimodal interaction in age-friendly product design. Mech. Design. **37**(9), 112–116 (2020)
13. ISO 9241-210:2019: Ergonomics of Human-System Interaction. ISO, Geneva (2019)
14. Alibaba Artificial Intelligence Laboratory: Usage Behaviors of Elderly People in Smart Homes in China. Alibaba Research Institute, Hangzhou (2022)
15. Xiaomi Technology: Design Specifications for Elderly-Friendly UI of Mi Home (Internal Document). Xiaomi User Experience Center, Beijing (2021)

Author Index